Communications
in Computer and Information Science   1925

Rationale

The CCIS series is devoted to the publication of proceedings of computer science conferences. Its aim is to efficiently disseminate original research results in informatics in printed and electronic form. While the focus is on publication of peer-reviewed full papers presenting mature work, inclusion of reviewed short papers reporting on work in progress is welcome, too. Besides globally relevant meetings with internationally representative program committees guaranteeing a strict peer-reviewing and paper selection process, conferences run by societies or of high regional or national relevance are also considered for publication.

Topics

The topical scope of CCIS spans the entire spectrum of informatics ranging from foundational topics in the theory of computing to information and communications science and technology and a broad variety of interdisciplinary application fields.

Information for Volume Editors and Authors

Publication in CCIS is free of charge. No royalties are paid, however, we offer registered conference participants temporary free access to the online version of the conference proceedings on SpringerLink (http://link.springer.com) by means of an http referrer from the conference website and/or a number of complimentary printed copies, as specified in the official acceptance email of the event.

CCIS proceedings can be published in time for distribution at conferences or as postproceedings, and delivered in the form of printed books and/or electronically as USBs and/or e-content licenses for accessing proceedings at SpringerLink. Furthermore, CCIS proceedings are included in the CCIS electronic book series hosted in the SpringerLink digital library at http://link.springer.com/bookseries/7899. Conferences publishing in CCIS are allowed to use Online Conference Service (OCS) for managing the whole proceedings lifecycle (from submission and reviewing to preparing for publication) free of charge.

Publication process

The language of publication is exclusively English. Authors publishing in CCIS have to sign the Springer CCIS copyright transfer form, however, they are free to use their material published in CCIS for substantially changed, more elaborate subsequent publications elsewhere. For the preparation of the camera-ready papers/files, authors have to strictly adhere to the Springer CCIS Authors' Instructions and are strongly encouraged to use the CCIS LaTeX style files or templates.

Abstracting/Indexing

CCIS is abstracted/indexed in DBLP, Google Scholar, EI-Compendex, Mathematical Reviews, SCImago, Scopus. CCIS volumes are also submitted for the inclusion in ISI Proceedings.

How to start

To start the evaluation of your proposal for inclusion in the CCIS series, please send an e-mail to ccis@springer.com.

Tran Khanh Dang · Josef Küng · Tai M. Chung
Editors

Future Data and Security Engineering

Big Data, Security and Privacy, Smart City
and Industry 4.0 Applications

10th International Conference, FDSE 2023
Da Nang, Vietnam, November 22–24, 2023
Proceedings

 Springer

Editors
Tran Khanh Dang ⓘ
Ho Chi Minh City University of Industry
and Trade
Ho Chi Minh City, Vietnam

Josef Küng
Johannes Kepler University of Linz
Linz, Austria

Tai M. Chung
Sungkyunkwan University
Suwon-si, Korea (Republic of)

ISSN 1865-0929   ISSN 1865-0937 (electronic)
Communications in Computer and Information Science
ISBN 978-981-99-8295-0   ISBN 978-981-99-8296-7 (eBook)
https://doi.org/10.1007/978-981-99-8296-7

This Springer imprint is published by the registered company Springer Nature Singapore Pte Ltd.
The registered company address is: 152 Beach Road, #21-01/04 Gateway East, Singapore 189721, Singapore

Paper in this product is recyclable.

Preface

In CCIS volume 1925 we present the accepted contributions for the 10th International Conference on Future Data and Security Engineering (FDSE 2023). The conference took place during November 22–24, 2023, on the main campus of Da Nang University of Science and Technology (DUT) -The University of Da Nang, Vietnam. Besides DBLP and other major indexing systems, the FDSE proceedings have also been indexed by Scopus and listed in the Conference Proceedings Citation Index (CPCI) of Thomson Reuters.

The annual FDSE conference is a premier forum designed for researchers, scientists, and practitioners interested in state-of-the-art and state-of-the-practice activities in data, information, knowledge, and security engineering to explore cutting-edge ideas, to present and exchange their research results and advanced data-intensive applications, and to discuss emerging issues on data, information, knowledge, and security engineering. At FDSE, researchers and practitioners are not only able to share research solutions to problems of today's data and security engineering themes but are also able to identify new issues and directions for future related research and development work.

The two-round call for papers resulted in the submission of 135 papers. A rigorous single-blind peer-review process was applied to all of them. This resulted in 46 accepted papers (an acceptance rate of 34%) for CCIS volume 1925, which were presented at the conference. Every paper was reviewed by at least three members of the international Program Committee, who were carefully chosen based on their knowledge and competence. This careful process resulted in the high quality of the contributions published in this volume. The accepted papers were grouped into the following sessions:

- Big Data Analytics and Distributed Systems
- Security and Privacy Engineering
- Machine Learning and Artificial Intelligence for Security and Privacy
- Smart City and Industry 4.0 Applications
- Data Analytics and Healthcare Systems
- Short Papers: Security and Data Engineering

In addition to the papers selected by the Program Committee, five internationally recognized scholars delivered keynote speeches:

- **Dieter Kranzlmüller**, Ludwig Maximilian University of Munich, Germany
- **Tai M. Chung**, Sungkyunkwan University, South Korea
- **Josef Küng**, Johannes Kepler University Linz, Austria
- **Manuel Clavel**, Eastern International University, Vietnam
- **Sadok Ben Yahia**, Southern Denmark University, Denmark

The success of FDSE 2023 was the result of the efforts of many people, to whom we would like to express our gratitude. First, we would like to thank all authors who submitted papers to FDSE 2023, especially the invited speakers for the keynotes. We would also like to thank the members of the committees and additional reviewers for their timely reviewing and lively participation in the subsequent discussion in order to select the high-quality papers published in this volume. Last but not least, we thank the Organizing Committee members and the host institute, DUT, for their great support of FDSE 2023.

November 2023

Tran Khanh Dang
Josef Küng
Tai M. Chung

Organization

Honorary Chairs

Nguyen Xuan Hoan   Ho Chi Minh City University of Industry and Trade, Vietnam

Nguyen Huu Hieu   Da Nang University of Science and Technology - The University of Da Nang, Vietnam

Program Committee Chairs

Tran Khanh Dang   Ho Chi Minh City University of Industry and Trade, Vietnam

Josef Küng   Johannes Kepler University Linz, Austria

Tai M. Chung   Sungkyunkwan University, South Korea

Steering Committee

Artur Andrzejak   Heidelberg University, Germany

Manuel Clavel   Eastern International University, Vietnam

Dirk Draheim   Tallinn University of Technology, Estonia

Johann Eder   Alpen-Adria-Universität Klagenfurt, Austria

Dinh Nho Hao   Institute of Mathematics, Vietnam Academy of Science and Technology, Vietnam

Dieter Kranzlmüller   Ludwig Maximilian University of Munich, Germany

Erich Neuhold   University of Vienna, Austria

Silvio Ranise   Fondazione Bruno Kessler, Italy

Makoto Takizawa   Hosei University, Japan

A Min Tjoa   TU Wien, Austria

Program Committee

Artur Andrzejak   Heidelberg University, Germany

Phan Thanh An   Ho Chi Minh City University of Technology, Vietnam

Hoang Xuan Bach	Ho Chi Minh City University of Industry and Trade, Vietnam
Pham The Bao	Saigon University, Vietnam
Hyunseung Choo	Sungkyunkwan University, South Korea
Manuel Clavel	Eastern International University, Vietnam
H. K. Dai	Oklahoma State University, USA
Vitalian Danciu	Ludwig Maximilian University of Munich, Germany
Quang-Vinh Dang	Industrial University of Ho Chi Minh City, Vietnam
Nguyen Tuan Dang	Saigon University, Vietnam
Tran Tri Dang	RMIT University, Vietnam
Thanh-Nghi Do	Can Tho University, Vietnam
Thanh-Dang Diep	Ludwig Maximilian University of Munich, Germany
Dirk Draheim	Tallinn University of Technology, Estonia
Johann Eder	Alpen-Adria-Universität Klagenfurt, Austria
Jungho Eom	Daejeon University, South Korea
Duc Tai Le	Sungkyunkwan University, South Korea
Ngo Duong Ha	Ho Chi Minh City University of Industry and Trade, Vietnam
Nguyen Hoang Ha	Hue University of Sciences, Vietnam
Trung Ha Le Hoai	University of Information Technology, Vietnam
Raju Halder	Indian Institute of Technology, Patna, India
Kha-Tu Huynh	International University - VNUHCM, Vietnam
Ngo Thanh Hung	Ho Chi Minh City University of Industry and Trade, Vietnam
Lam Son Le	Vietnamese-German University, Vietnam
Trung-Hieu Huynh	Industrial University of Ho Chi Minh City, Vietnam
Kien Huynh	Stony Brook University, USA
Mohand Tahar Kechadi	University College Dublin, Ireland
Nhien-An Le-Khac	University College Dublin, Ireland
Duy Ninh Khanh	Da Nang University of Science and Technology - The University of Da Nang, Vietnam
Tomohiko Igasaki	Kumamoto University, Japan
Nguyen Le Hoang	Ritsumeikan University, Japan
Hoang Duc Minh	National Physical Laboratory, UK
Tuan Pham Minh	Da Nang University of Science and Technology - The University of Da Nang, Vietnam
Nguyen Thai-Nghe	Can Tho University, Vietnam
Trung Viet Nguyen	Can Tho University of Technology, Vietnam

An Khuong Nguyen	Ho Chi Minh City University of Technology, Vietnam
Duy Ngoc Nguyen	Deakin University, Australia
Alex Norta	Tallinn University of Technology, Estonia
Eric Pardede	La Trobe University, Australia
Vinh Pham	Sungkyunkwan University, South Korea
Nguyen Van Sinh	International University - VNU-HCM, Vietnam
Erik Sonnleitner	Johannes Kepler University Linz, Austria
Ha Mai Tan	National Taiwan University, Taiwan
Michel Toulouse	Hanoi University of Science and Technology, Vietnam
Duc Le Tran	Da Nang University of Science and Technology - The University of Da Nang, Vietnam
Le Hong Trang	Ho Chi Minh City University of Technology, Vietnam
Tran Minh Quang	Ho Chi Minh City University of Technology, Vietnam
Tran Van Hoai	Ho Chi Minh City University of Technology, Vietnam
Pham Cong Thang	Da Nang University of Science and Technology - The University of Da Nang, Vietnam
Tuan Phat Tran-Truong	Ho Chi Minh City University of Industry and Trade, Vietnam
Takeshi Tsuchiya	Tokyo University of Science, Japan
Le Pham Tuyen	Kyunghee University, South Korea
Hau Pham Xuan	Quang Binh University, Vietnam
Viet Le Xuan	Qui Nhon University, Vietnam
Trung Pham Van	Pham Van Dong University, Vietnam
Edgar Weippl	SBA Research, Austria
Wolfram Wöss	Johannes Kepler University Linz, Austria
Kok-Seng Wong	VinUni, Vietnam

Local Organizing Committee

Tran Khanh Dang	Ho Chi Minh City University of Industry and Trade, Vietnam
Nguyen Tan Khoi	Da Nang University of Science and Technology - The University of Da Nang, Vietnam
La Hue Anh	Ho Chi Minh City University of Technology, Vietnam
Nguyen Le Hoang	Ritsumeikan University, Japan
Josef Küng	Johannes Kepler University Linz, Austria

Pham Cong Thang	Da Nang University of Science and Technology - The University of Da Nang, Vietnam
Thai Doan Thanh	Ho Chi Minh City University of Industry and Trade, Vietnam
Nguyen Hai Binh	Ho Chi Minh City University of Industry and Trade, Vietnam
Nguyen Van Tung	Ho Chi Minh City University of Industry and Trade, Vietnam
Trung-Hieu Huynh	Industrial University of Ho Chi Minh City, Vietnam

Additional Reviewers

Manh-Tuan Nguyen
Huu Huong Xuan Nguyen
Lai Trung Minh Duc
Phu H. Phung
Le Duc Anh
Le Thi Kim Tuyen
Ai Thao Nguyen Thi
Hung Tran Manh

Host and Sponsors

Contents

Data Analytics and Healthcare Systems

Short Papers: Security and Data Engineering

Big Data Analytics and Distributed Systems

Three-Dimensional Visualization of Legal Acts: Concept and Prototype

Ermo Täks[✉][iD], Helina Kruuk, and Dirk Draheim[iD]

Information Systems Group, Tallinn University of Technology,
Akadeemia tee 15a, 12618 Tallinn, Estonia
{ermo.taks,helina.kruuk,dirk.draheim}@taltech.ee

Abstract. Legal documents, including laws, regulations, norms, and general legal texts, exert a significant influence on many aspects of our daily lives. They establish the parameters for business operations, interpersonal interactions, and serve as the cornerstone for the functionality of the state. Modern society is constantly evolving, increasing the need for various relationships to be legally regulated. As behavioral rules change throughout society's development, so does the content of legal acts. Over time, legal documents become more and more extensive, complicated, harder to maintain and harder to review. Comprehending legal texts is often a huge challenge. Here, our working hypothesis is that visualization can significantly increase the processing of information by humans. With our research, we aim at utilizing data visualization to simplify the understanding of legal acts, both in regard of their content and changes made to them. In this paper, we elaborate a concept for the visualization of the Estonian State Gazette, which encompasses the complete corpus of Estonian legal acts together with their entire version history. As an evaluation of the concept, we provide a prototypical implementation of the suggested concept. We provide an exhaustive discussion of the motivation, concept, implementation and implications of our approach.

Keywords: Legal acts · e-law · data visualization

1 Introduction

A significant portion of a lawyer's workload involves conducting legal research. In the Republic of Estonia, the primary repository of legal information is the State Gazette (Riigi Teataja)[1] information system. According to a survey conducted among Estonian lawyers [1], the process of searching for legal sources within the State Gazette database and other sources can consume two to four hours of their daily workload. Nearly half of a lawyer's work is dedicated to locating pertinent legal references, and any tool that assists in pinpointing relevant legal norms holds significant potential to enhance the efficiency of their work.

As described [2–4], legal search can be complicated and tedious. Furthermore, legal text is not static but changes over time. This undermines previously

---

[1] https://www.riigiteataja.ee/en/.

obtained legal knowledge and forces lawyers to continuously validate specific legal norms over longer time periods. Furthermore, often changes in legal texts are accepted by institutions but not yet implemented, so lawyers have to take into account applying in the future.

A closer look to changes of legal text reveals their complex nature. Changes in legislation can happen over time due to the change of society. For example, the meaning of a specific notion with legal relevance might change over time, such as the term "marriage". Two hundred years ago it was used specifically to mark a union between a man and a woman, today it is more understood as the formally recognized union of two people as partners in a personal relationship, no matter of gender.

Our working hypothesis is that visualization can significantly increase the processing of information by humans. With our research, we aim at utilizing data visualization to simplify the understanding of legal acts, both in regard of their content and changes made to them.

In this paper, we contribute:

- A concept for the visualization of the Estonian State Gazette, which encompasses the complete corpus of Estonian legal acts together with their entire version history.
- An evaluation of the concept, we provide a prototypical implementation of the suggested concept[2].

We provide an exhaustive discussion of the motivation, concept, implementation and implications of our approach.

In Sect. 2, we discuss related work. In Sect. 3, we introduce our concept of visualizing data of the Estonian State Gazette. In Sect. 4, we describe the Web application prototype of our solution. We provide a discussion of our solution including future work in Sect. 5 and finish the paper with a conclusion in Sect. 6.

2   Related Work

2.1   Visualisation in the Legal Domain

Data visualization are used in many different areas of life. For example, it has found good use in marketing to evaluate popularity of advertisements or measure the traffic changes on web pages. It has been used extensively in sales to demonstrate sales results, identify popular products or analyze sales trends. Logistics departments use visualization for planning and monitoring shipping and delivery times, stock capacity, number of shipments, delivery routes.

Data visualization involves representing data through images or graphics, and its significance grows as data complexity and volume increase. Presently, data visualization is an evolving discipline that blends elements of both science and art. The foremost priority in visualization is to accurately convey the data

---

[2] https://cs.taltech.ee/research/projects/leseterevi/.

without introducing any misinterpretations or distortions. As the saying goes, 'a picture is worth a thousand words,' highlighting the power of effective visuals.

Information visualization is concerned with exploiting the cognitive capabilities of human visual perception in order to convey meaningful patterns and trends hidden in abstract datasets [5, 6]. An idea to visualize the law or the legislation as guiding tool is not new, tracing back to 1998 [7]. Visualisation of the law can be expanded into numerous directions, as demonstrated by many cases. For example, the visualisation attempt has been used for:

- revealing internal references within the legal act [8];
- illustrating citation networks [9];
- illustrating connections between different legal acts within the legislation [1, 8, 10];
- educational purposes [11];
- geo-temporal narratives in Law Enforcement [12];
- legal document content mapping [13].

Advantages of data visualization in legal domain are following. It benefits from the comprehensibility of information - graphic presentation allows visualizing a large amount of data, making it comprehensible and better understood The human brain grasps the image much faster than the text. It also helps of making connections - A pure sequence of numbers or a big portions of text are not easy to understand. Visualization helps to represent the relationships between the data and the operations and results performed with them.

Visualization is useful for identifying patterns - visualization allows users to identify patterns and trends in the data that are difficult to read from the original data. Patterns can be visualized on many levels: through colors, text fonts and images. Visualisation supports also interactivity - Visualization allows users to access data in an interactive way. Visuals use dynamic charts, colors, and shapes that change based on user input. It allows users to explore, manipulate and interact with data.

2.2   Temporal Aspects of Law

Regarding to the governments transition toward a digital model, undergoing digitization and transformation phases, they investigate the use of information and communication technologies to enhance the internal processes and operational methods within government structures.

Temporal aspects of the law has been researched because of the development of international digital legal systems standards like Akoma Ntoso. Akoma Ntoso establishes a standardized, technology-agnostic electronic representation (in XML format) for parliamentary, legislative, and judiciary documents, aimed at ensuring machine readability. Its primary goal is to create a framework for exchanging machine-readable documents within these domains. The purpose is to harness the potential of information and communication technologies (ICTs) to enhance efficiency and accountability within parliamentary, legislative, and judiciary contexts [14].

Akoma Ntoso is largely based on Bologna University researchers work, who also dedicated a lot of time for temporal aspects of the law [15]. According to their work, the legal domain requires at least tree axis of time dimensions: time of in force, time of efficacy and time of application of the norms [16]. Such an approach allows design legislative temporal aspects and evaluate rules legal validity with needed clarity.

2.3   Visualizing Estonian Legislation Semantic Temporal Behaviour

The Estonian State Gazette (Riigi Teataja) serves as the official online publication where legal documents gain their legal validity. Since June 1, 2010, the State Gazette has been exclusively available online, hosting an extensive collection of over 13,300 legal acts [17]. The majority of documents from the 1990s are accessible within this information system. These documents are officially authenticated and come with a digital stamp, ensuring the permanence of the act after publication.

For every modification, an updated complete text that incorporates the changes is meticulously prepared and published alongside the amending act. Each version of the full text is interconnected with its previous and subsequent revisions. This system allows for a comparison between two revisions within the same legislation, clearly displaying the specific changes made to the legislation.

Nonetheless, the process of comparing editorials can be inconvenient and time-consuming, and there's a risk of overlooking changes, especially when dealing with extensive legislation. In some cases, legislation undergoes such a substantial number of revisions over the years that it becomes impractical to discern the evolution of certain sections merely by comparing revisions. For instance, the Obligations Act and the Penal Code have seen 42 and 92 amendments, respectively, since their inception. Moreover, examining the complete text doesn't offer a swift and lucid overview of the legislation's intricacies, especially when it comes to sections, paragraphs, and clauses.

The aim of this paper is to describe a develop of the web application for visualizing both the complete text of legislative documents and the modifications made to that text. The entire text is presented in the form of a three-dimensional tree structure, resembling a fir tree. Spruce branches correspond to sections, subsections, and points within the legal act and are represented using various colors. The specifics of this tree structure are elaborated further in latter sections. The web application should enable users to select from a range of legal acts and display both the tree structure of the current version and the tree structure depicting the alterations made to the legal act.

Additionally, this document offers an insight into the essence of visualization and its utilization in presenting legislative content. The subsequent section outlines the technologies employed and the rationale behind their selection. Following that, the document delves into the process of developing the web application, while the final section assesses the finalized web application and suggests potential future enhancements.

3   Concept for Estonian State Gazette Data Visualization

The Estonina State Gazette (Riigi Teataja) is the official online publication of the Republic of Estonia, which publishes legislation and other documents listed in § 2 of the Riigi Teataja Act. The full text shall reflect all amendments made to the act. Since 1 June 2002, when the electronic version of the Official Gazette was introduced, the Official Gazette contains all the current versions of the full texts of all Acts and nationwide regulations.

Based on the review of related work (see Sect. 2), we phrase the challenge as a series of hypotheses as follows:

- Legal text changes have semantic value and are made at a specific time, therefore legal semantics have temporal properties.
- Temporal aspects of legal semantics can be made visible through references between specific changes of specific legal text over time (temporal semantic references).
- Temporal aspects of legal semantics can be visualized on a time scale, using temporal semantic references.

3.1   Tree Map Diagram

The emphasis is placed on presenting solution that illustrate individual legal acts rather than illustrating the relationships between various legal acts. A tree map diagram offers a visual method for depicting hierarchical structures. Typically, this involves displaying data as a set of rectangles, with each rectangle's size representing the proportion of the total data it represents. By incorporating color schemes and interactive features, it becomes feasible to depict multiple levels effectively.

Legal documents often contain a substantial volume of pages and intricate hierarchical structures, including chapters and paragraphs. Analyzing such content can be quite daunting. However, employing a tree map diagram enables the visualization of extensive legislation on a single page. This method allows one to begin with an overarching view of the legislation and then delve deeper into various hierarchical levels [18].

Norma-Simplex is a project dealing with the improvement and evaluation of the texts of regulations and laws. The main tasks of the project are related to document modeling. NSM is a set of tools and applications developed within the Normal-Simplex project. These tools include NSM Viz, which can be used to view visualizations completed within the project [19].

3.2   Tree Structure

A tree is a hierarchical data structure that organizes information in a hierarchical manner. It comprises vertices connected by edges. When legal documents are formatted in XML, they can be represented as a tree structure. An XML document inherently follows a tree structure, with the root element positioned at the top and child elements branching from it.

3.3   Force Directed Graph

Force-directed graphs allow you to visualise a graph in an aesthetically pleasing way. Their aim is to arrange the nodes of the graph so that all edges are more or less equal in length and there are as few intersecting edges as possible. Force-directed graphs are often used to model physical objects such as gravitationally responsive molecules or interactions. Harry Surden, Associate Professor of Law at the University of Colorado, developed an application that visualizes the United States Copyright and Patent Code [20]. The visualization uses a force-directed graph, and the hierarchy of the code is displayed using a hub and spoke layout [20].

3.4   A Word Cloud

A word cloud is a collection or cluster of words of different sizes. The word cloud provides a visual picture of the vocabulary used in the text. The most popular approach is to resize the words, where the most frequently occurring words are visualised larger than the less represented words. This provides a quick overview of the topics covered in the document and which words are most prominent [18].

4   Web Application Prototype

We have specified the functional requirements of the prototype as follows:

- The user can select the legal act from which they want to generate the tree structure.
- The user is presented with the tree structure as a spruce.
- The user can view the metadata of the act (date of entry into force, date of adoption, etc.).
- The user can zoom in and out with the camera.
- The user can rotate and move the camera.
- The user can reset the camera position.
- The user can get information about the colours of the tree structure.
- The user can view the tree structure of the changes in the legislation.
- The user can view all the valid versions in the legislative changes tree.
- The user can view the timeline in the legislative changes tree.
- The user can view the annual accounts from the first version to the present day on the timeline of legislative amendments.

The data used in this work are the full texts of laws from the online edition of the Estonian State Gazette (Riigi Teataja), which are used in the application in XML format. The current version of the full text is used as a tree structure to visualise the full text, and the older versions are compared with each other to find the exact changes in the full texts. The changes found are also visualised as a separate tree structure.

Metadata, paragraphs, sections and clauses are read from the XML of the legal act. The legal metadata used in the web application are:

- Issuer of the act
- Type of act
- Type of text
- Date of adoption
- Date of entry into force
- Date of entry into force of the drafting
- Date of expiry of the drafting

Paragraphs in a piece of legislation are stored as a list, where each item in the list is a paragraph object. Each section object has a section number, a valid value, a section title, paragraphs and bullet points. Some paragraphs also have a body text. Paragraphs and bullet points are stored as an object, similar to a paragraph, with the parameters number, validity value and body text. If a paragraph has points, these are shown below it.

The prototype uses the full text of the current Employment Contracts Act [21]. Colours are used in the practical part to distinguish the different parts. Paragraphs are in brown, paragraphs in green and points in yellow.

Technologies used for developing prototype were WebGL [22], Three.js [23], JavaScript and HTML.

4.1   Visualization of the Section Structure

The section structure is visualized as follows:

- *Sections Without Subsections and Clauses:* Sections without subsections and clauses are visualised as a single straight line between two points. The current section is coloured brown. An invalid section or a section that has been deleted is in red, see Fig. 1
- *Section with Subsections:* A straight line part of a section sis divided into parts. A straight line of a section of legislation emerges from each part. Section number 1 is always at the end of the straight section, see Fig. 2
- *Section with Subsections and Clauses:* A straight line part of a section is divided into parts. A straight line of a section of legislation emerges from each part. If the section of the enacting terms has clauses, the straight line of the section is divided into parts. From each straight section a straight section of a point emerges, see Fig. 3.
- *Section Only With clauses:* A straight line part of a paragraph is divided into parts. A straight line, marked in yellow, emerges from each section, see Fig. 4.
- *Sections With Superscripts:* Sections defined by superscripts emerge from a single trunk point at a given height, see Fig. 5.

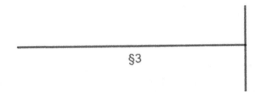

Fig. 1. Employment Contracts Act § 3 represented as fir tree branch. (Color figure online)

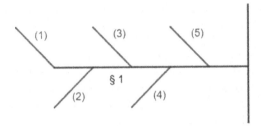

Fig. 2. Employment Contracts Act § 3 Subsects. 1 to 5.

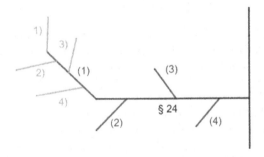

Fig. 3. Employment Contracts Act § 3 subsections and clauses

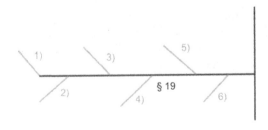

Fig. 4. Section with clauses only. (Color figure online)

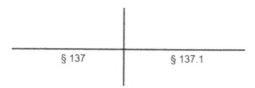

Fig. 5. Section with superscripts.

4.2   Visualization of the Whole Legislation as a Tree Structure

The Employment Contracts Act as a whole, with its sections, subsections and clauses, is depicted as a tree, see Fig. 6

The tree structure is drawn starting from the trunk. The trunk consists of points with xyz coordinates. A prerequisite for drawing parenthesis is the existence of stem points. One or more sections are drawn from each stub. The current sections are coloured brown. The drawing of section shall start with the section with the highest number. Sections, which are invalid or have been omitted from the full text are in red. A section is a straight line, the starting point of which is the stem.

Sections are drawn along the z-axis from the bottom to the top, and § 1 is always the uppermost straight section of the tree.

The endpoints of the straight lines of the segments are located around the trunk (see Fig. 6). Points A and B are the trunk points and C and D are the end points. Point D is rotated 90° clockwise from point C. To rotate the points, the three.js class Quaternion is used. The Quaternion has a method setFromAxisAngle(), which takes as parameters the unit vector of the axis and the angle in radians, and changes the coordinates of the end point xyz according to the given values. To find the rotation angle, the random() method is used, which generates an arbitrary number in the range [0, 360]. The angle in degrees is converted to radians, see Fig. 7.

4.3   Amendments to the Legislative Texts

The changes made to the legislation are found by comparing the two versions. A comparison is made between the previous and the next version, and the result is a list of which sections, subsections or clauses of the act have changed. The changes made to an act are:

- Amendment of the title of a paragraph
- Amendment of the substantive text of a paragraph, subparagraph or clause.
- Amendment of the wording of a paragraph, subparagraph or clause, or of the heading of a paragraph, subparagraph or clause.
- Amendment of the wording of a paragraph, subparagraph or clause, or of the wording of a paragraph, subparagraph or clause.

The amendments found are displayed in the timeline.

Fig. 6. Employment Contracts Act visualized as a fir tree. (Color figure online)

4.4 Creating a Timescale

The timescale is a 360-degree circle, divided into sectors by year (see Fig. 8). The very first sector represents the year in which the legislation came into force and each subsequent sector is a year ahead. The last sector represents the current year. Each version has its own date of entry into force and a specific place on the time scale. The changes found when comparing the older and newer versions are displayed with the newer date of entry into force on the timeline, see Fig. 8.

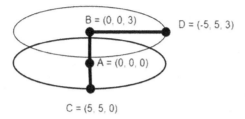

Fig. 7. Rotation of sigmoid end-points.

Fig. 8. Time scale of amendments.

4.5 View to the Amendments

Knowing the angle of the sector, the number of changes obtained by comparing the versions and their structure, the changes can be represented as a tree structure, see Fig. 9.

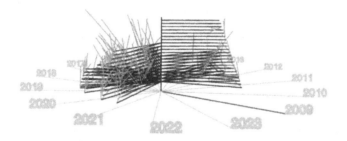

Fig. 9. The amendments view within the time scale.

4.6 Online Version of the the Prototype

The prototype is accessible from here[3]. The official name of the visualisation is Legal Semantic Temporal References Visualisation.

---

[3] https://cs.taltech.ee/research/projects/leseterevi.

5   Discussion

In the practical part of this work, the web application developed was tested by two individuals whose job responsibilities require knowledge of legal acts and their handling. One of the testers was a practicing lawyer, and the other was a legal services manager. The feedback received indicated that the idea of visualizing legal acts is very interesting, and there is potential for further development of such an application.

Both testers pointed out that this visualisation would be of great benefit to legal practitioners, who would be able to look at the normative side of the equation, to see which area is regulated and how precisely. The more sections there are, the more detailed the area covered. Since the degree of regulation is considered in a cross-college context, analysts or even postgraduates could here prove the hypothesis whether more detailed legislation is more effective than less detailed legislation, or whether more paragraphs means better legislation.

From the perspective of application functionality, it was suggested that it would be beneficial to see which paragraph has undergone the most changes since the adoption of amendments. Such a feature would immediately highlight potential areas of concern to lawmakers. Additionally, it was suggested that clicking on the branches of the tree structure could display the content of the legal act.

From a visual perspective, it was noted that the overall visualization as a tree structure is pleasing. It compactly displays which legal acts are more extensive and which ones have undergone the most changes. It was also mentioned that as a fun diversion, enthusiasts could experiment to see which law resembles a Christmas tree the most.

Regarding the hypothesises, all three of them were considered to be success-fully proven.

We identify potential future work as follows:

– *Displaying the Textual Content of the Legal Act:* Display the content of the legal act within the web application. When hovering the mouse cursor over any straight segment or clicking on it, the selected straight segment's textual content will be displayed. The content would include the title, identifier, and text of the paragraph, subsection, or point. In the case of changes in the revision tree structure, also display the content before and after the modification.
– *All Views in One Format:* Merge the existing revision tree structure and the change tree structure into a single view. The common view would include a timeline, the original text of the legal act, and the modified parts of the law would be highlighted. The highlighted sections could be examined in more detail in a separate view. This requires a thorough analysis
– *Expanding the Number of Legal Acts:* Increase the number of legal acts available to the application by creating a database that stores the complete texts of all laws of the Republic of Estonia, along with their valid and invalid revisions.

– *Integration:* Vertical integration of legal document visualization into e-court systems [24–26] and horizontal integration into interoperable e-government services [27] such as e-health systems [28].

6   Conclusion

As society and its structures continue to evolve, the significance of legally regulating various relationships becomes increasingly important. In the midst of this ongoing transformation, rules of conduct undergo modifications, resulting in corresponding changes to legislation. Legal documents expand with new provisions, remove outdated ones, and receive supplementary details. Over time, these documents become more extensive and intricate. It is crucial to preserve these alterations in legislation and enable retrospective reference. It is a well-established fact that the human brain processes visual information much faster than text. This is where visualization comes into play, simplifying the comprehension of legislative content and the visualization of legislative amendments.

The aim of this development was to create a web application that allows for the visualization of the complete text of a legal act and the changes made within the complete text. As it became evident from the work, legal acts are often challenging to comprehend, but visualization enables a better understanding of complex aspects.

As a result of the work, a prototype of a web application was developed, which allows for the visualization of the complete texts of legal acts from the Estonina State Gazette (Riigi Teataja) online edition and the changes made within the complete text as a three-dimensional tree structure. The completed web application fulfills both the functional requirements outlined in the analysis. A feedback survey was conducted for the completed web application with individuals whose job responsibilities require knowledge of legal acts and their handling. The feedback revealed that the visualization of legal acts would be beneficial for legal professionals involved in legislation, who could use it for analytical purposes.

References

1. Täks, E.: An automated legal content capture and visualisation method. Ph.D. thesis, Tallinn University of Technology (2013)
2. Klock, M.: Finding random coincidences while searching for the holy writ of truth: specification searches in law and public policy or cum hoc ergo propter hoc. Wisconsin Law Rev. **2001**, 1007–1064 (2001)
3. Livermore, M.A., Beling, P., Carlson, K., Dadgostari, F., Guim, M., Rockmore, D.N.: Law search in the age of the algorithm. Wisconsin Law Rev. **2020**(5), 1183–1240 (2021)
4. Wyner, A., Mochales-Palau, R., Moens, M.-F., Milward, D.: Approaches to text mining arguments from legal cases. In: Francesconi, E., Montemagni, S., Peters, W., Tiscornia, D. (eds.) Semantic Processing of Legal Texts. LNCS (LNAI), vol. 6036, pp. 60–79. Springer, Heidelberg (2010). https://doi.org/10.1007/978-3-642-12837-0_4

5. Vande Moere, A., Tomitsch, M., Wimmer, C., Christoph, B., Grechenig, T.: Evaluating the effect of style in information visualization. IEEE Trans. Vis. Comput. Graph. **18**(12), 2739–2748 (2012)
6. Hicks, T.A.: Information visualization: perception for design. J. Bus. Tech. Commun. **20**(1), 105–109 (2006)
7. McCloskey, M.J.: Visualizing the law: methods for mapping the legal landscape and drawing analogies. Washington Law Rev. **73**(1), 163–189 (1998)
8. Liiv, I., Vedeshin, A., Täks, E.: Visualization and structure analysis of legislative acts: a case study on the law of obligations. In: Proceedings of the 11th International Conference on Artificial Intelligence and Law, ICAIL 2007, pp. 189–190. Association for Computing Machinery, New York (2007)
9. Bommarito, M.J., Katz, D.M., Zelner, J.: Law as a seamless Web? Comparison of various network representations of the United States Supreme Court corpus (1791–2005). In: Proceedings of the 12th International Conference on Artificial Intelligence and Law (ICAIL 2009). ACM (2009)
10. Boulet, R., Mazzega, P., Bourcier, D.: Network analysis of the French environmental code. In: Casanovas, P., Pagallo, U., Sartor, G., Ajani, G. (eds.) AICOL -2009. LNCS (LNAI), vol. 6237, pp. 39–53. Springer, Heidelberg (2010). https://doi.org/10.1007/978-3-642-16524-5_4
11. Colbran, S.E., Gilding, A.: An authentic constructionist approach to students' visualisation of the law. Law Teach. **53**(1), 1–34 (2019)
12. Cunningham, A., Walsh, J., Thomas, B.: Immersive visualisation of geo-temporal narratives in law enforcement. In: Proceedings of BDVA 2018 - The 4th International Symposium on Big Data Visual and Immersive Analytics, pp. 1–8. IEEE (2018)
13. McLachlan, S., Kyrimi, E., Dube, K., Fenton, N., Webley, L.C.: Lawmaps: enabling legal AI development through visualisation of the implicit structure of legislation and lawyerly process. Artif. Intell. Law **31**(1), 169–194 (2023)
14. Akoma Ntoso Group: Akoma Ntoso. XML for parliamentary, legislative and judiciary documents. https://www.akomantoso.org/. Accessed 13 Sept 2023
15. Palmirani, M., Governatori, G., Contissa, G.: Modelling temporal legal rules. In: Proceedings of the 13th International Conference on Artificial Intelligence and Law, ICAIL 2011, pp. 131–135. Association for Computing Machinery, New York (2011)
16. Palmirani, M., Governatori, G., Contissa, G.: Temporal dimensions in rules modelling. In: Proceedings of the 2010 Conference on Legal Knowledge and Information Systems: JURIX 2010: The Twenty-Third Annual Conference, NLD, pp. 159–162. IOS Press (2010)
17. Riigi Teataja: Riigi Teataja website. https://www.riigiteataja.ee/. Accessed 12 Sept 2023
18. Carvalho, N.R., Barbosa, L.S.: Transforming legal documents for visualization and analysis. In: Proceedings of the 11th International Conference on Theory and Practice of Electronic Governance, ICEGOV 2018, pp. 23–26. Association for Computing Machinery, New York (2018)
19. NSM Home: Norma simplex models. https://nsm.nrc.pt/index.html. Accessed 13 Sept 2023
20. Surden, H.: Data visualization projects. https://www.harrysurden.com/wordpress/projects. Accessed 20 May 2020
21. Riigi Teataja: Töölepingu seadus. https://www.riigiteataja.ee/akt/122122012030?leiaKehtiv. Accessed 13 Sept 2023
22. WebGL: WebGL Fundamentals. https://webglfundamentals.org/webgl/lessons/webgl-fundamentals.html. Accessed 13 Sept 2023

23. Three.js: Three.js manual. https://threejs.org/manual/. Accessed 13 Sept 2023
24. Ahmed, R., Muhammed, K., Pappel, I., Draheim, D.: Impact of e-court systems implementation - a case study. Transforming Gov.: People Process Policy **15**(2), 108–128 (2021)
25. Ahmed, R., Ahmed, O., Pappel, I., Draheim, D.: e-Court system evaluation through the user's perspective: applying the end-user computing satisfaction (EUCS) model. In: Proceedings of DGO 2022 - The 23rd Annual International Conference on Digital Government Research. ACM (2022)
26. Ahmed, R.K., et al.: A legal framework for digital transformation: a proposal based on a comparative case study. In: Kö, A., Francesconi, E., Kotsis, G., Tjoa, A.M., Khalil, I. (eds.) EGOVIS 2021. LNCS, vol. 12926, pp. 115–128. Springer, Cham (2021). https://doi.org/10.1007/978-3-030-86611-2_9
27. Saputro, R., Pappel, I., Vainsalu, H., Lips, S., Draheim, D.: Prerequisites for the adoption of the X-Road interoperability and data exchange framework: a comparative study. In: Proceedings of ICEDEG 2020 - The 7th International Conference on eDemocracy & eGovernment, pp. 216–222. IEEE (2020)
28. Metsallik, J., Ross, P., Draheim, D., Piho, G.: Ten years of the e-health system in Estonia. In: Rutle, A., Lamo, Y., MacCaull, W., Iovino, L. (eds.) CEUR Workshop Proceedings, 3rd International Workshop on (Meta)Modelling for Healthcare Systems (MMHS), vol. 2336, pp. 6–15 (2018)

An Enhanced Incentive Mechanism for Crowdsourced Federated Learning Based on Contract Theory and Shapley Value

Tran Khanh Dang[1($\boxtimes$)], Phat T. Tran-Truong[1,2($\boxtimes$)],
and Nguyen Thi Huyen Trang[2]

[1] Ho Chi Minh City University of Industry and Trade, Ho Chi Minh City, Vietnam
khanh@hufi.edu.vn
[2] HCMC University of Technology, VNU-HCM, Ho Chi Minh City, Vietnam
{tttphat.sdh20,ngthtrang}@hcmut.edu.vn

Abstract. Federated learning is a recently dominant learning method for crowdsourced learning systems with diverse scales. It plays a pivotal role in smart city operation technologies, such as cross-organization (e.g., hospitals, banks, etc.), Mobile Ad hoc networks (MANETs), Mobile Edge Computing (MEC), Vehicle Ad hoc Networks (VANETs), and Internet of Things (IoTs). Specifically, this method aggregates a global model from local models trained on the private data of clients. To achieve high accuracy and collaborate effectively, federated learning-based crowdsourced systems need to attract sufficient quality clients. Therefore, a proper incentive mechanism is essential to motivate clients to join and contribute to the best of their ability. However, it is challenging to design such a mechanism due to the fact that each client has different system resources, data size, and effort. This implies that if the incentive mechanism is not well-designed, it will lead to a moral hazard situation, where clients may free-ride and the overall accuracy of the global model will undergo a downward spiral. Furthermore, the clients who contribute most to the accuracy of the global model are not necessarily those with the most decorated power and dedicated work. To address these challenges, we propose a joint optimization mechanism that leverages contract theory and Shapley value. This mechanism helps to reveal private information about clients and quantify their contribution to the global model, so that a suitable and equitable incentive can be constituted for each client.

Keywords: Federated Learning · Incentive Mechanism · Contract Theory · Shapley Value

1 Introduction

In recent years, our society has witnessed incredible researches and applications of Artificial Intelligence (AI) and deep learning techniques on an unprecedented scale. Having been gained significant interest from the research community since 2006, contemporarily AI becomes an umbrella term for smart applications that have a plethora of features, ranging from predicting, providing insights, recommending to users to generating artifacts according to users' needs and reasoning. Regarding to large-scale crowdsourced systems that are ubiquitous in the case of smart city management and operation, AI is also key levers in the "smart" components. It can be exemplified by crowdsourced systems such as: IoTs devices [1], smart monitoring systems [2] or vehicular network [3] that need to be equipped with AI-powered architectures. However, in these contexts, typical AI and deep learning training techniques, which is usually central trained, can not make impact on their strengths. One of the reasons for that is efficiency. Specifically, it takes colossal amount of communication cost and computing power. Additionally, it also needs long time to train that is not suitable for precision healthcare-related crowdsourced systems [4] and haptics-related crowdsourced systems [5] which are also omnipresent due to the advances of virtual/augmented reality (VA/VR) [6] and metaverse [7].

Besides, when it comes to large-scale crowdsourced systems, data privacy of each party is a prime hindering factor. If we train merely by a central server, which means that we need to collect all data from clients to a central server for training, it will violate the data privacy of each party. Indeed, data privacy is an itchy issue that currently gains attraction to model and regulate, for example, Canada's Digital Charter Implementation Act in Consumer Privacy Protection Act (CPPA)[1] in 2022 and Europe's General Data Protection Regulation (GDPR)[2] in 2018. Data minimization herein is a key principle to comply. It advocates that service providers should collect data strictly and selectively to meet specified and necessary purposes.

To tackle these aforementioned problems, we need other training techniques rather than the typical ones. One considered solution is that we train models distributedly. There are two usual ways to distribute tasks: data parallel [8] and model parallel [9]. Regarding to the former, this approach relies on multiple training severs running same models on each shard of data. Albeit by this way, it can accelerate training processes and boost efficiency, it still needs to collect data to a single source before dividing for each server and still faces privacy-related issues [10]. Regarding to the latter, models are trained on same dataset with distinct stages. Specifically, models are split into several part comprising group of layers for distributed training on different servers. Spit learning [9] is a

---

[1] C-27, An Act to enact the Consumer Privacy Protection Act, the Personal Information and Data Protection Tribunal Act and the Artificial Intelligence and Data Act and to make consequential and related amendments to other Acts [First Reading 2022] available at https://www.parl.ca/legisinfo/en/bill/44-1/c-27.

[2] Regulation (EU) 2016/679 of the European Parliament and of the Council of 27 April 2016 on the protection of natural persons with regard to the processing of personal data and on the free movement of such data, and repealing Directive 95/46/EC (General Data Protection Regulation) [2016] OJ L 119/1 available at http://eur-lex.europa.eu/legal-content/EN/TXT/?qid=1416170084502&uri=CELEX:32014R026,2014.

promising technique following this pattern. However, due to the fact that deep learning models are complicated connection of neutrons and layers, it seem to be hard to split network into separate parts. Another approach that is feasible is federated learning-based system [14].

Federated learning is a novel learning paradigm introduced by Google in 2016 [15] that allows to train high-quality centralized models with distributed models on each client's local dataset. The key point of federated learning is that data is retained locally in-devices or clients' storage and servers have no privileges to access clients' data directly. The implication of this is that the technique protects data privacy in term of data minimization principle. To be more specific, each client request to the server to download an initialized model that has been pre-trained on same data distribution. Then, each client fine-tunes the received model on its local private data without sharing them with any other party. After finishing this procedure, they send gradients or weights for server to update. This process is looped until the global model converges (Fig.1).

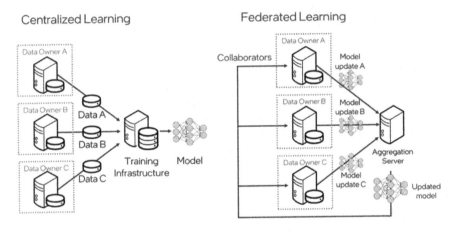

Fig. 1. Central Learning versus Federated Learning

Regarding to the first issue with crowdsourced systems, by leveraging the computation power of each client, federated learning shows its strength to solve the problem of efficiency. Additionally, because of keeping each client's data locally, it also address the data silo problem that each client is not willing to share directly with the others. Regarding to data privacy concerns, notwithstanding that the server can not access to the raw data of clients, it still faces the possibility of breaching data privacy [16]. However, the technique can play as a pivotal data-compliance infrastructure to incorporate with the other privacy-preserving techniques such as [17,18]: differential privacy [19], homomorphic encryption and secure multi-party computation [20]. Thus, federated learning-based systems satisfy requirements of stakeholders in crowdsourced learning systems context.

With aforementioned strength points, federated learning has been an application-rich paradigm for crowdsourced systems. Chief among these is vehicular networks [21]. In the next decade, it is anticipated that society has witnessed a boom of electric cars (EVs) argumented with autonomous features that can make decisions in real-time and near real-time scenarios. In which AI-powered systems are indispensable and federated learning-based is a best-fit solution. Another illustration is analysis of healthcare informatics [22]. Individual's health data is considered as extremely sensitive that easily infringes privacy when being collected and analyzed. If the data do not need to be in motion and the analytic result is still convincing, the cumbersome can be evaded. The other federated learning-based crowdsourced systems can be nobly mentioned are mobile applications - Google Gboard [23], finance [24], IoTs [1], unmanned aerial vehicles (UAVs) [25], MEC infrastructure [26], etc.

Albeit these above potentials, federated learning techniques still face profusion of challenges for mass adoption [13]. Firstly, the federated optimization methods that can work well in the environment of data and system heterogeneity among clients, are still an active research [27]. Besides, achieving high degree of accuracy is not only a prime factor, but also the efficiency of resources related to computing and communication is worthy to ponder [14]. Next, security and privacy issues also raise concern for widespread application [11,16]. The challenges that how to design federated learning architectures incorporated with secure and privacy-preserving techniques effectively and efficiently, have gained attention but still much more holistic research [12,17]. Additionally, motivating clients to join and contribute at their best to overarching federated learning system is another grand conundrum. This implies that designing a suitable incentive mechanism is of paramount importance.

Regarding to model incentive mechanisms for federated learning crowdsourced systems' rewards, there are several major approaches including Stackelberg games [32], auction theory [33], contract theory [28,29] and Shapley value [30,31]. However, each theory-based solution has its own strengths and weaknesses. In this paper, we analyze the current state-of-the-art incentive mechanisms for crowdsourced federated learning-based systems and propose a novel mechanism that fairly allocates rewards among clients and maximizes utility based on the following criteria: computing and communication cost, local accuracy, data size, and contribution to the global model. Specifically, our proposed solution leverages contract theory to make clients reveal their private information and preferences and Shapley value to measure the contribution of each client in the global model. By joint optimization of utility modeled from contract theory and Shapley value, our solution is holistic in term of fairness, group rationality, individual rationality and incentive compatibility. Besides, due to take into consideration multi-factors, our proposal solution helps to motive clients engage in training procedures and avoid "free-rider" phenomenon.

The main contributions of this paper are summarized as follows:

- We present and analyze the strengths and weaknesses of existing solutions for incentivizing and motivating clients to engage in federated learning-based crowdsourced systems.
- We sketch a novel mechanism that has strength points of the existing and remedies the weaknesses simultaneously. This proposed mechanism is based on Shapley value and contract theory.

The rest of the paper is organized as follows: in Sect. 2, we will explain some backgrounds used in our proposed solutions including: federated learning, contract theory and Shapley value. After that, we will review some related works that pinned research directions in Sect. 3. Then, we will display our proposed solution in Sect. 4 and draw conclusions in Sect. 5.

2   Preliminary

2.1   Federated Learning

A standard federated learning procedure usually comprises 4 steps. On the first step, server and clients handshake with others. In this step, if the training task satisfies both a client and server, a secure connection is established with a specific cryptographic protocol to recognize each other and maintain security [20]. In the second step, server transfers model to synchronize among stakeholders. When received the models, each client fine-tunes it on their own local data in step 3. On step 4, clients upload their training weights or gradients for server to aggregate. The server usually generates output according to FederatedAveraging (FedAvg) [14] (Fig. 2) or FedProx [34] algorithm.

Algorithm 1 FederatedAveraging. The K clients are indexed by k; B is the local minibatch size, E is the number of local epochs, and η is the learning rate.

Server executes:
  initialize w_0
  for each round $t = 1, 2, \ldots$ **do**
    $m \leftarrow \max(C \cdot K, 1)$
    $S_t \leftarrow$ (random set of m clients)
    for each client $k \in S_t$ **in parallel do**
      $w_{t+1}^k \leftarrow$ ClientUpdate(k, w_t)
    $w_{t+1} \leftarrow \sum_{k=1}^{K} \frac{n_k}{n} w_{t+1}^k$

ClientUpdate(k, w): *// Run on client k*
  $\mathcal{B} \leftarrow$ (split $\mathcal{P}_k$ into batches of size B)
  for each local epoch i from 1 to E **do**
    for batch $b \in \mathcal{B}$ **do**
      $w \leftarrow w - \eta \nabla \ell(w; b)$
  return w to server

Fig. 2. Federated learning procedure [14]

The last three steps will iterate a number of times until the global model reaches converge.

2.2   Contract Theory

Contract theory [36,37] is a branch of economics and game theory that studies how parties in a transaction can design contracts to protect themselves from opportunistic behavior. It is based on the idea that parties to a contract have different information and incentives, and that this can lead to problems such as moral hazard and adverse selection.

Contract theory provides tools for designing contracts that can mitigate these problems and ensure that both parties to the contract are better off than they would be without the contract. It has been used to design contracts for a variety of transactions, including insurance contracts, loan contracts, and employment contracts.

Here are some of the key concepts in contract theory:

– **Moral hazard:** This occurs when one party to a contract has more information than the other party, and this information asymmetry can lead to the first party taking actions that are not in the best interests of the second party. For example, if an insurance company does not have accurate information about the riskiness of a driver, it may be more likely to issue a policy to a high-risk driver.
– **Adverse selection:** This occurs when one party to a contract has more information about their own characteristics than the other party, and this information asymmetry can lead to the first party being selected for the contract even though they are not the best fit. For example, if a bank does not have accurate information about the creditworthiness of a borrower, it may be more likely to lend money to a risky borrower.
– **Incentive compatibility:** This refers to the ability of a contract to motivate parties to act in a way that is in the best interests of both parties. For example, an insurance contract should be incentive compatible so that the insured party has an incentive to take actions that reduce the risk of loss.
– **Renegotiation:** This refers to the ability of parties to a contract to change the terms of the contract after it has been signed. Renegotiation can be a problem if it allows one party to take advantage of the other party.

Contract theory is a complex and evolving field, but it has become an essential tool for understanding and designing contracts. It has been used to improve the efficiency of a wide variety of transactions, and it is likely to continue to play an important role in the future.

2.3   Shapley Value

The Shapley value [35] is a solution concept in cooperative game theory that assigns a value to each player in a game based on their marginal contribution to the grand coalition. It is named after who introduced it - American mathematician and economist Lloyd Shapley. Specifically, for N players, the Shapley value of the player i is defined as

$$s_i = \sum_{S \subseteq I \setminus i} \frac{1}{N \binom{N-1}{|S|}} [U(S \cup i) - U(S)] \tag{1}$$

The Shapley value has several desirable properties, including:

- **Efficiency:** The sum of the Shapley values for all players is equal to the value of the grand coalition. This properties can be regarded as group rationality due to the fact that all utility will be equitable allocation among players with no remaining reward.
- **Symmetry:** If two players have the same marginal contribution to the grand coalition, then they will receive the same Shapley value. This properties ensure the fairness between two players.
- **Dummy player:** A player who does not contribute to the grand coalition will receive a Shapley value of zero. The Shapley value is often used to allocate resources in cooperative games, such as in federated learning. In federated learning, a group of clients work together to train a machine learning model. The Shapley value can be used to allocate the rewards for participating in the training process.
  The Shapley value can also be used to explain the predictions of machine learning models. In this case, the Shapley value for each feature is the average increase in the model's prediction accuracy when the feature is included.
  The Shapley value is a powerful tool that can be used to allocate resources and explain the predictions of machine learning models. It is a fair and efficient way to distribute rewards and can help to ensure that all players in a game are treated fairly.

The Shapley value is a powerful tool that can be used in a variety of applications. It is a fair and efficient way to distribute rewards, ensure fairness, and explain the predictions of machine learning models. On the other hand, it has a drawback that it is so expensive to compute [30].

3   Related Work

3.1   Equal Amount Allocation Approaches

Beside the approaches based on contract theory and Shapley value, there are other popular themes in literature. For the very first approach, it is allocation of equal amount for each client. This approach also motivates clients for contributing to reap the profit and has the advantages of simplicity since the coordiation server only needs to distribute the total reward by N division for each client. However, in the long run, the approach fails due to the phenomenon of moral hazard and it is even worse with the present of free-riders for the reason that they only need to engage in the system to receive the reward, but not have requirements to preform tasks. The other noble approaches are Stackelberg game-based and auction theory-based approaches.

3.2   Stackelberg Game-Based Approaches

A Stackelberg game is a type of game in which one player, called the leader, moves first and the other player, called the follower, moves second. The leader takes into account the follower's reaction when making their decision, and the follower takes into account the leader's decision when making their decision. Stackelberg games are named after Heinrich Freiherr von Stackelberg, who first studied them in the 1930s. They are often used to model situations where one company has a first-mover advantage over another company. For example, a company that introduces a new product before its competitors can have a significant advantage in the market. In a Stackelberg game, the leader's goal is to maximize their profit, while the follower's goal is to minimize their losses. The leader's strategy is to choose a quantity to produce, and the follower's strategy is to choose a price to charge. The leader's optimal strategy can be found by backward induction. This means that the leader first considers the follower's reaction to all possible quantities that they could produce. Then, the leader chooses the quantity that maximizes their profit given the follower's reaction. The follower's optimal strategy can be found by considering the leader's reaction to all possible prices that they could charge. Then, the follower chooses the price that minimizes their losses given the leader's reaction.

3.3   Auction Theory-Based Approaches

Auction theory is a branch of economics that studies the strategic interactions between buyers and sellers in an auction. It is based on the idea that buyers and sellers have different preferences and information, and that this can lead to different outcomes in an auction.

Auction theory has been used to design auctions for a variety of goods and services, including spectrum licenses, oil leases, and artworks. It has also been used to study the behavior of buyers and sellers in auctions.

Here are some of the key concepts in auction theory:

- Bidders: These are the participants in an auction who are willing to pay for the good or service being auctioned.
- Sellers: These are the participants in an auction who are willing to sell the good or service being auctioned.
- Bidding strategy: This is the plan that a bidder uses to determine how much to bid in an auction.
- Nash equilibrium: This is a situation in which no bidder can improve their outcome by changing their bidding strategy, given the bidding strategies of the other bidders.
- Winner's curse: This is a situation in which the bidder who wins an auction pays more than the value of the good or service being auctioned.

Here are some of the types of auctions: English auction, Dutch auction, Sealed-bid auction and Vickrey auction. In the designs of auction theory-based approaches, the clients will bid (or submit) their information for applying to be a candidate in federated learning training procedure. The server receive these information and decide which clients to be chosen. However, the auction theory shows the weakness that the server can not verify the information in the bidding strategy. Thus, the overall results of global model can be passive affected by those stealthy clients.

4   System Design

4.1   System Overview

A typical federated learning-based crowdsourced systems includes 8 steps (Fig. 3). Firstly, it starts from a group of users or task requester that have a demand to train and predict a task which they have a description about data distribution. These users have a budget to reward all the participants for training a model for them. When received the task information, the coordination server will generate contract types based on utility maximization. After sketching these contract types, the server publishes them for all widespread clients.

For the clients' side, if they have the same or approximate distribution of the server, each will predict the profit and fine if it accepts to perform the local training tasks. These anticipations of the clients come from their system resources: the transmission bandwidth, transmission power, CPU cycle frequency, number of CPU cycles,.etc; their data resources such as: data size; and the local accuracy that it can ensure for a local training iteration. Here, the phenomenon of moral hazard comes from because on the server's side, it can not verify these private information of the clients. Thus, those approaches based on Stackelberg game and auction theory fail to model the cases.

By leveraging contract theory, our proposed solution helps the server to reveal these private information of the clients. Specifically, each contract types comprise of a tuple $(P_i, R_i(P_i))$. In which, P_i presents for the penalty amount of value the client will be charged if it can not fulfill the contract type requirement and the reward $R_i(P_i)$ it can be given if it meets the requirement. This leads to the fact that rational clients will choose that contract type that is suitable with their private information and even, for the reason of loss aversion of slashing penalty, they will choose underestimated contract types.

Specifically, the penalties, rewards and requirement of contract types will be characterized based on Shapley value. The reason for that is to ensure the fairness among the clients in term of the variety of criteria. The existing solutions based on such as the local accuracy or system resources of the clients are not equitable since the fact that the clients with high local accuracy can achieve it by training only small amount of local data and the clients with strong system resources can not ensure the corresponding contribution to the global models. The detail will be presented in Subsect. 4.3. Besides, rational clients would like to receive a positive amount of profit with effort that they have put into. We denote the utility of the client i by U_i ($U_i > 0$) and it is defined by expected reward of the client i minus cost it has spent. We describe meticulously those costs in Subsect. 4.2. In along slide, the rational server also needs to reap profit for attendance in training coordination. Those next two subsections, we also model it.

After signing a contract with the server, all of the clients will stake an amount equalizing to the penalty value and be transfered a model for fine-tuning on their local data. Then, they will submit local trained models to the server for aggregation and evaluation. If the evaluation results show that a local model passes the test, the corresponding client will receive the pre-defined self-chosen reward and the returned stake. Otherwise, it will be lost the deposit.

The above procedures continue until the task requests satisfy or the aggregated model is convergence. The final model will be delivered to the customers.

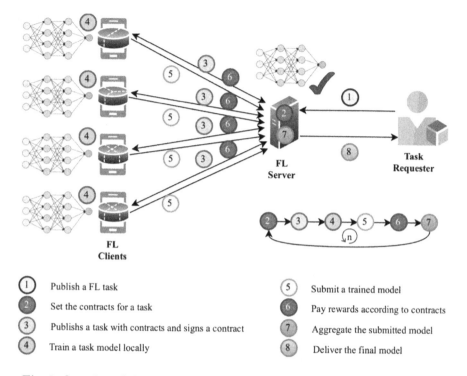

Fig. 3. Overview of the contract theory based federated learning procedure [29]

4.2   Cost Model

Regarding to cost incurrence of both server and clients, it can be decomposed into two kinds: communication an computation cost.

4.2.1   Communication Cost Model

For B is the transmission bandwidth and ρ_i is the transmission power of the data owner i. h_i is the channel gain of peer-to-peer link between client i and the server. N_0 is the background noise. The transmission rate of client i is characterized by:

$$r_i = Bln(1 + \frac{\rho_i h_i}{N_0})$$

(2)

Considering the data size of a local model update σ to be a constant with the same value for all data owners. The transmission time of a local model update of client i is:

$$T_i^{com} = \frac{\sigma}{Bln(1 + \frac{\rho_i h_i}{N_0})} \tag{3}$$

Here, the communication cost of client i is:

$$C_i^{com} = T_i^{com} * \rho_i = \frac{\sigma \rho_i}{Bln(1 + \frac{\rho_i h_i}{N_0})} \tag{4}$$

The communication time of server with each client i is relative with communication time of client i and local accuracy of client i denoted by θ_i. Therefore, it is

$$T_{G_i}^{com} = (1 + \theta_i) * T_i^{com} \tag{5}$$

4.2.2   Computation Cost Model For each client i using m_i local data to train, let f_i be CPU cycle frequency and the number of CPU cycles for training by a single data sample is c_i. Then, we have the computation time of a local iteration [38]:

$$T_i^{comp} = \frac{c_i m_i}{f_i} \tag{6}$$

The computation cost of client i with ζ be the effective capacitance parameter of the computing chipset and local accuracy θ_i is:

$$C_i^{comp} = log(\frac{1}{\theta_i}) * \zeta c_i m_i f_i^2 \tag{7}$$

The server only needs to perform the aggregation phrase. The computation cost of server regarding to client i hereby is:

$$T_{G_i}^{comp} = log(\frac{1}{\theta_i}) * \frac{c_i m_i}{f_i} \tag{8}$$

From Eq. 4 and Eq. 7, we have total cost of client i for a round of local training is:

$$C_i = C_i^{com} + C_i^{comp} = \frac{\sigma \rho_i}{Bln(1 + \frac{\rho_i h_i}{N_0})} + log(\frac{1}{\theta_i}) * \zeta c_i m_i f_i^2 \tag{9}$$

4.3   Proposed Mechanism

For the sake of resolving the problem of moral hazard, we need to design a solution with adverse selection from the clients. Thus, we will design k types of contract including penalty and reward corresponding to penalty. These are $(P_1, R_1(P_1)), (P_2, R_2(P_2)), ..., (P_k, R_k(P_k))$ contract type. These contracts have a property that R has a monotonic relationship with P. This means if $P_1 < P_2 < ... < P_k$, then $R_1 < R_2 < ... < R_k$ correspondingly.

By this approach, if a client i wants to join, it needs to stake a P_i corresponding to its choose. If the client completes the mission by the contract agreement according to contract type, this client will receive the corresponding reward R_i and return P_i. Otherwise, it will be charged P_i and receive no reward. This leads to that a standard quality is ensured. Specifically, in this situation, a client has been given a "stick and carrot" by virtue of the stochasticity of learning procedures, they can be one hundred percent confidence of the output results. Thus, all of the clients when having joined will try their best in order to receive the reward and evade the situation of slashing the P_i value.

Meanwhile, $(P_i, R_i(P_i))$ is calculated based on Shapley value. If $P_1 < P_2 < ... < P_k$, then the Shapley value of them $s_1 < s_2 < ... < s_k$. This also implies that $R_1 < R_2 < ... < R_k$ and $s_1 < s_2 < ... < s_k$ correspondingly. Let $G(\theta_G)$ be the monetary amount that users pay for the federated learning-based crowdsourced system with the global model having accuracy θ_G and U_G be the server's utility, then we have:

$$\sum_{i=1}^{N} s_i = G(\theta_G) \tag{10}$$

Thus, our solution will allocate the rewards to each client as:

$$R_i(P_i) = \frac{s_i}{G(\theta_G)}(G(\theta_G) - U_G) \tag{11}$$

Assuming that the client i signs a contract $(P_i, R(P_i))$ with corresponding s_i, let s_{actual_i} be the actual Shapley value of a training round of client i, then the utility of client i on each round will be:

$$U_i = \begin{bmatrix} R_i - C_i & , \text{ if the } s_{actual_i} >= s_i \\ -C_i - P_i & , \text{ otherwise} \end{bmatrix} \tag{12}$$

From Eq. 9, we have:

$$U_i = \begin{bmatrix} R_i - \left[\dfrac{\sigma \rho_i}{Bln(1+\frac{\rho_i h_i}{N_0})} + log(\frac{1}{\theta_i}) * \zeta c_i m_i f_i^2\right] & , \text{ if the } s_{actual_i} >= s_i \\ -\left[\dfrac{\sigma \rho_i}{Bln(1+\frac{\rho_i h_i}{N_0})} + log(\frac{1}{\theta_i}) * \zeta c_i m_i f_i^2\right] - P_i & , \text{ otherwise} \end{bmatrix} \tag{13}$$

Let α_i $(0 < \alpha_i < 1)$ be the probability that client is successful to pass the Shaley value-based contribution test. Then, we have:

$$U_i = \alpha_i * R_i - \left[\frac{\sigma \rho_i}{Bln(1 + \frac{\rho_i h_i}{N_0})} + log(\frac{1}{\theta_i}) * \zeta c_i m_i f_i^2\right] - (1 - \alpha_i) * P_i \tag{14}$$

From the server's perspective, let ω be satisfaction degree parameter of the server. Then, regarding to a specific type with Eq. 5 and Eq. 8, the server has the cost:

$$C_{G_i} = \omega(T_{G_i}^{comp} + T_{G_i}^{com}) + R_i$$
$$= \omega(1 + \theta_i) * \frac{\sigma \rho_i}{Bln(1+\frac{\rho_i h_i}{N_0})} + \omega log(\frac{1}{\theta_i}) * \frac{c_i m_i}{f_i} + R_i \tag{15}$$

However, this cost of server will exclude the quantity of R_i if the client i can not meet the requirement and the value of server will increase a quantity of P_i for penalizing the client i.

When considering the case that all client i fulfill their duties, we have the utility of server:

$$U_G = G(\theta_G) - \sum_{i=1}^{N}\left[\omega(1+\theta_i)*\frac{\sigma\rho_i}{Bln(1+\frac{\rho_i h_i}{N_0})} + \omega log(\frac{1}{\theta_i})*\frac{c_i m_i}{f_i} + R_i\right] \quad (16)$$

Correspondingly, the utility of the client i when satisfying its choose:

$$U_i = R_i - \left[\frac{\sigma\rho_i}{Bln(1+\frac{\rho_i h_i}{N_0})} + log(\frac{1}{\theta_i})*\zeta c_i m_i f_i^2\right] \quad (17)$$

Meanwhile, corresponding to the client's utility in Eq. 14, we have the the utility of server:

$$U_G = G(\theta_G) - \sum_{i=1}^{N}\left[\omega(1+\theta_i)\frac{\sigma\rho_i}{Bln(1+\frac{\rho_i h_i}{N_0})} + \omega log(\frac{1}{\theta_i})\frac{c_i m_i}{f_i} + \alpha_i R_i - (1-\alpha_i)P_i\right] \quad (18)$$

Thus, our proposed solution needs to solve:

$$\max_{(P_i,R_i(P_i))}(U_G) = max\left[G(\theta_G) - \sum_{i=1}^{N}\left[\frac{\omega(1+\theta_i)\sigma\rho_i}{Bln(1+\frac{\rho_i h_i}{N_0})} + \omega log(\frac{1}{\theta_i})\frac{c_i m_i}{f_i} + \alpha_i R_i - (1-\alpha_i)P_i\right]\right] \quad (19)$$

s.t.

Individual rationality (IR):

$$U_i \geq 0 \iff \alpha_i * R_i - \left[\frac{\sigma\rho_i}{Bln(1+\frac{\rho_i h_i}{N_0})} + log(\frac{1}{\theta_i})*\zeta c_i m_i f_i^2\right] - (1-\alpha_i)*P_i \geq 0 \quad (20)$$

Individual compatibility (IC):

$$\alpha_i * R_i - \left[\frac{\sigma\rho_i}{Bln(1+\frac{\rho_i h_i}{N_0})} + log(\frac{1}{\theta_i})*\zeta c_i m_i f_i^2\right] - (1-\alpha_i)*P_i \geq$$
$$\alpha_i * R_j - \left[\frac{\sigma\rho_i}{Bln(1+\frac{\rho_i h_i}{N_0})} + log(\frac{1}{\theta_j})*\zeta c_i m_i f_i^2\right] - (1-\alpha_i)*P_j, \quad (21)$$
$$\forall j \neq i, i, j \in \overline{1, N}$$

The first condition (Eq. 20) is to ensure that clients when registering to engage in training procedures are rational. The implication of this is that when scrutinizing the cost and contract types (reward and penalty), it makes the decision after calculating positive utility. The individual compatibility condition (Eq. 21) means that if the client i chooses the suitable contract type i, they will reach the maximum utility, albeit the fact that it can train better results than the contract agreement.

5 Conclusion

In conclusion, we present and analyze the strengths and weaknesses of existing incentive mechanisms for motivating clients to participate in federated learning-based crowdsourced systems. We then sketch a novel mechanism that leverages the strengths of existing mechanisms and addresses their weaknesses. In next the step, we will solve the formula for the mechanism and prove its properties. Finally, we will design experiments to demonstrate the effectiveness of the mechanism.

References

1. Nguyen, D.C., Ding, M., Pathirana, P.N., Seneviratne, A., Li, J., Poor, H.V.: Federated learning for internet of things: a comprehensive survey. IEEE Commun. Surv. Tutor. **23**(3), 1622–1658 (2021)
2. Luckey, D., Fritz, H., Legatiuk, D., Dragos, K., Smarsly, K.: Artificial intelligence techniques for smart city applications. In: Proceedings of the 18th International Conference on Computing in Civil and Building Engineering: ICCCBE 2020, pp. 3–15 (2021)
3. Tang, F., Kawamoto, Y., Kato, N., Liu, J.: Future intelligent and secure vehicular network toward 6G: machine-learning approaches. Proc. IEEE **108**(2), 292–307 (2019)
4. Fernández-Caramés, T.M., Froiz-Míguez, I., Blanco-Novoa, O., Fraga-Lamas, P.: Enabling the internet of mobile crowdsourcing health things: a mobile fog computing, blockchain and IoT based continuous glucose monitoring system for diabetes mellitus research and care. Sensors **19**(15), 3319 (2019)
5. Yang, T.H., Kim, J.R., Jin, H., Gil, H., Koo, J.H., Kim, H.J.: Recent advances and opportunities of active materials for haptic technologies in virtual and augmented reality. Adv. Func. Mater. **31**(39), 2008831 (2021)
6. Zhang, Z., Wen, F., Sun, Z., Guo, X., He, T., Lee, C.: Artificial intelligence enabled sensing technologies in the 5G/internet of things era: from virtual reality/augmented reality to the digital twin. Adv. Intell. Syst. **4**(7), 2100228 (2022)
7. Hwang, G.J., Chien, S.Y.: Definition, roles, and potential research issues of the metaverse in education: an artificial intelligence perspective. Comput. Educ. Artif. Intell. **3**, 100082 (2022)
8. Li, S., et al.: Pytorch distributed: Experiences on accelerating data parallel training. arXiv preprint arXiv:2006.15704 (2020)
9. Verbraeken, J., Wolting, M., Katzy, J., Kloppenburg, J., Verbelen, T., Rellermeyer, J.S.: A survey on distributed machine learning. ACM Comput. Surv. (CSUR) **53**(2), 1–33 (2020)
10. Tran-Truong, P.T., Dang, T.K.: pPATE: a pragmatic private aggregation of teacher ensembles framework by sparse vector technique based differential privacy, paillier cryptosystem and human-in-the-loop. In: Dang, T.K., Küng, J., Chung, T.M. (eds.) FDSE 2022. Communications in Computer and Information Science, vol. 1688, pp. 332–346. Springer, Singapore (2022). https://doi.org/10.1007/978-981-19-8069-5_22
11. Ha, T., Dang, T.K., Le, H., Truong, T.A.: Security and privacy issues in deep learning: a brief review. SN Comput. Sci. **1**(5), 253 (2020)

12. Dang, T.K., Truong, P.T.T., Tran, P.T.: Data poisoning attack on deep neural network and some defense methods. In: 2020 International Conference on Advanced Computing and Applications (ACOMP), pp. 15–22. I (2020)
13. Kairouz, P., et al.: Advances and open problems in federated learning. Found. Trends ® Mach. Learn. **14**(1–2), pp. 1–210 (2021)
14. McMahan, B., Moore, E., Ramage, D., Hampson, S., Arcas, B.A.: Communication-efficient learning of deep networks from decentralized data. In: Artificial Intelligence and Statistics, pp. 1273–1282. PMLR (2017)
15. Konečný, J., McMahan, H.B., Yu, F.X., Richtárik, P., Suresh, A.T., Bacon, D.: Federated learning: Strategies for improving communication efficiency. arXiv preprint arXiv:1610.05492 (2016)
16. Nasr, M., Shokri, R., Houmansadr, A.: Comprehensive privacy analysis of deep learning: passive and active white-box inference attacks against centralized and federated learning. In: Proceedings of the 40th IEEE Symposium on Security and Privacy (SP), pp. 739–753 (2019)
17. Truex, S., et al.: A hybrid approach to privacy-preserving federated learning. In: Proceedings of the 12th ACM Workshop on Artificial Intelligence and Security, pp. 1–11 (2019)
18. Bonawitz, K., Kairouz, P., Mcmahan, B., Ramage, D.: Federated learning and privacy. Commun. ACM **65**(4), 90–97 (2022)
19. Abadi, M., et al.: Deep learning with differential privacy. In: Proceedings of the 2016 ACM SIGSAC Conference on Computer and Communications Security, pp. 308–318 (2016)
20. Bonawitz, K., et al.: Practical secure aggregation for privacy-preserving machine learning. In: Proceedings of the 2017 ACM SIGSAC Conference on Computer and Communications Security, pp. 1175–1191 (2017)
21. Pokhrel, S.R., Choi, J.: Federated learning with blockchain for autonomous vehicles: analysis and design challenges. IEEE Trans. Commun. **68**(8), 4734–4746 (2020)
22. Rieke, N., et al.: The future of digital health with federated learning. NPJ Digit. Med. **3**(1), 119 (2020)
23. Hard, A., et al.: Federated learning for mobile keyboard prediction. arXiv preprint arXiv:1811.03604 (2018)
24. Yang, W., Zhang, Y., Ye, K., Li, L., Xu, C.-Z.: FFD: a federated learning based method for credit card fraud detection. In: Chen, K., Seshadri, S., Zhang, L.-J. (eds.) BIGDATA 2019. LNCS, vol. 11514, pp. 18–32. Springer, Cham (2019). https://doi.org/10.1007/978-3-030-23551-2_2
25. Mowla, N.I., Tran, N.H., Doh, I., Chae, K.: Federated learning-based cognitive detection of jamming attack in flying ad-hoc network. IEEE Access **8**, 4338–4350 (2019)
26. Lim, W.Y.B., et al.: Federated learning in mobile edge networks: a comprehensive survey. IEEE Commun. Surv. Tutorials **22**(3), 2031–2063 (2020)
27. Konečný, J., McMahan, H.B., Ramage, D., Richtárik, P.: Federated optimization: Distributed machine learning for on-device intelligence. arXiv preprint arXiv:1610.02527 (2016)
28. Kang, J., Xiong, Z., Niyato, D., Yu, H., Liang, Y.C., Kim, D.I.: Incentive design for efficient federated learning in mobile networks: a contract theory approach. In: 2019 IEEE VTS Asia Pacific Wireless Communications Symposium (APWCS), pp. 1–5 (2019)

29. Liu, Y., Tian, M., Chen, Y., Xiong, Z., Leung, C., Miao, C.: A contract theory based incentive mechanism for federated learning. In: Federated and Transfer Learning, pp. 117–137 (2022)
30. Jia, R., et al.: Towards efficient data valuation based on the Shapley value. In: The 22nd International Conference on Artificial Intelligence and Statistics, pp. 1167–1176 (2019)
31. Ghorbani, A., Zou, J.: Data Shapley: equitable valuation of data for machine learning. In: International Conference on Machine Learning, pp. 2242–2251 (2019)
32. Khan, L.U., et al.: Federated learning for edge networks: resource optimization and incentive mechanism. IEEE Commun. Mag. **58**(10), 88–93 (2020)
33. Le, T.H.T., et al.: An incentive mechanism for federated learning in wireless cellular networks: an auction approach. IEEE Trans. Wirel. Commun. **20**(8), 4874–4887 (2021)
34. Li, T., Sahu, A.K., Zaheer, M., Sanjabi, M., Talwalkar, A., Smith, V.: Federated optimization in heterogeneous networks. Proc. Mach. Learn. Syst. **2**, 429–450 (2020)
35. Roth, A.E. (ed.): The Shapley Value: Essays in Honor of Lloyd S. Cambridge University Press, Shapley (1988)
36. Grossman, S.J., Hart, O.D.: An analysis of the principal-agent problem. In: Dionne, G., Harrington, S.E. (eds.) Foundations of Insurance Economics. Huebner International Series on Risk, Insurance and Economic Security, vol. 14, pp. 302–340. Springer, Dordrecht (1992). https://doi.org/10.1007/978-94-015-7957-5_16
37. Holmstrom, B., Milgrom, P.: Multitask principal-agent analyses: incentive contracts, asset ownership, and job design. J. Law Econ. Organ. **7**(special_issue), pp. 24–52 (1991)
38. Tran, N.H., Bao, W., Zomaya, A., Nguyen, M.N., Hong, C.S.: Federated learning over wireless networks: Optimization model design and analysis. In: IEEE INFOCOM 2019-IEEE Conference on Computer Communications, pp. 1387–1395 (2019)

Biggest Margin Tree for the Multi-class Classification

Tri-Thuc Vo[1(✉)] and Thanh-Nghi Do[1,2]

[1] College of Information Technology Can Tho University, Cantho 92000, Vietnam
{vtthuc,dtnghi}@cit.ctu.edu.vn
[2] UMI UMMISCO 209 (IRD/UPMC) Sorbonne University, Pierre and Marie Curie
University - Paris 6, Paris, France

Abstract. In this paper, we propose the random forest algorithm of biggest margin trees $RF-BMT$ for the multi-class classification. The novel algorithm enhances the classification of chest X-ray images, specifically for distinguishing between normal, covid-19, edema, mass-nodule, and pneumothorax cases. Our approach combines contrastive learning with our proposed algorithm to improve performance and address the limitation of labeled data by leveraging a large amount of unlabeled data for learning features. We propose training the $RF-BMT$ algorithm on the features extracted from the linear fine-tuned model of Momentum Contrast (MoCo), which is trained on Resnet50 architecture. The $RF-BMT$ algorithm plays a role as a replacement for softmax in deep networks. Based on the empirical results, our proposed $RF-BMT$ algorithm demonstrates substantial improvement compared to solely fine-tuning the linear layer both the ImageNet pretrained model and the MoCo pretrained model, reaching an impressive accuracy rate of 88.4%.

Keywords: Biggest margin tree · Multi-class · Self-supervised learning

1 Introduction

The lungs, a vital organ in the human body, play a crucial role in maintaining overall health. Lung diseases can have severe implications, potentially leading to death. In 2017, lung-related diseases were responsible for claiming the lives of over 3.3 million individuals, 3.23 million in 2019, according to the World Health Organization (WHO, source: https://www.who.int). Furthermore, the ongoing Covid-19 pandemic has tragically caused more than 6.95 million deaths and nearly 768 million infections globally (WHO), as of July 05, 2023. For diagnosing lung diseases, chest X-rays are not only the most cost-effective diagnostic tool but also a widely used method for screening and diagnosis. However, accurately interpreting lung diseases based on chest X-ray images requires the expertise of highly skilled radiologists. The subjective nature of lung disease detection using X-ray images can introduce the possibility of inaccurate diagnostic results, thereby potentially compromising the effectiveness of patient treatment. Therefore, building a system capable of assisting in the diagnosis of chest radiographs

T. K. Dang et al. (Eds.): FDSE 2023, CCIS 1925, pp. 34–48, 2023.
https://doi.org/10.1007/978-981-99-8296-7_3

would offer significant advantages to patients. Such a system would not only help reduce treatment costs but also contribute to improving the physical and mental well-being of individuals affected by lung diseases.

In recent years, deep learning has been widely adopted to address challenges related to medical image data, including X-rays, computed tomography (CT), and magnetic resonance imaging (MRI). These efforts have yielded promising results, as demonstrated in various studies [3,7,13,25,28]. However, deep learning heavily relies on large volumes of annotated data, which poses a significant challenge in the medical domain. Limited availability of labeled medical data can be attributed to factors such as domain expertise, privacy regulations, cost, and time constraints associated with the data labeling process. To overcome these limitations, self-supervised learning has emerged as an alternative approach. This method leverages the abundance of unlabeled data to learn representations or features without explicit human annotations. By utilizing unlabeled data, self-supervised learning has achieved remarkable outcomes, enabling the generation of pretrained models that can be fine-tuned with a limited amount of labeled data [10–12,20]. The construction of these pretrained models involves maximizing agreement between different views of the same image while minimizing agreement between different images based on a specific loss function. Compared to traditional supervised learning on labeled data, self-supervised learning demonstrated improved accuracy in various studies [10–12,20,36]. This showcases the potential and effectiveness of self-supervised learning in medical image analysis tasks, where limited labeled data is a common challenge.

In this study, a new algorithm $RF-BMT$ is proposed to improve the efficiency of multi-class classification. Our proposal involves combining the self-supervised learning with our proposed algorithm to enhance the performance of classifying X-ray images of lung diseases; namely normal, Covid-19, edema, mass nodule, and pneumothorax. The linear fine-tuned MoCo pretrained model and ImageNet pretrained model are employed as feature extractors on labeled X-ray images. Classifiers are trained on the extracted features. Our classification algorithm $(RF-BMT)$ demonstrates higher performance compared to other algorithms such as SVM [37], LightGBM [24], XGBoost [9], and CatBoost [18].

The structure of this paper is as follows: Sect. 2 provides a brief overview of the related research on the classification of lung diseases using X-ray images. Our proposed algorithm is presented in Sect. 3. The method for the X-ray image classification is illustrated in part 4 .The experimental results are presented in Sect. 5. Finally, Sect. 6 encompasses the conclusion of our study along with future directions for research.

2 Related Work

Disease detection from chest X-ray images has been extensively employed using deep learning techniques. In a study [33], Rajpurkar et al. introduced a CNN architecture named CheXNeXt, designed to classify 14 distinct pathologies based on chest X-ray images. A novel approach was suggested by the authors in [41], involving local variance analysis and probabilistic neural networks to solve the problem of lung carcinomas classification, attaining a performance accuracy of 92%. Convolutional Neural Networks (CNNs) were proposed to address the challenge of X-ray image classification, achieving an impressive accuracy 86% for twelve classes [27]. Furthermore, a transfer learning approach using two popular CNN models, VGG16 and InceptionV3, was applied in [42] for pneumonia classification from chest X-ray images. Researchers in [14] proposed the combination of five deep learning models with transfer learning for pneumonia detection from chest X-ray images. Through their ensemble model, they achieved an experimental accuracy of 96.4%. To detect lung abnormalities from chest X-ray and CT images, the authors [4] put forth a modified AlexNet deep learning framework combined with SVM, achieving a notable accuracy 92%.

Since the onset of the Covid-19 pandemic, numerous studies have focused on employing deep learning techniques to diagnose Covid-19 using chest X-ray images. In [2], the authors presented a model framework called COVID-CAPS, based on Capsule Networks, for the diagnosis of Covid-19 from X-ray images. The COVID-CAPS model exhibited promising results with an overall accuracy of 95.7%. Hemdan et al. introduced a novel deep learning framework named COVIDX-Net in [22]. The authors employed seven architectures of deep network models to construct this framework, enabling the classification of X-ray images into negative and positive cases of Covid-19. Notably, the COVIDX-Net framework achieved exceptional accuracy, with f1-scores of 89% and 91% for normal cases and Covid-19 cases, respectively. In a study conducted by Tulin Ozturk et al. in [30], the DarkCovidNet model was introduced to enable automated Covid-19 diagnosis using X-ray images. It achieved 98.08% accuracy in binary (Covid-19 and No-Findings) classification and 87.02% accuracy in multiclass classification including Covid-19, No-Findings, and pneumonia. Researchers in [16] introduced a novel approach by integrating SVM with deep networks for the detection of Covid-19 from chest X-ray images. Their proposed method achieved an impressive accuracy of 96.16%. In [8], Chakraborty et al. proposed a deep learning method including segmentation and training deep neural network model to detect Covid-19 using chest X-ray images.

The machine learning community has recently shown a great deal of interest in self-supervised learning. This approach has gained attention due to its ability to leverage unlabeled datasets for training models, resulting in improved performance in downstream tasks such as fine-tuning with labeled data. The utilization of self-supervised learning offers a promising avenue for enhancing the capabilities of machine learning models and unlocking their potential through the utilization of unannotated data. Researchers in [10,11] introduced the SimCLR framework, which is a self-supervised learning algorithm that was developed to enhance ImageNet performance. In [12,20], the authors presented Momentum Contrast as a contrastive learning approach and demonstrated its effectiveness by achieving competitive results through fine-tuning a linear model on the ImageNet dataset. In [36], Sowrirajan et al. proposed a classification method called MoCo-CXR, which utilizes the contrastive learning technique Momentum Contrast for classifying X-ray images. This approach aimed to identify various lung diseases including Pleural Effusion, Tuberculosis, and Atelectasis. Experimental results demonstrated that the MoCo-CXR method outperformed the approach of solely fine-tuning the ImageNet pretrained model, showcasing its superior performance.

3   Random Forest of Biggest Margin Trees

Algorithm 1: RF-BMT$(D, p', \epsilon, \omega)$ for the multi-class classification

---

   input :

        D: training dataset of n datapoints in p dimensions with c classes

        $ntree$: number of random large margin trees

        p': number of random dimensions used for oblique splits $(p' < p)$

        ϵ: error tolerant acceptance at terminal nodes

        ω: minimum size of terminal nodes

   output:

        $RF-BMT$ model

1 **begin**

2     $RF-BMT = \{\}$

3   **for** $t \leftarrow 1$ **to** $ntree$ **do**

4   Bootstrap B_t is created by random sampling with replacement n datapoints from the original training set D

5         $BMT_t = BMT(B_t, p', \epsilon, \omega)$

6         $RF-BMT.append(BMT_t)$

7   **end**

8 **end**

Our random forest algorithm $RF-BMT$ (as illustrated in Algorithm 1) learns an ensemble of biggest margin trees for the multi-class classification. Instead of performing uni-variate splitting like in the decision trees [6,32] of classical random forests [5], the biggest margin tree algorithm (denoted by BMT as illustrated in Algorithm 2) uses support vector machines (SVMs [37]) for multi-variate splitting, thereby taking into account the dependencies between dimensions. It increases the strength of the trees within our random forest $RF-BMT$.

The biggest margin tree algorithm BMT learns the classification model BMT_t from the bootstrap B_t which is created by random sampling with replacement n datapoints from the original trainset D. The partitioning process of the algorithm is described as follows. A data partition D consists of n datapoints in p dimensions with c classes. If the number of datapoints n is smaller than the minimum size ω or the error rate is smaller than the error tolerant acceptance

---

Algorithm 2: BMT$(D, p', \epsilon, \omega)$ for the multi-class classification

---

    input :

        D: learning dataset of n datapoints in p dimensions with c classes

        p': number of random dimensions used for oblique splits ($p' < p$)

        ϵ: error tolerant acceptance at terminal nodes

        ω: minimum size of terminal nodes

    output:

        LMT model

1   **begin**

2   Computing the *error_rate* of D upon the majority class in D

3   **if** *(n $\leq$ ω) or (error_rate $\leq$ ϵ)* **then**

4   Assigning the majority class in D to the terminal node L

5   Return the terminal node L

6   **else**

7   Biggest margin $\gamma = -\infty$

8   Optimal hyper-plane $H^* = null$

9   Randomly sampling p' dimensions

10   **for** $c_i \leftarrow 1$ **to** c **do**

11             $H_i = SVM(D, p', c_i)$ (class c_i versus All)

12   **if** $margin(H_i) > \gamma$ **then**

13                 $\gamma = margin(H_i)$

14                 $H^* = H_i$

15   **end**

16   **end**

17   H^* splits D into D_{pos} (positive part) and D_{neg} (negative part)

18   **BMT**$(D_{pos}, p', \epsilon, \omega)$

19   **BMT**$(D_{neg}, p', \epsilon, \omega)$

20   **end**

21   **end**

ϵ, then data partition D becomes a leaf node labeled as the majority vote of the classes within data partition D. Otherwise, the training BMT algorithm learns c binary SVMs using p' random dimensions where the ith one separates the ith class from the rest (i.e. H_1, H_2, H_3 in Fig. 1). After that, the BMT algorithm selects the binary SVM model H^* (i.e. H_1 in Fig. 1) corresponding to the biggest margin, to partition D into the positive part D_{pos} and the negative part D_{neg}. Furthermore, when training binary SVMs, it is essential to assign error weights to datapoints that are inversely proportional to the total number of datapoints in their class. The BMT algorithm continues recursively partitioning the positive part D_{pos} and the negative part D_{neg}. In such a way the BMT algorithm will reach terminal-nodes (leaves). The error bound and the algorithmic complexity of $RF-BMT$ have been studied in a such approach [17].

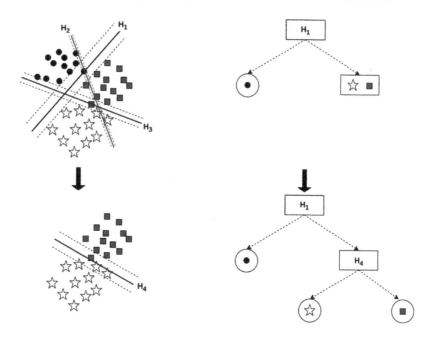

Fig. 1. Biggest margin tree for the multi-class classification

4   Methodology for the X-Ray Image Classification

4.1   Chest X-Ray Image Data Set

For our study, we collected a real chest X-ray image dataset from publicly available sources. The CheXpert X-ray dataset [23] served as the unlabeled dataset for training the contrastive learning model using MoCo. This dataset was originally published by the research team at Stanford University in 2019. In our training process, we utilized a total of 120,000 images from the CheXpert dataset to train the MoCo model.

The dataset used in our study consists of five labels aimed at identifying different conditions: normal cases representing healthy individuals, positive Covid-19 infected patients, lung diseases unrelated to Covid-19 such as edema, mass nodule, and pneumothorax. We gathered this dataset from various published sources [15, 19, 23, 26, 29, 34, 35, 38–40, 43], and in total, it comprises 98,996 images. Each X-ray image was assigned to one of the five classes. To ensure consistency, all images in the dataset were resized to dimensions of 224×224. The labeled dataset was divided into three subsets: a train set (70%), a valid set (15%), and a test set (15%). Further details about the dataset can be found in Table 1. Additionally, Fig. 2 provides visual examples of chest X-ray images belonging to each of the five classes.

Table 1. Dataset of chest X-ray.

Label	Trainset	Validset	Testset
Normal	18.425	3.949	3.948
Covid19	14.252	3.054	3.054
Edema	23.240	4.980	4.980
Mass-nodule	4.077	873	874
Pneumothorax	9.303	1.993	1.994

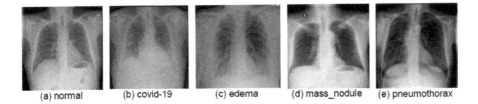

(a) normal   (b) covid-19   (c) edema   (d) mass_nodule   (e) pneumothorax

Fig. 2. Sample of chest x-ray images.

4.2   MoCo Self-supervised Learning

Momentum Contrast (MoCo) [8, 14] is self-supervised learning techniques that demonstrated promising outcomes. These techniques utilize unlabeled data to generate pretrained models by training a visual representation encoder with a loss function. The pretrained models are then fine-tuned using labeled data. MoCo is specifically known for its ability to construct large and consistent dictionaries for learning from unlabeled data, employing a contrastive loss function called InfoNCE. This loss function measures the agreement between positive image pairs and negative images. Positive image pairs are obtained by applying two data augmentation operators in the same image. A queue-based dictionary is utilized for storing samples with updates performed by enqueuing the current mini-batch and dequeuing the oldest mini-batch.

The flowchart for the classification of lung diseases based on X-ray images is depicted in Fig. 3. The first step involves training the MoCo architecture using the CheXpert dataset [23]. The backbone of the MoCo architecture is ResNet50 [21] that is initialized with parameters from ImageNet. Subsequently, the backbone is trained using MoCo with contrastive learning, which involves applying image rotation and image flip transformations. MoCo incorporates various data augmentation techniques on unlabeled data to generate positive image pairs. These techniques include random crop, grayscale, jitter, horizontal flip (MoCo v1 [20]), and Gaussian blurring (MoCo v2 [12]). However, we employed two specific data augmentation techniques: random rotation ($10°$) and horizontal flip. These techniques were used to create pairs of positive images through the contrastive learning approach, using a loss function similar to the one described by the authors in [36]. The training model for contrast learning on MoCo involves

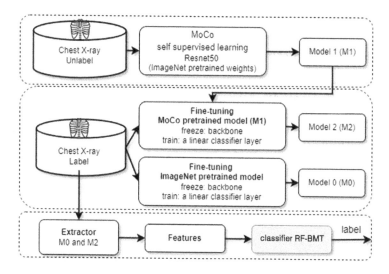

Fig. 3. Diagram for classifying chest X ray images.

the following parameters: batch size of 32, learning rate of 10^{-3}, momentum of 0.9, weight decay of 10^{-3}, optimizer as Adam, and 20 epochs. The outcome obtained from this initial step using MoCo is referred to as Model 1.

The second step involves supervised learning on labeled dataset, where Model 1 is fine-tuned by freezing all layers of the backbone model and training only the linear classifier layer, resulting in Model 2. Moreover, we also conduct experiments by fine-tuning the linear classifier on the ImageNet pretrained model, getting in Model 0. The parameters are set as follows: epochs=100, batch size=32, learning rate=30, momentum=0.9, and optimizer=Adam.

The third step, our objective is to leverage the linear fine-tuned model, known as Model 0 and Model 2, to enhance X-ray image classification by integrating it with our classifier. Essentially, we aim to replace the softmax layer in deep networks with $RF-BMT$ classifier. To achieve this, we propose utilizing Model 0 and Model 2 as feature extractors. The labeled dataset is considered as input to the Model 0 and the Model 2 to extract features (representations). Subsequently, we train our proposed algorithm $(RF-BMT)$. Furthermore, other classification algorithms such as SVM [37], LightGBM [24], XGBoost [9], and CatBoost [18] are also trained on these features to compare the results with our proposed algorithm. Experimental results on the testset, our $RF-BMT$ algorithm showcased superior classification performance when compared to the other four classification algorithms. Additionally, it achieved a significant improvement in accuracy compared to solely fine-tuning a linear layer on both the ImageNet pretrained model and the MoCo pretrained model. Detailed experimental results are presented in Sect. 5.

5 Results

5.1 Experimental Setup

We have successfully deployed a program for the purpose of classifying lung diseases in X-ray images. We have utilized various libraries such as Keras, Tensorflow [1], Scikit-learn [31], and Pytorch. All the experimental outcomes were obtained by executing the program on a computer system with the following architecture: Operating system (Ubuntu 20.04.5), CPU: Intel(R) Core^{TM} i5-10400 CPU @ 2.90GHz × 12, GPU: the NVIDIA GeForce RTX 3060 12GB GDDR6 - 3584 CUDA cores, and RAM: 16 GB.

5.2 Classification Results

Table 2. Classification accuracy on the test set.

No	Method	Accuraccy(%)
1	Model0(M0)	82.9
2	Features(M0) + SVM	83.7
3	Features(M0) + LightGBM	84.4
4	Features(M0) + CatBoost	83.2
5	Features(M0) + XGBoost	84.4
6	**Features(M0) + *RF-BMT* (our)**	**86.2**
7	Model2(M2)	84.8
8	Features(M2) + SVM	87.7
9	Features(M2) + LightGBM	87.4
10	Features(M2) + CatBoost	86.3
11	Features(M2) + XGBoost	87.3
12	**Features(M2) + *RF-BMT* (our)**	**88.4**

Table 3. Accuracy improvement of five classifiers compare to the linear fine-tuned ImageNet pretrained model (M0).

No	Method	Improved Accuraccy(%)
1	Features(M0) + SVM	+0.8
2	Features(M0) + LightGBM	+1.5
3	Features(M0) + CatBoost	+0.3
4	Features(M0) + XGBoost	+1.5
5	**Features(M0) + *RF-BMT* (our)**	**+3.3**

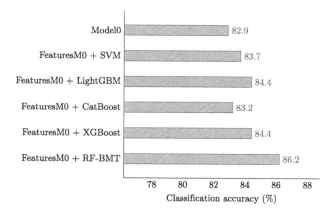

Fig. 4. Classification accuracy based on features extracted from the ImageNet-pretrained model

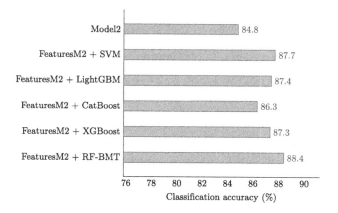

Fig. 5. Classification accuracy based on features extracted from the MoCo-pretrained model

Table 4. Accuracy improvement of five classifiers compare to the linear fine-tuned MoCo pretrained model (M2).

No	Method	Improved Accuraccy(%)
1	Features(M2) + SVM	+2.9
2	Features(M2) + LightGBM	+2.6
3	Features(M2) + CatBoost	+1.5
4	Features(M2) + XGBoost	+2.5
5	**Features(M2) + *RF-BMT* (our)**	**+3.6**

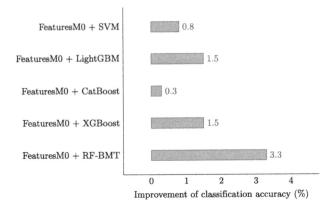

Fig. 6. Accuracy improvement of five classifiers compare to the linear fine-tuned ImageNet pretrained model (M0)

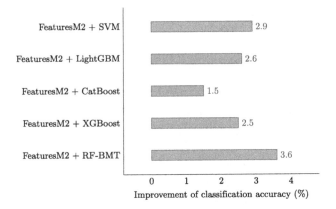

Fig. 7. Accuracy improvement of five classifiers compare to the linear fine-tuned MoCo pretrained model (M2)

The experimental results are illustrated in Table 2, Fig. 4, and Fig. 5. Model 0 (M0) is created by fine-tuning a linear layer on the labeled dataset from an ImageNet-pretrained model. On the other hand, Model 2 (M2) is obtained by fine-tuning the linear layer on MoCo model using chest X-ray images. We conducted experiments involving feature extraction from both M0 and M2 models, as well as training the classifier using various methods, including $RF-BMT$, SVM [37], LightGBM [24], XGBoost [9], and CatBoost [18]. Based on the experimental results, our proposed algorithm achieves the highest classification accuracy when compared to four other classification algorithms. The superior performance of our algorithm ($RF-BMT$) is observed based on features extracted from both the linear fine-tuned ImageNet pretrained model and the linear fine-tuned MoCo pretrained model.

After extracting features from the linear fine-tuned ImageNet pretrained model, we evaluated the performance of several classifiers. The $RF-BMT$ classifier achieved the highest accuracy of 86.4%, making it the top-performing classifier. Following closely behind, we have LightGBM and XGBoost with an accuracy of 84.4%. SVM performed slightly lower with an accuracy of 83.7%, while CatBoost achieved the lowest accuracy of 83.2%. By extracting features from M2 and training them on five classifiers, we achieved impressive accuracies exceeding 86%. Our algorithm exhibited the highest accuracy of 88.4%, while CatBoost obtained the lowest accuracy of 86.3%. SVM ranked second with an accuracy of 87.7%, closely followed by LightGBM at 87.4% and XGBoost at 87.3%. These results demonstrate the effectiveness of our algorithm in accurately classifying the data.

Details of the accuracy improvement are shown in Table 3, Table 4, Fig. 6, and Fig. 7. Our proposed algorithm showcases remarkable efficiency in X-ray image classification, surpassing the accuracy obtained through solely linear fine-tuning on ImageNet pretrained and MoCo pretrained models. The $RF-BMT$ algorithm demonstrates superior improvement compared to the other four classifiers, achieving an increase of 3.3% for M0 and 3.6% for M2. This highlights the effectiveness and superiority of the $RF-BMT$ algorithm in enhancing the performance of the classification models.

6   Conclusion and Future Works

We introduced a novel algorithm called $RF-BMT$ (Random Forest with Biggest Margin Trees) designed to enhance the performance of multi-class classification. Our algorithm experimented the classification of chest X-ray images, specifically focusing on distinguishing between normal, Covid-19, edema, mass-nodule, and pneumothorax cases. We leveraged contrastive learning to learn features from unlabeled data, enhancing data efficiency and addressing limited labeled data in X-ray images. Our contributions encompass two key aspects. Firstly, we propose the $RF-BMT$ algorithm, which significantly improves the efficiency of multi-class classification. Secondly, we gather two datasets: an unlabeled dataset and a labeled dataset, categorized into five classes. The experimental results demonstrate the superior performance of $RF-BMT$ in comparison to the other four classifiers when trained on features extracted from both the linear fine-tuned ImageNet pretrained model and the linear fine-tuned MoCo pretrained model. Our algorithm achieved the highest accuracy of 88.4% in X-ray image classification, representing a significant improvement of +3.6% compared to solely fine-tuning the linear classifier layer on the MoCo pretrained model.

In the near future, we plan to collect more chest X-ray images with various lung diseases. We'll experiment with different self-supervised learning techniques and deep networks, combined with classifiers to compare their performance.

Acknowledgements. This work has been funded by the STARWARS project (STormwAteR and WastewAteR networkS heterogeneous data AI-driven management). The authors would like to particularly thank for the STARWARS' support.

References

1. Abadi, M., et al.: Tensorflow: large-scale machine learning on heterogeneous distributed systems. arXiv preprint arXiv:1603.04467 (2016)
2. Afshar, P., Heidarian, S., Naderkhani, F., Oikonomou, A., Plataniotis, K.N., Mohammadi, A.: COVID-caps: a capsule network-based framework for identification of COVID-19 cases from x-ray images. Pattern Recogn. Lett. **138**, 638–643 (2020)
3. Akkus, Z., Galimzianova, A., Hoogi, A., Rubin, D.L., Erickson, B.J.: Deep learning for brain MRI segmentation: state of the art and future directions. J. Digit. Imaging **30**, 449–459 (2017)
4. Bhandary, A., et al.: Deep-learning framework to detect lung abnormality-a study with chest x-ray and lung CT scan images. Pattern Recogn. Lett. **129**, 271–278 (2020)
5. Breiman, L.: Random forests. Mach. Learn. **45**(1), 5–32 (2001)
6. Breiman, L., Friedman, J.H., Olshen, R.A., Stone, C.: Classification and Regression Trees. Wadsworth International (1984)
7. Castiglioni, I., et al.: Ai applications to medical images: from machine learning to deep learning. Physica Med. **83**, 9–24 (2021)
8. Chakraborty, S., Murali, B., Mitra, A.K.: An efficient deep learning model to detect COVID-19 using chest x-ray images. Int. J. Environ. Res. Public Health **19**(4), 2013 (2022)
9. Chen, T., Guestrin, C.: XGBoost: a scalable tree boosting system. In: Proceedings of the 22nd ACM SIGKDD International Conference on Knowledge Discovery and Data Mining, pp. 785–794 (2016)
10. Chen, T., Kornblith, S., Norouzi, M., Hinton, G.: A simple framework for contrastive learning of visual representations. arXiv preprint arXiv:2002.05709 (2020)
11. Chen, T., Kornblith, S., Swersky, K., Norouzi, M., Hinton, G.: Big self-supervised models are strong semi-supervised learners. arXiv preprint arXiv:2006.10029 (2020)
12. Chen, X., Fan, H., Girshick, R., He, K.: Improved baselines with momentum contrastive learning. arXiv preprint arXiv:2003.04297 (2020)
13. Chlap, P., Min, H., Vandenberg, N., Dowling, J., Holloway, L., Haworth, A.: A review of medical image data augmentation techniques for deep learning applications. J. Med. Imaging Radiat. Oncol. **65**(5), 545–563 (2021)
14. Chouhan, V., et al.: A novel transfer learning based approach for pneumonia detection in chest x-ray images. Appl. Sci. **10**(2), 559 (2020)
15. Cohen, J.P., Morrison, P., Dao, L., Roth, K., Duong, T.Q., Ghassemi, M.: COVID-19 image data collection: Prospective predictions are the future. arXiv preprint arXiv:2006.11988 (2020)
16. Do, T.N., Le, V.T., Doan, T.H.: SVM on top of deep networks for COVID-19 detection from chest x-ray images. J. Inf. Commun. Converg. Eng. (2022)
17. Do, T., Lenca, P., Lallich, S.: Classifying many-class high-dimensional fingerprint datasets using random forest of oblique decision trees. Vietnam J. Comput. Sci. **2**(1), 3–12 (2015)
18. Dorogush, A.V., Ershov, V., Gulin, A.: CatBoost: gradient boosting with categorical features support. arXiv preprint arXiv:1810.11363 (2018)
19. Haghanifar, A., Majdabadi, M.M., Ko, S.: COVID-19 chest x-ray image repository (2021). https://figshare.com/articles/dataset/COVID-19/_Chest/_X-Ray/_Image/_Repository/12580328

20. He, K., Fan, H., Wu, Y., Xie, S., Girshick, R.: Momentum contrast for unsupervised visual representation learning. In: Proceedings of the IEEE/CVF Conference on Computer Vision and Pattern Recognition, pp. 9729–9738 (2020)

21. He, K., Zhang, X., Ren, S., Sun, J.: Deep residual learning for image recognition. In: Proceedings of the IEEE Conference on Computer Vision and Pattern Recognition, pp. 770–778 (2016)

22. Hemdan, E.E.D., Shouman, M.A., Karar, M.E.: COVIDX-Net: a framework of deep learning classifiers to diagnose COVID-19 in x-ray images. arXiv preprint arXiv:2003.11055 (2020)

23. Irvin, J., et al.: CheXpert: a large chest radiograph dataset with uncertainty labels and expert comparison (2019)

24. Ke, G., et al.: LightGBM: a highly efficient gradient boosting decision tree. In: Advances in Neural Information Processing Systems, vol. 30 (2017)

25. Ker, J., Wang, L., Rao, J., Lim, T.: Deep learning applications in medical image analysis. IEEE Access 6, 9375–9389 (2017)

26. Kermany, D.S., et al.: Identifying medical diagnoses and treatable diseases by image-based deep learning. Cell 172(5), 1122–1131 (2018)

27. Kesim, E., Dokur, Z., Olmez, T.: X-ray chest image classification by a small-sized convolutional neural network. In: 2019 Scientific Meeting on Electrical-Electronics & Biomedical Engineering and Computer Science (EBBT), pp. 1–5. IEEE (2019)

28. Liang, C.H., Liu, Y.C., Wu, M.T., Garcia-Castro, F., Alberich-Bayarri, A., Wu, F.Z.: Identifying pulmonary nodules or masses on chest radiography using deep learning: external validation and strategies to improve clinical practice. Clin. Radiol. 75(1), 38–45 (2020)

29. Nguyen, H.Q., et al.: VinDR-CXR: an open dataset of chest x-rays with radiologist's annotations. Sci. Data 9(1), 429 (2022)

30. Ozturk, T., Talo, M., Yildirim, E.A., Baloglu, U.B., Yildirim, O., Acharya, U.R.: Automated detection of COVID-19 cases using deep neural networks with x-ray images. Comput. Biol. Med. 121, 103792 (2020)

31. Pedregosa, F., et al.: Scikit-learn: machine learning in python. J. Mach. Learn. Res. 12, 2825–2830 (2011)

32. Quinlan, J.R.: C4.5: Programs for Machine Learning. Morgan Kaufmann, San Mateo, CA (1993)

33. Rajpurkar, P., et al.: Deep learning for chest radiograph diagnosis: a retrospective comparison of the cheXNeXt algorithm to practicing radiologists. PLoS Med. 15(11), e1002686 (2018)

34. Saltz, J., et al.: Stony brook university COVID-19 positive cases. Cancer Imaging Archive 4 (2021)

35. Shiraishi, J., et al.: Development of a digital image database for chest radiographs with and without a lung nodule: receiver operating characteristic analysis of radiologists' detection of pulmonary nodules. Am. J. Roentgenol. 174(1), 71–74 (2000)

36. Sowrirajan, H., Yang, J., Ng, A.Y., Rajpurkar, P.: MoCo pretraining improves representation and transferability of chest x-ray models. In: Medical Imaging with Deep Learning, pp. 728–744. PMLR (2021)

37. Vapnik, V.: The Nature of Statistical Learning Theory, 2nd edn. Springer, Berlin (2000)

38. Vayá, M.D.L.I., et al.: BIMCV COVID-19+: a large annotated dataset of RX and CT images from COVID-19 patients. arXiv preprint arXiv:2006.01174 (2020)

39. Wang, X., Peng, Y., Lu, L., Lu, Z., Bagheri, M., Summers, R.M.: ChestX-ray8: hospital-scale chest x-ray database and benchmarks on weakly-supervised classi-

fication and localization of common thorax diseases. In: Proceedings of the IEEE Conference on Computer Vision and Pattern Recognition, pp. 2097–2106 (2017)

40. Winther, H., et al.: Dataset: COVID-19 Image Repository. Hannover Medical School, Hannover, Germany (2020)

41. Woźniak, M., Połap, D., Capizzi, G., Sciuto, G.L., Kośmider, L., Frankiewicz, K.: Small lung nodules detection based on local variance analysis and probabilistic neural network. Comput. Meth. Programs Biomed. **161**, 173–180 (2018)

42. Yadav, S.S., Jadhav, S.M.: Deep convolutional neural network based medical image classification for disease diagnosis. J. Big Data **6**(1), 1–18 (2019)

43. Zawacki, A., et al.: SIIM-ACR pneumothorax segmentation (2019). https://kaggle.com/competitions/siim-acr-pneumothorax-segmentation

Maintenance Algorithms for 0-Complete Trees with Improved Space Utilization

H. K. Dai[1(✉)] and K. Furusawa[2]

[1] Computer Science Department, Oklahoma State University, Stillwater, OK 74078, USA
dai@cs.okstate.edu
[2] Department of Computer Science, University of North Dakota, Grand Forks, ND 58202, USA

Abstract. A compact 0-complete tree is an indexing mechanism that can be effectively used for large databases with long and variable-size keys. Compared to B-trees, compact 0-complete trees eliminate search values from secondary indices altogether. They are replaced with small surrogates whose relatively short representation is adequate for most practical key lengths. Hence the secondary indices are simply hierarchical collections of (surrogate, pointer)-pairs. However, the overall storage performance of a compact 0-complete tree structure suffers from its dependency on the distribution of keys. We complete our previous study of structural modification of 0-complete trees, which improves their space utilization by reducing page-underfilling, with the design and implementation of coupled retrieval and maintenance algorithms. This is achieved by introducing the notion of a sequence set that is analogous to that of B^+-trees.

Keywords: index structure · B-tree · 0-complete tree

1 Introduction

B-trees provide a general and practical solution to the problem of indexing large files [1]. Their effectiveness and widespread use as index structures, are a consequence of their support of relatively fast and balanced access, good storage utilization (at least 50%), gradual expansion and shrinking, ordered sequential access to data items, insurance against the catastrophic behavior, and ease of implementation. Comparing B-tree retrieval to extendible hashing techniques [4], the former does not depend on storage of data in particular locations. Consequently, B-trees can be used to support secondary access paths. B-trees naturally tend to be the method of choice, since they provide both satisfactory primary and good secondary access to data sets.

However, unlike extensible hashing or compact 0-complete trees, B-tree index structures must duplicate the indexed attribute values of the keys. The replication of many secondary index values results in an index structure whose size may exceed that of the database itself. The inclusion of search values within pages of B-trees may significantly decrease the branching factor of the page, and increase tree-depth and retrieval time.

Compact 0-complete trees are introduced in [7], and are studied and analyzed in [9–11], and [8]. These index structures eliminate search values from secondary indices altogether: they are replaced with small surrogates whose typical eight-bit length will be adequate for most practical key lengths. Hence the secondary indices are simply hierarchical collections of (surrogate, pointer)-pairs. This organization reduces the size of the secondary index structure by 50–80% and increases the branching factor of the trees, thus providing a reduced number of disk accesses per exact-match query.

Although compact 0-complete trees provide an attractive alternative, there are two shortcomings which the other commonly used index structures such as B-tree do not have:

1. Page-underfilling after split, and
2. Empty nodes inserted at the leaf-level.

The cause of the two problems is that the overall performance of a compact 0-complete tree structure heavily depends on the key distribution and could possibly create many underfilled pages and empty leaf-nodes. Although the expected storage utilization in compact 0-complete trees is much better compared to B-trees and prefix B-trees, some particular non-uniformly distributed data could seriously degrade storage utilization. The empirical study in [7] demonstrates that a compact 0-complete tree structure behaves as theoretically predicted when input record keys are uniformly distributed over the key space.

Although compact 0-complete trees analytically outperform other commonly used index structures such as B-trees and prefix B-trees, the above-mentioned shortcomings could be a barrier in practice since real key distributions tend to be rather skewed. It is a well-known fact that for B-trees and prefix B-trees, index size and storage utilization are independent from the key distribution. That is, storage utilization for B-trees is guaranteed to be at least 50% for all key distributions.

In our previous work in [2] and [3], we study a structural modification of 0-complete trees that improves their space utilization by reducing page-underfilling. In this article, we focus on: (1) algorithmic details and implementations of the modified retrieval and maintenance algorithms for searching, insertion, and deletion, and (2) the correctness of the maintenance algorithms for modified 0-complete trees by implementing two modules of maintenance algorithms for B-trees and modified 0-complete trees for empirical studies.

2   0-Complete Trees and Their Structural Modification

We present in this section an overview of 0-complete trees and a brief development of the structural modification of 0-complete trees that improves their space utilization by: (1) designing an index-page splitting algorithm that reduces page-underfilling, (2) introducing the notion of a sequence set, and (3) providing semantic changes in parallel to the structural changes on 0-complete trees.

2.1   0-Complete Trees: An Overview

We introduce a variant of binary tries, called a 0-complete tree, which serves as the conceptual index structure that mirrors the actual retrieval structure, and study its compact representation — the practical index structure. Then we examine maintenance operations on compact 0-complete trees: searching, insertion, and deletion, and comment on the performance and storage utilization of compact 0-complete trees as index structures.

A *binary trie* structure can be transformed into a compact 0-complete tree, which is a compact multi-way search tree. A *trie* [6] is a multi-branching edge-labeled tree in which data items to be retrieved are stored at its leaves. Retrieval is achieved by successively comparing symbols in the search key with edge labels and following the indicated path to the desired leaf.

A binary trie is a trie structure with binary edge-labels — every edge is labeled with either 0 or 1. In a binary trie T, a node v is called a *0-node* (*1-node*) if the in-edge of v is labeled by 0 (respectively, 1). The *discriminator* of a node v is the string $D_v \in \{0,1\}^*$ such that $D_v = xy$ where x labels the path from the root of T to v, and $y = 0^{depth(T)-length(x)}$.

A *0-complete tree* is a binary trie T such that (1) the sibling of every 0-leaf must be present in T, and (2) the number of 1-nodes in T is one less than the number of leaves in T.

A *complete binary tree* is a binary tree in which every node has either 0 or 2 immediate descendants. It was proved in [11] that every complete binary tree satisfies the two conditions for the 0-completeness.

The nodes in a 0-complete tree T can be topologically ordered by the common pre-order traversal of the tree. The immediate successors of leaves in the pre-order traversal of T are called *bounding nodes* in T. We note that a 0-complete tree T with N leaves has $N-1$ bounding nodes, which are precisely the 1-nodes in T.

Discriminators and bounding nodes in a 0-complete tree T can be used to establish a partition of the *key space*, in which each *key interval* corresponds to each leaf in T. Denote by:

$$u_1, v_1, \ldots, u_2, v_2, \ldots, u_{N-1}, v_{N-1}, \ldots, u_N$$

the pre-order traversal of a 0-complete tree T with N leaves, where u_i's are leaves and v_i's are bounding nodes in T.

The key space is partitioned as:

$$[D_{u_1}, D_{v_1}), [D_{u_2}, D_{v_2}), \ldots, [D_{u_N}, 1^{depth(T)})$$

Observe that $D_{v_1} = D_{u_2}, D_{v_2} = D_{u_3}, \ldots, D_{v_{N-1}} = D_{u_N}$.

The significance of the bounding nodes is two-fold: (1) knowledge of the discriminators of bounding nodes is sufficient to identify the appropriate key interval of any data item with any given key, using a B-tree-like search operation, and (2) knowledge of the depths of bounding nodes can be used to compute the partition (key intervals) of the key space as follows.

Let M denote the (maximum) key length. Let D_i denote the discriminator of the ith bounding node in the pre-order traversal of a 0-complete tree of N leaves, where $i = 1, 2, \ldots, N - 1$ ($D_0 = 0^M$, and $D_N = 1^M$). Assuming knowledge of the depth sequence:

$$(d_i \mid d_i \text{ is the depth of the } i^{\text{th}} \text{ bounding node})_{i=1}^{N-1},$$

then the term D_i in the sequence $(D_i)_{i=1}^{N-1}$ can be computed inductively (hence the key intervals):

> algorithm *compute_discriminators*
>   set the d_i^{th} bit in D_{i-1} to 1
>   set all subsequent (lower-order) bits in D_{i-1} to 0
> end *compute_discriminators*

A compact representation of a 0-complete tree T, called a C_0-tree, is a hierarchical structure of index nodes (index pages). Each index page corresponds to a 0-complete subtree T' of T and contains the sequence of ordered pairs (depth$_i$, pointer$_i$), where (1) the ith bounding node in the pre-order traversal of T' is denoted by u_i, (2) depth$_i$ denotes the depth of u_i, and (3) pointer$_i$ points to the index page for the 0-complete subtree of T' rooted at u_i, or to the leaf page preceding u_i.

The 0-complete tree for an indexed file serves as a conceptual index structure, whereas the C_0-tree for the underlying 0-complete tree serves as a practical index structure for the file organization.

Retrieval, insertion, and deletion operations depend on the search operation for a given search key. A naive algorithm for the search operation on compact 0-complete trees, based on applying the algorithm *compute_discriminators* on the depth sequence in an index page of the C_0-tree, is to compute the partition of key intervals and choose the appropriate key interval for continuing search. This approach suffers the inefficiency of the recurrence in the algorithm *compute_discriminators*.

A more efficient implementation of the search operation reduces to comparisons of small integers, regardless of the key length or key type. In this algorithm, an array of increasing 1-bit positions in the search key is first computed, and then those positions are compared with the depth field of the index page one by one. Thus, the key comparison time for any access is significantly reduced.

Reflecting the practical compact C_0-representation onto its conceptual 0-complete model, the coupled maintenance algorithms (retrieval together with insertion/splitting and deletion/concatenation) are developed to preserve the 0-completeness of the conceptual tree. Their algorithmic details and performance in storage utilization are provided in [2] and [3].

2.2 Structural Modification of 0-Complete Trees

In this section, we provide a brief development of the desired structural modification of 0-complete trees with: (1) an index-page splitting algorithm that reduces page-underfilling, (2) the notion of a sequence set, and (3) semantic changes in parallel to the structural changes on 0-complete trees.

Index-Page Splitting Algorithm. The basic idea of optimized splitting in the original 0-complete tree [7] is that the depth of the splitting point must be the minimum of all the depths in the first page after the split, and the index that is the closest to the middle of the page is chosen as long as the first condition is met. A problem arises if entries with minimum depths appear near the beginning of index pages.

The worst case occurs when all the minimum depths happen to be at the beginning of the page in increasing order when overfilling occurs in a leaf index page. The problem is that more than one dummy node may be inserted in increasing order for a single insertion — the index page might split again and again until the last page is no longer overfilled. Under uniform key distribution, those underfilled pages are expected to be filled eventually. However those pages may not be filled under some skewed key distribution, such as keys always starting with a 1-bit.

The key idea of our modified index-page splitting algorithm is to choose a splitting index point with the minimum depth within a certain range to prevent underfilling of pages. It also simplifies the implementation by guaranteeing index page splitting into no more than two pages.

Notice that we may modify the original splitting algorithm so that an overfilled index page is split exactly in half, however such modification may induce unwanted side-effects such as appearance of dummies in upper layers of C_0-trees. Note that the tighter the index range to choose for a splitting point, the more is the chance that many dummies are inserted in index pages. Hence, our structural modification aims to prevent page-underfilling by selecting an index range that is not close to the beginning nor the ending of the index page.

The algorithmic details about insertion of nil-pointers in upper layers of C_0-trees are provided in Subsect. 3.2: Insertion.

Sequence Set Blocks. The sequence set [5] is based on the idea of grouping the records into blocks and then maintaining the blocks as records are added and deleted. The purpose of the index is to guide us to the block in the sequence set that contains the record. Note that the index set itself does not contain data, it contains only information about where to find the data. B^+-trees and prefix B^+-trees are examples of similar modifications of B-trees, with prefix B-trees using sequence set blocks. The advantage is a smaller index structure and fast sequential access.

With a sequence set, the number of the dummy entries in the leaves of index pages depends on how we select splitting points from the sequence set blocks.

In an original 0-complete tree where we have no control over key distribution, we can not reduce dummy entries since the conceptual 0-complete tree structure is fixed with the keys inserted in a given order. By using a sequence set, we can manipulate dummy entries in the upper level (leaves of the index structure). For example, by choosing the index with the minimum depth from a sequence set block (the minimum-depth computation runs in linear time — by comparing consecutive entries), the number of the dummy nodes can be minimized. However, the tradeoff is a higher chance of the underfilling of sequence set blocks, and that is certainly not a good choice. Therefore the splitting algorithm for the sequence set blocks has the same principle as the one for index pages.

The algorithmic details about splitting algorithms are provided in Subsect. 3.2: Insertion.

Semantic Changes. So far, the structural changes made from the original 0-complete tree are:

1. Entries with nil-pointers appear not only in the leaves of the index page but also in upper levels of the index structure.
2. The purpose of the index set is to provide access to the correct sequence set block that includes keys and the records.

Note that some semantics are also changed along with the structural changes above. In the original 0-complete tree structure, each entry presents a certain key range (that is computed by the depth) and an entry with a nil-pointer simply means that no key is in that range. On the other hand, in the modified index-page splitting algorithm, an entry with a nil-pointer does not represent any key range, and keys in that range are found at nearest entry below which has non-nil-pointer.

There are some similarities between C'-Trees [7] and the modified 0-complete tree structure developed in this paper. In a C'-Tree, the leaves of the index structure contain depth-pointer pairs, which point to data blocks containing sequential records.

Note that C'-trees do not strictly follow the property of the original 0-complete trees. In a C'-tree, a key that belongs to a missing 1-leaf can be stored in the immediately preceding leaf page (according to the pre-order traversal) as long as space is available. However, a new page must be created for a key that belongs to a 0-leaf with a nil-pointer, which is not the case for the modified 0-complete tree structure.

The empirical study in [7] shows that a C'-tree, when compared to the original 0-complete tree, would yield better retrieval performance only for small records whose length is at most 20 bytes because of the storage overhead caused by underfilled blocks. In the modified 0-complete trees, underfilled blocks are further reduced.

3   Coupling Modified Maintenance Algorithms

Having developed the structural modification of 0-complete trees in the previous section, we will present modified maintenance algorithms for searching, insertion, and deletion.

3.1   Searching

A search is performed by: (1) searching the index page, and then (2) searching the sequence set block located by the index search.

The same search algorithm for the original 0-complete tree can be used with a slight modification. Modifications come from the semantic change of the 0-complete tree structure (Subsect. 2.2: Structural Modification of 0-Complete Trees: Semantic Changes). That is, the search algorithm does not simply return the index if it is a nil-pointer, as the original search algorithm does. The index must be incremented until the algorithm finds an entry with a non-nil-pointer. After the index search, a straightforward binary search is performed on a sequence set block.

The search algorithm in Fig. 1 derives from the original index search algorithm in [9] with the modifications underlined. The modification (2) in Fig. 1 increments the index until the entry with a non-nil-pointer is encountered. The modification (1) is to update the value of $first$, which is the index of the array of sorted 1-bit positions in the search key, to pass to the lower page of the index structure correctly for further search. Figure 2 illustrates an example.

We trace the modified search algorithm in Fig. 1 on the example in Fig. 2. In searching for the key 01100101, the array b is computed to be $[2, 3, 6, 8, 9]$, and the identifier $first$ is set to zero, so the index k of the array b is zero. Note that the example in Fig. 2 has a depth sequence $d = [2, 3, 5, 6, \ldots]$. Before entering the second while-loop (modification (2)), the index j is two ($d[2] = 5$) and the index k of the array b is two ($b[2] = 6$). Since $p[j] = nil$, j is incremented until $p[j] \neq nil$. Therefore after the second while-loop (modification (2)), index j becomes 3 ($d[3] = 6$, $p[3] \neq nil$) and further search will continue in a sequence set block with the implied key range of $[01100000, 01101100)$. In this particular case, the identifier $first$, which is passed to the lower level of the index page for further searching, has the same value as the index k ($k = 2$, $b[k] = 6$).

However this might not be the case for other keys. Suppose that the key is 01101001, b is computed to be $[2, 3, 5, 8, 9]$, and $first$ is set to zero. Before entering second while-loop (modification (2)), the index j of the depth sequence is three ($d[3] = 6$). In this case j is not incremented before returning, since $p[j] \neq nil$. Therefore further search will continue in the same lower index page as the case above with implied key range $[01100000, 01101100)$. This time, the value of $first$ to be passed for searching the lower level index page must be two ($b[2] = 5$). But k is further incremented in the first while-loop (modification (1)), when the index $j = 2$ and $k = 2$ ($d[2] = b[2] = 5$). Therefore the value of k can not simply be the value of $first$ in the modified search algorithm. Modification (1) in Fig. 1 correctly updates the value of $first$.

algorithm *search*
input:
1. An array b of sorted 1-bit positions in the search key K, appended with the value $M + 1$, where M is the maximum key length.
2. An integer *first* that denotes the index in the array b (usually 0) at which to begin bit-comparison.
3. A sequence d of depths of the bounding nodes in a page.
4. A sequence p of pointers in a page.

output:
1. The index j of the entry whose key interval contains the key K.

$$j \leftarrow 0$$
$$k \leftarrow first$$

while $(b[k] \leq d[j])$
    if $b[k] = d[j]$ then
        $k \leftarrow k + 1$

        if $p[j] \neq nil$ then   – (1)
          $first \leftarrow k$

    $j \leftarrow j + 1$

  while $(p[j] = nil)$ – (2)
    $j \leftarrow j + 1$

  return j
end *search*

Fig. 1. A search algorithm for modified 0-complete trees.

depth	page-pointer	implied key range of child index page
2	$\xrightarrow{nil}$	
3	$\longrightarrow$	$[00000000, 01100000)$
5	$\xrightarrow{nil}$	
6	$\longrightarrow$	$[01100000, 01101100)$
$\vdots$		

Fig. 2. An index page in a modified 0-complete tree.

3.2 Insertion

An insertion is performed after the search algorithm has found the correct location in the sequence set block. If the key is absent in the sequence set block, the new key and its record are simply inserted at the location. Note that an insertion does not require any operation related to the 0-complete tree structure unless the block is overfilled.

Splitting a Sequence Set Block. When the sequence set block is overfilled, it is split into two and new entries and possibly some dummy nodes are inserted in the leaf index page. The number of dummy nodes is minimized if the splitting point is the index with the minimum depth. However, underfilling of a sequence set block depends on the location of the minimum index. In the modified split algorithm, the minimum and maximum indices are set and the splitting point is the index of the entry with the minimum depth between them. Figure 3 shows an example of this approach.

depth	block-pointer	sequence set block		
1	$\xrightarrow{nil}$			
		starting key range: 00000000		
		depth	record	
4	$\longrightarrow$	$\vdots$		
		1	00001000	
		–	10000000	
		starting key range: 10010000		
		depth	record	
		2	10010000	
		6	11000001	
		3	11000100	← minimum index
0	$\longrightarrow$			← splitting point
		6	11100011	← next_key
		5	11100110	
		4	11101000	← maximum index
		5	11110000	
		–	11111001	

Fig. 3. An overfilled sequence set block after insertion.

In Fig. 3, the index with the minimum depth among all the entries is the first entry (depth = 2, key = 10010000), which causes underfilling of the second sequence set block if it is chosen as a splitting point. According to the modified split algorithm, the minimum splitting point is at the third entry (depth = 3, key = 11000100), since the depth of 3 is the minimum among the depths between "minimum index" and "maximum index". This depth is computed by comparing the key 11000100 and "next_key" 11100011 — the depth of the third entry is 3, since the third bit is the leftmost bit at which these two keys differ. The depths for all entries can be stored as shown in Fig. 3. Note that the last record in a sequence set block does not need a depth value since it is used only to determine the splitting point, and a block will never be split at the last index. An alternative computation of the splitting point, if the depth sequence is not stored in the block, is to generate the depth sequence by comparing consecutive keys whenever a block is searched — the current depth entry is the position of the leftmost bit at which the current and next keys differ.

After the split, a new entry, which points to the newly created first part of the split block, along with dummy nodes, is inserted in the index page. The depth of the new entry is the depth of the entry at the splitting point, which is the position of the leftmost bit at which the key at the splitting point and the next key differ. Before inserting the new entry, dummy-node pairs of (depth, nil-pointer) must be inserted. The depths of the dummy entries are part of the 1-bit array in the next key (that is, $[1, 2, 3, 7, 8]$ for "next_key" in Fig. 3). The starting index of the 1-bit array in the next key can be computed easily if the starting range of the keys in each block is stored. This is done when the new sequence set block is created. Note that the starting range never changes once the block is created. The starting index of the next key for dummy insertion is simply the leftmost index at which the starting range and the next key differ. Insertion of dummy nodes ends when the next index is the same as the depth of the new entry. Figure 4 illustrates an example of the split and insertion of a new entry with a dummy node.

In Fig. 3, the depth of the new entry is the depth of the splitting point, which is at the third entry (depth $= 3$, key $= 11000100$) before the split. Dummy nodes are part of the 1-bit array of the next key (key $= 11100011$, 1-bit array $= [1, 2, 3, 7, 8]$). The starting range of the block before the split is 10010000 (1-bit array $= [1, 4]$). The starting index to insert dummy nodes is 2, since it is the leftmost position with the bit changing from 0 to 1 when comparing with the starting range. Insertion of dummy nodes ends since the next index is three, which is equal to the depth of the new entry. The result is depicted in Fig. 4.

The example in Fig. 3 has no dummy node between the entry pointing to the overfilled sequence block and the entry pointing to the previous sequence block. Therefore it is obvious where to insert new dummy-node entries. If dummy nodes already exist between the two delimiting entries in the index page, the depths of these two entries and the depths of the new dummy-node entries must be compared one-by-one to determine the location to insert. Figure 5 shows the algorithm that locates and inserts the new entry and dummy nodes in a leaf index page.

More examples that show possible scenarios and facets of insertions with splitting a sequence set block are provided in the full version of this article.

Splitting an Index Page. The algorithm of splitting an index page is analogous to that of splitting a sequence set block. An overfilled index page consists

depth	block-pointer	sequence set block	
1	$\xrightarrow{nil}$		
4	$\longrightarrow$	starting key range: 00000000	
		depth	record
		$\vdots$	
		1	00001000
		–	10000000
2	$\xrightarrow{nil}$		
3	$\longrightarrow$	starting key range: 10010000	
		depth	record
		2	10010000
		6	11000001
		–	11000100
0	$\longrightarrow$	starting key range: 11100000	
		depth	record
		6	11100011
		5	11100110
		4	11101000
		5	11110000
		–	11111001

Fig. 4. An index page and a sequence set block after splitting.

of depth-pointer pairs whereas an overfilled sequence set block consists of depth-key-record 3-tuples (the depth field is optional as stated in Subsect. 3.2: Insertion: Splitting a Sequence Set Block). The difference between the two insert/splitting algorithms comes from the fact that no key is stored in the index page.

Note that the last entry of each index page always has a non-nil-pointer to prevent an extra disk access in the search procedure. If we allow the last entry to have a nil-pointer, the search procedure needs to find the correct entry in the sibling of the index page when it reaches the last entry.

Figures 6 and 7 show an algorithm that locates and inserts the new entry and dummy nodes in a parent index page. The key idea is that the search to locate the insertion point is performed upwards by comparing the depth sequences of the parent index page and the child index page. Once it is located, the new entry, and then dummy nodes, are inserted. The (strictly) decreasing sequence of depths in the child index page corresponding to the depths of the existing dummy nodes are matched one-by-one in the search process.

Examples that show possible scenarios and facets of insertions with splitting an index page are provided in the full version of this article.

algorithm *split_sequence_set_block*
input:
    1. A sequence d_1 that is a slice of the depth sequence in a leaf index page parenting an overfilled sequence set block. The range of d_1 covers from the non-empty sequence set block preceding the overfilled one (exclusive) to the overfilled sequence set block (inclusive). Hence all but the last of d_1 correspond to empty sequence set blocks.
    2. A sequence d_2 of depths for dummy nodes and then the new entry to be inserted in d_1.
    3. An integer *last* that denotes the index of the last entry position in d_2.

output:
    1. Insert necessary dummy nodes and the new entry in d_2 in the leaf index page of d_1.

```
i ← 0
j ← 0

while (1)
        if d₁[i] = d₂[j] then
                if j = last then
                        /* change pointer from nil to the newly created block */
                        point_to_new_block(d₁, i)
                        exit
                else
                        i ← i + 1
                        j ← j + 1

        if d₁[i] < d₂[j] then
                /* insert d₂ in d₁ */
                for (; j ≤ last; j + +)
                        d₁[i] ← d₂[j]
                        i ← i + 1
                        j ← j + 1

                /* change pointer from nil to the newly created block */
                i ← i - 1
                point_to_new_block(d₁, i)
                exit
end split_sequence_set_block
```

Fig. 5. An algorithm for locating and inserting the new entry and dummy nodes in a leaf index page.

algorithm *split_index_page*
input:
1. A sequence d_1 of depths in a parent index page.
2. A sequence d_2 of depths in an overfilled index page.
3. An index *split_point* that denotes the splitting index position in d_2 at which the overfilled page will be split.
4. An integer *depth* that stores the updated depth.

output:
1. Insert the new entry and necessary dummy nodes in the parent index page of d_1.

set i to be the index of the entry in the parent index page of d_1,
        which points to the overfilled child index page of d_2
set j to be the index of the last entry in the child index page of d_2
$depth \leftarrow d_2[j]$

/* compute the index to split */
$split\_point \leftarrow find\_split\_point(d_2)$

while (1)
      if $j = split\_point$ then
           /* place to start insertion */
           $i \leftarrow i + 1$

           /* insert the new entry */
           $d_1[i] \leftarrow d_2[j]$

           /* insert all the depths of dummy nodes in $d_1[i]$ */
           $insert\_dummies(i, j)$
           exit

      if $d_1[i] = d_2[j]$ then
           /* $d_2[j]$ is the corresponding depth of $d_1[i]$ */
           $i \leftarrow i - 1$

           /* update index j and *depth* */
           while ($d_2[j] \geq depth$ or $j = split\_point$)
               $j \leftarrow j - 1$

           $depth \leftarrow d_2[j]$
end *split_index_page*

Fig. 6. An algorithm for locating and inserting the new entry and dummy nodes in a parent index page.

algorithm *insert_dummies* (integer i, integer j)

> while (1)
>> /* update index j and *depth* */
>> while ($j > 0$ and $d_2[j] \geq depth$)
>>> $j \leftarrow j - 1$
>>
>> $depth \leftarrow d_2[j]$
>>
>> if $d_2[j] > d_1[i-1]$ then
>>> /* insert dummy nodes */
>>> $d_1[i] \leftarrow d_2[j]$
>> else if $d_2[j] = d_1[i-1]$ then
>>> exit
>
> end *insert_dummies*

Fig. 7. An auxiliary algorithm for *split_index_page*.

3.3 Deletion, and Suite of Modified Maintenance Algorithms

A deletion is performed after the search algorithm has correctly located the key in one of the sequence set blocks. If the key is present in the sequence set block, the key and its record are simply deleted from the location. The depth of the previous key must be updated if depth sequence is stored in the sequence set block. The deletion algorithm is simpler than for original 0-complete trees as long as the merge procedure is not invoked.

The correctness of coupled maintenance algorithms for modified 0-complete trees has been tested by implementing two modules of maintenance algorithms for B-trees and modified 0-complete trees.

The algorithmic details of deletion and merging (sequence set blocks and index pages) algorithms and the implementation details of the two modules and the empirical test result are provided in the full version of this article.

4 Concluding Remarks

The modified 0-complete tree index structure coupled with retrieval and maintenance algorithms presented here reduces the number of underfilled index pages caused by a non-uniform key distribution. A side-effect of the modification may be the existence of dummy nodes in upper layers of index pages, whereas for original 0-complete-trees, dummy nodes exist only in the leaves. The size of the index structure is expected to be greatly reduced by introducing a sequence set. A smaller index structure reduces the number of disk accesses. The introduction of a sequence set in an index structure facilitates a fast sequential access of the keys.

The main results of the article are based on the structural modification of 0-complete trees in [2] and [3] that improves their space utilization by reducing page-underfilling, and provide the design and implementation of coupled retrieval and maintenance algorithms.

Complete algorithmic details and implementations of the modified retrieval and maintenance algorithms for searching, insertion, and deletion are presented in the full version of this article.

Future directions for research include the worst-case and expected-case analyses and comparisons for the original and the modified 0-complete tree structures. The expected-case behavior of the original 0-complete trees is detailed in [7]. Simulations of different index structures including 0-complete trees, modified 0-complete trees, B-trees, and prefix B-trees may also be of interest. However, the outcome may heavily depend on key distributions that may not be realistic.

References

1. Comer, D.: The ubiquitous B-tree. ACM Comput. Surv. **11**(2), 121–137 (1979)
2. Dai, H.K., Furusawa, K.: Improving the storage utilization of 0-complete trees as index structures. In: Dang, T.K., Kung, J., Chung, T.M. (eds.) Future Data and Security Engineering. Big Data, Security and Privacy, Smart City and Industry 4.0 Applications. FDSE 2022. CCIS, vol. 1688, pp. 88–102 Springer, Singapore (2022). https://doi.org/10.1007/978-981-19-8069-5_6
3. Dai, H.K., Furusawa, K.: On the storage utilization of 0-complete trees as index structures. Computer Science Department, Oklahoma State University, Technical report TR-23-01, October 2023
4. Fagin, R., Nievergelt, J., Pippenger, N., Strong, H.R.: Extendible hashing – a fast access method for dynamic files. ACM Trans. Database Syst. **4**(3), 315–344 (1979)
5. Folk, M.J., Zoellick, B.: File Structures, Second Edition. Addison-Wesley, Boston (1992)
6. Fredkin, E.: Many-way information retrieval. Commun. ACM **3**, 490–500 (1960)
7. Orlandic, R.: Design, analysis and applications of compact 0-complete trees. PhD thesis, Department of Computer Science, University of Virginia (1989)
8. Orlandic, R., Mahmoud, H.M.: Storage overhead of O-trees, B-trees and prefix B-trees: a comparative analysis. Int. J. Found. Comput. Sci. **7**(3), 209–226 (1996)
9. Orlandic, R., Pfaltz, J.L.: Compact 0-complete trees. In: Proceedings of the Fourteenth Conference on Very Large Databases, pp. 372–381. Association for Computing Machinery and IEEE Computer Society, August 1988
10. Orlandic, R., Pfaltz, J.L.: Q_0-tree: a dynamic structure for accessing spatial objects with arbitrary shapes. Institute for Parallel Computation, University of Virginia, Technical Report IPC-TR-91-010, December 1991
11. Orlandic, R., Pfaltz, J.L.: Compact 0-complete trees: a new method for searching large files. Institute for Parallel Computation, University of Virginia, Technical report IPC-TR-88-001, January 1988

Robust Vietnam's Motorcycle License Plate Detection and Recognition Using Deep Learning Model

Duc Hoa Le[1], Debarshi Mazumder[2], Luyl-Da Quach[3], Shreya Banerjee[4(✉)], and Vinh Dinh Nguyen[2(✉)]

[1] Bosch Global Software Technologies Company Limited, Ho Chi Minh city, Vietnam
hoa.leduc@vn.bosch.com
[2] School of Computing and Information Technology, Eastern International University, Thu Dau Mot, Vietnam
{debarshi.mazumder,vinh.nguyen}@eiu.edu.vn
[3] Department of Software Engineering, FPT University Can Tho City, Can Tho, Vietnam
daql@fpt.edu.vn
[4] Department of Computer Science and Engineering, Manipal Institute of Technology Bengaluru, Manipal Academy of Higher Education, Manipal, India
shreya.banerjee@manipal.edu

Abstract. Nowadays, driving fast is an emergency state in many countries in the world and Vietnam in particular, and the consequence is really cruel when an accident occurs. Therefore, it is very important to control the speed of vehicles. Motorcycle license plate recognition (MLPR) is one of many methods. If any motorcycle drives above the speed limit on the road that has a speed camera, a ticket will be sent to your living address. This research proposes a method that can automatically detect license plates (LP) and extract their data. The highest mAP achieved after three hundred epochs is 93% with Yolov8. There are three stages to extracting the LP's data, the first is detecting the motorcycle, the second is detecting the LP in the motorcycle's bounding box, and the third is LP recognition using Yolov8 also.

Keywords: Yolov8 · Deep Learning · License Plate Recognition

1 Introduction

Motorcycle License Plate Recognition (MLPR) holds significant significance in the domains of Intelligent Transportation and Surveillance. It possesses numerous practical and pertinent applications, including automated enforcement of traffic laws, identification of stolen vehicles, detection of toll violations, and traffic flow management. Despite the existence of various approaches, License plate recognition (LPR) using machine learning techniques continues to be a persistent

T. K. Dang et al. (Eds.): FDSE 2023, CCIS 1925, pp. 64–75, 2023.
https://doi.org/10.1007/978-981-99-8296-7_5

challenge due to the wide range of diversity in image acquisition conditions. Factors such as lighting conditions, capture angles, distance from the camera, and the varying layouts of license plates across different countries contribute to the complexity of the task. The challenge of MLPR can be divided into three main components: License Plate Detection (LPD), License Plate Segmentation (LPS), and Character Recognition (CR). These components represent the sequential steps involved in the license plate recognition process. LPD focuses on locating the license plate within an image, LPS aims to separate individual characters within the detected plate, and CR involves recognizing and interpreting the characters to extract the license plate information. Addressing these components collectively is crucial for achieving accurate and reliable license plate recognition. These components form the standard sequence of tasks for ALPR systems as described in various studies [1]. Many existing studies have primarily focused on one or two of these components [2]. Additionally, License Plate Segmentation (LPS) and Character Recognition (CR) are closely related to Optical Character Recognition (OCR), which is a well-established research field in computer vision. OCR techniques have been extensively studied and various solutions have been proposed to address the challenges in accurately segmenting characters from license plates and recognizing them. The advancements in OCR methodologies contribute to improving the performance of LPS and CR components in license plate recognition systems [3–6].

Vietnam has witnessed a significant number of motorcycles being utilized as common means of transportation, including by students commuting to school. However, this trend has also led to a rise in reckless driving behaviors and a consequent increase in the occurrence of accidents. Consequently, there is a pressing need to prioritize road safety enforcement in order to mitigate the risks posed by irresponsible motorists [22]. The purpose of this study is to utilize deep learning techniques to effectively identify motorcycle license plates in Vietnam. While previous research has employed various robust methods, deep learning has emerged as a highly acclaimed approach in the field of pattern recognition. Although most MLPR studies in Vietnam have focused on recognizing car license plates, numerous algorithms for character recognition have been explored in the literature. Several approaches have been successfully applied to address the challenges of License Plate Segmentation (LPS) and Character Recognition (CR) in different license plate recognition systems. Some notable methods include Hidden Markov Models (HMM), hybrid discriminative Restricted Boltzmann Machines (RBM), and Support Vector Machines (SVM).

Template matching, on the other hand, is a suitable technique for recognizing characters with specific properties such as a single font, non-rotated orientation, and fixed size. In addition to the mentioned techniques, artificial neural networks have gained significant attention for their remarkable capability to classify license plates. Neural networks, particularly deep learning models like Convolutional Neural Networks (CNNs), have demonstrated impressive performance in license plate recognition tasks. Their ability to learn complex features from images and effectively classify license plates has made them a popular choice among researchers in the field. The use of artificial neural networks has significantly contributed to advancements in license plate recognition systems.

The subsequent sections of our paper are structured as follows:

In section two, we conduct a comprehensive review of the existing methods in the field of Machine Learning-based License Plate Recognition (MLPR) and provide a detailed discussion of them.

Our proposed robust MLPR method, which utilizes Yolov8, is presented in section three. We explain the details and advantages of our approach.

To evaluate the effectiveness of our proposed method, we perform experiments on diverse datasets, and the results are discussed in section four.

Finally, in section five, we present the conclusions drawn from our research and discuss potential directions for future work.

2   Related Work

In recent times, numerous researchers have successfully addressed the issue of identifying license plates for motorcycles (LPM). The recognized aspect ratio is one of the prominent identifying features frequently associated with the geometric form of an LPM detection. In prior research, specifically referenced as [7] and [8], the vertical Sobel operator was utilized to detect vertical edges. Following this edge detection, the plates were then verified by considering the width and height with an aspect ratio. However, it has been observed that the boundary-based approach is more susceptible to detecting undesired edges, as mentioned in the literature [9]. Some LPs exhibit distinct colors that serve to differentiate vehicle ownership.

Several researchers have extensively investigated the application of Convolutional Neural Networks (CNNs) for object recognition in the detection stage of License Plate (LP) identification. Silva and Jung [10] discovered that the Fast-Yolo model [11], when applied to LP recognition without prior vehicle detection, yielded a low recognition rate. In order to achieve high precision-recall rates on a dataset consisting of Brazilian License Plates (LPs), the researchers employed a cascaded structure of the Fast-Yolo model. The model first detected the top view of automobiles and subsequently identified the LPs within the designated regions.

Yolo is considered the cutting-edge real-time object detection algorithm that is currently available. Yolo operates as a unified convolutional neural network, allowing it to make predictions for multiple bounding boxes and classes for the entire image in a single pass. Taking inspiration from the GoogLeNet model, which is commonly used for image classification, Yolo integrates 24 convolutional layers and two fully connected layers into its architecture. A notable aspect of Yolo is its utilization of 1×1 reduction layers, which are subsequently followed by 3×3 convolutional layers. Presently, there are eight iterations of Yolos: from yolov1 to yolov8. Yolov2, an improved version of Yolov1, maintains the speed advantages while introducing enhancements such as batch normalization, anchor boxes, and a high-resolution classifier. These additions contribute to the overall performance and accuracy of the network. Yolov3 introduces an enhanced feature extractor by integrating 53 convolutional layers that have been trained on the ImageNet dataset. This augmentation in the network architecture helps to improve the model's ability to extract relevant features from the input images. While Yolov3 exhibits superior accuracy compared to Yolov2, it operates at a slower pace due to the increased number of layers in its architecture.

3 Materials and Proposed Methods

3.1 Yolov8 Architecture

Yolov8 (You Only Look Once) is the latest Yolo version by Ultralytics, released in January 2023 [12]. It's a cutting-edge and state-of-the-art (SOTA) model, Yolov8 builds on the strengths of previous versions specific is Yolov7, designed faster and more accurately, and usable for real-time detection problems. Yolov8 also supports the latest computer vision algorithms such as instance segmentation, able to detect multiple objects in an image, video, and streaming also [15]. Figure 1 shows the detail of Yolov8's architecture. Yolov8 uses a new backbone, a variant of the CSPDarkNetBackbone architecture, with some changes on the CSPLayer, now called the C2f module. The first 6×6 Conv has been replaced by 3×3 Conv in the Backbone, replaced the first 1×1 Conv by 3×3 Conv in the Bottleneck [13]. With Yolov8, it applied a new solution that is predicted directly to the center of the object instead of the offset known from the anchor box, called anchor-free detection. It reduces the number of the predicted bounding box which speeds up Non-Maximum Suppression (NMS).

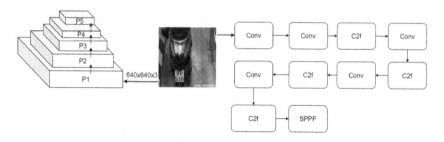

Fig. 1. Overall model structure of Yolov8 detection models [12]

Yolov8 uses an anchor-free model with a decoupled head to independently process objectness. With new architecture, it allow each branch to focus on its task and improves the accuracy of the model [13].

3.2 Transfer Learning

This research applied the transfer learning method to increase the accuracy of the best model, after experimenting with many versions of Yolo, detail shown in Fig. 4. Based on learning the advantage of the pre-train model ability, the model can reduce the training time, and require less data from the knowledge transferred. Transfer learning is a useful way to re-train the model on new data without re-training the entire network shown in Fig. 2. Instead, part of the initial weights are frozen in place, and the rest of the weights are used to compute loss and are updated by the optimizer [12].

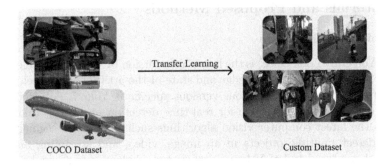

Fig. 2. Simulation process of transferring knowledge from COCO dataset to custom dataset [17]

3.3 Dataset

The dataset for motorcycles and motorcycle license plates has been collected from Roboflow [14] and motorcycle parking place, with 3600 images total, the combination of 2000 images for motorcycles, and 1600 images for license plates. Decide this dataset into three sub-set including training, testing, and validating with a ratio is 60%–20%–20% (Fig. 3).

Fig. 3. Sample of digit, motorcycle, and LP dataset [14, 21]

3.4   Training Environment

All eight experiments have been trained in cloud environment. The first is Google Colab Pro, with system RAM up to 84 GB, 40 GB of GPU RAM, and 166.8 GB of disk size, GPU includes A100, V100, and T4. The second environment is Kaggle, which supports GPU P100 with 16 GB of RAM, system RAM maximum is 13 GB, currently, Kaggle enables the option for multiple GPU - T4x2.

3.5   Proposed Methods - Detection Model

Our research uses experiments and customizes the hyperparameters to find the optimal parameter for Yolov8. Applied image augmentation while training such as image rotation $30°$, $45°$, $60°$, $90°$, image flipping, scaling, cropping, blurring, optimizer used Adam, batch sizes is 256.

Transfer learning has been applied with 5 layers of freeze. It makes the model learn new knowledge on these layers and increases the accuracy significantly.

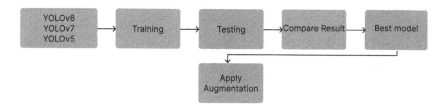

Fig. 4. Process of comparing and choosing the best model [16]

After training the model with optimal hyper-parameter, compare the result together, figure out the best model is Yolov8, and start applying augmentation for it to improve the accuracy and adapt to other conditions such as the motorcycle in a parking slot, it will rotate with random degree, in lack of light condition, etc.

There are three stages of our methodology shown in Fig. 5. The first is motorcycle detection, the second is license plate detection, and the third is license plate recognition.

For the motorcycle detection stage, used Yolov8 to perform it. The input is the raw image or the raw frame of video, already tried with Yolov5 and Yolov7 but the result doesn't as expected. After finding out the optimal hyperparameters group as above, and applying transfer learning technique with 5 layers of freeze, the mAP50 achieve 89% for training set, decide applied augmentation for training process, the mAP50 increased to 93% after 300 epochs.

For the license plate detection, one time again, Yolov8 surpassed all our expectations, the mAP50 result achieved 93% for specific LP class. The input of this stage comes from the previous stage, after motorcycle detects successfully, the result returns the coordinates of motorcycle's bounding box, crops the image base on the bounding box, and performs LP detection on new cropped range. This solution enhanced the velocity and correctness of LP detection stage.

For the license plate recognition, trained the Yolov8 with digit dataset to perform the digit recognition, both of train and validation achieved 99% accuracy, quite high because the data has been cropped, resize, and remove the background. After performing the LP detection, the input is the cropped license plate number (LPN). There are two small stages, we combined object detection and classification. The first step involves detecting and cropping a line of text, followed by detecting and classifying individual characters within cropped images (Fig. 6).

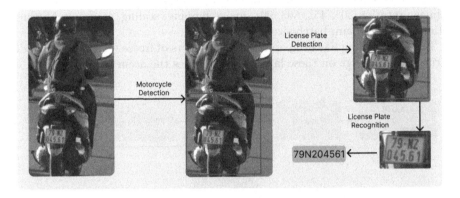

Fig. 5. Pipline of processing from raw image/frame to final license plate number

Fig. 6. Sample image of successful detection and recognition

4 Result

4.1 Experiment 1: License Plate Detection Using Yolo Version 8

In this experiment, Yolov8 achieved the highest mAP50 93% for the transfer learning and augmentation dataset, 89% with the original dataset and without the frozen layer, recorded after finished 300 epochs. Fine-tuning hyperparameters including batch-size tried are 16, 32, 64, 128, 256, 512, and 1024, optimizer tried with Adam and Adamax, applied image augmentation with many ways such as image flipping only for motorcycle, scaling, cropping, blurring, Random-Contrast (0.5, 1.5), RandomRotate (degrees = 10), RandomBrightness (0.5, 1.5), RandomSaturation (0.5, 1.5), image size are 640 and 1024.

4.2 Experiment 2: License Plate Detection Using Yolo Version 7

In this experiment, Yolov7 achieved the highest mAP50 81% for base architecture and transfer learning is 85%. After applied with 5 layers of freeze, the accuracy improved by four percent. This result was recorded after 300 epochs of training.

4.3 Experiment 3: License Plate Detection Using Yolo Version 5

In this experiment, Yolov5 achieved the highest mAP50 88% for base architecture and transfer learning after 300 epochs. Trained with original dataset, original architecture of Yolov5, fine-tuning hyperparameters including batch-size tried are 16, 32, 64, 128, 256, 512, and 1024, optimizer tried with Adam and Adamax, image size are 640 and 1024.

4.4 Evaluation of Results

After training with three versions of Yolo, we can see the improvement from Table 1 and Table 2 with detailed results, Fig. 7 and Fig. 8 visualize the result of three stage experiment. The training process is performed in 300 epochs, during training progress, we base on the mAP50 value to decide whether to continue training the model or stop to change the parameters. Based on the visualization, we can see the accuracy of Yolov8 improved better than other versions when applying augmentation and fine-tuning the model. The increasement come from the architecture enhancement of Yolov8 as mentioned in Yolov8 architecture above. YOLOv8 uses the CIoU and DFL loss functions, as well as BCE for class loss. These losses have been proven to increase object identification performance, especially with tiny objects.

Besides of that, our research has higher accuracy than research in the same field as LP recognition with Random Forest Classifier [18], processing vehicle's rear or front image and four steps are Pre-Processing, Number plate localization, Character segmentation, and Character recognition and the accuracy of this method is 90.9%. Apply deep learning to recognize LP in the parking system with accuracy is 92.16%, used the system called SHINE, which uses the deep

Table 1. Comparison between Yolov5, Yolov7, Yolov8, and applied augmentation for Yolov8 with transfer learning technique.

	Stage	Model	precision	recall	mAP50	mAP50-95
Transfer learning	Train	Yolov5	0.80	0.85	0.88	0.58
		Yolov7	0.75	0.8	0.85	0.54
		Yolov8	0.9	0.84	0.89	0.62
		Yolov8 with augmentation	0.94	0.80	0.93	0.64
	Validate	Yolov5	0.82	0.83	0.88	0.58
		Yolov7	0.8	0.77	0.84	0.55
		Yolov8	0.84	0.82	0.89	0.62
		Yolov8 with augmentation	0.94	0.81	0.93	0.63

Table 2. Comparison between Yolov5, Yolov7, Yolov8, and applied augmentation for Yolov8 when using the default architecture.

	Stage	Model	precision	recall	mAP50	mAP50-95
Base architecture	Train	Yolov5	0.83	0.81	0.88	0.6
		Yolov7	0.78	0.79	0.81	0.53
		Yolov8	0.83	0.82	0.88	0.62
		Yolov8 with augmentation	0.84	0.84	0.89	0.64
	Validate	Yolov5	0.82	0.83	0.88	0.58
		Yolov7	0.77	0.8	0.81	0.53
		Yolov8	0.85	0.83	0.89	0.64
		Yolov8 with augmentation	0.83	0.82	0.88	0.62

learning-based object detection algorithm for detecting the vehicle, license plate, and disability badges [19]. With the none Latin character of LP like Inranian also applied to perform recognition in this research [20], their process is similar to Fig. 5 and an average accuracy achieved 75.14% for the end-to-end process.

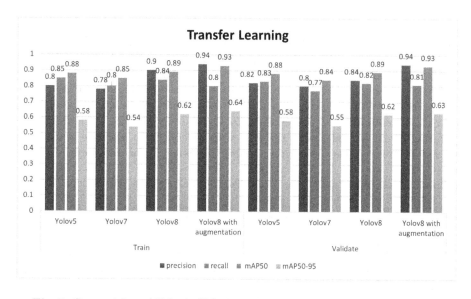

Fig. 7. Comparision of Yolov5, Yolov7, and Yolov8 for transfer learning stage

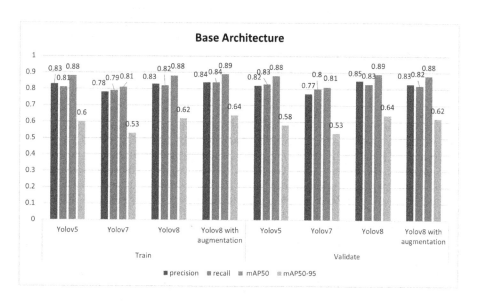

Fig. 8. Comparision of Yolov5, Yolov7, and Yolov8 original architecture model

5   Conclusion

Our research explores the training technique with custom hyperparameters, applied transfer learning with 5 freeze layers on the Yolov8, and image augmentation techniques. Perform motorcycle detection used for input of LP recognition step, minimal recognize scope in the image. After many experiments, the final result has been improved from 89% to 93% based on mAP50 and shown in Experiment 1. With this achievement, this research can contribute to making the ratio of accidents in Vietnam decrease, accidents due to driving without license, operating a vehicle while under the influence of alcohol, etc. Because we can use this model to recognize the license and get the owner of this motorcycle.

Acknowledgments. The authors would like to thank Eastern International University (EIU) Vietnam for funding this research.

References

1. Du, S., Ibrahim, M., Shehata, M., Badawy, W.: Automatic license plate recognition (ALPR): a state-of-theart review. IEEE Trans. Circuits Syst. Video Technol. **23**(2), 311–325 (2013)
2. Gonçalves, G.R., Menotti, D., Schwartz, W.R.: License plate recognition based on temporal redundancy. In: IEEE 19th International Conference on Intelligent Transportation Systems (ITSC2016), pp. 2577–2582 (2016)
3. Rahman, C.A., Badawy, W., Radmanesh, A.: Deep automatic license a real time vehicle's license plate recognition system. In: IEEE Conference on Advanced Video and Signal Based Surveillance (AVSS'03), pp. 163–166 (2016)
4. Nguyen, M.T.T., Nguyen, V.D., Jeon, J.W.: Real-time pedestrian detection using a support vector machine and stixel information. In: International Conference on Control, Automation and Systems (ICCAS), Jeju, Korea (South), pp. 1350–1355 (2017). https://doi.org/10.23919/ICCAS.2017.8204203
5. Chau, D.H., et al.: Plant leaf diseases detection and identification using deep learning model. In: Hassanien, A.E., Rizk, R.Y., Snasel, V., AbdelKader, R.F. (eds.) The 8th International Conference on Advanced Machine Learning and Technologies and Applications (AMLTA2022). AMLTA 2022. LNDECT, vol. 113, pp. 3–10. Springer, Cham (2022). https://doi.org/10.1007/9783031039188_1
6. Nguyen, V.D., Trinh, T.D., Tran, H.N.: A robust triangular sigmoid pattern-based obstacle detection algorithm in resource-limited devices. IEEE Trans. Intell. Transp. Syst. **24**(6), 5936–5945 (2023). https://doi.org/10.1109/TITS.2023.3253509
7. Badr A., Abdelwahab, M.M., Thabet, A.M., Abdelsadek, A.M.: Automatic number plate recognition system. Ann. Univ. Craiova - Math. Comput. Sci. Ser. **38**(1), 62–71 (2011)
8. Zheng, D., Zhao, Y., Wang, J.: An efficient method of license plate location. Pattern Recognit. Lett. **26**(15), 2431–2438 (2005). https://doi.org/10.1016/j.patrec.2005.04.014
9. Du, S., Ibrahim, M., Shehata, M., Badawy, W.: Automatic license plate recognition (ALPR): a state-of-the-art review. IEEE Trans. Circuits Syst. Video Technol. **23**(2), 311–325 (2013)

10. Silva, S.M., Jung, C.R.: Real-time Brazilian license plate detection and recognition using deep convolutional neural networks. In: Conference on Graphics, Patterns and Images (SIBGRAPI), pp. 55–62, October 2017

11. Redmon, J., Divvala, S., Girshick, R., Farhadi, A.: You only look once: Unified, real-time object detection. In: IEEE Conference on Computer Vision and Pattern Recognition (CVPR), June 2016, pp. 779–788 (2016)

12. Jocher, G., Chaurasia, A., Qiu, J.: Ultralytics Yolov8 (2023). https://docs.ultralytics.com/models/Yolov8/

13. Terven, J., Cordova-Esparza, D.: A comprehensive review of yolo: from yolov1 and beyond, 09 June 2023. arXiv. http://arxiv.org/abs/2304.00501. Accessed 05 July 2023

14. Motorcycle License Plate Detection - v8 2022–08-27 Roboflow. https://universe.roboflow.com/motorcycle-9gyny/motorcycle-license-plate-detection/dataset/8

15. Aboah, A., Wang, B., Bagci, U., Adu-Gyamfi, Y.: Real-time multi-class helmet violation detection using few-shot data sampling technique and Yolov8, 13 April 2023. arXiv. http://arxiv.org/abs/2304.08256. Accessed 08 July 2023

16. Duc, H.L., Minh, T.T., Hong, K.V., Hoang, H.L.: 84 Birds classification using transfer learning and EfficientNetB2. In: Dang, T.K., Kung, J., Chung, T.M. (eds.) Future Data and Security Engineering. Big Data, Security and Privacy, Smart City and Industry 4.0 Applications. FDSE 2022. CCIS, vol. 1688, pp. 698–705. Springer, Singapore (2022). https://doi.org/10.1007/978-981-19-8069-5_50

17. Hong, K.V., Minh, T.T., Duc, H.L., Nhat, N.T., Hoang, H.L.: 104 Fruits classification using transfer learning and DenseNet201 fine-tuning. In: Barolli, L. (eds.) Complex, Intelligent and Software Intensive Systems. CISIS 2022. LNNS, vol. 497, pp. 160–170. Springer, Cham (2022). https://doi.org/10.1007/978-3-031-08812-4_16

18. Akhtar, Z., Ali, R.: Automatic number plate recognition using random forest classifier, 26 March 2023. arXiv. https://doi.org/10.48550/arXiv.2303.14856

19. Neupane, D., Bhattarai, A., Aryal, S., Bouadjenek, M.R., Seok, U.-M., Seok, J.: SHINE: deep learning-based accessible parking management system, 28 April 2023. arXiv. https://doi.org/10.48550/arXiv.2302.00837

20. Hatami, S., Sadedel, M., Jamali, F.: Iranian license plate recognition using a reliable deep learning approach, 03 May 2023. arXiv. https://doi.org/10.48550/arXiv.2305.02292

21. MNIST Dataset > Overview, Roboflow. https://universe.roboflow.com/popular-benchmarks/mnist-cjkff

22. Nguyen, D.V.M., Vu, A.T., Ross, V., Brijs, T., Wets, G., Brijs, K.: Small-displacement motorcycle crashes and risky ridership in Vietnam: findings from a focus group and in-depth interview study. Saf. Sci. **152**, 105514 (2022). https://doi.org/10.1016/j.ssci.2021.105514

Structuring of Discourse and Annotation Method for Contribution Assessment in Collaborative Discussions

Takeshi Masuda[1]([✉]), Hiroo Hirose[1]([✉]), and Takeshi Tsuchiya[2]

[1] Graduate School of Engineering and Management, Suwa University of Science,
5000-1 Toyohira, Chino, Nagano, Japan
{GH22701,hirose}@ed.sus.ac.jp
[2] Institute for Data Science Education, Tokyo International University, 1-13-1 Matobakita,
Kawagoe, Saitama, Japan
ttsuchi@tiu.ac.jp

Abstract. Human resource training, screening, and recruiting processes all require low-cost individual evaluation of participants in group discussions. This study aims to explore efficient ways to evaluate verbal discussions based on transcription data in an objective and multi-angle perspective to structure and annotate discussions for quantitative evaluation of the contribution from participants. Using two discussion data sets, this study conducted an experiment in which discussions were classified into a multi-layered discussion structure, and then annotations were further assigned within each layer and evaluated using a rating formula. In this experiment, we evaluated each participant in five evaluation dimensions and the result shows that they can be evaluated from multiple aspects as in conventional evaluation by observers. In addition, we also found that evaluation can be shown in a continuous scoring scope different from the five-point rating scale in conventional evaluation by observers. As only manual annotation is used in this study, it is believed that evaluation can be executed at an even lower cost by automated annotation in future studies.

Keywords: Collaborative discussion · Contribution assessment · Learning analytics · Information Visualization

1 Introduction

Group discussion is a common method adopted by the business sector for ability assessment for member selection and recruitment interviews. Individual performance and business skills such as leadership become visible and audible as concrete actions during discussions but not in written tests. Evaluation is usually done by assessors through observation so inconsistent judgment and bias must be eliminated if at all possible. A fair result can only be attained if the assessors are highly experienced. Moreover, since the number of participants each assessor can observe is limited, a huge number of assessors is, thus, necessary for large groups. The evaluation cost soars considering the difficulties of training and recruiting assessors equipped with experience and skills. Business enterprises, thus, long for evaluations only with inexperienced personnel officers but still be objective to a certain extent so they can stop relying on the skill set of assessors.

Face-to-face discussions and interactions are studied through multimodal learning analytics based on verbal and physical expressions recorded by cameras and sensors [1–3]. Detailed analysis including investigations on the emotions of participants is feasible, but the method is not widely adopted for the complicated installation of cameras and sensors along with the limitations of venue selection.

Researchers also extend their study interest to written posts on online forums instead of only real-time, verbal discussions through summarization based on the extraction of key posts from forum threads [4, 5]. Yet, the evaluation of individual participants is not multi-faceted. There are also studies on automated evaluation of text data such as thesis and essays [6, 7]. The evaluation of essays is highly individual but there are, after all, no interactions so interpersonal skills are not evaluated.

Conventional evaluation of individual data of participants in verbal discussions involves the time and effort-consuming processes of preparing microphones and transcribing audio data so the method is not well penetrated. Nevertheless, online meetings have taken the world by storm in recent years, and recording a discussion has become much easier. The accuracy of auto transcription has been improved significantly, too.

This study aims to develop an objective and multi-aspect evaluation based on the transcription of verbal discussions. We are convinced that the evaluation cost would be enormously reduced with no adverse influence on objectiveness and fairness when evidence is based on discussion record data instead of the observation of a small group of qualified assessors. It would be a much easier evaluation of multiple target participants when compared with the conventional method contributing to the exploration of talents. This thesis focuses on the following research question-

How can we evaluate, from multiple angles, the ability of discussion participants based on the transcription of audio records?

This thesis is structured in this way - the second section is a review of previous studies, followed by the definition of the target discussion structure and a description of the multi-angle evaluation of participants in the third section. The fourth section reveals the experiment result based on two sets of discussion samples. The fifth section elaborates findings of the experiment, followed by the conclusion in the sixth section.

2 Literature Review

Research on structuring discussions has been around for a long time. In the 1970s, Kunz and Rittel [8] proposed IBIS (Issue-Based Information Systems) in which discussions are structured for decision-making by the decomposition into logical elements such as issue, position, and argument. Based on IBIS, gIBIS [9, 10] has been proposed to display the structure of arguments on a computer. Various other frameworks for structuring and representing arguments have also been proposed [11, 12].In addition to structuring and visualizing discussion, researchers also focused on the creation of summaries [13].

There were also studies called Argument Mining with structure identification and extract from discussion in natural language. As Lawrence and Reed [14] pointed out, discussions applicable to Argument Mining include claims, evidence, counterarguments, preconditions, and conclusions. Alsinet et al. [15], on the other hand, visualized in a concrete model the extent of disagreement between online discussions and the aggressive relationship among comments. Studies have also been conducted to model essays (written texts) as argument structures [16, 17]. Stab and Gurevch [16] visualized the core claim, assumptions, and supporting/objecting elaborations in essays through annotation and sentence models.

These previous studies all focused on discussions and written texts with clear arguments and confrontational structures, such as debates; many of them structure arguments based on the logical notion of the remarks such as arguments/counterarguments. This study focuses on group discussions for training, screening, and recruiting in the real business world with no clear arguments or a confrontational structure, which is called Collaborative Discussion [18]. The purpose of this study is to evaluate how participants contribute to the discussion as a whole through collaborative dialogues. For this, information other than annotations indicating logic, such as arguments and counterarguments, is needed as indications of the overall collaborative discussion structure.

Speech annotation can be done in different ways [19–23] and analysis can be based on the role classification of the participants instead of individual speeches [24, 25]. Pianesi et al. [26] and Fujimoto [27] previously classified participants into the two areas of "task" and "socio-emotional" by their respective functional roles as evaluation should also be done in the individual performance in terms of their roles in the discussion group instead of the content of their speech alone. Examples include the role of a "listener" who does not speak much and the role of a "summarizer" who summarizes the discussion. Role-focused evaluation is also important in real-world individual evaluation situations.

The focus of conventional speech analysis in discussions was the details of individual opinions as elements contributing to affecting the discussion direction in terms of the decision-making process and speeches that influence other participants. Considering Bartel's statement [28] that the mood of the group can influence individual performance, we realized that conventional discussion analysis focused merely on the contents and that evaluation of the mood of the discussion is insufficient.

There are also studies on asynchronous online forums. Klaas [4] put the relationship between comments and their replies in online forums as a graph structure consisting of nodes and edges for studies on extracted important comments. The TextRank model is sometimes used to determine the importance of nodes in the graph structure for keyword extraction [29]. Murakami [30] illustrated how to assign a useful comment indicator value to comments from the thread structure of online forums.

All in all, the methodology and the study purpose of synchronous verbal discussions differ from those of asynchronous textual debates in online forums. As simultaneous textualization for synchronous verbal discussions is now possible, it has become practical to apply the analysis methods of asynchronous online forums to verbal discussions.

This study aims to evaluate the individual performance of participants based on textualized contents of verbal discussions through the record and transcription functions of some widely used online meeting systems, the approach is much more practical when compared with those on discussions in previous studies with the installation of microphones, cameras, and sensors. Furthermore, much greater contributions are expected for a thorough, integrated evaluation of participants' abilities for candidate selection and training purposes through the multi-angle analysis of speech data in discussions instead of merely on the logical flow of the interaction.

3 Methodology

3.1 Structuring Discussions

In this research, a discussion is depicted as a speech network illustrated in a graph structure in which the speeches are shown as nodes and connections between them are as edges Fig. 1. A speech starting a new cluster without referring to other speeches is called a parent speech, and those connected with a parent speech are called child speeches.

In Fig. 1, speeches B and C are based on A while E, F, and G are based on speech C. Speeches H and I are based on G. As a result, speech I is not directly but just indirectly based on A, it is, still, influenced by A indeed.

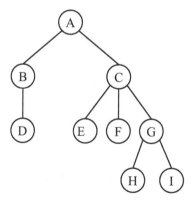

Fig. 1. Graph structure of speeches

The following hypotheses of our research are set for assessors with no advanced assessment skills to conduct evaluations based on data.

Hypothesis 1) Evaluation is feasible based on speech structure without any detailed assessment of the contents and importance of the speeches.

Based on hypothesis one, this research adopts an evaluation algorithm that highly evaluates speeches provoking replies and those with a longer sub-speech string. In Fig. 1, C scores higher than B's because C received more replies and the child speeches lasted longer. However, if this algorithm is applied to all speeches, speeches located upstream will be evaluated more highly than necessary, so the decay rate is applied to the chain of speeches so that the effect of speeches that are too far apart will not be too great.

In previous studies, all speeches in verbal discussions were lumped together for evaluation. Annotations were assigned to claims, opinions, and counterarguments that influence the conclusion of the discussion and were structured. Short responses and jokes with no expressions of opinions are not annotated. Therefore, short responses were excluded from the evaluation. This study is, instead, also based on the following hypothesis for the focus of evaluation on collaborative discussions instead of discussions consisting of a concrete decision-making process and debates.

Hypothesis 2) The classification of speech types according to their speech type also contributes to the evaluation of speeches other than those that constitute the logic of the discussion.

Based on hypothesis two, this study defines the three layers of speech structure in discussions as illustrated in Fig. 2.

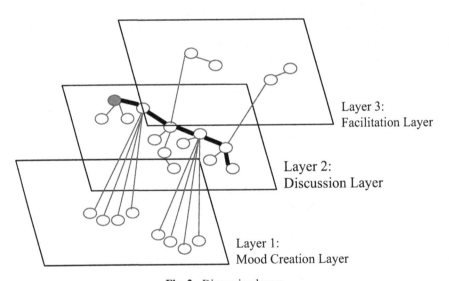

Layer 3:
Facilitation Layer

Layer 2:
Discussion Layer

Layer 1:
Mood Creation Layer

Fig. 2. Discussion layers

The discussion layers shown in Fig. 2 were selected from the elements that evaluators often emphasize when evaluating discussions. The main part of the discussion consists of utterances that form the logical line of the discussion, such as expressing opinions, presenting new ideas, and providing additional information and additions to these ideas. In addition, facilitation, such as encouraging other participants to speak and summarizing previous discussions, also takes place among the participants in the discussion. Because a facilitator is not predetermined in collaborative discussions, the evaluator is highly interested in who among the participants spontaneously provides facilitation. In addition, the act of agreeing with others' statements through a verbal expression or gesture is also evaluated as an indication of interpersonal communication skills. On this basis, the three discussion layers are defined as follows.

The first layer is the "Mood Creation Layer," which is rather crucial for the constitution of mood in which participants cooperate in the desired atmosphere of a collaborative discussion including speeches to assist others to air their views in a harmonized atmosphere. Examples include agreement, short responses, compliments, greetings, jokes, and laughter.

The second layer is the "Discussion Layer" accommodating speeches to constitute the discussion logic, which was the focus of conventional discussion analysis. They are a declaration of stance, a statement of new ideas, additional information for previous speeches (from both the own statement and other participants), and questions.

The third layer is the "Facilitation Layer" accommodating facilitation stemmed from a macro point of view for a smooth discussion. For example, this layer includes comments that expand the discussion to include other ideas, converge the discussion, or invite passive participants to talk.

We then performed annotations to speeches in these layers according to their categories. Annotation labels are shown in Table 1.

Table 1. Speech classification

Discussion Layer	Speech Category	Speech details
Facilitation	Facilitation	Diverging, converging, summarizing, moderating, and facilitating discussions
Discussion	Opinion	Declaration of stance/statement of new ideas
	Argument Reinforcement	Extra information for previous speeches (from both the own statement and other participants)
	Argument Development	Confirmation/questions of existing speeches, replies, and statements of related information
Mood Creation	Warm Up	Greetings, short responses, jokes, and laughter
	Agreement	Agreement with other participants
	Admiration	Compliment/gratitude to others

In the annotation process, multiple labels can be put on the same speech as some of them can be a facilitation in the first half followed by the statement of stance in the second half.

3.2 Quantitative Evaluation of Speech

The quantitative evaluation of each speech of the discussion, which is divided into layers by structuring the discussion into a speech graph structure and further assigning annotations of speech categories to each node of the discussion, is performed as follows.

The Speech Evaluation of the Discussion Layer
Speeches in the discussion layer are evaluated using the speech structure graph and annotations. The evaluation formula is an improved formula based on a previous study [30] that aimed to extract useful comments in asynchronous discussions as shown below.

$$cv_{(p)} = \left(sv_{(p)} + \sum_{i=0}^{N-1} cf_{(p_i)} \times cv_{(p_i)} \times af^i \right) \times cr_{(p)} \tag{1}$$

The score for speech p in the discussion is $cv_{(p)}$ as calculated from (1) above.

$sv_{(p)}$ is the self-remark score, which is the initial value of speech.
N is the number of chain speeches including the speech to be evaluated.
$cf_{(p)}$ is the category coefficient, whose value depends on the speech category assigned to the child speeches.
af is the attenuation coefficient to minimize the influence when the structure goes deep.
$cr_{(p)}$ indicates the category probability as the weight of the target speech categories.

As mentioned, multiple labels might be given to the same speech for the co-existence of speech categories. For example, if the speech is categorized both as an opinion on the discussion layer and facilitation on the facilitation layer, the weights of the respective categories are $cr_{(p)}$ for the calculation of the opinion score of the discussion layer and the facilitation score on another layer. As a result, a speech can appear on multiple layers with different scores.

The Speech Evaluation of the Facilitation Layer
The evaluation score is the number of speeches corresponding to this layer.

The Speech Evaluation of the Mood Creation Layer
Similarly, the evaluation score is the number of speeches corresponding to this layer.

Each speech has the attributes of the participant, their speech category, and evaluation score (if multiple speech categories are assigned, multiple speech categories and evaluation scores for each category).

3.3 Evaluation of Individual Participants

The total evaluation scores of individual participants and speech categories were then added up. We also standardized the score of the respective layers (by calculating their T-scores) for the evaluation of the speeches of the participants in different layers. Table 2 shows the evaluation dimensions of the individual participants, which are partial combinations of the annotated speech categories.

Table 2. Evaluation Dimensions

Items for Evaluation	Overview
Opinion	Indicator of the strength of the impact of the statement that presented a claim or new idea on the discussion
Argument Reinforcement	Indicator of the ability to supplement and reinforce the statements of others and self
Argument Development	Indicator of the ability to develop discussion through questions and confirmation of statements
Mood Creation	Indicator of the ability to create an atmosphere conducive to speaking up by empathizing, praising, or joking with others
Facilitation	Indicator of the ability to oversee the discussion and encourage and summarize comments

This study then assesses individual participants with the above annotations according to the speech layers and the structure of the replying relationships of the speeches. By doing so, this study performs quantitative evaluations using simple annotations without looking into the contents of the speech based on advanced assessment techniques. Furthermore, the annotation of this study assesses participants from multiple angles in collaborative discussions without any concrete points of argument or conclusions.

3.4 Experiment

This section describes the discussion data used in this study.

Our discussion involved six male and female participants about workstyle. The discussion was divided into two sessions - the first one was a 15-min discussion about the merits of working from home followed by the second one - a 10-min discussion about the merits of reporting duty at offices. The participants in both sessions were all the same. As the stance of all participants was the same in both discussions so that they communicated on the same ground, it could be regarded as a "collaborative discussion."

The discussions were held online through the meeting system Zoom and the audio was recorded. The audio data was then transcribed by API auto-transcription with manual post-editing. Audible speeches were all textualized including fillers like "um..." and short responses like "oh, yes." Attained data consisted of four elements - speech ID, speech time, speaker, and the text of the speech details.

Each speech was treated as a node, and edges were added to represent the referencing relationships between speeches. The assignment of edges was accomplished by specifying the reference of a given speech to another speech using their respective identification numbers. In this experiment, the task of assigning edges was performed manually by experts experienced in discussion assessment.

The annotation of the speeches in the textualized discussion was all manually performed according to their categories as shown in Table 1 by three annotators. The chief annotator is an experienced and professional discussion assessor who also provided guidelines for the other two assisting annotators. In the annotation process, 423 labels were given to the two discussion sessions.

41% of the labels given by the three annotators were the same and 48% of them were the same between the two of them, making up a total of 89% of the labels in alignment with at least two annotators. The alignment rate of the annotation was directly used as the variable of the category probability. For example, for a statement with all three annotators labeled "facilitation" and two out of the three annotated "opinion," the category probability for facilitation is 1 and that for opinion is 0.67. Speeches out of the mood creation, discussion, and facilitation layers are excluded from the assessment process.

After the annotation, the evaluation score of the speeches was calculated using the formula shown in the previous section about the quantitative evaluation of speeches.

4 Results

The parameters adopted for the calculation of the evaluation scores are shown in Table 3.

Table 3. Parameters

Parameter	Discussion Layer	Speech Category	set value
$sv_{(p)}$			0.5
$cf_{(p)}$	Facilitation	Facilitation	0.75
	Discussion	Opinion	1.0
		Argument Reinforcement	1.25
		Argument Development	0.75
	Mood Creation	Warm Up	0.5
		Agreement	1.0
		Admiration	1.25
af			0.3

The parameter values were set concerning previous studies. Opinions, which are utterances that constitute the main storyline of the discussion, were set to a base value of "1", and the score was set so that the more agreement and reinforcement of the opinion by others gathered on that opinion, the higher the score. The coefficient for mood creation, which is often a short utterance, was made relatively small.

Evaluation scores are shown in Table 4 and Table 5. The six participants are referred to as A to F.

Table 4. Discussion Session 1 Evaluation scores (based on the calculation of this study)

Evaluation dimensions	A	B	C	D	E	F
Opinion	45.19	69.12	37.22	48.26	64.83	50.10
Argument Reinforcement	40.90	62.99	37.22	56.24	62.99	46.42
Argument Development	38.44	57.47	37.83	52.56	48.88	43.35
Mood Creation	38.15	48.61	38.15	50.17	60.63	64.29
Facilitation	39.27	58.21	37.38	56.31	63.89	44.95

Table 5. Discussion Session 2 Evaluation scores (based on the calculation of this study)

Evaluation dimensions	A	B	C	D	E	F
Opinion	54.51	74.10	37.72	50.31	54.51	48.91
Argument Reinforcement	46.11	65.70	37.72	44.71	58.71	44.71
Argument Development	43.31	57.31	37.72	41.91	41.91	60.11
Mood Creation	43.30	49.18	35.95	51.14	51.63	68.79
Facilitation	52.93	58.78	29.51	52.93	58.78	47.07

Figure 3 is a part of the speech graph structure of the discussion data in this research. The size of the node represents the assessment score of the respective speeches; NetworkX of the Python library is adopted for plotting the speech graph structure.

Fig. 3. Visualized speech graph structure

As shown in the figure, speeches with more child speeches/longer child speeches score higher.

For comparison purposes, these scores were put together with a 5-point rating from professional and experienced assessors with assessment techniques through conventional observation on the same sets of textual discussion data with criteria shown in Table 6. The results of the 5-point rating are shown in Tables 7 and 8.

Table 6. The 5-point rating scheme for assessor

Score	Criteria
5	Contributing enormously to the discussion
4	Contributing to the discussion
3	Natural/neither
2	Contributing only a little to the discussion
1	No notable contribution/no speeches

Table 7. Discussion Session 1 Evaluation scores from the assessor

Evaluation dimensions	A	B	C	D	E	F
Opinion	3	5	1	3	4	4
Argument Reinforcement	4	4	1	3	5	2
Argument Development	1	3	1	3	3	2
Mood Creation	4	4	2	4	4	5
Facilitation	2	3	1	3	4	2

Table 8. Discussion Session 2 Evaluation scores from the assessor

Evaluation dimensions	A	B	C	D	E	F
Opinion	3	5	1	3	4	3
Argument Reinforcement	3	4	1	3	4	3
Argument Development	2	3	1	2	2	2
Mood Creation	4	4	1	4	4	5
Facilitation	3	4	1	2	4	2

Figures 4 and 5 show the comparison of the assessment scores of this study and the conventional method as radar charts for participants. As illustrated, the assessment scores of this study have the same tendency as the conventional observation by the assessor.

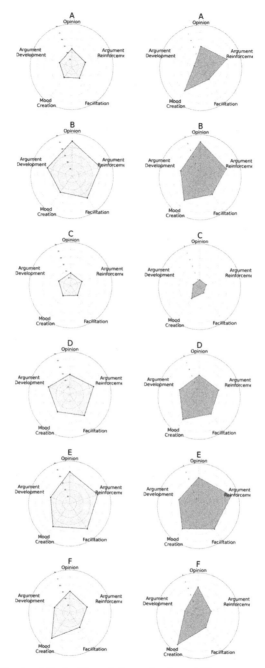

Fig. 4. Discussion Session 1 Radar Chart (left - evaluation of this research; right - conventional method)

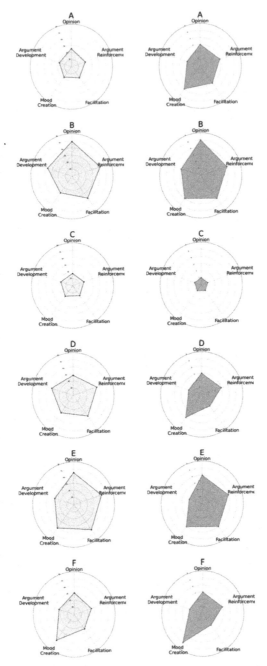

Fig. 5. Discussion Session 2 Radar Chart (left - evaluation of this research; right - conventional method)

5 Discussion

This study showed that it is possible to evaluate discussion participants using the structure of the speeches and the annotations assigned to each discussion layer; the performance of participants can thus be evaluated from multiple angles without the presence of assessors with advanced techniques. In conventional discussion analysis, structuring methods have been adopted only for debates with clear argument points and conclusions while this study found the discussion layers that can be not only to clarify the logical structure of an argument, but also evaluate its contribution to facilitation such as efforts to smoothen the discussion or creating a mood to invite other participants to air their views. In this study, only the Discussion layer was evaluated by the score of its speeches calculated with the use of a formula, the Facilitation layer and Mood Creation layer were both evaluated merely using the number of their speeches. All evaluations except for that of the Discussion layer were hence rather straightforward. Still, we witnessed a very much similar result when compared with the conventional evaluation by experienced assessors. This in turn proved that the evaluation method can be applied to the different evaluation algorithms in different layers of a discussion. The evaluation method is, in fact, highly practical and applicable to different situations as the assessment purpose is flexible.

Additionally, while conventional argument analysis assigns annotations suitable for logical discussions, this study proposes annotations suitable for collaborative discussions without an opposing structure or a concrete conclusion. The method is relatively detailed and thorough when the scores are expressed as T-scores converted using this annotation. Conventional manual assessments were often 5-point or 7-point ratings with separate consecutive grades so no fine distinctive differences could be expressed between the scores, such as between "3" and "4". It also fails to show extreme results such as those above the upper limit of "5" in a 5-point rating. This new assessment visualizes the T scores based on the calculation using a formula telling the tiny little differences could not be revealed by manual assessments.

On the other hand, the links of the referential relationship among speeches and annotations of the speeches in manual processes should also be automated in the future as this study. Since this study aims to reduce the cost and improve the processing power of the assessment work, there is still room for improvement in this respect. It does not require as much skill as assessment, which involves examining and evaluating the content of statements, and is not as costly as conventional methods because it can be done with simple annotation work. However, manual annotation becomes a bottleneck, making it difficult to evaluate a large number of discussions in a short period. Therefore, in the future, we will consider automating the part of the process. As targets for automation, we would like to examine the possibility of using natural language models and deep learning to stratify and annotate the structure of discussions and to add reference relations for creating a graph structure of statements.

6 Conclusion

This study aims to develop a multi-angle and objective evaluation method based on the transcription data of verbal discussions contributing to structuring and annotating collaborative discussions for a quantitative evaluation. We have divided speeches in discussions into three layers and annotated them according to their functions in a collaborative discussion for evaluation in which we successfully proved the method does contribute to evaluating participants from multiple aspects in a continuous scoring scheme that could not be revealed in the conventional and manual assessments by assessors. The method does not rely on professional assessors equipped with specific advanced skills, and evaluations are all based on the discussion data, so it is both fair and objective to a certain extent. The method is, at the same time, cost-saving.

It is essential to automate the manual annotation and layer division processes for future studies as having more automated processes and fewer manual processes encourages usage for large-group discussions such as in the practical situations of human resource training, staff selection, appraisal meetings, and recruitment for locating capable beings in the private business sector.

References

1. Okada, S., et al.: Estimating communication skills using dialogue acts and nonverbal features in multiple discussion datasets. In: Proceedings of the 18th ACM International Conference on Multimodal Interaction, pp. 169–176. Association for Computing Machinery, New York (2016)
2. Avci, U., Aran, O.: Predicting the performance in decision-making tasks: from individual cues to group interaction. IEEE Trans. Multimed. **18**, 643–658 (2016). https://doi.org/10.1109/TMM.2016.2521348
3. Murray, G., Oertel, C.: Predicting group performance in task-based interaction. In: Proceedings of the 20th ACM International Conference on Multimodal Interaction, pp. 14–20. Association for Computing Machinery, New York (2018)
4. Klaas, M.: Toward indicative discussion fora summarization. UBC CS TR-2005. 4 (2005)
5. Sharifi, B., Hutton, M.-A., Kalita, J.K.: Experiments in microblog summarization. In: 2010 IEEE Second International Conference on Social Computing, pp. 49–56. ieeexplore.ieee.org (2010)
6. Snow, E.L., Allen, L.K., Jacovina, M.E., Crossley, S.A., Perret, C.A., McNamara, D.S.: Keys to detecting writing flexibility over time: entropy and natural language processing. Learn. Anal. **2**, 40–54 (2015). https://doi.org/10.18608/jla.2015.23.4
7. Ke, Z., Ng, V.: Automated essay scoring: a survey of the state of the art. In: Proceedings of the Twenty-Eighth International Joint Conference on Artificial Intelligence. International Joint Conferences on Artificial Intelligence Organization, California (2019)
8. Kunz, W., Rittel, H.W.J.: Issues as elements of information systems. Institute of Urban and Regional Development, University of California at Berkeley Working Paper **131**, 14 (1970)
9. Conklin, J., Begeman, M.L.: GIBIS: a hypertext tool for exploratory policy discussion. ACM Trans. Inf. Syst. Secur. **6**, 303–331 (1988). https://doi.org/10.1145/58566.59297
10. Burgess Yakemovic, K.C., Conklin, E.J.: Report on a development project use of an issue-based information system. In: Proceedings of the 1990 ACM Conference on Computer-Supported Cooperative Work, pp. 105–118. Association for Computing Machinery, New York (1990)

11. van Gelder, T.: Enhancing deliberation through computer supported argument visualization. In: Kirschner, P.A., Buckingham Shum, S.J., Carr, C.S. (eds.) Visualizing Argumentation: Software Tools for Collaborative and Educational Sense-Making, pp. 97–115. Springer, London, London (2003). https://doi.org/10.1007/978-1-4471-0037-9_5

12. Selvin, A., et al.: Compendium: making meetings into knowledge events (2001)

13. Barker, E., Gaizauskas, R.: Summarizing multi-party argumentative conversations in reader comment on news. In: Proceedings of the Third Workshop on Argument Mining (ArgMining2016), Berlin, Germany, pp. 12–20. Association for Computational Linguistics (2016)

14. Lawrence, J., Reed, C.: Argument mining: a survey. Comput. Linguist. Assoc. Comput. Linguist. **45**, 765–818 (2020). https://doi.org/10.1162/coli_a_00364

15. Alsinet, T., Argelich, J., Béjar, R., Martínez, S.: Measuring user relevance in online debates through an argumentative model. Pattern Recogn. Lett. **133**, 41–47 (2020). https://doi.org/10.1016/j.patrec.2020.02.008

16. Stab, C., Gurevych, I.: Annotating argument components and relations in persuasive essays. In: Proceedings of COLING 2014, the 25th International Conference on Computational Linguistics: Technical Papers, Dublin, Ireland, pp. 1501–1510. Dublin City University and Association for Computational Linguistics (2014)

17. Stab, C., Gurevych, I.: Parsing argumentation structures in persuasive essays. Comput. Linguist. Assoc. Comput. Linguist. **43**, 619–659 (2017). https://doi.org/10.1162/coli_a_00295

18. Sawyer, R.K.: Creative teaching: collaborative discussion as disciplined improvisation. Educ. Res. **33**, 12–20 (2004). https://doi.org/10.3102/0013189X033002012

19. Alexandersson, J., et al.: Dialogue acts in VERBMOBIL-2 (1997)

20. Renals, S., Hain, T., Bourlard, H.: Recognition and understanding of meetings the AMI and AMIDA projects. In: 2007 IEEE Workshop on Automatic Speech Recognition & Understanding (ASRU), pp. 238–247 (2007)

21. Fang, A., Cao, J., Bunt, H., Liu, X.: The annotation of the Switchboard corpus with the new ISO standard for dialogue act analysis. In: Workshop on Interoperable Semantic Annotation, p. 13. sigsem.uvt.nl (2012)

22. Sinclair, J., Coulthard, M.: Towards an analysis of discourse. taylorfrancis.com (2013)

23. ISO 24617-2:2020. https://www.iso.org/standard/76443.html

24. Benne, K.D., Sheats, P.: Functional roles of group members. J. Soc. Issues **4**, 41–49 (1948). https://doi.org/10.1111/j.1540-4560.1948.tb01783.x

25. Salazar, A.J.: An analysis of the development and evolution of roles in the small group. Small Group Res. **27**, 475–503 (1996). https://doi.org/10.1177/1046496496274001

26. Pianesi, F., Zancanaro, M., Lepri, B., Cappelletti, A.: A multimodal annotated corpus of consensus decision making meetings. Lang. Resour. Eval. **41**, 409–429 (2007). https://doi.org/10.1007/s10579-007-9060-6

27. Fujimoto, M.: Team roles and hierarchic system in group discussion. Group Decis. Negot. **25**(3), 585–608 (2015). https://doi.org/10.1007/s10726-015-9453-7

28. Bartel, C.A., Saavedra, R.: The collective construction of work group moods. Adm. Sci. Q. **45**, 197–231 (2000). https://doi.org/10.2307/2667070

29. Mihalcea, R., Tarau, P.: TextRank: bringing order into text. In: Proceedings of the 2004 Conference on Empirical Methods in Natural Language Processing, Barcelona, Spain, pp. 404–411. Association for Computational Linguistics (2004)

30. Murakami, A., Nasukawai, T., Nakagawa, H.: Extracting useful remarks in online discussions. In: Proceedings of the Fourteenth Annual Meeting of the Association for Natural Language Processing, pp. 352–355 (2008). (in Japanese)

Removal of Various Noise Types and Voice-Based Gender Classification for Dubbed Videos

Hai Thanh Nguyen[1], Toan Khanh Do[1], Khoa Viet Le[1,2],
Tong Thanh Nguyen[1], and Huong Hoang Luong[3(✉)]

[1] Can Tho University, Can Tho, Vietnam
nthai.cit@ctu.edu.vn
[2] CanTho Radio and Television Station, Can Tho, Vietnam
[3] FPT University, Can Tho, Vietnam
huonghoangluong@gmail.com

Abstract. Gender classification based on voice is an important area of research with numerous applications in various fields. It is commonly used in speech recognition, forensic science, and social sciences. In the film industry, using both female and male voices in a dubbed movie can provide a more realistic and diverse experience for the audience. However, noise can cause errors in speech recognition software. Therefore, noise removal is crucial in generating accurate subtitles for audio or video content, often used to generate subtitles automatically. Our study evaluates the effectiveness of different techniques for removing noise on different types of noises, such as crowded places, motorcycle sounds, engine running, etc. In addition, we have leveraged machine learning algorithms to perform voice-based gender classification. The experiments found that DeepFilterNet was the most effective noise removal technique, with a similarity score of 0.8442, followed by Noisereduce with 0.7339. In addition, Support Vector Machines (SVM) and K-Nearest Neighbor (KNN) are more effective in gender classification using voice-based signals with a mean accuracy of 0.8715 and 0.7773, respectively, than the Logistic Regression and Random Forest. The work is expected to produce dubbed videos using female and male voices.

Keywords: noise reduction · dubbed videos · subtitle-generator · voice classification · film industry

1 Introduction

Video has become popular for daily communication, entertainment, and information sharing. However, text extraction from video, noise reduction, and voice gender classification are still difficult in speech processing and computer vision due to multiple noise sources and complex video content. Recent works [1,2] demonstrate the importance of text retrieval. [3,4] studies show the importance of noise cancellation and audio-to-text recognition to create a highly accurate captioning engine. The results of this study aim to address the fundamental problems and challenges of video processing, such as speech detection and recognition and speech gender classification noise reduction using machine learning methods. The method of building subtitles for a video is intended to help the audience better understand the content of the video. Male and female voice recognition is important in distinguishing and providing accurate subtitles. Some methods of voice gender classification are as follows [5–7] determining the speaker's gender will help in creating subtitles and voiceovers video becomes more accurate, helping viewers understand the content of the video most clearly. In addition, male and female voice recognition can also assist in creating suitable subtitle versions for foreign-language audiences, enhancing the audience's experience and improving communication efficiency information of the video, making the video's content more vivid and accessible. Therefore, the research and development of technologies in this field are being invested heavily to bring the best experiences to viewers. The proposed method offers a promising solution to these challenges, providing high-quality video content with subtitles.

Various tools have been used in speech-to-text applications to support research and learning. However, automated speech-to-text systems are often significantly affected by noise. Noise can be generated from the media or channel and degrade the performance of the speech-to-text system. This unwanted noise can change the main characteristics of a voice signal and degrade the quality of the information contained therein. Such damage can cause significant harm to human-computer interaction systems. Therefore, noise reduction methods have been created. At radio and television stations, producers usually leverage both female and male voices in dubbed videos to convey a broader range of emotions and increase interest in the film or video-based newsletters. Besides, automatic subtitle generators combining text-to-speech can help automatically quickly produce dubbed videos. However, the accuracy of subtitle generators can be affected by noises. Our study evaluates the efficiency of some noise removal techniques on natural speeches recorded and leveraged some learning algorithms to perform gender classification to support producing dubbed videos with the significant contributions as follows:

- We have recorded voices from Can Tho University, Vietnam students, and collected more data from several sources for evaluations in various scenarios.
- We have examined some noise removal techniques to evaluate their efficiency. In addition, we also evaluate their performance in various noisy environments such as crowded places, coffee shops, engine running, raindrops, and motorcycle sounds.
- We have performed the gender classification with various classical algorithms to see that SVM outperforms other considered algorithms. Combined with noise removal techniques, this task is expected to support producing dubbed videos.

The remaining is organized as follows. In Sect. 2, we review the most advanced techniques currently recommended by researchers for text and gender recognition in video. We describe the dataset used in our study and explain our workflow in detail in Sect. 3. We present our test results, which demonstrate the effectiveness of our framework in Sect. 4. Finally, we summarize our work and discuss potential future directions in Sect. 5.

2   Related Work

In recent years, much research has been done on video text processing. This study's noise reduction component, which entails eliminating superfluous or disruptive components from the captioning process, is a crucial component [4,8]. A variety of machine-learning techniques have been employed for this.

2.1   Research on Text Recognition in Video

The authors in [9] reviewed some approaches to the video-to-text problem aiming to associate an input video with its textual description. The survey was done on twenty-six benchmark datasets, analyzing the drawbacks and strengths of each problem.

Some subsequent research has explored automatic captioning tools, like Ruiz Domingo and his team's work [10]. They developed a system called FILENG: An Automatic English Subtitle Generator from Tagalog Videos, which can generate English subtitles from Tagalog videos. The researchers used sphinx4 as a tool for speech-to-text extraction, and the output includes timestamps. The system achieved an accuracy of 79%, and the study used accuracy, coverage, and F-measure to evaluate the collected data. Further research should consider system improvements.

Microsoft's automatic captioning tools were implemented and evaluated in the Yim project [11], demonstrating the growing interest in automatic captioning applications. Additionally, in the study by Halpern. [12], the authors showed that the efficiency of a contextual hypothesis in speech recognition is relatively high. This method allows training relatively small context models that are still effective in speech recognition.

2.2   Machine Learning for Gender Recognition Based on Audio Signals

Acoustic-based gender classification apps are used in [5,13,13–16] focuses on relationships relationship between health and gender-based on gender identity and speech classification. This study used a general health survey by telephone. Interviewers classified transgender women (n = 722) and transgender men (n = 446) by gender based on their assumptions after hearing the person's voice. Research shows that transgender men and women have different health assessments based on gender classification. Transgender black men were likely to be ranked the most inappropriate for their gender. This study may provide helpful information on the impact of gender on transgender health. However, careful consideration of the methodology and completeness of the data is needed to ensure the accuracy and reliability of the results.

More recently, a method of gender recognition through audio signals presented in the study [16] has given quite impressive results. Specifically, E. Priya et al. used the spectral and temporal properties of audio signals to determine gender. Spectral features include spectral energy density, focus, currents, and roll. Time characteristics include energy, zero crossing rate, square root mean, and peak amplitude. Features were checked for statistical consistency by t-test. The classification is based on the graph of the Mel spectral features. This study can also be expanded to compare with other methods to analyze and evaluate which method of gender determination is more appropriate in each specific case.

3   Methods

The general procedure for reducing noise and captioning a video, as shown in Fig. 1, includes the following steps. First, we collect videos for the experiments. Then, we use FFmpeg Library to extract audio from video files. Next, to enhance the subtitle generator, we choose DeepFilterNet [17] or Noisereduce [18] to remove noise in audio files. Then, we convert the audio file format from WAV to FLAC to comply with Speech-to-Text API requirements. Finally, we evaluate the similarities between the generated subtitle and the original text. Also, we perform voice-based gender classification to support dubbed videos for further processing.

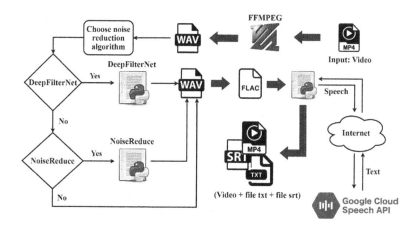

Fig. 1. The proposed workflow.

3.1   Data Collection

This section presents details on our study's initial data collection process, as outlined in Table 1. Our dataset consists of 1923 female and 1743 male voice recordings, including diverse ages and various voice types. We sourced these recordings from students enrolled at Can Tho University. To supplement our primary dataset, we also incorporated data from the Common Voice (Mozilla) [19] dataset, which is a comprehensive collection of audio samples gathered from volunteers across global locations. This extensive dataset serves as a valuable resource for training speech recognition models that recognize different languages. All voice samples included in our study are meticulously categorized by gender, age, language, and the location where they were collected. Our meticulous data collection approach ensures the highest accuracy and reliability of our study, making our results significant and applicable to a broader context.

Table 1. Samples distributions according to Gender

Type	Number of samples
Female voice	1923
Male voice	1743
Natural voice	81
Machine-based voice	102

Our study used eight different datasets for our speech-to-text recognition method. These datasets include audio recordings from various sources, including male and female Vietnamese (VI) and English (EN) voices. In addition, the datasets were divided into five groups based on the number of words in each record: less than 50 words, 50 to 100 words, 100 to 300 words, 500 to 1000 words, and over 1000 words. The above sample numbers are randomly selected according to the five noise types described in Scenario 1. Furthermore, by comparing the performance of the speech-to-text recognition method among different groups of users with different record lengths, we can conclude the effectiveness of this method. However, in the experimental process, gender and language did not affect the speech-to-text conversion process. Table 1 presents the number of samples classified by agents as natural and machine voices in the last two rows.

3.2   Noise Removal Techniques

Noisereduce: Noisereduce [18,20] is a Python-based noise reduction algorithm that reduces noise in time domain signals, such as speech, bioacoustics, and physiological signals. It utilizes a technique called "spectral gating", which is a form of noise gate. The algorithm calculates the spectrogram of a signal (specifically, noise), estimates the noise threshold for each signal's frequency band, and uses it to calculate a mask. This mask is important in preventing the noise from falling below the frequency change threshold. Below are the steps of the Fixed Noise Reduction Algorithm:

- Calculate a spectrum on the noisy sound clip.
- Compute statistical information on the spectrum of the noise (by frequency)
- Determine a threshold based on the statistical information of the noise and desired sensitivity of the algorithm.
- Calculate a spectrum on the signal.
- The mask is determined by comparing the signal's spectrum with the threshold.
- The mask is smoothed by time- and frequency-domain filtering.

- The mask is applied to the signal's spectrum, and if no noise signal is provided, the algorithm assumes the signal is a noise clip and tends to work correctly.

DeepFilterNet: DeepFilterNet [17] is a two-stage speech enhancement the framework that utilizes the "Deep Filtering" feature. DeepFilterNet enhances the spectral envelope in the first stage using an Equivalent Rectangular Bandwidth (ERB) model that mimics human frequency perception. The ERB bandpass filter bank reduces the input and output dimensions to only Thirty-two frequency bands, allowing fast encoding/decoding in the internal network. However, since the minimum bandwidth obtained from 100 Hz to 250 Hz (depending on the Fast Fourier Transform (FFT) size) is often insufficient to enhance periodic components, the second stage enhancement relies on deep filtering. In the second stage, deep filtering is used to enhance the periodic components of speech. The encoding process is streamlined in DeepFilterNet2 with only linear layers grouped on the frequency axis via single matrix multiplication. The hidden dimension of GRU is reduced to 256 to simplify grouping. Temporary downsampling is applied by replacing 2×3 convolutions with 1×3 to reduce bandwidth usage. Parameter redundancy and FLOP are decreased by grouping residual connections with 1×1 PConv layers. Finally, post-filtering reduces excessive noise in TF bins while preserving beneficial information. This is achieved by utilizing predicted gains in the first stage of post-processing.

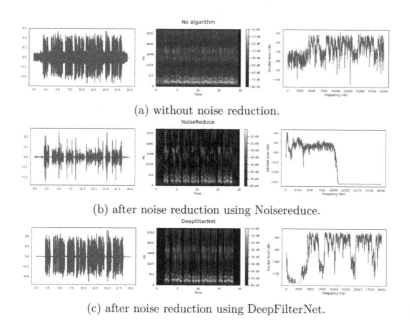

(a) without noise reduction.

(b) after noise reduction using Noisereduce.

(c) after noise reduction using DeepFilterNet.

Fig. 2. Visualization of an audio sample.

Fig. 2a exhibits the audio waveform before using any noise reduction algorithm. Noise waves look a lot and affect the sound quality. Further observation in Fig. 2b The results show that the number of interference waves has been significantly reduced, and this method reduces the noise significantly. However, the sound quality is also reduced to the 2b image. We can easily see that the audio volume is also significantly reduced. This process will make the video subtitles disappear. Figure 2c shows the sound wave after applying the deepfilterNet method. The results show that this method has eliminated most of the noise, leaving only some purple wave points but with a minimal amount, and it is also easy to see that the sound volume is not reduced.

3.3   Voice Classification

Finding the best classification model, which supports identifying test patterns based on unknown characteristics and labels, requires classifier learning algorithms. Different learning methods can be mathematically modeled to represent knowledge. To provide diversity in the use of different types of sound-based gender classification techniques will be introduced in this section, and the classifiers selected include SVM, logistic (L), Random Forest (RF), and KNN.

Fig. 3. General gender recognition framework.

To build a high-quality model and voice gender recognition, as shown in Fig. 3. In particular, each classification technique is used to build a set of hypothetical models and select the most optimal model. We have proposed a specific dataset in Table 1. This model classifies unknown voice labels by getting voice features and voice gender classification.

4   Experimental Results

4.1   Environmental Settings and Metrics

Test results are run on Windows 11 with CPU configuration Intel i7-10750H 2.60 GHz 2.59 GHz, RAM 8.00 GB (7.83 GB available). Results also depend on network speed (required by Google API Speech-To-Text). The program setup environment is Python with FFmpeg, Numpy, Autosrt, Librosa, Tensorflow, and other libraries.

For Scenario 1, we measure the similarity between the original text (ground truth) and the detected text (predicted results). We calculate the similarity of the text detected from the audio and original files. Referring to the speech-to-text conversion model illustrated in Fig. 1, when performing speech recognition on a FLAC audio file, three files are generated, including an SRT file, an MP4 file, and an MP4 file. TXT file. Based on the TXT file, we can calculate similarity by comparing two documents with an extension, i.e., TXT. This is a method to represent vectors in a two-vector model. We use the measure of similarity of a scalar space between two vectors, A and B, as shown in Eq. 1 with θ as the angle between A and B, to quantify their similarity. For example, if the dot product of two vectors forms a 90-degree angle, then the similarity between the two vectors is 0 ($\cos(90) = 0$), which proves that the two documents are not identical. Conversely, if the dot product of two vectors is 1 ($\cos(0) = 1$), the similarity between the two scripts is perfect. The cosine similarity metric is particularly well suited to non-negative spaces, with results strictly limited to the range [0, 1]. For classification tasks in Scenario 2, we use Precision, Recall, and F1-score to evaluate the performance.

$$\mathrm{Sin}(A, B) = \cos(\theta) = \frac{A \cdot B}{\|A\|\|B\|} \qquad (1)$$

4.2 Experiment 1: Performance Comparison of Noise Removal Techniques

The results shown in the several tables in this section shed important light on how noise affects speech-to-text translation and the effectiveness of different noise reduction methods. The number of words measures the lengths in all tables.

Table 2 shows that when no noise reduction is applied, despite the relatively high similarity for all noise types, the number of detected words is lower than the actual number of words. This has shown that noise can significantly reduce the accuracy of speech-to-text conversion. However, Table 3 demonstrates that applying the NoiseReduce technique improves the number of detected words and maintains reasonable similarity for all noise types. This suggests that noise reduction techniques can partially mitigate the detrimental effect of noise on speech-to-text accuracy.

Table 2. Average results without using noise reduction.

Type of noises	Length of original script	Detected Length	Similarity score
Crowded places	836	480	0.8928
Engine running	411	123	0.6235
In the coffee shop	155	91	0.7615
Motorcycle sound	70	37	0.6773
Sound of raindrops	46	26	0.6897

Table 3. Average results with NoiseReduce.

Type of noises	Length of original script	Detected Length	Similarity score
Crowded places	836	537	0.7942
Motorcycle sound	70	42	0.6789
In the coffee shop	155	106	0.7239
Engine running	411	199	0.7539
Sound of raindrops	46	32	0.7406

Table 4. Average results with DeepFilterNet.

Type of noises	Length of original script	Detected Length	Similarity score
Crowded places	836	604	0.9004
Motorcycle sound	70	54	0.8227
In the coffee shop	155	120	0.8320
Engine running	411	163	0.7848
Sound of raindrops	46	41	0.8917

Furthermore, the results presented in Table 4 highlight the remarkable performance of the DeepFilterNet technique in reducing noise and improving speech-to-text conversion accuracy. This technique achieves the highest number of detected words and gives the highest similarity for all noise types compared to the other two techniques. In summary, as exhibited in Table 5, these findings suggest that noise reduction techniques such as NoiseReduce or DeepFilterNet can significantly improve speech-to-text conversion accuracy in noisy environments.

Table 5. Results Comparison of noise removal algorithms

Algorithms	Length of original script	Detected Length	Similarity score
Do not use	283	142	0.7266
Noisereduce	283	171	0.7339
Deepfilternet	283	184	0.8442

The same classification results show that machine-based voices achieve higher accuracy than natural speech (Table 6). For example, the classification similarity of the machine-based speech agent is 0.8173, while the score of the natural speech agent is only 0.7066. This suggests that machine-based speech can provide more accurate and reliable similarity classification results than natural speech. The advantages of machine-based speech agents include the ability to read standard pronunciations and intelligibility, thereby providing results with the same accuracy.

Table 6. Results of various voice types

	Length of original script	Detected Length	Similarity score
Natural voice	23949	13767	0.7066
machine-based voice	27900	16598	0.8173

4.3 Experiment 2: Voice-Based Gender Recognition

Table 7 and Fig. 4 exhibit the average results of SVM, KNN, logistic regression, and Random Forest with accuracy ranging from 0.7075 to 0.8656. We can see the highest average accuracy is 0.8715, where the accuracy, recall, and f1 scores for both men and women are quite high. KNN also gives quite good results with an average accuracy of 0.7773. However, the f1 scores of the Female and Male classes are low. Logistic and Random Forest methods give relatively close results with an average accuracy of 0.7500 and 0.7075, respectively. However, their accuracy, recall, and f1 scores were lower than those of SVM and KNN. Overall, the SVM and KNN methods appear more effective than logistic regression and Random Forest in sound-based gender classification. It should be noted that this result is evaluated on a specific data set and should be tested on other data sets to ensure the generalizability of the results.

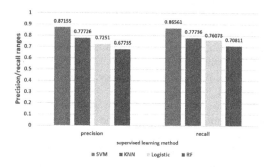

Fig. 4. Voice-based Gender classification with different algorithms

Table 7. The average result of voice-based gender classification using SVM

	Precision	Recall	F1-score
Female	0.84590	0.91720	0.88071
Male	0.89719	0.81402	0.85258
accuracy			0.86556
macro avg	0.87155	0.86561	0.86615
weighted avg	0.86737	0.86556	0.86593

5 Conclusion

This study presented the evaluation of the efficiency of removal techniques. We compared and examined the effects of such techniques on various common noise types. These noises can appear in numerous movies and affect the accuracy of subtitle generators. As shown from experiments, Deepfilternet revealed the best performance with a similarity score of 0.8442 compared to the original text. In addition, the noise removal technique significantly improved the noise generated by the sound of raindrops. In addition, the results showed that voices created by a machine such as Google text-to-speech could quickly generate subtitles. In contrast, natural voices directly collected from interviewees are still challenging. Another point related to gender classification based on classic machine learning is that SVM achieved the best among considered machine learning while Random Forest showed the worst. The experimental results also revealed that female voice recognition could be challenging compared to males.

After generating subtitle and gender classification, translator tools can be applied to translate the subtitle and choose appropriate voices with the detected gender to produce dubbed videos with more emotions. In addition, although classic machine learning can provide reasonable performance, future work should explore deep learning architectures for comparison. Finally, further studies can collect more types of noise to provide and evaluate more diverse perspectives.

References

1. Lei, J., Yu, L., Berg, T.L., Bansal, M.: TVR: a large-scale dataset for video-subtitle moment retrieval. In: Vedaldi, A., Bischof, H., Brox, T., Frahm, J.-M. (eds.) ECCV 2020. LNCS, vol. 12366, pp. 447–463. Springer, Cham (2020). https://doi.org/10.1007/978-3-030-58589-1_27
2. Elshahaby, H., Rashwan, M.: An end to end system for subtitle text extraction from movie videos. J. Ambient Intell. Humaniz. Comput. **13**(4), 1853–1865 (2021). https://doi.org/10.1007/s12652-021-02951-1
3. Tassano, M., Delon, J., Veit, T.: DVDNET: a fast network for deep video denoising. In: 2019 IEEE International Conference on Image Processing (ICIP). IEEE (2019). https://doi.org/10.1109/icip.2019.8803136
4. Nguyen, H.T., Thanh, T.N.L., Ngoc, T.L., Le, A.D., Tran, D.T.: Evaluation on noise reduction in subtitle generator for videos. In: Barolli, L. (ed.) IMIS 2022. LNNS, vol. 496, pp. 140–150. Springer, Cham (2022). https://doi.org/10.1007/978-3-031-08819-3_14
5. Alnuaim, A.A., et al.: Speaker gender recognition based on deep neural networks and ResNet50. Wirel. Commun. Mob. Comput. **2022**, 1–13 (2022). https://doi.org/10.1155/2022/4444388
6. Ertam, F.: An effective gender recognition approach using voice data via deeper LSTM networks. Appl. Acoust. **156**, 351–358 (2019). https://doi.org/10.1016/j.apacoust.2019.07.033
7. Kabil, S.H., Muckenhirn, H., Magimai-Doss, M.: On learning to identify genders from raw speech signal using CNNs. In: Interspeech, vol. 287, p. 291 (2018)

8. Shrawankar, U., Thakare, V.: Noise estimation and noise removal techniques for speech recognition in adverse environment. In: Shi, Z., Vadera, S., Aamodt, A., Leake, D. (eds.) IIP 2010. IAICT, vol. 340, pp. 336–342. Springer, Heidelberg (2010). https://doi.org/10.1007/978-3-642-16327-2_40

9. Perez-Martin, J., Bustos, B., Guimarães, S.J.F., Sipiran, I., Pérez, J., Said, G.C.: A comprehensive review of the video-to-text problem. Arti. Intell. Rev. **55**(5), 4165–4239 (2022). https://doi.org/10.1007/s10462-021-10104-1

10. Domingo, I.V.R., Mamanta, M.N.G., Regpala, J.T.S.: FILENG: an automatic English subtitle generator from Filipino video clips using hidden Markov model. In: The 2021 9th International Conference on Computer and Communications Management. ACM (2021). https://doi.org/10.1145/3479162.3479172

11. Yim, J.: Design of a subtitle generator. In: Advanced Science and Technology Letters. Science & Engineering Research Support soCiety (2015). https://doi.org/10.14257/astl.2015.117.17

12. Halpern, Y., et al.: Contextual Prediction models for speech recognition. In: Proceedings of the Interspeech 2016, pp. 2338–2342 (2016)

13. Lagos, D.: Hearing gender: voice-based gender classification processes and transgender health inequality. Am. Sociol. Rev. **84**(5), 801–827 (2019). https://doi.org/10.1177/0003122419872504

14. Harb, H., Chen, L.: Gender identification using a general audio classifier. In: Proceedings of the 2003 International Conference on Multimedia and Expo, ICME 2003 (Cat. No.03TH8698). IEEE (2003). https://doi.org/10.1109/icme.2003.1221721

15. Mamyrbayev, O., Toleu, A., Tolegen, G., Mekebayev, N.: Neural architectures for gender detection and speaker identification. Cogent Eng. **7**(1), 1727168 (2020). https://doi.org/10.1080/23311916.2020.1727168

16. Priya, E., Reshma, P.S., Sashaank, S.: Temporal and spectral features based gender recognition from audio signals. In: 2022 International Conference on Communication, Computing and Internet of Things (IC3IoT). IEEE (2022). https://doi.org/10.1109/ic3iot53935.2022.9767929

17. Schroter, H., Escalante-B, A.N., Rosenkranz, T., Maier, A.: DeepFilterNet: a low complexity speech enhancement framework for full-band audio based on deep filtering. In: ICASSP 2022–2022 IEEE International Conference on Acoustics, Speech and Signal Processing (ICASSP). IEEE (2022). https://doi.org/10.1109/icassp43922.2022.9747055

18. Sainburg, T., Thielk, M., Gentner, T.Q.: Finding, visualizing, and quantifying latent structure across diverse animal vocal repertoires. PLOS Comput. Biol. **16**(10), e1008228 (2020). https://doi.org/10.1371/journal.pcbi.1008228

19. Ardila, R., et al.: Common voice: a massively-multilingual speech corpus (2019). https://arxiv.org/abs/1912.06670

20. Sainburg, T.: timsainb/noisereduce: v1.0 (2019). https://zenodo.org/record/3243139

Apply Multivariate Time Series Approaches for Forecasting Vietnam Index 30

Noi Thanh Nguyen, Huy Quang Vo, Nhut Minh Nguyen,
and Thuan Dinh Nguyen[✉]

University of Information Technology - VNUHCM, Ho Chi Minh City, Vietnam
{19521979,19521640,17520867}@gm.uit.edu.vn, thuannd@uit.edu.vn

Abstract. The stock market is an attractive channel for many investment funds. The stock indices of several largest capitalized companies are the key indicators of the status of the economy. The VN 30 Index in Vietnam is calculated from the top 30 enterprises with the largest capitalization and liquidity. Forecasting for these market indices is always a stubborn challenge but rewarding. With recent research, many univariate models including LSTM, and GRU are proposed to achieve great performance in extracting temporal trends. However, the stock indices are affected by many factors that univariate is not able to represent all the information. Therefore, this paper studies multivariate time series with different approaches from statistical models, and machine learning regression to deep learning models to predict the VN 30 Index with the support from multivariate time series of the largest and most influenced stocks in the current Vietnam stock market.

Keywords: multivariate · stock index · VN30 Index · deep learning · machine learning

1 Introduction

The economic health and growth of a nation can be measured by its stock market indices. This paper examines Vietnam, a developing country that has made impressive strides in economic and social development in the last 30 years. The stock market in Vietnam has undergone significant changes since its inception in 2000 and currently, the stock is one of the most attractive channels for investment and asset accumulation. The main indicator of the Vietnamese stock market is the Ho Chi Minh 30 Index (VN-30), which represents the 30 largest capitalization and liquidity companies in the Ho Chi Minh Stock Exchange in Vietnam. The index is based on the FTSE Frontier Vietnam Index, which includes the Vietnamese equity market as part of the global frontier markets. The VN-30 Index is a common reference for investors and fund managers who want to invest in the Vietnamese stock market. Predicting the trends of stock indices, especially forecasting, can help investors, policymakers, and researchers make better decisions and plans.

T. K. Dang et al. (Eds.): FDSE 2023, CCIS 1925, pp. 104–117, 2023.
https://doi.org/10.1007/978-981-99-8296-7_8

With the advancement of technology and research nowadays, many models based on statistics and computer science theory show great performance on univariate time series forecasting for Vietnam stock index [9]. However, the stock market indices are influenced by many factors including economic status, exchange rates, inflation, interest rates, market capitalization and other microeconomic components. To improve the accuracy of our predictions through extraction of the hidden relationship between these factors, forecasting models can use these factors as multivariate time series for constructing the model patterns. The goals of the multivariate time series models are capturing the dependencies between variables and generating the temporal forecasting results. Furthermore, the mechanism to eliminate irrelevant time series variables must also be considered to avoid noise information and achieve desirable results for the models.

In this paper, our goal is to apply different approaches for multivariate time series models to improve the prediction of the VN 30 Index through relationship with other factors. The microeconomic and macroeconomic factors consisting of government policy, and investor psychology, however, have difficulty transforming into numeric metrics due to their abstraction. Therefore, in this research, we are considering using the closing price from the companies with the largest capitalization, and liquidity in the market and have a long history of development as the direct factors to inspect the relationship between the VN-30 Index and these stock prices. We collect daily data from 2015 to the end of 2022, covering the close price of VN 30 itself and these stocks and compare the performance with different approaches including the multivariate deep learning models LSTNet [11], MTGNN [25]; statistical model Vector Autoregression [1]; machine learning regression approaches with two popular XGBoost Regressor [22] and Random Forest Regressor [3]; and lastly Nonlinear Autoregression Exogenous approach with Dual Stage Two Phase Attention-based [12] model. Our work is in terms of accuracy and reliability. We evaluate the performance between these models from different approaches and compare them to the univariate LSTM [20] model in terms of accuracy and reliability.

2   Literature Review

There is plenty of research and related work that approach to tackle the forecasting the future data problem. Due to the statistical properties as well as the well-known Box-Jenkins methodology [14], Autoregressive Integrated Moving Average (ARIMA) [1] and its variants including autoregression (AR), moving average (MA), autoregressive moving average (ARMA) are the most classic methods for time series forecasting. Despite their effectiveness in real world applications, ARIMA is rarely used for high dimensional multivariate time series due to the high computational cost. On the other hand, Vector Autoregression (VAR) [1,5] is widely used for multivariate time series due to its simplicity, which is the extension of autoregression for multivariate time series in combination. There are multiple research projects relied on VAR for analysis of causality of economic factors including banking field [15] and financial field [21]. With the advancement of machine learning methods, regression models including Random Forest Regression [3], XGBoost [22,24], Support Vector Regression [17,23] are modified to make regression result as prediction value.

Deep learning grows exponentially in modern research fields, including time series forecasting. Recurrent neural networks (RNNs) [10] models show great performance for the temporal dependencies for time series. Recurrent neural network variants include LSTM [20] leveraging multiple gates structure including forget gate, input gate, output gate and GRU [8] with faster and less memory recurrent network with reset and update gate. LSTM [20] and GRU [8] have solved the vanishing gradient problem of their predecessor and been applied to financial forecasting with stock and bitcoin price [7,16] and some use case for Vietnam stock price [9,18]

The recurrent neural layer is only used for capture time dependencies, so other components need to be implemented for extracting spatial relationship of multivariate. LSTNet [11] introduces the convolution neural network (CNN) for capturing dependencies of multivariate and use recurrent skip [6] component which is designed for capturing long and short-term temporal patterns. MTGNN [25] uses graph structure to represent the relationship between time series and have great performance on prediction of temperature, traffic flow from different places through geometric relationship. Dual Stage Recurrent Neural Network (DA-RNN) [19] of NARX (Nonlinear autoregression Exogenous) takes advantage of the addictive attention [2] to capture both spatial between exogenous series and temporal patterns for prediction of American Stock Indices. Dual State Two Phase Attention-based Recurrent Neural Network (DSTP) [12] is a variant of DA-RNN with additional phase to capture attention weight between exogenous factors and target series.

3   Methedology

3.1   Problem Statement

Our aim in our paper is to forecast the future value one step ahead of VN-30 Index regardless of the number of variables in the output result of the models. The multivariate models have different approaches for the output result including the prediction of all variables or the prediction for a single target variable.

In the original multivariate problem statement, the output consists of all variables to be predicted at once. Giving the series $X = x_1, x_2, \ldots, x_L \in R^{L \times d}$ where L is the input sequence length, d is the number of the multivariate time series, the goal of our model is to predict the next values, which is denoted as:

$$\hat{x}_{L+1} = F(x_1, x_2, \ldots x_L) \tag{1}$$

where F(.) is our nonlinear mapping model we aim to study on the paper for multivariate time series.

The prediction result for multivariate models can be a vector for all variables at once indicated in Eq. (1). However, with some approaches including ARX

(Autoregressive Exogenous Model) or NARX (Nonlinear Autoregressive Exogenous), the model only focuses on a target time series and treats other variables as exogenous time series. Giving exogenous time series $X_e x = x_1, x_2, \ldots, x_L \in R^{L \times (d-1)}$ and target series $Y = y_1, y_2, \ldots, y_L \in R^L$, the prediction is described as follows equation:

$$\hat{y}_{L+1} = F(x_1, x_2, \ldots x_L, y_1, y_2, \ldots y_L) \tag{2}$$

3.2 MTGNN

One of the popular approaches for multivariate time series forecasting is leverage on Graph Neural Network. In graph-based perspective, every variate, and their relationship to each other are described as nodes and edges in a graph structure respectively. The structure of graph is formed as adjacency matrix to represent graph in model. Multivariate Graph Neural Network (MTGNN) [25] is a popular graph-based deep learning model for spatial time series forecasting. Each variate in multivariate time series is treated as a node in graph. However, in most of the circumstances including stock market data, the adjacency matrix for the graph structure is not given explicitly and therefore the model needs a layer to construct the graph through learning process. The MTGNN model consists of three main components: Graph Learning Layer, Graph Neural Network and Temporal Convolution Layer. The architecture of MTGNN for each learning step includes a layer to construct the adjacency matrix first. The next component is the stack of k layers. For each layer, the Temporal Convolution captures the temporal dependencies and Graph Neural Network uses the representation value from convolution and the adjacency matrix to extract spatial relationships.

Graph Learning Layer. The purpose of the Graph Neural Network is to generate graph structure throughout the learning iteration. Graph learning layer is formulated as:

$$M_1 = tanh(\alpha E_1 W_1) \tag{3}$$

$$M_2 = tanh(\alpha E_2 W_2) \tag{4}$$

$$A = ReLU(tanh(\alpha M_1 M_2{}^T - M_2 M_1{}^T) \tag{5}$$

With E_1, E_2 are the random embedded nodes, α is the hyper parameter modified for saturation rate of activation function. M_1, M_2, which is regularized linear transformation from embedded nodes, are used to create asymmetric adjacency matrix through subtraction Eq. (5).

Furthermore, authors of MTGNN also select the k closest neighbors for each node to enhance the sparsity of adjacency matrix and therefore reduce the computation cost. The remaining neighbors from each node are set to zero which indicates as nodes without connection.

Graph Convolution Network is applied to capture the dependencies between nodes in the graph structure and therefore learn the spatial relationship of multivariate through the process of passing information between node's neighbors. For each node, the information transmitted in and out to its neighbors is captured by two separate mix-hop propagation.

The mix-hop propagation proposed by the authors of MTGNN consists of two main steps, information propagation step and information selection step.

The information propagation step is defined to propagate information node information throughout the graph structure. The information propagation step is defined as follow equation:

$$H^k = \beta H_i + (1 - \beta)\tilde{A}H^{k-1} \tag{6}$$

where H_k is the embedded of input data from a convolution layer. β is the hyper parameter in order to retain the state of the origin nodes in graph because of the convergence for node hidden states to a single data and there would be the total loss of origin node information when number of layers increases to a threshold.

After the information propagation step is completed, the information selection step is used to prevent or reduce effects of the noisy information from neighboring nodes through aggregation. The information selection step uses a fully connected linear layer for each neighboring node as feature selection matrix. Therefore, the irrelevant features or variates are less likely to affect the spatial dependencies captured.

$$H_out = \sum_{i=0}^{k} H^k W^k \tag{7}$$

where H_{out} is the output hidden state for the current layers, H^k is the hidden state for each of the k-depth propagation, is the learnable parameter for feature selection layer.

Temporal Convolution Component has the goal to extract the temporal dependencies through convolution layers. The authors for MTGNN use the stack of two dilation inception layers including the filter convolution with tangent hyperbolic activation function and the gate convolution with sigmoid output function as the controller for the amount of the filter information to pass through the next layers or output.

The dilation inception layer is the stacking of multiple convolutions with different kernel sizes with adoption of dilation convolutions. The concept of inception is introduced to solve the problem of difficulty when choosing the suitable kernel size for capturing temporal dependencies. In the circumstances when kernel size is too small, it is hard for the model to extract enough information for medium to long pattern formulization. With too large kernel size, the model is not able to capture the short-term trends and therefore it will miss the local short-term pattern. Dilation is the technique to expand the kernel size by skipping pixel in between its elements with the aim for the kernel to reach out larger range. With the adoption of dilation, the inception dilation convolution layers reduce the computational expense.

3.3 LSTNet

LSTNet [11] is the deep learning model for multivariate time series forecasting. LSTNet is the combination of Convolution Neural Network and Recurrent Neural Network for capturing the dynamic dependencies between variables and leveraging these hidden relationships to enhance the forecasting result. Furthermore, the authors of LSTNet also applied different components to refine the ability to extract long-term dependencies through Recurrent Skip Layer, Autoregressive Component and Temporal Attention Component.

Convolution Layer is the main component in LSTNet with the mission to capture the dynamic dependencies in multivariate time series. The dynamic dependencies extracted through convolution layer include the hidden relationship from different variables at different timestamps and the local temporal patterns. The convolution filter with kernel size of width w and height n with n is the number of time series variates and w is the period of time for each filter calculate convolution operation. For each filter k, the convolution process is formulated as:

$$h_k = ReLU(W_h * X + b_k) \tag{8}$$

where h_k is the convolution output vector for filter k, $(*)$ is denoted as convolution operation, X is the time series input. The convolution output is regularized by rectified linear unit (ReLU) activate function after the convolution.

Recurrent Layer. After the convolution layer, the calculated output is then used to extract the temporal dependencies with Recurrent Neural Network. In the proposed paper for LSTNet, the Gated Recurrent Unit (GRU) is chosen as the Recurrent component due to its low computation cost in both memory and processing.

Recurrent-Skip Layer (Optional). For origin recurrent neural network methods including LSTM and GRU, they are designed to capture historical information. However, due to the purpose of vanishing gradient elimination, these models fail to extract the long dependencies. The authors of LSTNet propose the Recurrent-skip layer [6] to solve the problem of capture the long-term patterns. The recurrent-skip layer has the same structure and equation as its original recurrent component, except for hidden state used in updating process. Instead of using direct previous hidden state h_{t-1}, the recurrent skip uses the hidden state h_{t-p}.

3.4   Temporal Attention Layer (Optional)

In addition to the recurrent-skip layer, the authors of LSTNet also provide another approach for capturing the long-term dependencies. With the recurrent-skip component the hyperparameter of skip period p needs to be well-chosen which is a difficult task and for some non-periodic data, the p is dynamic changed over time. The attention mechanism is used to calculate the weight of hidden state for every window timestamp.

$$a_t = Att(H_t^R, h_{t-1}^R) \tag{9}$$

where a_t calculate the weight of hidden state, $H_t^R = [h_{t-q}^R, \dots h_{t-1}^R]$ is the matrix of every hidden state of previous time stamp from recurrent component. Attention formular in Eq. (9) depend on the attention score function such as dot product, scale dot product, cosine similarity,...

The context vector $c_t = H_t a_t$ is the weighted hidden states, and is used to concatenate with last window hidden state h_{t-1}^R to get the prediction output through linear projection:

$$h_t^D = W[c_t, h_{t-1}^R] + b \tag{10}$$

where h_t^D is the prediction output, W and b are the learnable parameters weight and bias for linear projections.

Autoregressive Component. In order to maintain the scale of the inputs to the prediction output, the Autoregressive component is added to the LSTNet model as the linear part. The final prediction for LSTNet model is the decomposition of the linear part from the local scaling and the non-linear part from the recurrent neural network components. Autoregressive component is defined as a fully connected linear layer as below equation

$$h_{t,i}^L = \sum_{k=0}^{(} q - 1) + b_{ar} \tag{11}$$

3.5   Multivariate Regression Approaches

Differencing for Time Series. Because the traits of the stock time series forecasting are non-stationary, the statistical regression models with moving average and auto regression are unable to forecast precisely. With the other methods of regression, which are unaware of trend and or temporal pattern, the future outbound values in the stock market may cause difficulties for these models to extract the patterns. Therefore, in order to apply regression model into non-stationary time series in general, differencing must be taken into account for data preprocessing. The differencing preprocessing is described as

$$diff_t = x_t - x_{t-1} \tag{12}$$

where x_t is the time series data at time t. Differencing transforms time series into stationary state, which make the statistical methods viable. Furthermore, the processed time series where trend is eliminated through differencing become better data to feed into regression models.

Vector Autoregression (VAR) is the statistical model forecasting the multivariate time series data. VAR is the combination of univariate autoregression (AR) and simultaneous equations (SEs), which defines that every variable has linear dependencies on its lag version and other variables' lags. The general forecasting formular of VAR is defined as:

$$\tilde{x}_t = \sum_{i=1}^{p} A_i x_{t-i} + c + e \tag{13}$$

where $x_t \in R^d$ is the data at time t, d is the number of variables in multivariate time series. A_i, c are the learnable weight and bias, e is the error term, p is the maximum lag or the window size. The value of p in VAR is determined through information criterions including BIC (Bayesian information criterion), AIC (Akaike information criterion) [5].

Machine Learning Regression often work with tabular data. Therefore, with the multivariate time series data, data must be differenced and then flatten into attributes where n is the variate in time series, p is the time window. Each attribute represents for variable at a timestamp so that the prediction for regression can capture the dependencies of every variable at every timestamp.

3.6   Dual Stage Two Phase Attention Model

Another variant of multivariate time series is Nonlinear Autoregression Exogenous (NARX) model which differs from original version that NARX treats one time series as the target time series and others as exogenous factors to enhance the target prediction. The output of NARX is the prediction of only target variable instead of all variates in ordinary multivariate models.

Dual Stage Two Phase Attention model (DSTP) is one of NARX models which leverages the attention mechanism and encoder-decoder architecture to capture both spatial and temporal dependencies. For encoder, its main purpose is to extract the relationship between exogenous variables and between exogenous variables with target variables. Decoder receives context vector as output of encoder and uses it for temporal attention.

Global Attention. The attention mechanism used throughout the model is global attention. The global attention mechanism leverages the hidden states and the cell states of recurrent layer to calculate the alignment score as the weight for attention output. The process of global attention is formulated through these following steps:

$$f_t^k = v_f^T tanh(W_f[h_{t-1}^f; s_{t-1}^f] + U_f x^k + b^f) \qquad (14)$$

$$a_t^k = \frac{exp(f_t^k)}{\sum_{j=1}^n exp(f_t^j)} \qquad (15)$$

$$c_t = (a_t^1 x_t^1, a_t^2 x_t^2, \dots a_t^n x_t^n) \qquad (16)$$

where $[*; *]$ denotes for concatenation operation, h_{t-1}^f, s_{t-1}^f, are the hidden state and cell state of previous LSTM layer, other parameters are the learnable parameters to refine the model. For later usage, the sequences of above Eqs. (23) (24) (25) are denoted as $GlobalAtt(x)$

Spatial Attention Encoder. DSTP uses an encoder to capture the spatial relationship. The spatial attention encoder consists of two main phases. The first phase is to capture the dependencies between exogenous variables and the second phase to capture the relationship between exogenous series with target series.

Exogenous time series is fed into global attention. The first phase attention output is defined as below equation

$$\tilde{x} = GlobalAtt(x) \qquad (17)$$

where x is the exogenous series. The result from first phase attention $\tilde{x}$ is then concatenated with target series to get the input for second phase attention. The second phase attention's main purpose is to generate dependencies between the target series and other exogenous data.

$$z = [\tilde{x}; y] \qquad (18)$$

$$\tilde{z} = GlobalAtt(z) \qquad (19)$$

While calculate the output $\tilde{z}$ of weighted spatial vector, the hidden states of the last phase h^S is saved to feed as the input for the decoder.

Temporal Attention Decoder extracts the temporal dependencies through the hidden states of second phase spatial attention.

$$\tilde{h}^S = GlobalAtt(h^S) \qquad (20)$$

The context vector, which is the fuse of all hidden states from encoder input, is concatenated with input series and fed into separate recurrent layer.

$$c_t = \sum_{j=1}^T \tilde{h}_j^S \qquad (21)$$

$$\tilde{y}_t = \tilde{W}^T[y_t; c_t] + b \qquad (22)$$

$$d_t = f_d(d_{t-1}, \tilde{y}_{t-1}) \tag{23}$$

where $f_d(.)$ is the recurrent layer, d_t is the hidden state for recurrent layer at timestamp t. The final output for prediction is the linear projection from the concatenation result between context vector and the hidden state from temporal decoder.

$$\hat{y}_{t+1} = W_y[d_t; c_t] \tag{24}$$

4 Experiment

For the experiment in the paper, we have applied the multivariate time series forecasting models from different approaches including linear statistical method Vector Auto regression, machine learning regression methods with XGBoost Regression and Random Forest Regression, deep learning approach with graph-based model MTGNN, multiple layer combination model LSTNet, Nonlinear Autoregression Exogenous approach as DSTP model on the dataset of Vietnam 30 Index. We also add a baseline of LSTM with the univariate setting to compare the effectiveness of the multivariate time series when compared to univariate. The result of predicting of VN30 index at the next day is evaluated and compared with each other's to bring the deep analysis of high-performed multivariate forecasting model.

4.1 Dataset

The VN30 dataset contains the close price of 21 largest stocks in the VN30 basket and the close index of VN30 itself. The stocks included in our dataset are BID, BVH, CTG, FPT, GAS, HPG, KDH, MBB, MSN, MWG, NVL, PDR, PNJ, REE, SBT, SSI, STB, TCH, VCB, VIC, VNM.

Table 1. Data plit information.

Data purpose	From	To	Number of data points
Train	12-30-2016	8-11-2020	900
Validation	8-12-2020	10-21-2021	150
Test	10-22-2021	12-30-2022	150

Data ranges from the date 12-30-2016 to 12-30-2022 with 1500 data points. Data is collected from the website investing.com - one of the reliable financial data providers. We split the dataset into training, validation and test set of ratios 6/2/2 in time order as Table 1.

4.2 Hardware

We trained our models mostly on one machine with the operating system Ubuntu 22.04.2 LTS, CPU Intel Core i5-5300U with 2 cores-4 threads and 8 Gb of RAM.

4.3 Evaluation Metric

The metrics we use to evaluate the effectiveness and the accuracy of the models include Root Mean Square Error (RMSE), Mean Absolute Error (MAE) and Mean Absolute Percentage Error (MAPE) and Correlation Coefficient (CORR). The metrics RMSE, MAE, MAPE with the lower values and CORR with higher values indicate the better prediction model.

4.4 Models

The models which we use in the experiment are VAR, XGBoost Regressor, Random Forest Regressor, LSTNet, MTGNN. Furthermore, we also add the univariate LSTM model for comparison.

4.5 Model Training Settings

The training process uses the ADAM optimizer with MSE Loss and learning rate of 0.001, batch size of 64, number of epochs 1000 for deep learning methods include MTGNN, LSTNet, DSTP. The univariate time series LSTM model will have the same setting as other deep learning methods.

For the regression approach, the data is preprocessed as discussed in Section regression approaches, differencing and scaling is applied before the training the regression models including Vector Autoregression, XGBoost Regression, Random Forest Regression.

4.6 Result

Table 2. Metric table data.

	MAPE	MAE	RMSE	CORR
VAR	1.13%	14.2216	19.9501	99.48%
XGBoost	1.27%	16.0431	21.7196	99.38%
Random Forest	1.17%	14.6459	20.206	99.46%
LSTNet	**1.12%**	**14.1026**	**19.6988**	**99.5%**
MTGNN	4.4%	30.0711	51.0711	97.35%
DSTP	1.64%	21.0864	26.7603	99.33 %
Univariate LSTM	2.01%	26.397	31.3855	99.29%

As shown from Table 2, the model with the best prediction result is LSTNet with the smallest MAPE of 1.12% and highest CORR of 99.5% among all models in experiment. LSTNet has 0.01% better at MAPE and 0.02% CORR better than the second-best model Vector Autoregression and outperform other deep learning and machine learning models.

Surprisingly, the multivariate approaches for machine learning regression and statistical regression model show good performance on predicting the VN Index 30 and even outperform other deep learning models except LSTNet. The effectiveness of models with linear pattern extraction on this dataset causes the direct effect of stock price with high capitalization and liquidity to the market indices. Stock indices are calculated through the combination of every stock within their basket followed by ratios but changes over time. Therefore, linear pattern can also represent the relationship between market index and its component stocks in short term.

With the graph-based approach, MTGNN is shown as the model with the lowest performance in this experiment. Previous work of MTGNN focused on variables with spatial correlation as geometric relationships including solar energy or traffic flow. Therefore, with the complicated structure of stock markets, the traditional graph is not suitable to represent the stock interconnection. Despite performing better than the MTGNN model, DSTP still yields results inferior to simpler models with less complexity like tree-based regression models or vector autoregression. This indicates that linear models with proper settings and preprocessing data can still achieve forecasting outcomes for specific time series like VN Index 30.

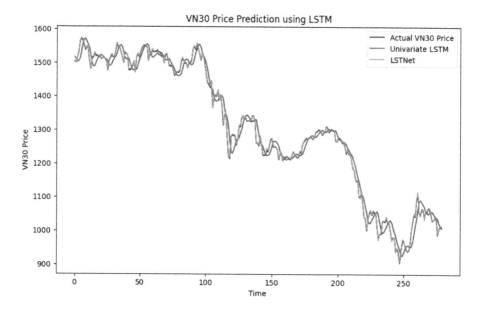

Fig. 1. Prediction result for univariate LSTM and multivariate LSTNet model.

When comparing to the univariate LSTM, most of the multivariate models show better results than LSTM except for the MTGNN model. Figure 1 demonstrates that the one day ahead predictions of LSTNet closely align with the actual data to a greater extent than the univariate LSTM model.

5   Conclusion and Future Work

This paper studies multivariate forecasting models with different approaches in financial markets. Our work applied LSTNet, MTGNN, DSTP, VAR, XGBoost Regressor and Random Forest Regression to forecast the VN Index 30 and make comparison with each other's and with the univariate approach. The result shows that the LSTNet has the best performance in forecasting VN 30 Index through its historical data and stock price of tickers within VN 30 basket. In the relationship between stocks and their basket index, we found that the regression approaches also have great performance, and even outperform some deep learning model with much more complex structures. In addition, most of the multivariate time series have slightly better accuracy than univariate approaches due to the utility of more information fed into model. However, with the fluctuation and affected by exogenous factors in stock market, there still needs time to research to enhance the multivariate forecasting models. One of the ideas for future work is enriching the multivariate data with microeconomic and macroeconomic attributes including government interest rate, the greediness of investors through sentiment analysis.

References

1. Anderson, O.D.: Time series analysis: forecasting and control. J. Franklin Inst. **310**(2), 144 (1980)
2. Bahdanau, D., Cho, K., Bengio, Y.: Neural machine translation by jointly learning to align and translate. arXiv preprint arXiv:1409.0473 (2014)
3. Breiman, L.: Random forests. Mach. Learn. **45**, 5–32 (2001)
4. Broyden, C.G.: A class of methods for solving nonlinear simultaneous equations. Math. Comput. **19**(92), 577–593 (1965)
5. Burnham, K.P., Anderson, D.R.: Multimodel inference: understanding AIC and BIC in model selection. Sociol. Methods Res. **33**(2), 261–304 (2004)
6. Campos, V., et al.: Skip RNN: learning to skip state updates in recurrent neural networks. arXiv [cs.AI] (2017). https://arxiv.org/abs/1708.06834
7. Cao, J., Li, Z., Li, J.: Financial time series forecasting model based on CEEMDAN and LSTM. Phys. A: Stat. Mech. Appl. **519**, 127–139 (2019)
8. Chung, J., et al.: Empirical evaluation of gated recurrent neural networks on sequence modeling. arXiv [cs.NE] (2014). https://arxiv.org/abs/1412.3555
9. Co, N.T., Son, H.H., Hoang, N.T., Lien, T.T.P., Ngoc, T.M.: Comparison between ARIMA and LSTM-RNN for VN-index prediction. In: Ahram, T., Karwowski, W., Vergnano, A., Leali, F., Taiar, R. (eds.) IHSI 2020. AISC, vol. 1131, pp. 1107–1112. Springer, Cham (2020). https://doi.org/10.1007/978-3-030-39512-4_168
10. Connor, J.T., Martin, R.D., Atlas, L.E.: Recurrent neural networks and robust time series prediction. IEEE Trans. Neural Netw. **5**(2), 240–254 (1994)

11. Lai, G.: Modeling long-and short-term temporal patterns with deep neural networks. In: The 41st International ACM SIGIR Conference on Research & Development in Information Retrieval, pp. 95–104 (2018)

12. Liu, Y., et al.: DSTP-RNN: a dual-stage two-phase attention-based recurrent neural network for long-term and multivariate time series prediction. Expert Syst. Appl. **143**, 113082 (2020)

13. Luong, M.-T., Pham, H., Manning, C.D.: Effective approaches to attention-based neural machine translation. arXiv [cs.CL] (2015). https://arxiv.org/abs/1508.04025

14. Makridakis, S., Hibon, M.: ARMA models and the box-Jenkins methodology. J. Forecast. **16**(3), 147–163 (1997)

15. Marcucci, J., Quagliariello, M.: Is bank portfolio riskiness procyclical?: evidence from Italy using a vector autoregression. J. Int. Finan. Markets. Inst. Money **18**(1), 46–63 (2008)

16. Moghar, A., Hamiche, M.: Stock market prediction using LSTM recurrent neural network. Procedia Comput. Sci. **170**, 1168–1173 (2020)

17. Müller, K.-R., Smola, A.J., Rätsch, G., Schölkopf, B., Kohlmorgen, J., Vapnik, V.: Predicting time series with support vector machines. In: Gerstner, W., Germond, A., Hasler, M., Nicoud, J.-D. (eds.) ICANN 1997. LNCS, vol. 1327, pp. 999–1004. Springer, Heidelberg (1997). https://doi.org/10.1007/BFb0020283

18. Ngoc Hai, P., et al.: An empirical research on the effectiveness of different LSTM architectures on vietnamese stock market. In: Proceedings of the 2020 1st International Conference on Control, Robotics and Intelligent System, pp. 144–149 (2020)

19. Qin, Y., et al.: A dual-stage attention-based recurrent neural network for time series prediction. arXiv preprint arXiv:1704.02971 (2017)

20. Sepp, J.: Long short-term memory. Neural Comput. **9**, 1735–1780 (1997)

21. Shan, J.: Does financial development 'lead' economic growth? A vector autoregression appraisal. Appl. Econ. **37**(12), 1353–1367 (2005)

22. Chen, T., Guestrin, C.: XGBoost: a scalable tree boosting system. arXiv [cs.LG] (2016). https://arxiv.org/abs/1603.02754

23. Trafalis, T.B., Ince, H.: Support vector machine for regression and applications to financial forecasting. In: Proceedings of the IEEE-INNS-ENNS International Joint Conference on Neural Networks, IJCNN 2000. Neural Computing: New Challenges and Perspectives for the New Millennium. Proceedings of the IEEE-INNS-ENNS International Joint Conference on Neural Networks, IJCNN 2000. Neural Computing: New Challenges and Perspectives for the New Millennium. IEEE (2000)

24. Wang, Y., Guo, Y.: Forecasting method of stock market volatility in time series data based on mixed model of ARIMA and XGBoost. China Commun. **17**(3), 205–221 (2020)

25. Wu, Z., et al.: Connecting the dots: multivariate time series forecasting with graph neural networks. In: Proceedings of the 26th ACM SIGKDD International Conference on Knowledge Discovery & Data Mining, KDD 2020: The 26th ACM SIGKDD Conference on Knowledge Discovery and Data Mining. ACM, New York (2020)

26. Zilly, J.G., et al.: Recurrent highway networks. arXiv [cs.LG] (2016). https://arxiv.org/abs/1607.03474

Efficient Mining of Top-K Cross-Level High Utility Itemsets

Nguyen Tuan Truong[1], Nguyen Khac Tue[1], Nguyen Duc Chinh[1], Le Dinh Huynh[1], Vu Thu Diep[2(✉)], and Phan Duy Hung[1(✉)]

[1] Computer Science Department, FPT University, Hanoi, Vietnam
{truongnthe150138,tuenkhe150066,chinhndhe150974}@fpt.edu.vn,
{huynhld3,hungpd2}@fe.edu.vn
[2] Hanoi University of Science and Technology, Hanoi, Vietnam
diep.vuthu@hust.edu.vn

Abstract. High utility itemset (HUI) mining extracts frequent itemsets with high utility values from transactional databases. Traditional algorithms have limitations in detecting relationships between items and categories across multiple levels of a taxonomy-based database. Cross-level algorithms have been proposed to address this issue while top-k algorithms find the top-k HUIs with the highest utility values. Fast and Efficient Algorithm for Cross-level high-utility Pattern mining (FEACP) and Top-K Cross-level high utility itemset mining (TKC) algorithms were proposed for HUI mining with high efficiency. However, they suffer from scalability and efficiency issues when dealing with large datasets. To overcome these limitations, we propose a new algorithm called TKC-E (Efficient Top-K Cross-level high utility itemset mining), which combines the strengths of FEACP and TKC while applying efficient strategies to identify cross-level HUIs in taxonomy-based databases, resulting in significantly improved scalability and efficiency. Experimental results show that TKC-E outperforms TKC in terms of processing speed and memory usage, with up to 2.4 times memory and 60 times runtime improvements on sparse and dense datasets, respectively.

Keywords: TKC-E · High utility itemset · Top-k · Cross-level · Taxonomy

1 Introduction

Data mining is crucial for knowledge discovery. It extracts valuable insights from large datasets, revealing patterns and relationships. It aids decision-making, enhances understanding, and uncovers hidden knowledge in various domains. By analyzing the characteristics of a dataset, data mining algorithms can reveal useful information for users. Frequent itemset mining (FIM) and association rule mining (ARM) are two important algorithms in the field of data mining related to the relationships between items in a dataset. FIM is the process of finding sets of items that frequently appear together in transactions of a dataset [1]. These sets are called frequent itemsets. ARM is the process of finding association rules between items in frequent itemsets, providing recommendations or information related to the dataset [2]. Although FIM and ARM have been widely

© The Author(s), under exclusive license to Springer Nature Singapore Pte Ltd. 2023
T. K. Dang et al. (Eds.): FDSE 2023, CCIS 1925, pp. 118–131, 2023.
https://doi.org/10.1007/978-981-99-8296-7_9

used in many fields and have many effective applications, they only focus on searching for frequent itemsets and association rules, while ignoring the utility value of items in those frequent itemsets. Therefore, high utility itemset mining (HUIM) was developed to focus on finding frequent itemsets with high utility value based on information related to value, quantity, or the combination of items.

HUIM is a data mining method for mining a set of items that, when purchased together, provide higher utility value than buying individual items. Utility value can be measured using metrics such as total revenue, profit, or number of products sold [3]. The high utility itemset mining algorithm can be performed using methods such as FHM [4], UP-Growth [5], and HUI-Miner [6]. Although most of these algorithms are effective, they overlook the fact that items in transactional databases are often organized into categories and subcategories of classifications.

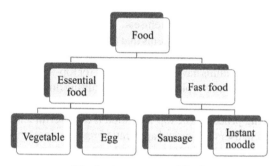

Fig. 1. A taxonomy of food.

Figure 1 shows that a taxonomy can classify items in a database into categories and subcategories. For example, in a supermarket database, items can be classified into categories like Food, Essential food (e.g. vegetables, eggs), and Fast food (e.g. sausages, instant noodles). Traditional frequent itemset mining algorithms can only find itemsets at the lowest level (e.g. vegetable, egg, sausage, instant noodle). They miss more general itemsets like Food, Fast food, Essential food. Recent studies have proposed algorithms to find frequent itemsets at multiple levels and across levels, such as ML-HUI Miner [7], CLH-Miner [8], and FEACP [9].

ML-HUI Miner was proposed by Cagliero et al. in 2017 [7]. ML-HUI Miner uses a hierarchical method to separate the multi-level database into separate layers, thereby providing sets of high-value items on each separate layer. Additionally, the algorithm uses several new techniques to improve data mining efficiency, including using a combined value function with a utility function to evaluate the value of an itemset, and using a dynamic filtering technique to eliminate unimportant items and reduce processing time.

However, a problem with the ML-HUI mining algorithm is that it cannot find itemsets with items from different classification levels (cross-level HUIs). Therefore, it may miss some interesting HUIs. Furthermore, the ML-HUI mining tool does not rely on classification to reduce search space, as it mines each separate classification level individually.

Recently, in 2020, Fournier-Viger et al. proposed a new algorithm called CLH-Miner to address these limitations [8]. This algorithm uses a cross-level method to combine itemsets from different levels to provide sets of high-value items at a new level. CLH-Miner proposes new upper bounds on utility and effective pruning strategies while allowing an itemset to combine items from different abstraction levels. Continuing the improvement of CLH-Miner in 2022, N.T. Tung et al. proposed the FEACP algorithm [9]. FEACP is an algorithm for mining high-level cross-utility itemsets in quantitative databases. This algorithm operates by scanning the database three times, from general computation to classification, while applying search space reduction techniques. To find all Cross-Level HUIs, FEACP performs a deep search based on DFS to recursively traverse the search space and expand the initial frequent itemset. This algorithm relies on "local utility" and "sub-tree utility" techniques to calculate the utility value for itemsets and their sub-branches. By using upper bounds on utility as pruning strategies, FEACP can reduce the number of itemsets to be considered in the search space, increase mining efficiency, and find useful information itemsets.

Top-k high utility itemset is a set of items that appear in the transactions of a database, having the highest utility values and belonging to the top-k itemsets with the highest utility values. Several algorithms have been developed for top-k HUIM, such as TKU [10] and TKO [11]. These algorithms typically operate by cutting down the search space based on utility constraints, reducing the computational cost effectively and improving the efficiency of the mining process. The top-k method is a powerful and flexible technique that can handle different user options and application requirements in high utility itemset mining. However, both TKU and TKO have the drawback of using non-categorical data structures. This limits their ability to mine High Utility Items across different data levels, reducing the effectiveness of extracting complex patterns and potentially missing out on opportunities to exploit potential data patterns.

To address this problem, in 2020, Fournier-Viger et al. proposed a new algorithm called TKC [12]. TKC uses a data structure called Tax-utility-lists, which consists of a list of itemsets sorted in a similar order to the taxonomy table and containing information about the utility value and utility limit of each itemset. Using tax-utility-lists allows for quick calculation of the utility value of itemsets without having to scan the database, which speeds up the mining process and reduces processing time. The TKC algorithm starts searching from single items and uses a priority queue to keep track of the current top-k patterns found. When a new cross-level HUI is found, it is inserted into the priority queue, and if the queue contains at least k patterns, the min-utility threshold is increased to the utility value of the k-th pattern in the queue. All patterns that do not meet the new min-utility threshold are removed from the queue. Optimization is used to increase the speed of increasing the min-utility value by raising the threshold with the k-th highest utility value in the priority queue.

Although traditional HUIM algorithms can find interesting patterns, they encounter difficulties in setting appropriate minimum utility thresholds. Therefore, the Top-K algorithm is proposed, which allows users to specify the number k of patterns to be found instead of setting a minimum utility threshold. In addition, the problem of mining cross-level HUIs is also of great interest as it can reveal many different aspects of the data. To address these issues, the TKC algorithm was proposed based on the CLH-Miner algorithm. However, the runtime and memory usage of TKC are almost no different, and in fact, TKC usually consumes more memory than CLH-Miner [12]. In this paper, we propose a new algorithm called TKC-E, which inherits the advantages from FEACP - an improved version of CLH-Miner [9] and TKC. Experimental results demonstrate that TKC-E significantly improves performance compared to TKC on real datasets and is confirmed to be effective in mining cross-level high-utility itemsets across different datasets.

2 Methodology

2.1 Preliminaries and Problem Definition

The type of databases considered in this paper are quantitative transaction databases with a taxonomy that is used in retail stores.It's quite general and can be used to represent data in many other applications.In this section, we first define the problem and main definition for cross level HUIM.

Definition 1 (Transaction database): Let I be a finite set of items $I = \{i_1, i_2,..., i_m\}$. A transaction database, denoted as $D = \{T_1, T_2,..., T_m\}$ is a collection of transactions. Each transaction T_c in the database consists of a set of items i that belong to the item set I. Each transaction T_c is uniquely identified by a transaction ID (TID) denoted as c. Additionally, each item i from the item set I is associated with a positive value p(i), which represents its external utility or in other words, it's unit profit. For each item i in T_c there is a positive number $q(i, T_c)$ associated with it, which represents its internal utility or purchase quantity in that transaction.

Example 1: Consider the database in Table 1, which will be used as the running example. It contains seven transactions $(T_1, T_2, ..., T_7)$. Transaction T_2 show that items a, c, e and g are present in this transaction, with internal utility values of 2, 6, 2, and 5, respectively. According to Table 2, the external utility values for these items are 5, 1, 3, and 1, respectively.

<table>
<tr><td colspan="2">**Table 1.** A transaction database</td><td colspan="2">**Table 2.** External utility values</td></tr>
<tr><td>TID</td><td>Transaction</td><td>Item</td><td>Unit Profit</td></tr>
<tr><td>T1</td><td>(a, 1), (c, 1), (d, 1)</td><td>a</td><td>5</td></tr>
<tr><td>T2</td><td>(a, 2), (c, 6), (e, 2), (g, 5)</td><td>b</td><td>2</td></tr>
<tr><td>T3</td><td>(a, 1), (b, 2), (c, 1), (d, 6), (e, 1), (f, 5)</td><td>c</td><td>1</td></tr>
<tr><td>T4</td><td>(b, 4), (c, 3), (d, 3), (e, 1)</td><td>d</td><td>2</td></tr>
<tr><td>T5</td><td>(b, 2), (c, 2), (e, 1), (g, 2)</td><td>e</td><td>3</td></tr>
<tr><td>T6</td><td>(a, 2), (c, 6), (e, 2)</td><td>f</td><td>1</td></tr>
<tr><td>T7</td><td>(c, 1), (d, 2), (e, 1)</td><td>g</td><td>1</td></tr>
</table>

Definition 2 (Taxonomy): A taxonomy τ is a tree(a directed acyclic graph) defined for a transaction database D. Leaf nodes of the taxonomy represent the different items of I, while internal nodes represent categories of items, which are called generalized items or abstract items. Generalized items represent an abstract category that groups all descendant leaf nodes(items) or all descendant categories into one higher-level category. In the context of τ, a child-parent edge connecting two (generalized) items i and j signifies an "is-a" relationship.

Definition 3 (The sets of generalized items and all items): The set containing all these generalized items is denoted as GI, and the set containing both generalized and leaf items is denoted as $AI = GI \cup I$.

Definition 4 (Generalization relationship): Let there be a relation $LR \subseteq GI \times I$ such that $(g, i) \in LR$ if there is a path from g to i. And, let there be a relation $GR \subseteq AI \times AI$ such that $(d, j) \in GR$ if there is a path from d to j.

Definition 5 (Descendant): Consider a taxonomy τ and a generalized item g in τ. The leaf items of a generalized item g are all leaves that can be reached by following paths starting from g defined as $Leaf(g, \tau) = \{i \mid (g, i) \in LR\}$. The descendant items of a (generalized) item d is the set $Desc(d, \tau) = \{j \mid (d, j) \in GR\}$. The level denotes the number of edges to be traversed to reach an item d starting from the root node of τ.

Example 2: In the taxonomy of Fig. 2, we can see that $Leaf(\{X\}, \tau) = \{a, b, c\}$ and $Desc(\{X\},\tau) = \{Y, a, b, c\}$, the itemset $\{Y, d\}$ is a descendant of $\{X, Z\}$, and $level(c) = 2$.

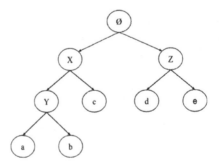

Fig. 2. A taxonomy of items.

Definition 6 (Utility of an item/itemset): The utility of item i in transaction T_c is defined as $u(i, Tc) = p(i) \times q(i, T_c)$. Similarly, the utility of an itemset P (a group of items $i \subseteq I$) in transaction Tc is defined as $u(P,) = \sum_{i \in P} u(i, T_c)$. Finally, let g(P) is the set of transactions containing X in D, the utility of an itemset X in a database is defined as $u(P) = \sum_{T_c \in g(P)} u(P, T_c)$.

Example 3: The utility of a in T_1 is $u(a, T_1) = 1 \times 5 = 5$. The utility of $\{a, c\}$ in T_2 is $u(\{a, c\}, T_2) = u(a, T_2) + u(c, T_2) = 2 \times 5 + 6 \times 1 = 16$. The utility of $\{b, c\}$ in the database D is $u(\{b, c\}) = u(\{b, c\}, T_3) + u(\{b, c\}, T4) + u(\{b, c\}, T_5) = 5 + 11 + 6 = 22$.

Definition 7 (Utility of a generalized item/itemset): The utility of generalized item g in transaction T_c is defined as $u(g, T_c) = \sum_{i \in Leaf(g,\tau)} p(i) \times q(i, T_c)$. Similarly, let $g(GP)$ is the set of transactions containing P in D, the utility of a generalized itemset GP in a transaction T_c is calculated by $u(GP, T_c) = \sum_{d \in GP} u(d, T_c)$. The utility of an itemset P in a database is calculated by $u(GP) = \sum_{T_c \in g(GP)} u(GP, T_c)$ where $g(GP) = \{T_c \in D \mid \exists P \subseteq Tc \land P \text{ is a descendant of } GP\}$.

Example 4: In the taxonomy of Fig. 1, Z is a generalized item and $u(Z, T_4) = u(d, T_4) + u(e, T_4) = 3 \times 2 + 1 \times 3 = 9$. The utility of the generalized itemset $\{Z, b\}$ in T_4 is $u(\{Z, b\}, T_4) = u(Z, T_4) + u(b, T_4) = (6 + 3) + 8 = 17$. The utility of the generalized itemset $\{Z, b\}$ in the database is $u(\{Z, b\}) = u(\{Z, b\}, T_3) + u(\{Z, b\}, T_4) + u(\{Z, b\}, T_5) = 17 + 19 + 7 = 43$.

Definition 8 (Cross-level high utility mining): The problem of cross-level high utility mining is defined as finding all cross-level high-utility itemsets(CLHUIs). A (generalized) itemset X is called a CLHUI if $u(X) \geq \mu$ where μ is minutil threshold.

Example 5. If $\mu = 70$, the cross-level high utility itemsets in the database of the running example are: $\{X,e\}$, $\{Z, X\}$, $\{Z, Y\}$, $\{Z, Y, c\}$, $\{Z, c, a\}$,$\{e, Y, c\}$ with respectively a utility of 81, 111, 84, 103, 70,77.

Definition 9 (Top-K cross-level high utility mining): Consider a transaction database D and a user-defined parameter k which indicates the desired number of cross-level high utility itemsets. An itemset $X \subseteq AI$ is called a top-k cross-level high utility itemset (top-k CLHUI) if X in k-th itemsets in D whose utilities are largest. Mining top-k cross-level high utility itemsets consists of identifying top-k CLHUI having the highest utility in database D.

Example 6: If k = 3, the top-k cross-level high utility itemsets are: $\{Z, X\}$, $\{Z, Y, c\}$, $\{Z, Y\}$ with a utility of 111, 103, and 84.

2.2 Proposed Algorithm

2.2.1 Search Space Exploration and Pruning Techniques

To be able to explore the search space of all itemsets in a systematic way, a processing order $\succ$ is defined on items of AI. According to that total order, two distinct items a, b $\in AI$ are ordered as $a \succ b$ if $level(a) < level(b)$, or if $level(a) = level(b) \land GTWU(a) > GTWU(b)$. The arrangement of levels in a specific order within the algorithm ensures that generalized items are considered before their descendant items. This order is crucial as it facilitates the pruning of itemsets in the search space. The ordering is determined based on the GTWU (Generalized Total Weighted Utility) measure, which defines the prioritization of items within each level.

Definition 10 (Generalized Transaction Weighted Utilization – GTWU): A transaction T_c has its transaction utility defined as $TU(T_c) = \sum_{i \in T_c} u(i, T_c)$. For an itemset $P \subseteq I$, the GTWU is computed as $GTWU(P) = \sum_{T_c \in g(P)} TU(T_c)$. Similarly, an itemset $GP \subseteq GI$, the $GTWU$ is computed as:

$$GTWU(GP) = \sum_{T_c \in g(i \in Leaf(GP, \tau))} TU(T_c).$$

Example 7: The TU values of transactions T_1 to T_7 for Table 1 are: 8, 24, 30, 20, 11, 22 and 8, respectively. $GTWU(\{a\}) = TU(T_1) + TU(T_2) + TU(T_3) + TU(T_6) = 8 + 24 + 30 + 22 = 84$, $GTWU(\{Y\}) = TU(T_1) + TU(T_2) + TU(T_3) + TU(T_4) + TU(T_5) + TU(T_6) = 8 + 24 + 30 + 20 + 11 + 22 = 115$.

Definition 11 (Extension): An extension of an itemset P is an itemset obtained by adding an item i to P. The set of all extensions of P is defined as $E(P) = \{i \mid i \in AI \wedge i \succ w \text{ and } \forall\, w \in P, i \notin Desc(w, \tau)\}$.

Definition 12 (Remaining utility): The remaining utility of an itemset P in a transaction T_c is defined as $re(P, T_c) = \sum_{i \in T_c \wedge i \in E(P)} u(i, T_c)$.

Definition 13 (Utility-list): The utility-list of an itemset X in a database D is a set of tuples such that there is a tuple $(c, iutil, rutil)$ for each transaction containing X. The iutil and rutil elements of a tuple respectively are the utility of X in T_c $(u(X, T_c))$ and the remaining utility of X in T_c $(re(X, T_c))$.

Definition 14 (Local utility): Let P be an itemset. Consider an item $i \in E(P)$. The local utility of i w.r.t itemset P is defined as $lu(P, i) = \sum_{T_c \in g(P \cup \{i\})} [u(P, T_c) + re(P, T_c)]$. Similarly, if item z is a generalized item in taxonomy, the local utility of z w.r.t itemset P is calculated as $lu(P, z) = \sum_{T_c \in g(P \cup j \in Leaf(z, \tau))} [u(P, T_c) + re(P, T_c)]$.

Example 8. Consider the running example and $P = \{c\}$. We have that $lu(P, a) = 8 + 27 + 30 + 22 = 87$, $lu(P, d) = 8 + 30 + 20 + 8 = 66$ and $lu(P, e) = 115$.

Theorem 1: (Pruning an item from all sub-trees using the local utility): Let be an itemset P and an item $i \in E(P)$. If $lu(P, i) < \mu$, then all extensions of P containing i are low-utility. So, item i can be ignored when exploring all sub-trees of P.

Definition 15 (Sub-tree utility): Let P be an itemset. Consider an item $i \in E(P)$. The local utility of i w.r.t itemset P is defined as follows:

$$su(P, i) = \sum_{T_c \in g(P \cup \{i\})} [u(P, T_c) + u(i, T_c) + \sum_{j \in T_c \wedge j \in E(P \cup \{i\})} u(j, T_c)]$$

Similarly, if item z is a generalized item in taxonomy, the local utility of z w.r.t itemset P is calculated as follows:

$$su(P, z) = \sum_{T_c \in g(P \cup j \in Leaf(z, \tau))} [u(P, T_c) + \sum_{j \in Leaf(z, \tau)} u(j, T_c) + \sum_{j \in T_c \wedge j \in E(P \cup \{z\})} u(j, T_c)].$$

Example 9: Consider the running example and $P = \{c\}$. We have that $su(P, a) = 8 + 21 + 27 + 16 = 72$, $su(P, d) = 6 + 22 + 17 + 5 = 50$ and $su(P, e) = 115$.

Theorem 2: (Pruning a sub-tree using the sub-tree utility): Let be an itemset P and an item $z \in E(P)$. If $su(P, z) < \mu$, then the single item extension $P \cup \{z\}$ and its extensions are low-utility. In other words, the sub-tree of $P \cup \{z\}$ in the set-enumeration tree can be pruned.

Definition 16 (Primary and secondary items): Let be an itemset P. The primary items of P is the set of items defined as $Primary(P) = \{z \mid z \in E(P) \wedge su(P, z) \geq \mu\}$.

The secondary items of P is the set of items defined as $Secondary(P) = \{z \mid z \in E(P) \wedge lu(p, z) \geq \mu\}$. Because $lu(p, z) \geq su(P, z)$, $Primary(P) \subseteq Secondary(P)$.

2.2.2 TKC-E Algorithm

The proposed TKC-E algorithm is presented in Algorithm 1. It accepts three input parameters that are a database D, a taxonomy τ, and the user-defined number of patterns to be found k.

Algorithm 1: The TKC-E algorithm

---

input: D: a transaction database, τ: a taxonomy, k: the number of patterns to be found.
output: the top-k cross-level HUIs.
1. Initializes $\mu = 0$, $P = \{\varnothing\}$ a priority queue Q with the top-k cross-level HUIs from AI;
2. Read τ and D and use a utility-bin array to calculate to compute $lu\ (P, z)$ of each (generalized) item $z \in AI$;
3. $Secondary(P) = \{z \mid z \in AI \wedge lu(P, z) \geq \mu\}$;
4. Compute $\prec$, the total order on items from Level and $GTWU$ values on $Secondary(P)$;
5. Scan D to store each generalized item $g \in Secondary(P)$ in each transaction, discard every item $i \notin Secondary(P)$ from transactions, sort items in each transaction, delete empty transactions, and then build and store the utility-list of each generalized item;
6. Compute the sub-tree utility $su(P, z)$ of each item $z \in Secondary(P)$;
7. $Primary(P) = \{z \mid z \in AI \wedge su(P, z) \geq \mu\}$;
8. SEARCH $(P, D, Primary(P), Secondary(P), k, \mu, Q, UtilityList)$;

The overall process is done as follows:

Line #1: Initializes $\mu = 0$, the current itemset P to the empty set ($\varnothing$) and priority queue Q. In the case $GTWU(Y) = lu(P, z)$.

Line #2: Scan taxonomy τ and database D to calculate to compute $lu(P, z)$ of each (generalized) item $z \in AI$ and store it using a utility-bin array.

Line #3: The algorithm compares the local utility of each item to construct the set of all secondary items of P.

Then line #4: P is sorted based on the total order $\prec$ of levels and the GTWU.

At line #5 of the algorithm, another scan of the database D is conducted using the taxonomy τ. This scan aims to identify all generalized items that correspond to secondary items within each transaction. Any items i that do not belong to the Secondary(P) set are removed from the transactions to optimize memory usage. Subsequently, the items within each transaction are sorted, and any empty transactions are deleted. The algorithm then proceeds to construct and store the utility-list of each generalized item from the database in a variable called UtilityList.

Line #6 performs a third scan of the database and taxonomy to compute the sub-tree utility of every item in Secondary(P) using Definition 13.

Based on Definition 16, line #7 constructs the primary set with respect to the itemset P; Primary(P).

With all the necessary information gathered, the DFS-based Search procedure (Algorithm 2) is executed at line #8 to traverse the search space recursively and extend the initial itemset P to find all top-k CLHUIs.

Algorithm 2: The SEARCH procedure

---

input: P: itemset, D_P: P-projected database, Primary(P): primary items of P, Secondary(P): secondary items of P, k: the number of patterns to find, μ: the
internal threshold, Q: the top-k patterns until now.
output: Q is updated with top-k CLHUIs that are transitive extensions of P.
FOR EACH item z ∈ Primary(P) DO:
    1. $N = P \cup \{z\}$, Secondary(P)' = {x ∈ Secondary(P) | x ∉ Desc(z, τ)};
    2.   Scan D_P to determine u(N), construct D_N, remove every item ∈ Desc(z, τ) and remove empty transactions;
    3.   IF u(N) > μ THEN Insert z into Q;
    4.   IF Size of Q > k THEN:
        Raises to the k-th largest utility value in Q;
        Remove from Q all patterns with utility less than μ;
    5.   Scan D_N to compute su(N,w), lu(N,w) for every item w ∈ Secondary(P)';
    6.   Primary(N) = {x ∈ Secondary(P)' ∧ su(N, z) ≥ μ};
    7.   Secondary(N) = {x ∈ Secondary(P)'∧ lu(N, z) ≥ μ};
    8.   SEARCH (N, D_N, Primary(N) , Secondary(N) , k, μ , Q);
END

Algorithm 2 accepts seven arguments as input: an itemset P to be extended, the projected database D_P of P, the set of primary and secondary items of P, the minimum utility threshold, the number of patterns to find k. The details of the depth-first search process to further explore a given itemset are described as follows.

Lines #1 to #8 form a loop to examine every single-item extension of P using each item $z \in$ Primary(P) base on Definition 8, that is of the form $N = P \cup \{z\}$, which is given in line #1.

Lines #2: Perform a database scan to determine the utility of N and construct N's projected database D_N remove every item ∈ Desc(z, τ) and remove empty transactions.

Line #3 and #4 Check whether N has a utility greater than μ. If so, then N is added in priority queue Q. If size of $Q > k$ then raises to the k-th largest utility value in Q and removes from Q all patterns with utility less than μ.

In this case, D_N is scanned once more at line #5 to determine the sub-tree and local utility of each item w that could be used to extend N. This step is required to construct *Primary(N)* and *Secondary(N)* at lines #6 and #7, respectively.

At line #8, the Search algorithm is then recursively invoked to continue exploring the search space to extend N.

3 Experiments and Results

3.1 Data Collection

Various categories of actual data sets were utilized in the experiments (Table 3). Liquor and Fruithut are sparse databases. It contains transactions from US liquor stores and grocery stores. The next two databases are Chess and Accident. In comparison to the previous database, all of them exhibit a higher level of data density.

Table 3. Database characteristics

Database	|D|	|I|	|GI|	MaxLevel	|T_MAX|	|T_AVG|	Density
Liquor	9284	4026	78	7	11	7.87	Spare
Fruithut	181.970	1.265	43	4	36	3.58	Spare
Chess	3.196	75	30	3	37	37.00	Dense
Accident	10.000	468	216	6	51	33.80	Dense

The Table 3 includes various parameters such as transaction count of D represented by $|D|$, number of distinct items represented by $|I|$, generalized item count represented by $|GI|$, maximum traction length represented by $|T_{MAX}|$, average transaction length represented by $|T_{AVG}|$ maximum level in each database represented by MaxLevel and the density of each database represented in the last column.

3.2 Experiments

In this section, we evaluate the performance of the proposed algorithm. We do the experiments on a computer with an Intel Core-i7™ processor clocked at 4.5GHz and 16 GB of RAM, running on the Windows 11 operating system. We compared the performance of the algorithm in terms of execution time and peak memory usage for mining our proposed algorithm and TKC algorithm. The compared algorithms were implemented using the Java programming language with version JDK 11, the runtime and memory usage were measured using the Java API.

3.3 Result and Analysis

First, we evaluated how the runtime and memory of each algorithm are influenced by the K threshold on the test datasets for various K threshold values. The results show that TKC-E has better performance than TKC for almost all K threshold values. The Fig. 3 is represented for the two first datasets Liquor and Fruithut. These are sparse databases. When it comes to the first K threshold values, such as 50 and 100, the efficiency of the two algorithms is almost the same. Both algorithms use approximately 500MB of memory and 20 s to process the datasets. The main difference between the two algorithms is evident in the next K values, the reasoning behind this is evidently rooted in the definitions of sub-tree utility and local utility. For example, with Liquor data set on price K = 1000, the runtime of TKC-E is 2.3 times shorter than that of TKC. The same execution time reduction can be seen on the Fruithut database. And with the Fig. 3a, thanks to the effective use of upper bounds to prune the search space, the memory usage of TKC-E is less than the unoptimized one. The memory of TKC-E is cut by 50% with the value K = 1000 when compared with TKC. The same memory usage reduction is also observed on the Fruithut dataset (Fig. 3c). It is concluded that TKC-E is an efficient algorithm because it had a better performance compared with TKC on both runtime and memory usage.

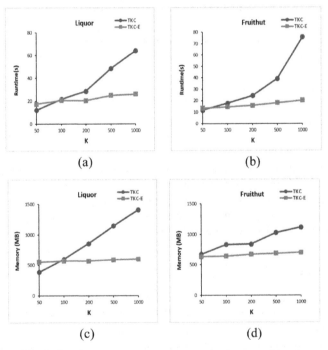

Fig. 3. Runtime, memory usage comparion in spare datasets.

Next, we show the performance on the Chess and Accident database. They all have high density compared to the previous dataset. The outcomes are depicted in Fig. 4, illustrating the findings visually. TKC-E's execution time has a huge efficiency with TKC on the Chess (Fig. 4b) The maximum point of TKC-E is 100 times higher than the one from TKC. The same execution time improvement can be seen in the Accident dataset. The performance of TKC-E is 2–3 times better compared to the TKC. TKC-E has shown its effectiveness with its tight sub-tree utility pruning with extremely low runtime. Therefore, the TKC-E can eliminate many candidates found in the dense datasets, and significantly reduce the mining time. According to this assessment, the TKC-E algorithm demonstrates the most efficient mining performance when applied to dense databases. When it comes to the memory path, the result has a slight difference. Both in Chess and Accident datasets, the memory usage of TKC-E is a little bit more compared to TKC. Although at the first K threshold, the TKC-E algorithm is still limited in that it uses a lot of memory, the trade-off with it is the processing time of the algorithm. The reason is that it applies efficient pruning strategies to keep the average memory usage low by eliminating unpromising candidates from the search space when mining cross-level itemset.

Overall, the test results have shown that the TKC-E algorithm we developed is time-efficient and also optimal in terms of memory usage. TKC-E has achieved a substantial speed boost and has more effective memory consumption. The reason is that it applies efficient pruning strategies to keep the average memory usage low by eliminating unpromising candidates from the search space when mining cross-level itemset.

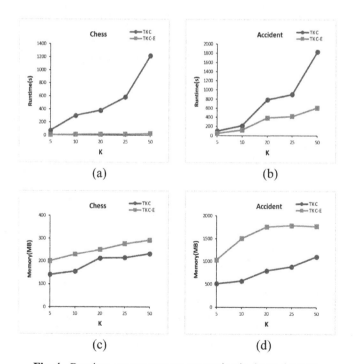

(a)   (b)

(c)   (d)

Fig. 4. Runtime, memory usage comparion in dense datasets.

4   Conclusion and Future Works

In this work, a novel algorithm called TKC-E was presented to efficiently discover cross-level high-utility itemsets in transaction databases. The algorithm takes as input a transaction database with an item taxonomy that describes categories and subcategories of items. TKC-E uses the method of keeping items in a priority queue of the TKC algorithm and the min utility threshold strategy to quickly eliminate patterns and narrow the search space. Additionally, we combined a new pruning strategy from FEACP that uses local utility and sub-tree utility techniques to create upper bounds for each category in the classification system, which significantly improves the time required to search for HUIs. Experimental evaluations demonstrated that TKC-E outperforms its predecessor, the TKC algorithm, in terms of time and memory consumption. The runtime and memory consumption were improved up to 4 times on sparse datasets. However, on dense datasets, TKC-E exhibited higher from 1.5 to 2.0 times memory usage than TKC. Nevertheless, TKC-E was up to 60 times more efficient than TKC in terms of runtime on dense datasets. For future work, we will focus on improving the memory usage of TKC-E for both sparse and dense datasets. Parallel computing frameworks will be studied to reduce mining time, as well as enable computation with larger databases. The paper can be a good reference for data mining problems [13–17].

References

1. Agrawal, R., Srikant, R.: Fast algorithms for mining association rules in large databases. In: Proceedings of the 20th International Conference on Very Large Data Bases, San Francisco, pp. 487–499 (1994)
2. Agrawal, R., Imielinski, T., Swami, A.: Mining association rules between sets of items in large databases. ACM SIGMOD Rec. **22**(2), 207–216 (1993)
3. Fournier-Viger, P., Chun-Wei Lin, J., Truong-Chi, T., Nkambou, R.: A survey of high utility itemset mining. In: Fournier-Viger, P., Lin, J.-W., Nkambou, R., Vo, B., Tseng, V.S. (eds.) High-Utility Pattern Mining. SBD, vol. 51, pp. 1–45. Springer, Cham (2019). https://doi.org/10.1007/978-3-030-04921-8_1
4. Fournier-Viger, P., Cheng-Wei, Wu., Zida, S., Tseng, V.S.: FHM: faster high-utility itemset mining using estimated utility co-occurrence pruning. In: Andreasen, T., Christiansen, H., Cubero, J.-C., Raś, Z.W. (eds.) ISMIS 2014. LNCS (LNAI), vol. 8502, pp. 83–92. Springer, Cham (2014). https://doi.org/10.1007/978-3-319-08326-1_9
5. Tseng, V.S., Wu, C.-W., Shie, B.-E., Yu, P.S.: UP-growth: an efficient algorithm for high utility itemset mining. In: Proceedings of the 16th ACM SIGKDD International Conference on Knowledge Discovery and Data Mining, pp. 253–262. Association for Computing Machinery, New York (2010)
6. Liu, M., Qu, J.: Mining high utility itemsets without candidate generation. In: Proceedings of the 21st ACM International Conference on Information and Knowledge Management (CIKM 2012), pp. 55–64. Association for Computing Machinery, New York (2012)
7. Cagliero, L., Chiusano, S., Garza, P., Ricupero, G.: Discovering high-utility itemsets at multiple abstraction levels. In: Kirikova, M., Nørvåg, K., Papadopoulos, G.A., Gamper, J., Wrembel, R., Darmont, J., Rizzi, S. (eds.) ADBIS 2017. CCIS, vol. 767, pp. 224–234. Springer, Cham (2017). https://doi.org/10.1007/978-3-319-67162-8_22

8. Fournier-Viger, P., Wang, Y., Lin, J.-W., Luna, J.M., Ventura, S.: Mining cross-level high utility itemsets. In: Fujita, H., Fournier-Viger, P., Ali, M., Sasaki, J. (eds.) IEA/AIE 2020. LNCS (LNAI), vol. 12144, pp. 858–871. Springer, Cham (2020). https://doi.org/10.1007/978-3-030-55789-8_73

9. Tung, N.T., Nguyen, L.T.T., Nguyen, T.D.D., Fourier-Viger, P., Nguyen, N.-T., Vo, B.: Efficient mining of cross-level high-utility itemsets in taxonomy quantitative databases. Inf. Sci. **587**, 41–62 (2022). https://doi.org/10.1016/j.ins.2021.12.017

10. Wu, C.W., Shie, B.-E., Tseng, V.S., Yu, P.S.: Mining top-K high utility itemsets. In: Proceedings of the 18th ACM SIGKDD International Conference on Knowledge Discovery and Data Mining, KDD 2012 (2012)

11. Tseng, V.S., Wu, C.-W., Fournier-Viger, P., Yu, P.S.: Efficient algorithms for mining top-K high utility itemsets. IEEE Trans. Knowl. Data Eng. **28**(1), 54–67 (2016)

12. Nouioua, M., Wang, Y., Fournier-Viger, P., Lin, J.C.-W., Wu, J. M.-T.: TKC: mining top-K cross-level high utility itemsets. In: Proceedings of the International Conference on Data Mining Workshops, Sorrento, Italy, pp. 673–682 (2020)

13. Tram, N.N., Hung, P.D.: Analysing hot Facebook users posts' sentiment using deep learning. In: Hassanien, A.E., Bhattacharyya, S., Chakrabati, S., Bhattacharya, A., Dutta, S. (eds.) Emerging Technologies in Data Mining and Information Security. AISC, vol. 1300, pp. 561–569. Springer, Singapore (2021). https://doi.org/10.1007/978-981-33-4367-2_53

14. Phan, D.H., Do, Q.D.: Analysing effects of customer clustering for customer's account balance forecasting. In: Nguyen, N.T., Hoang, B.H., Huynh, C.P., Hwang, D., Trawiński, B., Vossen, G. (eds.) ICCCI 2020. LNCS (LNAI), vol. 12496, pp. 255–266. Springer, Cham (2020). https://doi.org/10.1007/978-3-030-63007-2_20

15. Hai, P.N., Hieu, H.T., Hung, P.D.: An empirical examination on forecasting VN30 short-term uptrend stocks using LSTM along with the Ichimoku cloud trading strategy. In: Sharma, H., Shrivastava, V., Kumari Bharti, K., Wang, L. (eds.) Communication and Intelligent Systems. LNNS, vol. 461, pp. 235–244. Springer, Singapore (2022). https://doi.org/10.1007/978-981-19-2130-8_19

16. Hung, P.D., Son, D.N., Diep, V.T.: Building a recommendation system for travel location based on user check-ins on social network. In: Joshi, A., Mahmud, M., Ragel, R.G. (eds.) ICTCS 2022. LNNS, vol. 623, pp. 713–724. Springer, Singapore (2023). https://doi.org/10.1007/978-981-19-9638-2_62

17. Nam, L.H., Hung, P.D., Vinh, B.T., Diep, V.T.: Practical fair queuing algorithm for message queue system. In: Joshi, A., Mahmud, M., Ragel, R.G. (eds.) ICTCS 2021. LNNS, vol. 400, pp. 421–429. Springer, Singapore (2023). https://doi.org/10.1007/978-981-19-0095-2_40

Security and Privacy Engineering

Web Browsers' Support for Managing Cookies. An Experiment Report

Ngoc Chau Lam[1(⊠)] and Manuel Clavel[2]

[1] University of Information Technology, Ho Chi Minh City, Vietnam
chauln.14@grad.uit.edu.vn
[2] Eastern International University, Binh Duong, Vietnam
manuel.clavel@eiu.edu.vn

Abstract. In this paper we analyze the support currently provided by the most-widely used web browsers for managing cookies. To carry out our study we have first designed an experiment, and then we have carried out this experiment in each of the selected web browsers—or, more precisely, in each of the configurations related to cookies currently supported by each of the selected web browsers. The main take-away from this experiment is that the current trend among web browsers of leaving the responsibility of handling cookies to the browsers' end-users is not practical (and, therefore, not effective), simply because the understanding required for setting up the browsers' configurations related to cookies is beyond what can be reasonably expected from typical browsers' end-user. In addition, we have carried out a survey whose preliminary results seem to validate the main conclusion from our experiment.

1 Introduction

Along with the growth of the Internet, data is becoming the new *oil* of the 21st century. Indeed, being able to *mine* and analyze data can provide key information to understand and even predict human behavior at all levels: individual, group, and global.

In the Internet context, the term "usage data" refers to the data generated by the end-users when using the web browsers—e.g., the websites that they have visited; the topics that they have searched for; or the time that they have spent visiting a website. Usage data is usually collected without end-users' explicit consent. In fact, end-users are typically unaware about the usage data that is collected while they browse the Internet, and even less about the purpose for which this data is collected.

Internet "cookies" are pieces of data that are created by websites and are stored in the web browsers. In principle, a web browser will *attach* all the cookies created by a website, which are stored in the browser, to every request submitted to the website.

In recent years cookies have been the basic technology used to collect usage data [2,20,23]. In fact, it can be argued that the main usage of Internet cookies

T. K. Dang et al. (Eds.): FDSE 2023, CCIS 1925, pp. 135–152, 2023.
https://doi.org/10.1007/978-981-99-8296-7_10

nowadays is to *track* users as they browse the Internet, so as to customize with personalized ads (e.g., Google Ads) the websites that they visit, based on their past web searches, likes and dislikes, etc.

Background

In 1989, Tim Berners-Lee created the Hyper Text Markup Language (HTML) as a language for publishing documents in the Web [1]. A key idea behind HTML—inherited from its predecessor, the Standard Generalized Markup Language (SGML)—was that the language should be independent of the "formatter", i.e., of the software in charge of rendering the document. The key novelty of HTML was the so-called "hypertext links", which allowed the users to *click* their way from document to document.

"Web browsers" are software applications that render documents to be published in the Web. Depending on the web browser, a document may be displayed differently in different computers. The first prototype of web browser for HTML documents was developed by Tim Berners-Lee on a NeXT computer in 1990 [1]. In May 1991, Nicola Pellow developed the line-mode browser [10]. In 1993, Mosaic became the first browser that supported the IMG-tag [3]. The idea of this tag was to display images along with the text—instead of in separate windows—, without requiring users to click on links to view the images. In effect, the IMG-tag introduced for the first time *subresources* in the HTML language.[1]

A "subresource" is a resource (e.g., an image) that is requested to be embedded or executed in the context of another resource (e.g., an HTML document). A subresource can be "internal" (if it is stored in the same server that the requesting resource) or "external" (if it is stored in a different server that the requesting resource). Subresources gave then rise to the so-called "cross-origin requests", in which a browser fetches a subresource from an URL that does not coincide with the browser's top navigation URL.

2   Cookies

History. The standard protocol for the Web is the HyperText Transfer Protocol (HTTP). In its origin, HTTP was a simple protocol: the *client* will send a request for a file to the *server*, and the *server* will send back the file to the *client*, and then close the connection.

In June 1994, Louis J 'Lou' Montulli invented the HTTP cookies [18] with the clear purpose of enabling e-commerce websites with the capability of remembering customers' preferences: e.g., the items that the customers bought before.[2]

---

[1] Following the IMG-tag, other tags were later added to HTML in order to embed or execute different types of subresources in the context of a document, including: script, frame, video, audio, iframe, link, and form.

[2] The name "cookie" was chosen after the Computer Science term *magic cookie*. A "magic cookie" is some information passed between routines or programs that enables the *receiver* to perform some operation, which could not be performed without it.

Privacy Concerns. However, cookies have been used in the past with other purposes in mind.[3] In particular, cookies have been used in ways that (potentially, at least) violate browsers' end-users' *privacy rights* [24–26, 28].

The now infamous "third-party" cookies are a prime example of this problematic usage of the cookies. The typical third-party cookie scenario is the following. A website B (third-party) installs in a user's browser a cookie ck that contains the usage data generated by the user when visiting a website A (first-party).[4] From the point of view of the end-user's privacy rights, the problem is that the end-user is unaware of the fact that the website B is collecting usage data that belongs to him/her; and, of course, the end-user is equally unaware of which usage data is being collected, and for which purpose is being collected.

Different from third-party cookies, the so-called "first-party" cookies are cookies that are installed in a user's browser by the same website that the user is visiting. From the point of view of the end-user's privacy rights, first-party cookies are less problematic than third-party cookies, since the end-user is, in principle, aware of the website that he/she is visiting. Nowadays, websites routinely use first-party cookies to remember users' identities and preferences.

Other Security-Related Concerns. Nevertheless, privacy-concerns—and, in particular, *cross-site tracking*—are not the only concerns caused by cookies. *Cross-site request forgery* (CSRF) is a well-known security-attack based on cookies and cross-origin requests. When a victim visits the attacker's website, an HTTP request is triggered to the vulnerable website. Unless prevented, the victim's browser will automatically attached all the cookies associated with vulnerable website to the attacker's request. If the cookies include, for example, the victim's credentials, the vulnerable website will process any request as it would have been made by the victim itself.

Technical Considerations. The `Set-Cookie` HTTP response *header* is used to send a cookie from the server to the browser, so that the browser can send it back to the server later.

Cookies may have, among others, the following *attributes:*[5]

- ⟨*cookie-name*⟩ = ⟨*cookie-value*⟩. It defines the cookie name and its value. It is the only required attribute.

---

[3] In 1996, the media started reporting on the cookies potential threat to privacy. The concerns rightly raised from the fact that cookies were storing private information on the users' computers without their knowledge or consent.

[4] There are different methods for the website B to install the third-party cookie ck in the user's browser when the user is visiting the website A. The basic method, however, consists in the website A making a request (JavaScript files, images, fonts, CSS files, etc.) to the website B when the user is visiting the website A. Along with the response, the website A will receive from the website B the "third-party" cookie ck, which will be then installed in the user's browser.

[5] We discuss here only the attributes that are used later on in the experiment. See [8, 22] for the complete list of available cookies attributes, as well as for the current browsers compatibility.

– `Domain` = ⟨*domain-value*⟩. It defines the host to which the cookie will be sent. If omitted, this attribute defaults to the host of the current document URL, not including subdomains. If a domain is specified, then subdomains are always included.
– `HttpOnly`. It forbids JavaScript from accessing the cookie.
– `Max-Age` = ⟨*number*⟩. It indicates the number of seconds until the cookie expires. A zero or negative number will expire the cookie immediately.
– `Path` = ⟨*path-value*⟩ It indicates the path that must exist in the requested URL for the browser to send the Cookie header.
– `SameSite` = ⟨*samesite-value*⟩ It controls whether or not a cookie is sent with cross-site requests, providing some protection against cross-site request forgery attacks (CSRF). The possible attribute values are:
  • `Strict`. The browser sends the cookie only for same-site requests, that is, requests originating from the same site that set the cookie.
  • `Lax`. The cookie is not sent on cross-site requests, except when the user is navigating to the origin site from an external site (for example, when following a link). This is the default behavior if the `SameSite` attribute is not specified.
  • `None`. The browser sends the cookie with both cross-site and same-site requests. The `Secure` attribute must also be set when setting this value. If `Secure` is missing an error will be logged.
– `Secure` The cookie is sent to the server only when a request is made with the `https:` scheme (except on localhost).

3   Experiment

As a response to customers' and regulators' privacy concerns, web browser vendors are now providing end-users with different configurations to manage cookies, in general, and third-party/cross-site tracking cookies, in particular.[6] At the time of writing, Apple has set the option of blocking third-party cookies, by default, in its Safari browser [4], and Google has promised to phase out third-party cookies by the end of 2024 in its Chrome browser [27]. We have compiled in Appendix A a brief description of the configurations currently supported by the most-widely used web-browsers for managing cookies.

To analyze the level of protection against cookies currently provided by the most-widely used web browsers, we have designed the following experiment.

Web Servers. For our experiment, we need two web servers running on two different machines/domains, as shown in Fig. 1.

---

[6] As it is well-known, CPPA [15], ePR [12], and GDPR [13] impose serious penalties to the websites that fail to notify their visitors of the usage of cookies. More specifically, they require the websites to inform their visitors about the data that will be collected using cookies, and about the websites with which the data will be shared using the cookies.

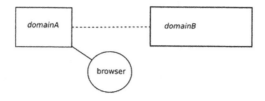

Fig. 1. Deployment Diagram

Web Application. For our experiment, we have developed a simple web application, depicted in Fig. 2, with the following functionality:

- By clicking on different HTML-elements in the upper part of the web page (white part), the user triggers different requests to *domainB*. Each request is responded then by *domainA* with a different type of cookie, i.e., with a cookie with different attributes.
- By clicking on different HTML-elements in the lower part of the web page (grey-colored part), the users triggers also different requests to *domainB*. Each request is responded then by *domainA* with the list of cookies that has received attached to this request.

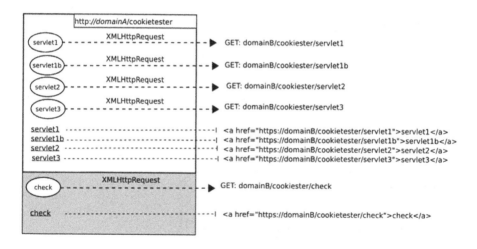

Fig. 2. Web-UI Diagram

Servlets. In our experiment, the different requests to *domainB* are handled by different servlets. In particular, requests to

```
/cookiester/servlet1, /cookiester/servlet1b,
/cookiester/servlet2, /cookiester/servlet3,
/cookiester/servlet2lk, /cookiester/servlet3lk
```

are handled, respectively, by the servlets `servlet1`, `servlet1b`, `servlet2`, `servlet3`, `servlet21k`, and `servlet31k`. Each of these servlets is a different instance of the servlets template shown in Fig. 3. Basically, each servlet differs from the others in the type of cookies that it attaches to its response. Table 1 shows the relationship between the servlets and the cookies that they attach to their respective responses.

```
@WebServlet(..., urlPatterns = {"/servlet"},...)
public class CookieServlet extends HttpServlet {
...
  public void doGet(HttpServletRequest request, HttpServletResponse response)
  ...{
    response.addHeader("Access-Control-Allow-Credentials", "true");
    response.addHeader("Access-Control-Allow-Origin", domainA);
    response.setHeader("Set-Cookie", "cookie= value; Domain=domainB; Path=path;
        SameSite= same_site; [secure]; [http_only]; Max-Age=max_age;");
    ...
  }
}
```

Fig. 3. Servlets template

Moreover, requests to `/cookiester/check` are handled by the servlet `check`, which is (partially) shown in Fig. 4. Basically, this servlet responds with the list of cookies that were attached to the request.

```
@WebServlet(name = "Check", urlPatterns = { "/check" }, ...)
public class ServletCheck extends HttpServlet {
...
  public void doGet(HttpServletRequest request, HttpServletResponse response)
  ... {
    ...
    response.addHeader("Access-Control-Allow-Credentials", "true");
    response.addHeader("Access-Control-Allow-Origin", domainA);
    StringBuilder reqCookies = new StringBuilder();
    Cookie ck[] = request.getCookies();
    if (ck != null) {
      for (int i = 0; i < ck.length; i++) {
        reqCookies.append(ck[i].getName() + "; ");
      }
    } else {
      reqCookies.append("No cookies");
    }
    PrintWriter writer = response.getWriter();
    writer.println(reqCookies.toString());
    ...
  }
}
```

Fig. 4. Servlet check

Table 1. Relationship between servlets and cookies, with *path* = `cookiester`.

Servlet	Cookie	Domain	Path	Max-Age	HttpOnly	Secure	SameSite
`servlet1`	`cookie1`	*domainB*	*path*	600	false	false	None
`servlet1b`	`cookie1b`	*domainB*	*path*	600	false	true	None
`servlet2`	`cookie2`	*domainB*	*path*	600	false	true	Lax
`servlet3`	`cookie3`	*domainB*	*path*	600	false	true	Strict
`servlet2lk`	`cookie2lk`	*domainB*	*path*	600	false	true	Lax
`servlet3lk`	`cookie3lk`	*domainB*	*path*	600	false	true	Strict

Web Browsers. According to [30], in May 2023, the 5 most-widely used web browsers (considering desktops, tablets, and mobiles together) are the browsers shown in Fig 5. As expected, they are the web browsers that we have selected for our experiment.

Web Browser	Market Share
Chrome	62.85%
Safari	20.72%
Edge	5.31%
Opera	2.82%
Firefox	2.77%

Fig. 5. Browser market share world (May 2023)

Runs. For each of the web-browsers, and for each of the configurations provided by the browser, we have run the following experiment:

- **Step 1**. We delete all the cookies installed in the web browser.
- **Step 2**. We click on buttons `servlet1`, `servlet1b`, `servlet2`, and `servlet3`.
- **Step 3**. We click on the links `servlet2lk` and `servlet3lk`.
- **Step 4**. We click on the button `check` and record the list of cookies displayed.
- **Step 5**. We click on the link `check` and record the list of cookies displayed.
- **Step 6**. We enter the URL *domainB*/`cookiestester/check` in the top navigation bar and record the list of cookies displayed.

Results. In Tables 2, 3, 4, 5 and 6 we show the results obtained in our experiment. Each table shows, for each of the browser's configurations and for each of the cookies, whether, after completing **Step 1**, **Step 2**, and **Step 3**, the cookie is attached (✓) or not (✗) to the corresponding request, in each of the following situations/methods:

- Method "xhr:get". By clicking on the button `check`, we triggered a JavaScript XMLHttpRequest to *domainB*/`cookiestester/check` (**Step 4**).

- Method "⟨a⟩:href". By clicking on the link check, we triggered a request to *domainB*/cookiestester/check (**Step 5**).
- Method "url:top". By entering the URL *domainB*/cookiestester/ check in the top navigation bar, we triggered a request to *domainB* /cookiestester/check (**Step 6**).

As mentioned before, in Appendix A we have compiled a short description of each of the browser's configurations that we have considered in our experiment. Also, remember that in Table 1 we have summarized the key attributes of the cookies that we have used in our experiment.

Analysis. A preliminary analysis of the results obtained in our experiment allows us to draw the following remarks about the current state of the web browsers' support for managing cookies.

Table 2. Chrome Web Browser. Experiment results

Chrome Version 114.0.5735.133 (Official Build) (64-bit)

Configuration	method	cookie1	cookie1b	cookie2	cookie2lk	cookie3	cookie3lk
Allow all cookies	xhr:get	✗	✓	✗	✗	✗	✗
	⟨a⟩:href	✗	✓	✗	✓	✗	✗
	url:top	✗	✓	✗	✓	✗	✓
Block third-party cookies	xhr:get	✗	✗	✗	✗	✗	✗
	⟨a⟩:href	✗	✗	✗	✓	✗	✗
	url:top	✗	✗	✗	✓	✗	✓
Block all cookies	xhr:get	✗	✗	✗	✗	✗	✗
	⟨a⟩:href	✗	✗	✗	✗	✗	✗
	url:top	✗	✗	✗	✗	✗	✗

Table 3. Firefox Web Browser. Experiment results

Firefox (114.0.2)

Configuration	method	cookie1	cookie1b	cookie2	cookie2lk	cookie3	cookie3lk
Standard	xhr:get	✓	✓	✗	✗	✗	✗
	⟨a⟩:href	✗	✗	✗	✓	✗	✗
	url:top	✗	✗	✗	✓	✗	✓
Strict	xhr:get	✓	✓	✗	✗	✗	✗
	⟨a⟩:href	✗	✗	✗	✓	✗	✗
	url:top	✗	✗	✗	✓	✗	✓
[Block] Cross-site tracking cookies	xhr:get	✓	✓	✗	✗	✗	✗
	⟨a⟩:href	✓	✓	✗	✓	✗	✗
	url:top	✓	✓	✗	✓	✗	✓
[Block] Cross-site tracking cookies, and isolate other cross-site cookies	xhr:get	✓	✓	✗	✗	✗	✗
	⟨a⟩:href	✗	✗	✗	✓	✗	✗
	url:top	✗	✗	✗	✓	✗	✓
[Block] All cross-site cookies	xhr:get	✗	✗	✗	✗	✗	✗
	⟨a⟩:href	✗	✗	✗	✓	✗	✗
	url:top	✗	✗	✗	✓	✗	✓
[Block] All cookies	xhr:get	✗	✗	✗	✗	✗	✗
	⟨a⟩:href	✗	✗	✗	✗	✗	✗
	url:top	✗	✗	✗	✗	✗	✗

Table 4. Safari Web Browser. Experiment results

Safari version 16.4 (18615.1.26.110.1)	Cookies						
Configuration	method	cookie1	cookie1b	cookie2	cookie2lk	cookie3	cookie3lk
Allow all cookies	xhr:get	✓	✓	✗	✗	✗	✗
	⟨a⟩:href	✓	✓	✗	✓	✗	✗
	url:top	✓	✓	✗	✓	✗	✓
Prevent cross-site tracking	xhr:get	✗	✗	✗	✗	✗	✗
	⟨a⟩:href	✗	✗	✗	✓	✗	✗
	url:top	✗	✗	✗	✓	✗	✓
Block all cookies	xhr:get	✗	✗	✗	✗	✗	✗
	⟨a⟩:href	✗	✗	✗	✗	✗	✗
	url:top	✗	✗	✗	✗	✗	✗

Table 5. Edge Web Browser. Experiment results

Edge Version 114.0.1823.58 (Official build) (x86_64)	Cookies						
Configuration	method	cookie1	cookie1b	cookie2	cookie2lk	cookie3	cookie3lk
Allow sites to save and read cookies data + Block third-party cookies	xhr:get	✗	✗	✗	✗	✗	✗
	⟨a⟩:href	✗	✗	✗	✓	✗	✗
	url:top	✗	✗	✗	✓	✗	✓
Allow sites to save and read cookies data	xhr:get	✗	✓	✗	✗	✗	✗
	⟨a⟩:href	✗	✓	✗	✓	✗	✗
	url:top	✗	✓	✗	✓	✗	✓
Not allow sites to save and read cookies data and no tracking prevention	xhr:get	✗	✗	✗	✗	✗	✗
	⟨a⟩:href	✗	✗	✗	✗	✗	✗
	url:top	✗	✗	✗	✗	✗	✗

Table 6. Opera Web Browser. Experiment results

Opera One Version: 100.0.4815.21 (x86_64)	Cookies						
Configuration	method	cookie1	cookie1b	cookie2	cookie2lk	cookie3	cookie3lk
Allow all cookies	xhr:get	✗	✓	✗	✗	✗	✗
	⟨a⟩:href	✗	✓	✗	✓	✗	✗
	url:top	✗	✓	✗	✓	✗	✓
Block third-party cookies	xhr:get	✗	✗	✗	✗	✗	✗
	⟨a⟩:href	✗	✗	✗	✓	✗	✗
	url:top	✗	✗	✗	✓	✗	✓
Block all cookies	xhr:get	✗	✗	✗	✗	✗	✗
	⟨a⟩:href	✗	✗	✗	✗	✗	✗
	url:top	✗	✗	✗	✗	✗	✗

– *Different browsers offer different configurations for managing cookies.* Except for Chrome and Opera, which are both Chromium-based browsers, each of the selected browsers supports a different set of configurations for managing cookies. These configurations are not only *nominally* different (i.e., they have different *titles*), but also they are different in the level of protection that they offer against cookies.

- *The different configurations for managing cookies offered by the different browsers target different security-concerns.* Firefox, Safari, and Edge are explicitly concerned about users *tracking*, while Chrome and Opera are concerned about third-party cookies. Third-party cookies are "cross-site" cookies, and may be used for "users tracking". However, whether a third-party cookie is considered a "cross-site tracking" cookie or not depends on the (concrete and dynamic) definition/list of cross-site tracking cookies used by each web browser (in our case, Firefox, Safari, or Edge).[7] As expected, Firefox, Safari and Edge consider the cookies generated by third-party advertising and analytics sites as cross-site tracking cookies. In our experiment, since *domainB* is not a third-party advertising or an analytical site (as mentioned before, it is our own domain: only use for this experiment), Firefox does not "block" the cookies "servlet1" and "servlet1b" (third-party cookies) with the configuration "[Block] cross-site tracking cookies". but it does "block" them with the configuration "[Block] all cross-site cookies".

- *There is not an obvious mapping/translation across the different browsers with respect to the level of protection against cookies offered by their different configurations.* This is a natural consequence of the different security-concerns addressed by the different browsers. Except for "block all cookies" or (when applicable) "allow all cookies", there is no other level of protection against cookies that is obviously *common* to Chrome, Firefox, Safari, Edge, and Opera. Of course, "block all cookies", although offering *full protection* against cookies, it is not really an option (and it is not recommended by the browsers), since it will dramatically affect the possibility for the end-user to access many websites. A similar remark can be made of "allow all cookies", but for the opposite reason.

- *In particular, the "default" configurations of the different browsers offered a different level of protection against cookies.* The "default" configurations for Chrome, Firefox, Safari, Edge, and Opera in normal windows—i.e., no *incognito* or *private* windows—are, respectively, "block third-party cookies", "standard", "prevent cross-site tracking", "tracking prevention: balance"[8], and "allow all cookies". A quick inspection to the tables containing the results of our experiment shows that, the "default" configurations of the different browsers provide different level of protection against cookies.

4 Survey

Based on our experiment, we have the (strong) impression that *the technical knowledge required to understand the level of protection against cookies provided*

---

[7] From the Mozilla Web Docs [21]: "Firefox ships with a list of sites which have been identified as engaging in cross-site tracking of users. When tracking protection is enabled, Firefox blocks content from sites in the list." From Safari's Help [5]: "Some websites use third-party content providers. A third-party content provider can track you across websites to advertise products and services.".

[8] In Edge, the configuration "tracking prevention: balance" sets on the option "allow sites to save and read cookie data" and off the option "block third-party cookies".

by each of the configurations offered by the different web browsers is far beyond what can be expected in an average end-user. However, to validate this conclusion, we have carried out a preliminary survey. The interested reader can find in Appendix B the questions that were asked in our survey. The survey was available both in English and in Vietnamese.

We report below the main result of our survey. In a nutshell, for a population of users that regularly access the Internet, have experienced "cross-tracking" of some sort or another, are mostly reluctant to share their "usage data" across web-sites, the understanding of the level of protecting offered by the different browsers' configurations is mostly wrong. More specifically: *only 22,9% of Google Chrome's respondents, 22.6% of Safari's respondents, and 20% of Mozilla Firefox's respondents are able to correctly identify the "privacy setting" that will allow their browers to install only cookies that are created by the website that they are visiting (first-party cookies).*

- The survey was available online from May 2023 to June 2023.
- We received 158 complete responses.
- The respondents were mostly from Vietnam (89.3%).
- The majority of our respondents were in the age range 18–35.
- 46.3% use the Internet at least once a week.
- 20.4% use the Internet at least once a day to buy items.
- 30.9% report that they always feel that the website that they visit "knows" about their past browing activity.
- 67.9% report that they occasionally feel that the website that they visit "knows" about their past browing activity.
- 45.7% are unwilling to share information about their "usage data" with other websites.
- 43.8% are only willing to share information about their "usage data" with other websites with explicit permission.
- 50.8% report that they have no idea what "usage data" is being collected with they visit a website.
- 23.5% report that the information provided by the websites about the "usage data" that is being collected is too complicated for them to read.
- 23.9% are mostly concerned about being watched or followed in their browing activity.
- 23.4% are mostly concerned about ther information begin stolen.
- 33.3% know how to delete cookies.
- 53.7% believe that they could learn about how to delete cookies.
- Only 22,9% of Google Chrome's respondents, 22.6% of Safari's respondents, and 20% of Mozilla Firefox's respondents are able to correctly identify the "privacy setting" that will allow their browers to install only cookies that are created by the website that they are visiting (first-party cookies).

5   Related Work

[6,7] provides a clear, standarized definition of cookies. About privacy-violations related to cookies, [14,20] reports about the usage of cookies for linking users'

browsing history accross different websites. Other security-related misuses of cookies are reported in: [9] (information leakage), [17] (information sharing), [19] (cross-site request forgery), [2] (ever-cookies), [29] (super-cookies or flash cookies). From the legal standpoint, [16], CPPA [15], ePR [12], and GDPR [13] define the current regulatory framework. To comply with this new regulatory framework, among other actions, browsers vendors are banning third-party cookies and adding settings to protect users' privacy. However, [11] has recently pointed out that banning third-party cookies does not completely eliminate the possibility of using cookies to track users. [31], on the other hand, stresses the benefits of allowing the users to control when and where cookies are sent, instead of simply "blocking" the installation of cookies. Finally, [11,14] report on experiments related to cookies, but with a different methodology (crawling the sites) and scope (counting, analyzing the cookies). In our case, our experiment focuses on analyzing the different configuration offered by the most-widely used web browser for managing cookies.

6   Conclusions and Future Work

In this paper we have analyzed the support currently provided by different web browsers for managing cookies. To carry out our analysis, we have set up an experiment consisting on a simple web application that responds to different request with different cookies, or, more precisely, with cookies with different attributes/properties.

To analysis how web browsers manage cookies, we basically check whether the cookies generated by our web application are send back to our web server on subsequent requests. To be more precise: for each of the web browsers considered in our analysis, we perform the aforementioned check for each of the (cookies-related) configurations currently available in the browser, and for each of the following scenarios: (i) the users clicks on an HTML-button element that triggers a JavaScript `GET-XMLHttpRequest` to our web server; (ii) the users clicks on a HTML-link-element with a `HREF`-attribute that references to our web server; (iii) the users types in the URL of our web server in the browser's top navigation bar.

The main results of our analysis are the following. Currently,

– Different browsers offer different configurations for managing cookies.
– The different configurations offered (for managing cookies) by the different browsers target different security-concerns and/or different group of end-users.
– There is not an obvious mapping/translation across the different browsers with respect to the level of protection against cookies offered by their different configurations.
– In particular, the "default" configurations of the different browsers offered a different level of protection against cookies.

The consequence of the current state-of-affairs with respect to how web browsers manage cookies is easy to draw. From the point of view of the end-users, to navigate the Internet with a consistent response/behavior with respect to cookies:

– They need to understand the level of protection provided by each of the configurations available in each web browser that they use, since these configurations are not consistent/standardized across web browsers.
– They need to set up in each of the web browsers that they use the required configuration, since not even the "default" configuration offered the same level of protection across web browsers.

However, based on our experiments, we are lead to conclude that:

– The technical knowledge required to understand the level of protection offered by each of the configuration available in each of the web browsers is far beyond what can be expected in an average end-user.

To validate this conclusion, we have carried out a preliminary survey. The main outcome of this survey is that, even for a population of users that regularly access the Internet, have experienced "cross-tracking" of some sort or another, are mostly reluctant to share their "usage data" across web-sites, the understanding of the level of protecting offered by the different browsers' configurations is mostly wrong.

As a consequence of this state-of-affairs, we can expect that typical end-users either (i) do not modify the "default" configuration (which, as we pointed out above, do not offer the same level of protection across web browsers), or (ii) do modify the "default" configuration but to a less-protective configuration, when the former renders unusable the site that they want to visit (without really understanding the level of protection offered by the later). In either case, the pursued goal of putting the protection against (bad) cookies in the hands of the end-users reveals to be ineffective: the end-users is not prepared to use the tools (configurations) provided by the web browsers to protect themselves against (bad) cookies.

In this unsettling situation, we find the Edge's configuration requiring the end-user's explicit consent before *sending* a cookie to a web site that the end-user is visiting as particularly promising. The reason is the following. A typical end-user will easily give consent when asked if he/she is willing to accept cookies to be installed in his/her browser in order to access a web site he/she wants to visit, even if these cookies (i) may contain information about his/her current browsing activity, and (ii) may be created by web sites different from the one he/she wants to visit. After all, if the cookies are safely stored in his/her browser, what can be "dangerous" in accepting these cookies? However, we argue, a typical end-user will not so easily give consent when asked if he/she is willing to send cookies installed in his/her browser in order to access a web site he/she wants to visit, knowing that these cookies (i') may contain information about his/her past browsing activity, and (ii') may be forwarded to other web sites different from the one he/she wants to visit. Still, it is up for discussion whether the aforementioned Edge's configuration is, in practice, effective, in the sense of being actually used by the end-users, despite the fact that will required from them a constant interaction, which may hinder their usual browsing activity.

A   Web-Browsers' Configurations for Managing Cookies

The content of this Appendix is a compilation of the information provided by the browsers themselves. We do not claim any authorship with respect to the content of this Appendix. We include this Appendix only to facilitate the readers the understanding of our experiment.

A.1   Chrome and Opera

It currently provides the following basic configurations:

- **Allow all cookies.** Sites can use cookies to improve the browsing experience, for example, to keep the user signed in or to remember items in the user's shopping cart. And the sites can use cookies to see the user's browsing activity across different sites, for example, to personalize ads.
- **Block third-party cookies in Incognito.** (or Private Mode in Opera) Sites in "normal" mode can use cookies to improve the user's browsing experience, for example, to keep the user signed in or to remember items in the user's shopping cart. While in the "Incognito" mode or "Private" mode, sites can't use cookies to see the user's browsing activity across different sites, for example, to personalize ads. Features on some sites may not work.
- **Block third-party cookies.** Block all cookies which have different origins than the current top navigation. "Has different origins" means that the requests comes from a URL different from the current top navigation, even if the cookie is associated with the target of the request.
- **Block all cookies.** Block all the cookies no matter where it comes from.

A.2   Firefox

It currently provides the following basic configurations:

- **Standard.** Block social media trackers, cross site tracking cookies, cross site cookies in "Private" windows, tracking content in "Private" windows, cryptominers, and fingerprinters.
- **Strict.** Block social media trackers, cross site cookies in all windows (includes tracking cookies), tracking content in all windows, cryptominers, fingerprinters.
- **Custom.** The user can choose among the following "customized" configurations:
  - Block cross-site tracking cookies;
  - Block Cross-site tracking cookies and isolate other cross-site cookies;

- Block cookies from unvisited website: Block all the third-party cookies from sites you have not visited as a first-party.
- Block all third-party cookies
- Block all cookies

Enhanced Tracking Protection. To enhance privacy protection for users but limit the effect on users' experience, Firefox also provides a function, namely Enhanced Tracking Protection. With this feature on, when a user access a website, all the "tracking" sites are blocked (e.g., tracking content, fingerprinters, social media trackers, cross-site tracking cookies, and cryptominers) Users can have the information of these blocked sites. This feature was included in the Standard mode (only in Private Windows), Strict mode (in all windows) and Custom mode (in all windows or in Private Windows). However, if the site can not work, you can turn off this feature only for your visiting site.

This feature is easy to use and does helpful for protecting user privacy. However, compared to the Edge, this one has a bit less security. Though users can see the information of every "tracking" things, but they only can choose to allow all or reject all by turning on or turning off the Enhanced Tracking Protection, respectively.

A.3 Safari

It currently provides the following basic configurations:

- **Prevent cross-site tracking.** Unless you visit and interact with the third-party content provider as a first-party website, their cookies and website data are deleted.
- **Block all cookies** (also Prevent cross-site tracking). Select "Block all cookies" to disable cookies. This may prevent some websites from working properly.
- **Allow all cookies** (deselect Prevent cross-site tracking and deselect Block all cookies). Websites, third parties, and advertisers can store cookies and other data on your Mac.

A.4 Microsoft Edge

It currently provides the following basic configurations:

- **Allow sites to save and read cookie data.** When on, sites can store and read cookies on your PC.
- **Allow sites to save and read cookie data + Block third-party cookies.** When on, sites cannot use cookies that track you across the web. Features on some sites may break.
- Besides these basic configurations, user can choose one of the following **tracking prevention** option:
  - **Basic**: Allow most trackers cross all sites and blocks know harmful trackers
  - **Balanced**: Block trackers from sites you haven't visited. Blocks know harmful trackers
  - **Strict**: Blocks a majority of trackers from all sites. Blocks known harmful trackers

B   Survey's Questions

1. What is your age group?
2. How much familiar are you with the Internet?
3. How often (on average) do you use the Internet to look for information (including news, places, promotions, events, etc.)
4. How often do you use the Internet to buy items? (foods,products, tickets, items, etc.,)
5. Have you ever had the feeling that a website you are visiting "knows" about your past Internet activities (including some information that you looked for, some items that you bought, some messages that you sent, etc.)
6. Do you agree if a website shares information about your "usage data" (i.e., your browser activity when visiting the website) with other websites?
7. When you visit a website, do you know what "usage data" about you that they are collecting?
8. When a website you visit asks you to allow cookies, which option do you usually select?
9. If you want to delete the cookies installed on your computer, do you know how to do it?
10. What issue worries you the most when using the Internet?
11. Do you always use the same browser (Chrome, Firefox, Safari, Edge, etc.) on all your devices (desktop, laptop, mobile, tablet, etc.)?
12. What is the "privacy setting" you usually select in your browsers?
13. Do you normally use any of the following browsers on any of your devices?
14. If you want your browser to install cookies on your computer only when they are created by a website that you directly visit, which option in the "privacy settings" will you select?
15. If you want your browser to install any cookies in your computer, even if they are created by a website that you do not directly visit, what option in the "privacy settings" do you have to select?

References

1. Raggett on Html 4. Addison Wesley Longman
2. Acar, G., Eubank, C., Englehardt, S., Juarez, M., Narayanan, A., Diaz, C.: The web never forgets: persistent tracking mechanisms in the wild. In: Proceedings of the ACM Conference on Computer and Communications Security, pp. 674–689. Association for Computing Machinery (2014). https://doi.org/10.1145/2660267.2660347
3. Andreessen, M.: NCSA Mosaic for X 0.10. https://groups.google.com/g/comp.windows.x/c/fMl2xRqLvRk/m/58RdTW0v3n8J
4. Apple Developer Documentation: Safari 13.1 release notes (2020). https://developer.apple.com/documentation/safari-release-notes/safari-13_1-release_notes
5. Apple Support: Prevent cross-site tracking in Safari on Mac (2021). https://support.apple.com/en-vn/guide/safari/sfri35610/mac

6. Barth, A., Westhoff, D., Wilton, M.: HTTP state tokens (2019). https://datatracker.ietf.org/doc/draft-ietf-httpbis-rfc6265bis/12/
7. Barth, A., Westhoff, D., Wilton, M.: HTTP state tokens (2023). https://datatracker.ietf.org/doc/draft-ietf-httpbis-rfc6265bis/10/
8. Barth, A.: HTTP state management mechanism. Technical report RFC 6265, RFC Editor (April 2011), https://datatracker.ietf.org/doc/rfc6265/
9. Cahn, A., Alfeld, S., Barford, P., Muthukrishnan, S.: An empirical study of web cookies. In: Proceedings of the 25th International Conference on World Wide Web - WWW '16, pp. 891–901 (2016). https://doi.org/10.1145/2872427.2882991
10. CERN Accelerating Science: Line mode browser available at CERN. https://timeline.web.cern.ch/line-mode-browser-available-cern
11. Demir, N., Theis, D., Urban, T., Pohlmann, N.: Towards understanding first-party cookie tracking in the field, February 2022. https://arxiv.org/abs/2202.01498
12. European Commission: Proposal for a regulation of the European Parliament and of the Council concerning the respect for private life and the protection of personal data in electronic communications and repealing Directive 2002/58/EC (Regulation on Privacy and Electronic Communications), January 2017. https://eur-lex.europa.eu/legal-content/EN/TXT/?uri=CELEX:52017PC0010
13. European Parliament and Council of the European Union: Regulation (eu) 2016/679 of the European Parliament and of the Council of 27 April 2016 on the protection of natural persons with regard to the processing of personal data and on the free movement of such data, and repealing Directive 95/46/EC (General Data Protection Regulation), April 2016. https://eur-lex.europa.eu/legal-content/EN/TXT/?uri=CELEX/3A32016R0679
14. Gomez, G., Yalaju, J., Garcia, M., Hoofnagle, C.: Cookie blocking and privacy: first parties remain a risk. Ptolemy Project (2010). https://ptolemy.berkeley.edu/projects/truststc/education/reu/10/Papers/GomezG,YalajuJ_paper.pdf
15. Innovation, S., Canada, E.D.: Consumer privacy protection act (2022). https://ised-isde.canada.ca/site/innovation-better-canada/en/consumer-privacy-protection-act. Accessed 04 Jan 2023
16. JISC Legal Information: EU Cookie Directive - Directive 2009/136/EC, April 2010. https://www.jisc.ac.uk/guides/eu-cookie-directive
17. Krishnamurthy, B., Wills, C.: Privacy diffusion on the web: a longitudinal perspective. In: Proceedings of the 18th International Conference on World Wide Web, pp. 541–550. ACM (2009)
18. Lou, M.: Persistent client state in a hypertext transfer protocol based client-server system. https://worldwide.espacenet.com/publicationDetails/biblio?locale=en_EP&FT=E&CC=US&NR=5774670&KC=
19. Mao, Z., Li, N., Molloy, I.: Defeating cross-site request forgery attacks with browser-enforced authenticity protection. Technical report, Purdue University, February 2009. https://www.cs.purdue.edu/homes/ninghui/papers/csrf_fc09.pdf
20. Mayer, J.R., Mitchell, J.C.: Third-party web tracking: policy and technology. In: Proceedings of the 2012 IEEE Symposium on Security and Privacy, pp. 413–427. IEEE Computer Society (2012)
21. Mozilla Developer Network: Firefox tracking protection (2021). https://developer.mozilla.org/en-US/docs/Web/Privacy/Firefox_tracking_protection
22. Mozilla Developer Network: Set-cookie (2021). https://developer.mozilla.org/en-US/docs/Web/HTTP/Headers/Set-Cookie
23. Çınar, N., Ateş, S.: Data privacy in digital advertising: towards a post third-party cookie era. In: Filimowicz, M. (ed.) Privacy: Algorithms and Society. Routledge (2022). https://papers.ssrn.com/sol3/papers.cfm?abstract_id=4041963

24. Rosenberg, M., Confessore, N., Cadwalladr, C.: How Trump consultants exploited the Facebook data of millions, March 2018. https://www.nytimes.com/2018/03/17/us/politics/cambridge-analytica-trump-campaign.html
25. Satariano, A.: Google is fined \$57 million under Europe's Data Privacy Law. The New York Times, January 2019. https://www.nytimes.com/2019/01/21/technology/google-europe-gdpr-fine.html
26. Schneider, J.: Verizon's 'custom experience' will now track you unless you opt out, January 2022. https://petapixel.com/2022/01/05/verizons-custom-experience-will-now-track-you-unless-you-opt-out/
27. Schuh, J.: An update on testing the privacy sandbox to sustain a healthy web, August 2021. https://blog.google/products/chrome/update-testing-privacy-sandbox-web/
28. Singer, N., Conger, K.: Google is fined \$170 million for violating children's privacy on YouTube (2019). https://www.nytimes.com/2019/09/04/technology/google-youtube-fine-ftc.html
29. Soltani, A., Canty, S., Mayo, Q., Thomas, L., Hoofnagle, C.J.: Flash cookies and privacy, August 2009. https://papers.ssrn.com/sol3/papers.cfm?abstract_id=1446862
30. Statcounter Global Stats: Desktop browser market share worldwide (2023). https://gs.statcounter.com/browser-market-share/desktop/worldwide
31. Wang, X., Wang, H., Chen, S.: Cookie poisoning in web based applications. In: Proceedings of the 2005 IEEE International Conference on e-Technology, e-Commerce and e-Service, pp. 258–263. IEEE (2005)

Authenticating Parties in Blockchain-Enabled Inter-Organizational Processes with Configurable Challenge-Sets

Chibuzor Udokwu[1]([envelope]) [iD], Stefan Craß[1], and Alex Norta[2,3] [iD]

[1] ABC-Research, Favoriten 111, 1100 Vienna, Austria
{chibuzor.udokwu,stefan.crass}@abc-research.at
[2] Tallinn University, Tallinn, Estonia
alex.norta.phd@ieee.org
[3] Dymaxion OÜ, Tallinn, Estonia

Abstract. Blockchain has shown potential in enabling trustable and transparent executions of business collaborations between organizations. Blockchain provides a decentralized network for storing data associated with different collaboration use cases, and smart contracts ensure that specified business rules and conditions can be automatically executed without depending on a centralized entity. Still, it is important to correctly identify parties in different organizations and the roles they play in executing various functions in interorganizational collaboration use cases deployed on a blockchain. This is particularly crucial in public blockchains where privacy concerns and user-management issues have slowed the adoption of interorganizational use cases in such networks. Hence, enterprises opt for permissioned networks to deploy decentralized applications. Smart contracts are computer programs running on blockchains that execute specified business rules and conditions in an immutable and transparent manner. However, the state of any organization and parties within such organizations are dynamic. Thus, it is necessary to apply secure, configurable, and flexible mechanisms for authenticating individuals within organizations before executing functions in inter-organizational collaboration (IoC) processes on a blockchain. This research explores the use of concepts defined in the multifactor challenge set self-sovereign identity authentication (MFSSIA) in verifying and validating parties in IoC using nonfungible token (NFT)-based luxury-asset authentication as a running case. The main results of this paper show a set of configurable challenges represented by an organizational chart for authenticating members of an organization and the necessary steps required for integration into an existing DApp that executes IoC.

Keywords: Blockchain · multi-factor · identity · authentication · non-fungible token · decentralized application

1 Introduction

Several research works have shown the increasing importance of executing inter-organizational collaborations (IoCs) on blockchain due to the decentralised

T. K. Dang et al. (Eds.): FDSE 2023, CCIS 1925, pp. 153–170, 2023.
https://doi.org/10.1007/978-981-99-8296-7_11

nature, immutability, and transparency that blockchain provides [1,8] Blockchain is a distributed network that allows participants to add information to the network ledger with formalized consensus mechanisms cryptographically ensuring that the information stored in a ledger remains correct and consistent [25]. Various research works have also demonstrated several use cases of IoC on blockchains such as supply chains of various goods and services demonstrated in sectors such as agriculture, healthcare, construction etc. [1].

Blockchain networks are largely grouped into public networks and permissioned. As the name implies, the former does not restrict users who can access the network, while the latter is a private network where access is restricted to specific known parties [25]. Previous research [26] identifies public networks as the choice to experiment with blockchain use cases. However, for prototyped applications that enable IoC, a permissioned network is the preferred choice. This has also been validated by the continued rise in Hyperledger Fabric (HLF) network applications for DApps used in business collaboration contexts [11]. HLF is a permissioned blockchain network that provides architecture and blockchain infrastructure to execute and validate business logic contained in on-chain codes in private peer-to-peer networks called channels [3]. The low number of blockchain applications that allow IoC to be implemented on a public blockchain can be related to the privacy and user management issues common to applications prototyped on public networks. These problems have been well addressed on private blockchains with private data collections that ensure the privacy of information shared between collaborating parties and organizations' certificate authorities to manage users' access to specific functions by issuing and removing certificates [15].

Still, there is a need to apply flexible and configurable identity mechanisms to authenticate organizations and parties within an organization when IoC is executed on public blockchains. This is because organizations are usually dynamic; individuals within any particular organization change, as well as the role such individuals play. For instance, during the onboarding phase in some blockchain applications, functions and roles are associated (or hardcoded) with specific keys during deployment and instantiation of the contract, especially for public blockchains. When executing interorganizational collaborations on a blockchain, the keys represent users specific to particular organizations and the tasks they perform. Smart contracts that are computer programs running on a blockchain are immutable. Modifying the on-chain code to reflect the changes that occur within an organization is not possible [25].

Researchers have proposed several solutions for authenticating information assets and managing users' access to functions specified in public blockchain applications. Role-based access control (RBAC) systems have also been applied in managing and restricting user access to certain functions in blockchain applications [10,22]. In addition, concepts of self-sovereign identity such as decentralized identifiers (DID) that contain cryptographically signed verifiable credentials (VC) [19,23], and other forms of SSI authentication mechanisms [4] have been proposed. SSI provides models for managing digital identities so that individuals and parties within organizations have control over their personal identity data, and therefore they decide how their data are shared and used [4]. Token-based systems have also been proposed to verify users and their properties in blockchain applications [18,28]. The research work [21] presents an SSI system referred to as MFSSIA that is based on issuing configurable challenge sets by a party, organization or object that wishes to be authenticated. The MFSSIA is expressed as a configurable challenge-response system where external agents are used to check the validity of responses and thereby authenticate the user. These related research works in user authentication on public blockchains are further expanded in the literature review section.

The goal of this paper is to adapt and apply challenge-response concepts to authenticate parties within organizations and the roles they play in the execution of IoC functions within public blockchains. Hence, MFSSIA concepts are applied to an existing blockchain application that enables IoC to authenticate the parties within such collaboration and improve the security of information assets exchanged in the collaboration process. Thus, the main research question for this paper is How to design a configurable challenge-set mechanism for authenticating organizations and parties in executing IoC on blockchains? To establish a separation of concerns, the main research question is used to derive the following research questions: What is the current process depicting a decentralized application for executing IoC on blockchains? What are the useful sets of challenges for verifying parties within organizations? What are the necessary integration steps of challenges sets for verifying parties in organizations when executing IoC on blockchains?

The remainder of this paper is structured as follows. Section 2 provides the background for this work. Section 3 provides the answer to the first research question by describing a sample business process of an existing DApp that enables organizational collaboration on a blockchain. Section 4 provides the answer to the second research question by proposing a set of challenges that can be used to improve the authentication of parties in the outlined business collaboration. Section 5 answers the third research question by adapting the collaborative process by integrating configurable challenge sets and blockchain oracles to improve user authentication in blockchain-based collaborative processes. Section 6 shows the evaluation of this work by assessing existing blockchain technology stacks for the implementation of the proposed system and providing a comparative analysis of the authentication system described in this work and other related works. The conclusion of this research and future work are presented in Sect. 7.

2   Background

2.1   Blockchain Concepts

This section provides a literature definition of the main concepts in blockchain applications commonly encountered to execute IoC. These concepts include decentralized storage, consensus mechanisms, public-key cryptography (PKC) and digital signatures, smart contracts, and blockchain oracles.

Decentralized Storage: Data stored on blockchain networks are replicated across the nodes of parties (and organizations) that participate in collaborative processes executed on a blockchain. This ensures that there is no single point of failure, no single authority relying on to access data associated with a collaborative process, thus providing interoperability of data between participating organizations [26]. Due to limitations in blockchain storage spaces and associated costs, distributed data storage systems such as interplanetary file (IPFS) systems are also integrated into blockchains to address storage limitations [5]. Data stored in blockchains are organized in blocks and cryptographically linked to ensure immutability [25].

Consensus Mechanisms: This is an agreement mechanism for verifying, validating, and adding new information represented as transactions to a blockchain network. Consensus mechanisms are largely divided into proof-based and voting-based consensus systems. In the former, proof is required to be obtained by a participant, allowing such a party to aggregate and add a new block of transactions to the network. For example, in proof of work, the selected participant is required to have solved a difficult mathematical task. In the latter, a new block of transactions added to the network is determined based on a majority vote. Most voting-based consensus systems are adapted from Byzantine fault tolerant systems [25].

Public Key Cryptography (PKC) and Digital Signatures: Participants in collaborative processes executed on a blockchain are identified by their key pairs; public and private keys [26]. The public key is derived from the private key and can be used to identify users. Private keys allow users to cryptographically sign transactions they publish to a blockchain network, generating a unique digital signature for each published transaction. In private blockchains such as HLF, the keys are issued by certificate authorities while they are automatically and individually generated in public networks [3, 25].

Smart Contracts and Oracles: These are computer programs that run on a blockchain network such that specific business logic can be encoded in them. Hence, business conditions specific to a collaboration context can be executed automatically without being dependent on a central organizational entity. Since the blockchain is generally a closed system, smart contracts can access only data stored on a blockchain. Yet, with decentralized software agents with blockchain capabilities, referred to as oracles, external data can be introduced into a blockchain system as inputs for smart contracts in a transparent and trustable manner [2, 26].

Tokenization: Tokens provide a mechanism for rewarding users and also provide utility value while performing functions within applications deployed on blockchains [12]. These are commonly referred to as utility tokens. Thus, values can be exchanged between parties in IoC by transferring tokens among them. Another type of token commonly used in DApps is non-fungible tokens (NFT) that provide a unique representation for digital assets represented on a blockchain [12]. Other types of tokens include identity tokens such as soulbound tokens that are non-transferrable, providing a unique representation for users in blockchain applications [28]. Additionally, a special type of token called governance tokens has been proposed and applied to democratic governance blockchain applications [12].

2.2   Related Literature Review

Access control mechanisms provide means for restricting access to functions and data in different applications of the information system. Research [18] proposes a token-based and flexible mechanism to enforce access control on on-chain resources in blockchain applications. A smart contract uses a token service to grant or deny access to a client who wishes to access a smart contract function. The tokens are classified into various permission levels, thereby, determining the type of resources or functions that can be accessed by the client users.

The Role-Based Access Control (RBAC) system is another approach to managing access to smart contract functions executed on a blockchain. However, these roles are not further configurable and remain immutable once the smart contract application is instantiated. The research work in [10,22] shows that conventional smart contract applications can also incorporate predefined roles such that access to specific functions is limited to users with the assigned roles. Research [9] extends the RBAC system by addressing the need to apply democratic concepts in managing and modifying user roles in decentralized applications. In the IoC context, the method developed and implemented in [9] ensures that parties who approve certain business process workflows have the required role based on the policy defined in the organization. This is achieved by ensuring that tasks involving administrative decisions have a specified number of approvals by users within the admin role for the task to be executed.

SSI-based authentication schemes provide approaches for managing identities and users when performing functions in blockchain applications. DIDs are frequently used SSI verification mechanisms [7,23]. DIDs are universal resource identifiers that connect a party or an entity to a document, thereby enabling trustable interaction such that a party can digitally prove ownership of a particular document [23]. VCs provide a standardized data format for cryptographically verifiable digital credentials, such that the credentials are issued by a DID to a party proving ownership of a document or asset [19]. The DID system defines three main roles: issuer, receiver, and verifier. The issue creates a cryptographically signed VC for a particular DID that is handed over to a receiver. The verifier checks the digital signature contained in the VC linked to a DID document to verify that the credentials are generated by a particular issuer. The verifier also checks that the signature is still valid and has not been revoked. Some privacy issues could arise by applying the DID/VC systems for implementing user access control in smart contracts. Yet, this can be addressed using oracles to perform the verifications [29].

Another example of an SSI-based user authentication scheme is the soulbound token (SBT). Unlike DID-based verifiable credentials, an SBT is a non-transferable unique token used to digitally represent a person or an entity such as a business organization [28]. The features of the SBT can be used to capture entity properties, such as historical activities or records linked to a person or entity. Several SBTs can be linked to a single user, such that they provide transparent provenance of the behaviors and reputations associated with the entity. Although SBT can be used to represent organizations such as decentralized autonomous organizations, the current specification does not show how different roles can be assigned to individuals representing the same organization. Theoretically, a multi-party wallet can be used to capture the ownership of SBT. Still, the problem of role configurability remains since organizations are generally dynamic entities.

The self-configurable challenge-response system has also been used to demonstrate SSI in blockchain applications [17, 20]. The authcoin system described in [17] proposes a challenge-response system that allows two parties to authenticate each other by posing challenges where both parties know the correct responses to the challenges. The result of the response check is stored on a blockchain so that both parties have access to the status of the authentication. The paper [20] shows the implementation of MFSSIA that extends the authcoin protocol. The extension is achieved by providing a challenge-response system that allows parties executing interorganizational processes to check and verify the business conditions before a particular business process task is executed. Challenges and correct responses are initially known by both parties so that the correct responses are hashed and stored on chain. However, if the business conditions change, the parties will have to deploy new challenges and responses. Otherwise, the authentication will not be successful. This ensures that parties executing autonomous inter-organizational processes on blockchain have a common understanding and overview of the business conditions before they are executed.

However, in permissioned blockchains, such as HLF, the user authentication system is based on PKC. Here, the organizational-level certificate authority that issues and revokes user certificates are specified. The certificates can contain information such as the organizational name, units/departments, and user roles. Therefore, at the chain code (smart contract) level, the client identity function can be used to check and limit which users have access to a particular function based on the role and departments listed in the user certificate [3, 16].

2.3   Running Case

The previous work [27] shows the design of a blockchain application to authenticate luxury assets using NFTs. NFTs are used to provide a digital representation of a luxury asset, thereby providing immutable historical transparency as the luxury item moves across the production to the customer end of the supply chain. The main stakeholders comprise the organization brand that produced the luxury item, approved retailers that sell the luxury items, and customers that purchase and resell the items among each other. Luxury products are digitally mapped to NFTs using the unique identity of the physical item, such as serial number and product IDs, to map them to an NFT. The authenticity of a luxury item is proven by the digital signature associated with the Genesis transaction on the NFT published on-chain. Still, further improving the security of the NFT minting process is necessary by introducing configurable challenge sets concepts described in MFSSIA [20].

3 Luxury Asset Authentication in a Collaborative Context

This section presents the AS-IS process of a blockchain application that enables the authentication of luxury products with NFTs. Section 3.1 introduces the IoC AS-IS process that employs NFT-based identity authentication. Next, Sect. 3.2 discusses the security issues related to the NFT minting process.

3.1 AS-IS Process of NFT-Based Authentication

Figure 1 shows the process of authentication and verification of luxury items using NFTs in the LogisticsBDT[1] DApp. The process comprises four (4) process groups and four (4) process lanes. The first subprocess is brand registration, which verifies luxury brands responsible for creating the NFTs linked to an actual physical product produced by the brand. The second subprocess is the NFT minting process. Hence, luxury items are authenticated by the verified brand digital signature associated with the genesis transaction on the NFT, that is, the minting transaction. The rest of the subprocesses show the NFT transfer between the brand and the retailer, and between the retailer and the customer. An additional subprocess can be added to show the transfer of the NFT between customers for use cases involving the trading of pre-owned luxury items, which is out of focus for the current paper.

The first lane of the process shows a set of conditions for registering luxury brands, minting NFTs, and transferring NFTs. These conditions are contained within the DApp algorithms. The second subprocess shows the activities that are specific to the luxury brand, the third shows the activities that are specific to the retailer, and the last lane shows the activities that are specific to the customers.

To register a brand, the application checks the email and host address supplied by the brand to check if it matches. The application also uses a random string token to check whether the authenticated party belongs to the specified host organization. To mint an NFT, the application checks if the minter has a valid key from a verified luxury brand. To transfer an NFT, the application checks if the key of the executor of the function matches the key of the last owner. An NFT is uniquely connected to a physical luxury item by mapping the distinctive ID such as serial number or product id number to the metadata of the NFT's digital identity.

---

[1] LogisticsBDT Luxury Assets Authentication Platform: https://www.logistics-bdt.com/.

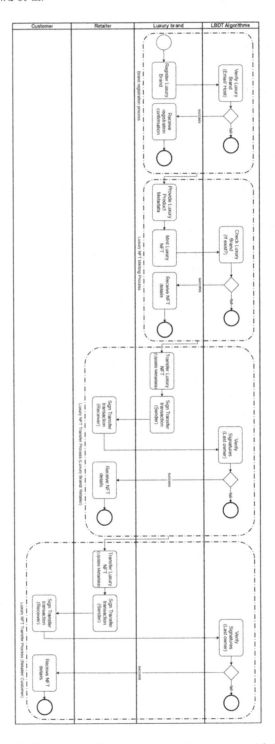

Fig. 1. AS-IS process of luxury asset authentication with NFTs.

3.2   Security Issues of the NFT Minting Process

By qualitatively analyzing the authentication processes for verifying luxury assets in the presented DApp, we identify weaknesses in the application's brand registration and the NFT minting process. The issues identified can also apply to other similar DApps that enable organizations to collaborate in verifying physical/ digital assets.

- *Security Weaknesses in Brand Verification:* The current process relies on simple verification of the email / host in addition to a random token challenge. This implies that any individual within the brand organization can register and represent the organization in the DApp.

- *Scalability Issues*: Since each organization is represented by a single key pair, this implies that the entire organization has to rely on a single individual to digitize its physical assets as NFT. For smaller organizations, the process can run to completion. Still, for larger organizations for which specific departments and individuals focus on a single process, multiple key pairs must be assigned to the luxury NFT minting process.

- *Access Control Problems*: In the current process of brand registration and NFT minting, user roles cannot be defined within organizations to perform specific tasks in the NFT minting process. For example, a role assigned as *administrator* can be required to complete the brand registration on behalf of the organizations, while other roles can be defined to perform the minting tasks. Besides, organizations are generally dynamic, and the current set-up of the problematic processes does not address the changes that occur in the organizations such as individuals leaving the organization or changing roles.

4   Challenge-Sets for Securing Parties Within Organizations

This paper proposes administrative-administered challenges for securing parties and functions executed in blockchain-based organizational collaborations using information about the organization. Since the state of any organization is dynamic, information about such an organization is also dynamic, such that only individuals within the organization have access to complete information. Thus, by posing questions about the organization as challenges and providing correct responses, functions can be executed in a collaborative business process without hardcoding any key pair to a specific organization.

- *Organizational Challenge-Sets*: Figure 2 shows the chart of an organization, containing general information about the organization, departments, and products they offer, and specific information about individuals in the organization such as a passphrase. This set of information is posed as challenges while the answers to these questions are hashed and stored in a decentralized database. Any party that wishes to execute a function in a blockchain-based IoC will face

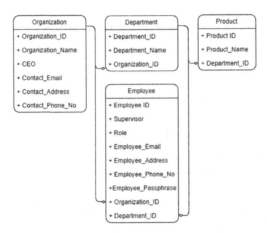

Fig. 2. Challenge-sets for verifying members of an organization.

random challenges. An external oracle collects the responses from the parties executing the functions and compares the response hashes with the hashes stored on-chain. The oracle checks are executed in a confidential manner, ensuring that there is no user information leakage to the oracle operators. Therefore, individuals are authenticated if the responses they provide match the hashes stored in a decentralized database. The challenges are randomly generated, and the number of challenges posed depends on the level of importance of the IoC function executed.

- *Administering Challenges*: The challenges are deployed by a role *administrator* and the administrator updates the challenges when there is any change in the state of the organization represented. The administrator also ensures regular updates to the challenge answers when there is a change in the organization's state, thereby preventing individuals who have left the organization from executing IoC functions on its behalf. Furthermore, the admin can selectively deploy only hashes of challenge answers specific to certain departments or certain products to ensure role-based access control on the IoC functions. The passphrase can be included as a mandatory part of randomly generated challenges to prevent information leakage between members of organizations from different departments. The passphrase is unique to each member of the organization and can be graphically linked to specific departments and roles. Furthermore, scalability is ensured by linking challenges to departments and products, such that individuals working in certain departments/ products can be assigned to execute IoC functions for the organization on a blockchain. Hence, key pairs are directly linked to any functions, but rather to individuals that are capable of providing the correct responses to the challenges.

-*Registering an Admin that Deploys Challenges*: Given the crucial responsibility of the organization administrator in managing and maintaining the challenges and their corresponding answers, it is essential to present a challenge during the brand registration process that can only be successfully answered by genuine administrators of the organization. Therefore, only registered administrators can deploy and update challenges for any given organization. We propose that organizational admins are requested to provide their host domain and email address, and a random token is generated, then encrypted with the RSA key linked to the organizational host domain. Since only the administrators of an organization have access to the private keys of their organization's host address, correctly returning the original token confirms the party as a legitimate administrator.

5 Challenge-Set Integration into the NFT-Based Luxury Asset Authentication System

We present the integration of the challenge-set concepts described in the previous section into the process of authentication of luxury assets with NFT. The AS-IS process contains four subprocesses, of which only two require a challenge-set integration for the improvement of the entire process. Thus, the TO-BE processes presented in this section contain the adapted brand registration and luxury NFT minting processes. The changes due to the integration of a configurable challenge set into the luxury-asset NFT authentication are marked with the green process tasks.

5.1 Brand Admin Registration and Challenge-Set Deployment

Figure 3a shows the TO-BE process for brand admin registration and the deployment of configurable challenge sets for NFT minting tasks. The process started with a brand administrator providing the email and host address of the organization. The DApp algorithm checks if the host/email address matches and then proceeds to generate a random token string. The DApp algorithm further crawls the public Internet to locate the RSA public key of the host address provided. The generated random token is encrypted with the public key of the host address and sent to the email address provided by the admin. The administrator decrypts the token to return the original token. The DApp algorithm checks if the token provided by the administrator matches the initially generated random token. The brand (admin) is registered if the token response matches the encrypted token challenge.

On successful registration, the admin deploys the challenge sets to authenticate the members of the registered organization before they can proceed to mint luxury NFT. To deploy the challenges, the admin selects the relevant challenges from the challenge-set library such that the correct answers to the challenges are hashed information representing the state of the organization at the given time. The DApp algorithm checks if the key of the user deploying the challenge sets is registered as the brand administrator. If the check is positive, the challenges and the hashed responses are stored in a decentralized database that can be accessed using decentralized oracles.

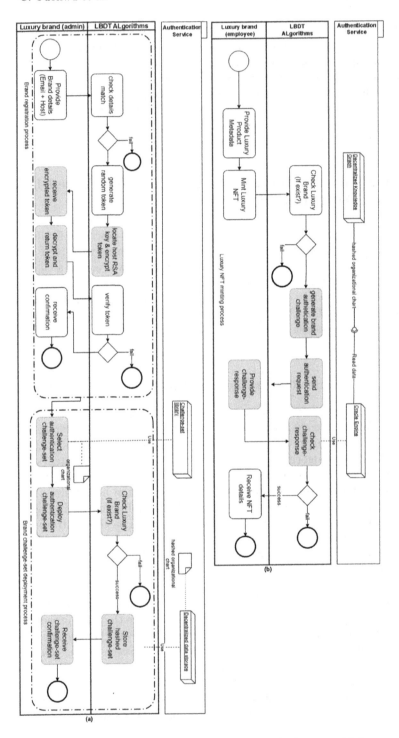

Fig. 3. TO-BE a) Admin registration and challenge-set deployment, b) Luxury NFT minting that includes configurable challenge sets.

5.2 Secured Luxury NFT Minting Process

Figure 3b shows the TO-BE process to produce luxury NFTs. The process starts with a representative of a luxury brand, such as an employee, providing the details about a luxury asset. The information is represented as the NFT metadata showing the brand name, asset name, and other attributes specific to the asset. A unique ID is used to represent the asset digitally and the NFT representation is temporarily created for the asset. The DApp algorithm checks if the brand information contained in the metadata is already a registered organization with challenge sets deployed. If the check is successful, the algorithm generates random questions based on the challenges already implemented for the employee representing the brand organization. A decentralized oracle verifies whether the response provided by the NFT minter matches the hashed data stored in the decentralized database, which represents the current state of the organization. If the response is validated successfully, the minting process for the luxury NFT is complete. Otherwise, the minting process fails.

6 Evaluation and Discussion

We evaluate and discuss the results obtained from this work. First, Sect. 6.1 shows an assessment of the existing blockchain-based technology stacks that can be used to realize the TO-BE processes depicted in Figs. 3a and 3b Then Sect. 6.2 provides a comparative assessment of the user authentication system presented in this work with similar works.

6.1 Technology Stacks for Realizing the Authentication Design

We refer to the extended MFSSIA for authenticating organizations and their parties developed in this paper as the organizational configurable challenge set system (org-ccs). The authentication design developed in this paper requires additional technology stacks, such as decentralized storages and oracles, for implementation. Some of the existing tools for implementing decentralized oracles include ChainLink [6] and iExec oracle factory [13]. The iExec Oracle system is selected as the preferred choice since it provides a trusted execution environment (TEE). The TEE defines an area of the processor such that tasks are executed securely without information leakage to other parts of the computing unit [24]. Therefore, tasks processed by iExec oracles are executed confidentially. Thereby, ensuring zero-knowledge proof such that operators of decentralized oracles have no access to authentication information provided by the users of the proposed system described in this paper.

Some of the decentralized storage systems used for blockchain applications include the Interplanetary File System (IPFS) [5] and Origin trail network [14]. The origin trail storage system is selected to store challenge sets for the proposed system described in this paper because it uses a decentralized knowledge graph mechanism to establish relationships between the various properties described for the information assets stored in the network. This ensures that graph-based relationships can be established for every hashed organizational chart containing various subcomponents of the organizational states.

6.2 Comparative Assessment of the Authentication Design

To assess the authentication approach outlined in this paper, we apply a set of properties when comparing the former with other existing solutions. HLF as a permissioned blockchain provides a well-defined user management system for implementing authentication and access control at the organizational level [3]. Thus, the HLF user management system provides the basis for assessing the Org-CSS system developed in this paper. We also include the SBT system as an additional solution for comparison, since the former provides techniques for defining and verifying user identity properties in decentralized applications [28]. The collaborative administration of RBAC (CA-RBAC) presented in [9] is included in the related works examined. Three main criteria are used for the evaluation such as the existence of certificate authority, role configurability, and flexibility of the authentication approaches. The certificate authority criteria help in assessing whether the system is capable of issuing and revoking certificates to parties/organizations within the decentralized application. The role configurable checks whether the system can be configured to set up admin roles and other roles within a given organization that participates in blockchain-based collaborative processes. Lastly, the flexibility property checks the automation of onboarding organizations in the set-up process and the ease of updating the authentication system to reflect the changes that occur within the organization.

Table 1. Assessment of authentication approaches.

Authentication comparison	Property	HLF	SBT	Org-CCS	CA-RBAC
Certificates Authority	Issuing certificates	++	+	+	+
	Revoking certificates	++	+	+	+
Role Config-urability	Admin roles	++	-	++	++
	Other user roles	++	-	+	+
Flexibility	Automated setup	++	++	++	+
	Ease of update	+	+	++	-

++ highly applicable, + somewhat applicable, - not applicable

Table 1 shows the result of the comparative assessment of the authentication approach designed. HLF has a well-defined approach for issuing and revoking certificates using certificate authorities. It also provides automated onboarding of organizations using root certificates generated by the member organizations. Although the authentication approach described in this paper expressly does not provide certificate authority, the concepts of issuing and revoking certificates can also be represented by an administrator deploying or updating the hashed organizational chart that contains information about specific members of the organization. In that case, only the specified members of the organization can provide correct and valid responses to the challenge questions (such as the user passphrase) used in the authentication. In the CA-RBAC system, although there is the absence of certificate authority, issuing and revocation of certificates can be achieved by simply configuring user roles in the smart contract.

Regarding the ease of updating to reflect the changes within the organizations, in the configurable challenge approach, both the admin and the roles can be updated by providing the correct challenge responses for the admin registration. Still, in HLF, the member of an organization that controls the root certificate indefinitely controls the user authentication system within the particular organization. In SBT, a community-based approach is used to update and remove specific elements that are used to define the properties of an authenticated individual. Regarding role configurability, in HLF, admin and other user roles can easily be specified in the policy document. Yet, in the organizational challenge-set approach, only the administrator can be automatically configured directly, while the rest of the roles can be indirectly specified as organizational members that have their challenge-response information deployed in the authentication system. The SBT offers a well-defined setup mechanism and ease of update. Still, the current design of the SBT lacks the ability to define specific roles within an organization. In CA-RBAC, the admin roles are well defined, so an automated voting system can be used to administer the other roles. Still, other user roles in the CA-RBAC cannot be updated once the roles have been assigned. For initial admin roles, the CA-RBAC follows a semi-automated approach.

7   Conclusions and Future Work

This paper seeks to adapt and apply a challenge-response mechanism, such as the MFSSIA, to authenticate parties within different organizations when executing collaborative processes on a blockchain. The necessity for such a study is due to the dynamics of representing the state of organizations that undergo many changes over time. Hence, there is a need to apply configurable and flexible authentication mechanisms to verify parties that execute IoC functions on behalf of organizations. To address this problem, we apply MFSSIA concepts to identify suitable authentication challenges to verifying parties and integrate such a challenge-response system into an existing blockchain application that allows IoC. The result of the paper, first, outlines the AS-IS process that represents blockchain-based IoC using a running case of an NFT-based luxury-asset authentication system in the format of the LogisticsBDT DApp.

The second part of the result of this work shows a set of challenges for authenticating parties. Challenges are expressed as information on the current state of an organization. The correct responses are hashed and stored on-chain so that only the current members of the organization are capable of providing the right response to the specific challenges. Furthermore, an additional challenge with a higher level of difficulty is used to register the organizational administrators that deploy and update the challenges to reflect the changes that occur in the organization. The last part of the result shows the necessary steps in integrating the designed challenge-response system into an existing DApp that is already specified in the AS-IS process.

In the latter part of the article, an evaluation is conducted to assess and recommend suitable blockchain technology stacks for implementing the designed authentication system. The Origin Trail DKG system is proposed as a suitable choice for implementing the on-chain storage of challenge sets, while the iExec system is recommended as a suitable oracle system for the confidential execution of the challenge-response checking mechanism. Furthermore, a comparative assessment of the designed approach with the alternative approaches is conducted to determine the presence of certification authority, configurability, and flexibility of the authentication systems. The designed authentication system is highly flexible due to the ability to automatically set up an admin and easily deploy challenge sets during the organizational onboarding process. The roles in the designed system are also highly configurable due to the presence of admins and the configurability of challenges to represent specific members or parts of an organization.

The future work for this research is a prototype implementation and evaluation of the designed artefact. Hence, the experimental parts of this work will be properly analyzed and presented in more detail to confirm the novelty of this research.

Acknowledgment. This research is partially funded by the Estonian "Personal research funding: Team grant (PRG)" project PRG1641 and within the framework of the COMET center ABC, Austrian Blockchain Center by BMK, BMAW and the provinces of Vienna, Lower Austria and Vorarlberg. The COMET program (Competence Centers for Excellent Technologies) is managed by the FFG.

References

1. Akram, S.V., Malik, P.K., Singh, R., Anita, G., Tanwar, S.: Adoption of blockchain technology in various realms: opportunities and challenges. Secur. Priv. **3**(5), e109 (2020)
2. Al-Breiki, H., Rehman, M.H.U., Salah, K., Svetinovic, D.: Trustworthy blockchain oracles: review, comparison, and open research challenges. IEEE Access **8**, 85675–85685 (2020)
3. Androulaki, E., et al.: Hyperledger fabric: a distributed operating system for permissioned blockchains. In: Proceedings of the Thirteenth EuroSys Conference, pp. 1–15 (2018)

4. Baars, D.S.: Towards self-sovereign identity using blockchain technology. Master's thesis, University of Twente (2016)
5. Benet, J.: IPFS-content addressed, versioned, P2P file system. arXiv preprint arXiv:1407.3561 (2014)
6. Breidenbach, L., et al.: Chainlink 2.0: next steps in the evolution of decentralized oracle networks. Chainlink Labs **1**, 1–136 (2021)
7. Brunner, C., Gallersdörfer, U., Knirsch, F., Engel, D., Matthes, F.: DID and VC: untangling decentralized identifiers and verifiable credentials for the web of trust. In: 2020 the 3rd International Conference on Blockchain Technology and Applications, pp. 61–66 (2020)
8. Centobelli, P., Cerchione, R., Del Vecchio, P., Oropallo, E., Secundo, G.: Blockchain technology for bridging trust, traceability and transparency in circular supply chain. Inf. Manage. **59**(7), 103508 (2022)
9. Craß, S., Lackner, A., Begic, N., Mirhosseini, S.A.M., Kirchmayr, N.: Collaborative administration of role-based access control in smart contracts. In: 2022 4th Conference on Blockchain Research & Applications for Innovative Networks and Services (BRAINS), pp. 87–94. IEEE (2022)
10. Cruz, J.P., Kaji, Y., Yanai, N.: RBAC-SC: role-based access control using smart contract. IEEE Access **6**, 12240–12251 (2018)
11. Dasaklis, T.K., Voutsinas, T.G., Tsoulfas, G.T., Casino, F.: A systematic literature review of blockchain-enabled supply chain traceability implementations. Sustainability **14**(4), 2439 (2022)
12. Di Angelo, M., Salzer, G.: Tokens, types, and standards: identification and utilization in Ethereum. In: 2020 IEEE International Conference on Decentralized Applications and Infrastructures (DAPPS), pp. 1–10. IEEE (2020)
13. Fedak, G., Bendella, W., Alves, E.: iExec: blockchain-based decentralized cloud computing (2018)
14. Ferdous, M.S., Biswas, K., Chowdhury, M.J.M., Chowdhury, N., Muthukkumarasamy, V.: Integrated platforms for blockchain enablement. In: Advances in Computers, vol. 115, pp. 41–72. Elsevier (2019)
15. George, J.T.: Hyperledger fabric. In: Introducing Blockchain Applications: Understand and Develop Blockchain Applications Through Distributed Systems, pp. 125–147. Springer, Cham (2021)
16. Hyperledger. Identity (2021). https://hyperledger-fabric.readthedocs.io/en/release-2.5/identity/identity.html. Accessed 12 July 2023
17. Leiding, B., Cap, C.H., Mundt, T., Rashidibajgan, S.: Authcoin: validation and authentication in decentralized networks. arXiv preprint arXiv:1609.04955 (2016)
18. Liu, B., Sun, S., Szalachowski, P.: SMACS: smart contract access control service. In: 2020 50th Annual IEEE/IFIP International Conference on Dependable Systems and Networks (DSN), pp. 221–232. IEEE (2020)
19. Mukta, R., Martens, J., Paik, H.Y., Lu, Q., Kanhere, S.S.: Blockchain-based verifiable credential sharing with selective disclosure. In: 2020 IEEE 19th International Conference on Trust, Security and Privacy in Computing and Communications (TrustCom), pp. 959–966. IEEE (2020)
20. Norta, A., Kormiltsyn, A., Udokwu, C., Dwivedi, V., Aroh, S., Nikolajev, I.: A blockchain implementation for configurable multi-factor challenge-set self-sovereign identity authentication. In: 2022 IEEE International Conference on Blockchain (Blockchain), pp. 455–461. IEEE (2022)
21. Norta, A., Matulevičius, R., Leiding, B.: Safeguarding a formalized blockchain-enabled identity-authentication protocol by applying security risk-oriented patterns. Comput. Secur. **86**, 253–269 (2019)

22. OpenZeppelin. Access control. https://docs.openzeppelin.com/contracts/4.x/access-control. Accessed 12 July 2023

23. Reed, D., et al.: Decentralized identifiers (DIDs) v1. 0: core architecture, data model, and representations. W3C Working Draft, 8 (2020)

24. Shepherd, C., et al.: Secure and trusted execution: past, present, and future-a critical review in the context of the internet of things and cyber-physical systems. In: 2016 IEEE Trustcom/BigDataSE/ISPA, pp. 168–177 (2016)

25. Sheth, H., Dattani, J.: Overview of blockchain technology. Asian J. Converg. Technol. (AJCT) (2019). ISSN-2350-1146

26. Udokwu, C., Kormiltsyn, A., Thangalimodzi, K., Norta, A.: The state of the art for blockchain-enabled smart-contract applications in the organization. In: 2018 Ivannikov Ispras Open Conference (ISPRAS), pp. 137–144. IEEE (2018)

27. Udokwu, C., Zimmermann, R., Norta, A., Brandtner, P., Kormiltsyn, A., Aroh, S.M.: Exerting qualitative analytics and blockchain requirement-engineering in designing and implementing a luxury products authentication system. Inventions 8(1), 49 (2023)

28. Weyl, E.G., Ohlhaver, P., Buterin, V.: Decentralized Society: Finding Web3's Soul. SSRN 4105763 (2022)

29. Xiong, Y., Yao, S., Li, P.: D2CDIM: did-based decentralized cross-domain identity management with privacy-preservation and Sybil-resistance. In: Chen, J., He, D., Lu, R. (eds.) EISA 2022. Communications in Computer and Information Science, vol. 1641, pp. 191–208. Springer, Cham (2022). https://doi.org/10.1007/978-3-031-23098-1_12

Differential Privacy for Consumer Data in Retail Data Partnerships

Tran Khanh Dang[1]([✉]) [ID] and Lai Trung Minh Duc[2] [ID]

[1] Ho Chi Minh City University of Industry and Trade, Ho Chi Minh City, Vietnam
khanh@hufi.edu.vn
[2] Ho Chi Minh City University of Technology, VNU-HCM, Ho Chi Minh City, Vietnam
duc.lai.imp20@hcmut.edu.vn

Abstract. In the context of Industry 4.0 within the retail sector, the pursuit of improved customer experiences through data partnerships has become crucial. Unfortunately, existing frameworks and privacy models do not adequately address consumer privacy protection at the granular level of receipt data. This research paper aims to investigate and propose a privacy-preserving model designed explicitly for retail data partnerships, focusing on receipt data at the multi-granular level. Leveraging the principles of Differential Privacy, we explore techniques to ensure the confidentiality and privacy of sensitive consumer information. Additionally, we delve into selecting an appropriate global sensitivity value, seeking a balance between accuracy and privacy preservation. By addressing the existing gaps in privacy protection within retail data partnerships, this study contributes to establishing robust privacy frameworks and enabling secure collaboration in the retail industry.

Keywords: Privacy-preserving data partnership · Differential privacy · Retails industry · Data management · Machine Learning privacy · Deep Learning privacy

1 Introduction and Motivation

The advent of Big Data and AI Analytics in the context of Industry 4.0 has ushered in a prominent trend, necessitating the implementation of multiple behavioral analyses to enhance customer experiences. This imperative is particularly salient within the retail and Fast-Moving Consumer Goods (FMCG) sectors. However, the disparity in data availability among companies poses a challenge in unlocking the potential of analytics. In response, the concept of data partnership emerges, wherein multiple entities collaborate and pool their data resources. Nevertheless, the absence of comprehensive legal and compliance guidelines has impeded the progression of data partnerships, particularly concerning the sensitive domain of individual privacy data, encompassing details such as customer demographics and purchase receipts. The apprehension of infringing upon privacy regulations, with its attendant financial and reputational ramifications, underscores the caution exhibited by corporations.

© The Author(s), under exclusive license to Springer Nature Singapore Pte Ltd. 2023
T. K. Dang et al. (Eds.): FDSE 2023, CCIS 1925, pp. 171–183, 2023.
https://doi.org/10.1007/978-981-99-8296-7_12

To align analyses with contemporary business operations, data is consistently captured in a temporal format, encompassing data streams such as receipt records (including timestamps and item breakdowns) and check-in/check-out logs. While these data are invaluable for analysis, the intricate management of data privacy during sharing presents significant challenges.

Given the urgent requirement for expedited data partnerships to facilitate swift analytics implementation while concurrently safeguarding corporate reputation by upholding customer privacy, this paper seeks to make the following contributions: firstly, the exploration and application of methodologies centered around differential privacy, tailored to time-series data to balance between privacy and performance; and secondly, the proposal of an approach to estimate the global sensitivity of datasets. Through these contributions, this research aims to provide a roadmap for initiating data partnerships that enable efficient analytics deployment while ensuring robust privacy protection measures, thus striking a balance between innovation and ethical considerations.

2 Related Work

Several prominent methodologies have emerged throughout the historical progression of privacy-preserving data publishing (PPDP), including generalization, suppression, perturbation, and encryption. These techniques have been instantiated as concepts such as k-anonymity, l-diversity, t-closeness, and delta-presence [2]. These methods have been instrumental in enhancing privacy levels in published datasets. However, their effectiveness becomes limited when dealing with intricate data structures, particularly in time-series data, where dynamic attributes and correlations are pivotal in privacy preservation [4].

In recent years, other approaches have used Machine Learning or Deep Learning models, especially the usage of Generative Adversarial Networks (GAN) to fit the time-series attributes into and regenerate synthesis time-series from that model [15]. This approach utilizes the ability to capture, memorize, and generalize the whole data series. However, Khanh and Trung [13, 14] have mentioned the potential risks of reidentification of GAN.

Fortunately, a pivotal advancement in the realm of privacy protection emerged in 2006 with the inception of Differential Privacy, spearheaded by Professor Cynthia Dwork [6]. This innovation has paved the way for developing numerous novel privacy protection methodologies tailored to specific use cases. Differential Privacy operates on the foundational principle that alterations to individual data records, whether through addition or removal, should not yield discernible changes in the aggregated outcomes of statistical databases. Crucially, Differential Privacy is grounded in mathematical principles. This mathematical foundation implies that any novel approach demonstrating adherence to Differential Privacy principles can be confidently employed in real-world production data scenarios.

The Differential Privacy paradigm's significance lies in its ability to harmonize statistical accuracy and privacy preservation, overcoming the limitations of traditional PPDP techniques. By ensuring that privacy breaches are statistically improbable, Differential Privacy presents a potent solution to the challenges of intricate data structures, thereby bolstering privacy protection in modern data publishing practices.

The Differential Privacy formula:

$$Pr[M(D_1) \in S] \leq e^{\varepsilon} * Pr[M(D_2) \in S] \tag{1}$$

where M is the mechanism, D1 and D2 are the neighbor database, ε is the privacy loss.

Following the inception of Differential Privacy, several pioneering methods emerged that effectively uphold its principles when applied to time-series data. Notably, these novel techniques have garnered substantial attention for their adeptness in reconciling privacy preservation and statistical accuracy. Among these methods, the Laplace Perturbation Algorithm (LPA) and Fourier Perturbation Algorithm (FPA) were introduced by Rastogi [3] in 2007. These methodologies have demonstrated their capacity to satisfy Differential Privacy requirements while operating within the dynamic landscape of time-series data.

In 2012, L. Fan and L. Xiong [5] proposed the FAST framework, offering a distinctive approach for the real-time release of aggregated statistical values. This innovation further expanded the repertoire of methods capable of preserving privacy while accommodating the necessities of time-series data.

In 2021, Q. Ye et al. [1] introduced the Temporal Local Differential Privacy (TLDP) concept to enhance privacy within the temporal dimension. By centering on the perturbation of the temporal aspect, TLDP represents an innovative stride towards safeguarding sensitive time-series data.

A noteworthy advancement in this domain materialized in 2022 with Kim et al.'s [8] development of the STL-DP framework. This approach capitalizes on the Fourier Perturbation Algorithm (FPA) and applies it to the decomposition features of time-series data. This methodological amalgamation showcases the evolution of Differential Privacy's application within the temporal context.

Collectively, these novel methodologies underscore the malleability of Differential Privacy, as they cater to the intricate demands of time-series data while ensuring robust privacy preservation. This progression exemplifies the ongoing commitment to advancing privacy-preserving techniques in the ever-evolving data analytics landscape.

3 Differential Privacy in Retail Data Partnership

3.1 Problem Setup

This paper delves into a specific facet of data privacy protection, concentrating on the preliminary stages that transpire before the actual sharing of data occurs. The focus is directed toward data providers, primarily encompassing retailer corporations and data consumers, comprising Fast-Moving Consumer Goods (FMCG) companies and suppliers. This preliminary phase is situated within the broader framework of Data Management, occurring before obtaining legal approvals and eventual data [9] (Fig. 1).

Notably, this paper strictly adheres to the technical realm and refrains from venturing into the realm of business perspectives or scenario planning. The delineation of business implications is deemed beyond the purview of this study's technical objectives. By narrowing its scope to the technical intricacies of data privacy protection within the pre-sharing phase, this paper aims to contribute to a comprehensive understanding of the mechanisms and considerations that underpin the safeguarding of sensitive data in the complex landscape of data exchange.

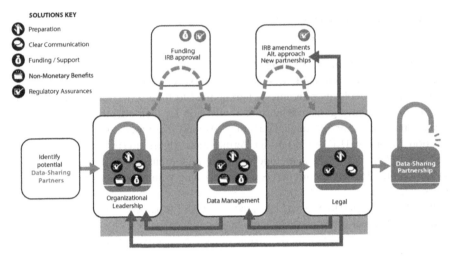

Fig. 1. Data Partnership Process – extracted from [9]

3.2 Scope of the Proposal

Dataset

Usually, the receipt data from the retail corporates to their partners should be in this format at basic level (Table 1):

Due to the clearly concern of multiple FMCG competitors can learn very detail on how the consumer choosing products, the data provider intends to provide the aggregation data level into "PurchaseDate" and "ProductCategory" level, which means: for each user at each day:

- if they buy multiple products inside one category, then only one aggregated record gets exported.
- if they buy in one store, multiple times per day, then only one aggregated record gets exported.

Data provider also concern about the "Gender", "YearOfBirth", and "LoyaltyRank" that can disclose user information, so they also want to remove it. Therefore, the suggested data structure will be (simplified from receipt data) (Table 2):

From this data structure, we build a synthesis dataset leverage from our experimental data generation model using GAN and the Faker library combined with insights from supermarket product categories in the retail market.

Use-Case Evaluation

Based on the provided data schema and analytics requirements, two common use-cases can be chosen to evaluate the impact of privacy protection algorithm on the published dataset:

- Use-case 1: Consumer segmentation (using RFM – Recency Frequency Monetary method) to find good/bad/churn customer groups.

Table 1. Data Partnership requirement for publishing Retail receipts

Field name	Data type	Remarks
PseudoUserID	String (GUID)	PseudoID for marking user and their purchase behavior. It's completely not a national ID/ royalty ID, or any ID that can identify user directly
YearOfBirth	Integer	
Gender	String	Male/Female/Others
RoyaltyRank	String	Bronze/Silver/Gold/Platinum/Diamond
LocationID	Integer	
OrderDateTime	DateTime	
PseudoBillingID	String (GUID)	
PaymentMethod	String	
ProductCategory	String	
ProductName	String	
ProductListPrice	Float	
ProductDiscountPrice	Float	
ProductUOM	String	
ProductQuantity	Float	

Table 2. Data Partnership requirement for publishing Retail receipts (simplified)

Column name	Data type	Note
PurchaseDate	String	Format: YYYYMMDD
LocationID	String	In real shared dataset, this field will transparently share
PseudoUserID	String	Pseudo User ID – anonymize from real user-id inside the system
ProductCategory	String	Serving the mentioned purpose
Quantity	Integer	Aggregate volume in each category
TotalAmount	Integer	Aggregate volume in each category of pair Quantity * Price

- Use-case 2: Forecast by each consumer group and each product category.

Evaluation Metrics

The data utility after applying Differential privacy can be seen as the usefulness of the analytics. Therefore, the methodology to consider can be:

- Number of correct consumers in the segmentation before and after the perturbation.
- The accuracy of the forecast model on original data and on perturbed data (method forecast: Simple Linear Regression)

We will use the RMSE (Root Mean Squared Error) to calculate accuracy, one of the standard error metrics that is familiar in the data science community.

$$RMSE = \sqrt{\sum_{i=1}^{n} \frac{\left(y_{pred} - y_{actual}\right)^2}{n}} \qquad (2)$$

The privacy level of the perturbed dataset can be audited with a couple of approaches:

- Privacy loss: By evaluating the typical ε range and measuring the noise output.
- Simulation evaluation: Re-attack the perturbation dataset with data analysis techniques to see if the victim (or the specialty group) could be found or not. This

3.3 Methodologies and Approach

Privacy Protection Strategy

Based on the requirements, we intend to perturb the dataset using three approaches: Laplace mechanisms (LPA), Fourier Perturbation Algorithm (FPA), and STL-DP. The Threshold mechanism and other temporal-related methods will not be used in this particular use case, as value perturbation is deemed sufficient given the sales volume.

To apply these algorithms, it is necessary to plan out the prerequisite components:

- ε: The suggested ε values by Dwork [6] are $\{0.01, 0.1, \ln 2, \ln 3\}$, by Boenisch [7] are $\{5, 10\}$. ε is a parameter that determines the level of privacy protection, with smaller values providing stronger privacy guarantees.
- *Sensitivity:* The sensitivity of the data is calculated as suggested by Rastogi [3])

$$GS = M\sqrt{Tk} \qquad (3)$$

where M represents the maximum bound in the data domain, T is the size of the time series, and k is the coefficient length in the Fast Fourier Transform (FFT). Sensitivity is a measure of how much the output of an algorithm can change in response to changes in the input data.

By determining the appropriate values for ε and sensitivity, we can apply the Laplace mechanisms, FPA, and STL-DP to perturb the time-series data, ensuring privacy protection and data utility.

Maximum Data Domain Estimation for Global Sensitivity

To determine a suitable value for the maximum data domain that adds a reasonable amount of noise when applying Differential Privacy mechanisms, there are a couple of approaches that can be considered:

- *Domain Knowledge*: Utilizing domain knowledge specific to the problem can provide valuable insights. For example, in the case of Differential Privacy on Short-term Energy Forecasting [10], knowledge about household power consumption in Germany could be used. By considering factors such as the electrical capacity of a typical household, nominal voltage, and acceptable over-voltage, it is possible to estimate the maximum power consumption. This domain knowledge can provide a realistic upper bound, ensuring that the sensitivity value used is higher than the actual peaks of power demand.

- *Assumption with Data Analytics*: Another approach involves making assumptions based on data analytics. Given the large dataset available, statistical techniques such as the interquartile range (IQR) can be employed to estimate the maximum data domain value. The IQR helps identify the centralization of data candidates and detect outliers. In this context, the 50th percentile (Q2), 75th percentile (Q3), and the upper quantile (Q3 + IQR) can be considered as candidates for the maximum data domain value (M).

By leveraging either domain knowledge or data analytics techniques like the IQR, it becomes possible to determine appropriate values for the maximum data domain. These values will ensure the addition of a reasonable amount of noise while preserving privacy through Differential Privacy mechanisms.

Experiment Approach
In the RFM analysis use-case, we utilize a uniform 5-level scale (1-Very Low, 2-Low, 3-Medium, 4-High, 5-Very High) for each R-F-M column to derive insights into consumer group characteristics. Following this, we conduct RFM analysis on the original and privacy-protected datasets generated using various Differential Privacy methods. Subsequently, we compare the outcomes and calculate accuracy, as outlined in the evaluation metrics section (Fig. 2).

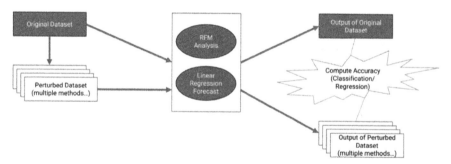

Fig. 2. Experiment process of privacy protection methods and accuracy compute

Upon completing the RFM analysis, we aggregate sales volume at the segmentation group level and apply an algorithm (in this case, Linear Regression Forecast) for forecasting instead of directly at the individual customer level, which may involve sparse and discrete intermittent data points. From a data analytics perspective, this approach provides a better understanding of the potential and behavior of each group, enabling adequate preparation for promotions and revenue enhancement.

3.4 Solution Implementation

See Fig. 3.

```
1   DF['PurchaseDate'] = pd.to_datetime(DF['PurchaseDate'], format='%Y%m%d')
2   DF['PurchaseWeek'] = DF['PurchaseDate'].dt.week
3   pd.pivot_table(DF, index='PurchaseWeek', columns='ProductCategory',
4                   values='Quantity', aggfunc='sum').plot(figsize=(10,5))
```

<Axes: xlabel='PurchaseWeek'>

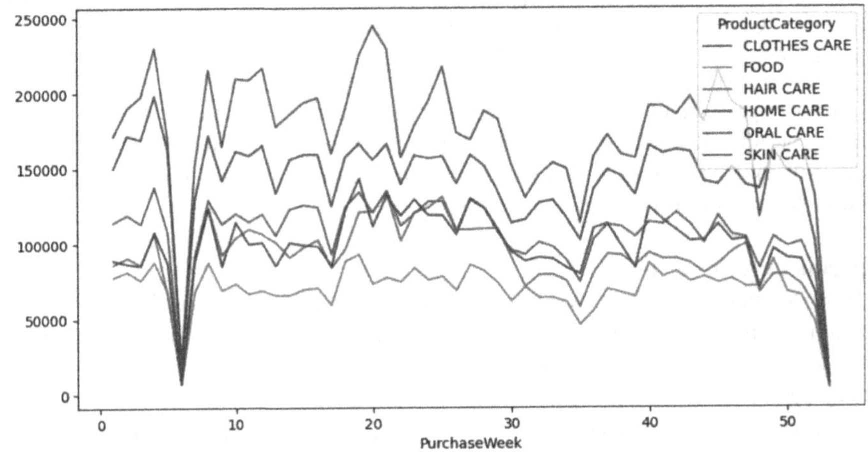

Fig. 3. Visualization of dataset by Purchase Week and Sales Volume groupby Product Category

Dataset Quick Summary

Synthesis dataset contains:

- Daily data from 2021–01-01 to 2021–12-31 (full year 2021)
- More than 1,000,000 rows and 7 columns (follow the required structure)
- 15 supermarkets
- Nearly 5,000 consumers
- 6 distinct product categories.

Maximum Data Domain Estimation

By leveraging the IQR and quantiles rule from the mentioned strategy above on each of the categories, we get this concrete table (Table 3):

The calculated values can be used as the maximum domain value, in terms of their statistical meaning to evaluate the perturbation algorithm accuracy and performance.

Table 3. Summary candidates for Maximum Data Domain estimation for each category

Category	Q2	Q3	Q3 + IQR
CLOTHES CARE	28	51	108
FOOD	24	40	85
HAIR CARE	17	34	73
HOME CARE	30	51	105
ORAL CARE	36	55	110.5
SKIN CARE	20	36	78

4 Implementation Environment and Tools

To conduct the demonstration, we use Python 3.9 with standard data science libraries *(pandas, numpy, scipy, statsmodels)*, the differential privacy library from IBM *(IBM diffprivlib)*, and the state-of-the-art parallel engine named Ray Framework from UC Berkeley RISE Lab. Running on Databricks 11.3 LTS ML with 32 CPUs cluster helped me to speed up the result generating well.

To build the LPA, FPA, STL-DP methods, we follow the architecture mentioned in papers [5] and [8] (Fig. 4).

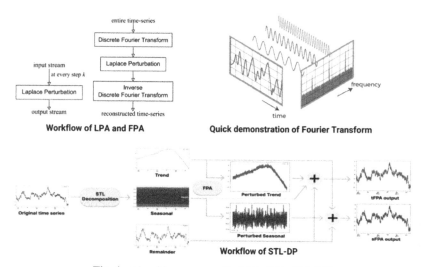

Fig. 4. Algorithms process for LPA, FPA, STL-DP

Source-code and full outputs are given in this repository.[1]

---

[1] Github link: https://github.com/LAITRUNGMINHDUC/DP_ConsumerData_RetailIndustry.

4.1   Solution Evaluation

Use Case 1 Evaluation
From this table, we recognize most of the LPA methods create an incorrect classification for the dataset (with accuracy lower than 70%), except for the level of $\varepsilon = \{5, 10\}$ and sensitivity $= Q2$, then it gets the result quite good. The FPA and STL-DP methods share similar results (STL-DP also gets slightly higher than FPA), ranging from 70% to 77% depending on the sensitivity and ε, respectively (Table 4).

Table 4. Summary of output result for Use-case 1 (TOP 5 best and TOP 3 worst accuracy)

METHOD	Total User	Count True	ACCURACY
Quantity_sFPA_Q2_10	4914	3826	77.90%
Quantity_FPA_Q2_10	4914	3719	75.70%
Quantity_sFPA_Q2_5	4914	3562	72.50%
Quantity_sFPA_Q3_10	4914	3560	72.40%
Quantity_tFPA_Q2_10	4914	3540	72.00%
Quantity_LPA_Q2_0.01	4914	105	2.10%
Quantity_LPA_Q3_0.01	4914	57	1.20%
Quantity_LPA_Q2_ln2	4914	36	0.70%

Use Case 2 Evaluation
Looking at and comparing the accuracy order of this prediction use-case, we can recognize the non-consistent between two use-cases. For TOP 10 methods, both use-case show the similar results. However, take an example of the method "Quantity_LPA_Q3_10", in RFM use-case, it's ranks 13, but in Prediction, it's rank 5 (Table 5).

Table 5. Summary of output result for Use-case 2 (TOP 5 best and TOP 4 worst RMSE)

METHOD	RMSE_SUM	RMSE_MEAN	RANK_PREDICTION	RANK_RFM
Quantity_tFPA_Q2_10	8207	21	1	5
Quantity_FPA_Q2_10	8261	21	2	2
Quantity_FPA_Q3_10	14703	39	3	8
Quantity_sFPA_Q2_10	14705	38	4	1
Quantity_tFPA_Q3_10	15443	41	5	13
Quantity_FPA_Q3 + IQR_0.01	47798869	128837	69	51
Quantity_sFPA_Q3 + IQR_0.01	47905850	129126	70	49
Quantity_LPA_Q2_0.01	50934082	509340	71	70
Quantity_LPA_Q3 + IQR_0.01	2.24E + 08	801595	72	58

Privacy Loss Evaluation

From previous related data (RMSE accuracy of the forecast solution), these figures below will show and confirm with you the trade-off between data utility (RMSE metrics) and data privacy (changes in E and Sensitivity value).

We all agree when the ε is 0.01, all the methods and sensitivity values create very huge errors (too much noise), and the LPA has suffered from it the most.

Although the concept of Differential Privacy assures within the ε range of 0 to 1, it is essential to acknowledge that the data utility of these methods tends to be quite low. On the other hand, when the ε value exceeds 1, it is considered "better than not applied" in terms of privacy protection (Fig. 5).

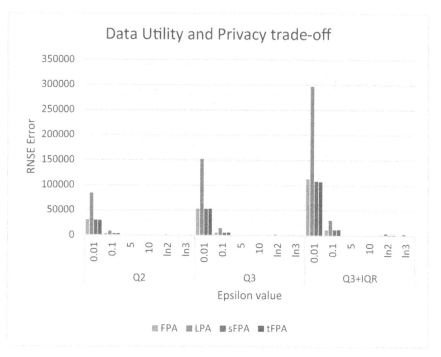

Fig. 5. Relationship between Error and Privacy Level

Recommendation

Based on the extensive analysis, it is evident that there is no definitive solution for ensuring data privacy, including Differential Privacy. While the concept of Differential Privacy is mathematically proven, further research is required to develop appropriate solutions for specific use cases. Considering this, the following recommendations are proposed:

- Each use case should employ a tailored mechanism, as no one-size-fits-all solution exists.

- Leverage domain knowledge to define the properties of Differential Privacy accurately.
- Define the acceptable error range to select proper parameters.
- When perturbing time-series data, experiment with various parameters for techniques such as FPA and STL-DP.
- Select the methods that balance accuracy and privacy for all analytics use cases.

By adhering to these recommendations, organizations can enhance data privacy protection while still achieving accurate results for their specific analytical requirements.

5 Conclusion

This paper extensively explored Differential Privacy, its mechanisms, and its application to time-series data by synthesizing Retail Data Partnership use cases. The findings emphasize the potential of Differential Privacy, especially in corporate settings. Notably, applying the Laplace mechanism directly to time-series data can introduce excessive noise, rendering results unusable. However, the Fourier Perturbation Algorithm and STL-DP promise to reduce noise while preserving data utility for modeling and analysis.

Despite its contributions, this paper acknowledges certain limitations. Firstly, determining suitable values for ε and sensitivity remains somewhat biased and lacks precise translation into human language. Secondly, while the synthesis use-case aimed for naturalness and impartiality, there is room for improvement, especially when incorporating transaction detail-level data, which poses privacy challenges. Some of the approaches using Deep Learning and Generative Adversarial Networks (GAN) data generation with Differential Privacy from Khanh et al. in [11] and [12] can be candidates to tackle this constraint.

Future work should address these limitations and develop enhanced techniques for adequate data protection with Differential Privacy. Overcoming these challenges will strengthen the foundation for privacy-preserving methodologies in the field.

References

1. Ye, Q et al.: Beyond value perturbation: local differential privacy in the temporal setting. In: IEEE INFOCOM 2021 - IEEE Conference on Computer Communications, Vancouver, BC, Canada, pp. 1–10 (2021). https://doi.org/10.1109/INFOCOM42981.2021.9488899
2. Wong, R.C., Fu, A.W.: Privacy-Preserving Data Publishing: An Overview. Morgan and Claypool Publishers, San Rafael (2010)
3. Rastogi, V., Nath, S.: Differentially private aggregation of distributed timeseries with transformation and encryption. In: ACM SIGMOD International Conference on Management of data, Indiana, USA, pp. 735–746 (2010)
4. Fung, B.C.M., Wang, K., Chen, R., Yu, P.S.: Privacy-preserving data publishing: a survey of recent developments. ACM Comput. Surv. **42**(4), 1–53 (2010)
5. Fan, L., Xiong, L.: Real-time aggregate monitoring with differential privacy. In: Proceedings of the 21st ACM International Conference on Information and Knowledge Management, Maui, Hawaii, USA, pp. 2169–2173 (2012)

6. Dwork, C.: Differential privacy: a survey of results. In: Agrawal, M., Du, D., Duan, Z., Li, A. (eds.) TAMC 2008. LNCS, vol. 4978, pp. 1–19. Springer, Heidelberg (2008). https://doi.org/10.1007/978-3-540-79228-4_1
7. Boenisch, F.: Differential privacy: general survey and analysis of practicability in the context of machine learning. M.Sc. thesis, Freie Universität Berlin (2019)
8. Kim, K., Kim, M., Woo, S.: STL-DP: differentially private time series exploring decomposition and compression methods. In: ACM CIKM22-PAS: The 1st International Workshop on Privacy Algorithms in Systems, Georgia, USA (2022)
9. Wiehe, S.E., et al.: A solutions-based approach to building data-sharing partnerships. EGEMS 6(1), 20 (2018). https://doi.org/10.5334/egems.236
10. Eibl, G., Bao, K., Grassal, P.W., Bernau, D., Schmeck, H.: The influence of differential privacy on short-term electric load forecasting. Energy Inform. 1 (Suppl 1), 48 (2018). https://doi.org/10.1186/s42162-018-0025-3
11. Ha, T., Dang, T.K., Le, H., Truong, T.A: Security and privacy issues in deep learning: a brief review. SN Comput. Sci. 1(5), 253 (2020)
12. Ha, T., Dang, T.K.: Investigating local differential privacy and generative adversarial network in collecting data. In: ACOMP, pp. 140–145 (2020)
13. Ha, T., Dang, T.K.: Inference attacks based on GAN in federated learning. Int. J. Web Inf. Syst. 18(2/3), 117–136 (2022)
14. Ha, T., Dang, T.K., Nguyen-Tan, N.: Comprehensive analysis of privacy in black-box and white-box inference attacks against generative adversarial network. In: Dang, T.K., Küng, J., Chung, T.M., Takizawa, M. (eds.) FDSE 2021. LNCS, vol. 13076, pp. 323–337 (2021). https://doi.org/10.1007/978-3-030-91387-8_21
15. Yoon, J., Jarrett, D., van der Schaar, M.: Time-series generative adversarial networks. In: Proceedings of the 33rd International Conference on Neural Information Processing Systems, Curran Associates Inc., Red Hook, NY, USA, Article 494, 5508–5518 (2019)

Using Transformer Technique
for Intrusion Detection

Quang-Vinh Dang[(✉)] [iD]

Industrial University of Ho Chi Minh City, Ho Chi Minh City, Vietnam
dangquangvinh@iuh.edu.vn

Abstract. Intrusion detection is indeed a crucial research topic in the
cyber-security domain. Researchers have recently explored many supervised machine-learning algorithms to detect intrusions in computer networks. However, recent attention-based algorithms have not yet attracted
enough attention from the research community. As attention-based algorithms have achieved impressive results in other domains, particularly
natural language processing, we believe that they have the potential to
be applied to intrusion detection problems. In this paper, we develop a
transformer-based algorithm to detect intrusion. We evaluated our algorithm using a famous dataset called CICIDS-2017. We compared the
transformer-based techniques with standard techniques in the literature.
We observed that transformer-based techniques have some advantages
compared to other supervised tree-based algorithms.

Keywords: intrusion detection · cybersecurity · transformer

1 Introduction

Cyber-crime is a crucial threat to modern organizations. According to the Cyber
Warfare Report [18], cyber-crime will cost the world about 10.5 trillion USD per
year. This staggering figure underscores the urgency and importance of developing robust cyber-security measures.

Intrusion detection is an essential research topic in the cyber-security domain
[12]. Over the years, researchers have developed multiple techniques to detect
intrusions effectively [2]. Traditional techniques, such as signature-based and
anomaly-based methods, have their strengths but also come with limitations [21].
Signature-based methods, while highly effective against known threats, struggle
to detect novel attacks. Anomaly-based methods, on the other hand, can identify
new and unexpected intrusions but often suffer from high false positive rates.

With the rise of deep learning and its successes in various domains like natural
language processing and image recognition [11], there is a growing interest in
applying these techniques to intrusion detection. The Transformer architecture,
introduced by Vaswani et al. [22], has revolutionized the field of natural language
processing with its self-attention mechanism. This architecture enables the model
to weigh the importance of different input data points relative to each other,
making it particularly suitable for sequences and time series data.

© The Author(s), under exclusive license to Springer Nature Singapore Pte Ltd. 2023
T. K. Dang et al. (Eds.): FDSE 2023, CCIS 1925, pp. 184–196, 2023.
https://doi.org/10.1007/978-981-99-8296-7_13

Given the sequential nature of network traffic data, the Transformer technique has the potential to capture intricate patterns and dependencies that might be missed by traditional methods. The dataset CICIDS 2017 [20] is a comprehensive benchmark for intrusion detection, encompassing a wide variety of attack scenarios and normal behaviors. Leveraging this dataset provides a rigorous evaluation ground for any new technique.

The motivation behind this paper is to explore the feasibility and efficacy of the Transformer technique for intrusion detection using the CICIDS 2017 dataset. Specifically, we aim to answer the following research questions:

- How does the Transformer-based approach compare to traditional intrusion detection techniques in terms of accuracy, false positive rate, and computational efficiency?
- What are the unique patterns and features that the Transformer model can capture from the network traffic data that might be overlooked by other methods?
- Can the self-attention mechanism of the Transformer provide interpretable insights into the detected intrusions, aiding analysts in understanding and mitigating threats?

2   Related Works

2.1   Rule-Based Approaches

Rule-based intrusion detection systems (IDS) [14, 23] leverage a set of predefined rules to analyze network traffic or system behavior. For a given data input x, a rule R is applied, and if the rule conditions are satisfied, an alert is triggered. Mathematically, this can be represented as:

$$f(x) = \begin{cases} 1 & \text{if } R(x) \text{ is true} \\ 0 & \text{otherwise} \end{cases}$$

where $f(x)$ is the alert function. These systems are adept at catching known threats but may struggle against novel attack vectors.

While rule-based methods seems to be very simple, it is still being used widely in industrial-based systems[1]. The main reasons include a fast execution speed and easy to understand [4]. The first reason is important for engineering department, and the second reason is important for operational/business development departments.

2.2   Signature-Based Approaches

Signature-based detection can be viewed as a specialized rule-based method [13]. It operates by maintaining a database of known attack signatures. Each

---

[1] https://support.kaspersky.com/KICSforNetworks/2.9/en-US/171090.htm.

incoming packet is compared against this database. If a match M is found, an alert is raised. This can be represented as:

$$f(x) = \begin{cases} 1 & \text{if } x \in M \\ 0 & \text{otherwise} \end{cases}$$

The primary challenge is the continuous updating of the signature database to account for emerging threats. The challenges can be solved partly using a fuzzy algorithm [16].

2.3 Supervised Machine Learning Approaches

Supervised ML techniques for IDS rely on a labeled dataset $\mathcal{D} = \{(x_i, y_i)\}$, where x_i represents the data input and y_i is the corresponding label (benign or malicious). The goal is to learn a function $h : x \to y$ that maps inputs to their appropriate labels. Commonly used algorithms like Support Vector Machines (SVM) find a hyperplane that maximizes the margin between two classes:

$$y = \mathbf{w} \cdot \mathbf{x} + b$$

where $\mathbf{w}$ is the weight vector and b is the bias.

In the work of [2], the authors evaluated multiple supervised machine-learning algorithms. The result has been extended in the following research studies [3,5–9].

2.4 Reinforcement Learning-Based Approaches

In reinforcement learning, an agent interacts with an environment to maximize some notion of cumulative reward. The primary components are the state s, action a, and reward r. The agent follows a policy π to decide actions based on states. The goal is to optimize:

$$\max_{\pi} \mathbb{E} \left[\sum_{t=0}^{\infty} \gamma^t r_t | \pi \right]$$

where γ is the discount factor. IDS agents can use such policies to decide whether to flag traffic as malicious or benign [10].

2.5 Deep Learning-Based Approaches

Deep learning techniques automatically learn representations from data.

Multi-layer Perceptrons (MLP). MLPs consist of layers of nodes (or neurons) connected by weighted edges. Given an input vector $\mathbf{x}$, the output $\mathbf{y}$ is computed as:

$$\mathbf{y} = \sigma(\mathbf{W}\mathbf{x} + \mathbf{b})$$

where σ is an activation function, $\mathbf{W}$ is the weight matrix, and $\mathbf{b}$ is the bias vector.

MLP has been studied in several search studies for the problem of intrusion detection [1,19].

Convolutional Neural Networks (CNN). CNNs use convolutional layers to automatically and adaptively learn spatial hierarchies from data. The convolution operation is represented as:

$$\mathbf{y}(i,j) = \sum_m \sum_n \mathbf{W}(m,n) \cdot \mathbf{x}(i-m, j-n) + b$$

where $\mathbf{W}$ is the filter and b is the bias.

We refer the audience for a recent survey for further details of using CNN for the problem we are discussing [17].

Long Short-Term Memory (LSTM). LSTMs are a special kind of RNNs designed to learn long-term dependencies [15]. Their core idea is the cell state, which can be written, read, and modified by three gates: input, forget, and output gate. The state update can be represented as:

$$\mathbf{c}_t = \mathbf{f}_t \odot \mathbf{c}_{t-1} + \mathbf{i}_t \odot \tanh(\mathbf{W}_c[\mathbf{h}_{t-1}, \mathbf{x}_t] + \mathbf{b}_c)$$

where $\odot$ denotes element-wise multiplication and $\mathbf{f}_t, \mathbf{i}_t$ are the forget and input gates, respectively.

3 Methodology

This study employs four sophisticated algorithms to tackle intrusion detection: LightGBM, XGBoost, CatBoost, and the multi-head self-attention transformer. In this section, we provide an exhaustive overview of each method, emphasizing their mathematical foundations, principles, and training processes.

3.1 LightGBM

LightGBM, standing for Light Gradient Boosting Machine, is an advanced gradient boosting framework that employs tree-based learning algorithms. It's optimized for speed and is particularly useful for large-scale data.

Algorithm Principle: The core of the LightGBM model is its additive training process. For a defined objective function $\mathcal{L}(\cdot)$, the algorithm seeks the function $F(x)$ that minimizes:

$$\mathcal{L}(y, F(x)) = \sum_i \mathcal{L}(y_i, F(x_i))$$

Each iteration introduces a new tree that fits the negative gradient of the loss function, akin to residual fitting.

Tree Growth Strategy: LightGBM's unique approach is its leaf-wise tree growth strategy, as opposed to level-wise growth. This strategy prioritizes splitting the leaf that contributes the most to the loss reduction.

Training Process: The training process iteratively adds trees while minimizing the loss, and regularizes the process by considering both the number of leaves and the leaf weights.

3.2 XGBoost

XGBoost, denoting eXtreme Gradient Boosting, is a potent gradient boosting algorithm known for its performance and speed.

Algorithm Principle: The objective function for XGBoost combines a loss term and a regularization term:

$$\mathcal{J}(\Theta) = \sum_i \mathcal{L}(y_i, \hat{y}_i) + \sum_k \Omega(f_k)$$

Here, $\mathcal{L}$ represents the training loss, and Ω is the regularization term which penalizes the complexity of the model.

Training Process: During training, XGBoost iteratively adds new functions that predict the residuals or errors of prior functions. The objective in each iteration is to find the best function that, when added to the existing functions, minimizes the overall objective.

3.3 CatBoost

CatBoost is a gradient boosting algorithm with a focus on efficiently handling categorical features.

Algorithm Principle: Like other boosting methods, CatBoost iteratively adds trees to the model. The distinct aspect is its treatment of categorical variables. CatBoost encodes these variables based on the target variable, ensuring minimal loss during encoding.

Ordered Boosting: CatBoost's ordered boosting reduces overfitting by processing each object in the training dataset using only information from preceding objects.

Training Process: Training in CatBoost involves building a series of decision trees, where each tree corrects the errors of its predecessor. The categorical features are transformed using various techniques, with mean encoding being predominant.

While 3 boosting machines are quite similar in the principle ideas, they have some difference mainly in how to grow trees. The process is visualized in Fig. 1.

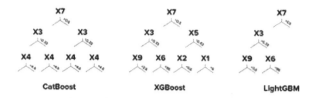

Fig. 1. Difference in growing trees of 3 boosting algorithms

3.4   Multi-head Self-attention Transformer

Transformers, with their multi-head self-attention mechanism, have gained significant traction in numerous fields.

Self-attention Mechanism: For a set of input vectors $\mathbf{Q}$, $\mathbf{K}$, and $\mathbf{V}$, the attention scores are computed as:

$$\text{Attention}(\mathbf{Q}, \mathbf{K}, \mathbf{V}) = \text{softmax}\left(\frac{\mathbf{Q}\mathbf{K}^{\mathbf{T}}}{\sqrt{d_k}}\right)\mathbf{V}$$

This mechanism allows the model to weigh the importance of different input data points relative to each other.

Multi-head Attention: The multi-head variant of the attention mechanism allows the model to focus on different parts of the input for different tasks or representations:

$$\text{MultiHead}(\mathbf{Q}, \mathbf{K}, \mathbf{V}) = \text{Concat}(\text{head}_1, \ldots, \text{head}_h)\mathbf{W}_O$$

Training Process: The training of transformers involves feeding sequences into the model and optimizing the weights based on the prediction error for tasks like sequence classification or sequence-to-sequence prediction. The backpropagation algorithm, combined with optimization methods like Adam, adjusts the model weights.

The architecture of multi-head self-attention is visualized in Fig. 2.

4   Results

4.1   Dataset

The CICIDS 2017 dataset was created by the Canadian Institute for Cybersecurity (CIC)[2]. It's a comprehensive dataset for evaluating intrusion detection systems (IDS) and includes a wide variety of intrusions simulated in a testbed reflecting a real-world scenario. The dataset provides a detailed view of modern network traffic, which can be used for various tasks beyond just intrusion detection, such as network traffic characterization and network forensics.

---

[2] https://www.unb.ca/cic.

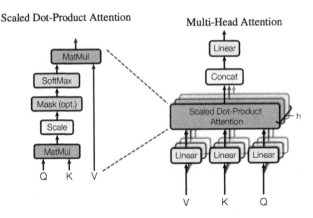

Fig. 2. Multi-head self-attention

The dataset was generated over a week, and each day contains different attack scenarios mixed with benign traffic. Some of the attack categories present in the dataset include Brute Force, Heartbleed, Botnets, DoS/DDoS, Infiltration, and more. The dataset is available to download at https://www.unb.ca/cic/datasets/ids-2017.html.

The dataset provides a myriad of features extracted from the traffic flows, including basic features like source and destination IP addresses, ports, timestamps, and other more advanced features derived from the packet data.

Table 1. Attack Categories Distribution in CICIDS 2017

Attack Category	Count
BENIGN	2,095,057
DoS Hulk	172,846
DDoS	128,014
PortScan	90,694
DoS GoldenEye	10,286
FTP-Patator	5,931
DoS slowloris	5,385
DoS Slowhttptest	5,228
SSH-Patator	3,219
Bot	1,948
Web Attack - Brute Force	1,470
Web Attack - XSS	652
Infiltration	36
Web Attack - Sql Injection	21

The distribution of classes in the dataset is presented in Table 1. The dataset is severely imbalanced, with most of the packets are benign packets. The dataset is organized in 8 CSV files that are ready to be loaded and transformed.

We keep out of 20% of the dataset as the test-set.

4.2   Results

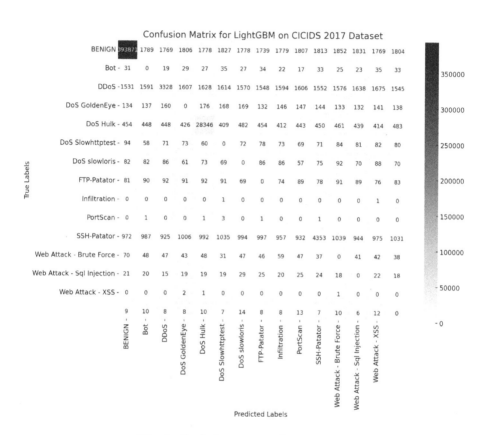

Fig. 3. Confusion matrix of LightGBM

In our comprehensive analysis of intrusion detection methods utilizing the CICIDS 2017 dataset, we rigorously evaluated four state-of-the-art machine learning algorithms. Their respective performance metrics are pictorially presented through confusion matrices in Figs. 3, 4, 5, and 6. Figure 3 delineates the outcomes for the LightGBM model, which displayed a commendable capability in discerning benign traffic, albeit with certain shortcomings in detecting

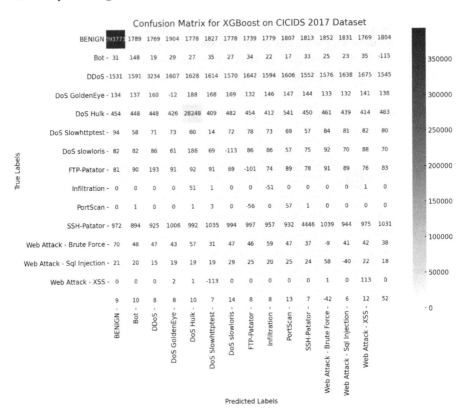

Fig. 4. Confusion matrix of xgboost

specific attack types. A nuanced enhancement in these areas is noticeable in the XGBoost model, as portrayed in Fig. 4. Progressing to Fig. 5, the CatBoost algorithm further refines the detection capabilities, particularly accentuating its prowess in identifying intricate attack patterns. The climax of our exploration is embodied in Fig. 6, where the Transformer architecture, with its inherent attention mechanisms, not only underscores its potential in the domain of intrusion detection but also demonstrates a marked improvement in performance relative to its gradient-boosted counterparts. Collectively, these visual representations offer invaluable insights into the strengths and potential avenues for enhancement for each algorithm in the intricate landscape of intrusion detection.

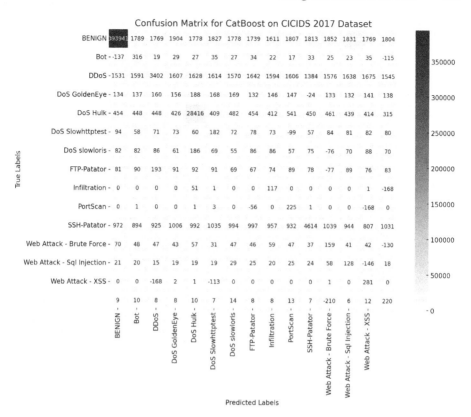

Fig. 5. Confusion matrix of catboost

Table 2 provides a succinct summary of the performance metrics for the four machine learning algorithms evaluated on the CICIDS 2017 dataset. The metrics encompass accuracy, macro precision, macro recall, training time, and inference time. Notably, while gradient boosting methods such as LightGBM, XGBoost, and CatBoost exhibit commendable accuracy levels, the Transformer architecture, albeit marginally, outperforms them with an accuracy of 0.8674. This superiority is further highlighted in the macro precision score of 0.2696. Additionally, the training time for the Transformer is considerably lower than XGBoost, making it a favorable choice considering both efficiency and performance. While the current results are promising, it's pertinent to note that the Transformer's potential hasn't been fully realized. With further refinements and optimizations, its performance in intrusion detection is anticipated to further improve, setting new benchmarks in the cybersecurity domain.

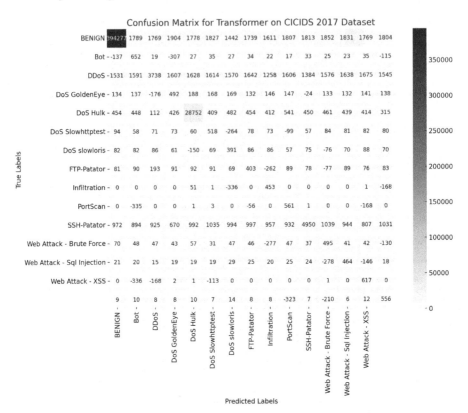

Fig. 6. Confusion matrix of transformer

Table 2. Summary of Model Performances on CICIDS 2017. Training time and inference time are measures in seconds.

Algorithm	Accuracy	Macro Precision	Macro Recall	Training	Inference
LightGBM	0.8571	0.176	0.137	60	2
XGBoost	0.8621	0.181	0.142	1800	2
CatBoost	0.8671	0.186	0.147	100	3
Transformer	0.8674	0.2696	0.162	1500	2

5   Conclusion

In the ever-evolving landscape of cyber threats, crafting robust and efficient intrusion detection systems remains paramount. This paper embarked on a comprehensive exploration of leveraging cutting-edge machine learning techniques, including boosting algorithms and the transformer architecture, to address intrusion detection using the CICIDS 2017 dataset.

While boosting algorithms like LightGBM, XGBoost, and CatBoost have been extensively employed in the domain of intrusion detection, their performance nuances, especially in tandem, are always worth revisiting given the dynamic nature of cyber threats. Our study underscored the strengths and potential areas of improvement of these algorithms, offering insights that could guide future research and practical implementations.

Perhaps the most distinctive contribution of this paper is our exploration of the multi-head self-attention transformer for intrusion detection. Transformers, which have revolutionized fields like natural language processing, are seldom utilized in the realm of intrusion detection. Our work stands as one of the pioneering efforts in this direction. The self-attention mechanism, inherent to transformers, allows the model to weigh the importance of different input data points relative to each other—a feature that could be instrumental in detecting intricate cyber threats.

In conclusion, while boosting algorithms continue to be a staple in the intrusion detection toolkit, there is substantial untapped potential in transformer architectures. As one of the maiden endeavors in marrying transformers with intrusion detection, we hope this paper serves as a catalyst for further research, fostering innovations that make our digital realms safer and more secure.

References

1. de Almeida Florencio, F., Moreno, E.D., Macedo, H.T., de Britto Salgueiro, R.J., do Nascimento, F.B., Santos, F.A.O.: Intrusion detection via MLP neural network using an Arduino embedded system. In: 2018 VIII Brazilian Symposium on Computing Systems Engineering (SBESC), pp. 190–195. IEEE (2018)
2. Dang, Q.-V.: Studying machine learning techniques for intrusion detection systems. In: Dang, T.K., Küng, J., Takizawa, M., Bui, S.H. (eds.) FDSE 2019. LNCS, vol. 11814, pp. 411–426. Springer, Cham (2019). https://doi.org/10.1007/978-3-030-35653-8_28
3. Dang, Q.V.: Evaluating machine learning algorithms for intrusion detection systems using the dataset CIDDS-002. In: Proceedings of the 4th International Conference on Computer Science and Software Engineering, pp. 112–118 (2021)
4. Dang, Q.V.: Improving the performance of the intrusion detection systems by the machine learning explainability. Int. J. Web Inf. Syst. **17**(5), 537–555 (2021)
5. Dang, Q.-V.: Studying the attack detection problem using the dataset CIDDS-001. In: Antipova, T. (ed.) DSIC 2021. LNNS, vol. 381, pp. 525–532. Springer, Cham (2022). https://doi.org/10.1007/978-3-030-93677-8_46
6. Dang, Q.V.: Detecting intrusion using multiple datasets in software-defined networks. In: Dang, T.K., Küng, J., Chung, T.M. (eds.) FDSE 2022. CCIS, vol. 1688, pp. 739–746. Springer, Singapore (2022). https://doi.org/10.1007/978-981-19-8069-5_55
7. Dang, Q.V.: Multi-layer intrusion detection on the USB-IDS-1 dataset. In: Abraham, A., Hong, T.P., Kotecha, K., Ma, K., Manghirmalani Mishra, P., Gandhi, N. (eds.) HIS 2022. LNNS, vol. 647, pp. 1114–1121. Springer, Cham (2022). https://doi.org/10.1007/978-3-031-27409-1_102
8. Dang, Q.V.: Using machine learning for intrusion detection systems. Comput. Inform. **41**(1), 12–33 (2022)

9. Dang, Q.V.: Learning to transfer knowledge between datasets to enhance intrusion detection systems. In: Shukla, A., Murthy, B.K., Hasteer, N., Van Belle, J.P. (eds.) Computational Intelligence. LNEE, vol. 968, pp. 39–46. Springer, Singapore (2023). https://doi.org/10.1007/978-981-19-7346-8_4

10. Dang, Q.-V., Vo, T.-H.: Reinforcement learning for the problem of detecting intrusion in a computer system. In: Yang, X.-S., Sherratt, S., Dey, N., Joshi, A. (eds.) Proceedings of Sixth International Congress on Information and Communication Technology. LNNS, vol. 236, pp. 755–762. Springer, Singapore (2022). https://doi.org/10.1007/978-981-16-2380-6_66

11. Goodfellow, I., Bengio, Y., Courville, A.: Deep Learning. MIT Press, Cambridge (2016)

12. Gümüşbaş, D., Yıldırım, T., Genovese, A., Scotti, F.: A comprehensive survey of databases and deep learning methods for cybersecurity and intrusion detection systems. IEEE Syst. J. 15(2), 1717–1731 (2020)

13. Hubballi, N., Suryanarayanan, V.: False alarm minimization techniques in signature-based intrusion detection systems: a survey. Comput. Commun. 49, 1–17 (2014)

14. Ilgun, K., Kemmerer, R.A., Porras, P.A.: State transition analysis: a rule-based intrusion detection approach. IEEE Trans. Softw. Eng. 21(3), 181–199 (1995)

15. Imrana, Y., Xiang, Y., Ali, L., Abdul-Rauf, Z.: A bidirectional LSTM deep learning approach for intrusion detection. Expert Syst. Appl. 185, 115524 (2021)

16. Masdari, M., Khezri, H.: A survey and taxonomy of the fuzzy signature-based intrusion detection systems. Appl. Soft Comput. 92, 106301 (2020)

17. Mohammadpour, L., Ling, T.C., Liew, C.S., Aryanfar, A.: A survey of CNN-based network intrusion detection. Appl. Sci. 12(16), 8162 (2022)

18. Morgan, S.: Special report: cyberwarfare in the C-suite (2021)

19. Rosay, A., Carlier, F., Leroux, P.: MLP4NIDS: an efficient MLP-based network intrusion detection for CICIDS2017 dataset. In: Boumerdassi, S., Renault, É., Mühlethaler, P. (eds.) MLN 2019. LNCS, vol. 12081, pp. 240–254. Springer, Cham (2020). https://doi.org/10.1007/978-3-030-45778-5_16

20. Sharafaldin, I., Lashkari, A.H., Ghorbani, A.A.: Toward generating a new intrusion detection dataset and intrusion traffic characterization. ICISSp 1, 108–116 (2018)

21. Suthishni, D.N.P., Kumar, K.S.: A review on machine learning based security approaches in intrusion detection system. In: 2022 9th International Conference on Computing for Sustainable Global Development (INDIACom), pp. 341–348. IEEE (2022)

22. Vaswani, A., et al.: Attention is all you need. In: Advances in Neural Information Processing Systems, vol. 30 (2017)

23. Yang, Y., McLaughlin, K., Littler, T., Sezer, S., Wang, H.: Rule-based intrusion detection system for SCADA networks (2013)

Machine Learning and Artificial Intelligence for Security and Privacy

A Siamese-Based Approach for Network Intrusion Detection Systems in Software-Defined Networks

Dinh Hoang Nguyen[1]([✉])(iD), Nam Khanh Tran[1](iD), and Nhien-An Le-Khac[2](iD)

[1] Le Quy Don Technical University, Hanoi, Vietnam
{hoangnd,khanhtn107195}@lqdtu.edu.vn
[2] University College Dublin, Dublin, Ireland
an.lekhac@ucd.ie

Abstract. Recently, a new approach to networking called Software-Defined Networking (SDN) has emerged based on the idea of separating the centralized control plane from the data plane, which simplifies network management and meets the needs of modern data centers. However, the centralized nature of SDN also introduces new security risks that could hamper widespread SDN adoption, such as single points of failure. The controller is a critical vulnerability since an attacker who compromises it can control traffic routing and severely disrupt the network. SDN is still an emerging technology, utilizing deep learning for Network Intrusion Detection Systems (NIDS) is an effective security solution that could enable more accurate and adaptive threat detection to against attacks targeting vulnerabilities introduced by centralized control. In this paper, we describe a Siamese-based method for NIDSs in SDN. When it comes to the process of training and testing models based on Siamese Networks, making effective pairs is a key strategy that can have a considerable impact on the outcome. To prevent overfitting, we enhance the data pairing both within and across classes. The findings of our methodology demonstrate a notable enhancement in the efficacy of NIDS, resulting in an accuracy rate of approximately 100%. This estimated accuracy exceeds that of baseline methods. The study's conclusions facilitate the development of reliable IDS systems tailored for SDN environments.

Keywords: Siamese Network · CNN · InSDN dataset · SDN · Machine learning · Deep learning · Intrusion Detection System · Prevent overfitting

1 Introduction

SDN represents a pioneering network architecture that effectively segregates the control and data planes within network devices. The conventional network architecture entails the presence of the control plane within individual network devices, which gives rise to various predicaments in terms of network administration and security. In contrast to traditional networking architectures, SDN

T. K. Dang et al. (Eds.): FDSE 2023, CCIS 1925, pp. 199–211, 2023.
https://doi.org/10.1007/978-981-99-8296-7_14

introduces a decoupling of the control logic from the physical infrastructure. This decoupling is achieved by implementing a centralized controller that governs the network devices. The process of centralization facilitates the ability of network administrators to effectively program and configure network devices by utilizing precisely defined Application Programming Interfaces (APIs) [1]. The holistic perspective offered by SDN serves to augment the flexibility, scalability, and efficiency of network management, thereby presenting novel avenues for enhancing network security. SDN has emerged as a catalyst for numerous applications within the realm of computer networks. These applications span a wide range, encompassing Network Virtualization, Traffic Engineering, and Quality of Service [2]. The advent of SDN has brought forth a multitude of benefits, yet it concurrently presents novel security considerations. The vulnerability of the control plane as a singular point of failure renders it susceptible to targeted attacks aimed at unauthorized access or the disruption of network operations. SDN attacks can be classified into distinct categories [3], including controller-based attacks, switch-based attacks, and data plane attacks. The primary objective of controller-based attacks is to undermine the integrity of the central controller, thereby granting malicious actors unrestricted authority over network devices. Switch-based attacks are a class of cyber threats that take advantage of inherent weaknesses present in individual switches. These vulnerabilities enable malicious actors to exert control over network traffic and enforce unauthorized policies without proper authorization. The present study investigates the potential of data plane attacks [4] for the purpose of intercepting, modifying, or blocking data packets within a network. These attacks have the capacity to cause network outages or enable unauthorized access to sensitive information.

The Intrusion Detection System (IDS) serves as a pivotal security mechanism, diligently observing network traffic and systems to detect any anomalous activities or plausible security breaches. The IDS assumes a pivotal function in the protection of networks through the meticulous examination of network packets, events, or behaviors, with the aim of promptly detecting and addressing potential security threats. The efficacy of traditional IDS has been well-documented in the context of conventional networks. However, the advent of SDN with its dynamic and flexible nature necessitates the exploration of novel approaches to intrusion detection. In the realm of SDN, it is imperative for IDS to acclimatize themselves to the distinctive attributes inherent in SDNs. These attributes encompass dynamic network topology, programmable policies, and centralized control. In order to tackle the aforementioned challenges, novel methodologies such as the Siamese-based technique have been put forth to amplify the precision and efficacy of identifying network attacks within SDN environments.

The contribution of this paper includes the following:

- We present a novel approach for IDS by leveraging the Siamese Network architecture. Our proposed IDS utilizes the Siamese Network, a deep learning model that has shown promising results in various domains.

- We employed a methodology involving the creation of pairs to address the issue of overfitting. Therefore, our proposed model exhibits notable efficacy in the detection of novel intrusions that were not encountered during the training phase.
- We used the recently generated InSDN dataset [5] to ensure an accurate evaluation, as it represents attacks specific to SDN environments. The performance of intrusion detection systems relies heavily on the quality of the training datasets. This is significant as existing IDSs do not accurately reflect SDN environments or have limitations with the datasets used for classification.

The rest of this paper is organized as follows: Sect. 2 provides a brief background about the CNN, Siamese Network. Section 3 gives an overview of the existing machine learning and deep learning techniques that are currently used to monitor and detect threats in SDNs. The proposed model including the evaluation dataset and the experimental setup are provided in Sect. 4. The obtained experimental results are discussed in Sect. 5. Finally, Sect. 6 discusses and concludes the paper.

2 Background

2.1 Convolutional Neural Networks

Convolutional Neural Networks (CNNs) [6] represent a pivotal breakthrough in the field of computer vision and have become the backbone of state-of-the-art visual data analysis. These deep learning models are particularly designed to process and extract features from visual data, such as images and videos [7], making them exceptionally adept at understanding spatial relationships and patterns. The key innovation of CNNs lies in their architecture, inspired by the visual processing system in the human brain. At their core, they use convolutional layers, where a set of learnable filters convolve over the input data to capture local features and spatial information. The filters are learned during the training process, allowing the network to automatically identify critical characteristics, such as edges, textures, and shapes, directly from the data. Pooling layers are another integral component of CNNs. These layers systematically downsample the feature maps produced by the convolutional layers, retaining essential information while reducing the spatial dimensions. Pooling helps to make the model robust against translation and distortions, as well as reducing the computational complexity of the network. Furthermore, CNNs incorporate fully connected layers, which perform high-level reasoning and combine information from different parts of the visual input. These layers contribute to making the final predictions based on the learned features, enabling CNNs to excel in complex classification tasks.

2.2   Siamese Network

Siamese Networks are a class of neural networks that are specifically designed for tasks involving similarity or distance comparison. They were first introduced in the context of signature verification [8], but they have since found applications in various domains, including face recognition, image similarity, and network attack detection.

The key idea behind Siamese Networks is to learn embeddings, or feature representations, that can capture the similarity between pairs of input data points. The architecture of a Siamese Network consists of two or more identical subnetworks, known as "twins," that share the same set of parameters. Each twin processes one of the input data points independently.

The two data points to be compared (e.g., two images or network traffic data) are fed through their respective twins, producing two sets of embeddings in a common feature space. The embeddings are then compared using a similarity metric, such as Euclidean distance or cosine similarity, to determine the similarity or dissimilarity between the input data points.

During training, Siamese Networks are typically fed with pairs of data points and their corresponding similarity labels (e.g., similar or dissimilar). The network learns to minimize the distance between embeddings for similar pairs and maximize the distance for dissimilar pairs. Recently, Siamese Networks have been used for different purposes including image recognition [9], age estimation [10], gait recognition [11], object tracking, sentence similarity, etc.

3   Literature Review

In the following section, we present an overview of recent and popular research works in the field of anomaly detection in SDN environments.

Tang and Mhamdi [12] proposed an anomaly-based IDS tailored for SDN that solely leverages traffic features supplied by the SDN controller, in 2016. They benchmarked multiple machine learning algorithms, with deep neural networks comprising three hidden layers achieving the top accuracy of 75.75% on their evaluation dataset. However, specific details were not provided on the parameter configurations used for the learning algorithms. The lack of implementation specifics could hinder reproducing their architecture choices and identifying potential hyperparameter tuning improvements. More comprehensive reporting of model parameters would enable deeper analysis and building on their results to further enhance the accuracy of machine learning-based intrusion detection techniques customized for SDNs. In 2017, the article [13] proposed utilizing the SDN controller to extract flow features that are input to a voting ensemble of machine learning models including decision trees, random forests, XGBoost, SVM, and deep neural networks. The models are trained and tested on the NSL-KDD and KDDCup99 [14] intrusion detection datasets. Evaluations show deep neural networks achieve the highest accuracy around 83–99% depending on the dataset. However, combining the models in a voting system leads to a balanced trade-off improving the overall false positive rate to 0.03 while maintaining accuracy around 79%. The paper demonstrates how SDN can enable building intrusion detection systems that leverage controller telemetry data and machine learning without additional overhead. The voting ensemble approach allows tuning detection accuracy and false positives. Results are improved over past SDN IDS methods.

After that, another article presents a systematic study on using machine learning techniques for detecting attacks in SDN is [15]. It discusses two main approaches that have been explored - simulation-based machine learning where synthetic network data is generated for model training, and public dataset-based approaches that leverage existing labeled intrusion detection datasets. An analysis of the nonlinearity in the NSL-KDD dataset [14] feature space is provided using Andrews curves and t-SNE plots. Several classic machine learning algorithms including SVM, J48, Naive Bayes, and Random Forest are benchmarked on the NSL-KDD dataset, with J48 showing the best performance but overall accuracy limited to the 80–85% range due to issues like the relevance of the input features. The paper identifies the limitations of these classical machine-learning techniques in detecting modern sophisticated network attacks. To overcome these limitations, deep learning is suggested as a promising approach for developing more robust attack detection frameworks for SDNs, by automatically learning discriminative features from the network traffic data.

Mahmoud [16] proposed an anomaly detection model using LSTM autoencoder and One-Class SVM (OC-SVM) for intrusion detection in networks. The main idea is that only normal traffic data is used for the training model. In 2016, [17] also recommend SVM for detecting attacks in SDN Networks and got the result of detection rate in range 92–98%, but for Distributed Deny of Services (DDos) only. In the same context, the article [16] uses an LSTM-Autoencoder that learns compressed representations of input data. OC-SVM then detects anomalies in the compressed feature vectors from the LSTM-Autoencoder. It demonstrates a good performance with 90.5% accuracy, higher than just using OC-SVM to detect malicious data (87.5%). The model presented in paper [16] achieves considerably reduced training and testing times in contrast to using only OC-SVM, as indicated by the experimental results. The LSTM-Autoencoder-OC-SVM model yields highly encouraging results, especially when confronted with unseen data.

In [18], a deep learning-based intrusion detection and prevention system (DL-IDPS) for SDN networks is proposed, which focuses on detecting SSH brute force attacks and DDoS attacks based on traffic characteristics. The article evaluates multilayer perceptron (MLP), convolutional neural network (CNN), long short-term memory (LSTM), and stacked autoencoder (SAE) models. DL-IDPS mitigates attacks by blocking flows or dropping packets after MLP detection. Despite evidence that the proposed DL-IDPS [18] framework effectively mitigates DDoS attacks and reduces resource strain, further evaluation is required to determine its capability in detecting other network intrusion techniques like Probe, Botnet or Exploitation attacks. The experiments [18] are limited to DDoS, SSH brute force attacks only. This research did not mention unseen attack data.

A review of prior literature reveals several studies that have explored the application of machine learning [12,13,15,17] and deep learning [16,18] models for intrusion detection tasks in SDN environments, with some promising results reported. However, a deeper analysis suggests there is still substantial room for improving the performance of machine learning-based anomaly detection solutions on key metrics like accuracy, false positive rate, and generalization ability. The current results, while valuable, seem to fall short of fully realizing the potential gains machine learning methods could bring to network security in the emerging SDN paradigm.

4   Proposed Model

4.1   Dataset

We employ the recently updated InSDN dataset [5], a specific dataset designed for SDN attack evaluation, to assess the performance of our proposed model. This dataset is particularly valuable as it is one of the first comprehensive collections available for assessing Intrusion Detection Systems (IDSs) in SDN environments.

The InSDN dataset [5] comprises various types of normal traffic applications (HTTP, HTTPS, DNS, Email, FTP, and SSH) and includes common attacks found in conventional networks, as well as SDN-specific attacks. Attack types range from Probe, Botnet, DoS, DDoS, Exploitation, Brute force to Web attacks, originating from both internal and external sources to simulate real-world attack scenarios. The dataset is available in both PCAP and CSV formats and is divided into three groups: OVS group with external attacks, attacks against the Metasploitable 2 server, and a group representing normal traffic. The dataset contains a total of 343,939 samples, comprising both normal network traffic as well as malicious attack traffic. Out of these, 68,424 samples represent normal benign traffic, while the remaining 275,515 samples consist of various attack traffic instances. For more, the dataset boasts over 80 features generated using the CICFlowMeter tool [19]. However, not all of these features can be extracted inside the SDN environment. In SDN, only statistical features can be extracted from the SDN controller through OpenFlow calls to the SDN switches (e.g., flow duration, number of packets, number of bytes). For this goal, the same framework of [20] is used to find the sub-features, which are easily retrieved directly by the SDN controller quarries or by competition calculation of the flow statistics. The original framework [20] employed a selection of 50 features to accomplish their research goal. In this thesis, a reduced set of 48 features [5] is employed, with the exclusion of source and destination IPs from the experiments. These two attributes are subject to alteration across different networks, and malicious actors can employ genuine users' IP addresses. Consequently, training the classifier model with these attributes could introduce bias towards these socket features, leading to the issue of overfitting. To test the effectiveness of our model for anomaly detection, we use attack samples during testing that differ from those used in training.

4.2 Data Preparation

Initially, the normalization technique is applied to map the value of features between 0 and 1. Reshape the 1D-dimensional 48 network traffic features to create an image structure with dimensions of 8×6. This process helps to reduce the number of weights within a convolution layer through the parameter sharing concept. The symbolic features are converted into numerical data. The label column has several attack classes as well as the normal class. The normal label is assigned a value of 0, while all attack labels are set to 1. In all experiments, the pairing of data was done after dividing it into separate training and test sets to guarantee that there was no cross-contamination that could influence the outcomes.

The normal data was initially divided into two parts with a ratio of 7:3 for training and testing. Similarly, the attack data was split into two parts with a ratio of 7:3 for training and testing as well. Afterward, these parts were combined to create the training dataset and testing dataset, maintaining the same normal:attack ratio as in the original InSDN dataset [5].

We paired the data by sequentially combining each record with another. This made the pairing process very time-consuming, resulting in long training times. Moreover, after training the model on the data obtained from this pairing approach, we observed that the model suffered from overfitting, meaning it became overly specialized to the training data and did not generalize well to new data.

Therefore, we employed a different pair methodology. To create pairs of data within the same class, the normal data was divided into two equal parts with a ratio of 5:5. Each record in the first part was then paired with a random record from the second part. This ensures that each new pair consists of different records within the same class. The same process was applied to the attack data to create pairs within the attack class. This process generates new records with a label of 1, indicating that the records belong to the same class. To create pairs of data between distinct classes, each normal dataset record was paired with a random attack dataset record. This process produced new records with a label of 0, indicating that the records are from distinct classes. A record comprises of a pair of normal and attack samples, and a new record is created by exchanging attack and normal samples.

4.3 Experimental Setup

Our experimental environment is on a PC with the following configuration: Intel(R) Core(TM) i5-6200U CPU @ 2.30 GHz 2.40 GHz, 8 GB RAM. The experiment was designed and executed using Python programming language, where Keras with Tensorflow backend library is used for all proposed approaches. When we train the model, we use Python version 3.9.0, sci-kit learn 1.2.2, TensorFlow 2.12.0, numpy 1.23.5, pandas 2.0.3.

4.4 Building Model

This section introduces the architecture of the proposed model to learn and classify the network traffic. The network architecture of the model is depicted in Fig. 2. The model is designed to determine whether two grayscale images are similar or dissimilar based on their learned representations. The proposed architecture comprises two identical CNN branches, each processing one of the two input images. Model Architecture: The model begins with an Input Layer, accepting two grayscale images with spatial dimensions of 8×6 pixels. These images are subsequently fed into the shared Convolutional Neural Network, serving as the main feature extraction backbone. This shared CNN consists of two Convolutional layers with Rectified Linear Unit (ReLU) activation functions and two MaxPooling layers. The first Convolutional layer employs 32 filters of size 3×3, while the second Convolutional layer uses 64 filters of the same size. The MaxPooling layers with a pool size of 2×2 are incorporated to reduce spatial dimensions and capture significant patterns from the input images. Following the second MaxPooling layer, the output feature maps are flattened into a 1-dimensional vector, which is then passed through a Dense layer with 64 units and a ReLU activation function. This Dense layer acts as a fully connected layer to further process the extracted features from the CNN. A key element of the proposed architecture is the Siamese Architecture, where the two input images are simultaneously processed through the shared CNN. As a result, two feature vectors are generated, representing the learned representations of the two input images. To combine the information from both images effectively, the feature vectors from both branches are concatenated using the Concatenate layer. This concatenated feature vector contains essential information about the combined features from the input images. For higher-level abstraction learning, the concatenated feature vector is then fed through another Dense layer with 64 units and ReLU activation. The final decision on image similarity is made through a Dense layer with a single unit and a sigmoid activation function, resulting in a binary decision indicating whether the input images are similar or dissimilar (Fig. 1).

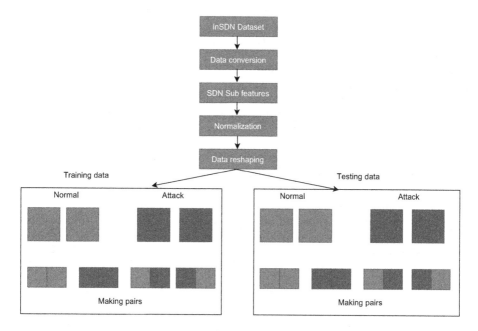

Fig. 1. Flow of Preprocessing data

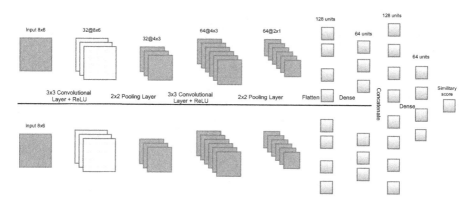

Fig. 2. Our proposed model for detecting attacks in SDN network.

After training phase, the model can compute the similarity score of two input images (between 0 and 1) The normal anchor is a sample that is used to compare with another sample to determine the similarity between them. The normal anchor is the mean or median of the normal training dataset. The normal anchor is calculated in two ways: - Mean: The average number; found by adding all data points and dividing by the number of data points. - Median: The middle number; found by ordering all data points and picking out the one in the middle (or if there are two middle numbers, taking the mean of those two numbers).

The normal anchor is the mean or median of the normal training dataset. The normal anchor is calculated in two ways:

- Mean: The average number; found by adding all data points and dividing by the number of data points.
- Median: The middle number; found by ordering all data points and picking out the one in the middle (or if there are two middle numbers, taking the mean of those two numbers).

The median (mean) sample is determined by calculating the median (mean) of each feature. Therefore, the normal anchor is the median or mean sample of the normal dataset. Both methods seek a center point or representation of "normal samples" from the normal training dataset. The similarity of a new sample to the normal anchor and attack anchor is then calculated to determine its class. If the similarity score of the sample with the normal anchor is greater than the similarity score of the sample with the attack anchor, then the sample is predicted as normal. On the contrary, if the similarity score with the attack anchor is greater, the sample will be predicted as an attack.

5   Evaluation Results

Our Siamese-based CNN model is assessed using four performance indicators: Accuracy (Acc), Precision (Pre), Recall (Rec), and F1 measure. These indicators are computed using mathematical representations specified in Eqs. 1, 2, 3, and 4, respectively.

$$Acc = \frac{TP + TN}{TP + TN + FP + FN} \tag{1}$$

$$Pre = \frac{TP}{TP + FP} \tag{2}$$

$$Rec = \frac{TP}{TP + FN} \tag{3}$$

$$F1 = \frac{2 \times Pre \times Rec}{Pre + Rec} \tag{4}$$

True Positive (TP) and True Negative (TN) denote a model's accurate predictions. On the other hand, False Positives (FP) and False Negatives (FN) refer to events that were incorrectly classified or predicted by the model.

Table 1. Performance metrics of different methods.

Method	Accuracy (%)	Precision (%)		Recall (%)		F1-score (%)	
		Normal	Attack	Normal	Attack	Normal	Attack
Logistic Regression	96.12	98.31	95.69	81.96	99.65	89.40	97.63
Decision tree	99.14	97.69	99.51	98.01	99.42	97.85	99.46
Random Forest	99.22	98.30	99.45	97.80	99.58	98.05	99.51
CNN	99.14	98.91	99.20	96.76	99.73	97.82	99.47
Siamese + Median anchor	**99.98**	**99.93**	**99.99**	**99.97**	**99.98**	**99.95**	**99.99**

In this evaluation, we contrast our model with a number of methods, such as CNN, Logistic Regression, Decision Tree, and Random Forest. The categorization metrics for the normal and attack classes are shown in Table 1, which also compares how well our model performs to the aforementioned traditional methods. The results reveal that the Siamese-based approach showcases exceptional capabilities in network attack detection within SDNs. The performance metrics illustrate not only the accuracy achieved by the proposed approach but also its consistency across multiple metrics, including precision, recall, and F1-score. While the achieved accuracy of 99.98% serves as a testament to the effectiveness of the proposed approach, it is important to scrutinize other metrics such as precision and recall. The proposed approach consistently achieves high precision values for both normal and attack classes, underscoring its ability to minimize false positives and false negatives. Similarly, the high recall values indicate the approach's proficiency in capturing a significant proportion of true positive instances. Although the proposed model achieves results above 99%, outperforming baseline methods by approximately 0.8%, the Siamese-based approach comes at the cost of sacrificing execution time (both during training and testing). The Siamese Network, while delivering impressive accuracy gains, demands longer training periods due to its need to compare each pair of data points for effective learning. This extended training time is a trade-off for the model's enhanced performance. Similarly, the testing phase also experiences increased time consumption as it involves comparing data pairs. In comparison to traditional methods like Logistic Regression, Decision Tree, Random Forest, and CNN, the proposed Siamese-based approach exhibits a notable advantage in network attack detection. The comprehensive analysis suggests that the Siamese architecture's focus on similarity comparison and feature extraction contributes to its superiority in handling complex and dynamic network traffic patterns. Furthermore, the approach's high precision in detecting both normal and attack instances indicates its potential to minimize the risk of misclassifications, thereby reducing the operational overhead associated with false alarms. This property can be particularly crucial in ensuring swift and accurate responses to potential security threats.

6 Conclusion

In this paper, we have conducted an in-depth examination of recent research efforts utilizing Siamese neural network architectures for intrusion detection tasks within SDN environments. We perform our benchmarking experiments on InSDN dataset. The proposed Siamese network-based NIDS method shows significant improvement in detection accuracy over conventional techniques, achieving near 100% accuracy on the evaluation dataset. Moreover, the model provides an effective deep learning approach customized for SDN environments using optimized data pairing to handle overfitting. And the results will facilitate the development of reliable anomaly detection systems tailored for securing next-generation SDN architectures against emerging threats.

In the future, we plan to evaluate the approach on real-world SDN systems to assess performance impacts like latency and expand the binary classification to identify specific attack types to provide granular actionable information. Furthermore, we will also investigate ensemble models combining Siamese networks with other deep learning architectures to further improve generalizability.

References

1. ONF. Software-Defined Networking (SDN) Definition. https://www.opennetworking.org
2. Karakus, M., Durresi, A.: Quality of service (QoS) in software defined networking (SDN): a survey. J. Netw. Comput. Appl. **80**, 200–218 (2017). https://doi.org/10.1016/j.jnca.2016.12.019. ISSN: 1084-8045
3. Alhaj, A.N., Dutta, N.: Analysis of security attacks in SDN network: a comprehensive survey. In: Sarma, H.K.D., Balas, V.E., Bhuyan, B., Dutta, N. (eds.) Contemporary Issues in Communication, Cloud and Big Data Analytics. LNNS, vol. 281, pp. 27–37. Springer, Singapore (2022). https://doi.org/10.1007/978-981-16-4244-9_3
4. Dargahi, T., Caponi, A., Ambrosin, M., Bianchi, G., Conti, M.: A survey on the security of stateful SDN data planes. IEEE Commun. Surv. Tutor. **19**(3), 1701–1725 (2017)
5. Elsayed, M.S., Le-Khac, N.-A., Jurcut, A.D.: InSDN: a novel SDN intrusion dataset. IEEE Access **8**, 165263–165284 (2020)
6. O'Shea, K., Nash, R.: An introduction to convolutional neural networks. arXiv preprint arXiv:1511.08458 (2015)
7. Li, Z., et al.: A survey of convolutional neural networks: analysis, applications, and prospects. IEEE Trans. Neural Netw. Learn. Syst. **33**(12), 6999–7019 (2021)
8. Bromley, J., et al.: Signature verification using a "siamese" time delay neural network. In: Advances in Neural Information Processing Systems, vol. 6 (1993)
9. Koch, G., Zemel, R., Salakhutdinov, R.: Siamese neural networks for one-shot image recognition. In: International Conference on Machine Learning, Lille, France, pp. 1–8 (2015)
10. Jeong, Y., Lee, S., Park, D., Park, K.H.: Accurate age estimation using multi-task siamese network-based deep metric learning for frontal face images. Symmetry **10**(385), 1–15 (2018)

11. Zhang, C., Liu, W., Ma, H., Fu, H.: Siamese neural network based gait recognition for human identification. In: International Conference on Acoustics, Speech and Signal Processing (ICASSP), Shanghai, China, pp. 2832–2836. IEEE (2016)
12. Tang, T.A., Mhamdi, L., McLernon, D., Zaidi, S.A.R., Ghogho, M.: Deep learning approach for network intrusion detection in software defined networking. In: 2016 International Conference on Wireless Networks and Mobile Communications (WINCOM), Fez, Morocco, pp. 258–263 (2016). https://doi.org/10.1109/WINCOM.2016.7777224
13. Abubakar, A., Pranggono, B.: Machine learning based intrusion detection system for software defined networks, pp. 138–143 (2017). https://doi.org/10.1109/EST.2017.8090413
14. Tavallaee, M., Bagheri, E., Lu, W., Ghorbani, A.A.: A detailed analysis of the KDD CUP 99 data set. In: Proceedings of the IEEE Symposium on Computational Intelligence for Security and Defense Applications, pp. 1–6. IEEE (2009)
15. Elsayed, M.S., Le-Khac, N.-A., Dev, S., Jurcut, A.D.: Machine-learning techniques for detecting attacks in SDN. In: 2019 IEEE 7th International Conference on Computer Science and Network Technology (ICCSNT) (2019). https://doi.org/10.1109/iccsnt47585.2019.8962519
16. Said Elsayed, M., Le-Khac, N.-A., Dev, S., Jurcut, A.D.: Network anomaly detection using LSTM based autoencoder. In: Proceedings of the 16th ACM Symposium on QoS and Security for Wireless and Mobile Networks (Q2SWinet 2020), pp. 37–45. Association for Computing Machinery, New York (2020). https://doi.org/10.1145/3416013.3426457
17. Li, D., Yu, C., Zhou, Q., Yu, J.: Using SVM to detect DDoS attack in SDN network. In: IOP Conference Series: Materials Science and Engineering, vol. 466, p. 012003 (2018). https://doi.org/10.1088/1757-899X/466/1/012003
18. Lee, T.-H., Chang, L.-H., Syu, C.-W.: Deep learning enabled intrusion detection and prevention system over SDN networks. In: 2020 IEEE International Conference on Communications Workshops (ICC Workshops), Dublin, Ireland, pp. 1–6 (2020). https://doi.org/10.1109/ICCWorkshops49005.2020.9145085
19. Draper-Gil, G., Lashkari, A.H., Mamun, M.S.I., Ghorbani, A.A.: Characterization of encrypted and VPN traffic using time-related. In: Proceedings of the 2nd International Conference on Information Systems Security and Privacy (ICISSP), pp. 407–414 (2016)
20. Krishnan, P., Duttagupta, S., Achuthan, K.: VARMAN: multi-plane security framework for software defined networks. Comput. Commun. **148**, 215–239 (2019)

An Efficient Machine Learning-Based Web Application Firewall with Deep Automated Pattern Categorization

Cong-Vu Trinh[1], Thien-Thanh Le[1], Minh-Khoi Le-Nguyen[1], Dinh-Thuan Le[1], Van-Hoa Nguyen[2], and Khuong Nguyen-An[1(✉)]

[1] Ho Chi Minh city University of Technology (HCMUT), VNU-HCM, Ho Chi Minh City, Vietnam
{vu.trinhmm64,thanh.le,1652318,thuanle,nakhuong}@hcmut.edu.vn
[2] Polaris Infosec Pte. Ltd., Ho Chi Minh City, Vietnam
hoanv@polarisec.com

Abstract. Web application firewalls (WAFs) are frequently utilized since they are simple services and offer considerable defense against various cyber attacks. However, based on rules and signatures, traditional WAFs have significant false positive rates (34%.

Keywords: Web Application Firewall · machine learning · network request categorizing · network request analyzing · ModSecurity

1 Introduction

Web applications are essential for various purposes, including social media, email, banking, online shopping, education, entertainment, etc. They have become necessities for every business, brand, institution, organization, and individual. However, these applications are attractive targets for remote attackers due to their publicity and accessibility. Cybercriminals can exploit flaws in web applications, such as programming faults, misconfigured servers, application design errors, and failure to validate forms, allowing adversaries to access databases containing sensitive information.

Therefore, WAFs are vital in organizational security systems. The challenge of enhancing and developing new techniques to improve the efficiency of WAF has been raised since the inception of WAF. Given that traditional WAFs like ModSecurity displayed several weaknesses, including high false positive rates—meaning legitimate traffic being mistakenly blocked and requiring constant manual updates and tweaks, alternative approaches leveraging machine learning have proven more effective in the current era.

Enhancing cybersecurity is imperative due to the potential consequences posed by cybercriminals. Given the pressing need for robust cybersecurity measures, our objective is to improve the capabilities of WAFs. Our approach involves

ⓒ The Author(s), under exclusive license to Springer Nature Singapore Pte Ltd. 2023
T. K. Dang et al. (Eds.): FDSE 2023, CCIS 1925, pp. 212–225, 2023.
https://doi.org/10.1007/978-981-99-8296-7_15

developing a machine learning-based web application firewall, focusing on mitigating the high false positive rate and intrinsic vulnerability of rule-based WAFs while ensuring the WAF's responsiveness. Our system uses two fast and simple machine-learning models. Each model will run independently to generate an output, then combine the result to achieve accuracy and time constraints sufficient for an effective WAF. The main obstacle in this work is balancing between time constraint, which is supposed to be in milliseconds, and the effectiveness of WAFs.

2   Related Works

Malicious request detection has been a focus of recent studies, with several systems being developed. They propose solutions for particular or different types of harmful requests. Existing malicious website detection approaches can be divided into two categories based on their architecture: machine learning-based WAFs, which only use machine learning models to detect abnormal requests, and machine learning-assisted WAFs to improve existing WAFs.

2.1   Machine Learning-Based WAF

WAF based on machine learning is a type of web application firewall built on machine learning techniques to detect and prevent attacks on web applications. It uses machine learning algorithms to analyze data from incoming requests and responses from web applications, thereby creating rules to identify and prevent attacks. With continuous learning, the machine learning-based WAF can automatically update new rules to detect new and more advanced attacks. This makes it possible for WAF to protect web applications against unknown attacks and ensure the safety of user and business data. Some significant articles have an approach to using machine learning to create a WAF.

A. Shaheed and M. Kurdy [1] proposed a model for a web application firewall that utilizes machine learning and features engineering to detect common web attacks. The model uses Naive Bayes with cross-validation to analyze incoming requests, extracting four features that describe HTTP request parts (URL, payload, and headers) and classifying normal or anomalous incoming requests. The model achieved a classification accuracy of 99.6% with research studies and 98.8% with real web server datasets.

I. Jemal et al. [2] developed a Smart Web Application Firewall (SWAF) using a Convolutional Neural Network (CNN) to detect malicious HTTP requests and reduce attack detection overhead time. They proposed compressing HTTP requests and reducing CNN neurons. They also used 5-fold cross-validation and ASCII embedding for better accuracy. Furthermore, they filtered CNN neurons to achieve a high attack detection rate of 98.1%.

B. Dawadi et al. [3] built a layered architecture of WAF using Long Short-Term Memory (LSTM) for detecting DDoS attacks, SQL injection, and XSS attacks. The first detection layer achieved 97.57% accuracy, while the second layer achieved 89.34% accuracy. Rather than training the module with the single dataset, training the module with separate datasets improves results, as data and attacks differ. Analysis of features and parameters reduces false positives during traffic filtering, proving the effectiveness of WAF.

S. Toprak and A. Yavuz [4] focus on WAF systems using single and stacked LSTM layers architecture to detect malicious HTTP web requests using hyper-parameter values. They trained a semi-supervised approach with the `PayloadAllTheThings` dataset and used normal payloads of HTTP Dataset CSIC 2010. The proposed model achieved high F1 scores and success in detecting and classifying attacks. The resulting models are promising for detecting specific attack types using a small attack payload dataset, but a dataset for sample payloads remains challenging.

B. Gogoi et al. [5] assessed the effectiveness of machine learning methods in detecting XSS attacks in web apps and websites using SVM. They developed a custom Apache webserver module and used 10-fold cross-validation to prevent overfitting. The results showed that linear and nonlinear SVMs successfully separated XSS attack inputs from benign web application inputs. However, nonlinear SVM performed better in accuracy and F1-score but required a longer time in model fitting.

T. A. M. Devi et al. [6] developed a machine learning-based approach for web application firewalls using logistic regression to classify legitimate and malicious queries. The study uses Jupyter Notebooks to convert data to numeric features and apply the N-Gram method and TF-IDF vectorizer. The results showed 99.93% accuracy, precision of 98.83%, and F1-score of 99%. However, the small dataset may limit the generalizability of the proposed method.

2.2 Improving Existing WAF by Using Machine Learning

While machine learning-based WAFs are effective, they demand heavy resources and require significant processing time. Some works have been implemented to tackle this problem; the most notable ones focus on compromising between a traditional rule-based WAF and small machine-learning models.

M.-T. Nguyen et al. [7] use machine learning methods to enhance WAF performance by detecting attacks on web applications using support vector machines (SVM) and HTTP requests analysis. The approach has an accuracy and F1-score of around 99.9% but is only effective for variable query length attacks and requires high computational power. Improvements include combining machine learning methods, increasing query quality attributes, and updating signature databases.

N.-T. Tran et al. [8] developed a WAF system using ModSecurity and ModSecurity CRS to lower false-positive rates. They combined ModSecurity and CRS with Decision Tree and Random Forest machine learning models. Experimental results showed a significant improvement in the false-positive rate but required a decrease in the true-positive rate to reach 1.26%. The trained model significantly reduced the false-positive rate in ModSecurity CRS's final decision formula, making it more suitable for real-world applications.

A. Alshammari and A. Aldribi [9] propose a detection architecture using multiple machine learning models for IDS to detect anomalous network traffic. The study uses a dataset of both malicious and legitimate traffic. The data preprocessing phase significantly influences the results, with Naive Bayes and SVM only having a 60% accuracy, while others reach approximately 100%. However, the large dataset and the need for real-time response affect the model's performance.

T.-C.-H. Nguyen et al. [10] proposed a machine learning approach using WAF rules to train a self-reliant decision model, resulting in neutral results. The module has been tested but has limitations such as a small dataset, skewed ML model, and limited testing of malicious request validators. This approach inspires our module. We aim to finalize this module but combine it with another machine learning model to specialize it to determine incoming requests independent of the WAF rule.

3   The Proposed Model

As processing time is our critical criterion, and computational resources are a luxury to most web owners, our work focuses on the machine learning-assisted approach. Figure 1 illustrates our proposed model for the machine learning-based WAF. The proposed model consists of four phases: feature preprocessing, feature extraction and representation, ensemble learning-based prediction, and decision-making. The first two phases will tokenize and vectorize the data once collected to feed it to the ensemble learning-based model. The ensemble learning-based prediction phase consists of two individual models, each being trained using different feature sets. In the last phase, the decision model will combine the two predictions from each smaller model in the third phase.

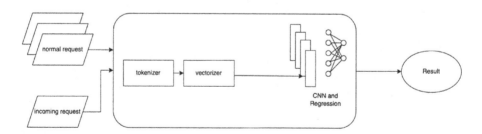

Fig. 1. Decision model for the combination of CNN and the Regression model

3.1   Phase 1: Feature Preprocessing (Tokenizer)

In this phase, the inputs were sanitized and normalized. The URL and the body of HTTP requests were preprocessed using Natural Language Processing (NLP) techniques. Since HTTP request bodies tend to contain not only words but also special characters and punctuation, the collected text data were normalized to reduce feature complexity and enhance the classification performance. The normalization procedure consists of tokenization and eliminating stop words, preparing the text for vectorization in the next phase.

3.2 Phase 2: Feature Extraction and Representation (Vectorizer)

The tokenized HTTP body and URL are vectorized using a standard word vectorizer (TF-IDF or word2vec). The model is trained using the structured language dataset itself. The output of the vectorizer is a list of vectors representing each word of the tokens.

3.3 Phase 3: Ensemble Learning-Based Prediction

Our proposed approach is explained as follows.

It is observed that when attackers attempt to breach a system, they must try to execute or inject something executable into the system. Malicious requests must, therefore, be script-based or written in computer languages. Most standard online applications and services, particularly API applications, appear to accept just plain text queries, i.e., requests in JSON or XML.

We aim to classify requests supplied as inputs to determine whether they are harmful or inoffensive. The requests then can be categorized into five categories, as inspired by [10]:

- **Plain text.** Request that contains data but does not trigger any machine execution, typically in HTML, JSON, XML, CSV, etc.
- **Client-side script.** Request in the form of programming languages or scripts that can be executed on the client's machine.
- **Server-side script.** Request in the form of programming languages (mostly back-end programming languages like PHP, java, python, and so on) that can change the behavior of the application or web.
- **Shell script.** Request in the form of shell scripts that can run jobs on the server or change the server's or operating system's behavior.
- **SQL script.** Request that, in the form of SQL, can be used to query data from the database.

As presented in [10], *normal requests to a server have the same category.* For example, a static web request may only contain plain text, API server requests are mostly JSON format, incoming queries to a database are SQL, or online compilers use programming language-format requests. A malicious request must be in a different category from the normal requests like a script request to a static web server or API server can be considered code injection or command injection, SQL requests to an API server may be SQLi, or script requests to a database is command injection or stored XSS attacks. We can determine if a request is 'normal' to a server by comparing the types of incoming suspicious requests to the average categories of regular requests. If the resemblance is low, we might presume that the origin of the inbound request is unusual. For instance, if a typical request to a secured server is in JSON format (plain text), but a suspicious request is in JavaScript (client-side script), we can deduce that the incoming Request is malicious. If a suspicious request is in XML format (plain text), we may assume that the user made a mistake and the alarm was false.

The second hypothesis can be presented as *all regular requests will have a similar pattern; the same goes for malicious requests*. For example, a request with a URL ending in.exe or.php is frequently malicious, and a request with work like "SELECT", "DROP", or "TABLE" is unquestionably an SQLi. By analyzing its content, we can implement logistic regression to identify if an incoming request is normal or abnormal.

We can create a CNN model from the hypotheses to detect the type of Request. Then, we compare the incoming requests with the "normal" corresponding category and decide whether the requests are malicious or not by using logistic regression.

3.4 Phase 4: Decision Model

Our architecture (illustrated in Fig. 2) suggests a reasonable decision model for the combined result: *when two predictions are the same, the result is straightforward*. When the logistic regression model decides that the Request is malicious, but the CNN model predicts the Request is normal, then the CNN is favored. Otherwise, the Regression model classified the Request as valid, but the CNN predicted it as abnormal. We'll select the regression. The decision model can be expressed in a table (Table 1).

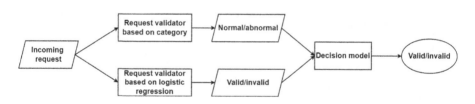

Fig. 2. Malicious request validator architecture

Table 1. Decision table of Regression model and CNN model

Regression model	CNN model	Result
Valid	Normal	Valid
Valid	Abnormal	Valid
Invalid	Normal	Valid
Invalid	Abnormal	Invalid

The request is routed through the module, which predicts the category. The category of suspicious requests is then compared with the standard category. Then, the Regression model will determine whether the request is good or bad, combined with the normal or abnormal status to decide the result.

4 Experiments and Evaluation

This section describes the used dataset, the experimental procedures, and the performance evaluation.

4.1 Sources and Preprocessing of Datasets

This research used the HTTP dataset CSIC 2010[1], which is publicly available. The dataset contains the generated traffic targeted to an e-commerce web application. The study also uses another publicly available malicious URL dataset[2]. The URLs in the dataset were categorized into normal and malicious requests, including attacks such as SQL injection, buffer overflow, information gathering, file disclosure, CRLF injection, XSS, server-side injection, parameter tampering, etc. The whole combined dataset consists of over 400,000 unique already labeled URLs.

For the CNN model, a sample of 400,000 chunks of code is randomly extracted[3], and only from the languages relevant to our classification in the proposed approach.

The dataset was split into training and testing sets with 80% for training and 20% for testing.

4.2 Experimental Procedures

In our model, TF-IDF weighted word2vec is used as the HTTP body vectorizer. The textual vector is implemented with a height of 150. The Limited Broyden-Fletcher-Goldfarb-Shanno (L-BFGS) is the optimization algorithm for the Logistic Regression model. L-BFGS is one of the variants of the gradient descent algorithm and has proven to have better accuracy than the plain gradient descent algorithm. For the CNN models, the structure is initialized as described in Fig. 3.

4.3 Performance Evaluation

To validate the detection performance of the proposed model, five performance measures were used: the overall accuracy, the detection rate (recall), the precision, the F1 score, the false-positive rate (FPR), and the false-negative rate (FNR). These performance metrics are frequently employed in the literature to

---

[1] Available at https://www.isi.csic.es/dataset/.

[2] Available at https://www.kaggle.com/datasets/antonyj453/urldataset.

[3] Available at https://www.kaggle.com/datasets/simiotic/github-code-snippets.

Fig. 3. Architecture of malicious request validator model.

assess the efficacy of malware detection technologies. The same machine-learning methods used to determine the associated malicious URL detection were also used to evaluate the suggested model.

This module validates machine learning WAFs; the main goal is to reduce the false positive rate of WAFs overall. Then, the exceptional true positive rate is our ultimate goal, especially on category *plain text*.

Another vital criterion is time efficiency. A WAF must respond immediately. Therefore, the time processing of each request in the model must be less than ten milliseconds.

4.4   Result and Discussion

The above dataset has validated the proposed machine learning-based WAF model and performance measures.

Logistic Regression Validator. The experimental results of logistic regression are presented in Fig. 4 with train accuracy 88.56% and test accuracy 86.89%. The detailed evaluation of the model is presented in Table 2.

Table 2. Logistic regression model evaluation

Label	Precision	Recall	F1-Score	Support
bad	0.52	0.86	0.65	1430
good	0.97	0.87	0.92	8568
Accuracy			0.87	9998
Macro avg	0.75	0.87	0.78	9998
Weighted avg	0.91	0.87	0.88	9998

The model has an excellent chance of detecting normal requests with a precision of 97%. However, it performs poorly in identifying malicious requests. The recall is not advised as a metric for evaluating malicious request detection since FP is more critical. This problem is not alarming, as we will discuss further in this article.

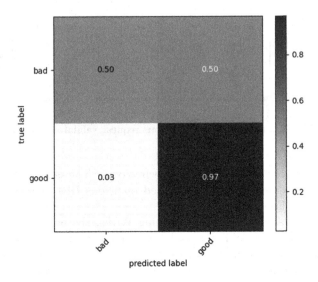

Fig. 4. Confusion matrix of logistic regression model

CNN Classifier. The CNN model is trained in 10 epochs with batch size 128. The precision metric and loss of the model during the training process are plotted in Fig. 5.

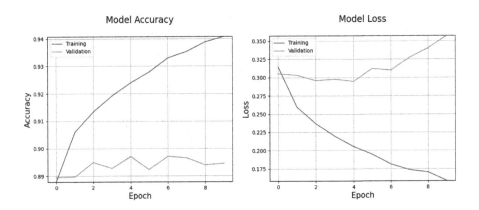

Fig. 5. The precision metric and loss of the model

It appears that the model's training and validation sets differ noticeably from one another. The loss of the training dataset decreases continuously, while the loss of the validation set decreases at early steps and starts increasing after a certain point. This demonstrates how "overfitting" our model was. The validation loss began below the training loss, then slightly decreased and increased after the fourth epoch. This leads to the stagnation of validation accuracy when the *val_accuracy* does not seem to increase. The confusion matrix is displayed in Fig. 6.

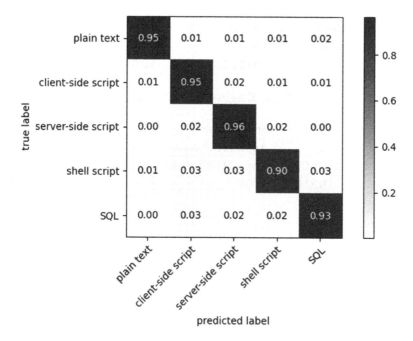

Fig. 6. Structural language classifier model trained

While the values for other categories are only from 90% to 95% corresponding-ingly, it appears that the model has a fair possibility of recognizing regular requests (plain text) with pretty good accuracy and a tiny chance of false alert or miss detection. As the following four categories are all programming languages, it is difficult for the model to separate them, and their weights are lower than plain text (one-fifth). Then, the model has succeeded in reducing the blocking of legitimate requests, i.e., reducing the false positive rate of WAF.

The evaluation metric of the model is presented in Table 3. It is notice-able that the model does not have the best accuracy (only 95.75% on the test set). However, because there are just two convolutional layers in the model, it processes requests on average in 29ms (with system specifications shown in Table 4), meaning that the response is returned nowhere instantly. That time is still acceptable despite not reaching our goal yet (since our model requires combining two different models to produce the desired result).

End-to-End Experiments. In these experiments, we consider the default structural language category as plain text, showing that our module is defending

Table 3. Evaluating the model by Precision, Recall, and F1-score.

Label	Accuracy	Precision	Recall	F1-score
Plain text	98.56%	0.95	0.99	0.97
Client-side script	97.91%	0.95	0.95	0.95
Server-side script	97.29%	0.96	0.99	0.97
Shell script	98.4%	0.9	0.36	0.52
SQL	99.34%	0.93	0.63	0.75

Table 4. System specifications.

Hardware	Specification
CPU	Apple M1 (8 cores)
GPU	Apple M1 8-core integrated GPU
RAM	16 GB

an API application (which accepts just plain text queries, i.e., requests in JSON or XML). We are using the CSIC 2010 dataset to test our model and compare our work with the related works that also train on the same dataset. The detailed results of the experiments are presented in Table 5 and Fig. 7.

Table 5. Evaluation of our WAF.

Label	Precision	1-Precision	Recall	1-Recall	F1-score
bad	0.7157	0.2843	0.9955	0.0045	0.8327
good	0.9966	0.0112	0.7686	0.2314	0.8679
Accuracy			0.8523		
Misclassification rate			0.1477		
Macro F1			0.8503		
Weighted F1			0.8549		

These experiments show that the WAF model performs excellently in correctly detecting normal requests with a 99.66% chance. This implies that it is incredibly uncommon for our WAF to intercept a legitimate request unintentionally. On the other hand, the WAF's performance in identifying malicious requests was found to be sub-optimal, with precision values of 0.7157. This seems to be a problem. But attack detection should not be emphasized because when a hacker targets a website, he must test out a wide range of attack techniques, from simple to complicated, and send many malicious requests quickly. As a result, this issue is not concerning. Only around 80% of incoming attacks need to be detected for a model to alert administrators to take action to prevent further attacks. The

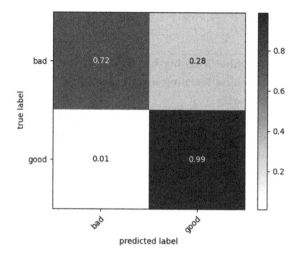

Fig. 7. End-to-end confusion matrix

extremely high precision in predicting normal requests also means that we have succeeded in reducing the FP rate in Traditional WAF. Therefore, the WAF has passed the FP rate criteria.

The evaluation of our models and other related works is presented in Table 6. Even though our WAF is still far from perfect, it has perfected the core elements of a WAF, such as accepting requests as input and returning whether or not the requests were denied. When our machine learning-based WAF is compared to traditional WAF, in this case, ModSecurity, it is clear that our WAF performs significantly better, with 85.23% accuracy compared to 51.46% of ModSecurity, on the same dataset. We also attempt to apply our machine learning models to ModSecurity to determine whether a machine learning-aided WAF may outperform a WAF under the same circumstances. In this instance, it is still insufficient to be compared to our WAF, thereby showing that, under the same conditions, machine learning-based WAF is better than the other two approaches. However, it is still insufficient for our WAF to be considered superior to other studies. It still has weaknesses that can be overcome in the future. In reality, if you look at it from the standpoint of an application, 99.66% of blocking the request is sufficient and even considered average. If a model has a precision in predicting a legitimate request of 99%, that means out of every 100 legitimate requests that pass through the WAF system on average (just counting different requests), one of them will be mistakenly labeled as an attack. If the WAF mentioned above is used to defend a customer website and even one request is unintentionally blocked, it may render the user useless. It will be even worse if customers are prevented from logging in or transacting on e-commerce websites. The accuracy required to forecast the "normal" class must, therefore, be extremely high (above 99.9%), but the accuracy needed to predict the "attack" class must be at a tolerable level (about 80%).

Table 6. Accuracy of our proposed model compared with related works.

Method	CSIC 2010
Our machine learning-based WAF	85.23%
Our machine learning-assisted WAF	66.98%
ModSecurity	51.46%
A. Shaheed et al. [1] (2022)	99.59%
I. Jemal et al. [2] (2022)	98.1%
S. Toprak et al. [4] (2022)	99.03%
T. A. M. Devi et al. [6] (2022)	99.93%

The weakness of this WAF is that it takes an average of 90ms to process a request, depending on the type of request. This is an unacceptable time for WAF. WAF must be able to handle thousands of requests per second. Otherwise, it will significantly affect the user experience. So, in the latency criteria, our WAF has failed to pass.

5   Discussion and Conclusion

Our dataset is small for the HTTP request vectorizer, which is the common problem of [6], but it was used to prove that our machine learning-assisted prototype is applicable. Of course, using a larger dataset definitely results in better results. Categorizing the data based on locale can give the model better insights into the requests and their language. Also, we can fine-tune the height of the output to find the best balance between precision and processing time, as well as optimize the vectorizer by trying other works on word vectorizers like fastText, BERT, t-SNE, etc., which can provide a better-vectorized output.

The structural language categorization module can benefit from other notable works. For example, guesslang[4] can provide a precise and rapid language categorization suitable for our work.

Finally, our decision model on validating requests (Table 1) is binary-based. We can improve the decision model by implementing a weighted approach to the decision model based on the relationship between the effects of our input models and the true positive results of our system. More studies can be conducted to find out the most suitable weight for this model.

Conclusion. This paper reports our work toward building a machine learning-based WAF with a network request categorizer and request content predictor. Our contributions focus on a new strategy of a machine learning-based WAF: combine a content predictor built from Logistic Regression with a request categorizer built from CNN to determine whether a request should be restricted. We have constructed a malicious request validator that can validate incoming

---

[4] Available at https://github.com/yoeo/guesslang.

requests. Our machine learning-based WAF succeeded in reducing the false positive rate by less than 1%. However, the response time of 90ms per request is still unsatisfactory for practical WAF. Based on the comparison of our machine learning-based WAF with others' works in the field, we can conclude that depending on the requirements, a machine learning-based WAF or machine learning-assisted WAF can be applied industrially.

Acknowledgment. We acknowledge Ho Chi Minh City University of Technology (HCMUT), VNU-HCM, for supporting this study.

References

1. Shaheed, A., Kurdy, M.-B.: Web application firewall using machine learning and features engineering. Secur. Commun. Netw. **2022** (2022). https://doi.org/10.1155/2022/5280158
2. Jemal, I., Haddar, M.A., Cheikhrouhou, O., Mahfoudhi, A.: SWAF: a smart web application firewall based on convolutional neural network, pp. 01–06 (2022). https://doi.org/10.1109/SIN56466.2022.9970545
3. Dawadi, B., Adhikari, B., Srivastava, D.: Deep learning technique-enabled web application firewall for the detection of web attacks. Sensors **23** (2023). https://doi.org/10.3390/s23042073
4. Toprak, S., Yavuz, A.: Web application firewall based on anomaly detection using deep learning. Acta Infologica (2022). https://doi.org/10.26650/acin.1039042
5. Gogoi, B., Ahmed, T., Saikia, H.: Detection of XSS attacks in web applications: a machine learning approach. Int. J. Innov. Res. Comput. Sci. Technol. **9**, 1–10 (2021). https://doi.org/10.21276/ijircst.2021.9.1.1
6. Devi, T.A.M., Kumar, B.A.: Machine learning with logistic regression for web application firewall. Int. J. Eng. Res. Technol. (IJERT) ICCIDT - 2022 **10** (2022). https://doi.org/10.17577/IJERTCONV10IS04059. ISSN 2278-0181
7. Nguyen, M., Truong, P., Hoang, T.: A new approach to improving web application firewall performance based on support vector machine method with analysis of http request. J. Sci. Technol. Inf. Secur. **1**, 62–73 (2022). https://doi.org/10.54654/isj.v1i15.842
8. Tran, N.-T., Nguyen, V.-H., Nguyen-Le, T., Nguyen-An, K.: Improving modsecurity WAF with machine learning methods. In: Dang, T.K., Küng, J., Takizawa, M., Chung, T.M. (eds.) FDSE 2020. CCIS, vol. 1306, pp. 93–107. Springer, Singapore (2020). https://doi.org/10.1007/978-981-33-4370-2_7
9. Alshammari, A., Aldribi, A.: Apply machine learning techniques to detect malicious network traffic in cloud computing. J. Big Data **8** (2021). https://doi.org/10.1186/s40537-021-00475-1
10. Nguyen, T.-C.-H., Le-Nguyen, M.-K., Le, D.-T., Nguyen, V.-H., Tôn, L.-P., Nguyen-An, K.: Improving web application firewalls with automatic language detection. SN Comput. Sci. **3**(6), 446 (2022). https://doi.org/10.1007/s42979-022-01327-2

Utilizing InfoGAN and PE Header Features for Synthetic Ransomware Image Generation: An Experimental Study

Viet Trung Le[1] , Phuc Hao Do[2] , Sylvestre Uwizeyemungu[3] ,
Thang Le-Dinh[3] , and Tran Duc Le[1,3(✉)]

[1] University of Science and Technology–The University of Danang, Danang, Vietnam
letranduc@dut.udn.vn
[2] Da Nang Architecture University, Danang, Vietnam
[3] Université du Québec à Trois-Rivières, Trois-Rivières, Québec, Canada

Abstract. Ransomware is a growing threat in the digital world, posing significant challenges to malware detection systems due to its rapidly evolving nature. Addressing this issue requires innovative approaches and robust datasets for training advanced machine learning models. This paper presents a method for generating synthetic ransomware image samples using the InfoGAN model in conjunction with Portable Executable (PE) Header features. The generated samples mimic real ransomware's structural characteristics, enhancing their realism and utility for model training. A detailed implementation of the Information Maximizing Generative Adversarial Network (InfoGAN) model and an evaluation of its performance in generating high-quality ransomware images are provided. The utility of the generated samples is further validated through classification experiments using a Convolutional Neural Network (CNN) model. The results demonstrate the promise of the proposed method in enhancing malware detection capabilities, particularly in the context of ransomware.

Keywords: GAN · InfoGAN · PE Header · CNN

1 Introduction

The integration of Artificial Intelligence (AI) is increasingly becoming a crucial determinant in the growth of any nation's digital economy, a subject of discussion in academia for many years [1]. In cybersecurity, recent years have seen concerted efforts toward developing AI-centric solutions [2]. One specific area in the cybersecurity field, malware analysis, stands to gain significantly from this computational assistance [3].

Malware analysis involves studying malware's behavioral patterns to detect and neutralize it. However, malware analysis faces challenges, such as the need for more automation and integrated tools, which makes tracking malware patterns over time and identifying connections and similarities among different malware families in large datasets difficult [4]. AI can deal with this difficulty.

T. K. Dang et al. (Eds.): FDSE 2023, CCIS 1925, pp. 226–239, 2023.
https://doi.org/10.1007/978-981-99-8296-7_16

However, real-world datasets are typically chaotic, disorganized, and unstructured, posing challenges to AI performance [5]. The success of an AI model heavily relies on the quantity, quality, and relevance of the dataset, but achieving the right balance is a challenging task. For specific problem statements, assembling a domain-specific dataset, cleaning, visualizing, and comprehending its relevance become essential to obtain desired outcomes [6].

One contemporary approach to address this issue involves employing AI models and algorithms to emulate real-world datasets. Such datasets are referred to as synthetic datasets. Generative Adversarial Networks (GANs) [7] are among the premier methods for creating these synthetic datasets. Based on neural network models, these architectures generate datasets that closely resemble real-world data. This characteristic renders GANs especially suitable for creating malware samples to serve AI or machine learning models in malware analysis and cybersecurity [8].

In this study, we use image processing capabilities to classify malware, emphasizing ransomware due to its increasingly prevalent and destructive nature [9]. It entails the conversion of malware samples from binary into image form, followed by applying machine learning models and AI methodologies to these converted images, as opposed to the direct application to the actual malware samples. The rationale behind this methodology of image-based analysis arises from several factors. Image representation of binary malware samples facilitates pattern recognition that may remain undetected in raw binary form. The features derived in this manner can be processed more efficiently by image-centric models. Furthermore, this approach offers an added layer of security as it mitigates the risk associated with the direct execution of malware. The method also accommodates applying transfer learning techniques using pre-existing, pre-trained AI models. Image data also offer opportunities for augmentation, thereby enhancing the robustness of the model. Consequently, the model's ability to classify various forms of malware is amplified.

Portable Executable (PE) Header features[1] are pivotal in this research. They represent the structural information of the executable files, providing valuable insights into the underlying behavior of the malware. PE Header features such as the image size, the number of sections, and the characteristics of these sections can serve as significant indicators of malware presence. In our study, these features are utilized as part of the input to the Information Maximizing Generative Adversarial Network (InfoGAN) model, guiding the generation process to produce synthetic ransomware samples that mimic the structural characteristics of the original ransomware. By doing so, we aim to enhance the realism and quality of the generated samples, thereby improving their utility for model training and testing in ransomware detection tasks.

Our main contributions are as follows:

- Utilizing the InfoGAN model to generate synthetic ransomware images from a specific ransomware family;
- Using Portable Executable features as input for generating the ransomware images with custom features;
- Validating the synthetic ransomware samples' utility through classification experiments with a CNN model.

---

[1] https://learn.microsoft.com/en-us/windows/win32/debug/pe-format.

The remaining part of this paper encompasses the presentation of several relevant studies in Sect. 2, followed by an overview of the GAN and InfoGAN models in Sect. 3. Section 4 will introduce the methodology, while the evaluation and results will be elucidated in Sect. 5. The final section will provide the conclusions.

2 Related Works

This section presents an extensive review of existing studies that align closely with the subject matter of this paper. It aims to explore and discuss key research efforts, methodologies, and outcomes in synthetic dataset generation using AI, with particular emphasis on applying GAN.

Moti et al. [10] developed a deep generative adversarial network to create signatures for potential future malware, enhancing classifier training. The method uses executable file headers and a neural network for feature extraction, improving classification accuracy by at least 1%. However, its effectiveness may be limited due to the diverse range of malware and insufficient header information. Classification is done using random forest, SVMs, and logistic regression. In the study [11], Ding et al. introduced a method for creating adversarial malware using feature byte sequences. The method outperforms random and gradient-based techniques but is effective only for CNN-based detectors and needs prior algorithmic knowledge.

In the study [12], Lu and Li used the Deep Convolutional Generative Adversarial Network (DCGAN) to create synthetic malware samples, boosting ResNet-18's accuracy by 6%. However, the method requires large datasets and lacks comparison with other classifiers.

In the study [13], Singh et al. developed a GAN-based model for creating labeled malware image datasets to improve classifier training. The method benefits from incorporating domain knowledge but requires such knowledge, which may not always be accessible. The study is limited to a single dataset, not covering all malware types.

In the study [14], Gao et al. presented the MaliCage framework for accurate malware classification. It has three main components: a packer detector, a deep neural network-based malware classifier, and a packer generative adversarial network. The framework identifies and classifies packed and unpacked malware using synthetic samples to improve training and accuracy. The evaluation shows that it effectively mitigates the impact of packed malware on machine learning models.

The use of Information Maximizing GAN (InfoGAN) [15] in creating malware images is an emerging field that improves malware detection and classification. Info-GANs generate images with specific features, allowing for exploring and analyzing different malware variants. This approach excels at identifying unique malware characteristics that traditional methods may miss, such as specific encryption or packing techniques.

3 Overview of GAN Models

Generative Adversarial Networks (GANs) consist of a generator network (G) and a discriminator network (D).

The generator network inputs a random noise vector and generates synthetic data (like images) from this noise. The generator aims to produce data indistinguishable from the real-world data it tries to mimic. On the other hand, the discriminator network takes both real-world data and the synthetic data produced by the generator as input. Its task is to distinguish between real and synthetic data. In other words, it tries to classify whether each input data is real or fake.

The Generator tries to fool the Discriminator by generating increasingly realistic data. In contrast, the Discriminator tries to better distinguish real data from the fake data produced by the Generator. This competition improves both networks, leading to the Generator producing highly realistic data. The mathematical formulation of the GAN model [15] can be written as:

$$\underset{G}{min}\,\underset{D}{max}\,V(D,G) = \mathbb{E}_{x \sim p_{\text{data}}(x)}[\log D(x)] + \mathbb{E}_{z \sim p_z(z)}[\log(1 - D(G(z)))] \qquad (1)$$

Here, $V(D,G)$ is the objective function of the GAN. The first term, $\mathbb{E}_{x \sim p_{\text{data}}(x)}[\log D(x)]$, is the expected log probability that the Discriminator correctly classifies real data (drawn from the true data distribution $p_{\text{data}}(x)$). The second term, $\mathbb{E}_{z \sim p_z(z)}[\log(1 - D(G(z)))]$, is the expected log probability that the Discriminator correctly classifies synthetic data (generated by passing noise z drawn from the noise distribution $p_z(z)$ through the Generator).

The loss function for the Discriminator can be derived from the objective function and is given by:

$$\mathcal{L}_D = -\mathbb{E}_{x \sim p_{\text{data}}(x)}[\log D(x)] - \mathbb{E}_{z \sim p_z(z)}[\log(1 - D(G(z)))] \qquad (2)$$

The loss function for the Generator is:

$$\mathcal{L}_G = -\mathbb{E}_{z \sim p_z(z)}[\log D(G(z))] \qquad (3)$$

Figure 1 shows the design of the GAN architecture.

Nevertheless, a conventional GAN is not intended for multiclass data and additional information. Therefore, we aim to employ InfoGAN, an improved version of GAN that incorporates a class label and extra information into the generative model.

InfoGAN aims to make the generated data more interpretable and meaningful. It maximizes the mutual information between a fixed small subset of the GAN's noise variables and the observations. These variables could represent specific, meaningful characteristics of ransomware that we want to vary in a controlled way, such as the type of encryption used, the type of files targeted, or the message displayed.

For the case of generating ransomware samples, the original GAN loss function is modified in InfoGAN to include an additional term that represents the mutual information between the generated ransomware samples and a subset of the input noise variables. It encourages the model to use these variables meaningfully, leading to more interpretably generated ransomware samples.

The objective function of InfoGAN [15] can be written as: $\underset{G}{min}\,\underset{D}{max}\,V(D,G) - \lambda I(c; G(z,c))$. Here, $V(D,G)$ is the original GAN objective function. The term $-\lambda I(c; G(z,c))$ encourages the Generator to use the variable c in meaningfully, leading to ransomware samples that vary in a controlled and interpretable way based on c. c is also called the interpretable latent code, learned by InfoGAN. It represents different aspects of the data that the GAN is trying to generate.

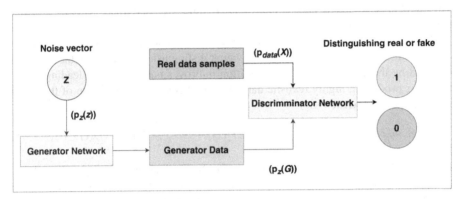

Fig. 1. Design of the GAN architecture.

The parameter λ is a hyperparameter that controls the trade-off between the original GAN objective and the mutual information term. A higher λ places more emphasis on maximizing mutual information.

The mutual information $I(c; G(z, c))$ can be difficult to compute directly, so in practice, an auxiliary distribution $Q(c \mid G(z, c))$ is introduced, and the mutual information is maximized by maximizing a lower bound:

$$I(c; G(z, c)) \geq \mathbb{E}_{c,z}[\log Q(c \mid G(z, c))] + H(c) \tag{4}$$

Here, $H(c)$ is the entropy of c, which is a constant with respect to Q so maximizing this lower bound is equivalent to maximizing the expectation $\mathbb{E}_{c,z}[\log Q(c \mid G(z, c))]$. It can be done using standard backpropagation and gradient ascent, like the rest of the GAN training process.

4 Methodology

The methodology employed in our research is a multi-step process revolving around using the InfoGAN model and PE features. Our approach encapsulates a comprehensive strategy from ransomware collection to testing synthesized images using a CNN classifier. The step-by-step procedure of the methodology is visually depicted in Fig. 2, providing a clear and concise overview of our research design.

In the initial phase, we collected ransomware samples as the primary data for our study. It served as the basis for our analysis and the foundation of our image dataset. Following the data collection, we performed two crucial steps. Firstly, the binary data of the ransomware were converted into images, and secondly, we extracted and selected the Portable Executable (PE) header features.

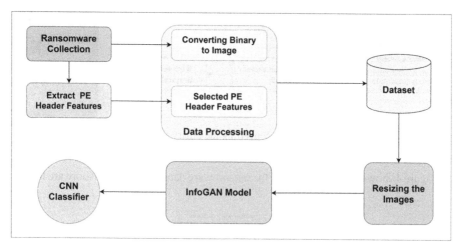

Fig. 2. Research flow.

After the conversion and selection, a dataset of these images for further processing was created. We then resized the images to ensure uniformity and consistency in the data, which is an essential pre-processing step in image analysis and processing tasks.

Having prepared our image dataset, we applied the InfoGAN model with multiple input values. The synthesized images generated by the InfoGAN model were then subjected to a CNN classifier for testing.

The details of each step, including the nuances of the InfoGAN model application and the CNN classifier testing, will be discussed in the subsequent sections.

4.1 Converting Binary to Image

Obtaining a comprehensive dataset of ransomware proved challenging, prompting the decision to create our own dataset, referred to as the *"ransomware dataset"*. We manually searched, downloaded, and classified the ransomware samples (only Windows executable binary files) from *Virusbay, Hybrid-analysis, Bazaar, Virusshare, GitHub, and Virustotal.*

Leveraging the *Dataloader* modules provided by *PyTorch*, we extracted images and labels from the ransomware executable files. Furthermore, the transform functions were employed to address our pre-processing requirements effectively.

At this phase, since the ransomware files are executable binaries, they can be converted into images using a similar approach as used in [16]. According to it, the binaries were converted into pixels, as described in Fig. 3. The samples belonging to the same variant will have similar pixel distribution. It should be noted that the pixel distribution may no longer accurately represent the variants of the samples due to the obfuscations introduced. Consequently, the reliability of the results for classifying malware variants may be compromised. To minimize this impact, we tested and removed obfuscated ransomware samples using *PEiD* and *Exeinfo PE* tools.

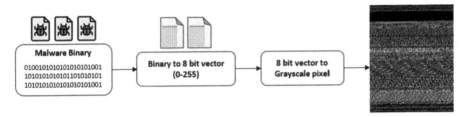

Fig. 3. Process of converting the binary file to image.

Figure 4 shows the distribution of the ransomware dataset in each ransomware family.

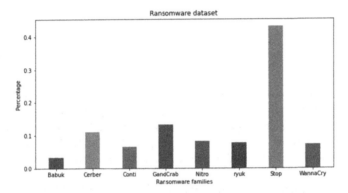

Fig. 4. Distribution of ransomware families in the dataset.

Table 1 presents the number of samples for each family. It is observed that the sample distribution within each family exhibits a relatively balanced distribution. The *Stop* family stands out with a notably higher sample count than the other families. In order to address the inherent data imbalance, we implemented shuffling of the data during the training phase and employed balanced accuracy as the evaluation metric during testing. This approach ensures that each class is equally represented during training, mitigating the potential bias introduced by the imbalanced data distribution. By utilizing balanced accuracy, we account for the disproportionate class sizes and comprehensively assess the model's performance across all classes.

When converting binary executable files into images, the selection of the image width is based on the corresponding file size range (Table 2). This choice aims to represent the original file effectively while balancing visual details and computational efficiency. By associating each file size range with a specific image width, we ensure that the resulting images accurately capture the essence of the files. Narrower images with lower pixel counts are assigned to smaller file sizes, while wider images with higher pixel counts represent larger file sizes. This approach successfully tra a diverse range of executable files into image representations, optimizing memory usage and computational resources.

Upon completing the transformation process, the images were resized to predetermined dimensions to create an input dataset tailored for training the model. This resizing

Table 1. Number of samples in each ransomware family.

Ransomware Families	Number of samples	Ransomware Families	Number of samples
Babuk	43	Nitro	104
Cerber	141	Ryuk	99
Conti	84	Stop	556
GandCrab	170	WannaCry	92

Table 2. Width (in pixel) of image based on the size of the binary.

File Size Range	Image Width	File Size Range	Image Width
<10 kB	32	100 kB–200 kB	384
10 kB–30 kB	64	200 kB–500 kB	512
30 kB–60 kB	128	500 kB–1000 kB	768
60 kB–100 kB	256	>1000 kB	1028

operation enabled us to obtain images that offer various scale views of the underlying data. Figure 5 exemplifies the diverse scale views captured by the images depicting a *Nitro* family.

4.2 Extract PE Header Features and Apply Them to the InfoGAN Model

Portable Executable Header features are a critical aspect of our methodology, serving as a key input for the InfoGAN model in generating synthetic ransomware samples. The PE Header, which forms the structural metadata of the executable files, provides crucial insights into the behavior of the malware. The use of PE Header features in this manner serves a dual purpose. Firstly, it enhances the quality of the generated samples, making them more representative of real ransomware. Secondly, it allows for the exploration of specific features and their variations in the generated samples, aiding in understanding their influence on ransomware detection.

In the first step, we extract the PE Header features from a dataset of known ransomware samples. This process is facilitated using a Python library named *pefile*, which parses the PE Header information from the binary executable files. Table 3 presents some important features of the PE Header derived from an analysis of a *WannaCry* ransomware sample.

Given the extensive number of PE feature values, an evaluation was conducted to assess the influence of these features through various models, thereby determining which values to use for training. Machine learning models, specifically *XGBoost* and *CatBoost*, were employed due to their superior performance in machine learning competitions hosted on Kaggle[2]. These models were used to assess the impact of features on the

---

[2] https://www.kaggle.com/code/nholloway/catboost-V-xgboost-V-lightgbm.

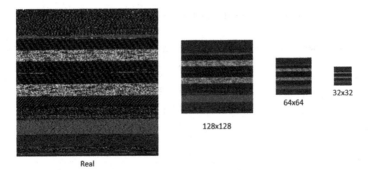

Fig. 5. Images of a *Nitro* family from other scale views.

Table 3. A short list of *Wannacry's* PE features.

PE Features	Size (Bytes)	PE Features	Size (Bytes)
Machine	2	BaseOfCode	4
SizeOfOptionalHeader	2	BaseOfData	4
Characteristics	2	ImageBase	8
MajorLinkerVersion	1	SectionAlignment	4
MinorLinkerVersion	1	DllCharacteristics	2
SizeOfCode	4	CheckSum	4
SizeOfInitializedData	4	FileAlignment	4
SizeOfUninitializedData	4	MajorOperatingSystemVersion	2
AddressOfEntryPoint	4	SizeOfStackCommit	8

ability to classify ransomware families. While the quantity of these features was not extensive, their impact on classification results and model accuracy was significantly superior to other features within the PE header. The average influence of the features was then calculated as presented in Table 4, incorporating the top five features that exert the greatest influence on the model. Nevertheless, in practice, the number of features may vary depending on the computational power of the hardware utilized and desired training time during the model training. The optimal determination of the number of features falls beyond the scope of this study and could be a prospective avenue for future research.

These selected features are then fed into the InfoGAN model as part of the input data, which also includes *Noise code*, *Ransomware Label*. In particular, the selected features are used as conditioning variables in the InfoGAN, influencing the generation process of the synthetic samples. By integrating the PE Header features, the InfoGAN model is guided to generate ransomware samples that appear realistic and mimic the original ransomware's structural characteristics. The model's output will be a ransomware variant learned by the model. The Implementation section will provide a more detailed presentation of the Generator and the overall InfoGAN model. This approach aligns with the primary objective of this study, which is to utilize image-processing capabilities for the classification of ransomware.

Table 4. The average influence of the five greatest features.

Features	Impact level (%)
CheckSum	12.51
SizeOfUninitializedData	11.23
SizeOfStackCommit	8.54
DllCharacteristics	7.35
MinorLinkerVersion	7.21

5 Evaluation and Results

In order to evaluate the image generation capabilities of the model, two groups of experiments are conducted:

- InfoGAN experiments: The application of the InfoGAN model was systematically examined through three distinct experiments, encompassing images of varying sizes: 32×32, 64×64, and 128×128 pixels.
- CNN experiments: The employment of the CNN model to differentiate the real and the synthesized ransomware samples generated by the InfoGAN model and PE header features.

5.1 InfoGAN Experiments

The application of the InfoGAN model was systematically examined through three distinct experiments, encompassing images of varying sizes: 32×32, 64×64, and 128×128 pixels. The dataset images were resized to the respective dimensions in each case to ensure uniformity. The InfoGAN model was trained over 1000 epochs with a batch size of 32, with each training process conducted on *Google Colab Pro* lasting approximately 10 h for the 32×32 and 64×64 image sets and about 12 h for the 128×128 image set.

Table 5 presents the mean loss values for each experiment conducted using InfoGAN. The results demonstrate a notable consistency, independent of the image dimensions.

As the image size increases, the average discriminator loss decreases while the average generator loss rises. This trend suggests that the InfoGAN model was able to generate more refined images as the size of the images increased. The discriminator model, tasked with distinguishing real images from synthesized ones, improved with the increase in image size. Conversely, the generator model, responsible for creating

Table 5. Average loss values of InfoGAN models.

Image Size	Average Discriminator Loss	Average Generator Loss	Average Information Loss
32 × 32	0.1899	0.5865	1.274
64 × 64	0.1212	0.7597	1.275
128 × 128	0.0525	0.9626	1.274

synthetic images, found the task progressively more challenging with the larger image size, as seen by the increase in loss.

Interestingly, the average information loss remained relatively constant across all image sizes. It indicates that the InfoGAN model preserved consistent information across all experiments, regardless of the image size.

These results collectively suggest a trade-off between the generator and discriminator performance as the image size increases. The increasing challenge for the generator, juxtaposed with the improved performance of the Discriminator, underscores the intricate dynamics at play within the GAN model. Despite this, the constancy in the information loss shows the model's stability across different image resolutions, reinforcing the versatility of the InfoGAN model for generating high-quality ransomware images.

Figure 6 demonstrates the visual comparisons of the original and synthesized images that share identical characteristics for the ransomware family, *GandCrab*. In the 32 × 32 pixel scenario context, the resolution appears to be suboptimal across all instances. However, in the cases involving 64 × 64 and 128 × 128 pixels, it becomes discernible that the synthesized samples, as generated by the InfoGAN, manifest a substantial degree of visual similarity to the original images. It indicates that the model can more accurately replicate the original image structure as the resolution increases, thus suggesting its potential efficacy in synthesizing high-resolution images for further studies.

5.2 CNN Experiments

In this section, we try to differentiate between real ransomware images and those synthesized by the InfoGAN model. The CNN model was employed, treating the original and synthesized images as separate classes within multiclass experiments. There are eight classes derived from the dataset. Therefore, this procedure results in 16 classes, each encompassing the eight original families and their corresponding synthesized classes. Subsequent sections will individually explore experiments for image sizes of 32 × 32, 64 × 64, and 128 × 128 pixels. Approximately 100 samples were generated per subclass for each case, resulting in a novel ransomware dataset of 800 synthetic images in conjunction with 1100 original images. Table 6 below delineates the accuracy scores attained on these test sets.

The accuracy is particularly high for ransomware families such as *Babuk, Conti, GandCrab, Nitro,* and *Stop*. These families exhibited accuracy values close to or at 100% in most test scenarios, showcasing the efficacy of both InfoGAN's ability to generate

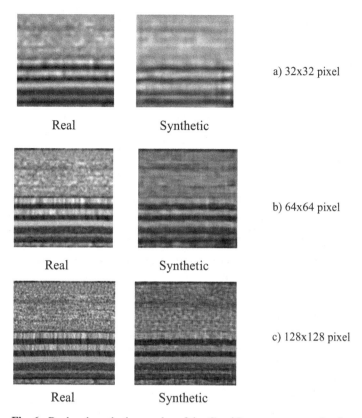

a) 32x32 pixel

Real   Synthetic

b) 64x64 pixel

Real   Synthetic

c) 128x128 pixel

Real   Synthetic

Fig. 6. Real and synthetic samples of the *GandCrap* ransomware family.

Table 6. Accuracy of test sets from prediction of CNNs model.

Class (Label)	Accuracy values of CNN model (%)					
	32 × 32 pixel images		64 × 64 pixel images		128 × 128 pixel images	
	Real	Synthesized	Real	Synthesized	Real	Synthesized
Babuk	100	93.8	100	93.8	100	98.8
Cerber	28.6	96	50	100	66.7	100
Conti	94.4	100	59.1	100	86.4	100
GandCrab	96.8	100	96.8	100	96.6	100
Nitro	100	90	94.7	100	95.2	98.7
Ryuk	33.3	96.4	100	96.4	33.3	96.7
Stop	100	100	95.8	100	97.9	100
WannaCry	91.7	85.7	57.1	100	54.5	100

high-quality synthetic ransomware images and CNN's ability to classify these images accurately.

On the other hand, the ransomware families *Cerber*, *Ryuk*, and *WannaCry* showed relatively lower accuracy rates, especially with real images at smaller resolutions (32×32 and 64×64 pixels). These discrepancies could be due to the inherent complexity of these particular ransomware families or limitations within the training data that may have resulted in less optimal feature learning.

The fluctuation in accuracy across different resolutions indicates the importance of image size in the training of the models. Larger image sizes might contain more detailed information that contributes to better feature learning and, thus, more accurate classification.

The results underscore the successful application of GANs, specifically the Info-GAN model, in generating synthetic ransomware images. The synthesized images were seemingly close enough to real images to be effectively utilized for model training and testing. It not only broadens the possibilities for data augmentation but also provides a safer and more efficient method for model training, as it mitigates the risks associated with the direct execution of malware.

6 Conclusions

In conclusion, this study has successfully demonstrated the potential of using the InfoGAN model and PE Header features for generating synthetic ransomware samples.

By leveraging PE Header features, the InfoGAN model could generate realistic samples that mimic the structural characteristics of real malware, thereby enhancing the quality and utility of the generated data.

Validation of the synthetic samples using a CNN model further underscored the realism and quality of the generated images. The high classification accuracy achieved by the CNN model on the synthetic samples attests to their potential as a valuable resource for training and testing malware detection models.

While the results of this study are promising, future work should focus on expanding the methodology to other types of malware and improving the generation process to produce more diverse samples. It would help further to enhance the generalizability and robustness of malware detection models.

References

1. Makridis, C.A., Mishra, S.: Artificial intelligence as a service, economic growth, and well-being. J. Serv. Res. **25**, 505–520 (2022)
2. Ansari, M.F., Dash, B., Sharma, P., Yathiraju, N.: The impact and limitations of artificial intelligence in cybersecurity: a literature review. Int. J. Adv. Res. Comput. Commun. Eng. (2022)
3. Majid, A.-A.M., Alshaibi, A.J., Kostyuchenko, E., Shelupanov, A.: A review of artificial intelligence based malware detection using deep learning. Mater. Today: Proc. **80**, 2678–2683 (2023)
4. Akhtar, Z.: Malware detection and analysis: challenges and research opportunities. arXiv preprint arXiv:2101.08429 (2021)

5. Halevy, A., Norvig, P., Pereira, F.: The Unreasonable effectiveness of data. IEEE Intell. Syst. **24**, 8–12 (2009)
6. Zhang, C., Bengio, S., Hardt, M., Recht, B., Vinyals, O.: Understanding deep learning (still) requires rethinking generalization. Commun. ACM **64**, 107–115 (2021)
7. Goodfellow, I., et al.: Generative adversarial nets. In: Advances in Neural Information Processing Systems, vol. 27 (2014)
8. Dutta, I.K., Ghosh, B., Carlson, A., Totaro, M., Bayoumi, M.: Generative adversarial networks in security: a survey. In: 2020 11th IEEE Annual Ubiquitous Computing, Electronics & Mobile Communication Conference (UEMCON), pp. 0399–0405. IEEE (2020)
9. Beaman, C., Barkworth, A., Akande, T.D., Hakak, S., Khan, M.K.: Ransomware: recent advances, analysis, challenges and future research directions. Comput. Secur. **111**, 102490 (2021)
10. Moti, Z., Hashemi, S., Namavar, A.: Discovering future malware variants by generating new malware samples using generative adversarial network. In: 2019 9th International Conference on Computer and Knowledge Engineering (ICCKE), pp. 319–324. IEEE (2019)
11. Ding, Y., Shao, M., Nie, C., Fu, K.: An efficient method for generating adversarial malware samples. Electronics **11**, 154 (2022)
12. Lu, Y., Li, J.: Generative adversarial network for improving deep learning based malware classification. In: 2019 Winter Simulation Conference (WSC), pp. 584–593. IEEE (2019)
13. Singh, A., Dutta, D., Saha, A.: MIGAN: malware image synthesis using GANs. In: Proceedings of the AAAI Conference on Artificial Intelligence, pp. 10033–10034 (2019)
14. Gao, X., Hu, C., Shan, C., Han, W.: MaliCage: a packed malware family classification framework based on DNN and GAN. J. Inf. Secur. Appl. **68**, 103267 (2022)
15. Chen, X., Duan, Y., Houthooft, R., Schulman, J., Sutskever, I., Abbeel, P.: InfoGAN: interpretable representation learning by information maximizing generative adversarial nets. In: Advances in Neural Information Processing Systems, vol. 29 (2016)
16. Nataraj, L., Karthikeyan, S., Jacob, G., Manjunath, B.S.: Malware images: visualization and automatic classification. In: Proceedings of the 8th International Symposium on Visualization for Cyber Security, pp. 1–7 (2011)

Enhancing Detection of Daily-Used Face Swap Applications by Using Focused Landmark Analysis

Minh-Khoi Nguyen-Nhat[1,2] ⓘ, Trung-Truc Huynh-Ngo[1,2] ⓘ,
Minh-Triet Tran[1,2(✉)], and Trong-Le Do[1,2]

[1] University of Science, VNU-HCM, Ho Chi Minh City, Vietnam
{19120020,19120040}@student.hcmus.edu.vn, {tmtriet,dtle}@hcmus.edu.vn
[2] Vietnam National University, Ho Chi Minh City, Vietnam

Abstract. The rapid evolution of user-friendly, high-quality face swap apps has raised security and privacy concerns, particularly on social media. This motivates our proposal of an efficient method to identify faceswap images. Our approach is based on Vision Transformer and exploits Facial Landmark Focusing Image (FAFI), designed to target regions adjacent to facial landmarks to identify anomalies. We conduct experiments on our dataset containing diverse faceswap videos from common applications, capturing real-life contexts. Experimental results demonstrate that FAFI exhibits superior generalization potential compared to Multi-scale Retinex, especially when using the Vision Transformer as a feature extractor, with the accuracy, precision, and recall of 95.29%, 96.45%, and 93.53%, respectively. Furthermore, the visualization using Grad-CAM also demonstrates that our method with Vision Transformer tends to emphasize intricate and detailed abnormal artifacts within the face, providing promising hints to users to identify potential suspected regions in a human face for further evaluation (Code and dataset are available at https://github.com/minhkhoi1026/face-spoofing-dection).

1 Introduction

The advancement of deepfake technology has led to significant improvements in output quality and accessibility. Today, anyone can easily create deepfake videos using mobile or PC applications, raising concerns about the potential for misuse and deception in various contexts [1,2,4].

The rapid advancement of user-friendly, high-quality face swap applications has raised significant security and privacy concerns, particularly within the realm of social media. In response to this pressing issue, we propose an efficient methodology for identifying faceswap images. We aim to enhance our investigation beyond the traditional use of a CNN-based feature extractor by integrating the Vision Transformer (ViT), a transformer-based backbone, into our approach. Our method centers around the utilization of the Vision Transformer and harnesses the power of the Facial Landmark Focusing Image (FAFI) [17], a specialized technique tailored to pinpoint irregularities in regions proximate to facial

T. K. Dang et al. (Eds.): FDSE 2023, CCIS 1925, pp. 240–254, 2023.
https://doi.org/10.1007/978-981-99-8296-7_17

landmarks. Our solution also utilizes a dual-stream approach with an attention fusion module to leverage both the original and feature images' information.

While the FaceForensics++ dataset [18] is often cited as one of the notable resources for face swap research, it has certain limitations. Most notably, it primarily consists of videos sourced from television, which limits its representation of real-world scenarios and individuals. Additionally, the dataset relies on outdated face swap methods that do not perform as well as modern techniques. Therefore, we addressed these limitations by creating a novel dataset [17] derived from commonly used deepfake applications. This dataset is first introduced in [17] and offers a more diverse and authentic benchmark for face swap detection, encompassing a wide range of manipulated facial images generated through popular deepfake applications.

Experimental results show that our proposed method achieves high accuracy, precision, and recall on the dataset with various real-life scenarios. We compare the results of our method with the solution using the well-known Multi-scale Retinex (MSR) feature [13] in the MobileNetV3 backbone setting. Leveraging the Vision Transformer's ability to capture detailed information and FAFI outperforms the MSR feature in this setting. Moreover, visual analysis reveals more reasonable regions of interest in the Vision Transformer setting than MobileNet when using MSR and FAFI features. This underscores the potential of combining FAFI with the Vision Transformer to improve generalization in face swap detection significantly.

Our main contributions in this paper are as follows. First, we propose a potential face swap detection method that incorporates a transformer-based feature extractor and a dual-stream architecture, taking advantage of the Facial Landmark Focusing Image (FAFI) to focus on irregularities in regions proximate to facial landmarks. Then we also develop "Face Sleuth", a user-friendly application equipped with advanced anti-face-swap models to help users detect and analyze face swap content in videos effectively.

The content of this paper is as follows. In Sect. 2, we briefly review existing methods related to our work. We present our frame-based face swap detection model, including the dual stream architecture with the attention-based feature fusion module and the new image feature in Sect. 3. Section 4 presents the dataset we curated [17], highlighting its unique characteristics, the experimental setup and results, demonstrating the effectiveness of our proposed model. Section 5 briefly introduces our application "Face Sleuth" to assist users in detecting face swap video. Finally, Sect. 6 concludes the paper, summarizing contributions and suggesting future research directions.

2   Related Work

2.1   Face Manipulation

The general face swap process involves four key steps. Firstly, it detects and crops the faces in input frames, ensuring relevant facial regions are processed. Next, it extracts intermediate representations from the detected faces, capturing

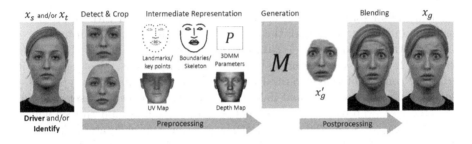

Fig. 1. General face swap framework [16]

essential facial features. These representations serve as the basis for generating a new face using a driving signal, mapping the features to desired characteristics. Finally, it seamlessly blends the generated face into the target frame, minimizing visual artifacts. This framework is depicted in Fig. 1.

Recent advancements in this field employ deep learning, often using two encoder-decoder pairs. An encoder extracts latent face features, followed by a decoder for reconstruction. After training, decoders are swapped so that a source image encoder and a target image decoder regenerate the target picture. Well-known applications like DFaker [3], DeepFaceLab [1], and more recently, [4], use this approach.

2.2 Facial Manipulation Detection

Several of the methods described utilize a **CNN-based frame-by-frame analysis**. One example is MesoNet, as proposed in [5]. It is a relatively straightforward CNN designed to detect manipulated faces. However, the authors have shown that XceptionNet, retrained for this purpose, outperforms MesoNet in performance. Another technique is **Long Short-Term Memory (LSTM)** analysis, which leverages the temporal evolution of video frames. This approach is employed in studies like [14], where frame-based features are extracted and combined using recurrent methods. It is worth noting that these methods often consume excessive memory without significantly enhancing accuracy compared to frame-by-frame techniques [22].

The frame-level approach is the most commonly used due to its memory and computational efficiency while maintaining effectiveness compared to video-level methods. On the FaceForensics++ dataset, the solution presented in [6] holds the state-of-the-art position. This approach explores the concept of using an ensemble of CNN-trained models and considers EfficientNetB4, proposing a modified version with an added attention mechanism and siamese training. The success of transformer-based models in this task [8] motivates further exploration in transformer-based method.

2.3   Face Swap Detection Dataset

With the proliferation of high-quality face modification methods, the need for image editing detection has grown. Notable face manipulation detection datasets like FaceForensics++ [18] have emerged in response.

FaceForensics++ (FF++) is one of the most renowned datasets for deepfake detection. It comprises four subsets: FaceSwap, DeepFake, Face2Face, and NeuralTextures, corresponding to specific generation methods. FF++ includes 1000 original videos and 3000 manipulated videos created using computer graphics and deepfake techniques. The dataset is available in both uncompressed and H264 compressed formats, facilitating evaluation on compressed and uncompressed videos.

Despite its contributions, FaceForensics++ has limitations. Its source videos primarily come from TV programs, resulting in limited contextual diversity, including restricted activities, backgrounds, age groups, and focus on frontal face poses. Additionally, the dataset's face swap tools are outdated, performing poorly compared to contemporary applications. These limitations motivate the development of a new dataset to address these issues.

3   Proposed Method

3.1   Backbone with Vision Transformer

The backbone plays a crucial role in extracting valuable information from the image, effectively transforming it into a feature vector within the latent space $\mathcal{R}^d$. In our face swap detection task, we choose two distinct backbones: MobileNetV3-Small [12] and Vision Transformer [11]. MobileNetV3-Small stands out as a lightweight convolutional neural network architecture that strikes an excellent balance between model size and accuracy. On the other hand, Vision Transformer offers a lightweight configuration that reduces the feature dimension while retaining the capability to facilitate direct information sharing between different parts of the image through self-attention techniques.

3.2   Facial Landmark Focusing Image

To improve a face detection model's focus on vital areas, we employ FAFI (**F**acial l**A**ndmark **F**ocusing **I**mage). We first presented this approach in [17]. The central aim of this feature is to enhance the model's attention to vital facial characteristics while minimizing interference from less important image components.

The process of generating FAFI (Facial Landmark Focusing Image) data involves a meticulous three-step procedure [17]. In the initial step, we embark on the task of Facial Landmark Detection. This crucial phase involves the identification of key facial landmarks within the image. These landmarks are categorized into distinct groups based on their types, encompassing features like the corners of the eyes, the tip of the nose, the contours of the lips, and more. These landmarks serve as indispensable reference points for the subsequent stages of our process.

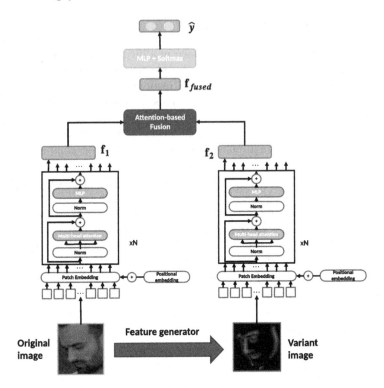

Fig. 2. Overview of dual stream architecture using Vision Transformer as a feature extractor.

The second phase entails Binary Mask Creation, where we construct a binary mask by connecting landmarks within the same groups. This resultant mask encapsulates a representation of the facial structure, effectively outlining the edges and boundaries of the identified landmarks. This serves as a robust means of capturing any potential discrepancies that may arise during the face-swapping process.

To further enhance the effectiveness of our method in identifying potential anomalies, we proceed to the third step known as Mask Dilation. Here, we employ a combination of dilation and Gaussian operations on the binary mask. Dilation expands the highlighted areas within the mask, encompassing additional pixels along the edges, while the Gaussian operation introduces a blur effect that accentuates pixels in proximity to the face more than those further away. This comprehensive approach helps broaden the regions of interest, leading to improved detection capabilities.

By employing this feature, we assist the model in directing its focus towards the critical areas of the face, resulting in more reasonable results.

3.3   Dual Stream Model with Attention-Based Feature Fusion

To enrich the model's capacity for handling intricate real-world scenarios, we employ the concept of feature attention fusion [7] in our approach. This innova-

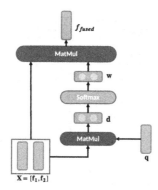

Fig. 3. Attention-based feature fusion module

tive approach empowers us to incorporate additional information into the model, thus enhancing its overall performance. Our proposal involves the integration of an additional model stream, tasked with extracting insights from a modified version of the original image. In this paper, we undertake experiments with two distinct variants: the Multi-scale Retinex Image as outlined in [7], and our Facial Landmark Focusing Image [17], which is summarized in Sect. 3.2.

Both the original image and its variants are independently processed through separate Vision Transformer backbones, yielding representation vectors commonly referred to as **features**. These feature vectors are subsequently merged into a unified feature representation using an attention-based fusion module. Finally, the resulting single feature representation undergoes transformation through a fully connected layer equipped with a softmax activation function, resulting in a probability vector of size 2. For a visual representation of our proposed architecture, please refer to Fig. 2. This dual-stream model harnesses the power of multiple data streams and attention-based fusion to enhance its ability to handle complex real-life scenarios effectively.

Attention-Based Feature Fusion: Our goal is to derive a set of weights $w_i, i = 1, \ldots, N$ from a given set of features $f_i, i = 1, \ldots, N$ to enable the calculation of a weighted sum feature v in the following manner:

$$v = \sum_{i=1}^{N} w_i f_i \tag{1}$$

The central focus of our work is the learning process for the weights w_i. Drawing inspiration from attention-based models, as described in [7], we propose the introduction of a kernel denoted as q. This kernel is designed to be the same size as the individual features f_i and plays a pivotal role in generating the weights based on its attention mechanism towards the features. The weight w_i is generated using the following equation:

$$w_i = \frac{e^{d_i}}{\sum_j e^{d_j}} \quad \text{with} \quad d_i = q^T f_i \quad \forall i = 1, \ldots, N \tag{2}$$

Fig. 4. Sample images from the FaceSwap dataset: (a) A wider range of ages by incorporating kids and older individuals. (b) More diverse backgrounds and daily life activities. (c) Enhanced variations in face poses and lighting conditions.

As a result, the only parameter to learn in the fusion module is a kernel q. Figure 3) shows the overview of this fusion module.

Loss Function: Throughout our training procedure, we implemented an enhanced variant of the Cross-Entropy Loss [9], known as Focal Loss [15]. The primary objective of Focal Loss is to tackle the challenge posed by imbalanced data in classification tasks. In such scenarios, certain classes may have a significantly smaller number of samples compared to others.

Focal Loss primarily deals with what are referred to as "difficult samples". These are instances that the model predicts incorrectly and assigns low confidence scores to. Focal Loss introduces a gamma parameter to amplify the significance of these challenging samples. This approach allows the model to prioritize learning from more informative examples while diminishing the impact of easily classifiable samples.

4   Experiment

4.1   FaceSwap Dataset

We curated a dataset specifically designed to address realistic scenarios in face-swap photos, first introduced in [17]. This dataset draws from diverse sources, including the Pexel website and FaceForensics++. While FaceForensics++ offers formal scenarios like TV programs, Pexel provides a broader context, enriching the dataset with varied backgrounds, activities, age groups, and facial poses. (see Fig. 4). This diversity challenges models to detect face swaps effectively.

We utilized two face-swap applications, the user-friendly *DeepFaker App* [2] and the open-source tool *Roop* [4], to generate 378 videos, comprising 189 face-swap videos from 51 participants and their corresponding original videos. These were divided into training, validation, and test sets, with different participants contributing to each set to ensure impartiality and robust evaluation.

Our dataset, balanced with both original and modified images, supports effective training and evaluation of image manipulation detection algorithms. We employed a frame-by-frame technique, processing videos to extract frames and applying face identification and landmark detection to over $170,000$ face images for thorough analysis.

4.2   Experiment Setup

To evaluate the effectiveness of our novel Facial Landmark Focusing Image technique, we conduct comparative experiments against baseline models that utilize the MobileNetV3-Small backbone [12] and Vision Transformer architecture [11]. These models are widely employed in various computer vision tasks, striking a balance between computational efficiency and performance. We harness the existing capabilities of the `timm` library [24], which offers pre-trained weights for both the `MobileNetV3-Small` and `ViT-tiny-patch16` (a vision transformer with a smaller configuration, dividing the image into 16×16 patches) models. These weights were pre-trained on the extensive ImageNet dataset [10].

The evaluation includes the examination of **two image variations**: we employ our novel Facial Landmark Focusing Image (FAFI) feature and a well-known feature called Multi-scale Retinex Image [7]. The FAFI feature serves to emphasize the facial structure, whereas the MSR feature highlights the underlying facial structure.

During the experiments, we trained the models using same configurations. All experiments share the optimizer parameters, batch size, input resolution, and early stopping settings. Furthermore, to ensure a consistent computing environment, the experiments were conducted on an NVIDIA GTX 3090 GPU with a substantial 20 GB of RAM, ensuring sufficient computational resources for model training and evaluation.

The evaluation of our face swap detection models will utilize the well-established metric commonly used in biometric systems - the Equal Error Rate (EER) [21]. The EER signifies the point at which the False Acceptance Rate (FAR) equals the False Rejection Rate (FRR), creating a balance where the rates of incorrectly accepting impostors and incorrectly rejecting legitimate users are identical. This equilibrium is essential for evaluating the model's ability to strike a balance between these two types of errors, effectively managing the risks associated with impostor acceptance and genuine user rejection. In addition to EER, we will also consider accuracy, precision, and recall to gain a more comprehensive and nuanced understanding of the model's performance.

4.3   Data Preprocessing and Augmentation

In **the preprocessing step**, we create a rectangular bounding box of the face ensuring the existence of face landmarks. This work involves two steps: first we need to perform face detection to get an initial box using Multi-Task Cascaded Convolutional Neural Networks (MTCNN) [20]. Then, we use the Face Mesh

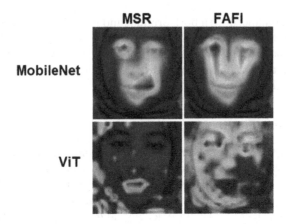

Fig. 5. Examples of Grad-CAM results

model from MediaPipe [23] to determine facial landmarks positions. Lastly, we use these landmarks to align the box produced from MTCNN.

During the preprocessing step, there are frames that two models failed to detect any human faces or landmarks. These frames are discarded to ensure that only frames containing human faces are included in our final dataset. Consequently, there is a difference in the number of extracted faces between manipulated and original videos, with manipulated videos typically containing fewer face images than original videos. This could potentially introduce data imbalance during the training phase. To mitigate this issue, we addressed the imbalance by oversampling the training set.

During the **data augmentation process**, we applied various techniques to introduce variations in the orientation, brightness, and spatial properties of the facial images. These techniques include:

- *Orientation augmentation*: We performed transformations on the face images to vary their viewing angles. To achieve this, we applied three main steps to each image: horizontal flipping, vertical flipping, and 90-degree rotation. Each augmentation is executed with a probability of 0.5.
- *Brightness augmentation*: We randomly adjusted the brightness of the images within a certain range. This creates diversity in the brightness of the data without affecting the important facial features. It is worth noting that we do not use contrast enhancement methods to ensure the accuracy and detection capability of the models.
- *Spatial augmentation*: We alter the spatial characteristics of the faces by applying translations (shifts) and resizing. These transformations are randomly applied within a specific range while ensuring that the significant facial features are not lost. Note that any empty areas resulting from these transformations were filled with black pixels to maintain the original frame size and aspect ratio.

4.4   Result and Discussion

With the above settings, our result is summarized in Table 1. The results obtained from our experiments provide valuable insights into the performance of different models when incorporating MSR (Multi-scale Retinex) features and the Facial Landmark Focusing Image (FAFI) technique for video deepfake detection.

Model MobileNet + FAFI attained an EER of 6.01% and an accuracy of 93.51%. While this model shows promising results in detecting face swaps, its performance is relatively lower than MobileNet + MSR.

In ViT + MSR config, the model achieved an EER of 5.47% and an accuracy of 93.42%. The combination of Vision Transformer (ViT) and MSR features shows potential in identifying face swap manipulations, although its performance is not as strong as MobileNet + MSR. ViT's ability to learn spatial structures in facial images and MSR features' capability to recognize complex facial expressions contribute to the model's overall performance.

In the same feature extractor setting, FAFI performs better than MSR in Vision Transformer. We have an EER of 3.81 of FAFI feature with ViT in comparison with 5.47 of its MSR counterpart. This indicates that FAFI features have the ability to effectively identify critical facial regions and unnatural expressions, resulting in better face swap detection.

For visual analysis of the model, we employed Grad-CAM [19] to determine the areas of focus during the analysis of manipulated faces. We use the library `pytorch-gradcam-model` to analyze the cumulative activation map of the two streams. Three key insights were extracted from the observation of the results (Fig. 5):

- ViT tends to emphasize intricate and detailed abnormal artifacts within the face, whereas MobileNet focuses more on specific regions. This phenomenon is possibly due to the distinct architectural characteristics of transformer-based and CNN-based models. The locality characteristic of CNNs originating from convolution is counterbalanced by the attention mechanism in transformers, allowing them to more freely connect various details. This indicates ViT's potential for improved face swap detection with more data and training, possibly surpassing MobileNet.
- Additionally, ViT concentrates on artifacts surrounding landmarks, whereas MobileNet primarily focuses on the central area of the face. This suggests

Table 1. Model Performance: include the settings of backbone and feature, respectively. All the entries measurement is %

Model Name	EER	Accuracy	Precision	Recall
MobileNet + MSR	**3.41**	**95.66**	**96.53**	91.45
MobileNet + FAFI	6.01	93.51	91.66	**94.87**
ViT + MSR	5.47	93.42	93.44	92.68
ViT + FAFI	3.81	95.29	96.45	93.53

that ViT is more adept at capturing new features (like FAFI) compared to MobileNet.

– In the same feature extractor setup, the FAFI feature yields more concise and relevant regions compared to the MSR feature. This distinction is particularly evident in the results of ViT. While ViT + MSR tends to focus on a small number of artifacts around the face, occasionally including unrelated artifacts, ViT + FAFI concentrates more on landmark regions for detection. This underscores the potential of FAFI features in conveying explicit information to the model.

The baseline model achieved a high level of accuracy on both the validation and test sets, affirming the feasibility of the proposed deepfake detection method.

5 Face Sleuth: An Application for Face Swap Detection

For better illustration and adaptability for regular users, we create *Face Sleuth* application. *Face Sleuth* is a powerful and intuitive application designed to assist users in detecting and analyzing face swap content in videos. The application employs a variety of anti-face-swap models to provide comprehensive and accurate insights into potential face manipulation.

Face Sleuth is designed to provide users with a comprehensive set of features that aid in analyzing videos and detecting face swapping using various anti-face-swap models. These features are intended to support users in identifying and combatting face-swap content effectively. However, it is essential to emphasize that the application is a tool for support and should not be considered a decision-maker on its own. In our application, users first upload the video they want to verify, then choose which type of face swap detector they want; the detector is named based on the face swap application they are trained on and the method they use. Finally, the user can click the submit button to get the result.

Fig. 6. Overview of application interface

Fig. 7. Overview of *Face Sleuth* result

Key features of the *Face Sleuth* include:

- **Video Upload**: Users can easily upload videos directly into *Face Sleuth* for analysis, supporting various video formats.
- **Model Selection**: *Face Sleuth* allows users to choose from a variety of anti-face-swap models using a detector list. Users can select multiple models simultaneously, enabling comprehensive analysis and comparison (Fig. 6).
- **Overall Fake Score**: *Face Sleuth* provides users with insightful information about the likelihood of face swapping in the uploaded video. Each selected model generates a score, indicating the probability of face swap manipulation.
- **Frame Investigation**: Users can delve deeper into the analysis results by exploring individual frames of the video. *Face Sleuth* allows users to select a specific model and observe the detection outcome for each frame. Detected faces are highlighted with bounding boxes, and corresponding scores are provided. Additionally, the application employs the Grad-CAM technique [?, ?] to indicate **where the model focuses** by highlighting the areas most influential in the classification score (Fig. 7).
- **Visual Representation**: To enhance the interpretation of analysis results, *Face Sleuth* offers visually appealing representations of face swap content

throughout the video. A bar plot illustrates the frame number and associated fake level, providing users with a comprehensive overview of the video's face swap activity. The application also generates a video with scores for each face and heat map visualization of where the model focuses, allowing for more straightforward observation (Fig. 7).

When used collectively, these features provide users with powerful capabilities to identify and evaluate face swap content in videos accurately. However, it is essential to reiterate that *Face Sleuth* serves as a support tool, and users are responsible for making informed decisions based on the results obtained.

Combining these features equips users with powerful capabilities to accurately identify and evaluate face swap content.

6   Discussion and Conclusion

In summary, we proposed a novel approach that utilizes Vision Transformer and critical facial landmarks in a dual stream network structure for enhancing the accuracy of face swap detection. This approach provides more informative cues for precise classification between authentic and manipulated content. We also developed the "Face Sleuth" application, a user-friendly and robust tool designed to aid individuals in detecting and analyzing face swap content within videos. This application harnesses multiple anti-face-swap models to deliver detailed and accurate assessments of potential face manipulation, making it a powerful and intuitive solution for users.

Nevertheless, the domain of face swap detection still offers opportunities for refinement. Our models exhibited limitations in detecting face swap under real-world conditions characterized by more significant uncertainty. Instances of erroneous predictions underscore the challenges posed by specific manipulation techniques. Consequently, further research and model refinement are imperative to enhance their resilience and generalizability. Moreover, exploring advanced methodologies to boost performance in demanding circumstances would yield valuable insights for the practical implementation of face swap detection strategies.

Acknowledgment. This research is funded by University of Science, VNU-HCM under grant number T2023-96.

References

1. Deepfacelab. https://github.com/iperov/DeepFaceLab
2. DeepFaker app on Google Play. https://play.google.com/store/apps/details?id=app.deepfaker.face_swap.ai_video_editor.gender_magic_face_merge_morph
3. Dfaker. https://github.com/dfaker/df
4. Roop. https://github.com/s0md3v/roop

5. Afchar, D., Nozick, V., Yamagishi, J., Echizen, I.: MesoNet: a compact facial video forgery detection network. In: 2018 IEEE International Workshop on Information Forensics and Security (WIFS), pp. 1–7. IEEE (2018)

6. Bonettini, N., Cannas, E.D., Mandelli, S., Bondi, L., Bestagini, P., Tubaro, S.: Video face manipulation detection through ensemble of CNNs. In: 2020 25th International Conference on Pattern Recognition (ICPR), pp. 5012–5019. IEEE (2021)

7. Chen, H., Hu, G., Lei, Z., Chen, Y., Robertson, N.M., Li, S.Z.: Attention-based two-stream convolutional networks for face spoofing detection. IEEE Trans. Inf. Forensics Secur. **15**, 578–593 (2020). https://doi.org/10.1109/TIFS.2019.2922241

8. Coccomini, D., Messina, N., Gennaro, C., Falchi, F.: Combining efficientnet and vision transformers for video deepfake detection. arXiv preprint arXiv:2107.02612 (2021)

9. De Boer, P.T., Kroese, D.P., Mannor, S., Rubinstein, R.Y.: A tutorial on the cross-entropy method. Ann. Oper. Res. **134**, 19–67 (2005)

10. Deng, J., Dong, W., Socher, R., Li, L.J., Li, K., Fei-Fei, L.: ImageNet: a large-scale hierarchical image database. In: 2009 IEEE Conference on Computer Vision and Pattern Recognition, pp. 248–255 (2009). https://doi.org/10.1109/CVPR.2009.5206848

11. Dosovitskiy, A., et al.: An image is worth 16×16 words: transformers for image recognition at scale. arXiv preprint arXiv:2010.11929 (2020)

12. Howard, A., et al.: Searching for MobileNetV3 (2019). https://doi.org/10.48550/arXiv.1905.02244

13. Jobson, D.J., Rahman, Z., Woodell, G.A.: A multiscale retinex for bridging the gap between color images and the human observation of scenes. IEEE Trans. Image Process. **6**(7), 965–976 (1997)

14. Korshunov, P., Marcel, S.: DeepFakes: a new threat to face recognition? Assessment and detection. arXiv preprint arXiv:1812.08685 (2018)

15. Lin, T.Y., Goyal, P., Girshick, R., He, K., Dollár, P.: Focal loss for dense object detection. In: Proceedings of the IEEE International Conference on Computer Vision, pp. 2980–2988 (2017)

16. Mirsky, Y., Lee, W.: The creation and detection of deepfakes: a survey. ACM Comput. Surv. **54**(1), 1–41 (2022). https://doi.org/10.1145/3425780

17. Nguyen-Nhat, M.K., Huynh-Ngo, T.T., Tran, M.T., Do, T.L.: Unmasking illusion of daily-used deepfake applications through landmark focused image. In: Proceedings of the 6th International Conference on Multimedia Analysis and Pattern Recognition (MAPR 2023) (2023)

18. Rossler, A., Cozzolino, D., Verdoliva, L., Riess, C., Thies, J., Nießner, M.: Faceforensics++: learning to detect manipulated facial images. In: Proceedings of the IEEE/CVF International Conference on Computer Vision, pp. 1–11 (2019)

19. Selvaraju, R.R., Cogswell, M., Das, A., Vedantam, R., Parikh, D., Batra, D.: Grad-CAM: visual explanations from deep networks via gradient-based localization. Int. J. Comput. Vis. **128**(2), 336–359 (2019). https://doi.org/10.1007/s11263-019-01228-7

20. Shi, W., Li, J., Yang, Y.: Face fatigue detection method based on MTCNN and machine vision. In: Abawajy, J.H., Choo, K.-K.R., Islam, R., Xu, Z., Atiquzzaman, M. (eds.) ATCI 2019. AISC, vol. 1017, pp. 233–240. Springer, Cham (2020). https://doi.org/10.1007/978-3-030-25128-4_31

21. Singh, M., Pati, D.: Replay attack detection using excitation source and system features, Chapter 2. In: Neustein, A. (ed.) Advances in Ubiquitous Computing, pp. 17–44. Advances in Ubiquitous Sensing Applications for Healthcare, Academic

Press (2020). https://doi.org/10.1016/B978-0-12-816801-1.00002-5. https://www.sciencedirect.com/science/article/pii/B9780128168011000025

22. Tolosana, R., Vera-Rodriguez, R., Fierrez, J., Morales, A., Ortega-Garcia, J.: Deep-Fakes and Beyond: A Survey of Face Manipulation and Fake Detection (2020)
23. Wachter, J.M.: Schwellwertanalyse bezüglich der Limitierung von MediaPipe Face Mesh anhand von informationsreduziertem Ausgangsmaterial. Ph.D. thesis (2022)
24. Wightman, R.: Pytorch image models (2019). https://github.com/rwightman/pytorch-image-models. https://doi.org/10.5281/zenodo.4414861

Differential Privacy Under Membership Inference Attacks

Trung Ha[1], Trang Vo[1], Tran Khanh Dang[2(✉)], and Nguyen Thi Huyen Trang[3]

[1] University of Information Technology, VNU-HCM, Thu Duc City, Vietnam
`trunghlh@uit.edu.vn, 20522043@gm.uit.edu.vn`
[2] Ho Chi Minh City University of Industry and Trade, Ho Chi Minh City, Vietnam
`khanh@hufi.edu.vn`
[3] HCMC University of Technology, VNU-HCM, Ho Chi Minh City, Vietnam
`ngthtrang@hcmut.edu.vn`

Abstract. Membership inference attacks are used as an audit tool to quantify training data leaks in machine learning models. Protection can be provided by anonymizing the training data or using training functions with differential privacy. Depending on the context, such as building data collection services for central machine learning models or responding to queries from end users, data scientists can choose between local and global differential privacy parameters. Different types of differential privacy have different epsilon values that reflect different mechanisms, making it difficult for data scientists to select appropriate differential privacy parameters and avoid inaccurate conclusions. The experiments in this paper show the relative privacy-accuracy trade-off of local and global differential privacy mechanisms under a white-box membership inference attack. While membership inference only reflects the lower bound for inference risk, and differential privacy formulates the upper bound, the experiments in this study with some datasets show that the trade-off between accuracy and privacy is similar for both types of mechanisms, although there is a large difference in their upper bounds. This suggests that the upper bound is far from the practical susceptibility to membership inference. Therefore, a small epsilon value in global differential privacy and a large epsilon value in local differential privacy lead to the same risk of membership inference. In addition, the risks from membership inference attacks are not uniform across all classes, especially when the training dataset in machine learning models is skewed.

Keywords: Member inference attack · black-box · white-box · differential privacy · shadow model

1 Introduction

Machine learning (ML) is increasingly being used in everyday life to make predictions about privacy-sensitive data. In recent years, major tech companies such as Google and Amazon have started offering machine learning models as a service to the public through their cloud platforms. While these systems can provide value and benefits in various

© The Author(s), under exclusive license to Springer Nature Singapore Pte Ltd. 2023
T. K. Dang et al. (Eds.): FDSE 2023, CCIS 1925, pp. 255–269, 2023.
https://doi.org/10.1007/978-981-99-8296-7_18

fields, machine learning models trained on sensitive data also pose two challenges. First, legal restrictions in some countries and regions may prohibit the collection, processing, and publication of certain data, such as National Health Service data. Secondly, membership inference (MI) attacks [8, 10, 14] and model decompilation attacks [5, 7] can identify and reconstruct training data based on information leaks from a trained neural network model that is publicly available. Both challenges can be mitigated by training an anonymous deep learning neural network model with differential privacy (DP). Currently, there are two types of mechanisms for differential privacy: local DP (LDP) [1] and central DP (CDP) [2]. LDP perturbs the training data before any processing takes place, while CDP perturbs the gradient update steps during training. The degree of perturbation, which affects the accuracy of the neural network model trained on experimental data, is adjusted for both DP categories by adjusting their respective privacy parameter ϵ. Choosing ϵ too large will not mitigate privacy attack risks such as MI effectively, while choosing ϵ too small will significantly reduce the accuracy of the model. Choosing ϵ too large will not mitigate privacy attack risks such as MI effectively, while choosing ϵ too small will significantly reduce the accuracy of the model. Therefore, balancing the trade-off between privacy and accuracy is a challenging task, especially for data scientists who are not experts in DP. Therefore, balancing the trade-off between privacy and accuracy is a challenging task, especially for data scientists who are not experts in DP [4, 9, 12, 25]. Yeom [9] demonstrated that DP training algorithms guarantee a theoretical upper bound for privacy leaks caused by MIA. This constraint was later improved by Erlingsson, providing strong protection at high DP levels (corresponding to small values of DP parameter ϵ), but quickly weakening for large ϵ values. However, empirical evaluations of MIA for DP-trained models [22] show that large values of ϵ, which are theoretically considered a low-privacy setting, provide sufficient protection against MIA in the real world. Motivated by these findings, Jayaraman [12] developed a tool to tune ϵ based solely on experimental performance by applying a black-box MI attack, while Nasr [14] established white-box attacks on datasets such as consumer matrices, social graphs, facial recognition, and health data. These MI attacks demonstrate a lower limit to the risk of inference attacks while DP guarantees an upper bound for the privacy parameter ϵ.

In summary, this work makes the following contributions:

- We compare the success of inference attacks using the Area Under the Curve (AUC) as a measure of privacy across different datasets and show that under this metric there is a trade-off between accuracy and privacy when changing the value of the privacy parameter.
- We show that DP mechanisms do not consistently achieve better trade-offs between privacy and accuracy.
- We analyze the relative trade-off between privacy and accuracy and show that it is not linear over ϵ. For each dataset, there are ranges where the relative trade-off favors protection against MI attacks over accuracy.

The remainder of this paper is structured as follows: Sect. 2 introduces the concepts of differential privacy and membership inference attacks. In Sect. 3, related work is reviewed. Section 4 describes and analyzes our experiments and datasets. Finally, Sect. 5 concludes the paper.

2 Background

Membership inference (MI) is a threat model used to quantify how accurately an honest-but-curious membership inference attacker can identify members of a training dataset in machine learning, as shown in Fig. 1. Membership inference attacks are of particular concern for members of a training dataset when the nature of the dataset is such that it reveals sensitive information. For example, a medical training dataset containing patients with different types of cancer or a training dataset used to predict weeks of pregnancy based on shopping cart data [3]. A related attack based on membership inference is attribute inference [9], where specific attribute values are inferred from records in the training dataset that are partially known to the attacker. In this research, we only consider membership inference that provides protection against MI and attribute inference. Let A_{MI} be an MI adversary, M be a differentially private learning algorithm, n be a positive integer, and Dist represent the distribution over data points (x,y). Sample D from $Dist^n$ and set $r = M(D)$. Consider data that is a member of the training set as follows [9]:

1. Sample z_D uniformly from D and z_{Dist} from Dist.
2. Randomly choose b from {0, 1} with equal probability.
3. Let

$$z = \begin{cases} z_D & \text{if } b = 1 \\ z_{Dist} & \text{if } b = 0 \end{cases}$$

4. The A_{MI} outputs $b' = A_{MI}(r, z, Dist, n, M) \in \{0,1\}$. If $b' = b$, then the A_{MI} is successful and the output of the experiment is 1; otherwise it is 0.

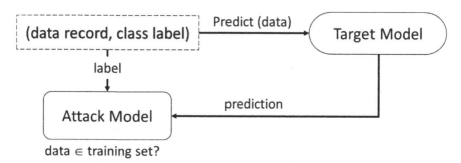

Fig. 1. Member Inference Attack

Specifically, this study examines the differences between black-box and white-box membership inference attacks in terms of what knowledge an attacker is assumed to possess about a machine learning model. In a black-box membership inference attack, an attacker is limited to external features of a machine learning model such as its loss function or predictive confidence during inference. In contrast, in a white-box membership inference attack an attacker also has access to internal features of a machine

learning model such as its gradients. Specifically, Shokri [6] and Yeom [9] have demonstrated membership inference attacks against centralized machine learning models, while
Nasr [14] has demonstrated membership inference attacks against both centralized and
federated neural networks. Membership inference attacks assume that an attacker has
access to the trained predictive function h(·), information about the machine learning
model's hyperparameters, and the differential privacy mechanism used during training.
The trained predictive function represents the target model and the training data as D_{target}^{train}.
Using this information, an attacker can build a binary classifier machine learning model,
known as an attack model, that can classify data as either members or non-members of
the dataset. This attack model can classify data from the training dataset of the target
model with high accuracy. The accuracy of the attack model is evaluated on a balanced
dataset consisting of all members (i.e., target model training data) and an equal number
of non-members (i.e., target model test data). This simulates a worst-case scenario where
an attacker checks membership for all records in the training dataset. The real membership can be inferred using a machine learning classifier such as a neural network (NN)
that tends to classify records d = (x,y) from the training dataset D_{target}^{train} with different
confidence p(x) given h(x) for features x and true label y than a record $d \notin D_{target}^{train}$.

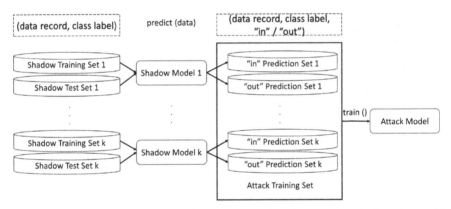

Fig. 2. Membership inference attacks observe the behavior of a target machine learning model

An attacker can obtain various types of information to attack ML models. There
are two types of information that are useful for an attacker to deploy MIA on ML
models: knowledge of the training data and knowledge of the target model. Knowledge
of the training data refers to its distribution. In most implementations of MIA, it is
assumed that the distribution of training data is available to the MIA attacker. This
means that an attacker can derive a shadow dataset containing data records from the
same distribution as the training records. This assumption is reasonable since shadow
datasets can be obtained through statistical-based aggregation when the data distribution
is known, and through model-based aggregation when it is unknown [8]. To conduct
a non-trivial MIA, it is generally assumed that the shadow dataset and the training
dataset are distinct. Information about the target model refers to its trained state (i.e., its
learning algorithm), its architecture, and its parameters, as shown in Fig. 2. Based on

an adversary's knowledge, we can categorize existing attacks into two levels of danger: black-box inference attacks and white-box inference attacks.

2.1 Black-Box Inference Attack

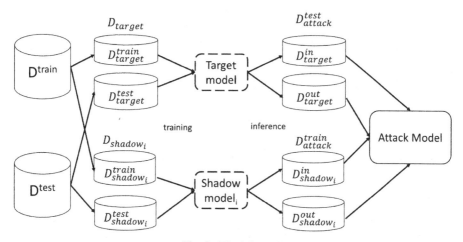

Fig. 3. Black-box MI

The black-box MI (BB) attack proposed by Shokri [6] is limited to external features of a trained machine learning model, as shown in Fig. 3.This would be the case, for example, when a model is exposed through an API call. The black-box membership inference attack exploits vulnerabilities in a machine learning model using a classifier such as a neural network (NN) that tends to classify a record d from its training dataset D_{target}^{train} with high softmax confidence p(x) given h(x) at its true y in than for record d $\notin D_{target}^{train}$. Therefore, A_{MI} consist of two steps. First, A_{MI} trains copies of the target model based on its structure and hyperparameters, known as shadow models, on data that is statistically similar to D_{target}^{train} and D_{target}^{test}. It applies that $\left|D_{shadow_i}^{train}\right| = \left|D_{shadow_i}^{test}\right| \wedge$ $D_{shadow_i}^{train} \cap D_{shadow_i}^{test} = \emptyset \wedge \left|D_{shadow_i} \cap D_{shadow_j}\right| \geq 0$ for all $i \neq j$. After training, each shadow model is invoked by A_{MI} to classify all corresponding training data (member records) and test data (non-member records), i.e. p(x), $\forall$ d $\in D_{shadow_i}^{train} \cup D_{shadow_i}^{test}$. Since A_{MI} has full control over $D_{shadow_i}^{train}$ and $D_{shadow_i}^{test}$, the output of each shadow model (p(x), y) is labeled 'in' if the corresponding record d $\in D_{shadow_i}^{train}$, Otherwise, its label is 'out'. Second, A_{MI} trains a binary classifier attack model for each target variable y $\in$ Y to map p(x) to an 'in' or 'out' data pair. The triple (p(x), y, in/out) serves as the training dataset for the attack model, i.e. D_{attack}^{train}. Therefore, the attack model exploits an imbalance between predictions on target d $\in D_{target}^{train}$ and d $\notin D_{target}^{train}$. Figure 3 illustrates a black-box inference attack setup. The features used to train the attack model are generated by passing shadow model training and test data again through the trained shadow model. The accuracy of the attack model is calculated based on features similarly extracted from the target model.

2.2   White-Box Inference Attack

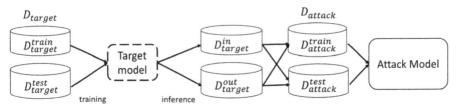

Fig. 4. White-box MI

White-box inference attacks [14] make two assumptions about A_{MI}. First, a white-box inference attack can observe internal features of an ML model in addition to its external features (i.e., its output). Internal features include observed losses $L(h(x; \theta))$, gradients $\delta L/\delta \theta$, and learned weights θ of $h(\cdot)$. Secondly, an attacker A_{MI} is assumed to have knowledge of a portion of D_{target}^{train} and D_{target}^{test}. Simultaneously, an attacker A_{MI} extracts internal and external features from a balanced set of records that have been identified as members or non-members. Figure 4 illustrates a white-box MI attack. Again, it is assumed that an attacker A_{MI} has knowledge of a portion of D_{target}^{train} and D_{target}^{test} and generates attack features by passing these records through the trained target model. An attacker A_{MI} trains a binary classifier attack model for each target variable $y \in Y$ to map $p(x)$ to an 'out' or 'in' indicator. The set $(L(h(x; \theta)), \delta L/\delta \theta, p(x), y, in/out)$ serves as the training dataset for the attack model, i.e., D_{attack}^{train}. Therefore, an MI attack model exploits imbalances between predictions on $d \in D_{target}^{train}$ and $d \notin D_{target}^{test}$. The accuracy of an attack model is also calculated based on features extracted from the target model.

3   Related Work

In this section, the paper focuses on introducing issues related to differential privacy in neural network models, attacking the security of the training data set, and introducing security measures of the neural network model. There are five types of membership inference attacks on the data security of the training dataset, including: membership inference attacks on classification models, on generative models, on the embedded models, on the linear models, and on the federated learning [24]. This paper focuses on types of attacks on classification and generative models.

3.1 Member Inference Attack on Classification Model

In the setup of membership inference attack on the classification model, there are two types: the white-box attack and the black-box attack.

In a black box attack setup, the attacker queries the target model with a pair of input and output data. From the dataset received after querying the target model, the attacker builds shadow models and performs membership inference attack on the target model. Shokri [8] proposed the first MIA on classification models. In this setup, the attacker has black box access (full feedback for all classes) to a model trained on a local dataset and to a public dataset that follows the same distribution as private datasets. The attacker performs membership inference using the black box output of the target model. To do this, the attacker simulates models by training shadow models on known discrete pieces of data from the public dataset. On these simulation models, an attacker can analyze output patterns that correspond to those from private training datasets and from target model's datasets. Salem [16] relaxes two main assumptions of shadow training technique in [8]: multiple shadow models and knowledge of training data distribution. They argue that these two assumptions are relatively strong, which greatly limits application scenarios of MIA to machine learning models. Also, shadow models are not required to have the same structure as target models. Besides extending binary classifier-based MIA existing in [8], they also propose two metric-based attacks that take advantage of highest confidence score and predictive entropy. Yeom [9] also proposed two metric-based MIAs: MIA based on prediction accuracy and MIA based on prediction loss. Yeom [9] also proposed two metric-based MIAs: MIA based on prediction accuracy and MIA based on prediction loss. Long [20] performs MIA on machine learning models that do not fit their training data. They propose a generalized member inference attack that can determine the membership of specific vulnerability records. Accordingly, some records have a unique effect on the target model, even if the model is well normalized. An attacker can exploit the unique effects of specific data records as an indicator of their presence in the training dataset.

In contrast to the black box attack setup, the attackers in the white box attack setup are provided with sufficient information about the target model to perform the attack inferring information about the member state of the record. Nasr [15] first proposed a membership inference attack in a white-box setup, where the attacker knows the internal parameters of the target model. The MIA in Nasr's white box setup can be considered an extension of the binary classifier-based MIA in the black box setup. Compared to black-box MIA, white-box MIA tries to improve attack performance by taking advantage of intermediate computations of input data through the target mode. They use slope of input's predicted attenuation relative to target model's parameters as additional features to infer membership of records in training dataset. The loss slope of a member in training dataset for model parameters can be distinguished from non-member data through training SGD algorithm. However, Leino and Fredrikson [19] pointed out that white box setting in Nasr [15] is too powerful, which is different from most MIA implementations in the real world. Nasr [15] assumes that the attacker knows a significant portion of the target model's private training dataset, while the attacker is usually given a shadow dataset separate from the target model's private training dataset. Therefore, Leino and Fredrikson propose a white-box MIA that does not require any information about records in any training dataset of the target model. This setting is often the same as in actual attack.

3.2 Member Inference Attack on the Generative Model

Besides previous models, MIA was also studied on generative models. Currently, MIA on generative models focuses on GANs compared to other types of generative models, as GANs are the most common generative pattern. Hayes [10] first introduced MIA on generative models in both black-box and white-box settings. The attack intuition is that a GAN discriminator is more confident in giving higher confidence values to training members, since it is trained to learn the statistical difference between the training data and generated data. In a white-box setting, an attacker who inputs all data records into a discriminator will receive a confidence score for each record corresponding to the probability of membership. The attacker sorts these probability values in descending order and chooses the first half of records as members. In a black box setting, the attacker collects records generated from the generative model and uses them to train a local GAN to mimic the target GAN [18]. After the local GAN has been trained, the attacker deploys MIA using the local GAN's discriminator in the same attack approach as in the white box setting. Hilprecht [11] proposed two MIA-based extensions of generative model attacks. One is a Monte Carlo integration attack designed for GANs in a black box setting and the other is a reconstruction attack designed for VAEs in a white box setting. The Monte Carlo integration attack exploits generated records located within a small distance from the target record to estimate the probability that this record is a member through Monte Carlo integration. The attack performed during GAN generation should be able to generate composite records close to training members if GAN is too coincident. The direct reconstruction attack uses loss function of VAE to compute reconstruction error of target member, and result of attack is that training members produce smaller reconstruction error than data whether or not member. In addition to MIA for record, Hilpreche [11] introduces the concept of set membership inference where an attacker tries to determine if a set of records belongs to a training dataset. Save [13] proposes co-membership inference which is essentially the same as set membership inference proposed by Hilpreche [11]. Liu [13]'s proposed attack starts with attacking a single target record then expands to a set of records. For a given record and generator of target GAN, the attacker first optimizes the neural network to reconstruct latent variables such that the generator can generate synthetic records closely matching destination record. The result of attack is that if record belongs to training dataset, then attacker can copy closely similar synthetic records to it. The attacker then measures L2 distance between aggregate record and target record and infers target record as member if distance is less than threshold. In addition, Chen [17] proposes a general member inference attack based on generative models that can be applied to all adversarial generative network model implementations, from black box to white box implementation. For the target record, the attacker tries to recreate the synthetic record closest to the target record. The attacker only needs to find the synthetic record generated by the generator if possible. On the other hand, the attacker uses optimization algorithms to reconstruct the synthetic record. The distance between the reconstructed record and target record is then used to calculate the probability that this target record is a member. The result of the attack is that the generation process will be able to generate more similar patterns for members than for non-member data. To perform a more accurate probability estimate, a generative adversarial network model is trained referentially with a related but discrete dataset and decides target record to be a member when corrected reconstruction error is smaller than threshold [21].

4 The Experimentation

We performed an experiment comparing the trade-off between accuracy and the privacy parameter ε in the presence of inference attacks and without inference attacks on datasets Texas Hospital. This dataset was trained on the models illustrated in Table 1. We chose these training datasets because the unbalanced number of training data per label leads to vulnerability to inference attacks. Besides the tabular dataset, an unstructured dataset is also considered, specifically the CIFAR dataset, which is trained on pre-built models such as ResNet-18, DenseNet-121 illustrated in Table 1.

Table 1. Overview of datasets considered in the evaluation

Dataset	Model
Texas Hospital Stays	Fully connected NN with three layers $(512 \times 128 \times m)$
Cifar 10	resnet 18
	densenet 121

4.1 Datasets

Purchases Shopping Carts dataset was of the unbalanced type and consists of binary vectors with 600 characteristics representing the customer's shopping cart [8]. However, a significant difference from the Texas Hospital Stays dataset is that this dataset has a nearly 90% lower feature count. Each vector is labeled with a customer group. The learning task is to classify the shopping cart by customer group using a fully connected neural network.

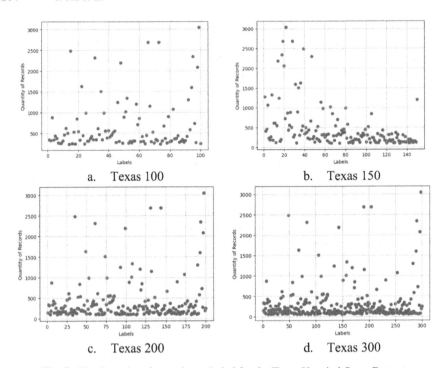

a. Texas 100   b. Texas 150

c. Texas 200   d. Texas 300

Fig. 5. The Quantity of records per Label for the Texas Hospital Stays Dataset

4.2 Experimental Results

A test environment was set up so that the experiments were performed using PyTorch on Google Colab platform running in a GPU. The attacks were performed on Texas Hospital Stays with a fully connected NN with three layers and CIFAR with ResNet-18, DenseNet-121.

Firstly, the target model was trained with 4 shadow models on the Texas Hospital Stays dataset with label numbers: 100, 150, 200, and 300 as shown in Fig. 5. The accuracy of the trained models is shown in Table 1. The model's accuracy decreased as the number of labels in the training dataset was increased. Only two special cases, shadow model 1 and shadow model 2, trained on the Texas Hospital Stays dataset with 150 classes, have higher accuracy than the remaining cases. Their accuracies are 93.044 and 88.85 respectively as shown in Table 2. During the training process of the victim model and shadow model, the accuracy of the models trained on the Texas Hospital Stays dataset with 100 labels always gave the highest accuracy, while the accuracy of the models trained on the Texas Hospital Stays dataset with 300 labels always gave the lowest accuracy. Machine learning models were set to train for 10 epochs. After 10 epochs, the model's accuracy no longer improved much compared to previous epoch runs as shown in Fig. 6. After the shadow models were trained, the target model was attacked by these models in both cases where the target model applied differential privacy and did not apply differential privacy. The results of the member inference attack were shown in Table 3.

Table 2. Results of training the victim model and attack shadow model on the Texas Hospital Stays dataset with the number of labels: 100, 150, 200, 300.

Model	Process	Texas100	Texas150	Texas200	Texas300
Victim Model	Train	**91.596**	87.098	77.967	**76.102**
	Test	59.828	58.699	52.84	48.236
Shadow model 0	Train	**87.913**	85.205	72.851	76.737
	Test	60.376	58.37	51.781	48.968
Shadow model 1	Train	85.259	**93.044**	80.416	80.706
	Test	60.013	58.309	52.942	48.785
Shadow model 2	Train	**88.223**	81.93	87.036	83.323
	Test	60.462	57.768	51.981	48.191
Shadow model 3	Train	84.493	**88.85**	77.325	82.17
	Test	59.696	58.011	52.364	48.79
Shadow model 4	Train	**82.42**	82.101	80.286	68.483
	Test	60.013	58.985	52.343	48.835

Table 3. The results of attacking the victim model when the victim model applied differential privacy ($\varepsilon = 0.1$) and does not apply differential privacy.

Dataset	Attack – NonDP	Attack - DP
Texas100	70.067%	66.206%
Texas150	69.413%	66.529%
Texas200	64.958%	64.384%
Texas300	67.94%	64.63%

Secondly, perform attacks on pre-built models on the CIFAR dataset. Before performing the attack, the CIFAR dataset is divided into two equal parts: one part for training the target model, and one part for training the shadow model. In each part, the dataset is divided into three parts: training (45%), validation (10%), and test (45%). The validation data set is used in cases where training needs to end when the models reach a certain threshold. Therefore, membership inference through random guessing yields an attack accuracy of 50% as illustrated in Table 4.

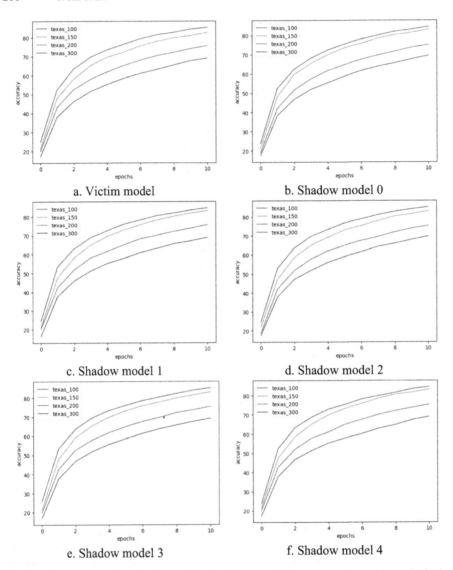

Fig. 6. The accuracy of the victim model and shadow models is measured over 10 epochs in the training process on the Texas Hospital Stays dataset with label numbers: 100, 150, 200, and 300.

Table 4. Results of training two victim models, ResNet-18 and DenseNet-121, and attacking the shadow model on the CIFAR data set.

Model	Process	Resnet-18	Densenet-121
Victim Model	Train	**98.63**	**98.437**
	Test	69.681	76.844
Shadow model 0	Train	98.526	98.793
	Test	**67.719**	74.637
Shadow model 1	Train	97.407	98.044
	Test	68.719	**74**
Shadow model 2	Train	97.637	98.385
	Test	68.563	74.659
Shadow model 3	Train	**99.259**	**99.593**
	Test	69.748	75.637
Shadow model 4	Train	97.756	96.259
	Test	68.022	74.363
Attack accuracy		65.13	61.863

5 Conclusions

By evaluating membership inference attacks on different numbers of classes on the same dataset, we highlight problems with a rapidly growing research series on membership inference. Typically, attack performance is evaluated using different types of models in the case of using and not using differential privacy. Experiments in the study show that when increasing the number of classes in the unbalanced dataset, the accuracy of the black-box attack method using shadow models increases. When applying differential privacy methods to the target model, it reduces the risk of being attacked. Currently, experiments in the study have only performed attacks on the target model Fully Connected Neural Network, while pre-built models such as DenseNet121, ResNet18, and VGG16 also have a high risk of being attacked by membership inference. In addition, the target model in the experiment has not been pruned, so considering models that use different pruning methods will affect its risk level by membership inference attacks. Next, the shadow attack model is trained on a homogeneous environment. If the shadow attack model is used in a heterogeneous environment, it will increase the level of attack success. Finally, this study uses the global differential privacy defense method, which is not enough because there is also a local differential privacy method. This method is often used in organizational training models, especially in federated learning models [23].

Acknowledgements. This research is funded by University of Information Technology-Vietnam National University Ho Chi Minh City under grant number D1–2023-42.

References

1. Warner, S.L.: Randomized response: a survey technique for eliminating evasive answer bias. J. Am. Stat. Assoc. **60**(309), 63–69 (1965)
2. Dwork, C., Kenthapadi, K., McSherry, F., Mironov, I., Naor, M.: Our data, ourselves: Privacy via distributed noise generation. In: Vaudenay, S. (ed.) EUROCRYPT 2006. LNCS, vol. 4004, pp. 486–503. Springer, Heidelberg (2006). https://doi.org/10.1007/11761679_29
3. Hill, K.: How target figured out a teen girl was pregnant before her father did. Forbes, Inc, vol. 7, pp.4–1 (2012)
4. Li, N., Qardaji, W., Su, D., Wu, Y., Yang, W.: Membership privacy: a unifying framework for privacy definitions. In: Proceedings of the 20th ACM SIGSAC Conference on Computer and Communications Security, pp. 889–900 (2013)
5. Fredrikson, M., Jha, S., Ristenpart, T.: Model inversion attacks that exploit confidence information and basic countermeasures. In: Proceedings of the 22nd ACM SIGSAC Conference on Computer and Communications Security, pp. 1322–1333 (2015)
6. Shokri, R., Shmatikov, V.: Privacy-preserving deep learning. In: Proceedings of the 22nd ACM SIGSAC Conference on Computer and Communications Security, pp. 1310–1321 (2015)
7. Tramèr, F., Zhang, F., Juels, A., Reiter, M.K., Ristenpart, T.: Stealing machine learning models via prediction {APIs}. In: Proceedings of the 25th USENIX Security Symposium, pp. 601–618 (2016)
8. Shokri, R., Stronati, M., Song, C., Shmatikov, V.: Membership inference attacks against machine learning models. In: Proceedings of the 38th IEEE Symposium on Security and Privacy, pp. 3–18 (2017)
9. Yeom, S., Giacomelli, I., Fredrikson, M., Jha, S.: Privacy risk in machine learning: analyzing the connection to overfitting. In: Proceedings of the IEEE 31st Computer Security Foundations Symposium (CSF), pp. 268–282 (2018)
10. Hayes, J., Melis, L., Danezis, G., De Cristofaro, E.: LOGAN: membership inference attacks against generative models. Proc. Priv. Enhancing Technol. (PoPETs) **2019**(1), 133–152 (2019)
11. Hilprecht, B., Härterich, M., Bernau, D.: Monte Carlo and reconstruction membership inference attacks against generative models. Proc. Priv. Enhancing Technol. **2019**(4), 232–249 (2019)
12. Jayaraman, B., Evans, D.: Evaluating differentially private machine learning in practice. In: Proceedings of the 28th USENIX Security Symposium (USENIX Security 2019), pp. 1895–1912 (2019)
13. Liu, K.S., Xiao, C., Li, B., Gao, J.: Performing co-membership attacks against deep generative models. In: Proceedings of the 19th IEEE International Conference on Data Mining (ICDM), pp. 459–467 (2019)
14. Nasr, M., Shokri, R., Houmansadr, A.: Comprehensive privacy analysis of deep learning. In: Proceedings of the 40th IEEE Symposium on Security and Privacy, pp. 1–15 (2019)
15. Nasr, M., Shokri, R., Houmansadr, A.: Comprehensive privacy analysis of deep learning: passive and active white-box inference attacks against centralized and federated learning. In: Proceedings of the 40th IEEE Symposium on Security and Privacy, pp. 739–753 (2019)
16. Salem, A., Zhang, Y., Humbert, M., Berrang, P., Fritz, M., Backes, M.: ML-leaks: model and data independent membership inference attacks and defenses on machine learning models. In: Proceedings of the 26th Network and Distributed Systems Security Symposium (2019)
17. Chen, D., Yu, N., Zhang, Y., Fritz, M.: GAN-leaks: a taxonomy of membership inference attacks against generative models. In: Proceedings of the 27th ACM SIGSAC Conference on Computer and Communications Security, pp. 343–362 (2020)
18. Ha, T., Dang, T.K., Le, H., Truong, T.A.: Security and privacy issues in deep learning: a brief review. SN Comput. Sci. **1**(5), 253 (2020)

19. Leino, K., Fredrikson, M.: Stolen memories: leveraging model memorization for calibrated {White-Box} membership inference. In: Proceedings of the 29th USENIX Security Symposium (USENIX Security 20), pp. 1605–1622 (2020)
20. Long, Y., et al.: A pragmatic approach to membership inferences on machine learning models. In: Proceedings of the 5th IEEE European Symposium on Security and Privacy, pp. 521–534 (2020). https://doi.org/10.1109/EuroSP48549.2020.00040
21. Ha, T., Dang, T.K., Nguyen-Tan, N.: Comprehensive analysis of privacy in black-box and white-box inference attacks against generative adversarial network. In: Dang, T.K., Küng, J., Chung, T.M., Takizawa, M. (eds.) FDSE 2021. LNCS, vol. 13076, pp. 323–337. Springer, Cham (2021). https://doi.org/10.1007/978-3-030-91387-8_21
22. Jayaraman, B., Wang, L., Knipmeyer, K., Gu, Q., Evans, D.: Revisiting membership inference under realistic assumptions. Proc. Priv. Enhancing Technol. **2021**(2), 348–368 (2021). https://doi.org/10.2478/popets-2021-0031
23. Ha, T., Dang, T.K.: Inference attacks based on GAN in federated learning. Int. J. Web Inf. Syst. **18**(2/3), 117–136 (2022)
24. Hu, H., Salcic, Z., Sun, L., Dobbie, G., Yu, P.S., Zhang, X.: Membership inference attacks on machine learning: a survey. ACM Comput. Surv. **54**(11s), 1–37 (2022)
25. Liu, L., Wang, Y., Liu, G., Peng, K., Wang, C.: Membership inference attacks against machine learning models via prediction sensitivity. IEEE Trans. Dependable Secure Comput. **20**(3), 2341–2347 (2022). https://doi.org/10.1109/TDSC.2022.3180828

Smart City and Industry 4.0 Applications

LAVETTES: Large-scAle-dataset Vietnamese ExTractive TExt Summarization Models

Ti-Hon Nguyen[1(✉)], Thanh Ma[1(✉)], and Thanh-Nghi Do[1,2]

[1] Can Tho University, Can Tho, Vietnam
{nthon,mtthanh,dtnghi}@ctu.edu.vn
[2] UMI UMMISCO 209, IRD/UPMC, Bondy, France

Abstract. The problem of text summarization has consistently been a significant and prominent challenge for a particular language. Each language's unique characteristics will reflect that country's identity, culture, and nuances. This paper introduces extractive text summarization models for Vietnamese documents. Our approach concentrates on discovering appreciative and plausible models by combining ML algorithms. Namely, we investigate three potential models, including a "G-global-hard-cluster" (with GloVe), "probability-cluster" (with LDA, Latent Dirichlet Allocation), and a "soft-specific" combination between SGD (Stochastic gradient descent) and $k$means. Moreover, we also provide experimental results to evaluate the quality of the summary and the consumption time. In particular, our approaches obtain the expected results with 51.49% ROUGE-1, 17.99% ROUGE-2, and 29.25% ROUGE-L. Finally, we discuss the promising results of the proposed models.

Keywords: Text summarization · Classification · Clustering · $k$means · LDA · SGD

1 Introduction

Automatic text summarization aims to produce a concise, straightforward, and articulate summary while preserving essential statement content and overall meaning [3]. The text summarization model can be classified by the number of input documents or by the specific strategy to construct the summary. We can recapitulate a document or multi-document. Naturally, the single-document text summarization model receives one input text. In contrast, the input of the multi-document text summarization model will be a set of documents. To this end, the extractive text summarization endeavors to select the input sentence for assembling the summary. Building an extractive text summarization system includes three essential steps: (1) constructing the dataset, (2) making a score of the candidate's sentences, and (3) joining the top-scored candidate sentences. Typically, the candidate's sentence scoring process ranks the importance or relevance of every input text sentence with the entire. Sentence scoring can be based

T. K. Dang et al. (Eds.): FDSE 2023, CCIS 1925, pp. 273–288, 2023.
https://doi.org/10.1007/978-981-99-8296-7_19

on word scoring [1,14,22], sentence feature [12,13,27], graph [5], classification model [4,9,18], and clustering [6,24,26]. The methods using word-scoring-based, sentence-feature-based, and graph-based can only use the information of the input text directly. On the other hand, the clustering-based techniques can use the input text information by training the clustering model of the input sentence [2,26,33] or pre-trained the clustering model on a training dataset [25]. Furthermore, in another approach, we can leverage the abstractive summarization technique to paraphrase the input knowledge into a refreshed outline [17].

Automatic text summarization (ATS) plays an essential part in natural language processing (NLP) and information retrieval (IR) tasks. ATS generates a straightforward summary covering the midpoint information of a passage or document, consisting of a few keywords and sentences. Taking advantage of deep neural network models for the ATS obtains impressive ROUGE scores [19]. Several successful models in this approach include MoCa [34], Pegasus 2B with SLiC [35], BRIO [20], Pointer-Generator with Coverage on the CNN/Daily Mail dataset [30]. From the general perspective, the cost of training the neural network is expensive. We have to furnish enormous GPU resources and a long duration [32]. Especially it will be a weighting challenge for the Vietnamese large-scale dataset. For the Vietnamese, the meaning of a "word" will be composed of many single words, i.e., "Cong vien" is a "park", "Sau rieng" is a durian, and "Chim go kien" is a woodpecker. Hence, it is challenging to determine a sentence's meaning if we only account for each single word. Another troubling point is that the same word combined with another single word has a different meaning, i.e., "*Van* hoa" and "*Van* phong" correspond to the culture and office, respectively. Besides, suppose we swap the position of two single words. In that case, they will be different meanings, i.e., "Ngu phap" and "Phap ngu" will be Grammar and French, respectively. Accordingly, the situations of "local" and "global" word are also challenges to be curiousness. Furthermore, we aim to explore simple methods but still ensure efficiency.

Realizing the above issues, we investigate a sequence/series of studies (using machine learning) related to the ATS for the Vietnamese large-scale dataset. The explorations include (i) "global-hard-cluster" model, (ii) "G-global-hard-cluster" model with Glove embedding, (iii) "probability-cluster" model, and (iv) SGD-local-kmeans-combination model. Particularly, our first work published a proposal of pre-training the $k$means [23] to cluster the large-scale dataset [25]. In detail, we use $k$means clustering to create the clusters on the Vietnamese large-scale dataset. Then, we take advantage of these clusters to extract the most relevant sentences on the single-document to produce the summary. We call this approach proposed named the "global-hard-cluster" summary model. In this paper, we discover three remaining approaches. They include: (1) *Utilizing GloVe embedding* [28], a more succinct vector embeds the association of the words to replace the Bag-of-Words representation [15] in the model published [25]. The primary idea is to cluster the documents across the entire dataset. We denote this as a "global-hard-cluster" model; (2) *Leveraging the LDA clustering model* [7] instead of $k$means improving the ROUGE score. However, since LDA can not work with GloVe, which has a negative value in vector elements (work in non-negative integers), we, therefore, operate Bag-of-Words for this approach. We call this a "probability-cluster" model; (3) *Inserting a classifier (using SGD* [11]*) to classify the input text* before handing it into the summarization model to improve the quality of the output summary. Note that this proposal utilizes $k$means (local) to cluster the training dataset. The primary idea is to take advantage of the class's information (classification) for exploring the local in each category.

In order to evaluate the quality of the summary, we compare all the models' ROUGE score and experiment time [26], and abstractive summarization models (the Pointer-Generator networks [30]). We conduct these approaches because they provide a potential picture of local-to-global clusters and combinations between machine learning techniques for improving summarization quality and consumption time. Most of our proposals have an expected outcome for a large-scale Vietnamese extractive text summarization.

The remainder of this paper is structured as follows: we briefly presents a fundamental background in Sect. 2. Next, Sect. 3 describes the proposed method. Then, Sect. 4 illustrates the experiment and the results of the summary models. Finally, Sect. 5 shows the conclusions and future work.

2   Background

In this section, we deliver the primary foundation for text summarization. First, we mention $k$means clustering, also known as "hard-cluster", will be the technique to gather the expressions (words, sentences, and documents) into a group for the large-scale dataset. Second, we present Latent Dirichlet Allocation (LDA) to conduct the second proposal; in particular, instead of leveraging "hard-cluster", we replace "$k$means" by the maximum probability. Third, we mention distance metrics to select the documents or sentences for the summary. Fourth, ROUGE metrics will be introduced to evaluate the quality of the resume. Fifth, we furnish the techniques to represent vectors from input text. Finally, an efficient algorithm (SGD) for topic classification to apply the third proposal will be introduced in this section.

2.1   The $k$means Clustering

The $k$means [21, 23, 29] clustering is a popular unsupervised machine learning algorithm used for data clustering and partitioning. It's a straightforward and efficient method to classify data into distinct groups or clusters based on similarity. We use the mini-batch $k$means [29], an improved version of $k$means, to work on the large-scale dataset, to implement the summary component. The details of the mini-batch $k$means are indicated in [29].

2.2   Latent Dirichlet Allocation

Latent Dirichlet Allocation (LDA) [7] is an efficient approximate inference technique based on variational methods and an EM algorithm [10] for empirical

Bayesian parameter estimation. The LDA model assigns a sample in the dataset to a group of topics. First, we conduct the LDA models on the training dataset. Then, in the summary step, because the implementation of the LDA module returns the set of probabilities to which the input sentence belongs, we used the cluster with max probability as the input sentence's primary cluster and the probability of that sentence with the corresponding cluster for scoring.

2.3   Distance Metrics

Distance metrics are the standard to measure how two vectors with similar dimensions are near each other. The main purpose is to determine the potential sentences for summarization models.

Given two vectors $a = [a_1, a_2, ..., a_n]$ and $b = [b_1, b_2, ..., b_n]$ with n dimensions. The **cosine** distance of a and b and the **Euclidean** distance d of a and b are illustrated by the equation as follows: $cosine\_distance(a, b) = 1 - cos(\theta) = 1 - \frac{a \cdot b}{\|a\|\|b\|} = 1 - \frac{\sum_{i=1}^{n} a_i b_i}{\sqrt{\sum_{i=1}^{n} a_i^2} \sqrt{\sum_{i=1}^{n} b_i^2}}$ and $d(a, b) = \sqrt{\sum_{i=1}^{n} (a_i - b_i)^2}$.

2.4   ROUGE Metrics

ROUGE [19] is the metric for evaluating the text summary model. ROUGE work by comparing the summary produced by the model (system summary) with reference summaries (the gold standard summary). In ROUGE, the "overlapping word" is visible in both the system and the reference summaries. The "overlapping word" is determined by the n-gram model in ROUGE-N and the longest common subsequence in ROUGE-L.

2.5   Text Representation Models

Typically, the input of ML algorithms is the numerical vectors. Consequently, we utilize the word presentation model to transform the text documents into numerical vectors before putting them into the machine learning model. Two methods of word presentation include *(1) term frequency* and *(2) word embedding*. Namely, Bag-of-Words (BoW) [15] is one of the term frequency word representations. In BoW, the vocabulary set is usually created by all terms (words) in the corpus. Therefore, one text document will be represented as a vector, with the elements being the term frequency of the document's words. The dimension of the term frequency vector will be the number of words in the vocabulary set. Second, GloVe [28], one of the word embedding models, is to present the dataset. The GloVe model considered the "global" relationship of the words in the input text and was introduced in 2014 by Pennington. It will be trained on the training dataset and used to create the input vector for our summary model.

2.6   Stochastic Gradient Descent (SGD)

Stochastic gradient descent (SGD) [11] is a simple but efficient algorithm for large-scale learning due to the computational complexity that corresponds to linear in the number of training data points [11]. Therefore, we use the SGD algorithm to implement the classification model. Given a classification task with the dataset $D = [X, Y]$ that includes m data points $X = \{x_1, x_2, \ldots, x_m\}$ in the input space n dimensional R^n, the corresponding labels $Y = \{y_1, y_2, \ldots, y_m\}$ being $\{cl_1, cl_2, \ldots, cl_p\}$.

The stochastic gradient descent (SGD) algorithm tries to find p separating planes for p classes (denoted by normal vectors $w_1, w_2, \ldots, w_p \in R^n$) in which the plane w_i separates the class cl_i from the rest. This is achieved by solving the unconstrained problem: min $\Psi(w_p, [X, Y]) = \frac{\lambda}{2}\|w_p\|^2 + \frac{1}{m}\sum_{i=1}^{m} L(w_p, [x_i, y_i])$ where the errors are measured by $L(w_p, [x_i, y_i]) = max\{0, 1 - y_i(w_p.x_i)\}$ and a positive constant λ is to control the regularization strength ($\|w_p\|^2$).

Studies in [8, 31] illustrate that the SGD algorithm solves the unconstrained problem by updating w in T epochs with a learning rate η. For each epoch t, the SGD uses a single data point (x_i, y_i) randomly in the mini-batch B_i to compute the subgradient $\nabla_t \Psi(w_p, [x_i, y_i])$ and update w_p as follows: $w_p = w_p - \eta \nabla_t \Psi(w_p, [x_i, y_i])$

3   Extractive Summary Models

For the summary models, two highlight approaches are (i) the abstractive summary model and (ii) the extractive summary model. We concentrate on the second direction to discover the summary models proposed (from global to local cluster and the flexible methods). To assess our investigation, we implement Pointer-Generator networks (a.k.a. abstractive summarization models) as a baseline to compare with our extractive summarization model on the Vietnamese large-scale dataset.

A series of the potential summary models explored are as follows: (1) **"Local-cluster" model.** To present continuity in the research series and to compare the results, we recall the summary model proposed (published in [25]). Namely, first, we used the $k$means to cluster on the training dataset. Then, in the summarizing stage, the clustered $k$means will be operated for ranking the sentences of the input text. Finally, the summary step details, which receive one document as the input and return a summary, are illustrated in Fig. 1; (2) **Leveraging GloVe embedding (Global-cluster).** This model has the exact overall and summary-step details as the previous model in (1). It has only improved by replacing the Bag-of-Words text representation with the GloVe embedding. This extension aims to reduce the length of the feature vector to speed up the training and summarizing processes. We represent this model in Fig. 1(a); (3) **Applying LDA (Probability-cluster).** This model has the overall same as the model proposed in (1). However, we take advantages of LDA, an topic modeling algorithm, instead of $k$means clustering. Therefore, it has some modification of the summarizing step as shown in the Fig. 1. This extension aims to improve the quality of the output summary based on the ROUGE score; (4) **An addition of an SGD.** Our proposal of this extension model is shown in the Fig. 1(b). We insert a SGD classification model before the summary period. The training dataset is also split into m subsets based on the specific classes. Then, we use $k$means to cluster in the m subsets. In the summary step, the summarization model selects the clustering model based on the label of input text, which the classifier predicts. The summary step details, which receive one document as the input and return a summary, are illustrated in Fig. 1 is the same as the previous model with $k$means algorithms.

Next, to pinpoint the expected and representative sentences for the summary outcome, two strategies for the summarizing process are as follows: (1) **Applying $k$means.** The primary summary process with the hard clustering model gets a text document, and the pre-trained $k$means clustering model with the set of centroids C as the inputs and returns the output summary (Fig. 1). First, the input text will be split into sentences and stored in set S. These sentences are then transformed into a matrix of numerical vector X based on a word representation model. After that, the summary model will find the closest cluster centroid $c \in C$ for every vector $x \in X$; this process will store the index of x in X and the distance of x with the corresponding cluster center into the set V. Then, set V will be sorted with the increase of the distance value in its elements. After that, the summary model gets the top n-sentence index with the lowest distance in V and selects the corresponding sentence in S to create the summary; (2) **Using LDA.** The primary summary process with the soft clustering model gets a text document, and the pre-trained LDA clustering model as the inputs and returns the output summary (Fig. 1). First, the input text will be split into sentences and stored in set S. These sentences are then transformed into a matrix of numerical vector X based on a word representation model. After that, for every vector $x \in X$, the summary model will find the max probability of it with the LDA; this process will store the index of x in X and the max probability of x with the LDA model. Then, set V will be sorted by decreasing the probability value in its elements. After that, the summary model gets the top n-sentence index with the highest probability in V and selects the corresponding sentence in S to create the summary.

4   Experiment and Results

In this section, we mention the information the Vietnamese dataset used during the experimental process. Additionally, the configurations and parameters to support the training is also presented. Moreover, we provide and discuss quantity and quality results.

4.1   Dataset and Configurations

The dataset **VNText** was built by collecting the articles from the Vietnamese online newspapers, the same approach as the **CNN/Daily Mail** dataset [16, 30] authors. The collected articles had the HTML form, so we cleaned up by eliminating HTML tags and unrelated information like links and advertising. The final VNText dataset has 1,101,101 documents, each including the title,

(1) The proposed summary model for single-document

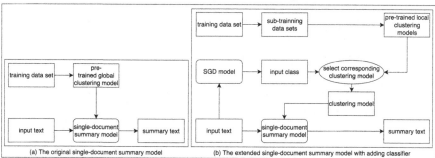

(2) The detail of the summary process

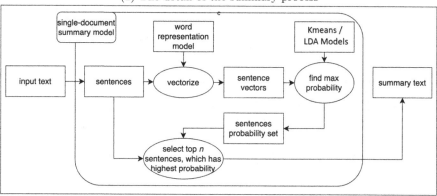

Fig. 1. Regarding (1), *(a)* and its extension model with an additional classification model *(b)*. (2) For two options including $k$means or LDA. A text is as input and returns the output summary.

subtitle, and main content. We use the subtitle as the reference summary and the main content as the input sample.

Next, we split the VNText into three subsets: the training, the validation, and the testing datasets with 880,895, 110,103, and 110,103 records, respectively (Table 1). After that, we use the training dataset to train the GloVe embedding, the $k$means, the LDA, and the SGD models. Then, we divide the training dataset into m sub-training datasets based on its sample class for preparing m $k$means models used in the summary model with SGD. And the validation set is used for tuning the parameters of these models. Finally, the testing dataset is used for evaluating and reporting the results.

In Table 1, #Words/Sent is the average number of words per sentence, #Words/Document is the average number of words per article, #Sents/Document is the average number of sentences per article.

In addition, to measure the time performance of the models, we use one computer configuration for all tasks of the extractive summary models in the experiments. It consists of CPU ARM model Neoverse-N1 4 cores 3.0 GHz, sin-

Table 1. Detail of the VNText

No	Information	Training	Testing	Validation
1	#Documents	880,895.00	110,103.00	110,103.00
2	#Sentences	18,738,333.00	2,342,296.00	2,333,519.00
3	#Words	452,686,377.00	56,563,630.00	56,417,036.00
4	#Words/Sent	24.16	24.15	24.18
5	#Words/Document	513.89	513.73	512.40
6	#Sents/Document	21.27	21.27	21.19

gle thread per core, RAM 24 GB, HDD read and write speed of about 150.34 MB/second. In addition, the baseline Pointer-generator network model is trained and inference on a computer with one V100, 16 GB GPU.

4.2   Training and Parameters

Kmeans, LDA, and SGD. We train the GloVe embedding, $k$means and LDA clustering, SGD classifier, and build Bag-of-Words vocabulary on the training dataset. The number of output sentences in all extractive models $n \in \{1, 2, 3, 4, 5\}$. The number of the cluster in $k$means and the topic number in LDA $k \in \{100, 500, 1000\}$. The number of words in the Bag-of-Words vocabulary is 121918, so we use sparse matrix types to adapt to our limited computing memory. The number of classes in our dataset is 16. SGD with number of $epoch = 20, alpha = 0.1, loss = "hinge"$. All models are trained on the entire training dataset, except the $k$means in the summary model with the addition of an SGD. In training that model, we created a 16 sub-set of the training dataset based on its record class and trained $m = 16$ $k$means model on these sub-training datasets.

GloVe Embedding. GloVe training parameters are chosen based on the GloVe paper [28] and held out on our dataset. There is the dimension of word vector $embedding\_len = 300$, number of epochs to train word embedding $epoch = 15$, size of the context windows $window\_size = 15$, kind of distributed representations model is $skip\_gram$.

Abstractive Summary. Similar to the training strategy of the author of the Pointer-generator networks, we first trained this model on our training set in $point\text{-}gen$ mode. We then used the last checkpoint to continue the training in the $coverage$ mode. However, because the VNText has approximately three times more records than the CNN/Daily Mail, we trained this model 10 epochs in $point\text{-}gen$ mode. After that, we continued training 2,000 iterations for the $coverage$ mode. In addition, we trained this model on a V100 GPU using default parameters.

4.3   Results and Discussion

Experimental Results. We obtain the summary length, F_1 score based on ROUGE-1, ROUGE-2, ROUGE-L, and experimentation time in Tables 2, 3, 4, 5, 6, respectively. The highest F_1 score in tables is bold-faced, and the second is in italics. These numerical test results are evaluated on the test dataset, which has $110, 103.00$ records.

The model name with *"bow-kms"* is the original model in [25], using $k$means clustering and BoW feature. The model name with *"bow-lda"* is the model using LDA clustering and BoW feature. The model name with *"glove-kms"* is the model using $k$means clustering and GloVe embedding. The model name with *"glove-sgd-kms"* is the model using $k$means clustering and GloVe embedding with an additional SGD. The cluster number in the clustering models is the suffix *"−100, −500, −1000"*. The model with the *star (*)* is the model presented in the paper [26], evaluated on the same dataset, *"glove-self-kms(*)"* is the model using $k$means clustering and GloVe embedding, this model run $k$means on the sentences of input text instead of pre-trained on the training dataset. The model name *point-gen(*)* and *coverage(*)* is the Pointer-generator network with *point-gen* mode and *coverage* mode, respectively.

Summary Length. The length of the output summary of extractive models is usually in the number of sentences, and the abstractive model is the max length. However, the number of words in sentences is generally different. Therefore, we suggest the average number of words per summary in our experimentation to observe more detail about output summaries. As shown in Table 2, the average words per summary is proportional to the increased number of output sentences. Almost the output of the extractive model is more prolonged than the comparative abstractive model. The models using GloVe embedding seem to produce a more extended summary than the others in case of the same number of clusters.

In ROUGE-1. The F_1 score of *glove-kms* models, the summary model with GloVe embedding, is higher than the previous model *bow-kms* [25] when $n = 1$, such as **51.35%** in comparison with 48.31%. However, when n from 2 to 5, the F_1 score of *glove-kms* is lower.

The F_1 score of *bow-lda* models, the summary model with LDA clustering, is lower than others when $n = 1$. But *bow-lda* models have significance higher F_1 than other extractive models when $n \in \{2, 3, 4, 5\}$ with 50.60%, 47.69%, 43.32%, 39.32%, respectively. The F_1 score of *glove-sgd-kms* models, the summary model with the addition of an SGD, is highest with **51.49%** compared with the model using pre-trained $k$means on the training dataset when $n = 1$, however, when $n \in \{2, 3, 4, 5\}$ the F_1 of *glove-sgd-kms* models are less than *bow-kms* models. The F_1 score of *glove-self-kms(*)*, proposed in [26], is highest with **51.91%** among extractive models when $n = 1$. However, when $n \in \{2, 3, 4, 5\}$ the F_1 of *glove-self-kms(*)* has the lowest trend.

The F_1 score of the Pointer-generator network has far different between the *point-gen* mode and the *coverage* mode. For example, all extractive models have F_1 scores **lower** than the *coverage* mode with **52.33%**. On the other hand, the

Table 2. Average words per summary

No	Model	n = 1	n = 2	n = 3	n = 4	n = 5
1	bow-kms-100	37.57	70.15	99.31	126.13	151.02
2	bow-kms-500	34.45	65.83	94.76	121.73	147.08
3	bow-kms-1000	35.86	67.26	96.19	123.23	148.50
4	bow-lda-100	28.44	53.57	77.36	100.30	122.57
5	bow-lda-500	27.42	52.68	76.99	100.65	123.51
6	bow-lda-1000	26.82	51.89	76.25	99.92	122.93
7	glove-kms-100	42.72	77.80	108.04	133.83	155.07
8	glove-kms-500	43.76	79.86	111.48	139.31	163.55
9	glove-kms-1000	44.14	80.48	112.56	141.15	166.54
10	glove-sgd-kms-100	44.35	80.08	109.79	133.37	150.86
11	glove-sgd-kms-500	45.04	81.75	113.85	141.91	166.02
12	glove-sgd-kms-1000	*45.24*	*82.17*	*114.58*	*143.17*	*168.14*
13	glove-self-kms(*)	**47.26**	**83.02**	**116.51**	**143.59**	**173.57**
14	point-gen(*) (*max_length* = 100)					41.38
15	coverage(*) (*max_length* = 100)					41.69

extractive model with GloVe embedding with $n = 1$ and the extractive with LDA clustering with $n = 2$ have F_1 score **larger than 50%** that is more significant than F_1 score of the *point-gen* mode with 49.60%. Especially, *bow-lda* models with $n = 2$ have the average number of words per summary greater than 51 words, which is longer 21.42% than that of one of the abstractive models, only less than 42 words.

In ROUGE-2. When $n \in \{1, 2, 3\}$, the F_1 score of *glove-kms* and *glove-sgd-kms* models are dominant, such as *glove-kms* with **17.85%** and *glove-sgd-kms* with **17.99%** when $n = 2$, but when $n \in \{4, 5\}$ the F_1 score of *bow-kms* and *bow-lda* are slightly higher. Especially, the F_1 score of the *bow-lda* models significantly changes from about 13% when $n = 1$ to more than 17% when $n = 5$. On the other hand, the *glove-self-kms(*)* have only the highest value of **17.45%** when $n = 1$ and goes down with the increasing n value. When $n >= 2$, all extractive models with pre-trained clustering have F_1 scores better than the abstractive model in both *point-gen* and *coverage* mode.

In ROUGE-L. When $n = 1$, the extractive models using GloVe embedding are better than those using Bag-of-Words. In contrast, when $n \in \{2, 3, 4, 5\}$, the extractive models using Bag-of-Words have better F_1 score. Thus, the *bow-lda* models are better than other extractive models with F_1 scores are **28.73%**, 27.60%, 25.98%, 24.44% when n from 2 to 5. However, the F_1 score of all extractive models is **less than** F_1 of the abstractive model with 32.59% in *point-gen* mode and 33.09% in *coverage* mode.

Table 3. F_1 based on ROUGE-1

No	Model	n = 1	n = 2	n = 3	n = 4	n = 5
1	bow-kms-100	48.31	48.65	43.58	38.84	35.05
2	bow-kms-500	44.13	48.56	44.47	39.76	35.80
3	bow-kms-1000	46.18	48.47	44.12	39.47	35.59
4	bow-lda-100	45.48	50.04	47.29	*43.23*	**39.32**
5	bow-lda-500	45.05	*50.21*	*47.41*	43.14	39.11
6	bow-lda-1000	45.31	**50.60**	**47.69**	**43.32**	*39.22*
7	glove-kms-100	51.22	47.69	41.74	37.39	34.55
8	glove-kms-500	51.35	47.34	41.18	36.57	33.39
9	glove-kms-1000	51.34	47.25	41.01	36.29	32.97
10	glove-sgd-kms-100	51.43	47.28	41.50	37.67	35.46
11	glove-sgd-kms-500	*51.49*	47.07	40.84	36.28	33.19
12	glove-sgd-kms-1000	*51.49*	46.99	40.72	36.09	32.89
13	glove-self-kms(*)	**51.91**	46.23	40.49	36.46	32.59
14	point-gen(*) ($max\_length = 100$)					49.60
15	coverage(*) ($max\_length = 100$)					**52.33**

Table 4. F_1 based on ROUGE-2

No	Model	n = 1	n = 2	n = 3	n = 4	n = 5
1	bow-kms-100	14.83	17.45	*17.70*	17.34	16.82
2	bow-kms-500	13.59	17.02	17.59	17.35	16.85
3	bow-kms-1000	14.28	17.19	17.63	17.34	16.84
4	bow-lda-100	13.21	16.49	17.42	17.52	17.24
5	bow-lda-500	13.04	16.49	17.47	*17.55*	*17.25*
6	bow-lda-1000	13.02	16.57	17.56	**17.62**	**17.28**
7	glove-kms-100	15.82	17.76	17.65	17.16	16.65
8	glove-kms-500	16.01	17.84	*17.70*	17.16	16.57
9	glove-kms-1000	16.05	17.85	17.68	17.12	16.51
10	glove-sgd-kms-100	16.22	17.93	**17.75**	17.26	16.84
11	glove-sgd-kms-500	16.32	**17.99**	**17.75**	17.15	16.55
12	glove-sgd-kms-1000	*16.33*	*17.97*	**17.75**	17.14	16.53
13	glove-self-kms(*)	**17.45**	16.97	16.47	16.09	15.60
14	point-gen(*) ($max\_length = 100$)					15.36
15	coverage(*) ($max\_length = 100$)					16.17

Table 5. F_1 based on ROUGE-L

No	Model	n = 1	n = 2	n = 3	n = 4	n = 5
1	bow-kms-100	28.08	28.08	26.20	24.38	22.82
2	bow-kms-500	26.02	28.08	26.52	24.73	23.11
3	bow-kms-1000	27.21	28.06	26.42	24.61	23.02
4	bow-lda-100	27.00	28.49	27.44	*25.94*	**24.44**
5	bow-lda-500	26.87	*28.55*	*27.47*	25.90	24.36
6	bow-lda-1000	27.02	**28.73**	**27.60**	**25.98**	*24.42*
7	glove-kms-100	29.10	27.69	25.51	23.78	22.55
8	glove-kms-500	29.16	27.58	25.33	23.50	22.11
9	glove-kms-1000	29.16	27.55	25.25	23.37	21.92
10	glove-sgd-kms-100	29.21	27.59	25.46	23.92	22.96
11	glove-sgd-kms-500	*29.24*	27.53	25.22	23.38	22.02
12	glove-sgd-kms-1000	**29.25**	27.49	25.17	23.31	21.90
13	glove-self-kms(*)	**29.65**	27.58	25.27	23.51	21.79
14	point-gen(*) (*max_length* = 100)					**32.59**
15	coverage(*) (*max_length* = 100)					**33.09**

Evaluation Time. The *bow-kms* is the fastest model in the training process, spending $0.61, 0.65$, and 0.71 h for the training model with $k \in \{100, 500, 1000\}$ clusters. On the other hand, the *bow-lda* model needs more training time with $4.26, 15.53$, and 22.94 h for the training model with $k \in \{100, 500, 1000\}$ clusters. The *glove-kms* model takes about three more times than the *bow-kms* models, with 1.50 h for the training of each model with $k \in \{100, 500, 1000\}$ clusters. It needs slightly extra time to train the SGD in *glove-sgd-kms* models and m $k$means models on m sub-training datasets, $1.51, 1.55$, and 1.63 h for the training model with $k \in \{100, 500, 1000\}$ clusters. The *glove-self-kms(*)* only needs time to train the GloVe model with 1.32 h. All extractive models need much less training time than the comparative abstractive model, with 129.63 h in training *point-gen* mode and 134.3 h for *coverage* mode.

In the summarization process, the *bow-kms* model needs a lot of time with 12.25 h when $k = 100$, 45.54 h when $k = 500$, and 86.12 h when $k = 1000$. The *bow-lda* model is better with 6.62 h when $k = 100$, 7.14 h when $k = 500$ and 7.83 h when $k = 1000$. The *glove-kms* models have the best summarizing time, only **0.20** h when $k = 100$, **0.33** h when $k = 500$, and **0.51** h when $k = 1000$. It is better than *glove-self-kms*, which needs **0.57** h. The *glove-sgd-kms* model needs more time than *glove-kms* model to predict the input class and choose the corresponding $k$means model, and they are also better than *glove-self-kms(*)* when $k = 100$ and $k = 500$ with 0.32 and 0.44 h. It is surprising when the abstractive model spends less time than the *bow-kms* model in the case of $k = 500$ and $k = 1000$, the *point-gen* mode needs 40.33 h, and the *coverage* mode needs 35.09 h. That is because of the dense BoW vector in implementing the summarizing process to adapt with the density vector of $k$means model centroids, which has 121918 dimensions.

In total experiment time on our VNText dataset, when $k \in \{100, 500\}$, the *glove-kms* model is the fastest, and the *glove-sgd-kms* is the second one. However, *bow-kms* and *bow-lda* models are also fast enough to summarize a large-scale dataset as VNText.

Table 6. Experiment time *(hour)*

No	Model	training	summarizing	calculate rouge	total
1	bow-kms-100	**0.61**	12.25	0.47	13.34
2	bow-kms-500	*0.65*	45.54	0.45	46.64
3	bow-kms-1000	0.73	86.12	0.46	87.31
4	bow-lda-100	4.26	6.62	0.38	11.26
5	bow-lda-500	15.53	7.14	0.38	23.05
6	bow-lda-1000	22.94	7.83	0.38	31.15
7	glove-kms-100	1.50	**0.20**	0.51	**2.21**
8	glove-kms-500	1.50	0.33	0.52	2.36
9	glove-kms-1000	1.50	0.51	0.53	2.55
10	glove-sgd-kms-100	1.51	*0.32*	0.51	*2.34*
11	glove-sgd-kms-500	1.55	0.44	0.38	2.37
12	glove-sgd-kms-1000	1.63	0.63	0.38	2.64
13	glove-self-kms(*)	1.32	0.57	0.59	2.48
14	point-gen(*)	129.63	40.33	0.69	170.65
15	coverage(*)	134.3	35.09	0.69	170.08

Discussion. In general, the SGD-kmeans-combinations (SKC) model achieves many better results than the other models with $n = 1$ for ROUGE-1 (obtain 51.49), $n = \{1, 2, 3\}$ for ROUGE-2 (obtain 17.99) and $n = 1$ for ROUGE-L (obtain 28.73). Since applying the "local-cluster" for the SKC and identifying the specific topics, the fewer summaries will give a better model ($n \leq 3$).

Regarding the probability-cluster model (PCM), it achieves the expected result with several summary sentences. Namely, the PCM obtains better outcomes with $n = \{2, 3, 4, 5\}$ for ROUGE-1, $n = \{4, 5\}$ for ROUGE-2, and $n = \{2, 3, 4, 5\}$ for ROUGE-L. To sum up, we might evaluate that this approach wins for all models with many summary sentences.

From the experimental results, the global-cluster model does not yield the expected summary results compared to other models. However, the global-cluster model obtains the best outcome for *the training and summarizing time*. Hence, if we concentrate on the computation time, the global-cluster model will be the reasonable selection. Otherwise, if we require a quality summary result, two methods including the PCM and SKC will be expected options.

The remarkable point is that we pay attention to investigating the summary solutions using machine learning. Here, we do not mention applying deep learning techniques in this paper because we expect to discover the power of ML algorithms with the Vietnamese large-scale dataset. The result of exploring DL techniques will be studied in the following works.

5   Conclusion and Future Work

We investigated the proposals using the pre-trained clustering model on the large-scale dataset for single document text summarization on the VNText dataset. An empirical test results are also presented. Our proposed model improves ROUGE-2 significantly with long output text and performs highly on large-scale datasets while maintaining low computing resources requirement. An example of the proposed approach's effectiveness on F_1 score is the *glove-sgd-kms* achieved with 17.99% with $n = 2$. An example of high performance is the *glove-kms* model with 500 clusters that can summarize $111,103$ documents five times ($n \in \{1, 2, 3, 4, 5\}$) in $0.33\,\mathrm{h}$ on a four-core ARM CPU. Future work will consider using the context vector for text representation to select more relevant sentences of the input for the summary.

References

1. Abuobieda, A., Salim, N., Albaham, A.T., Osman, A.H., Kumar, Y.J.: Text summarization features selection method using pseudo genetic-based model. In: 2012 International Conference on Information Retrieval & Knowledge Management, pp. 193–197. IEEE (2012)
2. Agrawal, A., Gupta, U.: Extraction based approach for text summarization using k-means clustering. Int. J. Sci. Res. Publ. **4**(11), 1–4 (2014)
3. Allahyari, M., et al.: Text summarization techniques: a brief survey. arXiv preprint arXiv:1707.02268 (2017)
4. Aone, C., Okurowski, M.E., Gorlinsky, J.: Trainable, scalable summarization using robust NLP and machine learning. In: 36th Annual Meeting of the Association for Computational Linguistics and 17th International Conference on Computational Linguistics, vol. 1, pp. 62–66 (1998)
5. Barrera, A., Verma, R.: Combining syntax and semantics for automatic extractive single-document summarization. In: Gelbukh, A. (ed.) CICLing 2012. LNCS, vol. 7182, pp. 366–377. Springer, Heidelberg (2012). https://doi.org/10.1007/978-3-642-28601-8_31
6. Barzilay, R., McKeown, K., Elhadad, M.: Information fusion in the context of multi-document summarization. In: Proceedings of the 37th Annual Meeting of the Association for Computational Linguistics, pp. 550–557 (1999)
7. Blei, D.M., Ng, A.Y., Jordan, M.I.: Latent Dirichlet allocation. J. Mach. Learn. Res. **3**, 993–1022 (2003)
8. Bottou, L., Bousquet, O.: The tradeoffs of large scale learning. In: Advances in Neural Information Processing Systems, vol. 20 (2007)

9. Conroy, J.M., O'leary, D.P.: Text summarization via hidden Markov models. In: Proceedings of the 24th Annual International ACM SIGIR Conference on Research and Development in Information Retrieval, pp. 406–407 (2001)
10. Dempster, A.P., Laird, N.M., Rubin, D.B.: Maximum likelihood from incomplete data via the EM algorithm. J. Roy. Stat. Soc.: Ser. B (Methodol.) **39**(1), 1–22 (1977)
11. Do, T.N., Tran-Nguyen, M.T.: ImageNet challenging classification with the Raspberry Pis: a federated learning algorithm of local stochastic gradient descent models. In: Dang, T.K., Küng, J., Chung, T.M. (eds.) FDSE 2022. CCIS, vol. 1688, pp. 131–144. Springer, Singapore (2022). https://doi.org/10.1007/978-981-19-8069-5_9
12. Fattah, M.A., Ren, F.: GA, MR, FFNN, PNN and GMM based models for automatic text summarization. Comput. Speech Lang. **23**(1), 126–144 (2009)
13. Gupta, P., Pendluri, V.S., Vats, I.: Summarizing text by ranking text units according to shallow linguistic features. In: 13th International Conference on Advanced Communication Technology (ICACT 2011), pp. 1620–1625. IEEE (2011)
14. Gupta, V., Lehal, G.S.: A survey of text summarization extractive techniques. J. Emerg. Technol. Web Intell. **2**(3), 258–268 (2010)
15. Harris, Z.S.: Distributional structure. Word **10**(2–3), 146–162 (1954)
16. Hermann, K.M., et al.: Teaching machines to read and comprehend. In: Advances in Neural Information Processing Systems, pp. 1693–1701 (2015)
17. Hovy, E., Lin, C.Y.: Automated text summarization and the SUMMARIST system. In: Proceedings of a Workshop, TIPSTER 1998, pp. 197–214. Association for Computational Linguistics (1998)
18. Lin, C.Y.: Training a selection function for extraction. In: Proceedings of the Eighth International Conference on Information and Knowledge Management, pp. 55–62 (1999)
19. Lin, C.Y.: Rouge: a package for automatic evaluation of summaries. In: Text Summarization Branches Out, pp. 74–81 (2004)
20. Liu, Y., Liu, P., Radev, D., Neubig, G.: Brio: bringing order to abstractive summarization. arXiv preprint arXiv:2203.16804 (2022)
21. Lloyd, S.: Least squares quantization in PCM. IEEE Trans. Inf. Theory **28**(2), 129–137 (1982). https://doi.org/10.1109/TIT.1982.1056489
22. Luhn, H.P.: The automatic creation of literature abstracts. IBM J. Res. Dev. **2**(2), 159–165 (1958)
23. MacQueen, J.: Classification and analysis of multivariate observations. In: 5th Berkeley Symposium on Mathematical Statistics and Probability, pp. 281–297 (1967)
24. McKeown, K., Klavans, J.L., Hatzivassiloglou, V., Barzilay, R., Eskin, E.: Towards multidocument summarization by reformulation: progress and prospects. In: Conference on Empirical Methods in Natural Language Processing (1999)
25. Nguyen, T.H., Do, T.N.: Extractive text summarization on large-scale dataset using k-means clustering. In: Fujita, H., Fournier-Viger, P., Ali, M., Wang, Y. (eds.) IEA/AIE 2022. LNCS, vol. 13343, pp. 737–746. Springer, Cham (2022). https://doi.org/10.1007/978-3-031-08530-7_62
26. Nguyen, T.H., Do, T.N.: Text summarization on large-scale Vietnamese datasets. Array (2022)
27. Nobata, C., Sekine, S., Murata, M., Uchimoto, K., Utiyama, M., Isahara, H.: Sentence extraction system assembling multiple evidence. In: NTCIR. Citeseer (2001)
28. Pennington, J., Socher, R., Manning, C.D.: Glove: global vectors for word representation. In: Proceedings of the 2014 Conference on Empirical Methods in Natural Language Processing (EMNLP), pp. 1532–1543 (2014)

29. Sculley, D.: Web-scale k-means clustering. In: Proceedings of the 19th International Conference on World Wide Web, WWW 2010, pp. 1177–1178. Association for Computing Machinery, New York (2010)

30. See, A., Liu, P.J., Manning, C.D.: Get to the point: summarization with pointer-generator networks. arXiv preprint arXiv:1704.04368 (2017)

31. Shalev-Shwartz, S., Singer, Y., Srebro, N.: Pegasos: primal estimated sub-gradient solver for SVM. In: Proceedings of the 24th International Conference on Machine Learning, pp. 807–814 (2007)

32. Wang, X., et al.: Lightseq2: accelerated training for transformer-based models on GPUs. arXiv preprint arXiv:2110.05722 (2021)

33. Zhang, P., Li, C.: Automatic text summarization based on sentences clustering and extraction. In: 2009 2nd IEEE International Conference on Computer Science and Information Technology, pp. 167–170. IEEE (2009)

34. Zhang, X., et al.: Momentum calibration for text generation. arXiv preprint arXiv:2212.04257 (2022)

35. Zhao, Y., Khalman, M., Joshi, R., Narayan, S., Saleh, M., Liu, P.J.: Calibrating sequence likelihood improves conditional language generation. arXiv preprint arXiv:2210.00045 (2022)

Exploring Links Between Personality Traits and Environmental Attitudes with GreenBig5 System

Binh Thanh Nguyen[1]([✉]), Bao Chung Hoang[2], Loc Nguyen Tien[2], Binh Ton That[2], and Huy Truong Dinh[2]

[1] IIASA, Laxenburg, Austria
nguyenb@iiasa.ac.at
[2] Duy Tan University, Danang, Vietnam

Abstract. The GreenBig5 system has been meticulously studied and developed with the aim of uncovering the intricate links between Big5 personality traits and their facets and environmental attitudes and behaviors. To achieve this, the GreenBig5 framework was initially rigorously formalized. Building upon this robust mathematical foundation, the GreenBig5 dashboard was designed and developed to model the intricate connections between personalities and environmental terminology. Subsequently, the dashboard generates tailored model-specific questions, which are then distributed to relevant target user groups via the GreenBig5 app. Following that, user answers are collected and stored in the GreenBig5 AnswerDB database. This system holds the potential to yield invaluable insights into the interplay between individual personality traits and environmental factors, carrying profound implications for the realms of environmental education and policy.

Keywords: Big5 traits · GreenBig5 · environmental attitudes and behaviors · dashboard · app

1 Introduction

Climate change is a global issue that requires effective policies and interventions to promote pro-environmental behavior. Understanding the links between personality traits and such behavior can help policymakers design more targeted and effective interventions [1, 3, 5, 19]. In this context, authors of [14] have suggested that personality traits play a crucial role in motivating our beliefs, values, and attitudes, and can influence individuals' likelihood of performing environmentally friendly behaviors. Consequently, numerous research studies have focused on identifying these links between personality traits and environmental attitudes and behaviors [14]. By doing so, policymakers can develop interventions that address specific barriers to desired outcomes and increase the likelihood of promoting sustainable behaviors.

Numerous studies have investigated the relationship between personality traits and pro-environmental attitudes and behaviors. While some studies have identified a significant correlation, others have not found any conclusive evidence. According to a study in

T. K. Dang et al. (Eds.): FDSE 2023, CCIS 1925, pp. 289–299, 2023.
https://doi.org/10.1007/978-981-99-8296-7_20

[2], conscientiousness, agreeableness, and openness to experience are positively associated with pro-environmental behavior. Another study in [16] found that individuals who scored high in conscientiousness exhibited more environmentally-friendly behaviors. On the other hand, [17] found that neuroticism was negatively associated with pro-environmental attitudes and behaviors.

According to various sources, predicting human personality and establishing its relationship with environmental impact requires significant resources in terms of both time and finances [4, 7, 8]. To address this challenge, leveraging our understanding of big data technologies, we have developed an intelligent data processing system that can operate on a website-based platform. The system is accompanied by an intuitive and user-friendly dashboard that facilitates ease of use [1].

Our research extends the existing body of knowledge in this domain by drawing upon prior studies [9, 10] and introducing the GreenBig5 system. This system effectively models and substantiates the relationships between Big5 personality traits and their facets and environmental terminology. Initially, we rigorously formalized the GreenBig5 concepts and the application framework. Subsequently, domain experts utilized the GreenBig5 dashboard to craft comprehensive models, enabling the establishment of meaningful connections between Big5 traits and facets and environmental keywords.

Following this, questions are generated by incorporating the model's Big 5 traits/facets and environmental keywords into predefined questionnaire templates. These questions undergo a rigorous review and adjustment process by experts before being dispatched to end users through the GreenBig5 app. To facilitate comprehensive user-context analysis, timestamps are meticulously assigned to these questions, and stored in the QuestionDB database. Within this framework, questions can be strategically disseminated at various time intervals to relevant target user groups, allowing for the thorough evaluation and collection of their responses and behaviors. Subsequently, user answers are annotated with timestamps and geographical coordinates, which assume significance in contextualizing user interactions.

Consequently, to assess the model's suitability across diverse user demographics, including age, income, and location, we devised a decision tree algorithm. Our research endeavors to provide psychologists with deeper insights into the alignment of personality traits with environmental attitudes and behaviors. This, in turn, can inform the creation of more efficient message delivery and behavioral models. Ultimately, these efforts have the potential to foster greater sustainability in both environmental attitudes and behaviors.

The rest of this paper is presented as follows: Sect. 2 introduces typical approaches and projects related to our work; after introducing the GreenBig5 concepts and application framework in Sect. 3, Sect. 4 will present our GreenBig5 application results. And lastly, Sect. 5 gives a summary of our achieved as well as future works.

2 Related Work

The relationship between personality traits and environmental attitudes and behaviors has been a topic of interest in psychology, with mixed findings [11, 13]. The Big Five model, which includes five broad dimensions of personality (openness, conscientiousness, extraversion, agreeableness, and neuroticism), is a commonly used framework for examining this relationship [15].

There is a growing body of research examining the links between personality traits and environmental attitudes and behaviors. Some studies have found that Conscientiousness and related traits are important predictors of pro-environmental behaviors [11], while others have identified the effects of traits related to Extraversion and Neuroticism [15].

For example, [1] found that individuals high in environmental concern tend to be more extraverted, conscientious, and mature than those low in environmental concern. Similarly, [14] discovered that pro-environmental attitudes were associated with Conscientiousness, self-confidence (a trait related to Extraversion), and sincerity.

Numerous studies have examined the connection between personality and environmental engagement, and some have discovered that broader personality dimensions are related to environmental values [16, 18]. For instance, [18] found that Eysenck's personality traits of Psychoticism and Neuroticism were associated with distinct aspects of environmental engagement. Specifically, higher levels of Psychoticism were linked to greater Utilization, an anthropocentric dimension that endorses the use of environmental resources; and higher levels of Neuroticism were linked to greater Preservation, a biocentric dimension that reflects attitudes relating to the appreciation of nature and conservation of resources [16, 18].

Overall, the link between personality and environmental engagement is complex and multifaceted, and further research is necessary to fully understand it. Nevertheless, the existing evidence suggests that personality traits may play an important role in shaping people's attitudes and behaviors towards the environment and should be taken into account in environmental education and communication efforts [16].

Despite the widespread use of Big Five personality models in various software products for decision-making, there has been a dearth of support for decision-making focused on environmental protection [6, 12]. To bridge this gap, the GreenBig5 system has been developed in this study offers a novel approach to exploring these links by modeling the connections between Big5 facets and environmental keywords and predicting user personality based on their responses. This system consists of the GreenBig5 dashboard, which models the links between personality traits and environmental factors, generates questions, and the GreenBig5 app, which collects user response data. As a result, the GreenBig5 system enables governments and organizations to identify users' personalities and their impact on the environment, allowing them to devise better solutions that minimize negative environmental impacts.

3   Concepts and Solutions

In this section, first we introduce the GreenBig5 concepts in term of formulars and their descriptions. Based on those just-specified formulars, we can introduce the GreenBig5 system, which is designed to model and validate associations between environmental terminology and specific facets of the Big5 personality trait. To accomplish this, we utilize the GreenBig5 dashboard, which enables us to create a model of these connections. Afterward, we create queries based on this model that are directed to the GreenBig5 App. Users' answers are recorded and kept in the GreenBig5 answer database. To evaluate the applicability of the model for diverse user groups, we employ a machine learning algorithm that considers various factors such as age, income, and location. Afterwards, the implementation results will be presented in Sect. 4 to prove our concepts.

3.1 GreenBig5 Concepts

In our previous studies [9, 10], a set of Big5 classifiers - agreeableness (A), conscientiousness (C), extraversion (E), neuroticism (N), and openness to experience (O) can be denoted as follows:

$$Big5Traits = \{O, C, E, A, N\} \tag{1}$$

Additionally, a set of Big5 facets can be specified as:

$$F = \{f_1^{t1}, f_2^{t1}, ..., f_m^{t5}\} \tag{2}$$

and a nested set of environmental keywords can be modeled as:

$$E = \{e_1, e_2, ..., e_n\} \tag{3}$$

We can then establish linkages between Big5 facets and environmental keywords as a set of linking models, denoted as:

$$M = <F, E>, where : \forall m_x \in M, m_x = linking(\{f_a, .., f_b\}, \{e_c, .., e_d\} > \tag{4}$$

Especially, a set of predefined question templates can be denoted as:

$$T = \{t_1, .., t_y\} \tag{5}$$

We can then generate a set of queries automatically by merging linked facets-environmental keywords of a model m_x with its relevant templates $T_r \subset T$

$$Q^{m_x} = \{q_1, ..., q_t\} \tag{6}$$

3.2 GreenBig5 System

The GreenBig5 system offers an expert tool to model and confirm correlations between environmental keywords and the facets of a personality trait within the GreenBig5 application framework as illustrated in Fig. 1.

The GreenBig5 dashboard forms the core of this system. It enables experts to create GreenBig5 models by linking GreenBig5 traits/facets (outlined in Formula 2) and environmental keywords (described in Formula 3) to define a specific model, m_x (per Formula 4). Following this, questions associated with the model are generated by integrating the chosen Big5 traits/facets and environmental keywords from the model m_x into the GreenBig5 questionnaire templates (described in Formula 5).

The just-generated questions (defined in Formula 6) are checked and modified by experts. Furthermore, a question-and-answer pathway between the GreenBig5 dashboard and app has been established. To enhance user-context analysis, timestamps are affixed to

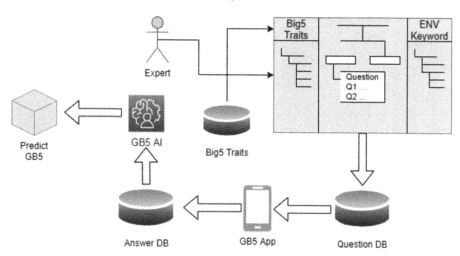

Fig. 1. GreenBig5 system architecture

these questions and subsequently stored in the QuestionDB database. Furthermore, each question can be sent to relevant target user groups at different time intervals, allowing for the assessment and accumulation of their responses and behaviors. Following this, user responses are marked with timestamps and geographical coordinates, imbuing them with importance in the contextualization of user interactions.

This process establishes a question-and-answer pathway between the app and the dashboard, which tailors the questions to the user's personality traits. The user's responses are then processed by AnswerDB, a database that enables AI algorithms to assess the user's suitability for different personality groups based on their age, income, and other factors.

Moreover, the aggregation of user answers results in expansive datasets, often referred to as "big data." These datasets are then utilized to deploy machine learning algorithms that draw on insights from variables encompassing the user's age, location, and other pertinent factors. In this manner, these algorithms play a pivotal role in assessing the user's alignment with different personality clusters.

By filtering the user's personality, the system gains a better understanding of their traits and identifies how they relate to their environment. This allows the system to develop a personalized view of the user's personality and establish connections between the user and their surroundings.

4   Application Results

The GreenBig5 dashboard was created using NodeJs [20], Python [23], and ReactJs [24] to visualize Big5 traits and facets, as well as environmental keywords in tree formats. The GreenBig5 database is built on MongoDB [21]and stores user personality traits, GreenBig5 questions and answers. To implement the GreenBig5 app, Flutter [22] was used. In the following sections, we will present the GreenBig5 workflow. The following figure describes how the GreenBig5 system has been developed.

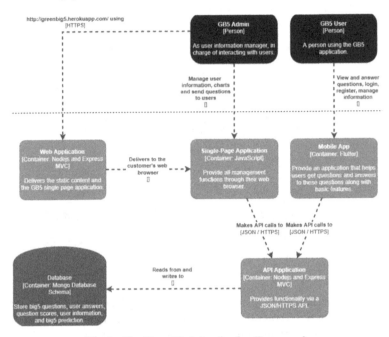

Fig. 2. The GreenBig5 Application Framework

As illustrated in Fig. 3, facet(s) of a trait and environmental keyword(s) can be selected by drag-and-drop into the main dashboard area, and then linked to define a specific model.

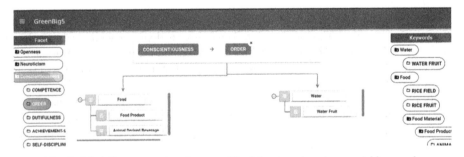

Fig. 3. Modeling connections between Big 5 facets and environmental keywords

Using the selected trait(s)- > facet(s), for example *Conscientious-* > *Order* and keywords, e.g. *Food*, a list of questions can be generated by merging these elements with questionnaire templates, as also shown in Fig. 4. Experts can define multiple models simultaneously and generate questions accordingly. The questions can be modified or corrected as needed.

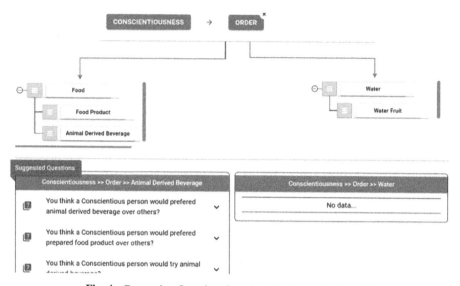

Fig. 4. Generating Questions based on the just-defined model

Following this, experts have the option to categorize user groups based on their personality traits by utilizing a scoring system and assigning labels such as "High" "Medium" and "Low" as outlined below (Fig. 5):

Fig. 5. Scoring and assigning labels such as "High" "Medium" and "Low" for Big5 traits of the example question

Moreover, experts have the authority to finely tailor the user context, considering factors such as geographical location (urban or rural), gender, age, and other relevant variables. This sophisticated level of customization is graphically presented in Fig. 6.

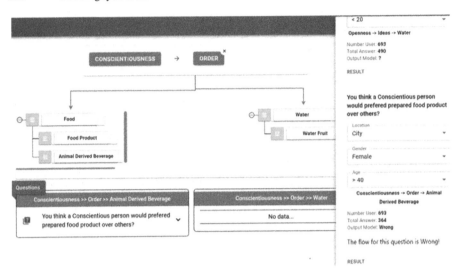

Fig. 6. Defining user contexts

After this meticulous contextualization, the crafted questions are transmitted to users via the GreenBig5 app. It is crucial to emphasize that both the questions themselves and their corresponding sending timestamps are meticulously archived within the QuestionDB database, which is built on top of the MongoDB as illustrated in Fig. 2.

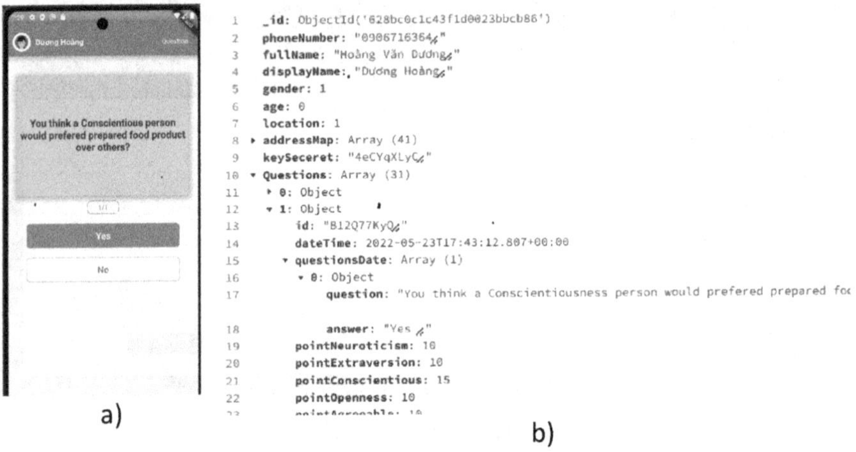

a)

b)

Fig. 7. User answer via GreenBig5 app

Figure 7a further provides an illustrative demonstration of the GreenBig5 app's intuitive functionality in receiving and addressing questions, fostering an effortless user experience. In this context, Fig. 7b shows an example of user answers which are represented in *json* format and will be stored in the AnswerDB.

AgeGroup	Gender	Location	SendingTime	ReceivingTime	Question	sO	sC	sE	sA	sN
>40	Male	City	6AM to 6PM	6PM to 12PM	You think a Censcientiousness person would prefered prepared food product over others?	920	470	260	650	110
30-40	Female	Country	6AM to 6PM	6AM to 6PM	You think a Censcientiousness person would prefered prepared food product over others?	440	840	210	820	430
<20	Male	Country	6AM to 6PM	6AM to 6PM	You think a Censcientiousness person would prefered prepared food product over others?	240	480	590	590	400
30-40	Male	Country	6AM to 6PM	6PM to 12PM	You think a Censcientiousness person would prefered prepared food product over others?	770	750	620	920	120
30-40	Male	Country	6AM to 6PM	6AM to 6PM	You think a Censcientiousness person would prefered prepared food product over others?	340	880	410	370	680
<20	Female	Country	6AM to 6PM	6PM to 12PM	You think a Censcientiousness person would prefered prepared food product over others?	180	250	630	800	220
20-30	Female	City	6AM to 6PM	6PM to 12PM	You think a Censcientiousness person would prefered prepared food product over others?	470	230	360	940	680
>40	Female	City	6AM to 6PM	After 6AM	You think a Censcientiousness person would prefered prepared food product over others?	590	460	750	800	250
20-30	Female	City	6AM to 6PM	After 6AM	You think a Censcientiousness person would prefered prepared food product over others?	190	540	600	780	600
>40	Female	Country	6AM to 6PM	6PM to 12PM	You think a Censcientiousness person would prefered prepared food product over others?	600	520	290	980	120
<20	Female	City	6AM to 6PM	6PM to 12PM	You think a Censcientiousness person would prefered prepared food product over others?	130	600	820	910	910
20-30	Male	City	6AM to 6PM	6PM to 12PM	You think a Censcientiousness person would prefered prepared food product over others?	450	620	1000	860	500
30-40	Male	Country	6AM to 6PM	6AM to 6PM	You think a Censcientiousness person would prefered prepared food product over others?	700	190	200	610	530
>40	Female	Country	6PM to 12PM	After 6AM	You think an Ideas person would try insect food product?	970	550	650	980	650
<20	Male	Country	6PM to 12PM	6PM to 12PM	You think an Ideas person would try insect food product?	230	710	910	910	780
>40	Female	Country	6PM to 12PM	6AM to 6PM	You think an Ideas person would try insect food product?	440	270	860	270	800
30-40	Male	Country	6PM to 12PM	6PM to 12PM	You think an Ideas person would try insect food product?	930	430	980	560	650
20-30	Female	City	6PM to 12PM	6PM to 12PM	You think an Ideas person would try insect food product?	280	480	230	840	240
30-40	Male	City	6PM to 12PM	After 6AM	You think an Ideas person would try insect food product?	230	460	880	790	680
30-40	Female	Country	6PM to 12PM	6PM to 12PM	You think an Ideas person would try insect food product?	190	220	540	770	700
20-30	Female	City	6PM to 12PM	6AM to 6PM	You think an Ideas person would try insect food product?	800	260	900	620	840
20-30	Male	City	6PM to 12PM	6PM to 12PM	You think an Ideas person would try insect food product?	200	690	130	790	940
30-40	Male	Country	6PM to 12PM	6PM to 12PM	You think an Ideas person would try insect food product?	320	920	110	630	960

Fig. 8. Example of collected answers with multiple user contexts

Figure 8 offers visual representations of answers, each accompanied by its corresponding user context. This context includes attributes like age, gender, location, and answer scores related to Big5 traits. Over an iterative cycle that involves sending a wide array of questions across diverse contexts and time frames, followed by the collection of responses and associated user attributes from a myriad of users, the AnswerDB database aggregates an extensive dataset, often referred to as "big data."

Table 1 also shows how Big5 trait score sO, sC, etc. columns of a question are calculated.

Table 1. An example of Big5 trait score calculations

ID	Openness	Conscientiousness	Extraversion	Agreeableness	Neuroticism	Answer	Big5_Env Keyword
1	10	10	20	15	10	Y	Extraversion - Activity - Food
2	15	10	20	10	10	N	Extraversion - Warmth - Food
3	20	10	15	10	10	Y	Openness - Ideas - Food
4	20	15	10	15	10	Y	Openness - Ideas - Water
5	10	15	10	20	15	N	Agreeableness – Trust - Food
Calculate	10+15+20* 2+20*2+10	10+10+10+15+15	20*2+20+15 +10+10	15+10+10+15 +20	10+10+10+10 +15	Openness	
Total	115	60	95	70	55		

As depicted in Fig. 9, an illustrative demonstration of the decision tree application result is presented. By leveraging this algorithmic analysis, the GreenBig5 system is adept at determining the precise user group(s) for which the expert model is applicable. This process of verification allows for a comprehensive understanding of the targeted user groups, ensuring optimal alignment between the expert model and its intended beneficiaries.

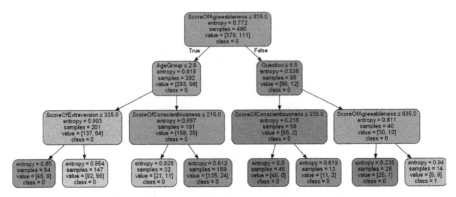

Fig. 9. Example of decision tree application result

5   Conclusion and Future Works

In conclusion, the GreenBig5 system is a novel and innovative approach to exploring the connections between personality traits and their facets and environmental attitudes and behaviors. By utilizing the GreenBig5 dashboard to model these links and generate questions for the GreenBig5 App, we can collect user answer data and gain insights into the relationship between personality and the environment. This system has the potential to inform environmental education and policy by providing valuable insights into how different personality traits may impact environmental attitudes and behaviors. Overall, the GreenBig5 system offers a promising tool for addressing the gap in decision-making support for environmental protection and represents a significant step forward in this area.

Future research could explore the practical applications of the GreenBig5 system and its potential impact on environmental decision-making at the organizational and governmental levels.

Acknowledgement. This work is fully supported by the Duy Tan university capstone project 2022.

References

1. Borden, R.J., Francis, J.J.: Personality and environmental concern. J. Pers. **46**(4), 603–616 (1978)
2. Díaz-Morales, J.F., Cohen, J., Delgado-Rodríguez, M.: Individual differences in pro-environmental behavior: a review and conceptualization. Curr. Opin. Psychol. **32**, 26–30 (2019)
3. Harari, G.M., Lane, N.D., Wang, R., Crosier, B.S., Campbell, A.T., Gosling, S.D.: Using smartphones to collect behavioral data in psychological science: opportunities, practical considerations, and challenges. Perspect. Psychol. Sci.: J. Assoc. Psychol. Sci. **11**(6), 838–854 (2016)

4. Homburg, A., Stolberg, A., Wagner, M.: Greening the service profit chain: the impact of environmental management practices. J. Bus. Res. **66**(8), 1038–1044 (2013). https://doi.org/10.1016/j.jbusres.2012.03.009

5. John, O.P., Srivastava, S.: The big five trait taxonomy: history, measurement, and theoretical perspectives. Handb. Pers.: Theory Res. **2**(1999), 102–138 (1999).

6. McCrae, R.R., John, O.P.: An introduction to the five-factor model and its applications. J. Pers. **60**(2), 175–215 (1992)

7. McCrae, R.R., Costa, P.T., Jr.: Personality in Adulthood: A Five-Factor Theory Perspective, 2nd edn. Guilford Press, New York City (2003)

8. Milfont, T.L., Sibley, C.G.: The big five personality traits and environmental engagement: Associations at the individual and societal level. J. Environ. Psychol. **32**(2), 187–195 (2012). https://doi.org/10.1016/j.jenvp.2012.01.002

9. Nguyen, B.T.: Dashboard for exploring personalities based on mobile user log data. J. Intell. Fuzzy Syst. **37**(6), 7503–7509 (2019)

10. Nguyen, B.T., Dung, D.N.: Big5 tool for tracking personality traits. In: Nguyen, N.T., Gaol, F.L., Hong, T.-P., Trawiński, B. (eds.) ACIIDS 2019. LNCS (LNAI), vol. 11431, pp. 726–736. Springer, Cham (2019). https://doi.org/10.1007/978-3-030-14799-0_62

11. Ones, D.S., Dilchert, S., Viswesvaran, C., Judge, T.A.: In support of personality assessment in organizational settings. Pers. Psychol. **60**(4), 995–1027 (2007)

12. Paunonen, S.V.: Big five factors of personality and replicated predictions of behavior. J. Pers. Soc. Psychol. **84**(2), 411–424 (2003)

13. Howlader, P., Pal, K.K., Cuzzocrea, A., Kumar, S.M.: Predicting Facebook-users' personality based on status and linguistic features via flexible regression analysis techniques. In: Proceedings of the 33rd Annual ACM Symposium on Applied Computing (SAC 2018). ACM, New York, NY, pp. 339–345 (2018)

14. Pettus, M.L., Giles, W.F.: Personality and environmental concern: reexamining the relationship. Soc. Behav. Personal. Int. J. **15**(2), 169–175 (1987). https://doi.org/10.2224/sbp.1987.15.2.169

15. Schultz, P.W., Gouveia, V.V., Cameron, L.D., Tankha, G., Schmuck, P., Franěk, M.: Values and their relationship to environmental concern and conservation behavior. J. Cross Cult. Psychol. **36**(4), 457–475 (2005)

16. Schultz, P.W., Oskamp, S., Mainieri, T.: Who recycles and when? A review of personal and situational factors. J. Environ. Psychol. **15**(2), 105–121 (1995)

17. Whitmarsh, L., O'Neill, S., Lorenzoni, I.: Public engagement with climate change: what do we know and where do we go from here? Int. J. Media Cult. Politics **11**(3), 217–234 (2015)

18. Wiseman, M., Bogner, F.X.: The influence of personality traits on environmental attitudes and behaviors: an application of the five-factor model. J. Environ. Psychol. **23**(4), 369–381 (2003)

19. https://en.wikipedia.org/wiki/Big_Five_personality_traits

20. https://nodejs.org/en

21. https://flutter.dev/

22. https://www.mongodb.com/

23. https://www.python.org/

24. https://react.dev/

Study on Web Based Virtualized Containers for Software Development Lectures in BYOD

Takeshi Tsuchiya[1]($\boxtimes$), Masami Matsunaga[2], Hiroo Hirose[2],
Tetsuyasu Yamada[2], Hiroshi Ichikawa[3], and Quang Tran Minh[4,5]

[1] Institute for Data Science Education, Tokyo International University,
Toshima, Tokyo, Japan
ttsuchi@tiu.ac.jp
[2] Suwa University of Science, Chino, Japan
{tsuchiya,hirose,yamada}@rs.sus.ac.jp
[3] Otsuma Women's University, Chiyoda, Tokyo, Japan
ichikawa.h@otsuma.ac.jp
[4] Faculty of Computer Science and Engineering,
Ho Chi Minh City University of Technology (HCMUT), 268 Ly Thuong Kiet,
District 10, Ho Chi Minh City, Vietnam
quangtran@hcmut.edu.vn
[5] Vietnam National University Ho Chi Minh City (VNU-HCM), Linh Trung Ward,
Thu Duc District, Ho Chi Minh City, Vietnam

Abstract. Virtualization technology is commonly employed to manage multiple computers within a shared environment. However, the growing prevalence of Bring Your Own Device (BYOD) practices, allowing users to utilize their personal computers, has presented challenges in achieving a standardized computing environment. To address this issue, study proposes a web service with the construction of a flexible software development environment for BYOD setups, leveraging container-based virtualization technology in the software development education domain. Specifically, the proposed solution enables the effortless creation of custom containers by selecting the necessary functionalities via a web interface. These containers can then be accessed and utilized by users through the web. Consequently, users can establish a containerized virtual environment in a BYOD context without relying on their own knowledge and expertise. Furthermore, the utilization of web-based tools is anticipated to enhance the maintainability and convenience of containers in this context.

Keywords: Educational Development Environment · Virtualization Environments · BYOD

1 Introduction

In recent years, information technology (IT) has become a vital infrastructure in our daily lives, and as technology continues to advance, it becomes crucial

T. K. Dang et al. (Eds.): FDSE 2023, CCIS 1925, pp. 300–311, 2023.
https://doi.org/10.1007/978-981-99-8296-7_21

to develop human resources capable of adapting to new technologies. In light of this, various measures are being implemented to foster IT literacy across society, including initiatives such as introducing programming to elementary school students and offering IT training for business professionals seeking to reskill. Traditionally, computers in companies and educational institutions have been built using uniform computer environments through hypervisor-based or host-based virtualization technologies. These methods allow for the separation of hardware and operating systems (OS) by installing virtualization control software, known as a hypervisor, or by setting up a virtualization software infrastructure on the host OS. As a result, it becomes possible to flexibly select the appropriate OS configuration and software for specific usage scenarios. Instead of individually configuring each host, the environment is distributed in the form of an OS image, which can be executed on multiple hosts, thereby creating several computers with the same environment. This approach enables users to access and experience the same environment on any of these computers at any given time. Furthermore, the system is designed to be user-friendly, eliminating the need for users to possess specialized skills to operate the environment effectively.

The growing popularity of Bring Your Own Device (BYOD) has been driven by the recent surge in remote work and an increased interest in learning programming, among other factors. However, the use of individual computers in a BYOD setting results in varying computer environments for each user, necessitating users to possess the knowledge and skills to manage their own machines. Additionally, the software development environment entails complex tasks such as installing multiple software environments and configuring the OS to work seamlessly with the installed software. To address these challenges, container-based virtualization technology has emerged in recent years for system development [2]. This technology enables the execution of a virtualized OS and software environment as application-level software running on top of a conventional OS. Containers encapsulate the entire system as a single application, inclusive of the OS. They can be distributed as pre-configured images or generated based on software and system settings. Regardless of the approach, the constructed container can be easily executed as an application. Consequently, container-based virtualization technology holds promise for resolving the complexities associated with deploying software development environments in BYOD setups. Furthermore, the use of containers is expected to rise due to their ability to harmonize system environments across diverse user setups.

Presently, lecturers are responsible for preparing and distributing containers to students. Subsequently, students receive these distributed containers along with configuration files and set them up in their respective environments. Consequently, lecturers are required to possess the expertise to construct and manage the latest containers, while students need to be get comfortable at container setup. Lecturers must independently manage the currency of the containers, and students must possess the necessary skills for container setup in addition to grasping the lecture content [1]. This collective requirement presents a challenging barrier for all students. As the utilization of container virtualization technology is anticipated to grow alongside the expansion of BYOD, it becomes imperative to develop a system operation approach that accommodates users without extensive knowledge or skills in the future.

A study on unifying the computer environment using container-based virtualization technology has been presented [5]. In this study, Docker container images are distributed to shared stand-alone computers, allowing the lecture environment to be used on individual computers. The shared computers are pre-configured with container-based virtualization technology. However, operating containers requires a certain level of computer knowledge and skills, such as configuring the CPU virtualization mode. To address this, the proposed solution suggests providing a virtualized container runtime environment on the server side via the web, which is more suitable for a BYOD environment. As users acquire knowledge and skills, they can migrate the containers executed on the server side to their own computers, thereby expanding the application range of the proposed system.

The proposed system is a web service that facilitates the configuration, execution, and connection of Docker [3] containers, a virtualization method. Specifically, users can input the configuration information of the desired containers, create containers, and control their execution through the proposed system. This enables users to utilize virtualized containers regardless of their level of knowledge and skills. Particularly in software development environments, the proposed system allows for the construction of a unified development environment even in a BYOD setting. As users gain proficiency in virtualization containers, they have the option to migrate the containers to their own computers. The proposed system proves effective in learning operational skills and management of container-based virtualization technology. To evaluate its efficacy, the paper implements the proposed system for evaluation purposes, assuming its operation in lectures, and investigates its availability and operational aspects within the lecture context.

2 Outline of the Proposal Model

The conventional process of constructing and running containers, including program development environments, typically involves several phases performed via the command line. These phases include setting up the virtualization software environment on each PC, configuring the container, generating the container, and finally running the container. To simplify this process, it is desirable for users to be able to operate virtualization containers through a web interface. This way, users can run the virtualized container on their own computers according to their specific needs, taking into account their level of knowledge and skills. Figure 1 provides an overview of the proposed system.

The proposed system can be categorized based on the functions it provides:

1. Container operations based on input information from users via the web: This category encompasses the functionality that allows users for visualizing their status running on the server (Web IF in Fig. 1): This category involves the

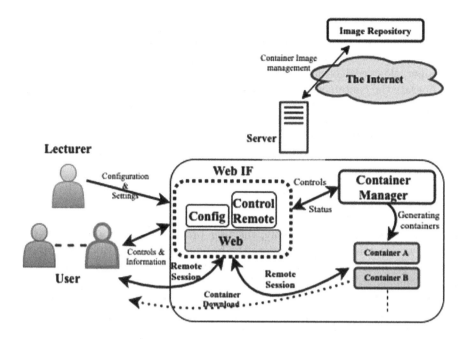

Fig. 1. Outline of Proposal System

interface functions that enable users to visualize the status of containers that are currently running on the server.

2. Container management functions for handling container generation and operation based on acquired information (Container Manager): This category includes the container management functions responsible for tasks such as generating and operating containers based on the information obtained from users.

3. Connecting function to virtualized containers via the web: This category covers the function that facilitates the connection to virtualized containers through the web interface.

By offering these functions, the proposed system aims to simplify the process of container operations, improve usability, and enhance the accessibility of virtualization containers through a user-friendly web interface.

2.1   Web Interface

The web interface provides the necessary configuration information for generating containers and the package information required for installation. The configuration of a container created with Docker [3] is described in YAML (YAML Ain't Markup Language) format, which is a simple text format that utilizes key-value pairs. The information input through the web interface can be converted to this YAML format. Thus, the basic configuration is written by converting the user-entered information into a standardized format. For more complex configurations, they can be uploaded to the server as separate files.

The web interface also offers users a display of the status of each generated container, along with basic controls for starting and stopping the container. Users can operate the containers through this web graphical user interface (GUI). The web interface sends control commands to the Docker program, while container status is retrieved from the standard output and displayed accordingly. Similarly, users can establish connections to the containers and download them using the information provided on the web GUI.

2.2 Manage Containers

The proposed system generates and executes containers based on the information entered via the web. Initially, the user provides the container name, OS, and network settings, which serve as the basic configuration. Subsequently, the software to be installed, package names, individual configurations, and processing commands are converted to YAML format and compiled into a Docker file. If more specific system or application settings are necessary, users can directly describe them in YAML format within the Docker file. Furthermore, users have the option to attach specific application configuration files as external files in the file system. This flexibility enables the deployment of containers without application-related constraints, providing greater versatility and customization options.

2.3 Remote Connection

Connections to the running containers are established through a web browser interface. Traditionally, SSH (Secure SHell) is widely used for remote connections. However, SSH may not be a familiar application for all users, and its usage is limited to a specific user base. To address this limitation, an SSH middleware is installed on the web server, which allows connections to be established via the web interface. In this setup, port forwarding and an SSH server must be installed and configured to initiate when all containers are generated.

Once the containers are generated, users have the option to download them to their own computers. As users acquire more computer knowledge and skills, they can utilize SSH to connect to the containers within their local environments. This enables users to adapt the container usage to their evolving proficiency levels and local settings.

3 Implementation

The above mentioned features are implemented as software on the server.

Table 1. System Environment

item	specification
Server	Intel Xeon Platinum 8176 × 2, Mem: 196 GB
OS	Ubuntu 18.04 LTS
Web Server	Flask 2.0
Virtualization	Docker 20.10.8
Container Management	Micro Kubernetes v.1.22.5
Development	Python 3.6.9

3.1 System Environment

Table 1 provides an overview of the server environment utilized for the implementation. The current implementation functions as an evaluation system and is designed to operate as a stand-alone server. However, the intended deployment involves constructing actual services on cloud platforms, allowing for scalability to accommodate an expanding user base and processing workload.

The proposed system, depicted in Fig. 1, is developed using Python, with the Python framework Flask [7] serving as the web server. Virtualization is achieved through the use of Docker containers, while container management on the servers is facilitated by the Kubernetes orchestration platform. Kubernetes [4] offers robust orchestration capabilities across multiple servers and can dynamically scale the number of containers to match user demand.

3.2 Container Management

The container configuration settings are converted to YAML format, and a Dockerfile is generated. Any errors that occur during container generation, such as configuration issues or additional input provided on the command line, are displayed as "status" on the web interface. Currently, it is necessary to modify the configuration file to handle errors that may arise during the container generation process.

Each user's containers are managed using MicroKubernetes (MicroK8s) [6], which is a single-node Kubernetes environment that can be easily set up. Each container image is loaded onto MicroKubernetes, and individual containers are managed as pods. These pods include execution parameters such as network settings and startup configurations. To enable external access to each pod, port forwarding is established using the server as a proxy. Users can then connect to the pods remotely via SSH.

3.3 Remote Connecting via Web

Users can establish connections to each container via a web interface. They can connect to the containers using SSH directly from their own computer environments, without the need to install any additional software. This functionality is made possible by installing the SSH-web framework, specifically the "Shell in a Box" [8], on the server side. Users also have the option to establish SSH connections from their local computers or connect through a web server acting as a proxy. To facilitate this setup, a Linux virtualization container is utilized, which is equipped several kinds of software development environment like Tomcat environment using J2EE or a Python Flask framework along with a MySQL environment and so on. This allows for flexible deployment options depending on the specific requirements of the users.

4   Evaluation

This section evaluates the proposed system through a questionnaire-based evaluation involving the intended users of the system.

4.1   Outline of Questionnaire

This evaluation involved conducting a questionnaire survey to assess the functionality of the proposed system. The targeted participants for the questionnaire were third-year undergraduate students studying computer science. These students possess basic knowledge and skills in computer operations and are expected to utilize the proposed system to construct web development environments for lectures covered in this paper. It is important to note that the participants have not undergone prior training in virtualization technology. The majority of users in this evaluation are using virtualization technology for either the first or second time. Thus, the users involved in the evaluation align with the intended users of the system proposed in this paper.

During the evaluation, users gained experience in installing an educational development environment using virtualization containers on their own computers and utilizing it in lectures. Drawing from this experience, a comparison was made between the characteristics of the proposed system and conventional virtualization containers. Subsequently, the effectiveness of the proposed system, particularly for users in the early stages of learning, was evaluated.

4.2   Questions

The following questions were asked in this questionnaire.

Cat. A Positioning of the user himself/herself
 Q.1 Computer skills (1: poor–5: good)
 Q.2 Interest in information systems development (1: none–5: strong)
 Q.3 Knowledge and skills in information systems (1: poor–5: good)
 Q.4 Understanding of virtualization technology through the introduction of virtualization containers (1: poor–5: good)
Cat. B Positioning of the user's development capabilities
 Q.5 User's knowledge and skills regarding his/her own virtualization technology (Docker) (1: poor–5: good)

Q.6 Understanding of the development environment provided by the user's containers (1: poor–5: good)

Q.7 Construction of development environment to user's real environment (1: difficult–5: easy)

Cat. C Positioning of the development environment

Q.8 Selection of real environment and virtualized container (1: container–5: real server)

Q.9 Connection to virtualized environment (1: SSH App–5: Web)

Q.10 Location of containers (1: local– 5: web)

Cat. D Other Comments (free descriptions)

The questionnaire is divided into three categories: own computer skills, understanding of virtualization technology (including containers), and use of the development environment. In the first category (Cat A.), students self-evaluate their knowledge and skills in information systems development related to the lectures. Then, the students also self-evaluate their understanding of the virtualization containers using in the lecture. The second category (Cat B.) is a self-evaluation of the understanding of the configuration of the virtualization containers currently used in the lectures. Then, the possibility of constructing the educational development environment used in the lecture on a real computer environment is compared with container. The third category (Cat C.) compares the web service type provided by the proposed system and the conventional method of connecting to the virtualized container via an application installed in the local environment.

4.3   Results and Considerations

The correlation coefficients between each questionnaire are shown in Table 2. The table above displays the correlation coefficients derived for the questions in the questionnaire, with each category representing a different aspect. The correlation coefficients are categorized as follows: a correlation between 0.3 and 0.5 is considered weak, between 0.5 and 0.7 is considered moderate, and between 0.7 and 0.3 is considered strong. Each question is rated on a 5-point scale. Based on the correlation coefficients, it can be observed that there is a moderate correlation (0.65) between computer skills (Cat. 1) and understanding of virtualization technology (Cat. 2) among the course attendees in this paper. However, computer skills do not show a significant correlation with the methods provided by the proposed system (Cat. 3). In evaluating the effectiveness of the proposed system, it may be more meaningful to consider the relationship between the aforementioned categories of questions rather than focusing solely on the correlation between individual questions.

Figure 2 and Figure 3 depict the correlation coefficients between Q.1 and Q.5 as shown in Table 2. Specifically, Fig. 2 shows the correlation between users' self-perception of their computer skills and another question. The graph reveals that Q.2 exhibits a moderate correlation, while Q.3 and Q.4 indicate a strong

Table 2. Correlations

	Q.1	Q.2	Q.3	Q.4	Q.5	Q.6	Q.7	Q.8	Q.9	Q.10
Q.1	1.00									
Q.2	0.38	1.00								
Q.3	0.88	0.43	1.00							
Q.4	0.46	0.45	0.57	1.00						
Q.5	0.57	0.25	0.52	0.65	1.00					
Q.6	0.59	0.40	0.76	0.65	0.74	1.00				
Q.7	0.70	0.36	0.78	0.52	0.67	0.77	1.00			
Q.8	−0.35	−0.28	−0.35	−0.42	−0.26	−0.15	−0.20	1.00		
Q.9	−0.07	−0.12	−0.08	0.01	−0.28	−0.24	−0.23	−0.23	1.00	
Q.10	−0.20	0.08	−0.25	0.16	0.09	−0.09	−0.14	−0.15	−0.30	1.00

correlation. This suggests that individuals' self-perception of computer skills significantly influences their interest and proficiency in information systems development and virtualization technology, which are considered as extensions of computer skills. Notably, users lacking sufficient computer skills exhibit diminished interest and proficiency in system development and virtualization technology, possibly attributable to certain personality traits.

There exists a correlation with the second classification, namely knowledge and skills in virtualization technology. Notably, a strong correlation is observed with the construction of the system development educational environment on a physical computer instead of using virtualization containers, as indicated by Q.7. To successfully establish a development environment on an actual device, understanding the current configuration of the virtualization container is crucial. Consequently, it can be inferred that users lacking sufficient skills struggle to comprehend the container's configuration, making it challenging for them to construct a development and education environment on a physical computer.

Furthermore, no correlation is observed between Q.1 and the third category. However, the correlation coefficient bears a negative value. This suggests that users select between the proposed web-based connection and the conventional method based on convenience and situational factors, irrespective of their computer skills.

Figure 3 exhibits the correlation coefficients with Q.5, which represents self-perception of virtualization technology skills. As previously mentioned, the correlation coefficient with Q.1 is essentially similar to that depicted in Fig. 2. Notably, a high correlation is observed for the question pertaining to constructing an educational development environment on a physical computer. This indicates a strong relationship between understanding the configuration of virtualization containers, proficiency in constructing a real environment, and the ability to construct it on a physical computer. Conversely, the correlation with the proposed system is low and aligns with the previously discussed findings. Additional

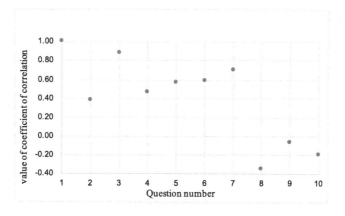

Fig. 2. Coefficient of correlation with Q1

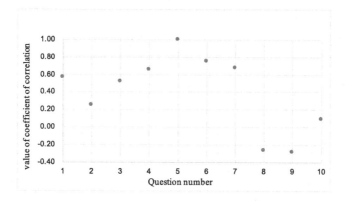

Fig. 3. Coefficient of correlation with Q5

information from free-text responses indicates that users opt for the conventional type over the web service type due to the capability to develop in an offline environment, such as while on the move. Furthermore, certain users prefer the web service type to alleviate concerns regarding local disk space. Moreover, a few comments express concerns about the convenience of virtualization, specifically uncertainty surrounding the ability to replicate the same environment in a physical setting.

5   Considerations and Future Work

Based on the results of the questionnaires in the previous section, the approach of the proposed system is verified. The current issues are then clarified.

5.1   Considerations

The aim of the proposed system in this research paper is to offer a standardized educational development environment for system development lectures. Based on the questionnaire evaluation results, it is evident that users possessing computer knowledge and skills also exhibit proficiency in virtualization technology. However, irrespective of their knowledge and skills, users make a choice between utilizing the proposed system or deploying the virtualization container on a traditional local computer, depending on convenience and specific usage scenarios. Consequently, it cannot be definitively asserted that the proposed system is inherently effective, but it can be concluded that it presents users with a novel alternative.

The proposed system proves particularly beneficial for students lacking sufficient computer knowledge and skills, as they can utilize the system without comprehending virtualization technology. To enhance the system's convenience, future efforts should focus on providing support for installing virtualization containers in the local environment. This can be achieved by packaging and delivering a comprehensive set of tools, including container downloads, verification of the virtualization platform's execution, and the establishment of a local web server.

5.2   Future Work

The proposed system necessitates a certain level of knowledge and skills regarding Docker containers, particularly when dealing with advanced settings or encountering errors. To address this, future considerations will involve incorporating forms and dropdown selections for Dockerfile generation, rather than relying on direct user input through the web interface. This approach aims to make the system applicable to a wider range of scenarios, eliminating the requirement for users to possess extensive system knowledge.

Currently, the system does not implement user management on an individual basis. Consequently, all containers are visible in the web browser interface. Introducing user management would resolve issues related to container management and enhance security for individual users. It is imperative to implement user management and swiftly apply it to system deployments.

6   Conclusion

This research paper introduces a software development education environment leveraging virtualization technology in a BYOD setting. The proposed system offers a comprehensive solution that spans from web browser interaction to container configuration, generation, and connection. It enables even novice students lacking computer knowledge and skills to independently install a unified system development and education environment on their personal computers. The implemented system has been successfully tested and verified in this study. Moving forward, there are several areas to address for further improvement. Firstly, a quantitative evaluation of the proposed system is deemed necessary. This evaluation will provide objective measures to assess its performance and effectiveness. Secondly, the generation of advanced containers should be explored, enabling the system to cater to more complex development scenarios. Lastly, enhancements to the web functions for debugging purposes should be considered to facilitate efficient troubleshooting and problem-solving. These issues will be key areas of focus for future development and refinement of the proposed system.

Acknowledgement. This research was partially supported by the Ministry of Education, Science, Sports and Culture, Grant-in Aid for Scientific Research (C), 2021–2023 21K11850, Takeshi TSUCHIYA.

References

1. Tsuchiya, T., Matsunaga, M., Yamada, T., Hirose, H.: Study on software development environment on BYOD for lectures. IEICE Technical report, vol. 123, no. 148, IN2023-19, pp. 13–16 (2023). (in Japanese)
2. Bhardwaj, A., Krishna, C.R.: Virtualization in cloud computing: moving from hypervisor to containerization—a survey. Arab. J. Sci. Eng. **46**, 8585–8601 (2021)
3. Reis, D., Piedade, B., Correia, F.F., Dias, J.P., Aguiar, A.: Developing docker and docker-compose specifications: a developers' survey. IEEE Access **10**, 2318–2329 (2022). https://doi.org/10.1109/ACCESS.2021.3137671
4. Islam Shamim, M.S., Ahamed Bhuiyan, F., Rahman, A.: XI commandments of Kubernetes security: a systematization of knowledge related to Kubernetes security practices. In: IEEE Secure Development (SecDev). Atlanta, GA, USA, pp. 58–64 (2020). https://doi.org/10.1109/SecDev45635.2020.00025
5. Sato, H.: Linux terminal system design for computer room by Docker. IPSJ SIG Technical report, 2017-SPT-25, vol. 25, no. 10, pp. 1–6 (2017). (in Japanese)
6. Koziolek, H., Eskandani, N.: Lightweight Kubernetes distributions: a performance comparison of MicroK8s, k3s, k0s, and Microshift. In: Proceedings of the International Conference on Performance Engineering, pp. 17–29. Association for Computing Machinery, New York (2023). https://doi.org/10.1145/3578244.3583737
7. Dwyer, G., Aggarwal, S., Stouffer, J.: Flask: Building Python Web Services. Packt Publishing (2017)
8. Morell, L., Jiang, C.: Using ShellInABox to improve web interaction in computing courses. J. Comput. Sci. Coll. **30**(5), 61–66 (2015)

Session-Based Recommendation System Approach for Predicting Learning Performance

Nguyen Xuan Ha Giang[1], Lam Thanh-Toan[1], and Nguyen Thai-Nghe[2(✉)]

[1] Faculty of Information System, Cantho University of Technology, Cantho, Vietnam
{nxhgiang,lttoan}@ctuet.edu.vn
[2] College of ICT, Cantho University, Cantho, Vietnam
ntnghe@cit.ctu.edu.vn

Abstract. The Intelligent Tutoring Systems (ITSs) are widely used, particularly in the context of the growing prevalence of online learning. A significant challenge in ITSs is performance prediction, specifically the ability to answer correctly at the first time, commonly referred to as CFA (Correct at First Attempt). This criterion serves as one of evaluation measures for learners' understanding and knowledge acquisition, enabling educational managers and teachers to adjust their teaching methods effectively to enhance learning outcomes. Because of the similarity between the prediction problem of learning performance and the session-based recommendation systems, this study proposes to experiment the application of session-based recommendation models, specifically LSTM (Long Short-Term Memory) in CFA prediction. In this research, two educational datasets, namely KDDCup 2010 and Assistment 2017, were employed for analysis and experimentation. The results indicate that the LSTM model outperforms other models, exhibiting a lower root mean square error (RMSE) value. Consequently, applying session data processing models to ITSs shows promise and potential for enhancing ITSs' performance.

Keywords: LSTM · Intelligent Tutoring Systems · Student's s performance prediction · Session-based recommendation system

1 Introduction

Intelligent Tutoring Systems (ITSs) [1, 2] are computer-based educational systems that offer personalized instruction by assessing learners' strengths and weaknesses. They provide customized learning experiences based on input data, previous outcomes, instructor assessments, and learner habits to enhance learning efficiency and effectiveness. ITSs recommend suitable materials, methods, assignments, and offer feedback on progress. Additionally, they support instructors in making teaching decisions, adjusting content, and employing methods tailored to individual learners' performance.

ITSs incorporate artificial intelligence techniques to operate and improve learners' educational performance, including: (1) Machine Learning: to analyze data, generate predictive models using data-driven learning capabilities, and automatically adapt parameters to improve forecasting results, thereby making automated decisions to appreciate

T. K. Dang et al. (Eds.): FDSE 2023, CCIS 1925, pp. 312–327, 2023.
https://doi.org/10.1007/978-981-99-8296-7_22

learning effectiveness. Machine learning techniques exploited in ITS encompass model of classification, clustering, regression, and reinforcement learning. (2) Data Mining: focus on encountering patterns and relationships within data. Data mining techniques enclose cluster analysis, multivariate analysis, quantitative analysis, and time series analysis. (3) Recommendation Systems: grant learning suggestions, materials, and activities that align with learners' preferences and requirements within ITSs. (4) Natural Language Processing: ITSs utilizes techniques such as parsing, grammartical and semantic analysis to understand and respond to user requests. (5) Expert advice: Expert knowledge can be directly given as consultation within ITS, offering accurate and contextually appropriate solutions for each specific case.

Recommendation systems (RSs) play a crucial role in supporting users and services in many fields, including education, business, finance, entertainment, culture, and decision-making processes faced with an overwhelming amount of information. The recommender techniques used in ITSs counting: (1) Collaborative Filtering leverages user ratings to identify other users with similar preferences and choices. (2) Content-based Filtering, which utilizes detailed information about questions and knowledge to make recommendations. (3) Knowledge-based Filtering employs knowledge and rules to generate suggestions. (4) Hybrid Recommender Systems combine multiple approaches. The flexible utilization of these techniques aims to enable ITSs to understand and proffer individual recommendations based on the individual learners' request, thereby enhancing their learning experience and effectiveness.

Recently, session-based recommendation systems (SBRSs) have emerged as a novel approach within the field of RSs. While traditional RSs rely on static content and colaborative filtering to model long-term user preferences, SBRSs capture short-term and contextually flexible user preferences within interactive sessions, suggesting more timely and accurate recommendations that adapt to session context changes. SBRSs aim to digest favour of user within the current session by leveraging associated sessions that have occurred during users' previous interactions. GRU-based RNN SBRS [3] operates on anonymous sessions, assuming that the ordered sessions in the dataset contain only one type of interaction (e.g., clicks) to predict the next items or videos. Hwangbo [4] introduced Feature-Weighted Session-Based Recommenders (FWSBRs), which blend items and attributes using various feature weighting techniques within an e-commerce dataset. This approach also factors in the sequence of session item occurrences to suggest upcoming fashion products. FWSBR addresses the cold-start item challenge, a known limitation of methods like Collaborative Filtering with Ratings and Item-Item Similarity-Based Recommender, by relying solely on item attributes for generating recommendations while maintaining recommendation quality.

Adventuring educational data for the purpose of serving, supporting, and improving RSs is an important approach that brings RSs closer to ITSs. Specifically, there have been numerous studies focusing on predicting learning results and assessing learners' abilities to identify early learning performance. Employing genuine data obtained from a multidisciplinary university, Li [5] conducted feature extraction and weight assignment to develop a neural network system distinguished by adaptable nodes and hidden layers, incorporating 1D CNN and LSTM. The efficiency of forecasting student performance in future courses, relying on their past course accomplishments, has been affirmed through the attained RMSE of 0.785. Pan [6] presents a framework for a multiview course recommendation system that relies on deep learning techniques for the purpose of extracting educational resources. This framework is designed with the intention of fostering increased collaboration between the machine learning community and the field of educational technology, with the aim of promoting and encouraging such engagement. Consequently, the interest in evaluating learners' level of understanding and knowledge exposure, which relates to achieving correct answers at the first attempt (CFA), has materialized. This result helps educational managers and teachers with appropriate solutions to strengthen the teaching activities and orient learning in the most suitable way for learners.

CFA refers to the accurate response tried by learners in their initial endeavor to address a question. CFA is a concept in the education field and achievement evaluation that is incorporated into several aspects: (1) Performance examination: CFA is used to measure learners' knowledge attainment. A high CFA indicator reflects a deep understanding and the ability to accurately resolve tasks on the opening effort. (2) Task design: The CFA index can review the appropriateness of exercises and questions. If the CFA is low, it exhibits that the problems are excessively difficult or unclear, preventing learners from correctly solving them on the first time. (3) Data analysis: CFA is an essential indicator in data-driven educating modeling, enabling teachers and researchers to understand the effectiveness of lecturing and the achievement of objectives through exercise design. (4) Teacher training: Evaluating and advancing the CFA score supports faculty members enhance their guiding methods and strengthen their instructional skills.

In this study, we propose the use of a Long Short-Term Memory (LSTM) session data processing model for multidimensional educational data. Our research specifically aims to predict learners' Correct First Attempt (CFA) scores based on their previous CFAs, and we compare this approach with other recommendation methods such as Matrix Factorization, User-based Collaborative Filtering, and User Average using two session datasets: KDDCup 2010 and Assistment 2017.

2   Related Works and Recommender Systems

2.1   Related Works in the Field of Predicting Academic Performance

Various methods and approaches have been investigated in educational data mining to survey and forecast dropout rates, knowledge, course consequence, and other indicators of learners. Regarding these activities, the research [7] this research investigates the influence of time on student performance projection in ITSs employing Bayesian Knowledge Tracing. The findings highlight the necessity of integrating time-related factors into educational models to enhance the precision of these prediction tasks. It demonstrated that predictive results have contributed to more diverse strategies in improving educational effectiveness. Yuan [8] conducted a predicting whether a student would answer correctly on their first experiment. This report uses each method separately or in combination with each other among the seven methods: Basic DecisionTree, Random Forest, AdaBoost, XGBoost, LightGBM, Gradient Boosting Decision Tree, and Logistic Regression. The observations demonstrate that, despite large-scale datasets, the author's approach combining these techniques achieves effectiveness. Measuring the error rate in the dataset with the lowest RMSE value when combining LightGBM with Random Forest is 0.3449. A study on Bayesian network models [9, 10], targeting to predict the first response of students taking the GRE (Graduate Record Examination) on the Assistment 2004–2005 dataset, represented the convincingness of different models.

Tatar [11] uses cumulative grade point average (GPA) and overall grade point average to assume student achievement and academic attainment. Thai-Nghe [12] demonstrated that predictive activities regarding learning outcomes can be improved, and students' knowledge can accumulate over time. By handling the matrix decomposition approach (Tensor Factorization) with the time factor, the authors perform specific student-level predictions. The study has been established the effectiveness and practical applicability. Zhang [13] announces a new model called STR-SA (Session-based Thread Recommendation - Self-attention), which applies a neural network combined with self-attention techniques to suggest academic topics. The STR-SA is built upon students' interest levels in the theme they have recently viewed in the current session. This model represents an extension of the applicability of neural networks in online learning environments. The aforementioned researches highlight the significance and practicality of implementing session data-based recommendation systems in educational contexts.

2.2 Models in Recommendation Systems

Long-Short Term Memory: LSTM is a widely-used deep learning method in forecasting models. LSTM is suitable for temporal-based data features, addressing the issue of long-term dependencies [14, 15]. Yu [16] introduced LSTM as an extended architecture of Recurrent Neural Network (RNN). Through various improvements, LSTM has become popular due to highly effective operation in numerous different issues.

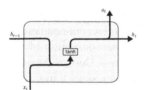
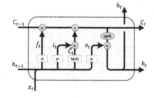

Fig. 1. Memory structure in RNN   **Fig. 2.** Memory structure in LSTM

Where

- h_t, c_t: *hidden state vector*
- x_t: *input vector*
- *f, i, c, o: bias vectors*
- W_f, W_i, W_c, W_o: *parameter matrices*
- σ, *tanh: sigmoid function*

The building of recurrent neural networks enables LSTM to retain multiple layers of information from previous computations. The current layer's result is a combination of the input data from the current layer and the computed output of the components from previous time steps. It is illustrated that LSTM's architecture (see Fig. 1) represents differently from and is the basis for enhanced memory capacity compared to RNN (see

Fig. 2). LSTM integrates a memory cell state structure, performed by the horizontal line running through the graph's vertices. The cell state is a conveyor belt-like structure that traverses the entire chain with only a few linear interactions, facilitating stable information propagation along the neural network graph. LSTM has the ability to erase and add information to the cell state, regulating these information flows through gates. Gates are a specialized mechanism synthesized by a hidden layer of a sigmoid activation function with a multiplication operator [17].

The proposed framework in this article utilizes a two-layer LSTM. The binary_crossentropy loss function in (Eq. 1) is deployed to measure the discrepancy, based on the probability distribution difference between the two discrete variables, namely the target value and the predicted value.

$$CE = -t_1 \log(f(s_1)) - (1 - t_1)\log(1 - f(s_1)) \tag{1}$$

where t represents the ground truth label (value of 0 or 1), and f(s) defined in (Eq. 2) is the sigmoid activation function to predict the probability for the output layer containing a node.

$$f(s_i) = \frac{1}{1 + e^{-s_i}} \tag{2}$$

The Adam Optimization algorithm [19] is exploited to optimize the model, automatically updating the learning rate for the parameters while reducing gradient fluctuations. This mechanism relies on the moving average moment between the current data moment and the closest data moment in the past [18].

User-Based Collaborative Filtering (User-Based CF): With the objective of sharing opinions with others, Collaborative Filtering (CF) is a filtering and evaluation process of items through the opinions of multiple individuals from a large interconnected community on the web. CF has significantly facilitated the filtering of large amounts of data. The collaborative filtering system supports predictions and recommendations for users to choose and rank multiple items. Ranking refers to the association of two components users and products, through numerical values. Figure 3. Depicts the user's ranking on products using a rating matrix structure. Each row represents a user, each column represents a specific product, and the rating value is located at the intersection.

	$Item_1$	$\cdots$	$Item_j$	$\cdots$	$Item_n$
$User_1$	$Rating_{1,1}$	$\cdots$	$Rating_{1,j}$	$\cdots$	$Rating_{1,n}$
$\vdots$	$\vdots$	$\vdots$	$\vdots$	$\vdots$	$\vdots$
$User_i$	$Rating_{i,1}$	$\cdots$	$Rating_{i,j}$	$\cdots$	$Rating_{i,n}$
$\vdots$	$\vdots$	$\vdots$	$\vdots$	$\vdots$	$\vdots$
$User_m$	$Rating_{m,1}$	$\cdots$	$Rating_{m,j}$	$\cdots$	$Rating_{m,n}$

Fig. 3. Illustration of a rating matrix [19]

A collaborative filtering system can: (1) Items recommendation: displaying a list of suggested items to the user, ordered by their perceived utility. This process typically involves first making predictions relied on item ratings, and then ranking the items according to these outputs. However, Schafer [20] conveys that some successful algorithms can make recommendations entirely without calculating predicted rank values. (2) Items prediction: selecting a specific item and weigh a estimated rating for that item. The challenge lies in how a system decides how to rate an item, when there are limited or no user reviews available on that particular item. (3) Suggestion: providing a list of recommended items. The task of CF is to forecast the votes and rankings of a specific user based on the voting and ranking database of other users. Breese [21] describes CF algorithm that can be categorized into two types:

Memory-Based Collaborative Filtering: This approach applies the past behavior of users. Guess determinations are made by enumerating the similarity between users or items based on their user ratings. This algorithm does not generate an explicit data model, but focuses on storing user-item interactions matrix and evaluating the similarity between users or items. Particularly, Memory-based CF can be divided into two popular approaches: User-based CF, which calculates the resemblance between users. The other is Item-based CF, which measures the similarity between items, to make predictions about user preferences on those items. This approach is computationally efficient and easy to implement but is suffered by sparse data and the cold-start problem.

In Memory-based CF, the data consists of a set of ratings, $v_{i,j}$ representing the rating of user i on item j. I_i is the item set that user i has voted, rated. The calculation of $\overline{v_i}$ in (Eq. 3) is the average of all ratings given by user i to all products j that user i has rated, denoted as:

$$\overline{v_i} = \frac{1}{|I_i|} \sum_{j \in I_i} v_{i,j} \tag{3}$$

$$w(a, i) = -\frac{\sum_j (v_{a,j} - \overline{v_a})(v_{i,j} - \overline{v_i})}{\sqrt{\sum_j (v_{a,j} - \overline{v_a})^2 \sum_j (v_{i,j} - \overline{v_i})^2}} \tag{4}$$

The distance, correlation index, or resemblance measure between item j and item k are expressed at weight w(j, k). Let n be the number of users in the database with a nonzero weight w(j, k). In collaborative filtering, the Pearson correlation coefficient [22] is used to assess the similarity between two users or two items based on ratings. (Eq. 4) captures the correlation coefficient between two users, a and i, for the items on which they have provided ratings. Predicting the rating of user i on item j, $p_{a,j}$ is is expressed according to (Eq. 5)

$$p_{a,j} = \overline{v_a} + k \sum_{i=1}^{n} w(a, i)(v_{i,j} - \overline{v_i}) \tag{5}$$

Model-Based Collaborative Filtering (CF): as a recommendation approach, involves constructing explicit data models using various machine learning algorithms. It analyzes the user-item interaction matrix to derive a lower-dimensional representation matrix containing latent factors. The objective is to build a guessing model for user preferences on items. Some machine learning models, such as linear regression, artificial neural networks, support vector machines (SVM), and Naive Bayes classifiers, are employed. This approach achieves higher accuracy, handles sparse data, but comes with increased computational complexity and the risk of overfitting.

This study experimentally investigates the collaborative filtering algorithm using the nearest neighbor-based approach (User-based CF). It measures the Pearson correlation coefficient (Eq. 4) and the accuracy of learner responses (Eq. 5) to estimate the effort of providing correct answers on the first attempt. The procedure advances using the following KNN algorithm (User-based CF):

Input:	R	User rating matrix. Each row represents a user (user_id), each column represents an item
	K	Number of nearest neighbors for prediction
	User	User for whom prediction is required
Output:	Rating	Predicted value for the user
Initialization:		• Initialize an empty list (Sorted_neighbors) to store the nearest users • Iterate over all (user_ids) in (R) • Calculate the similarity measure w(a,i) between user and (user_id) • Add (user_id, w(a,i)) to the (Sorted_neighbors)
Sorting neighbors:		Sort the (Sorted_neighbors) in descending order based on the similarity measure w(a, i)
Prediction:		• Create an empty list (Predictions) to store the predicted values • Iterate over the nearest users in (Sorted_neighbors): Check if reaching the (K- required Predictions) • If (K) have not been reached: Calculate the predicted value $p_{a,j}$ for the item not yet rated by the user • Add $p_{a,j}$ to the (Predictions)
Calculation:		• Calculate the average value of the predicted values in the (Predictions) • Return the predicted rating value for the user

Matrix Factorization (MF): as a successful technique of the latent factor model. MF is considered a state-of-the-art approach that addresses the sparsity issue in CF by employing matrix decomposition techniques. The latent rating values between users and items can be inferred from these previous values. The underlying idea of this technique is to disintegrate a large matrix X into two smaller matrices, W and H, such that reconstructing X from W and H yields a more accurate approximation of X. In other words, the aim is to optimize the reconstruction process of X using W and H, resulting in a better approximation [23].

$$\hat{r}_{ui} = \sum_{k=1}^{k} w_{ik} h_{ik} = w.h^T \tag{6}$$

$$e_{ui} = r_{ui} - \hat{r}_{ui} \forall u, i \in X \tag{7}$$

$$\text{RMSE} = \sqrt{\frac{1}{|D^{test}|} \sum_{(u,i,r \in D^{test})} \left(r_{ui} - \hat{r}_{ui}\right)^2} \tag{8}$$

Let $W \in |U| \times K$ be a matrix where each row u represents a vector of K latent factors describing user u. Similarly, let $H \in |I| \times K$ be a matrix where each row i represents a vector of K latent factors describing item i. Denote w_{uk} and h_{ik} as the corresponding elements of the two matrices W and H. Predicting of rating of user u on item i is determined using the following formula (Eq. 6). Let e_{ui} denote the training error of the (u, i) ranking. To Acquisition the submatrices W and H, the data error is minimized through (Eq. 8), which is also an optimization of the objective function in (Eq. 9).

$$O^{MF} = \sum_{u,i \in X} e_{ui}^2 = \sum_{u,i \in X} \left(r_{ui} - \hat{r}_{ui}\right)^2 = \sum_{u,i \in X} \left(r_{ui} - \sum_{k=1}^{k} w_{ui} h_{ui}\right)^2 \tag{9}$$

In RSs, this technique commonly handles stochastic gradient descent (SGD) as the optimization objective function. Processing SGD involves three steps, including (1): initializing random values for W and H; (2): iteratively calculating partial derivatives to reduce the stochastic gradient, while adjusting the values of W and H until the O_{MF} converges to the minimum value (Eq. 10) and (Eq. 11). (3): The elements of W and H are updated in the opposite direction of the derivative value in (Eq. 12) and (Eq. 13), where β represents the learning rate $(0 < \beta < 1)$.

$$\frac{\partial}{\partial w_{uk}} O^{MF} = -2\left(r_{ui} - \hat{r}_{ui}\right) h_{ik} \tag{10}$$

$$\frac{\partial}{\partial h_{ik}} O^{MF} = -2\left(r_{ui} - \hat{r}_{ui}\right) w_{uk} \tag{11}$$

$$w_{uk}^{new} = w_{uk}^{old} - \beta \frac{\partial}{\partial w_{uk}} O^{MF} = w_{uk}^{old} + 2\beta\left(r_{ui} - \hat{r}_{ui}\right) h_{ik} \tag{12}$$

$$h_{ik}^{new} = h_{ik}^{old} - \beta \frac{\partial}{\partial h_{ik}} O^{MF} = h_{ik}^{old} + 2\beta\left(r_{ui} - \hat{r}_{ui}\right) w_{uk} \tag{13}$$

This learning process continues until reaching the minimum of the objective function, which implies either achieving an acceptable error level or reaching a pre-defined number of iterations.

3 Proposed Method

3.1 The Correlation Between Predicting Academic Performance and SBRSs

Two datasets from ITSs were used in this study are namely KDDCup 2010[1] and Assistment 2017[2]. Each problem consists of multiple steps that a learner would either answer or skip to proceed to the next step (see Table 1). The system records the number of times learners utilize the assistance feature and request knowledge recommendations at each step.

The objective of forecasting learning outcomes in ITSs is to estimate whether the learner's CFA index at the current step will be correct or incorrect, and support appropriate knowledge components recommendations.

It is evident that this task shares several similarities with SBRSs. In this context, each problem can be considered as a transactional session consisting of multiple steps. When the learner performs an action (CFA-rating) on an answer (item), it forms a session. In SBRSs, each session is treated as a distinct data unit and an important entity. The boundary points marking the start and end of a session, generated over a continuous period, can be associated with user [24]. Interactions within a session is either sequential (ordered sessions) or non-sequential (unordered sessions). Each session consists of a set of characteristic attributes such as duration, time, date of occurrence, user information [19].

Table 1. Description of the extracted dataset from ITSs

User	Problem	Step	CFA	Knowledge Component (KC)	...
User 1	Problem 1	Step 1	0	KC1	...
User 1	Problem 1	Step 2	1	KC1	...
...	...	...	...	...	...
User n	Problem m	Step 1	1	KCn	...
User n	Problem m	Step 2	0	KCn	...
...	...	...	...	...	...

Through the analysis of the data features from the datasets, this study identified similarities and correspondences with session data in RSs. Consequently, the experiment employed session-based data processing models to address the research problem. In this context, the attribute student_ID/iTest_ID represents the user, problem_name/assignmentId corresponds to the item, and CFA/correct denotes the respective rating value.

The preprocessed datasets were selected, extracting the corresponding main features for each dataset and normalizing the input data for the learning models (see Fig. 4).

---

[1] https://kdd.org/kdd-cup/view/kdd-cup-2010-student-performance-evaluation/Data.

[2] https://sites.google.com/view/assistmentsdatamining/dataset.

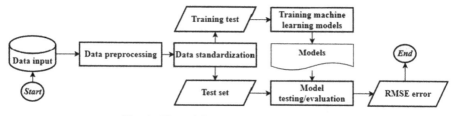

Fig. 4. The training and testing methodology

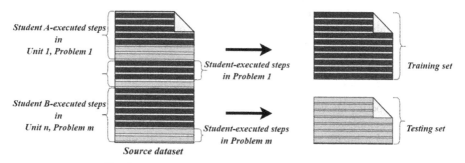

Fig. 5. Partitioning the training and testing dataset [25]

Each source set is organized according to the problems of each chapter, then each problem is divided into two distinct parts, aggregated correspondingly to collectively form the training set, accounting for 70% of the source data, and the testing set, representing the remaining 30% (see Fig. 5). The objective was to predict whether a learner would response correctly on their first attempt for each step of the problem or not. The rating value to be estimated is 1, indicating a correct answer, and 0, indicating an incorrect answer. For evaluating and comparing the performance of different models, the frequently employed metric is RMSE.

Table 2. Description of dataset configuration

Dataset	Number of steps/sessions		Features	Training features
	Training set	Testing set		
KDDCup 2010	59,864	33,331	23	3
Assistment 2017	154,204	77,199	76	3

Each dataset was meticulously chosen based on specific key features outlined in Table 2. The KDDCup 2010 dataset (as the KDD_training set) employed three distinctive features. (1) Anon Student Id: served as a unique identifier for learner. (2) Step_Name: feature captured the various steps within each exercise. For instance, a specific step within problem A001 was identified A0011 as "Find the length of side AB of rectangle

ABCD?". (2) Step_Name: was unique within each Problem_Name, overlaps across different Problem_Names. Consequently, to ensure distinct identification, a combination of the Problem_Name and Step_Name was deployed as the unique modifier for each step. (3) Correct_First_Attempt: indicated whether the learner's initial effort at decide a step was correct, with values of 1 and 0 denoting a correct or incorrect response respectively. Evaluating the model's performance on the KDDCup 2010 dataset, the testing set structure (as the KDD_test set) did not include the Correct_First_Attempt feature. Similarly, in the Assistment 2017 training set (Assistment_train set), the selected features include: (1) ITEST_id: representing the learner's identifier; (2) ProblemId: indicating the step within the problem; (3) Correct: assigning a value of 1 to indicate the correctness of the learner's initial attempt, and a value of 0 in the opposite scenario. The testing set (Assistment_test set) does not include the Correct feature.

3.2 Data Encryption

To conduct experiments with the LSTM model, the one-hot encoding data encoding technique was employed to convert each categorical value into a separate field. This process yielded a binary representation of either 0 or 1 to indicate the presence of a particular category. The application of the one-hot encoding method resulted in data sizes of (59864, 3) and (154204, 3) for the KDDCup 2010 and Assistment 2017 datasets, respectively.

3.3 Proposed Prediction Model

Figure 6 illustrates the architecture of the experimental model employed in this study. It is a multivariate input LSTM network that utilizes normalized input data, as described subsequently. This model utilizes sequential time data containing multiple input variables. The prediction technique, based on the sequential time factor, utilizes all prior data at time step $(t - 1)$ as input to forecast the current CFA (Cash Flow Analysis) value at the current time step (t).

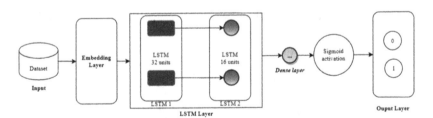

Fig. 6. The LSTM model's proposed architecture

Figure 7 provides a visual representation of the input dataset. Initially, the dataset is divided into training and testing portions, followed by a process of data filtration aimed at removing errors and missing information. Subsequently, the data is organized into a chronological sequence of steps $(t - 1, t - 2)$ and according to the specified problem_name.

Anon_Student_Id	Problem_Name	Step_Name	...	Correct_First_Attempt	...	KC(SubSkills)
stu_cc883f541b	WHOLENUMOPS1-083	Operation	...	1	...	identify operator
stu_cc883f541b	WHOLENUMOPS1-083	Digit1-1	...	0	...	
stu_cc883f541b	WHOLENUMOPS1-083	Digit2-1	...	0	...	
stu_cc883f541b	WHOLENUMOPS1-083	Digit2-2	...	1	...	
stu_cc883f541b	WHOLENUMOPS1-083	Digit2-3	...	1	...	

Anon_Student_Id	Problem_Name	Step_Name	...	Correct_First_Attempt	...	KC(SubSkills)
stu_cc883f541b	WHOLENUMOPS1-083	Operation	...		1	...	identify operator
stu_cc883f541b	WHOLENUMOPS1-083	Digit1-1	...		0	...	
stu_cc883f541b	WHOLENUMOPS1-083	Digit2-1		0		
stu_cc883f541b	WHOLENUMOPS1-083	Digit2-2				
stu_cc883f541b	WHOLENUMOPS1-083	Digit2-3				

Fig. 7. The multivariate input   **Fig. 8.** Predicting Correct First Attempt

The normalized input data comprises time step sequences that undergo feature selection, one-hot encoding, and hyperparameter tuning. Denoting t as the current step, the set of previous steps $(t-1, t-2, t-3)$ combined with step (t) attributes are input for the LSTM model. This input is used to predict the framed CFA value at step (t), (Fig. 8). The proposed LSTM network architecture consists of two layers, each consisting of 50 units, using the Keras library and the Sigmoid activation function (Eq. 2). Additionally, there is a single-unit Dense layer, producing predictions of 0 or 1.

To address overfitting, early stopping is used, reducing training time by halting after 5 consecutive epochs with loss fluctuations below 0.01, triggered by a Callback. Training can run for up to 100 epochs. Adam optimization with a learning rate of 0.0001 and batch size of 1 is applied, and model performance is evaluated with RMSE on the test dataset.

4 Experiments

4.1 Datasets

The KDDCup 2010 dataset employed in this study comprises 23 columns and 93,195 rows. These rows are divided into 59,864 instances allocated for training purposes and 33,331 instances reserved for testing. The dataset captures the actions undertaken by 70 users, functioning as learners, across a total of 6,666 problems. Additionally, the Assistment 2017 dataset encompasses data obtained from 276 users acting as learners. These users engaged in solving 204 problems and provided a total of 154,204 responses. The dataset encompasses a larger collection of records, amounting to 231,403 rows, with 154,204 rows, 76 columns designated for training and 77,199 rows designated for testing.

4.2 Evaluation Method

The Root-mean-square error metric is used to measure the error of the prediction model on the testing dataset. RMSE is calculated as the square root of the mean of the squared differences between the predicted values by the model and the actual values. A lower RMSE indicates a more accurate model with better predictive ability on new datasets. RMSE [26] is computed using the formula:

$$\text{RMSE} = \sqrt{\frac{1}{N_p} \sum_{u,i} (p_{ui} - r_{ui})^2} \qquad (15)$$

N_p denote the total number of predictions in the testing dataset, where p_{ui} represents the predicted rating proportion for user u on item i in the model, and r_{ui} represents the actual rating proportion. The RMSE is employed to assess the degree of overfitting in the model. If the RMSE calculated on the testing set surpasses the RMSE obtained on the training set, it signifies that the model has overfit the training data and necessitates appropriate adjustments during the training phase. By squaring the RMSE, greater emphasis is placed on larger errors before summing them, thereby amplifying the impact of significant errors.

4.3 Experimental Results

Ensuring objectivity in both the training and testing sets necessitates the utilization of random ratio splitting through the Cross-validation method [27]. However, due to the presence of time sequence features in both datasets, this study preserves the correct ordering of user interactions and refrains from employing Cross-validation. To augment the learning capability and encounter rating values in the training set, the data is organized based on the participating users. As mentioned, these two sets exhibit similar data characteristics, rendering them highly suitable for the application of specific data processing techniques in SBRSs.

Nevertheless, certain differences arise due to the collection of data from distinct educational platforms, thereby affecting the model execution process. In the KDDCup 2010, users are allowed to skip answering (rating) at any step, whereas Assistment 2017 mandates an answer of learner for progression to the subsequent step. Consequently, the KDDCup 2010 dataset exhibits a larger size in terms of the number of problems and steps compared to the other dataset. The LSTM encoding process for the KDDCup 2010 requires more time, and the resulting feature encoding matrix yields a significantly larger size. Consequently, the training time increases correspondingly.

The model's hyperparameters are tuned by randomly searching and selecting the optimal set using Bergstra's search technique [28]. This approach saves computational time by discretely selecting each sample and training the model on the training set, followed by prediction on the testing set, and finally calculating the error rate.

The experimental results obtained from the datasets reveal the RMSE difference values, which are presented in Table 3. The findings demonstrate that the MF method, currently considered the state-of-the-art in RSs, achieves the lowest RMSE error value of 0.418 and 0.472 on both datasets, respectively. The proposed model performs as the second-best with errors of 0.432 and 0.478. These outcomes indicate that there is still potential for improvement in the proposed model when compared to the current state-of-the-art method. However, in comparison to other popular methods such as CF and User average, the proposed model exhibits better suitability for datasets containing temporal sequence features (Figs. 9 and 10).

As our research advances, we are committed to expanding our endeavors towards enhancing the proposed model. Our primary goal is to integrate and synergistically incorporate additional temporal features, specifically the time interval between steps and learners' response time. By effectively integrating these features, we aspire to augment the model's performance across diverse data characteristics prevalent in both datasets. Consequently, we anticipate significant advancements in the efficacy and adaptability of our proposed model through these enrichments.

Table 3. Experimental results on the RMSE metric

Model	KDDCup 2010	Assistment 2017
LSTM	0.432	0.478
MF	**0.418**	**0.472**
CF	0.671	0.595
USER AVERAGE	0.876	0.588

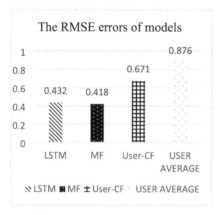

Fig. 9. RMSE in KDDCup 2010   **Fig. 10.** RMSE in Assistment 2017

5   Conclusion

Given the resemblance between the prediction of learning outcomes and SBRSs, this study proposes the adoption of session-based recommendation models (LSTM), to construct prediction models. The analysis and experimentation were conducted on two educational datasets, namely KDDCup 2010 and Assistment 2017. The findings reveal that while the LSTM model exhibits higher RMSE errors in comparison to the state-of-the-art Matrix Factorization method, it demonstrates potential for improvement when compared to other models. This highlights the viability of employing session-based data processing models, equipped with temporal sequence features, in ITSs.

In the future, our research will expand in various directions. This expansion will involve the integration of additional feature data and the refinement of alternative models within session-based recommendation systems. Furthermore, we will investigate and supplement one or more additional metrics to provide multiple perspectives for evaluating the prediction model, as well as assess the suitability of the data. These efforts are aimed at improving the error performance of prediction models, thereby fostering advancements in the field.

References

1. Almasri, A., et al.: Intelligent tutoring systems survey for the period 2000–2018 (2019)
2. Yuce, A., Abubakar, A.M., Ilkan, M.: Intelligent tutoring systems and learning performance: applying task-technology fit and IS success model. Online Inf. Rev. **43**(4), 600–616 (2019)
3. Hidasi, B., Karatzoglou, A.: Recurrent neural networks with top-k gains for session-based recommendations. In Proceedings of the 27th ACM International Conference on Information and Knowledge Management, pp. 843–852 (2018)
4. Hwangbo, H., Kim, Y.: Session-based recommender system for sustainable digital marketing. Sustainability **11**(12), 3336 (2019)
5. Li, S., Liu, T.: Performance prediction for higher education students using deep learning. Complexity **2021**, 1–10 (2021)
6. Pan, X., Li, X., Lu, M.: A MultiView courses recommendation system based on deep learning. In: 2020 International Conference on Big Data and Informatization Education (ICBDIE), pp. 502–506. IEEE (2020)
7. Pu, S., Converse, G., Huang, Y.: Deep performance factors analysis for knowledge tracing. In: Roll, I., McNamara, D., Sosnovsky, S., Luckin, R., Dimitrova, V. (eds.) AIED 2021, Part I. LNCS, vol. 12748, pp. 331–341. Cham, Springer, Cham (2021). https://doi.org/10.1007/978-3-030-78292-4_27
8. Yuan, K., Qi, Q.: KDD cup 2010: educational data mining challenge. Final Project Report (2019)
9. Feng, M., Heffernan, N.T., Mani, M., Heffernan, C.: Using mixed-effects modeling to compare different grain-sized skill models. In: Educational Data Mining: Papers from the AAAI Workshop. AAAI Press, Menlo Park (2006)
10. Pardos, Z.A., Heffernan, N.T., Anderson, B., Heffernan, C.L., Schools, W.P.: Using fine-grained skill models to fit student performance with Bayesian networks. In: Workshop in Educational Data Mining held at the 8th International Conference on Intelligent Tutoring Systems, Taiwan (2006)
11. Tatar, A.E., Düştegör, D.: Prediction of academic performance at undergraduate graduation: course grades or grade point average? Appl. Sci. **10**(14), 4967 (2020)
12. Thai-Nghe, N., Horváth, T., Schmidt-Thieme, L.: Factorization models for forecasting student performance. In: EDM, pp. 11–20 (2011)
13. Zhang, M., Liu, S., Wang, Y.: STR-SA: Session-based thread recommendation for online course forum with self-attention. In: 2020 IEEE Global Engineering Education Conference (EDUCON), pp. 374–381. IEEE (2020)
14. Dien, T.T., Luu, S.H., Thanh-Hai, N., Thai-Nghe, N.: Deep learning with data transformation and factor analysis for student performance prediction. Int. J. Adv. Comput. Sci. Appl. **11**(8) (2020)
15. Thai-Nghe, N., Thanh-Hai, N., Chi Ngon, N.: Deep learning approach for forecasting water quality in IoT systems. Int. J. Adv. Comput. Sci. Appl. **11**(8), 686–693 (2020)
16. Yu, Y., Si, X., Hu, C., Zhang, J.: A review of recurrent neural networks: LSTM cells and network architectures. Neural Comput. **31**(7), 1235–1270 (2019)
17. Gonçalves, P.J., Lourenço, B., Santos, S., Barlogis, R., Misson, A.: Computer vision intelligent approaches to extract human pose and its activity from image sequences. Electronics **9**(1), 159 (2020)
18. Kingma, D.P., Ba, J.: Adam: a method for stochastic optimization. arXiv preprint arXiv:1412.6980 (2014)
19. Isinkaye, F.O., Folajimi, Y.O., Ojokoh, B.A.: Recommendation systems: principles, methods and evaluation. Egypt. Inform. J. **16**(3), 261–273 (2015)

20. Schafer, J.B., Frankowski, D., Herlocker, J., Sen, S.: Collaborative filtering recommender systems. In: Brusilovsky, P., Kobsa, A., Nejdl, W. (eds.) The adaptive web. LNCS, vol. 4321, pp. 291–324. Springer, Heidelberg (2007). https://doi.org/10.1007/978-3-540-72079-9_9
21. Breese, J.S., Heckerman, D., Kadie, C.: Empirical analysis of predictive algorithms for collaborative filtering. arXiv preprint arXiv:1301.7363 (2013)
22. Cohen, I., et al.: Pearson correlation coefficient. Noise Reduct. Speech Process. 1–4 (2009)
23. Koren, Y.: Factor in the neighbors: scalable and accurate collaborative filtering. ACM Trans. Knowl. Discov. Data (TKDD) **4**(1), 1–24 (2010)
24. Quadrana, M., Karatzoglou, A., Hidasi, B., Cremonesi, P.: Personalizing session-based recommendations with hierarchical recurrent neural networks. In: Proceedings of the Eleventh ACM Conference on Recommender Systems, pp. 130–137 (2017)
25. Stamper, J., Pardos, Z.A.: The 2010 KDD cup competition dataset: engaging the machine learning community in predictive learning analytics. J. Learn. Anal. **3**(2), 312–316 (2016)
26. Chai, T., Draxler, R.R.: Root mean square error (RMSE) or mean absolute error (MAE)?– arguments against avoiding RMSE in the literature. Geosci. Model Dev. **7**(3), 1247–1250 (2014)
27. Kohavi, R.: A study of cross-validation and bootstrap for accuracy estimation and model selection. In: Ijcai, vol. 14, no. 2, pp. 1137–1145 (1995)
28. Bergstra, J., Bengio, Y.: Random search for hyper-parameter optimization. J. Mach. Learn. Res. **13**(2) (2012)

A Fuzzy Logic Model for Digital Transformation Assessment of Vietnamese Higher Education Institutions

Bach Hoang Xuan[1](✉) and An Nguyen Van[2]

[1] Institute of Digital Transformation, HCMC University of Industry and Trade,
Ho Chi Minh City, Vietnam
bach@idx.edu.vn

[2] Viettel Import Export Limited Company, Viettel Group, Hanoi, Vietnam

Abstract. A digital transformation assessment is a comprehensive review of an organization's current digital capabilities. It is used to identify areas where they need to invest in technology and strategy to become more competitive. In this paper, the researchers propose a fuzzy logic-based model that can be used to assist in determining digital maturity of Vietnamese higher education institutions. The fuzzy inference system (FIS) allows domain experts to present their knowledge in the form of fuzzy sets and fuzzy rules, thereby evaluating the criteria and degree of digital transformation. This model was implemented using Scikit-Fuzzy and can be applied to evaluate the degree of digital transformation in Vietnamese Higher Education Institutions.

Keywords: Fuzzy Logic · Fuzzy Inference System · Digital Transformation Assessment

1 Introduction

Digital transformation in higher education institutions is becoming a significant trend to enhance the learning experience and student management. In order to assess the level of digital transformation in higher education institutions, it is necessary to have a flexible, objective assessment method that accurately reflects the current situation [1]. The Ministry of Education and Training of Vietnam has issued a set of indicators and criteria for assessing digital transformation in higher education institutions in Decision No. 4740/QD-BGDDT dated December 30, 2022 [2]. The set of indicators is divided into two groups of criteria: "Digital transformation in training" and "Digital transformation in governance", including 52 evaluation criteria of different importance that are evaluated with the maximum score. Respective multi. This score evaluation will be difficult to do objectively, requiring a more effective method.

The proposed evaluation method uses fuzzy set theory, fuzzy inference system for objectively reflected results in the predictive model. Fuzzy logic can handle information that is imprecise or uncertain. This is important because assessing the digital transformation of higher education is a complex process and difficult to accurately measure.

T. K. Dang et al. (Eds.): FDSE 2023, CCIS 1925, pp. 328–340, 2023.
https://doi.org/10.1007/978-981-99-8296-7_23

2   Fuzzy Logic and Fuzzy Inference System

Fuzzy set theory was proposed by Professor Lotfi Aliasker Zadeh, University of California, Berkeley, in "L.A. Zadeh, Fuzzy Set Information and Control," 8, 338-353 (1965) [3]. Fuzzy set theory is a mathematical tool for solving problems of uncertainty because it can measure concepts that are subjectively ambiguous or unclear. Fuzzy logic is an approach based on human reasoning rather than hard computing. The inference method in fuzzy logic is more intuitive than classical logic. It allows us to better understand the imprecise and difficult to model natural phenomena based on the definition of rules and functions belonging to fuzzy sets.

A fuzzy set A on the universe X is usually represented as a membership function μ_A, which maps domain elements (x) with their respective degrees of belonging in the interval [0, 1]:

$$\mathbf{A} = \{(x, \mu_A(x)) | x \in X\}$$

Unlike crisp logic with only two values 0 and 1, fuzzy logic allows multi between 0 and 1 defined by membership functions.

The working of the Fuzzy Inference System (FIS) consists of the following steps [4].

- A fuzzification unit supports the application of numerous fuzzification methods, and converts the crisp input into fuzzy input.
- A rule base - collection of rule base and database is formed upon the conversion of crisp input into fuzzy input.
- The defuzzification unit fuzzy input is finally converted into crisp output (Fig. 1).

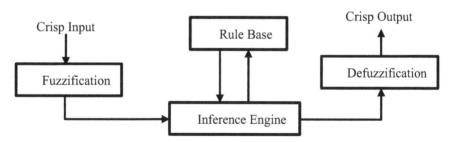

Fig. 1. Fuzzy Inference System

Following steps need to be followed to compute the output from this FIS.

- Step 1 − Set of fuzzy rules need to be determined in this step.
- Step 2 − In this step, by using the input membership function, the input would be made fuzzy.

- Step 3 — Now establish the rule strength by combining the fuzzified inputs according to fuzzy rules.
- Step 4 — In this step, determine the consequence of rule by combining the rule strength and the output membership function.
- Step 5 — For getting output distribution combine all the consequences.
- Step 6 — Finally, a defuzzified output distribution is obtained.

Fuzzy logic and FIS represent a powerful approach to scoring systems [5–8].

3   Fuzzy Logic Model for Digital Transformation Assessment

3.1   Evaluation Criteria and Software Tools

The proposed model does not change the evaluation framework provided in decision No. 4740/QD-BGDDT. The process of fuzzification of the evaluation criteria is carried out as follows.

- Mandatory criteria, not giving points, are fuzzified with two values in the interval [0,1], respectively: 0 - No (optional criteria); 1 - Yes (mandatory criteria).
- With the evaluation criteria by point scores, fuzzified on the interval [0.2] with three values: 0 - Not responsive (not meeting the criteria); 1 - Basic response and 2. Good response.

Python with scikit-fuzzy library is used to model and calculate output value of fuzzy system in this study (Figs. 2 and 3).

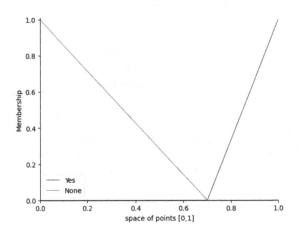

Fig. 2. Membership function of mandatory criteria

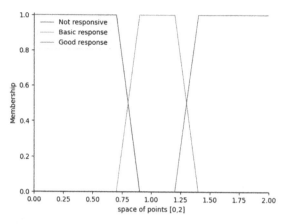

Fig. 3. Membership function of non-mandatory criteria

3.2   Inputs and Outputs of the Fuzzy Inference System

The set of indicators and criteria for evaluating the digital transformation of university institutions according to fuzzy logic is described in detail as follows.

Table 1. Criteria and fuzzification.

Item	Evaluation criteria	Universe of discourse
1	**Digital Transformation in Training**	**[0,2]**
1.1	Plan online training	[0,1]
1.2	There are regulations on training	[0,1]
1.3	Online training and management tools	[0,2]
1.3.1	There is live online training (via Teams, Zoom, and Google Meet software…)	[0,2]
1.3.2	Learners can self-study, evaluate, and grasp their learning progress and results	[0,2]
1.3.3	Higher education institutions manage grades, learners' learning progress, and activities of lecturers and academic advisors on the system	[0,2]
1.3.4	Provide exchange forums and other support tools for learners to interact with lecturers and departments of higher education institutions	[0,2]
1.3.5	Organize regular inspections and evaluation	[0,2]
1.4	Number of online courses (full content and training activities from enrollment to completion of a specific module) that have been evaluated and included in the training	[0,2]

(continued)

Table 1. (*continued*)

Item	Evaluation criteria	Universe of discourse
1.5	Deploying electronic/digital library applications	[0,2]
1.5.1	Number of publications available to meet training modules	[0,2]
1.5.2	Number of databases, specialized journals, that are connected and provide access to students	[0,2]
1.5.3	Promulgate regulations on management and use	[0,1]
1.5.4	Number of students who regularly use	[0,2]
1.5.5	Provide online borrow-return function	[0,2]
1.6	Implement digital transformation of testing work	[0,2]
1.6.1	Organizing exams and tests on computers (computer room with LAN connection)	[0,2]
1.6.2	Promulgating regulations on examinations and tests on computers	[0,2]
1.6.3	Percentage of subjects/modules that are held on computer-based exams	[0,2]
1.6.4	Have software to organize exams and tests on connected computers and exchange results with the school administration system	[0,2]
1.7	Developing human resources for digital transformation	[0,2]
1.7.1	Percentage of lecturers who can exploit and use software and tools to innovate teaching methods	[0,2]
1.7.2	Percentage of lecturers who can build digital learning materials and electronic lectures	[0,2]
1.8	Online training support system There is a studio for the production of learning materials (the studio includes a specialized room that is equipped with software and IT equipment used for building, editing, and publishing electronic learning materials)	[0,2]
1.8.1	The studio system is operated regularly	[0,2]
1.8.2	Quantity of quality self-produced learning materials	[0,2]
1.8.3	Instructors can use the studio to build learning materials	[0,2]
1.8.4	System of Lab rooms, multi-function IT rooms	[0,2]
2	**Digital transformation in management**	**[0,2]**
2.1	Higher education institutions set up a department to direct, be in charge of, and deploy IT applications and digital transformation (information: Full name; position; department; email; phone)	[0,1]

(*continued*)

Table 1. (*continued*)

Item	Evaluation criteria	Universe of discourse
2.2	Issuing a plan for IT application and digital transformation	[0,1]
2.3	Promulgating regulations on ensuring information security, restrictions on management, operation, and use of IT systems in higher education institutions	[0,1]
2.4	Having deployed higher education institution management software (provide information: solution name, self-build/rent/purchase)	[0,2]
2.4.1	Having deployed training management software (enrollment, training, degree-granting)	[0,2]
2.4.2	Have implemented human resource management software	[0,2]
2.4.3	Having deployed software to manage facilities and assets	[0,2]
2.4.4	Has implemented financial management software	[0,2]
2.4.5	Having deployed scientific research management software	[0,2]
2.4.6	Deployed electronic office (electronic documents, work records, digital signatures…)	[0,2]
2.4.7	Comply with the data specifications of the higher education sector database system; fully connect and exchange data with the HEMIS higher education database (managed by the ministry)	[0,2]
2.5	Deployment of online services	[0,2]
2.5.1	Having an electronic portal to provide adequate information as prescribed (Circular 15.2018/TT.BGDDT)	[0,2]
2.5.2	There is an application to connect students with the school (information via OTT - Over the top)	[0,2]
2.5.3	Services to serve learners (online enrollment, credit registration, learning results, tuition fees, etc.)	[0,2]
2.5.4	Services for lecturers, staff, and managers are deployed (Registration of work schedules, registration of leave, confirmation of records…)	[0,2]
2.5.5	Scientific research support services are deployed: registration, review, and approval of topics; Sign up for a study plan, course activities, etc.)	[0,2]
2.5.6	Is there a service to collect fees for education services in the form of not using cash?	[0,2]
2.6	IT technical infrastructure for administration	[0,2]

(*continued*)

Table 1. (*continued*)

Item	Evaluation criteria	Universe of discourse
2.6.1	Implement a master plan to ensure inheritance, connectivity, integration, sharing and communication, and data sharing among information systems in higher education institutions (Data connection systems). Data via LGSP; integrated data in a big data warehouse; SSO single sign-on account,)	[0,2]
2.6.2	Deploying solutions to ensure the security of information systems by level	[0,2]
2.6.3	Provide free internet access for students and faculty	[0,2]

According to the description of evaluation criteria in Table 1, the model includes 42 criteria and is divided into 11 groups of rules in Table 2, including 23 criteria for evaluating digital transformation in training and 19 criteria for evaluating digital transformation in training. Number change in administration, described in Table 3 (Fig. 4).

Table 2. Rule group table and input data for groups

No	Rules group	Input variables
1	Digital Transformation in Training **(1)**	(1.1); (1.2); (1.3); (1.4); (1.5); (1.6); (1.7); (1.8)
2	Online training and management tools **(1.3)**	(1.3.1); (1.3.2); (1.3.3); (1.3.4); (1.3.5)
3	Deploying electronic/digital library applications **(1.5)**	(1.5.1); (1.5.2); (1.5.3); (1.5.4); (1.5.5)
4	Implement digital transformation of testing work. **(1.6)**	(1.6.1); (1.6.2); (1.6.3); (1.6.4)
5	Developing human resources for digital transformation **(1.7)**	(1.7.1); (1.7.2)
6	Online training support system **(1.8)**	(1.8.1); (1.8.2); (1.8.3); (1.8.4)
7	Digital transformation in management **(2)**	(2.1); (2.2); (2.3); (2.4); (2.5); (2.6)
8	Having deployed higher education institution management software **(2.4)**	(2.4.1); (2.4.2); (2.4.3); (2.4.4); (2.4.5); (2.4.6); (2.4.7)
9	Deployment of online services **(2.5)**	(2.5.1); (2.5.2); (2.5.3); (2.5.4); (2.5.5); (2.5.6)
10	IT technical infrastructure for administration **(2.6)**	(2.6.1); (2.6.2); (2.6.3)
11	Evaluate the Digital Transformation	(1); (2)

Table 3. Input for the model

Criteria group	Input variables
Digital Transformation in Training	(1.1); (1.2); (1.4) (1.3.1); (1.3.2); (1.3.3); (1.3.4); (1.3.5) (1.5.1); (1.5.2); (1.5.3); (1.5.4); (1.5.5) (1.6.1); (1.6.2); (1.6.3); (1.6.4) (1.7.1); (1.7.2) (1.8.1); (1.8.2); (1.8.3); (1.8.4)
Digital transformation in management	(2.1); (2.2); (2.3) (2.4.1); (2.4.2); (2.4.3); (2.4.4); (2.4.5); (2.4.6); (2.4.7) (2.5.1); (2.5.2); (2.5.3); (2.5.4); (2.5.5); (2.5.6) (2.6.1); (2.6.2); (2.6.3)

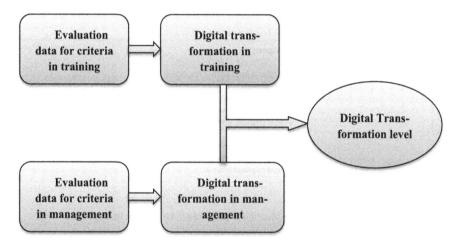

Fig. 4. Data presentation and assessment steps

3.3 Rule Base

The threshold for the membership functions corresponding to each evaluation criterion (not responsive, basic response, good response) requires industry experts to provide the corresponding threshold. Within the scope of this paper, the research team provides some hypothetical thresholds to test the operating model (Tables 4, 5 and 6).

Table 4. Rule table for evaluating the level of digital transformation

No	Digital Transformation in training	Digital transformation in management	Digital Transformation
1	Not responsive	Not responsive	Not responsive
2	Not responsive	Basic response	Not responsive
3	Not responsive	Good response	Not responsive
4	Basic response	Not responsive	Not responsive
5	Basic response	Basic response	Basic response
6	Basic response	Good response	Basic response
7	Good response	Not responsive	Not responsive
8	Good response	Basic response	Basic response
9	Good response	Good response	Good response

Table 5. Rule table for evaluating Digital Transformation in training

Input variables	Digital Transformation in Training
(1.1); (1.2); (1.3); (1.4); (1.5); (1.6); (1.7); (1.8)	**Not responsive:** - 1 of 2 criteria (1.1) or (1.2) none - 4 or more criteria are Not responsive **Basic response:** - 3 or more criteria are Basic response - 2 Base response criteria and 1 Good response criteria - 2 Good response criteria and 1 Base response criteria **Good response:** - 4 Good response criteria and 2 Base response criteria - 5 Good response criteria and 1 Base response criteria - 6 Good response criteria

Table 6. Rule table for evaluating Digital transformation in management

Input variables	Digital transformation in management
(2.1); (2.2); (2.3); (2.4); (2.5); (2.6)	**Not responsive:** - 1 of 3 criteria (2.1), (2.2) or (2.3) None - 2 Not responsive criteria **Basic response:** - 2 or more criteria are Base response - 1 Basic response criteria & 1 Good response criteria & 1 Not response criteria - 2 Good response criteria & 1 Not responsive criteria **Good response:** - 2 Good response criteria and 1 Base response - 3 Good response criteria

3.4 Simulated Evaluation Result

Model test evaluations according to the rules described in Sect. 3.3. are performed with samples 01, 02 and sample 03 below.

Sample 01

Item	Result of evaluation
1.1	Yes
1.2	Yes
1.3	Basic response
1.4	Not responsive
1.5	Basic response
1.6	Not responsive
1.7	Not responsive
1.8	Basic response

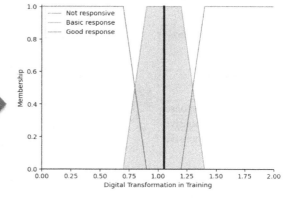

Item	Result of evaluation
2.1	Yes
2.2	Yes
2.3	Yes
2.4	Good response
2.5	Good response
2.6	Good response

Results of the assessment of the level of digital transformations

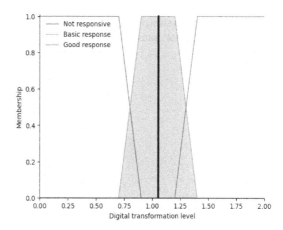

Sample 02

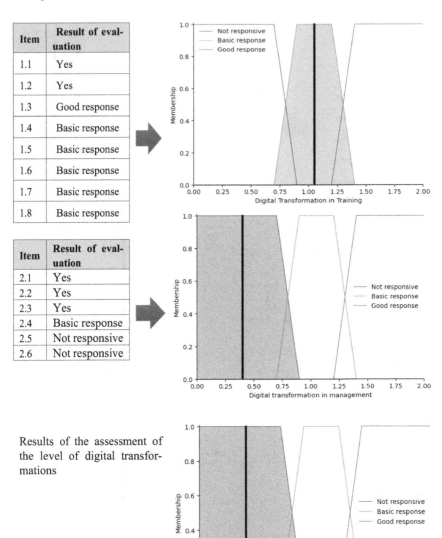

Item	Result of evaluation
1.1	Yes
1.2	Yes
1.3	Good response
1.4	Basic response
1.5	Basic response
1.6	Basic response
1.7	Basic response
1.8	Basic response

Item	Result of evaluation
2.1	Yes
2.2	Yes
2.3	Yes
2.4	Basic response
2.5	Not responsive
2.6	Not responsive

Results of the assessment of the level of digital transformations

Sample 03

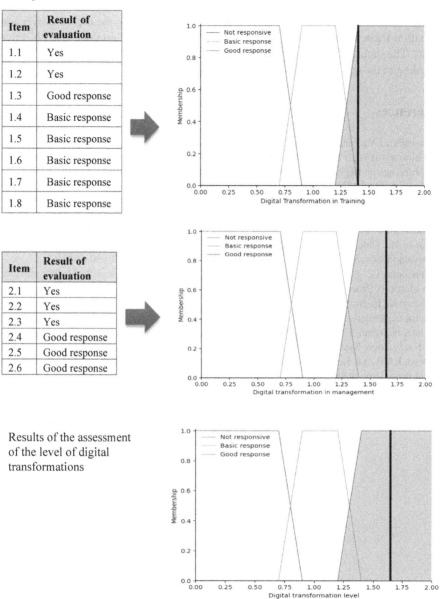

Item	Result of evaluation
1.1	Yes
1.2	Yes
1.3	Good response
1.4	Basic response
1.5	Basic response
1.6	Basic response
1.7	Basic response
1.8	Basic response

Item	Result of evaluation
2.1	Yes
2.2	Yes
2.3	Yes
2.4	Good response
2.5	Good response
2.6	Good response

Results of the assessment of the level of digital transformations

4 Conclusion

The scoring system in Decision 4740/QD-BGDDT to assess digital transformation in higher education institutions in Vietnam is difficult for experts to score, posing the problem of finding a more suitable model.

The purpose of this study is to propose a model to evaluate the degree of digital transformation using fuzzy logic. This method allows the evaluator to choose the appropriateness of each criterion more easily, without changing the digital conversion evaluation framework as prescribed, so it will also bring more accurate and objective results. The simulation results obtained in this study are in line with the expected results according to the evaluation framework in decision 4740/QD-BGDDT.

References

1. Carvalho, J.V., Pereira, R.H., Rocha, Á: A comparative study on maturity models for information systems in higher education institutions. In: Proceedings of the 2018 International Conference on Digital Science, Montenegro, pp. 150–158 (2018)
2. Decision No. 4740/QD-BGDDT. https://e-ict.gov.vn/laws/detail/Quyet-dinh-so-4740-QD-BGDDT-ngay-30-12-2022-Ban-hanh-Bo-chi-so-tieu-chi-danh-gia-chuyen-doi-so-co-so-giao-duc-dai-hoc-763. 30 Dec 2022
3. Zadeh, L.A.: Fuzzy sets. Inf. Control **8**, 338–353 (1965)
4. Carter, J., Chiclana, F., Khuman, A.S., Chen, T.: Fuzzy Logic Recent Applications and Developments. Springer, Cham (2021). https://doi.org/10.1007/978-3-030-66474-9
5. Bennouna, G., Tkiouat, M.: Fuzzy logic approach applied to credit scoring for microfinance in Morocco. Procedia Comput. Sci. **127**, 274–283 (2018)
6. Shang, K., Hossen, Z.: Applying fuzzy logic to risk assessment and decision-making. Casualty Actuarial Society, Canadian Institute of Actuaries, Society of Actuaries (2013)
7. Khan, N., Khan, F.: Fuzzy based decision making for promotional marketing campaigns. Int. J. Fuzzy Logic Syst. **3**, 64–77 (2013)
8. Dewi, I.A.P., AA Kompiang Oka Sudana SKom, M.T., SKom, I.K.G.D.P.: Comparing scoring and fuzzy logic method for teacher certification DSS in Indonesia. Int. J. Comput. Sci. Issues **9**(6), No 2, 309–316 (2012)

Digital Transformation Insights from an AI Solution in Search of a Problem

Richard Michael Dreyling III$^{(\boxtimes)}$ (iD), Tanel Tammet(iD), and Ingrid Pappel(iD)

Tallinn University of Technology, Ehitajate tee 5, 19086 Tallinn, Estonia
`richard.iii@taltech.ee`

Abstract. Countries are adopting artificial intelligence (AI) at a fast rate. This paper analyses the digital transformation lessons from a validation process for a design that proposes modifying an existing internal decision support system that currently aids counsellors internally at the Estonian Unemployment Insurance Fund into a public facing e-service through implementation with another AI enabled government application. The methodology is qualitative with document review, analysis of secondary data, and interviews with experts and stakeholders. The end results indicate that it would be possible to modify an existing system and integrate it to an already existing system in Estonia but that this may not have public value to the citizens. Authors provide an architectural recommendation and discuss the validation results which yield insight into the considerations of the Estonian Government's tactics and strategy for AI related digital transformation. Future research could include investigation of the digital transformation process of AI projects in Estonia.

Keywords: Digital Transformation · Artificial Intelligence · Machine Learning · Government Services · E-Government · E-Governance · Estonia · Decision Support System

1 Introduction

As governments continue to try to keep up with changes in technologies, they are increasingly forced to consider adopting new and less than proven technology sets. Sometimes the tech on the bleeding edge, like artificial intelligence technologies can have an issue of the solution in search of a problem otherwise known as technology push [1]. Within government technology push can cause agencies to focus on digital transformation projects that do not have public value [2]. One of the ways to decrease this is risk is to include stakeholders, especially users, in the design phase of a new technology to ensure that there is the need for the end product [3] and that it is designed to fit the specific purposes of users [4].

AI has a challenge of complexity that comes embedded in the nature of the technology [5]. Organizations considering AI adoption must consider many factors that can affect the readiness of the organization to adopt AI projects and pilots as well as the importance and ramifications of the project for public value [5, 6].

© The Author(s), under exclusive license to Springer Nature Singapore Pte Ltd. 2023
T. K. Dang et al. (Eds.): FDSE 2023, CCIS 1925, pp. 341–351, 2023.
https://doi.org/10.1007/978-981-99-8296-7_24

One area in which there is clear public value is employment related services. All countries depend on a robust labor market. Securing good industries which produces quality jobs leads to low unemployment and an ample tax base. Creating an environment where it is easy for citizens to find jobs is paramount for economies across Europe. However, the current system of finding a job often leaves jobseekers frustrated and employers searching for qualified people. At the same time, many countries are attempting to implement artificial intelligence-based solutions to increase the efficiency and effectiveness of public [7]. An AI enabled public service meant to help people find jobs for which they are qualified has the potential to help the efficiency of the labor market.

Governments lean into various economic solutions to unemployment, causing strain on the public sector to correct the problem. Jobseekers can use various government sponsored employment tools, EURES, ESCO, and state-run employment agencies for job search assistance. "The OECD's survey shows that 53% of countries in 2021 have increased support for jobseekers, and that 52% increased support for matching skill needs and talent." [8].

Some governments such as Estonia, are attempting to aid employment and labour market services by implementing AI based systems like decision support systems or direct public services [9]. The Estonian Unemployment Insurance Fund (UIF) has implemented a Decision Support System called "OTT" that helps identify those who are at risk for long term unemployment and to help balance caseloads for case workers. Were such a decision support system transitioned to a digital public service context it could help employed as well as unemployed individuals identify opportunities for upskilling and focusing their job searches while alleviating the need for some meetings with the EIUF counsellors.

This paper attempts to contribute to the literature by giving a specific example of the conception of an instance of technology push, describes the organizational and technical requirements that would be required to implement the proposed e-service, and explains the process through which similar organizations can prioritize AI related public service project. It answers the research questions, "How would an existing public service adopt AI enablement, and what are the key steps and challenges involved in this process?" and "What technical would AI enablement require?" The methodology employed is a qualitative study in which the researchers triangulate the academic literature, secondary document review, and qualitative interviews.

2   Background

Estonia, as a small country, has continually according to former Google CEO Eric Schmidt "punched above its weight" in the area of the use of technology in public service provision. Estonia has been one of the early countries to create a national Artificial Intelligence strategy. The country has piloted an application called Bürokratt, which at its core is a revolutionary new way to access government services through the use of virtual assistants. The program is currently under development and seeks to create a personalized virtual assistant for every citizen. The organization within the government of Estonia responsible for making "reusable building blocks" for AI use in government is the Ministry of Economic Affairs and Communication. Other departments and ministries are also sometimes able to make or procure their own AI systems.

In addition to Bürokratt, Estonia has implemented many "kratts" another term for an implementation of an algorithmic tool in government whose name is based on Estonian folklore. One kratt which has been deployed is a decision support and data analysis tool called "OTT." OTT, the acronym is derived from the Estonian language for "Decision Support" is implemented in the Estonian Unemployment Insurance Fund (UIF) and helps those delivering services to find the most difficult cases as well as to balance the workloads of case workers [MKM 2020]. OTT currently analyses 29 separate factors to aid case workers in predicting the most likely cases of leaving unemployed status within 180 days to identify those who require extra assistance. This solution is being used optionally internally but would need some changes to have it be implemented at scale as a customer facing tool to help the unemployed.

"OTT" the decision support system (DSS) used by the Estonian Unemployment Insurance fund is one of these systems. However, the vision of the Estonian AI strategy is to create a network of interoperable pieces to aid the vision of having government services accessible through virtual assistants. Bürokratt has been designed to be able to incorporate systems from other government authorities over time. This implies that it is possible at some point that DSS OTT could be retooled to create a customer facing public service.

3 Related Works

This Digital transformation is a complex topic and action that in practice requires stakeholders from many siloes to collaborate to solve a problem related to the sociotechnical system of the organization [11]. It has been identified that leadership is a very large factor in the success of digital transformations. Following the more practical definition of DT as digitalization of a process [2], the phenomenon of multistakeholder engagement also applies to those digital transformations in which organizations are attempting to adopt artificial intelligence to digitalize a process or service inside of an organization. There exists in the adoption of AI what [5]. Referred to as inherent complexity. If a routine digital transformation requires internal competence, it is reasonable to assume that it is at least as important in AI related projects to adhere to Luciano's recommendations of IT and business alignment and competence [2]. There are many academically published maturity models that look at various aspects to see where in the individual models the organization places [6]. The factors identified as omnipresent factors in the AI maturity models by Sadiq et al., are "Data, Analytics, Technology and Tools, Intelligent Automation, Governance, People, and Organization" [2021]. The successful implementation and public value creation from digital transformation initiatives can be dependent on the existence of certain skills inside an organization [2].

Even with the complexity, adoption of AI in government continues. The EU has been one of the governmental organisations which has sought to get ahead of the challenges posed by AI and ameliorate some of them. There have been an increasing number of Artificial Intelligence adoption cases in the EU. The EU is also a leader in attempting to ensure that the use of AI is conducted in a trustworthy manner. There are currently 143 AI use cases in the public sector available to be investigated on the AI Watch Github [12]. This does not mean that these are public services, but it shows a large adoption rate nonetheless.

Trustworthiness has an effect on optimizing the human computer interaction with AI systems and the adoption and acceptance of AI technologies. Avoiding black box reasoning and ensuring that the system has a high degree of usability are important for increasing acceptance among users [13]. The transparency of decision-making increases trust among the users and those who work with the AI system. In addition, the increased trust will aid optimization with the human operators of the system because they will know better when they should defer to the machine or when the decision could be faulty or biased.

The Estonian Government has participated in the formation of EU policy regarding Artificial Intelligence and has a stake in following the guidelines through which the EU attempts to protect residents and citizens. The Estonian national artificial intelligence strategy was originally implemented in 2019–2021. Since the beginning of that period, Estonia has greatly increased the number of implementations of AI in the government context. The current Estonian ecosystem for AI uses open-source components to build an "interoperable network of AI applications" [10]. Even though they can be developed by different organizations within the government with vary public private partnerships, the main goal in the end is to create a network of AI enabled services. The goal that there will be the open-source reusable components for government entities to use in order to build their own AI enabled projects.

In accordance with the legal framework development in Estonia at the current moment there are no purely machine decisions. It follows that any system that would be deployed in the country would have to adhere to principles for trustworthy and human centered AI. One of the chief goals of the AI strategy is to aid accessibility and usability of e-Governance services.

3.1 Existing Bürokratt Initiative

Bürokratt represents the future version of e-Governance services that will eventually be accessible from virtual assistants. On a step toward this goal, the Estonian government piloted Bürokratt as a proof-of-concept system that is designed as a network of chatbots. It does this to comply with the Estonian Personal Data Protection law which requires that data must reside where it is collected. If a query given to the chatbot is not answerable by a chatbot which is associated with a particular government authority and its databases, the query is passed to other chatbots until the query is able to be answered.

There currently available components to the architecture of Bürokratt include a translation engine that supports seven languages, a text analytics tool, a Speech synthesis tool that uses neural networks, a speech recognition tool, and the chatbot prototype [10].

The existing interface for citizens to use that has gone from proof of concept to initial implementation is a chatbot that is networked to ensure that data stays where it is captured. When the chatbot fields a question from the customer, it queries the connected database and training information associated with a particular data repository on the backend. Without changing the front end represented to the user, a classifier passes the query until it goes to the relevant authority. In this case, the recommendation engine OTT could potentially work on the backend to give the citizen information about their case and give recommendations that would normally be given to the Unemployment fund case worker.

3.2 Decision Support System OTT

Currently, a decision support system designed to help unemployment counsellors at the EUIF identify and provide additional aid to at risk unemployed individuals is in use. Repurposing this system, DSS OTT, into a customer facing e-service is a potentially cost-effective way to accomplish adding an e-service to aid unemployed workers and those seeking better employment. However, as with all AI projects, such a project would have to be approached with caution to minimize the risk that negative outcomes to humans result from the use of the technology.

Because of the emphasis which Estonia has put on making sure that no harm comes to the users of services that are powered by Artificial Intelligence, an analysis of the existing infrastructure surrounding the Decision Support System OTT must be conducted to have an idea of potential pitfalls.

The Estonian Unemployment Insurance Fund developed DSS OTT, a decision support system designed to enhance effectiveness and increase efficiency in the unemployment counseling process. It uses a "random walk" model that takes into account various factors and informs counsellors when those requesting services are at a high risk for remaining unemployed for an extended duration. This allows the counsellors to put more effort and time aside for those who will potentially need more services. The EUIF has used the system to ensure that workloads among counsellors are balanced in addition to the direct service-related role.

The technical system that OTT uses is a DSS architecture that uses a Random Forest based machine learning model. The number of variables that OTT uses has changed over time. According to [14] the number has gone from 63 and been reduced to 45. At the time of the writing of [15] the number of variables used was 40. The random forest walk model is one that is common among the employment prediction systems and OTT is modeled is in fact built in a very similar fashion to a Belgian system that operates in the public employment sector.

OTT uses ML algorithm to predict the chance that someone will gain employment within 180 days. The reasoning behind this use of AI being in the allowable aforementioned categories of trustworthy and human centered AI is two-fold. [16] argue that the idea of having algorithms and historic data that may discriminate or have biases against vulnerable populations in the case of the Belgian system which was discussed earlier, is not as much of a problem when the resulting services would add value to those who are high-risk or even misclassified as high-risk for not finding employment. Because the stakes in this case are increased services, there appears to be a net benefit for those who are considered high risk as long as the services are done well. The other part of this argument for OTT coincides with the Estonian stance toward human decision making and AI systems. According to these guidelines, even with all of the kratts, use cases deployed across the Estonian government there must always be a responsible human decision maker. The way this manifests in the process workflow of OTT is that there is always a human case worker who uses the output of the decision support system to inform the method through which they approach the specific case. They can decide to use the output to modify their approach to the unemployed individual's intervention or not to use it.

4 Methods and Approach

This piece of research is part of a larger research project aimed at investigating the digital transformation process surrounding the Bürokratt program and its development and adoption by various government entities. The primary data collection techniques are semi-structured interviews which are a good way to have the benefits while avoiding the pitfalls of structured interviews [17]. The research team has conducted workshops and interviews with six experts from academia, and the Ministry of Economic Affairs and Communication (MKM) team. The interviews and workshops were an average time of an hour and fifteen minutes. The team then transcribed the interview audio files and qualitatively coded to extract relevant data.

This paper began as a design science approach in which the research team conceived of a technology push initiative related to combining two existing AI related services to create an AI enabled public service. The design process began with understanding the potential needs of users, but quickly moved to designing a potential architecture in a workshop that would work for this purpose. The overall plausibility and technical function of the architecture was validated by discussions and whiteboard workshops with AI and ML experts inside academia. At this point, the architecture was discussed with those responsible for expanding Bürokratt's use in the government to elicit feedback.

5 Results

5.1 Proposed Integrative Architecture

Due to the existence of both a tested and functional customer interface through the networked chatbot architecture of Bürokratt, the expressed purpose of the initiative, and the functionality of DSS OTT, the possibility exists that DSS OTT could be brought into an implementation that allows customers to access the extrapolations from the random forest model through the currently available Bürokratt architecture.

The potential benefit of modifying an existing system to become a customer facing service has two plainly visible facets. One is that there is a new service that ought to be useful to some set of the populace. This could include unemployed individuals, or those who are seeking to learn their odds of having an extended period of unemployment if they lose their jobs. Some people are forever curious about what systems will say or recommend about them and would look regardless of utility. The other benefit is that it is difficult to bring AI projects to fruition and the modification of an existing system means that some subset of the data required to complete the system is known to exist. In the private sector when leaders want to complete an AI project, they tend to engage a consulting company like Microsoft or Deloitte. The consulting company would then complete a holistic readiness assessment and feasibility study to ensure that the technical social and organizational prerequisites are in place to increase the likelihood of project success. One of the key technical factors which the consultants will investigate is that the organization has suitable data for the AI implementation. On the other hand, the first step for organizations in the public sector is to procure a pilot. Sometimes, the pilots fail because the organization does not have data to make the implementation possible. By beginning with an existing system, although there are technical modifications to be made, the probability that the project will fail because the requisite amount of data does not exist is greatly reduced.

An additional benefit of using the Decision support system for a public facing service is that the interaction method of can itself become a source of data. It can become internally used information that speaks to the amount of use the service gets and that can be correlated with the outcomes of the individuals who use the service. In addition, the output of the citizen user interface (CUI) can be turned into data for the EUIF to inspect for utility to as a factor for the DSS. The output can be audited to check if it modifies the behavior of the humans who use the system. For example, if a person looking for upskilling opportunities queries the chatbot to reach the CUI and see what their current chance of being long-term unemployed is, and what ways the person could reduce that probability, the responding advice could potentially be monitored for follow up. Did the person take the recommended course? If a person uses the service, it could be used as a way to indicate the engagement on the part of the human in the process of finding employment or increasing employability.

In the proposed architecture shown in Fig. 1 the "citizen user interface" would act more as a data repository or service module access point associated with the UIF chatbot.

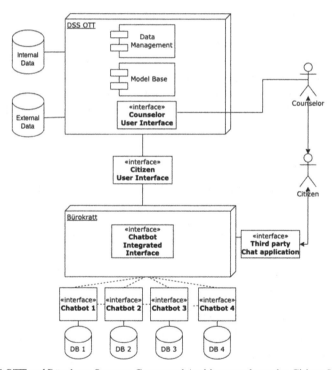

Fig. 1. DSS OTT and Bürokratt Systems Connected Architecture through a Citizen User Interface

As currently programmed, the interactions with chatbots are not stored when the networked chatbot exchanges the queries. But the opportunity exists for the interactions with the unemployed person who is accessing the service through a chatbot interface to be stored so as to be information for the caseworkers in the future. One way this could be helpful is if a person is flagged as a difficult case, the system would be able to indicate that it recommends the person contact a counsellor, as well as gives the counsellor a notification to contact the person.

Challenges may exist as to bias in the data or recommendations. However, following the principles of Trustworthy AI and HCAI as aforementioned may help ameliorate these challenges. The Estonian government uses a system of human decision makers in its AI augmented program. This means that there are no fully automated decision makers in practice. Audits could be augmented by ensuring that the system sends the complicated cases of unemployed workers to counsellors rather than making recommendations alone in the chatbot interface.

Architecturally speaking, the changes defined as necessary in Estonian CTO Kristo Vaher's vision paper [18] for the next generation of digital government would still need to be made. For example, when the Bürokratt chatbot POC was conducted, the developers used Apache Kafka to avoid the need to have an architectural change to the Data Exchange Platform X-Road. However, were OTT to go from an internal tool to a public facing service, the necessity arises to comply with the legal data exchange regulations when adding a data exchange element.

There would need to be additional work done in the area of classifying upskilling or career opportunities, to make data available for the citizen. Some measure of explainability could be added to give the citizen context as to why the system is recommending a certain path or upskilling opportunity. Were this the case, there would likely need to be an anonymization method to ensure that if a citizen is accessing comparative data through the chatbot, they are not privy personalized information from others. The decentralized nature of the architecture of Bürokratt may aid in the ability to implement the currently internal tool OTT to the more customer-friendly system.

5.2 Feedback and Insights

During a workshop related to adoption of Bürokratt, the researchers asked about the architecture in question and the concept of introducing an customer facing interface through which the citizens would be able to access the insights of the DSS OTT system through the Bürokratt chatbot function. The MKM employee confirmed that the approach to combining the two systems through a method in which there was an external customer (citizen) focused interface in which the data was appropriately sanitized is a valid approach. However, they pointed out several factors that simultaneously showed that the approach was not necessary and gave understanding of the approach used for the DT process within the government.

Essentially, DSS OTT at this point is under the organizational jurisdiction of EIUF. Firstly, it would take an initiative inside of UIF to see if they would like to develop the necessary customer interface that allows for both employed and unemployed persons to use the service and input relevant data. Secondly, the UIF may not want to make the tool customer facing because right now, the flow of work in which the counsellor uses the information to scope how much assistance to give keeps in place the concept of the human decision maker to ameliorate potential AI related issues. Thirdly, related to the way in which the Bürokratt program prioritises adoption cases, there are some services that although they could be addressed through integration with Bürokratt, the chatbot interface is not the best for the human computer interaction. The example given was the case of signing the papers when scheduling marriage related to the distribution of assets upon potential dissolution of the marriage. Even though one can envision a world in which the chatbot could send the individual provisions of the digitalized document in chat to the citizen and once the service module is implemented, have the citizen sign each provision, it is much easier to just have the person read the entire document and then sign each provision in the native digitalized format. In cases like this, the Bürokratt team, rather than reinventing the wheel, recommend that the chatbot just gives a link to the proper document.

Architecturally, the proposed solution would essentially function within the overall Bürokratt system as a localized UIF chatbot. On paper, this would work because the service module which is currently in development would be able to given the correct permissions pull the data from the person's UIF file once the authentication takes place. The Bürokratt architecture that has been implemented uses a containerized implementation that uses REST endpoints and the main logic is in business processes written into YAML files. The service module development is ongoing.

Another challenge for the proposed architectural function of having citizens access the projections that the system OTT made for them is in the unemployment fund. Due to the concern with ethical ramifications of allowing people to see their own projections, it does not appear that the UIF plans to make the results available to individual citizens. The counselors are able to use or disregard the feedback of DSS OTT. This coheres to the vision of the human in the loop decision making and values of the Estonian government as it pertains to use of AI.

The feedback given from the team indicates that the ministry responsible for the adoption across government of these AI functionalities within the Bürokratt program are considering not only the need to implement their software across ministries but keeping in mind the needs of the ministries involved and the citizen end user, even though it invalidated the need for the proposed architecture. The concern for the needs of the user is further substantiated by the study the ministry commissioned which asked for citizen input [19].

6 Limitations and Further Work

The study did not approach UIF prior to the conversations which took place at MKM. The study takes a limited scope of the problem of digital transformation and how AI related projects can be adopted in government. The design portion could have been strictly adherent to design science methodology.

Further work should investigate the DT process of AI projects deeper by interviewing many people on the topic from different stakeholder groups, including the residents of Estonia. Another area that could be of use is the design of an AI readiness assessment framework to aid in the adoption of AI related technologies in government services.

7 Conclusion

The complexity of AI projects and their adoption inside of governmental organizations is a relatively new field of study. This paper explains the design of an example of what could be called a "technology push architecture". Especially in an emerging area like artificial intelligence, such an example is worthwhile and pertinent to the academic community because the idea of engineers and others closely associated with the technology designing new ideas without necessarily grounding the use case in reality is a well known phenomenon. The insights from the validation process during this research indicate the necessity to consider the public value of a project. Beginning with a focus on the citizen, possibly with a co-creation method, could help avoid the issue of a solution in search of a problem.

From a practical perspective, ensuring that a system has a function and design that would add utility to people, especially in the public sector, has its own utility. In private companies, these control mechanisms reflect the constancy of the omnipresent profit and loss statement and other quantitative value measures that directly pertain to the adoption and development or scrapping of an idea. As discussed above, with the public sector, sometimes newer technology projects are adopted in and of themselves because a government wants to show that they can do new things and without a real conception of whether the project has the ability to come to fruition. Future research will focus on going deeper into understanding the digital transformation of the ministries involved in adopting AI through the Bürokratt initiative across the government, and not on combining two AI related systems because it would "be cool".

Acknowledgements. This work in the project "ICT programme" was supported by the European Union through European Social Fund.

References

1. Di Stefano, G., Gambardella, A., Verona, G.: Technology push and demand pull perspectives in innovation studies: current findings and future research directions. Res. Policy **41**(8), 1283–1295 (2020)
2. Luciano, E.M., Wiedenhöft, G.C.: The role of organizational citizenship behavior and strategic alignment in increasing the generation of public value through digital transformation. In: Proceedings of the 13th International Conference on Theory and Practice of Electronic Governance (2020)
3. Virkar, S., Alexopoulos, C., Tsekeridou, S., Novak, A.S.: A user-centred analysis of decision support requirements in legal informatics. Gov. Inf. Quart. **39**(3), 101713 (2022)
4. Distel, B.: Bringing light into the shadows: a qualitative interview study on citizens' non-adoption of e-government. Electron. J. e-Gov. **16**(2), pp98–105. (2018)
5. Jöhnk, J., Weißert, M., Wyrtki, K.: Ready or not, AI comes—an interview study of organizational AI readiness factors. Bus. Inf. Syst. Eng. **63**, 5–20 (2021)
6. Sadiq, R.B., Safie, N., Abd Rahman, A.H., Goudarzi, S.: Artificial intelligence maturity model: a systematic literature review. PeerJ Comput. Sci. **7**, e661 (2021)
7. Van Noordt, C., Misuraca, G.: Exploratory insights on artificial intelligence for government in Europe. Soc. Sci. Comput. Rev. **40**(2), 426–444 (2022)

8. Censorii, E.: The Job Market after Covid-19: OECD Employment Outlook 2021. Digital Skills and Jobs Platform, OECD (2021). https://digital-skills-jobs.europa.eu/en/inspiration/research/job-market-after-covid-19-oecd-employment-outlook-2021. Accessed 26 Aug 2021

9. Ministry of Economic Affairs and Communication (MKM). Decision support of the unemployment fund OTT (2020). https://www.kratid.ee/kasutuslood

10. Lopes Gonçalves, D.: Digital Public Services based on open source: Case study on Bürokratt. Joinup European Commission (2022). https://joinup.ec.europa.eu/collection/open-source-observatory-osor/document/digital-public-services-based-open-source-case-study-burokratt

11. Breaugh, J., Rackwitz, M., Hammerschmid, G.: Leadership and institutional design in collaborative government digitalisation: evidence from Belgium, Denmark, Estonia, Germany, and the UK. Gov. Inf. Q. **40**(2), 101788 (2023)

12. Hernandez, L.: Dataset with cases of Artificial Intelligence usage in the public sector available as Open data. Joinup European Commission (2021). https://joinup.ec.europa.eu/collection/elise-european-location-interoperability-solutions-e-government/news/143-ai-cases-public-sector-are-available-open-data

13. Shin, D.: The effects of explainability and causability on perception, trust, and acceptance: Implications for explainable AI. Int. J. Hum Comput Stud. **146**, 102551 (2021)

14. Leets, P.: Augmenting Public Sector Data-Driven Decision Support Systems With Expert Knowledge: Case Of Ott. University of Tartu, Tartu, Estonia (2022)

15. Pignatelli, F.: AI watch: European landscape on the use of artificial intelligence by the public sector annex II. In: JRC Science for Policy Report. European Commission. (2022)

16. Desiere, S., Struyven, L.: Using artificial intelligence to classify jobseekers: the accuracy-equity trade-off. J. Soc. Policy **50**(2), 367–385 (2021)

17. Yin, R.K.: Case Study Research Design and Methods, 5th edn. Sage, Thousand Oaks, CA (2014)

18. Vaher, K.: Next generation digital government architecture. Republic of Estonia GCIO Office (2020)

19. Teimuth, R., Kristiina Oll, K.: Functionalities of a bureaucrate user research: report. Civitta (2023)

Improving Human Resources' Efficiency with a Generative AI-Based Resume Analysis Solution

Thanh Tung Tran[1], Truong Giang Nguyen[1], Thai Hoa Dang[1], and Yuta Yoshinaga[2(✉)]

[1] Rikkeisoft Corporation, 21st Floor, Handico Tower, Pham Hung St., Nam Tu Liem District, Ha Noi, Vietnam
{tungtt3,giangnt4,hoa.dang}@rikkeisoft.com
[2] Rikkeisoft Japan Corporation, 3rd Floor, Fujishima Building, Tamachi 16 Str., 4-13-4 Shiba, Minato-ku, Japan
yoshinaga@rikkeisoft.com

Abstract. Reviewing resumes has been becoming essential during the hiring process up to now. Moreover, the company needs to continuously recruit for various technical positions to match job demands and requirements. This, in turn, created an influx of applications that needed to be managed by the Human Resources (HR) department. The first step of the resume management process was to enter the applicants' data from their resumes into the HR system. Because of the large number of applications received, this is a tedious and mind-numbing procedure for our employees, especially when the time and resources taken by it can be better used elsewhere. After data entry comes screening, analyzing, and matching the resumes to an available position. Like the previous step, the huge number of applications made it arduous and time-consuming to go through each application for vital information that would help place them in the right resume pile. In this paper, we introduce a solution to help the HR Department be more productive and efficient with resume analysis.

Keywords: Generative AI · Resume analysis · Human resources · Auto matching · ChatGPT

1 Introduction

The resume review process is an indispensable step in the recruitment process. Matching between the needs of businesses and candidates often takes a lot of time. Especially after Corona, job seekers and the demand for personnel by businesses have increased significantly, making the manual resume review process to be a bottleneck in recruitment.

Therefore, there have been many studies on how to improve the speed of resume review, such as deep Siamese Network [1], deep Collaborative Filtering Task [2], developing big data processing systems, parallel data processing, and analyzing data using AI. However, these methods only focus on evaluating the matching degree of job requirements and sentences extracted from resumes, without providing a comprehensive system

T. K. Dang et al. (Eds.): FDSE 2023, CCIS 1925, pp. 352–365, 2023.
https://doi.org/10.1007/978-981-99-8296-7_25

from resume analysis, and job description processing to searching for resumes that match the requirements. To deal with these problems, this paper describes implementing a Generative AI-based Resume Analysis & Matching Model to save them time and effort in sorting and matching resumes to compatible positions.

Firstly, Rikkei AI's model assists with data extraction from resumes. Applicants would send in their resumes via Rikkeisoft's recruitment website, which are then added to the Resume pool. From here, the AI model will categorize these resumes based on the information provided and extract the information to add to the HR database. This process is done automatically, freeing up human resources for other more demanding tasks.

After extraction, the resumes will be automatically matched to a position previously requested by Rikkeisoft's divisions. The HR executives will be notified of matches made by the AI model, to which they can give approval and have the resumes added to the in-house job request tool for divisions to contact.

2   Resume Analysis

Processing as the following Fig. 1:

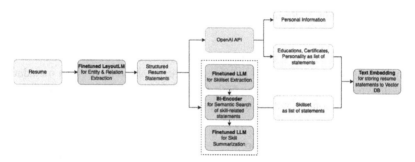

Fig. 1. Resume Analysis

2.1   Resume Layout Analysis via Entity and Relation Extraction

Resumes are typically stored as PDF files with various layouts (single-column, two-column, table format, timelines, etc.). Using PDF parsing libraries, we can identify the content, position, and formatting of individual text blocks, but determining the structure and relationships between these text blocks can be challenging. For example, it's difficult to discern which text block is the title and which one contains content related to that title.

The solution is to train a model based on the LayoutLM [3] architecture with input including:

- Content of each text block.
- 2D spatial position of each text block.

– Images of the PDF file divided into multiple patches.

The model will output:

– Classification of each text block (one of three types: Title, Metadata, Content).
– Dependency relationships between text blocks (which a text block belongs to).

For example, (see Fig. 2) red blocks represent Titles, green blocks represent Metadata, and black blocks represent Content. The black box to the right of each block indicates the block's order and the order of its 'parent' block (where order 0 represents the root of the PDF file).

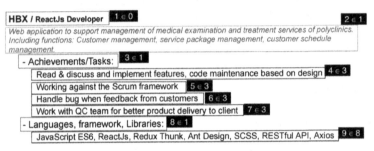

Fig. 2. Resume Layout Analysis (Color figure online)

From the model's results, the structure of the resume can be constructed as a tree. Each block of resume content will be stored in the database along with metadata and titles of their parent blocks, including both direct (level 1) and indirect (level 2, 3, …, n) parent blocks. This content will be used for the Skill and Experience Extraction step.

2.2 Basic Information Extraction

The information to be extracted in this step includes:

– Personal Information: Name, Date of Birth, Gender, Location, Position, Email.
– Education Information: Candidate's educational history.
– Certificates Information: Certifications received by the candidate.
– Personality Information: Personality traits mentioned by the candidate.

Among these, personal information will be stored as metadata of the resume. The remaining information will be passed to a model to calculate embedding vectors and stored in a Vector database (Vector DB), which will serve as a foundation for a search engine.

The solution involves using the OpenAI API and Prompt Engineering to request the extraction of this information based on the resume content. The output of the prompt should follow a predefined format for ease of further processing.

Specifically, the output is divided into four sections (**Information, Certificates, Educations** and **Personality**), each contains a list of relevant statements extracted from the resume in the following format:

```
<Section Title>:
- <Statement 1>
- <Statement 2>
- ...
```

2.3 Skill and Experience Extraction

Skills and Experience are two specific types of information that need to be extracted based on evidence from the resume and should be processed separately.

2.3.1 Extracting a List of Skills

- Utilize a Large Language Model (LLM) fine-tuned from LLama-2 [4].
- The input prompt will be the content of the Resume.
- The output will be a list of skill names mentioned by the candidate.

2.3.2 Finding Relevant Blocks

- The blocks from the Resume layout analysis via Entity and Relation Extraction step will be converted into embedding vectors and stored in a Vector DB.
- For each skill obtained in step 2.3.1, search the Vector DB for related blocks associated with that skill, including metadata and titles of parent blocks.

2.3.3 Aggregating and Evaluating Skills

- All the information retrieved in step 2.3.2 will be used as input in a prompt for an LLama2-based LLM.
- The LLM will generate a summarization statement for each skill. This statement will primarily include the skill name, years of experience, proficiency level, and relevant experience related to the corresponding skill.

2.3.4 Storing Skill Summarizations:

- The skill summarization statements will be transformed into embedding vectors and stored in the Vector DB (along with vectors related to Education, Certificates, Personality, as extracted in step 2.2).

After going through the Resume Analysis process, for each resume, we will have metadata and a list of embedding vectors representing the candidate's skills, experience, education, certificates, and personality traits. For each skill, we can also store related evidence (blocks) extracted from the resume.

3 Job Description Processing and Resume Search

Processing as the following Fig. 3:

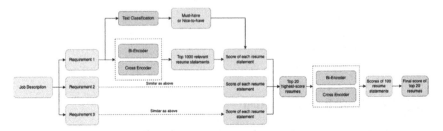

Fig. 3. Job description processing

3.1 Requirement Preprocessing and Classification

Each job description will have a list of requirements. Each requirement is processed to remove unnecessary characters (punctuation, leading and trailing spaces) and is then fed into a Text Classification model to be categorized into one of two types:

- Must-have: These are essential requirements that candidates must meet to be considered for the position. They are the core qualifications and skills required for the job.
- Nice-to-have: These are desirable but not mandatory requirements. Meeting these requirements can be advantageous, but they are not crucial for the candidate to be considered.

   This process helps in structuring and categorizing the requirements in job descriptions, making it easier to evaluate candidate suitability and match them with the right positions. The classification also assigns different levels of importance to each requirement type, with "Must-have" requirements typically carrying more weight in the evaluation process.

3.2 Search for Statements Matching Requirements

For each requirement, it is converted into a vector embedding and a search is conducted for the top-k statements in the Vector DB that have highest cosine similarity compared to the requirement (k = 1000). This is a Bi-Encoder-based search, where both the requirement and the statements are in vector embedding form [5]. Afterward, to enhance accuracy, the top-k statements along with the requirement are fed into a Cross-Encoder model to calculate the compatibility level of each requirement-statement pair for resume matching [6] (Fig. 4).

   The "Cross-Encoder Model" takes as input a pair of requirement and resume statements and outputs a score ranging from 0 to 1. After passing through the model, we obtain the top-k statements related to the requirement, sorted in descending order of compatibility [7, 8].

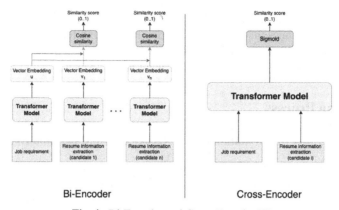

Fig. 4. Bi-Encoder and Cross-Encoder [5]

3.3   Aggregating Scores and Presenting Results

The scores obtained from each requirement-resume pair will be aggregated and used to calculate the average score for each resume. The top-n resumes with the highest scores will be selected (the value of n depends on the web page's pagination settings, typically displaying 20 resumes per page). Then, the process of Search for Statements Matching Requirements will be repeated but limited to these top 20 resumes instead of the entire database. This aims to mitigate any potential shortcomings in the initial search process. In step 2.2, only the top-k statements are selected, so there may be cases where a resume is in the top-n but its statements are not in the top-k for a specific requirement.

Finally, the scores are aggregated based on the search results and sorted in descending order of scores. A list of resumes is then provided, along with the following information:

- **Score:** The degree of compatibility between the resume and the job description, expressed as a percentage.
- **Information:** Extracted information from the resume, which typically includes personal details, education, work experience, certifications, and skills.
- **Requirement Qualification:** For each requirement, relevant statements from the resume are presented, along with any supporting evidence if available. Additionally, the candidate's qualification level for that specific requirement is indicated.

This process results in a ranked list of resumes, with each resume accompanied by its compatibility score, extracted information, and a breakdown of how well the candidate meets the specific requirements of the job description. This presentation format allows for easy assessment of candidate suitability for the job.

4   Detailed Analysis of Resume Suitability

This step is to create a comprehensive and detailed evaluation of how well a resume aligns with specific criteria or requirements, typically related to a job or position by taking all the information gathered from step 3 into the prompt and then using OpenAI API.

The information provided includes the content of the job description (JD) and relevant statements from resumes that were found during the "Search for relevant blocks" step 3.2. The system will then provide an analysis of the candidate's suitability for each requirement listed in the JD, along with explanations and evidence.

5 Training Process

5.1 Layout-Aware Segmentation Entity Recognition and Relation Extraction

Segmentation Entity Recognition (SER) and Relation Extraction (RE) are two common problems in the field of Visually rich Document Understanding (VrDU). Current models have achieved high accuracy in SER tasks by relying solely on the content and format information of text [9]. However, recent research indicates that information about the layout of text segments (such as the 2D position of a text segment in the document, the relative position between text segments) plays a crucial role in the RE problem, which has not been thoroughly solved [10].

Based on the observation, we have developed a layout analysis model using the pretrained model GeoLayoutLM [11], which has already incorporated the capability to learn document layout features during pre-training process. Experiments have shown that GeoLayoutLM achieves state-of-the-art results in both SER and RE tasks on popular benchmark datasets such as FUNSD [12] and CORD [13]. However, when applied to resume analysis, the model still exhibits numerous errors and requires fine-tuning with real-world resume data.

5.1.1 Data Preparation

We have collected 24,450 Resumes in PDF format in the fields of IT and Marketing, with various layouts, including single-column, double-column, table format, timeline, and more. Out of the total of 24,450 Resumes, 20,120 are native PDFs (created from a document file such as doc, docs, html), and 4,330 are scanned PDFs (created by scanning a paper document). Most of the Resumes are written in English, with only some place names, company names, and personal names in Vietnamese.

To extract information from native PDF files, we use the PyMuPDF library, which returns the content, format, and location of each text block in the file, as well as the position of each word within each block. For scanned PDF files, we use an Optical Character Recognition (OCR) engine to detect and recognize characters within each line of the image. In the end, each resume file is extracted for the following information:

– The image collection consists of snapshots, with each image representing a single page of a PDF document.
– One list of text blocks, each text block contains: Bounding box of the text block (absolute position on the image of the PDF page), content of the text block and content and bounding box of each word within each block.

We are labeling the entire resume dataset mentioned above, specifically, each text block will have the following labels:

- **Type of text block:** One of the 4 labels - Title, Metadata, Content, Other. (Blocks labeled as "Other" are usually headers and footers and will be skipped in subsequent processing steps.)
- **The relationship between a pair of text blocks:** There are two labeled relationships:

  - Belong: Text block A has a "Belong" relationship with text block B if B has the "Title" type, and the content of A is entirely within the section labeled as B.
  - Consequence: Text block A has a "Consequence" relationship with B if A and B have the same type, and the content of A follows B in a complete paragraph.

Figure 5 illustrates the four types of text blocks and the two types of relationships between a pair of text blocks. In this image, the red boxes represent the "Title" type, the green boxes represent the "Metadata" type, and the black boxes represent the "Content" type. The red arrows represent the "Belong" relationship between the block at the arrow's starting point and the block at the arrow's endpoint, while the green arrows represent the "Consequence" relationship between the block at the arrow's starting point and the block at the arrow's endpoint.

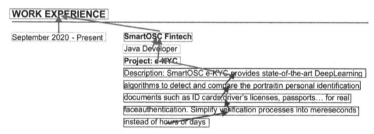

Fig. 5. Four types of text blocks and two types of relationships between a pair of text blocks (Color figure online)

5.1.2 Model Architecture

The pretrained GeoLayoutLM model is described as the following [11]:

- Input

  - Image of a PDF page
  - Bounding box for each text block in the page
  - Content of all text blocks tokenized into a list of token sequences, separated by a special token [SEP]
  - Relative order of each token within the text block
  - Relative order of each line in the page

- Output

  - An array of embedding vectors $\{H_i, i = 1..N\}$ where H_i is the embedding vector of the $i\text{-}th$ text block in the page and N is the number of text blocks.

We keep the GeoLayoutLM model architecture unchanged and add two corresponding heads for the SER (Semantic Entity Recognition) and RE (Relation Extraction) tasks.

- The SER (Semantic Entity Recognition) head consists of a linear layer corresponding to each embedding vector, and it outputs 4 predefined classes, as defined earlier. This is a typical 4-class classification problem.

$$P_i^{SER} = Softmax(Linear(H_i)) \tag{1}$$

With P_i^{SER} representing the probability of predicting the block type for the i-th block.

- The RE (Relation Extraction) head consists of a bilinear layer that takes input as a pair of embedding vectors from two text blocks and outputs 2 classes: Belong and Consequence relations.

$$P_{ij}^{RE} = Softmax\left(Bilinear\left(H_i, H_j\right)\right) \tag{2}$$

With P_{ij}^{RE} representing the probability of predicting the type of relationship between the i-th and j-th blocks.

We use the Cross-Entropy loss function for both tasks.

$$Loss = \sum\nolimits_{i=1..N} CrossEntropy\left(P_i^{SER}, Y_i^{SER}\right) + \sum\nolimits_{i,j=1..N} CrossEntropy\left(P_{ij}^{RE}, Y_{ij}^{RE}\right) \tag{3}$$

With Y^{SER} and Y^{RE} being the ground truth for the two tasks, SER and RE, respectively (Fig. 6).

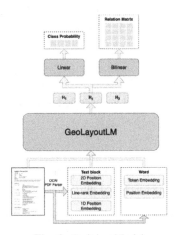

Fig. 6. Training Model

The Resume data is split into two parts, train and test, with an 8:2 ratio. The model is initialized with the weights of the pretrained GeoLayoutLM and fine-tuned for 10 epochs using the AdamW optimizer, a batch size of 6, and a learning rate of $2e-5$.

5.2   Cross Encoder

The Cross Encoder model provides a similarity score between a job requirement sentence and a skill summarization sentence, representing the degree of matching between the resume and the job requirement. The similarity score ranges from 0 to 1, indicating increasing levels of matching between the two sentences. Instead of using a heavier LLM for evaluating the similarity score, the Cross Encoder model has a lighter structure, allowing for faster inference while maintaining high accuracy.

The training data for the model is divided into two parts:

- **Job requirement:** A collection of sentences representing the requirements for each job position to be recruited.
- **Resume information extraction:** A collection of skill summarization sentences extracted from various resumes, corresponding to each job requirement sentence. Each job requirement sentence will have approximately 500–600 skill summarization sentences associated with it.

To reduce the labeling workload, we are using the Code Llama 34B Instruct [15] to rank the matching degree between a job requirement sentence and the sentences in the initial set of resume information extraction. This is done through the following steps:

- Step 1: From the initial set of resume information extraction corresponding to a job requirement sentence, use the LLM to compare the matching degree between each pair of skill summarization sentences and that job requirement sentence. Apply the quicksort algorithm to sort the resume information extraction set in descending order of matching with the job requirement sentence.
- Step 2: Manually categorize the sorted set of resume information extraction into four groups: "NotRelevant," "NotYetQualified," "NearlyQualified," and "Qualified." Each group will define a specific range of similarity scores, distributing the score ranges evenly based on the number of skill summarization sentences in each group. Assign the score values that have been divided into the skill summarization sentences. These four groups classify the skill summarization sentences into different levels:

  - **NotRelevant:** The statements in the resume do not contain any relevant information related to the job description requirements. (Similarity score: 0 -> 0.1)
  - **NotYetQualified:** The statement includes skills mentioned in the job description, but the proficiency level of these skills is not yet sufficient. (Similarity score: 0.1 -> 0.5)
  - **NearlyQualified:** The statement showcases skills at a level of proficiency that is close to meeting the job requirements. (Similarity score: 0.5 -> 0.8)
  - **Qualified:** The statement demonstrates skills at a proficiency level that fully meets the job requirements. (Similarity score: 0.8 -> 1)

In the end, we obtain the training dataset, which consists of a collection of (job requirement, skill summarization, similarity score) tuples. We use the pretrained MiniLM model [14] and fine-tune it with our training dataset, which contains 600,000 requirement-resume pairs. The training is performed on a single NVIDIA RTX GPU with 24 GB of memory.

5.3 Llama-Based LLM for Skill Set Extraction and Skill Summarization

Information Extraction and Text Summarization are two important and common applications of Large Language Models (LLMs). The Skill Set Extraction and Skill Summarization modules can be addressed by a powerful pretrained LLM like the OpenAI API, Llama 2 [4], or CodeLlama [15]. However, during usage, we have observed that these general-purpose LLMs occasionally produce results that do not conform to the required format and may include missing or redundant information. Additionally, high inference costs and latency are also disadvantages that need to be addressed. Therefore, we have decided to fine-tune a smaller LLM on specific resume data to improve the module's performance and optimize the cost and latency of the system.

5.3.1 Data Preparation

Following the concepts of Self-Instruct [17] and LIMA [16], fine-tuning a Large Language Model (LLM) with a small amount of high-quality data (around 1,000 - 10,000 samples) often yields better results than using a large but less controlled dataset. To achieve this, we have created a dataset of approximately 2,000 samples. This dataset was initially generated by Code Llama 34B Instruct [15] and then manually refined and curated to ensure its quality and relevance for our specific task.

Specifically, the steps for creating data for the Skill Extraction task are as the following:

- Randomly selecting 1,000 resumes from the dataset mentioned in 5.1
- Insert the content of the resume into the prompt and request LLM to extract a list of skills mentioned in the Resume.
- After receiving the output from the model, the labeler will review the list of skills and remove any duplicate, vague, or irrelevant skills. If the output format is not standard, the labeler will need to correct it. This process does not require the labeler to read the content of the resume, but only to know the position for which the candidate is applying.

For the Skill Summarization:

- Randomly select 1,000 resumes (not overlapping with the resume set for the Skill Extraction task).
- Proceed with the steps in Skill and Experience Extraction, including 2.3.2 and 2.3.3. Please note that among all these steps, use the Code Llama 34B Instruct [15] for steps requiring LLM.
- Labelers will be provided with text blocks related to skills and the summary of that skill. They will make corrections if the information in the summary is incorrect or lacks essential details. In most cases, errors are related to the incorrect number of years of experience or references to irrelevant information in the skill summary.

The result of the aggregation of these two processes is a dataset consisting of 2,000 samples, each sample in the format of Instruction-following [17].

5.3.2   Training Model

Due to hardware resource constraints, we have chosen to fine-tune the Llama 2 13B [14] model using the QLoRA [18] method on 6 Nvidia RTX 3090 GPUs with a batch size of 32. Fine-tuning a single model for both mentioned tasks aims to save model deployment costs and reduce inference time. Additionally, since these two tasks are somewhat interrelated, they do not significantly impact the model's learning process.

6   Experimental Results

We evaluate the performance of our Resume Analysis System on a private dataset consisted of approximately 6,000 resumes which are separated from any training sets mentioned above. As indicated in Fig. 7, the system possesses the ability to assess the qualification level of a resume with respect to each specific requirement given by employers, rendering it distinct from conventional keyword-based systems. Furthermore, the system aggregates and provides statements from resumes that is directly pertinent to the job description, thereby alleviating the need for recruiters to peruse the entire resume.

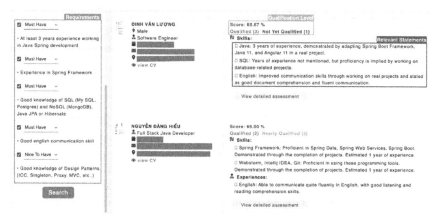

Fig. 7. Sample search results of Resume Analysis System. The left panel presents a list of requirements extracted from a real-world job description. The right panel contains a set of most relevant resumes returned by our system.

When incorporating this search engine into our internal resume screening process, HR personnel perceive this tool as more intuitive and efficient, with more than 60% reduction in time needed to analyze and match resumes.

7   Paper Solution Evaluation

The current system, although it has made progress in addressing the challenges of enterprise Resume search, still has untapped potential for further development:

- **Language Diversity:** Despite the system's architecture being designed to be language-agnostic, the reality is that AI models often struggle with non-English languages. This challenge is mainly due to data imbalances in the training of natural language processing (NLP) models, especially large language models (LLMs). For languages like Vietnamese, there are currently no high-quality open-source LLM models suitable for commercial use. However, the demand for local Resume search in these language communities is as significant as it is for English Resumes. In the future, there is hope for the creation of high-quality multilingual AI models to reduce language bias in the system.
- **Two-Sided Platform:** The current system caters to the Resume search needs of businesses. However, candidates also desire the ability to search for job descriptions that align with their skills and capabilities. In the near future, building on the existing technology platform, the goal is to address both aspects of the recruitment problem, creating a platform with depth that involves multiple stakeholders.
- **Specialized Fields:** Recruitment practices can vary significantly across different industries. While the current system is designed to handle a wide range of Resumes regardless of the field, it has been trained and tested primarily on data from the IT and Marketing sectors. As time progresses and more research is conducted in various industries, the system aims to adapt and meet the recruitment needs of all businesses.

Each field of recruitment comes with its unique characteristics, and it is hoped that with ample time for market research and in-depth exploration of each sector, the system can evolve to serve the hiring needs of all businesses effectively.

8 Conclusion

Currently, resume search systems primarily rely on keyword-based search algorithms and manually crafted templates. Our drawback is that we often fail to find the most suitable resumes for a job description in a large database and do not provide a visual and comprehensive view of the compatibility between a resume and a job description. Recruiters often spend a significant amount of time sifting through hundreds of resumes before selecting a few that fit their criteria.

Our system is overcoming these shortcomings but still ensures that search time is comparable to traditional search algorithms. By leveraging breakthroughs in Generative AI, the system can provide in-depth analyses of both job descriptions and resumes, on par with those performed by recruiters. This helps businesses save time and costs in recruitment campaigns, enhancing the user experience for recruiters on job search platforms.

References

1. Maheshwary, S., Misra, H.: Matching resumes to jobs via deep siamese network. In: WWW 2018: Companion Proceedings of the the Web Conference 2018, pp. 87–88. International World Wide Web Conferences Steering Committee, Republic and Canton of Geneva (2018)

2. Schmitt, T., Caillou, P., Sebag, M.: Matching jobs and resumes: a deep collaborative filtering task. In: Benzmüller, C., Sutcliffe, G., Rojas, R. (eds.) GCAI 2016. 2nd Global Conference on Artificial Intelligence, vol. 41, pp. 124–137 (2016)

3. Xu, Y., Li, M., Cui, L., Huang, S., Wei, F., Zhou, M.: LayoutLM: pre-training of text and layout for document image understanding. In: Computation and Language. Association for Computing Machinery, New York (2019)

4. Meta AI Homepage. https://ai.meta.com/research/publications/llama-2-open-foundation-and-fine-tuned-chat-models/. Accesed 23 Sept 2023

5. Reimers, N., Gurevych, I.: Sentence-BERT: sentence embeddings using siamese BERT-networks. In: Proceedings of the 2019 Conference on Empirical Methods in Natural Language Processing and the 9th International Joint Conference on Natural Language Processing, Hong Kong, China, pp. 3982–3992 (2019)

6. Nogueira, R., Cho, K.: Passage re-ranking with BERT. In: Information Retrieval arXiv:1901. 04085 (2019)

7. Zhao, W.X., Liu, J., Ren, R., Wen, J.-R.: Dense text retrieval based on pretrained language models: a survey. arXiv:2211.14876v1 [cs.IR] (2022)

8. Wang, K., Thakur, N., Reimers, N., Gurevych, I.: GPL: generative pseudo labeling for unsupervised domain adaptation of dense retrieval. In: Proceedings of the 2022 Conference of the North American Chapter of the Association for Computational Linguistics: Human Language Technologies, pp. 2345–2360 (2022)

9. Huang, Y., Lv, T., Cui, L., Lu, Y., Wei, F.: LayoutLMv3: pre-training for document AI with unified text and image masking. In: MM 2022: Proceedings of the 30th ACM International Conference on Multimedia, pp. 4083–4091. Association for Computing Machinery, New York (2022)

10. Li, Y., et al.: StrucTexT: structured text understanding with multi-modal transformers. arXiv: 2108.02923v3 [cs.CV] (2021)

11. Luo, C., Cheng, C., Zheng, Q., Yao, C.: GeoLayoutLM: geometric pre-training for visual information extraction. In: Proceedings of the IEEE/CVF Conference on Computer Vision and Pattern Recognition (CVPR), pp. 7092–7101 (2023)

12. Jaume, G., Ekenel, H.K., Thiran, J.-P.: FUNSD: a dataset for form understanding in noisy scanned documents. IEEE, Sydney (2019)

13. Park, S., et al.: CORD: a consolidated receipt dataset for post-OCR parsing. In: Computer Science, 33rd Conference on Neural Information Processing Systems (NeurIPS 2019), Vancouver, Canada (2019)

14. Wang, W., Wei, F., Dong, L., Bao, H., Yang, N., Zhou, M.: MINILM: deep self-attention distillation for task-agnostic compression of pre-trained transformers. In: NIPS 2020: Proceedings of the 34th International Conference on Neural Information Processing Systems, pp. 5776–5788. Curran Associates Inc., Red Hook (2020)

15. Rozière, B., et al.: Code llama: open foundation models for code. Computation and Language (2023)

16. Zhou, C., et al.: LIMA: less is more for alignment. arXiv:2305.11206v1 [cs.CL] (2023)

17. Wang, Y., et al.: Self-instruct: aligning language models with self-generated instructions. In: Proceedings of the 61st Annual Meeting of the Association for Computational Linguistics Volume 1: Long Papers, pp. 13484–13508. Association for Computational Linguistics, Toronto (2023)

18. Dettmers, T., Pagnoni, A., Holtzman, A., Zettlemoyer, L.: QLoRA: efficient finetuning of quantized LLMs. arXiv:2305.14314v1 [cs.LG] (2023)

LORAP: Local Deep Neural Network for Solar Radiation Prediction

Thanh-Tri Trang[1], Thanh Ma[1(✉)], and Thanh-Nghi Do[1,2]

[1] CICT, Can Tho University, Can Tho, Vietnam
{tritrang,mtthanh,dtnghi}@ctu.edu.vn
[2] UMI UMMISCO 209, IRD/UPMC, Paris, France

Abstract. Solar radiation directly affects human health and the surrounding environment. Therefore, scientists are paying much attention to this aspect to control the level of radiation. This paper introduces a new model to predict solar radiation using the collected dataset. Our approach focuses on predicting solar radiation frequency with a deep-learning network model. Instead of ideas directly indicating the outcome with one regression model (deep learning or machine learning), we take inspiration from the saying "divide and conquer" to propose a layered learning model. We implement classification models before building local regression models for classes. Our proposal obtains the expected results with 99% accuracy for the classification and an MAE of 17.8556 for the regression model. In this paper, we also compare our approach with existing models. Two highlights are: (1) our model is better than several approaches, and (2) it forecasts the ability of solar radiation in the next fifteen minutes based on the current information/data.

Keywords: Solar Radiation · Classification · Regression · Local Deep Neural Network

1 Introduction

In recent years, the energy sector's central focus has been reducing carbon emissions by transitioning to renewable energy sources. Excessive carbon emissions have a detrimental impact on the environment, leading to global warming and climate change. Furthermore, industrialization has significantly accelerated the world's energy demand, resulting in the depletion of non-renewable energy sources such as coal, natural gas, and oil, which are increasingly limited. In response to this situation, many countries have formulated and subsequently implemented policies and strategies related to the energy field. In 2015 [14], the United States and China jointly issued a statement addressing climate change issues [5]. The report emphasized new domestic policy commitments to achieve 90–100% reliance on renewable energy sources [18]. Moreover, the European Union plans to utilize renewable energy sources to generate 30–45% of electricity by 2030 and about 100% by 2050 [9,21].

T. K. Dang et al. (Eds.): FDSE 2023, CCIS 1925, pp. 366–380, 2023.
https://doi.org/10.1007/978-981-99-8296-7_26

Among the various promising types of renewable energy, solar energy is widely recognized and utilized worldwide. This situation is particularly true in economically developed countries [9]. Regarding integrating renewable energy sources into the power grid, most studies have focused on developing "photovoltaic" (PV) systems [25] rather than incorporating other forms of renewable energy, including wind energy, biomass, and others. However, the characteristics of solar energy, such as its uncertainty, variability, and randomness, can lead to dynamic instability and unpredictability of solar power output [1,33]. Faced with these challenges, pursuing accurate prediction techniques for solar radiation levels is imperative to provide crucial decision support for power distribution systems.

Indeed, solar energy [19] is becoming increasingly popular as a renewable energy source due to its environmental benefits and abundance. However, integrating solar energy into the power grid is challenging due to its discontinuous and uncertain nature. To accurately forecast solar radiation and PV power output, it is crucial to consider parameters such as spatial and temporal correlations that impact the accuracy of predictions [3]. Spatial correlation refers to the relationship between the geographic location of PV systems and the weather patterns of that area [31,40]. On the other hand, temporal correlation pertains to the time series relationship between solar radiation and PV power output data. Other parameters, such as cloud cover, atmospheric conditions, and time of day, can also influence the accuracy of forecasts. Hence, incorporating these parameters into forecasting models is highly significant.

Several vital techniques have been applied in forecasting studies, including statistical, physical, machine learning, and ensemble methods [35,37,41]. Typically, the performance of each strategy depends on the forecast horizon and input parameters [6]. Forecast analysis parameters like spatial-temporal correlations (where space and time correspond to spatial and temporal dimensions) are crucial in improving accuracy and require large-scale datasets [34,36]. More profound studies on spatial and temporal correlations, combined with other solar energy data sources, are essential for solar energy forecasting, such as PV power forecasting [16,22], as large datasets can lead to high accuracy despite their complexity.

Several forecasting models have been proposed in the literature targeting different prediction time-frames [17]: very short-term (within hours), short-term (within a day or the next day), medium-term (1 month), and long-term (1 year), each serving different applications. For instance, hourly and daily forecasts can be used for the real-time operation of the power system. Day-ahead predictions can be employed for scheduling purposes. Medium and long-term forecasts can serve maintenance and energy market purposes. Forecasting algorithms can be categorized into physical models, such as Numerical Weather Prediction (NWP) [24]; statistical models, such as AutoRegressive Moving Average (ARMA) [4] and AutoRegressive Integrated Moving Average (ARIMA) [8]; and data-driven models, such as Artificial Intelligence (AI) algorithms [23].

In this paper, our focus will primarily be on short-term prediction. We conduct radiation forecasting for the "very short term," specifically within the next

15 min. Our dataset will be collected at one-minute intervals. The rationale behind this choice aligns well with Vietnam's weather and climate conditions. Particularly in Vietnam and the wider Asian region, solar radiation levels are notably high. Furthermore, for a country prone to heavy rainfall and storms like Vietnam, efficiently managing the opening and closing of solar energy capacity over short durations becomes essential. To address the prediction task, we propose a novel approach named "local forecasting." Performing predictions over an extensive dataset poses challenges for classification and regression models. We formulate a fresh perspective inspired by the "Divide and Conquer" concept [32]. To this end, our core idea involves segmenting radiation ranges and constructing multiple forecasting models for these segments. Specifically, we partitioned the data into 14 subsets, each encompassing a radiation range of 100 units. Subsequently, we developed a classifier using these local subsets. Upon completing the classification, we train 14 regression models, each corresponding to one of the classes, to execute solar radiation predictions. It is important to note that one classification model will be performed before the regression (forecasting) process.

The remainder of this paper is structured as follows: we briefly present a fundamental background in Sect. 2. Next, Sect. 3 describes the proposed method. Then, Sect. 4 illustrates the experiment and the results of the DCNN models. Finally, Sect. 5 shows the conclusions and future work.

2 Background

In this section, we deliver the primary foundation for the classification and regression of a Deep convolutional neural network (DNN) [2, 20, 28]. First, we mention the classification model. Next, the following regression model is also reminded.

2.1 Classification Model

A classification model with Deep Neural Networks (DNNs) [27] utilizing ResNet-50V2 [26, 29, 30] refers to a specific approach in machine learning where a deep neural network architecture, particularly the ResNet-50V2 architecture, is employed for classification. Moreover, ResNet-50V2 (Residual Network-50 Version 2) is a specific convolutional neural network (CNN) architecture designed to address the vanishing gradient problem and improve the training of very deep neural networks. It includes a residual connection, which allows for the training of deeper networks while mitigating the degradation problem. In this paper, we use Resnetv2-50 to classify the radiation groups. The reason that we select this architecture are:

- Enhanced Depth Without Encountering the Vanishing Gradient Problem: ResNet-50V2 employs a residual block architecture, enabling deeper neural networks to learn complex features without encountering the issue of vanishing gradients. It facilitates the construction of deeper network models that can readily achieve high accuracy.

- Proficiency in Learning Deep Representations: ResNet-50V2 allows the acquisition of deep data representations through hidden layers, enabling the model
to comprehend intricate and abstract features from input images.
- Transfer Learning: ResNet-50V2 is pre-trained on extensive datasets like ImageNet, expediting knowledge transfer from this model to various image recognition tasks. It accelerates the training process and enhances the model's
generalization capabilities.
- Fine-Tuning Capability: Using ResNet-50V2, fine-tuning the model on a
smaller dataset to adapt to specific tasks becomes feasible. They conserve
time and resources compared to training a model from scratch.
- High Accuracy: Due to its adeptness in learning deep representations and
residual architecture, ResNet-50V2 consistently delivers impressive performance in image recognition tasks, achieving high accuracy across diverse test
datasets.

Furthermore, we have extensively experimented with this architecture, [11–
13]. Hence, we will leverage it for our approach. It should be noted that our focus
is not primarily on devising a proficient classification model; instead, our emphasis lies in employing the "divide and conquer" concept within our Framework to
address the regression forecasting problem.

2.2 Regression Model

A regression model with Deep Neural Networks (DNNs) [15,38] pertains to a
regression analysis methodology that adopts Deep Neural Networks as the foundational architectural framework. Regression analysis is a statistical procedure
utilized to anticipate continuous numerical outcomes (dependent variables) pred-
icated upon one or multiple input attributes (characterized as independent variables). Conversely, DNNs encompass artificial neural networks distinguished by
their profound structure, comprising multiple concealed layers between the input
and output strata. A DNN is meticulously engineered in regression modeling to
discern intricate associations between input attributes and the targeted outcome. Each latent layer within the DNN executes a sequence of mathematical
operations upon the input data, effectuating the extraction of progressively intricate and higher-level characteristics. Ultimately, the terminal output layer yields
forth the regression projection.

For the solar radiation forecasting task, a regression model is deemed appropriate. In this context, we utilize the ResNet50V2 architecture [39] to construct
the model. Our approach does not entail building a regression model across
the entire radiation spectrum; instead, we develop localized regression models
(within distinct groups). The forecast horizon encompasses 100 units for each
group. Given a radiation range of 1400, we establish 14 local regression models.
Next, we refer to solar radiation, which is the protagonist of this paper.

2.3 Solar Radiation

Solar radiation, commonly referred to as solar resource or sunlight, constitutes a broad nomenclature encompassing the electromagnetic radiation discharged by the Sun. The harnessing of solar radiation holds the potential to transform it into practical energy forms, including thermal and electrical, through diverse technological avenues. Nevertheless, the viability of implementing these technologies, both from a technical and economic standpoint, within a particular locale hinges upon the prevailing solar resource magnitude.

On the other hand, we also know that solar irradiance denotes the energy per unit area, expressed as surface power density, imparted by the Sun through electromagnetic radiation within a designated wavelength spectrum as dictated by the measuring apparatus. In the International System of Units (SI), solar irradiance is quantified in watts per square meter (W/m^2). A customary practice involves the temporal aggregation of solar irradiance over a specific interval, resulting in the quantification of the radiant energy emitted into the adjacent surroundings (in joules per square meter, J/m^2) during that stipulated timeframe. This amalgamated solar irradiance is termed solar irradiation, solar exposure, solar insolation, or simply insolation.

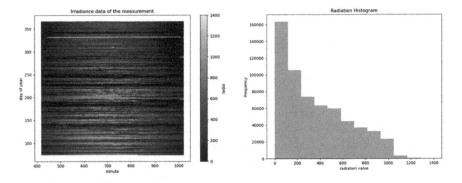

Fig. 1. Radiation distribution by year and minute (Location 1). High radiation data (1000–1400) occurs between 600–800 min (10:00 AM–13:30 AM) and in the first half of the year (from 1 to 250 days).

We deploy sensors to measure temperature, humidity, wind speed, wind direction, air pressure, and current radiation. Radiation data will be collected in minutes, radio ranges, and the number of days within a year (refer to Fig. 1 (left side)). Ordinarily, radiation values will progressively diminish from 0 to 1400, accompanied by their respective frequency of occurrence (as depicted in Fig. 1 (right side)).

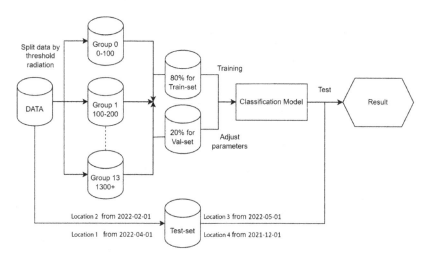

Fig. 2. Classification model for identifying the local radiation group

3 Framework of LORAP

To facilitate solar radiation forecasting, we propose a novel hierarchical prediction model. Our central vision involves segmenting the data range through classification and conducting predictions within these localized partitions. Analogously, when estimating an individual's age, we classify them into age ranges, such as under 18, 20–30, 30–40, 40–50, or above 50. Subsequently, we perform a refined age estimation within that local interval of, for instance, ten units. Expanding upon this notion, we construct a hierarchical prediction model. We develop a classification model in the first tier to identify the appropriate class. Subsequently, having determined the specific class, we implement regression modeling for solar radiation prediction within that localized group.

To accomplish this objective, we have constructed a classification model, as illustrated in Fig. 2. We establish a radiation threshold for data segmentation. Specifically, we partition the radiation spectrum into 14 distinct groups, each comprising 100 values, as elucidated in Fig. 2. i.e., groups 0: 0–99, 1: 100–199, and others. We have employed a deep neural network utilizing the ResNet50V2 architecture for this classification framework.

Subsequently, upon identifying the requisite class at the second tier, the system undertakes prediction through a regression model. The regression model in this strategy encloses 14 distinct models, each aligned with the class determined in the first tier, as illustrated in Fig. 3. All regression models are also constructed utilizing a deep neural network operating on the ResNet50V2 architecture, as depicted in Fig. 4.

The reason for subdividing the model into localized groups of 100 values each is that we tolerate an error margin of 50 for consecutive 15-s continuous prediction values. With a modest error of 50, the decision-making process remains

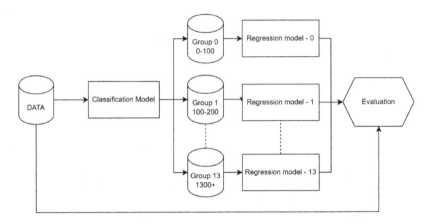

Fig. 3. Regression models for predicting the solar radiation

unaffected because it falls within an acceptable range for identifying high, low, and moderate radiation levels. However, as this is a flexible threshold, its establishment can be adapted based on specific regions. We have chosen a threshold of 100, which aligns well with the distinct solar radiation characteristics prevalent in the Southeast Asian area.

As presented in Subsect. 2.1, our chosen model architecture is a DNN model utilizing the ResNet50V2 architecture. Employing this architecture, we conducted experiments with various resized image dimensions. Building upon prior research, the ResNet50V2 model has demonstrated favorable performance with a resolution of 224×224, mainly when dealing with a limited number of classes, yielding high accuracy. We incorporated an averaging component for the final layer of ResNet50V2, employing Global Average Pooling before the process of classification and regression.

Subsequently, to evaluate our approach, the outcomes and discussions will be addressed in the following section.

4 Experiment and Results

This section delineates the dataset employed throughout the experimental phase. Furthermore, it elucidates the configurations and parameters essential for training support. A comprehensive analysis of quantitative and qualitative outcomes is also furnished and deliberated upon.

4.1 Dataset and Configurations

We collect data from four distinct locations across countries in Southeast Asia. To ensure an objective and equitable evaluation of outcomes, the dataset is acquired over diverse time frames and distributed across different periods throughout the year. A total of 524,520 images were gathered during the years

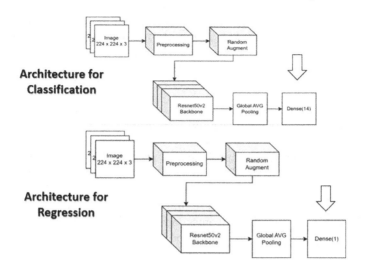

Fig. 4. Architectures for the DNN models

2021–2022. The dataset is partitioned into three subsets: Training, Testing, and Validation, as elaborated in detail in Table 1.

Table 1. Dataset of Solar Radiation collected

Area	Date/Time	Training	Testing	Validation	Total
Location 1	From 13:50:00, 15/3/2021 To 16:45:00, 31/5/2022	206,004	35,901	50,012	256,046
Location 2	From 07:00:00, 28/7/2021 To 16:45:00, 08/3/2022	52,259	20,719	12,437	64,726
Location 3	From 13:10:00, 08/7/2021 To 16:45:00, 31/12/2021	74,030	18,319	18,653	102,558
Location 4	From 11:29:00, 10/12/2021 To 16:45:00, 31/5/2021	81,156	18,508	19,671	101,190

The essential point is that the test data is entirely distinct from the training and validation data. We conducted the collection at different time points. Specifically, Location 1 was gathered on April 1st, 2022; Location 2 on February 1st, 2022; Location 3 on May 1st, 2022; and Location 4 on December 1st, 2021. It is noteworthy that we strategically selected test data "before" *(Location 4)*, "after" *(Location 3)*, and "within" *(Locations 1, 2)* the collection dates for training. The rationale behind this test data selection is to assess the stability of the data and ensure objectivity throughout the evaluation process.

In addition, to measure the time performance of the models, we use one computer configuration for classification and regression in the experiments. It consists of a CPU ARM model Neoverse-N1 with 4 cores at 3.0 GHz, a single thread per core, 24 GB of RAM, and an HDD read and write speed of about 150.34 MB/s.

In the next section, we will present the experimental results and refer to the parameters implemented.

4.2   Parameters and Experimental Results

Classification we train the dataset for 14 classes with the parameters as follows: Optimizer using Adam; Learning rate: 0.0001; Loss: Sparse Categorical Crossentropy; Batch size: 32; Early stopping: 200; and Epochs: 300. We employs *"early stopping"* to identify optimal results and prevent overfitting. With epochs ranging from 200 to 250, the outcomes were obtained as shown in Table 2. It is important to highlight that we conducted 10 experimental runs and calculated the average values for presentation in this paper.

Table 2. Accuracy of the classification model on our dataset collected

	Train	Validation	Testing
DCNN+Resnet50v2	From 99.24%	97.48%	99.19%

Across the board, the classification results demonstrate the compatibility of the DCNN-Resnet50V2 model with this image dataset, yielding a remarkable accuracy of 99.19%. Given the diverse nature of the test data and the high performance achieved, the outcomes of the first tier are scarcely anticipated to impact the forecasting process of the second tier significantly.

Regression parameters for the training dataset are as follows: Optimizer using Adam; Learning rate: 0.0001; Loss: Mean absolute error; Batch size: 32; Early stopping: 200; and Epochs: 300. Similarly, as aforementioned, we implement early stopping for the training process of the DCNN. The regression model outcomes for each localized group are presented in Table 2. Herein, we furnish the results using each model's Mean Absolute Error (MAE) metric [10]. This choice of metric is adopted as it directly corresponds to the loss function during the training procedure.

To evaluate the model, we compare it with the baseline results as presented in Fig. 5. We also provide assessments for both single images and image sequences. The results indicate that the image sequence (70.634) yielded a better MAE outcome than single images (79.917). The MAE result's models (single images and image sequences) are regression-based forecasting performed on the entire dataset without classification, following a different approach from our proposed methodology. When comparing this global model (79.917) to ours (17.8556), our model improves nearly fourfold. Additionally, we juxtapose our approach against other algorithms, such as Gru [7]. In essence, our proposed approach

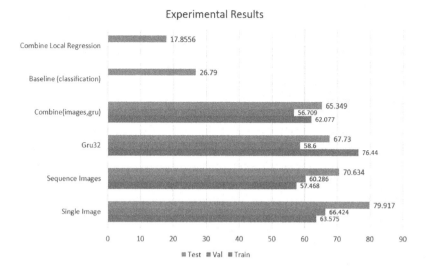

Fig. 5. Experimental results for the regression models

demonstrates enhanced outcomes, achieving an MAE value of merely 17.8556 (average of testing).

We will now provide a discussion of the results obtained as well as the issues worth considering in the next subsection.

Discussion. We have provided several charts for Locations 1, 2, and 3 to visualize the prediction outcomes. Examining the charts in Fig. 6, it is evident that the results for Location 2 closely match the test data. The deviation amplitude between the prediction curve and the target is minimal (around 50). However, at Location 1, there are instances where the results significantly deviate. Conversely, at Location 3, the majority of the predictions are accurate. However, fluctuations are observed during the time range from 12:00 to 13:00. In the event of considering an average over 15-min intervals. The outcomes likely exhibit improved accuracy.

Based on our results, typically, during the morning and afternoon, solar radiation is not significantly conducive to high-accuracy predictions. Some locations during midday exhibit substantial fluctuations in forecasting outcomes due to the intense solar radiation at that time, which is subject to various influencing factors. Aspects such as cloud cover, temperature, and humidity affect the prediction results. Nevertheless, overall, the forecasting outcomes remain acceptable and, in some locations, even favorable when disregarding the impact of these factors (Table 3).

For ease of tracking radiation results, we visualize the solar radiation prediction outcomes in Fig. 7. The image on the left depicts the collected data. In contrast, the image on the right illustrates the predicted solar radiation levels

Table 3. The results of the radiation prediction regression model for each data group

ID	Models	Train	Validation	Testing
1	Regression-class-0	13.9445	17.0080	14.2687
2	Regression-class-1	19.4748	20.7146	20.2085
3	Regression-class-2	19.9313	21.7013	20.8368
4	Regression-class-3	22.1949	22.5406	22.8055
5	Regression-class-4	17.6682	20.4956	18.5534
6	Regression-class-5	13.3054	19.4046	16.2311
7	Regression-class-6	15.0037	20.1935	15.5868
8	Regression-class-7	16.7431	19.8729	16.6200
9	Regression-class-8	16.6026	18.3221	15.8395
10	Regression-class-9	8.1358	16.3345	9.4007
11	Regression-class-10	14.0758	15.7202	11.0935
12	Regression-class-11	19.7640	20.8392	19.7840
13	Regression-class-12	9.1725	18.9882	16.0599
14	Regression-class-13	10.3365	14.6459	11.3998

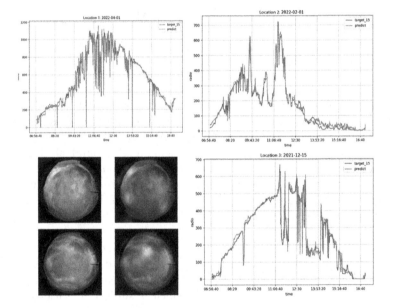

Fig. 6. Chart comparing results of 3 locations and visual prediction results (Color figure online)

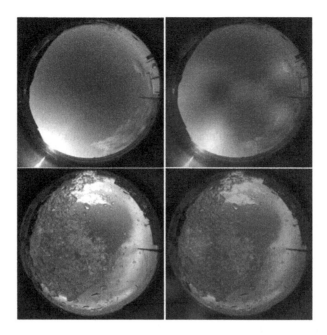

Fig. 7. Visualization of Solar Radiation using our approach (Color figure online)

through color representation. The color red signifies high solar radiation levels. Furthermore, as shown in Fig. 6, even under cloudy skies, the radiation results are still clearly depicted with distinct areas of red and green.

Our forecasting model primarily focuses on the upcoming 15-min intervals. As a result, it will exclude cases of short-lived heavy clouds and prolonged rain events. However, the data needs to be continuously updated to ensure minimal information discrepancies. Furthermore, given that our study region is Southeast Asia, where frequent rainstorms occur, real-time forecasting becomes crucial for effectively managing energy generation and consumption. Moreover, this approach extends to enhancing the protection of solar energy storage systems by providing more accurate near-term forecasts.

5   Conclusion and Future Work

We present a comprehensive solar radiation prediction framework for the dataset collected across multiple locations (Locations 1 through 4) utilizing advanced deep learning models. Our approach systematically divides the dataset into 14 distinct clusters, each corresponding to a specific solar radiation range. The framework facilitates automated image labeling by leveraging future radiation estimates, obviating the need for manual annotation.

In particular, we undertake a two-fold model development process. Initially, a classification model is trained to categorize the dataset into predefined clusters/groups. Following this, we introduce 14 localized regression models that predict solar radiation levels within a specific group. Fusing these classification and regression models culminates in a refined prediction process. Notably, the classification model's output aids in selecting the appropriate localized regression model for the final prediction. Empirical testing of our proposed methodology underscores its efficacy, as evidenced by achieving the lowest mean absolute error loss across the test dataset.

Our future endeavors involve refining our prediction model by incorporating observational data. This problem entails training localized regression models using observational inputs. Our ultimate vision encompasses the integration of both image-based localized regression and observation-based localized regression, thereby enhancing the precision and robustness of our final predictions.

References

1. Ahmed, R., Sreeram, V., Mishra, Y., Arif, M.: A review and evaluation of the state-of-the-art in PV solar power forecasting: techniques and optimization. Renew. Sustain. Energy Rev. **124**, 109792 (2020)
2. Aloysius, N., Geetha, M.: A review on deep convolutional neural networks. In: 2017 International Conference on Communication and Signal Processing (ICCSP), pp. 0588–0592. IEEE (2017)
3. Alqudah, M., Dokic, T., Kezunovic, M., Obradovic, Z.: Prediction of solar radiation based on spatial and temporal embeddings for solar generation forecast. arXiv preprint arXiv:2206.08832 (2022)
4. Benjamin, M.A., Rigby, R.A., Stasinopoulos, D.M.: Generalized autoregressive moving average models. J. Am. Stat. Assoc. **98**(461), 214–223 (2003)
5. Bodansky, D.: The Copenhagen climate change conference: a postmortem. Am. J. Int. Law **104**(2), 230–240 (2010)
6. Boland, J.: Spatial-temporal forecasting of solar radiation. Renew. Energy **75**, 607–616 (2015)
7. Boubaker, S., Benghanem, M., Mellit, A., Lefza, A., Kahouli, O., Kolsi, L.: Deep neural networks for predicting solar radiation at Hail Region, Saudi Arabia. IEEE Access **9**, 36719–36729 (2021)
8. Box, G.E., Pierce, D.A.: Distribution of residual autocorrelations in autoregressive-integrated moving average time series models. J. Am. Stat. Assoc. **65**(332), 1509–1526 (1970)
9. Das, U.K., et al.: Forecasting of photovoltaic power generation and model optimization: a review. Renew. Sustain. Energy Rev. **81**, 912–928 (2018)
10. De Myttenaere, A., Golden, B., Le Grand, B., Rossi, F.: Mean absolute percentage error for regression models. Neurocomputing **192**, 38–48 (2016)
11. Do, T.N.: Training neural networks on top of support vector machine models for classifying fingerprint images. SN Comput. Sci. **2**(5), 355 (2021). https://doi.org/10.1007/s42979-021-00743-0
12. Do, T.-N., Pham, T.-P., Pham, N.-K., Nguyen, H.-H., Tabia, K., Benferhat, S.: Stacking of SVMs for classifying intangible cultural heritage images. In: Le Thi, H.A., Le, H.M., Pham Dinh, T., Nguyen, N.T. (eds.) ICCSAMA 2019. AISC, vol. 1121, pp. 186–196. Springer, Cham (2020). https://doi.org/10.1007/978-3-030-38364-0_17

13. Do, T.N., Pham, T.P., Tran-Nguyen, M.T.: Fine-tuning deep network models for classifying fingerprint images. In: 2020 12th International Conference on Knowledge and Systems Engineering (KSE), pp. 79–84. IEEE (2020)
14. Dong, L.: The trump administration's decision to withdraw the United States from the Paris Climate Agreement. Chin. J. Popul. Resour. Environ. **15**(3), 183 (2017)
15. Du, J., Xu, Y.: Hierarchical deep neural network for multivariate regression. Pattern Recogn. **63**, 149–157 (2017)
16. Gupta, P., Singh, R.: PV power forecasting based on data-driven models: a review. Int. J. Sustain. Eng. **14**(6), 1733–1755 (2021)
17. Gutierrez-Corea, F.V., Manso-Callejo, M.A., Moreno-Regidor, M.P., Manrique-Sancho, M.T.: Forecasting short-term solar irradiance based on artificial neural networks and data from neighboring meteorological stations. Sol. Energy **134**, 119–131 (2016)
18. Herzog, A.V., Lipman, T.E., Kammen, D.M., et al.: Renewable energy sources. In: Encyclopedia of Life Support Systems (EOLSS). Forerunner Volume-Perspectives and Overview of Life Support Systems and Sustainable Development, vol. 76 (2001)
19. Kabir, E., Kumar, P., Kumar, S., Adelodun, A.A., Kim, K.H.: Solar energy: potential and future prospects. Renew. Sustain. Energy Rev. **82**, 894–900 (2018)
20. Kattenborn, T., Leitloff, J., Schiefer, F., Hinz, S.: Review on convolutional neural networks (CNN) in vegetation remote sensing. ISPRS J. Photogramm. Remote. Sens. **173**, 24–49 (2021)
21. Kumari, P., Toshniwal, D.: Long short term memory-convolutional neural network based deep hybrid approach for solar irradiance forecasting. Appl. Energy **295**, 117061 (2021)
22. Li, P., Zhou, K., Lu, X., Yang, S.: A hybrid deep learning model for short-term PV power forecasting. Appl. Energy **259**, 114216 (2020)
23. Long, H., Zhang, Z., Su, Y.: Analysis of daily solar power prediction with data-driven approaches. Appl. Energy **126**, 29–37 (2014)
24. Lorenc, A.C.: Analysis methods for numerical weather prediction. Q. J. R. Meteorol. Soc. **112**(474), 1177–1194 (1986)
25. Lupangu, C., Bansal, R.: A review of technical issues on the development of solar photovoltaic systems. Renew. Sustain. Energy Rev. **73**, 950–965 (2017)
26. Mascarenhas, S., Agarwal, M.: A comparison between VGG16, VGG19 and ResNet50 architecture frameworks for Image Classification. In: 2021 International Conference on Disruptive Technologies for Multi-Disciplinary Research and Applications (CENTCON), vol. 1, pp. 96–99. IEEE (2021)
27. Miller, D.J., Xiang, Z., Kesidis, G.: Adversarial learning targeting deep neural network classification: a comprehensive review of defenses against attacks. Proc. IEEE **108**(3), 402–433 (2020)
28. Onim, M.S.H., et al.: SolNet: a convolutional neural network for detecting dust on solar panels. Energies **16**(1), 155 (2022)
29. Phan, A.C., Nguyen, N.H.Q., Trieu, T.N., Phan, T.C.: An efficient approach for detecting driver drowsiness based on deep learning. Appl. Sci. **11**(18), 8441 (2021)
30. Prusty, S., Patnaik, S., Dash, S.K.: ResNet50V2: a transfer learning model to predict pneumonia with chest X-ray images. In: 2022 International Conference on Machine Learning, Computer Systems and Security (MLCSS), pp. 208–213. IEEE (2022)
31. Rodríguez, F., Martín, F., Fontán, L., Galarza, A.: Ensemble of machine learning and spatiotemporal parameters to forecast very short-term solar irradiation to compute photovoltaic generators' output power. Energy **229**, 120647 (2021)

32. Smith, D.R.: The design of divide and conquer algorithms. Sci. Comput. Program. **5**, 37–58 (1985)
33. Touti, E., Zayed, H., Pusca, R., Romary, R.: Dynamic stability enhancement of a hybrid renewable energy system in stand-alone applications. Computation **9**(2), 14 (2021)
34. Vignola, F., Grover, C., Lemon, N., McMahan, A.: Building a bankable solar radiation dataset. Sol. Energy **86**(8), 2218–2229 (2012)
35. Voyant, C., et al.: Machine learning methods for solar radiation forecasting: a review. Renew. Energy **105**, 569–582 (2017)
36. Walch, A., Castello, R., Mohajeri, N., Scartezzini, J.L.: A fast machine learning model for large-scale estimation of annual solar irradiation on rooftops. In: Proceedings of Solar World Congress 2019. International Solar Energy Society ISES (2020)
37. Wang, H., Lei, Z., Zhang, X., Zhou, B., Peng, J.: A review of deep learning for renewable energy forecasting. Energy Convers. Manag. **198**, 111799 (2019)
38. Xu, Y., Du, J., Dai, L.R., Lee, C.H.: A regression approach to speech enhancement based on deep neural networks. IEEE/ACM Trans. Audio Speech Lang. Process. **23**(1), 7–19 (2014)
39. Yuan, C., Marion, T., Moghaddam, M.: Leveraging end-user data for enhanced design concept evaluation: a multimodal deep regression model. J. Mech. Des. **144**(2), 021403 (2022)
40. Zang, H., Liu, L., Sun, L., Cheng, L., Wei, Z., Sun, G.: Short-term global horizontal irradiance forecasting based on a hybrid CNN-LSTM model with spatiotemporal correlations. Renew. Energy **160**, 26–41 (2020)
41. Zhou, Y., Liu, Y., Wang, D., Liu, X., Wang, Y.: A review on global solar radiation prediction with machine learning models in a comprehensive perspective. Energy Convers. Manag. **235**, 113960 (2021)

A Digital Therapeutics System for the Diagnosis and Management of Depression: Work in Progress

Yongho Lee[1,2] , Vinh Pham[1], Jieming Zhang[1] ,
and Tai-Myoung Chung[1,2(✉)]

[1] Department of Computer Science and Engineering, Sungkyunkwan University,
Suwon, Republic of Korea
{yohlee,vinhpham}@g.skku.edu, {jieming2021,tmchung}@skku.edu
[2] Hippo T&C Inc., Suwon, Republic of Korea
https://www.hippotnc.com

Abstract. Depression is a widespread and serious medical illness that negatively affects how you feel, think and act [1]. It impacts around 5% of the global adult population [2,3] and is the most common psychiatric disorder that is present in people that die by suicide [4]. Digital therapeutics are a promising new type of therapy that combines patient centric technologies with evidence-based medicine to deliver highly personalized care through programs to prevent, manage, or treat medical conditions [5]. This research aims to briefly review various past and current attempts at digital therapeutics, and share a work in progress that attempts to combine the strengths and negate the weaknesses of previous works with a focus on multimodal artificial intelligence powered digital therapeutics as a system for diagnosing and managing depression.

Keywords: Artificial Intelligence · Depression · Digital Therapeutics · Heart Rate Variability · Machine Learning · Voice

1 Introduction

Depression, or Major Depressive Disorder (MDD), is a highly prevalent mental disorder that induces a vicious cycle of negative reinforcement within the human cognition. It is known to cause a multitude of emotional and physical problems [1], and causes an non-trivial level of consequences including excessive mortality, disability, and secondary morbidity [6]. The fact that the recent COVID-19 pandemic has resulted in an estimated 27.6% increase in MDD prevalence worldwide [7] and that marginalized groups within society tend to be even more harshly impacted by MDD [8] also adds to the necessity of an effective solution to diagnose and manage MDD.

MDD is typically diagnosed by mental health practitioners by assessing the presence, severity, and duration of known traits of MDD [9]. To facilitate systematic diagnosis of MDD, mental health questionnaires such as the Public

Health Questionnaire-9 (PHQ-9) [10] and Beck Depression Inventory (BDI) [11] are often used by physicians along side in-person examination to diagnose a patient of MDD. However, the problem with the current approach of diagnosing MDD is that factors such as limited mental health knowledge, social stigma and embarrassment, perceptions of therapeutical relationships with professionals, and structural barriers and facilitators contribute to a suboptimal situation in which those who must visit a physician to help get diagnosed with and receive medical intervention for MDD often do not know that they should seek clinical attention, or are either not willing or unable to seek such attention [12]. This is where digital therapeutics may play a role in complementing the limitations of the current approach.

Digital therapeutics (DTx) are a category of digital health solutions that offer evidence-based software-driven therapeutic interventions for the prevention and management of medical disorders or diseases [13]. Thanks to its ubiquitous and non-physical nature, digital therapeutics are increasingly being used for a wide range of conditions, including but not limited to, MDD, Attention Deficit Hyperactivity Disorder (ADHD), and Post Traumatic Stress Disorder (PTSD). Also, given that humans tend to trust machine agents over human agents when disclosing personal information [14], the active application of DTx for the purpose of diagnosing and managing MDD is expected to yield promising results when it comes to digging into the actual reason a human diagnosed with MDD is facing cognitive distortion. Also, thanks to the digital nature of DTx, it becomes possible for MDD patients and those suspected of MDD to receive around-the-clock personalized diagnosis and management. Aided with data driven approaches made possible with the increased popularity in smart watches and smart phones capable of collecting physiological data such as photoplethysmography (PPG) and voice, the addition of artificial intelligence (AI) based models are widely believed to provide invaluable help to physicians in getting a better understanding of their patients.

This research will review existing DTx solutions and aim to propose, albeit a work in progress, a more comprehensive and robust system purposed with providing constant personalized diagnosis and management through AI based DTx, with a focus on MDD.

2   Related Works

There is no exact consensus on the definition of the term, DTx. However, many literature in the field [15–17] agree that DTx is a comprehensive term that includes a mixture of prevention, diagnosis, treatment and management of medical disorders through the use of digital tools. While it is difficult to point out the exact origins of DTx, it would be reasonable to say that the advent of DTx occurred along with the proliferation of smart devices and advances in technology. However, for purposes of clarity, the scope of this study will be limited to the diagnosis and management of MDD using DTx.

Christensen et al. performed multiple experiments where a web-based cognitive behavioral therapy (CBT) intervention (MoodGYM Mark I/II) consisted of five modules were provided to the public [18–20]. 19,607 visitors and 38,791 visitors registered and participated in the MoodGYM Mark I and II, respectively. Christensen's team was able to demonstrate that for registrants with initial depression scores above 2, the magnitude of improvement, measured in Goldberg Depression and Anxiety Scales [21], increased as a function of the number of CBT modules attempted. The work of Christensen's team was highly significant in that it was one of the earliest works that made use of digital technology to provide intervention for MDD, and was able to demonstrate its efficacy in treating MDD. However, Christensen's work is limited in that it only made use of one 18 question survey to assess the severity of MDD, and that recurring visits to an online website are quite tedious to follow through with. As CBT type interventions typically require repetitive application to take effect, it could reasonably be said that Christensen's experiment was meaningful in demonstrating the possibility of DTx, but was not designed for repeated usage under real life conditions. Since, repeated access was comparatively tedious, it would have been difficult to collect meaningful data from a given registrant for the purpose of reliably diagnosing and managing MDD.

The study by Lara et al. [22] is similar to that of Christensen et al. in that both research groups made use of web-based self-help interventions. Hence, they both share the same limitations due to the nature of web-based tools. One difference between the two is that Lara's experiment makes use of Center for Epidemiological Studies Depression Scale (CES-D) [23] to detect depressed participants.

The true power of utilizing smart devices for clinical applications is in that it brings a wide selection of sensors from the laboratory to our hands, wrists, and pockets. For example, starting from more "low-level" features to "higher-level" features, Zulueta et al. [24] were able to construct a statistically significant mixed-effects regression model ($R^2 = .63$, $P = .01$) that is able to predict Hamilton Depression Rating Scale (HDRS-17) scores based on mobile phone keystroke metadata.

Long et al. [25], Kontaxis et al. [26], and Mosche et al. [27] all utilize PPG based features to build models from smart phones and wearable devices to reliably predict MDD. While Cheng et al. [28] uses mobile app based lexicon development to screen for depression using 13 different categories.

Finally Joshi et al. [29] performed face analysis, upper body analysis, key interest point selection and bag of words approaches to detect depression.

While the authors of each of the above-mentioned previous works have found numerous significant features for the detection of depression, the authors of this research would like to propose an enhanced digital therapeutics system that benefits from the lessons given by these previous works through integration of multiple features into multimodal models that are able to learn from as much data as possible.

3   Dataset

Currently the authors make use of the Emognition dataset [30], Extended DAIC-WOZ dataset [31], and IEMOCAP dataset [32] to train and evaluate multimodal

AI models based on simulated voice and heart rate variability (HRV) data input. But during later stages of the project, the authors plan to test the mentioned AI models with custom collected datasets.

The Emognition dataset contains PPG, electroencephalogram (EEG), electrodermal activity measurement, accelerometer, and video data. For the purposes of our research, we will only be using the PPG and video data. The PPG data is numerical time series data that is used to extract HRV data. HRV data is the fluctuation in the time intervals between adjacent heartbeats [33]. The open source pyHRV library [34] will be used to extract HRV features.

The Extended DAIC-WOZ dataset consists of voice data collected from participants, along with a machine generated transcript from the given voice. Features are extracted from the voice data using the openSMILE library [35]. The voice data is time series data whose patterns may be exploited by using libraries such as openSMILE. While one might think that raw voice data may contain more data, a reduction in dimensionality is required to aid the learning process of AI models.

The IEMOCAP dataset contains the voice and facial expressions of actors trying to display between five specific emotions; happiness, anger, sadness, frustration, and neutral state. Both the voice and facial expression keypoints may be considered time series data.

4   System Design

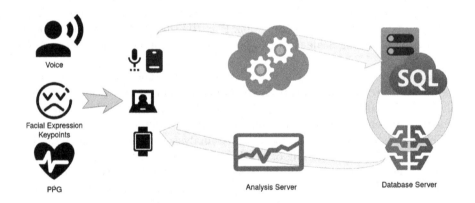

Fig. 1. System Design

As may be seen in Fig. 1, the authors propose a DTx system which collects voice, facial expression keypoints, and PPG using smart phones and smart watches. The facial keypoint data will be used to extract actions units in accordance with the Facial Action Coding System [36], and the openSMILE library will be used to extract AI friendly features such as log harmonics-to-noise ratio from the supplied voice instead of using the raw voice itself for analysis. pyHRV [34] will be used to extract HRV features from input PPG data. All raw data collected by sensors will be safely stored on the database server, while select features will be used to perform analysis on the analysis server. Since, the type of data stored is inherently relational, the database will take the form of an SQL server.

The voice and facial expression keypoints are planned to be collected by a custom developed Flutter app as in Fig. 2, and PPG data will be collected by a custom designed smart watch as in Fig. 3. The custom app shall also prepare a visual interface through which the user may observe his or her own personal baseline and any ensuing fluctuations.

5   Discussion

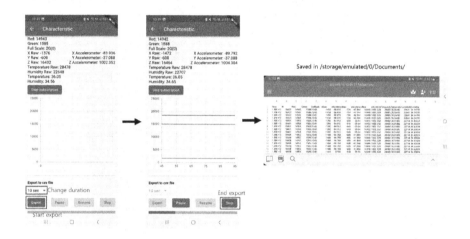

Fig. 2. Custom smart watch app

The main issue with the existing approaches concerning DTx systems for the diagnosis and managment of MDD is that most, if not all, previous works regarding this subject are generally centered around DTx systems that are either not scalable to service the needs of the population at large, or only exploit some physiological features for the diagnosis and management of MDD. However, albeit a work in progress, the authors' proposed DTx system makes use of all physiological features that are reasonably collectible from "low-level" to "high-level" using wearables and software that are not difficult to acquire or develop in real life. Also, the fact that the authors control every aspect of the proposed system, from custom app to backend server, means that the proposed system is also easily extensible should a different feature be found to have significant value in the diagnosis and management of MDD.

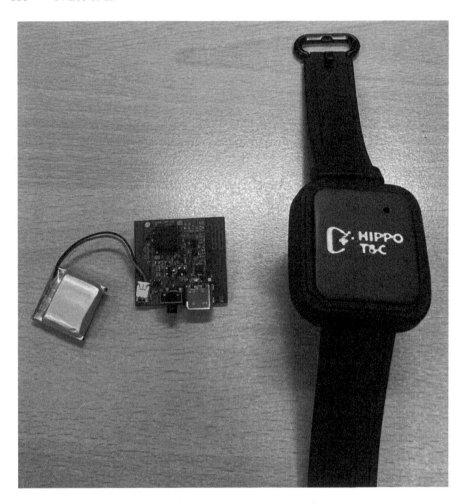

Fig. 3. Custom smart watch

The authors' proposed DTx system works around the limitations of web-based approaches by developing a custom Flutter app and a custom smart watch, facilitating around the clock monitoring and analysis of the subject's physiological conditions, making a highly personalized experience possible. It also does not stop at using one or two features, but makes use of as many features as reasonably extractable by the given hardware and software.

Also, the use of a multimodal AI model to analyze the many inputs together is expected to produce a much more robust model than others, that is capable of better learning the distribution of each of the input data in better context.

6 Conclusion

This research provided a review of DTx systems of the past and present that were aimed at the diagnosis and management of MDD. It also shared the concept of a DTx system designed to diagnose and manage MDD using the most features possible, while providing a highly personalized MDD diagnosis and management experience. Thanks to the ubiquitous nature of DTx, physicians are able to benefit from the insight provided by the continuous monitoring of MDD patients, and patients are able to enjoy a more accessible and objective method of managing their condition. Also, the fact that humans tend to disclose personal information more easily to machines instead of humans, mean that DTx makes it easier for MDD patients to speak their inner mind to the app, which the physician may use to complement the treatment of his or her patient.

Unlike existing research which mostly focus on using only a small number of features, the proposed DTx system tried to employ the most features extractable as possible in hope of creating a more accurate and robust multimodal AI model for the diagnosis and management of MDD. However, as the proposed system is still under active development, this research was limited in that it was only able to share the devised concept but not able to provide actual numbers that resulted from the use of the proposed system. In future works, the authors hope to be able to materialize the actual AI model that is supposed to handle the analysis. Also, the addition of a DTx treatment module for MDD would be greatly desirable so as to create a powerful end-to-end one stop solution for the diagnosis, management, and treatment of MDD. It should be noted that future works should incorporate factors which may maximize the "Therapeutic Alliance" [37] between the user and the system, for optimal results.

Acknowledgements. This work was supported by the Institute of Information & communications Technology Planning & Evaluation (IITP) grant funded by the Korea government (MSIT) (No. 2020-0-00990, Platform Development and Proof of High Trust & Low Latency Processing for Heterogeneous·Atypical·Large Scaled Data in 5G-IoT Environment) and the Technology Innovation Program (or Industrial Strategic Technology Development Program-Source Technology Development and Commercialization of Digital Therapeutics) (20014967, Development of Digital Therapeutics for Depression from COVID19) funded By the Ministry of Trade, Industry & Energy (MOTIE, Korea).

References

1. What is Depression? https://www.psychiatry.org:443/patients-families/depression/what-is-depression

2. Depressive disorder (depression). https://www.who.int/news-room/fact-sheets/detail/depression
3. GBD Results. https://vizhub.healthdata.org/gbd-results
4. Hawton, K., Casañas i Comabella, C., Haw, C., Saunders, K.: Risk factors for suicide in individuals with depression: a systematic review. J. Affect. Disord. **147**, 17–28 (2013)
5. DTA: Digital Therapeutics Industry Report 2018 (2018). https://dtxalliance.org/2018/10/23/dtaindustryreport2018/
6. Sartorius, N.: The economic and social burden of depression. J. Clin. Psychiatry **62**, 5400 (2001)
7. Santomauro, D.F., et al.: Global prevalence and burden of depressive and anxiety disorders in 204 countries and territories in 2020 due to the COVID-19 pandemic. Lancet **398**, 1700–1712 (2021)
8. Bailey, R.K., Mokonogho, J., Kumar, A.: Racial and ethnic differences in depression: current perspectives. Neuropsychiatr. Dis. Treat. **15**, 603–609 (2019)
9. Depression. https://www.nimh.nih.gov/health/publications/depression
10. Kroenke, K., Spitzer, R.L., Williams, J.B.W.: Patient health questionnaire-9 (2011)
11. Beck Depression Inventory-II. https://psycnet.apa.org/doiLanding?doi=10.1037%2Ft00742-000
12. Radez, J., Reardon, T., Creswell, C., Lawrence, P.J., Evdoka-Burton, G., Waite, P.: Why do children and adolescents (not) seek and access professional help for their mental health problems? A systematic review of quantitative and qualitative studies. Eur. Child Adolesc. Psychiatry **30**, 183–211 (2021)
13. Dang, A., Arora, D., Rane, P.: Role of digital therapeutics and the changing future of healthcare. J. Family Med. Primary Care **9**, 2207 (2020)
14. Sundar, S.S., Kim, J.: Machine heuristic: when we trust computers more than humans with our personal information. In: Proceedings of the 2019 CHI Conference on Human Factors in Computing Systems, CHI 2019, New York, NY, USA, pp. 1–9. Association for Computing Machinery (2019)
15. Hong, J.S., Wasden, C., Han, D.H.: Introduction of digital therapeutics. Comput. Methods Program. Biomed. **209**, 106319 (2021)
16. Wang, C., Lee, C., Shin, H.: Digital therapeutics from bench to bedside. NPJ Digit. Med. **6**, 1–10 (2023)
17. Ju, J.H., Sim, B., Lee, J., Lee, J.Y.: Reimbursement of digital therapeutics: future perspectives in Korea. Korean Circul. J. **52**, 265–279 (2022)
18. Christensen, H., Griffiths, K.M., Korten, A.: Web-based cognitive behavior therapy: analysis of site usage and changes in depression and anxiety scores. J. Med. Internet Res. **4**, e857 (2002)
19. Christensen, H., Griffiths, K.M., Korten, A.E., Brittliffe, K., Groves, C.: A comparison of changes in anxiety and depression symptoms of spontaneous users and trial participants of a cognitive behavior therapy website. J. Med. Internet Res. **6**, e124 (2004)
20. Christensen, H., Griffiths, K., Groves, C., Korten, A.: Free Range users and one hit wonders: community users of an internet-based cognitive behaviour therapy program. Aust. N. Z. J. Psychiatry **40**, 59–62 (2006)
21. Goldberg, D., Bridges, K., Duncan-Jones, P., Grayson, D.: Detecting anxiety and depression in general medical settings. BMJ **297**, 897–899 (1988)
22. Lara, M.A., Tiburcio, M., Aguilar Abrego, A., Sánchez-Solís, A.: A four-year experience with a Web-based self-help intervention for depressive symptoms in Mexico. Rev. Panamericana Salud Publica = Pan Am. J. Public Health **35**(5–6), 399–406 (2014)

23. The CES-D Scale: A Self-Report Depression Scale for Research in the General Population - Lenore Sawyer Radloff (1977). https://journals.sagepub.com/doi/10.1177/014662167700100306

24. Zulueta, J., et al.: Predicting mood disturbance severity with mobile phone keystroke metadata: a BiAffect digital phenotyping study. J. Med. Internet Res. **20**, e9775 (2018)

25. Long, Y., Lin, Y., Zhang, Z., Jiang, R., Wang, Z.: Objective assessment of depression using multiple physiological signals. In: 2021 14th International Congress on Image and Signal Processing, BioMedical Engineering and Informatics (CISP-BMEI), pp. 1–6 (2021)

26. Kontaxis, S., et al.: Photoplethysmographic waveform analysis for autonomic reactivity assessment in depression. IEEE Trans. Biomed. Eng. **68**, 1273–1281 (2021)

27. Moshe, I., et al.: Predicting symptoms of depression and anxiety using smartphone and wearable data. Front. Psychiatry **12**, 625247 (2021)

28. Cheng, P.G.F., et al.: Psychologist in a pocket: lexicon development and content validation of a mobile-based app for depression screening. JMIR Mhealth Uhealth **4**, e5284 (2016)

29. Joshi, J., Goecke, R., Parker, G., Breakspear, M.: Can body expressions contribute to automatic depression analysis? In: 2013 10th IEEE International Conference and Workshops on Automatic Face and Gesture Recognition (FG), pp. 1–7 (2013)

30. Saganowski, S., et al.: Emognition dataset: emotion recognition with self-reports, facial expressions, and physiology using wearables. Sci. Data **9**, 158 (2022)

31. Ringeval, F., et al.: AVEC 2019 workshop and challenge: state-of-mind, detecting depression with AI, and cross-cultural affect recognition (2019)

32. Busso, C., et al.: IEMOCAP: interactive emotional dyadic motion capture database. Lang. Resour. Eval. **42**, 335–359 (2008)

33. Shaffer, F., Ginsberg, J.P.: An overview of heart rate variability metrics and norms. Front. Public Health **5** (2017)

34. Gomes, P., Margaritoff, P., Silva, H.: pyHRV: development and evaluation of an open-source python toolbox for heart rate variability (HRV). In: Proceedings of the International Conference on Electrical, Electronic and Computing Engineering (IcETRAN), pp. 822–828 (2019)

35. Eyben, F., Wöllmer, M., Schuller, B.: Opensmile: the Munich versatile and fast open-source audio feature extractor. In: Proceedings of the 18th ACM International Conference on Multimedia, MM 2010, New York, NY, USA, pp. 1459–1462, Association for Computing Machinery (2010)

36. Ekman, P., Friesen, W.V.: Facial action coding system (2019)

37. Tremain, H., McEnery, C., Fletcher, K., Murray, G.: The therapeutic alliance in digital mental health interventions for serious mental illnesses: narrative review. JMIR Ment. Health **7**, e17204 (2020)

BERT-Based Sentence Recommendation for Building Vietnamese Universal Dependency Treebank

Tuyen Thi-Thanh Do[✉]

University of Information Technology, VNUHCM, Ho Chi Minh City, Vietnam
tuyendtt@uit.edu.vn

Abstract. A large Vietnamese universal dependency treebank is very important for creating Vietnamese universal dependency parser. However, the Vietnamese universal dependency treebank is small. In addition, there are not many skilled annotators for manually building Vietnamese universal dependency treebank. Therefore, a semi-automatic process, which predicts the high-quality dependency parse results for manual correction, should be used for speeding up the annotation process. This process is also used for beginner tutorials. In this paper, a BERT-based sentence recommendation is proposed for selecting sentences which are possibly predicted with high LAS using an inefficient dependency parser. These sentences should be predicted with high accuracy using a parser trained from the small Vietnamese universal dependency treebank. The experiments show that the recommended sentences are predicted with LAS above 87.1% when using a parser with LAS of 36.8%.

Keywords: Universal Dependency treebank · Universal Dependency Parsing · Sentence Similarity · BERT architecture

1 Introduction

Semantic dependency parse is an important structure in sentential semantic analysis. The research in Vietnamese sentential dependency parsing [1] shows that Vietnamese semantic dependency parses are possibly converted from dependency parses using the Vietnamese lexicon ontology (VLO) [2]. In [1], the dependency parses were generated by VnCoreNLP [3]. The dependency parser of VnCoreNLP was trained on a Vietnamese dependency treebank (DTB) [4] which was automatically converted from a Vietnamese constituency treebank [5] with about 10.200 annotated sentences. This parser has labeled attachment score (LAS) [6] of 73.5% which should be improved for practical applications. Therefore, a large DTB should be built using universal dependency (UD) [7] guidelines[1] for training more efficient Vietnamese dependency parsers.

When looking some skilled annotators from Vietnamese linguistic students for building a Vietnamese universal dependency treebank (UDTB) based on UD Vietnamese VTB

---

[1] https://universaldependencies.org/guidelines.html.

© The Author(s), under exclusive license to Springer Nature Singapore Pte Ltd. 2023
T. K. Dang et al. (Eds.): FDSE 2023, CCIS 1925, pp. 390–402, 2023.
https://doi.org/10.1007/978-981-99-8296-7_28

Treebank [8], it was not easy to find some annotators working with universal dependency. Thus, an important problem is to develop an annotation tool which is possibly provide sentences with predicted annotation. This tool can be used for both speeding up the annotation process and tutoring beginning annotators. The provided sentences should be predicted with high LAS by using a UD parser. These sentences may be used for training the annotators by requiring them to correct a few predicted errors using UD guidelines. The corrected results also enlarge the Vietnamese UDTB. When the annotators have more experience, they will work with more complex cases. All annotation results are used for updating the Vietnamese UD parser. The sentence recommendation problem is possibly solved with two phases. The first phase is to build a UD parser for predicting parses from sentences. The second phase is to build a model recommending sentences which will be predicted by the Vietnamese UD parser with high LAS.

This paper has two contributions. Firstly, it proposes a BERT-based sentence recommendation method which selects sentences being parsed with high LAS when using an inefficient UD parser. Secondly, it shows that the similarities of two sentences in their POS-tag chains and, in their semantics, may affect the similarity of their two UD parses. This means that the sentences, whose POS-tag chain similarity, and semantic similarity to a UD training set are equal or greater than threshold values, are parsed with high LAS when using a UD parser trained on a small UD training set.

This research of BERT-based sentence recommendation method is presented in five sections. The first section, introduction, introduces the problem in building a Vietnamese UDTB when there has been few skilled annotators and the solution to this problem. The second section, backgrounds, presents basic information about Vietnamese UDTB, UD parser and sentence retrieval to build a sentence recommendation component. The third section presents the solution for predicting UD parses in phase 1 and for sentence recommendation in phase 2. The experiments and evaluations of this solution are presented in the fourth section. In the fifth section some conclusions and future works for building a Vietnamese UDTB are provided.

2 Backgrounds

2.1 Vietnamese Universal Dependency Treebank

A Vietnamese universal dependency treebank, named UD Vietnamese VTB [8] with about 3200 parsed sentences, has been manually converted from a Vietnamese constituency treebank [5] with UD guidelines. UD has been proposed to unify the dependency annotation in many languages for sharing the common syntactic characteristics of different languages. UD has different POS tag and dependency label sets from Vietnamese dependency [4, 9]. This means a Vietnamese UDTB is possibly converted from a Vietnamese DTB automatically. However, the existing Vietnamese DTB was automatically converted from a Vietnamese constituency treebank thus the UD Vietnamese VTB [8] has been explored to check if the conversion is correct. As a result, there are two important notices about UD Vietnamese VTB [8].

The first is that UD Vietnamese VTB [8] has non-projective parses. There are five (0.36%) non-projective UD parses in the training set. Figure 1 Shows the UD parse of the sentence *"Kịch_bản này cần thêm một nhân_vật là người bạn giới_thiệu nhà."* (In English *"this script needs a character to whom you will show the house"*. In Fig. 1, the dependency *acl:subj(người, giới_thiệu)* is crossing two dependencies *appos:nmod(nhân_vật, bạn)* and *cop(bạn, là)*. Non-projective dependnecy parses are not possibly converted from constituency parses. This means the Vietnamese DTB may contain errors while being converted from a Vietnamese constituency treebank. Thus, a Vietnamese UDTB need to be manually built instead of being automatically converted from the Vietnamese DTB although the number of Vietnamese non-projective UD parses are small in UD Vietnamese VTB [8].

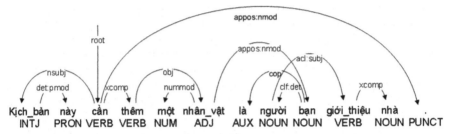

Fig. 1. A demonstration of a non-projective Vietnamese UD parse with the dependency parse of the sentence *"Kịch_bản này cần thêm một nhân_vật là người bạn giới_thiệu nhà."* (In English *"this script needs a character to whom you will show the house"*.

The second is that an adjective node may be in a *root* dependency. Figure 2 shows the UD parse of the sentence *"À, mà chuyện đó cũ hết rồi ..."* (in English: *"Ah, that stuff was already old ..."*). In Fig. 2, the word *"cũ"*, an adjective, is the dependent of the *root(ROOT, cũ)* dependency.

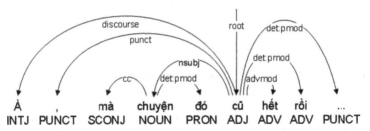

Fig. 2. A demonstration of a Vietnamese UD parse whose the *root(ROOT, cũ)* dependency containing an adjective node (*cũ/ADJ*).

2.2 Universal Dependency Parsing

UD is a dependency grammar. UD has been proposed to represent the dependency parses of many languages in a common fashion. Therefore, a UD parser is also a dependency parser, so a UD parser is possibly built by training a dependency parser with a UDTB. There are two types of dependency parsers: transition-based and graph-based.

Old transition-based parsers were not able to work with non-projective parses. However, new transition-based and graph-based parsers are now able to work with both projective and non-projective parses. In addition, the non-projective parses are rarely in DTB so any type of dependency parser may be used while the efficiency of parsing results will not change much.

Stanford neural network dependency parser is one of many efficient dependency parsers in parsing time and in LAS [10]. This parser is a transition-based one in which the oracle is a neural network classifier. A new oracle is possibly trained for this parser to work with another language by providing an appropriate DTB and the word embeddings of vocabulary of that language. The training process will learn the parameters of the oracle for choosing the right action of shift, arc-left or arc-right at every parsing step.

2.3 Sentence Similarity

Sentence similarity is the measure of how similar two sentences are with their semantic. Sentence similarity is important to the sentence retrieval problem. This problem is to identify the sentences related to a given sentence and then to rank these sentences by their similarity to the given sentence. Sentence similarity is possibly computed using sentence embedding. In this way, a semantic vector is approximated by a deep neural network (DNN) model for every sentence. The similarity of the two sentences is possibly the cosine similarity of their two semantic vectors. Other metrics, such as Jaccard or Euclidean distance, are possibly used to calculate the similarity in appropriate cases. In this approach, a similarity annotated dataset is needed. This dataset contains pairs of sentences which are annotated if two sentences are similar or are not. This dataset is used for training a model, such as a Siamese BERT model [11], for semantic vector approximation. Semantic vectors are used to calculate sentence similarity.

Sentence similarity is possibly computed in a logic approach also. In logic, given two propositions a and b, $a \equiv b$ if and only if $a \rightarrow b$ and $b \rightarrow a$. Therefore, DNN model for natural language inference (NLI) should be trained to predict if two sentences do make up an entailment pair or do not. The entailment scores from prediction are possibly used for sentence similarity calculation. In this approach, an NLI dataset for training an NLI model is also needed. This NLI model is used for calculating the similarity of sentence pairs.

3   Solution

The problem is to develop an annotation tool for building a Vietnamese UDTB while annotators are not familiar with UD annotation yet. This annotation tool must provide high-quality Vietnamese UD parses from given Vietnamese sentences for speeding up annotation and tutoring inexperienced annotators. Unfortunately, UD Vietnamese VTB is not large enough to train an efficient Vietnamese UD parser. Therefore, this paper proposes a solution of using an inefficient Vietnamese UD parser to provide high-quality Vietnamese UD parses. In this solution, a sentence recommendation component will select appropriate Vietnamese sentences for sample selection before giving the samples with their predicted parses to annotators. The Vietnamese UD parser and sentence recommendation component are presented as following.

3.1 Vietnamese Universal Dependency Parser

The Vietnamese UD parser has been built by training Stanford neural network dependency parser on the UD Vietnamese VTB [8] training set. The word embeddings of Vietnamese vocabulary were extracted from PhoBERT pretrained model [12] because of two reasons. Firstly, PhoBERT's vocabulary has been built from segmented words using VnCoreNLP therefore this vocabulary is suitable to UD Vietnamese VTB [8]. Secondly, PhoBERT's word embedding layer has been trained with a huge Vietnamese text collection and with many training epochs [12] that the quality of the word embeddings is high.

Our UD parser requires the input sentences presented in CoNLL-U format. In the preprocessing step, input sentences are first tokenized, and POS tagged using VnCoreNLP. Then, the POS labels from VnCoreNLP are programmatically converted to UD POS labels. Finally, these sentences are presented in columns ID, Text, From and UPOS of CoNLL-U format. Our UD parser only does shift-reduce actions based on predicted actions from the parser's oracle. Our UD parser has LAS of 53.2% and 36.8% when evaluating with test set and development set of the UD Vietnamese VTB [8] respectively.

3.2 BERT-Based Sentence Recommendation Component

The above Vietnamese UD parser has very low results therefore the annotating samples, which will be parsed using our parser with high LAS, should be selected for minimizing the number of parsing errors so that new annotators can do practice to improving their skills. There are two features affecting sentence similarity. The first feature is the POS tag chain similarity. If two sentences have similar POS-tag chains, then they will have similar UD parses. As an example, Fig. 3 shows the UD parses of two phrases a) "*Cuộc_đời dưới vành mũ thám_tử*" (in English: "*Life under the detective hat brim.*") and b) "*Chuông điện_thoại lúc nửa đêm.*" (In English: "*phone alarm at midnight.*"). These two phrases are in UD Vietnamese VTB [8]. In Fig. 3, the POS tag chains of phrase a) and phrase b) are respectively "*NOUN ADP NOUN NOUN NOUN PUNCT*" and "*NOUN NOUN NOUN NOUN PUNCT*". These POS-tag chains are very similar, and the UD parses of these phrases are also similar. Thus, the POS-tag chain similarity should be a good feature for the proposed solution.

In this paper, the similarity of two POS tag chains is computed with Levenshtein distance. Given s_1 and s_2 are two POS tag chains of two sentences, $d(s_1, s_2)$ is the Levenshtein distance of s_1 and s_2. The POS tag chain similarity of s_1 and s_2, denoted as $SimL(s_1, s_2)$, is calculated with formular (1). The $SimL(s_1, s_2)$ is in range [0, 1]. If s_1 and s_2 are identical then $SimL(s_1, s_2) = 1$ and if s_1 and s_2 are completely different then $SimL(s_1, s_2) = 0$. For example, in Fig. 3, the POS tag chain similarity of phrase a) and phrase b) is 0.909 because their Levenshtein distance is 1 (as shown in Fig. 4) and the length of a) and b) are 6 and 5 respectively.

$$SimL(s_1 s_2) = 1 - \frac{d(s_1 s_2)}{|s_1| + |s_2|} \tag{1}$$

The second feature is the semantic similarity of two sentences. This means that two phrases having the same POS tag chain may have different UD parses because the

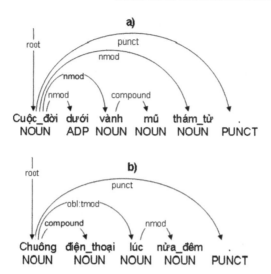

Fig. 3. The UD parses of two phrases a) *"Cuộc_đời dưới vành mũ thám_tử."* (In English: *"Life under the detective brim"*) and b) *"Chuông điện thoại lúc nửa đêm."* (In English: *"phone alarm at midnight"*)

PUNCT	6	5	4	3	2	**1**
NOUN	5	4	3	2	1	2
NOUN	4	3	2	1	1	2
NOUN	3	2	1	1	2	3
ADP	2	1	1	2	3	4
NOUN	1	0	1	2	3	4
#	0	1	2	3	4	5
	#	NOUN	NOUN	NOUN	NOUN	PUNCT

Fig. 4. The calculation of Levenshtein distance of phrase a) and phrase b) presented in Fig. 3

dependency label also depends on the meanings of head word and dependent word. For example, in Fig. 3, the phrase *"vành mũ"* (in English: *"hat brim"*) and the phrase *"lúc nửa_đêm"* (in English: *"at midnight"*) have the same POS tag chain "NOUN NOUN" but they have different parses which are respectively *compound(vành, mũ)* and *nmod(lúc, nửa_đêm)*. Therefore, the semantic similarity of two sentences should be computed for sentence selection. In this paper, the sentential semantic similarity is computed using an NLI model as mentioned in Sect. 2.3. Given p_1 is a Vietnamese sentence or phrase, p_2 is a candidate sentence or phrase to p_1, $SimS(p_2, p_1)$ is the score of the expression $p_2 \rightarrow p_1$ returned by the NLI model. This score is also used as the semantic similarity of the candidate sentence and the given sentence.

The PhoBERT$_{base}$ pretrained model has been fine-tuned on a mixed NLI dataset containing the training sets of VnNewsNLI [13] and of MultiNLI [14] translated into Vietnamese using Helsinki English-Vietnamese machine translation model[2]. The network architecture of our model is the BERT architecture for NLI problem [15]. The Vietnamese NLI model, named ViNLI, has been fine-tuned from 2 to 4 epochs to choose the best model with the accuracy of 0.95 on VnNewsNLI test set.

Our BERT-based sentence recommendation component selects samples with the Algorithm 1 Sentence recommendation. This algorithm recommends a group of sentences **RESLT** from an input sentence list **SENTs**. The criterion of choosing every sentence in **RESLT** list is that the sentence must be parsed with a high LAS when using a Vietnamese UD parser trained on a dataset **TRAIN**. This algorithm has three main steps. In the first step, the list of selecting sentences **SENTs** is word-segmented and POS-tagged with VnCoreNLP model and then it is converted to CoNLL-U format with the function *convertUPOS()*. In the second step, the POS chain similary and semantic similary of an any **TRAIN**'s sentence and an any **SENTs**' sentence are computed and then the POS chain similary and the semantic similarity of every **SENTs**' sentence to all **TRAIN**'s sentences are respectively identified as the maximum values of POS chain similarity and the semantic similarity of the **SENTs**' sentence and every **TRAIN**'s sentence. In the third step, the **SENTs**' sentences are selected if their POS chain similarity and semantic similarity are equal or greater than **MINSL** and **MINSS** respectively. The selected sentences are put into **RESLT** list. In Algorithm 1, **MINSL** and **MINSS** are chosen from experiments for good UD parsed results.

Algorithm 1 Sentence recommendation.

```
Input:
    TRAIN, a list of training sentences in CoNLL-U format.
    SENTs, a list of sentences being selected.
    ViNLI, a Vietnamese NLI model.
    VnCor, VnCoreNLP word segmentation with pos tagging model.
    MINSL, the minimum required POS chain similarity.
    MINSS, the minimum required semantic similarity.
Output:
    RESLT, a list of recommended sentences.

1    RESLT←∅
2    TEST←∅
3    for i←1 to |SENTs|  // converting SENTs to CoNLL-U format.
4        word_pos←convertUPOS(tags(VnCor, SENTs[i]))
5        TEST←TEST ∪ toCoNLLU(word_pos)
6    end for
7    TMP←∅
```

---

[2] https://huggingface.co/Helsinki-NLP/opus-mt-en-vi.

```
8   for i←1 to |SENTs|  // computes maximums of SimL and SimS
9      maxSimL←0          // of candidates. Priopritizing SimL in
10     maxSimS←0          // candidate selection.
11     poschain←getPOSChain(TEST[i])
12     words←getWords(TEST[i])
13     for j←1 to |TRAIN|
14        sl←getSimL(getPOSChain(TRAIN[j], poschain)
15        ss←getNLIScore(ViNLI, words, getWords(TRAIN[j]))
16        if sl > maxSimL then
17            maxSimL←sl
18            maxSimS←ss
19        else
20            if sl == maxSimL then
21                if ss < maxSimS then
22                  maxSimS←ss
23                end if
24            end if
25        end if
26     end for
27     TMP←TMP ∪ {(i, maxSimL, maxSimS)}
28  end for
29  for i←1 to |TMP|
30     if TMP[i][2]≥MINSL and TMP[i][3]≥MINSS then
31        RESLT←{TEST[TMP[i][1]]}
32     end if
33  return RESLT
```

4 Experiments

The experiments have been conducted with UD Vietnamese VTB [8]. The UD Vietnamese VTB training set is used for training Vietnamese UD parser and the two UD Vietnamese VTB development and test sets, respectively named as Dev and Test, are used for evaluation. A NVidia Tesla M40 24GB GPU has been used for fine-tuning ViNLI model and computing semantic similarity. For considering the effect of POS chain similarity to the LAS of UD parsed results, Dev and Test sets are divided in 20 groups and then the LAS of these groups are computed. These results are shown in Table 1. The results in Table 1 show that the LAS clearly decrease when the POS chain similarity values decrease in all two Dev and Test sets. This relation, illustrated in Fig. 5, show that the lower the POS chain similarity values, the lower the LAS of parsed sentences are.

Table 1. The effect of POS chain similarity to the LAS of UD parsed results (underlines mean there are not existing values)

Similarity range	Dev	Test	Similarity range	Dev	Test
0.95–1.00	71.43%	76.92%	0.45–0.50	36.00%	–
0.90–0.95	60.00%	75.41%	0.40–0.45	33.53%	–
0.85–0.90	30.77%	67.93%	0.35–0.40	34.96%	–
0.80–0.85	44.92%	63.55%	0.30–0.35	32.97%	–
0.75–0.80	37.11%	54.84%	0.25–0.30	–	–
0.70–0.75	41.94%	51.89%	0.20–0.25	–	–
0.65–0.70	42.07%	52.68%	0.15–0.20	–	–
0.60–0.65	39.38%	48.55%	0.10–0.15	–	–
0.55–0.60	37.36%	42.55%	0.05–0.10	–	–
0.50–0.55	35.04%	–	0.00–0.05	–	–

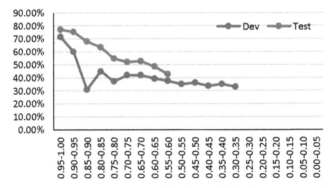

Fig. 5. The relation between POS chain similarity and LAS of recommended sentences

Similarly, for considering the effect of semantic similarity to the LAS of UD parsed results, Dev and Test sets are also divided into 20 groups and then the LAS of these groups are also computed. These results are shown in Table 2 indicating that the LAS do not clearly decrease when the semantic similarity values decrease in all two Dev and Test sets. This relation is illustrated in Fig. 6.

Table 2. The effect of semantic similarity to the LAS of UD parsed results (underlines mean there are not existing values)

Similarity range	Dev	Test	Similarity range	Dev	Test
0.95–1.00	66.67%	–	0.45–0.50	39.32%	57.89%
0.90–0.95	43.75%	–	0.40–0.45	39.13%	55.38%
0.85–0.90	40.15%	76.60%	0.35–0.40	36.72%	60.22%
0.80–0.85	40.75%	52.63%	0.30–0.35	34.62%	49.50%
0.75–0.80	41.50%	73.81%	0.25–0.30	35.52%	56.57%
0.70–0.75	35.51%	62.00%	0.20–0.25	35.57%	54.28%
0.65–0.70	37.11%	62.79%	0.15–0.20	36.23%	54.39%
0.60–0.65	37.60%	57.51%	0.10–0.15	38.35%	54.97%
0.55–0.60	39.66%	58.99%	0.05–0.10	37.48%	51.29%
0.50–0.55	36.70%	54.96%	0.00–0.05	34.40%	50.18%

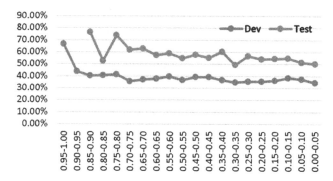

Fig. 6. The relation between semantic similarity and LAS of recommended sentences

The above results show that the semantic similarity may improve the LAS of recommended sentences while the POS chain similarity has an important role in sentence recommendation. Therefore, each sentence group having score in range [0.95, 1.0] in POS chain similarity is divided into 20 smaller groups by semantic similarity for considering the effect of these two features in LAS. The statistics of the LAS with these two features are shown in Table 3. Similarly, the statistics of the LAS with the two features where the POS chain similarity is in range [0.90, 1.0] are shown in Table 4.

The results in Table 3 and Table 4 show that the combination of two features POS-tag chain similarity and semantic similarity has affected in improving the result of sentence recommendation. If POS chain similarity and semantic similarity are high, the LAS of recommended sentences will be high. In addition, the required minimum POS chain similarity **MINSL** and the required minimum semantic similarity **MINSS** are respectively chosen of 0.95 and 0.65 according to Table 3 and Table 4. The LAS of recommended sentences of Dev set and Test set are 90.0% and 87.1% respectively.

Table 3. The effect of sentence similarity to the LAS of UD parsed results when the POS chain similarity is in range [0.95, 1.0] (underlines mean there are not existing values)

Similarity range	Dev	Test	Similarity range	Dev	Test
0.95–1.00	90.9%	–	0.45–0.50	71.4%	84.0%
0.90–0.95	90.9%	–	0.40–0.45	71.4%	84.0%
0.85–0.90	90.9%	83.3%	0.35–0.40	71.4%	80.5%
0.80–0.85	90.9%	83.3%	0.30–0.35	71.4%	80.5%
0.75–0.80	90.9%	86.5%	0.25–0.30	71.4%	76.7%
0.70–0.75	90.9%	86.4%	0.20–0.25	71.4%	76.9%
0.65–0.70	90.9%	87.1%	0.15–0.20	71.4%	76.9%
0.60–0.65	71.4%	87.9%	0.10–0.15	71.4%	76.9%
0.55–0.60	71.4%	87.5%	0.05–0.10	71.4%	76.9%
0.50–0.55	71.4%	87.5%	0.00–0.05	71.4%	76.9%

Table 4. The effect of sentence similarity to the LAS of UD parsed results when the POS chain similarity is in range [0.90, 1.0] (underlines mean there are not existing values)

Similarity range	Dev	Test	Similarity range	Dev	Test
0.95–1.00	66.7%	–	0.45–0.50	61.5%	77.4%
0.90–0.95	66.7%	–	0.40–0.45	63.6%	77.4%
0.85–0.90	66.7%	83.3%	0.35–0.40	63.6%	75.2%
0.80–0.85	66.7%	83.3%	0.30–0.35	63.6%	76.5%
0.75–0.80	66.7%	86.5%	0.25–0.30	63.6%	74.0%
0.70–0.75	66.7%	86.4%	0.20–0.25	63.6%	73.7%
0.65–0.70	66.7%	86.8%	0.15–0.20	63.6%	74.1%
0.60–0.65	61.5%	87.5%	0.10–0.15	63.6%	75.3%
0.55–0.60	61.5%	83.1%	0.05–0.10	63.6%	76.3%
0.50–0.55	61.5%	79.5%	0.00–0.05	63.6%	76.3%

These results show the efficiency of the sentence recommendation method in this paper. The recommended sentences are parsed with LAS above 87.1% when using a UD parser with LAS above 36.8%.

5   Conclusions and Future Works

In this paper, a BERT-based sentence recommendation method has been proposed for selecting sentences which will be parsed with high LAS when using an inefficient UD parser. According to the experiment results, the following conclusions may be drawn.

Firstly, the similarities of POS chain and of semantic of two sentences affect the similarity of two UD parses of these sentences. When using these two features for selecting sentences, the selected sentences are parsed with much higher LAS (above 87.1%) in comparison with the LAS (36.8%) of the parser itself. Secondly, The POS chain similarity has a stronger effect in sentence recommend than the semantic similarity. Thirdly, the reasonable values of POS chain similarity and of semantic similarity are respectively above 0.95 and above 0.65 when recommending sentences which will be parsed with higher LAS than LAS of the parser. These similarities are computed with the training set on which the UD parser was trained.

In future, this sentence recommendation method will be applied for providing UD annotators high-quality UD predicted sentences so that they can speed up the annotation process or they can learn the guidelines easily when they are beginners. All is for building a large and high-quality Vietnamese UDTB.

References

1. Do, T.T.-T., Nguyen, D.T.: Sentential semantic dependency parsing for Vietnamese. SN Comput. Sci. **2** (2021)
2. Do, T.T.-T., Nguyen, D.T.: VLO V1. 1-a Vietnamese lexicon ontology for universal dependency parsing. In: International Conference on Advanced Computing and Applications, pp. 94–100. IEEE (2020)
3. Vu, T., Nguyen, D.Q., Nguyen, D.Q., Dras, M., Johnson, M.: VnCoreNLP: a Vietnamese natural language processing toolkit. In: Conference of the North American Chapter of the Association for Computational Linguistics: Demonstrations, pp. 56–60. Association for Computational Linguistics, New Orleans (2018)
4. Nguyen, D.Q., Dras, M., Johnson, M.: An empirical study for Vietnamese dependency parsing. In: Australasian Language Technology Association Workshop, Melbourne, Australia, pp. 143–149 (2016)
5. Nguyen, P.-T., Vu, X.-L., Nguyen, T.-M.-H., Nguyen, V.-H., Le, H.-P.: Building a large syntactically-annotated corpus of Vietnamese. In: Third Linguistic Annotation Workshop, pp. 182–185. Association for Computational Linguistics, Suntec (2009)
6. Nivre, J., et al.: The CoNLL 2007 shared task on dependency parsing. In: Conference on Empirical Methods in Natural Language Processing and Computational Natural Language Learning, pp. 915–932. ACL (2007)
7. Schuster, S., Manning, C.D.: Enhanced English universal dependencies: an improved representation for natural language understanding tasks. In: International Conference on Language Resources and Evaluation, pp. 2371–2378 (2016)
8. Nguyễn, T.L., Hà, M.L., Lê, H.P., Nguyễn, T.M.H.: UD Vietnamese VTB (2018). https://uni versaldependencies.org/
9. Nguyen, D.Q., Nguyen, D.Q., Pham, S.B., Nguyen, P.-T., Le Nguyen, M.: From treebank conversion to automatic dependency parsing for Vietnamese. In: Métais, E., Roche, M., Teisseire, M. (eds.) NLDB 2014. LNCS, vol. 8455, pp. 196–207. Springer, Cham (2014). https://doi.org/10.1007/978-3-319-07983-7_26
10. Danqi, C., Manning, C.D.: A fast and accurate dependency parser using neural networks. In: Empirical Methods in Natural Language Processing, pp. 740–750 (2014)
11. Reimers, N., Gurevych, I.: Sentence-BERT: Sentence embeddings using Siamese BERT-networks. In: 2019 Conference on Empirical Methods in Natural Language Processing and the 9th International Joint Conference on Natural Language Processing, pp. 3982–3992. Association for Computational Linguistics, Hong Kong (2019)

12. Nguyen, D.Q., Nguyen, A.T.: PhoBERT: pre-trained language models for Vietnamese. In: Conference on Empirical Methods in Natural Language, pp. 1037–1042 (2020)
13. Nguyen, C.T., Nguyen, D.T.: Building a Vietnamese dataset for natural language inference models. SN Comput. Sci. **3**, 13 (2022)
14. Williams, A., Nangia, N., Bowman, S.R.: A broad-coverage challenge corpus for sentence understanding through inference. In: Conference of the North American Chapter of the Association for Computational Linguistics: Human Language Technologies, vol. 1, pp. 1112–1122. Association for Computational Linguistics, New Orleans (2018)
15. Devlin, J., Chang, M.-W., Lee, K., Toutanova, K.: BERT: pre-training of deep bidirectional transformers for language understanding. In: Conference of the North American Chapter of the Association for Computational Linguistics: Human Language Technologies, pp. 4171–4186. Association for Computational Linguistics (2019)

Evaluate the Efficiency of Hybrid Model Based on Convolutional Neural Network and Long Short-Term Memory in Information Technology Job Graph Network

Nguyen Minh Nhut[1,2], Dang Minh Quan[1,2], Le Mai Duy Khanh[1,2], and Nguyen Dinh Thuan[1,2(✉)]

[1] University of Information Technology, Ho Chi Minh City, Vietnam
thuannd@uit.edu.vn
[2] Vietnam National University, Ho Chi Minh City, Vietnam

Abstract. The advancement of technology has had a positive impact on the manner of life in society that offers more employment opportunities. It may have had an impact on Information Technology students' decisions about their ideal future careers. To help students majoring in Information Technology in Vietnam and the surrounding countries can connect and interact with recruiters to obtain jobs, we built an application called SmartCV, which uses Smart Contract in Blockchain Technology to create connection and store information. We also use several Machine Learning algorithms includes Convolutional Neural Network (CNN), Long Short-Term Memory (LSTM), Bidirectional Long Short-Term Memory (BiLSTM) to create a recommendation system that can assist individuals in choosing the right skill job. Moreover, we proposed a framework that combines Convolutional Neural Network (CNN) and Long Short-Term Memory (LSTM). The Hybrid CNN-LSTM model takes advantage of CNN's ability for feature extraction from input data and LSTM's ability for sequence learning. The dataset for training and testing is crawled from job search websites. We used classification performance metrics including Accuracy, Recall, Precision, Micro-F1 to evaluate the performance of machine learning algorithms. Final experiment results demonstrate that the Hybrid CNN-LSTM model has the highest level of accuracy.

Keywords: Recommendation System · Graph Network · IT students · Machine Learning · Job choice · CNN-LSTM

1 Introduction

Information Technology (IT) jobs are in high demand and significant in most aspects of daily life. Simultaneously, the demand for IT jobs is expanding in a broad and varied way. Recent university graduates or multi-skilled professionals find it challenging to decide which of the several IT-related job types now in demand would fit into best. Meanwhile, businesses and companies require more qualified and specialized IT jobs to meet their benefit needs. Understanding this problem, we decided to develop an application, called SmartCV, which uses Blockchain technology to connect students and businesses in a convenient and effective manner.

A blockchain is a distributed database or ledger shared among the nodes of a computer network. One key difference between a typical database and a blockchain is the way the data is structured. Blockchains collect information together in groups, called blocks, that contain sets of information. Blocks have a certain storage capacity and when filled are closed and linked to the previously filled block, forming a chain of data known as a blockchain. So, Blockchain ensures the truthfulness and security of data records and creates trust without the need for a trusted third party [1] (Fig. 1).

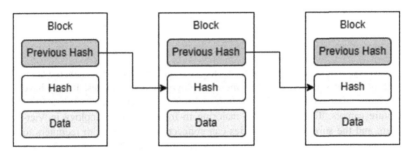

Fig. 1. Blockchain Structure.

Because of the fidelity and security of blockchain, we used it to build SmartCV application. SmartCV is a combirunsion of Smart Contracts of Block-chain Technology with each student's CV. Smart Contracts are simply programs stored on a blockchain that run when predetermined conditions are met [2]. We used Smart Contracts to build a Block-chain for data storage. In SmartCV, students fill in personal information and create their own CV. After that, student information is stored as blocks, closed and linked with previous data blocks to form a highly secure data chain (Blockchain). Additionally, we propose a recommendation system that uses machine learning algorithms to make predictions to help students choose their right job. The details on student's CV will be analyzed by the proposed system to make recommendations for suitable job. This will help the interaction between students and recruiters of the company to be more effective.

To build the proposed recommendation system, data were collected by a self-designed crawling system on job research websites in Vietnam. In previous research, we just collected data from TopDev website, this leads to lack of data. To make data more diverse and richer, in this research, we designed a crawling system to collect data from many websites like ITViec, VietnamWorks, Linkedin, … The data we collected includes IT job titles and required skills for IT jobs. We used the collected data for training and testing machine learning algorithms process. Several classification performance metrics like Accuracy, Recall, Precision and Micro-F1 are used to compare performance of models which have been trained from mentioned algorithms and our proposed hybrid framework. Our experiments demonstrate that the Hybrid CNN-LSTM model outperforms other models in the performance of job recommendation. The Hybrid

CNN-LSTM model gives the highest accuracy (96%). All experiments were conducted using the Python programming language.

2   Related Work

In our previous study [3], we proposed an application called SmartCV, which uses Smart Contract in Blockchain Technology to find jobs and connect with company recruiters for Information Technology students in Vietnam and the region. At the same time, we implemented a recommendation system using Ma-chine Learning and Statistical Analysis algorithms to help them choose a suitable job based on their skills. The experimental results of predicting students' jobs demonstrate that the Convolutional Neural Network Model (CNN) gives the highest accuracy.

Recent studies have shown an improvement in the effectiveness of combining models in predicting. To better mine the effective information contained in mas-sive data and improve the accuracy of short-term load forecasting, this paper [4] proposed a hybrid model based on convolutional neural network and long short-term memory network (CNN-LSTM) for short-term load forecasting (STLF). Convolutional neural network (CNN) is used to extract features and reshape them into vectors. The feature vectors are constructed in temporal and fed into long short-term memory network (LSTM) which is used to predict STLF. It was shown that the forecasting accuracy can be notably improved by CNN-LSTM hybrid model method.

Also, in this research [5], the suggested model merges two deep learning architectures, the long short-term memory (LSTM) and convolutional neural network (CNN) to make accurate photovoltaic power predictions. According to error metrics, MAE, MAPE, and RMSE, the suggested architecture CNN-LSTM performance exceeds standard machine learning and single deep learning models regarding prediction, precision, and stability.

Not only effective in prediction but this hybrid model is also used in recommender systems. With the ever-increasing use of the Internet and social networks that generate a vast amount of information, there is a severe need for recommendation systems. In this article [6], they proposed a hybrid movie recommender system, RSLCNet, which has been developed using CNN and LSTM architectures to simultaneously consider the users' ratings of the movies and the visual features of the movie poster and trailer. Or in this paper [7], to recommend songs based on emotions by suggesting music in keeping with the listeners' pervading mental and physical state, various deep learning models such as Long Short-Term Memory (LSTM), Convolution Neural network (CNN), CNN-LSTM, and LSTM-CNN Architectures were collated for detecting emotions such as anger, happiness, love, and sadness. The evaluation results show that the proposed approach's accuracy and effectiveness have improved compared to the best available methods.

Recently, Li, Jialin, Xueyi Li, and David He. Published an article [8] that proposes a directed acyclic graph (DAG) network that combines long short-term memory (LSTM) and a convolutional neural network (CNN) to improve the prognostic accuracy of accurate and timely prediction of remaining useful life (RUL). By comparing with existing methods using the same data set, it can be concluded that the prediction method proposed in this paper has better predictive ability.

3   Research Methodology

The proposed methodology in this study includes 3 main processes as follows: Crawl Data, Machine Learning and Blockchain. Crawl Data process involves collecting data from job seeker websites and preprocessing to get a clean dataset. Then, the models are trained and evaluated on the previously processed data set to come up with the best-performing model in the Machine Learning process. Finally, implement that model into SmartCV application. The process diagram of our research methodology is shown in Fig. 2, and the implementation and experimental study will be described below.

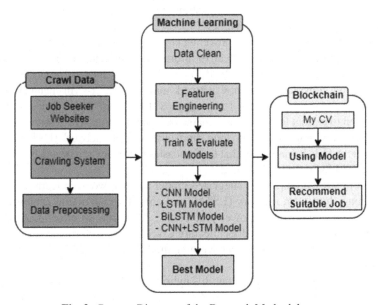

Fig. 2. Process Diagram of the Research Methodology.

3.1   Crawl Data Process

During this process, we continued to use the crawling system in the Python language designed in the previous study. This system still uses the Selenium library with XPath and adds Cascading style sheets (CSS) Selectors to increase data collection efficiency. Selenium is a web-based online testing tool. Using the Selenium web driver will reduce the time expended on crawling data. [9]. Therefore, we used it to collect a large amount of data in a short time (Fig. 3).

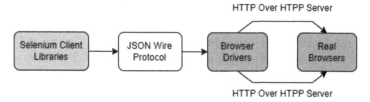

Fig. 3. Selenium WebDriver Architecture.

XPath in Selenium is a method that allows you to search and locate elements in the HTML structure of a web page. All major browsers support XPath. One of the advantages of using XPath is finding an element by its tag name using the find_element_by_xpath function [10] (Fig. 4).

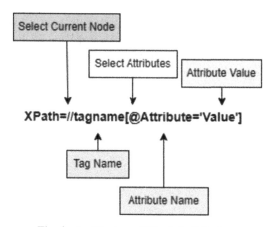

Fig. 4. Architecture of Xpath in Selenium.

Cascading style sheets (CSS) Selectors are patterns used to select HTML elements. They are often preferred in web data extraction because they are easy to prepare and have short expressions [11]. So, adding CSS Selectors and combining it with XPath in Selenium helps to find HTML tags for fast and accurate crawling (Fig. 5).

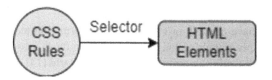

Fig. 5. Operation of CSS Selectors.

Because this article focuses on Information Technology Job Graph Network, we used this system to crawl data from reputable IT job search websites in Vietnam. In the previous study, we only collected data from TopDev - Top IT Jobs is a recruitment and employment platform dedicated to the IT field that owns 300,000 programmer profiles, with 5000 regular customers being technology companies in Vietnam and the region [12], so the number of IT jobs might not be many and diverse. Therefore, we decided to look for reputable and quality IT search websites such as ITViec, VietnamWorks, Linkedin, … to crawl richer and more diverse IT jobs for data collection. The collected data was preprocessed to get a clean dataset suitable for model building. We used Pandas - a Python library of rich data structures and tools for working with structured data sets common to statistics, finance, social sciences, and many other fields [13], to store tuples in a data frame and used functions like dropna(), drop_duplicates() to remove missing and duplicate values. In addition, we processed IT job titles by removing special words like "HOT", "Salary up to", … to reduce the number of unique IT job labels. The data preprocessing process finished with 7534 IT jobs, and the dataset used in the experiments contained 7534 records.

It can be said that the job of a developer is always the top concern of company recruiters and attracts young people who are passionate about the field of Information Technology. The career of a developer is always at the top of the most searched-for jobs on job recruitment sites. Figure 6 depicts the correlation ratio between jobs in the information technology job network.

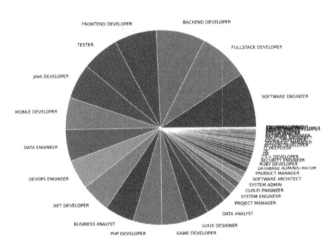

Fig. 6. Distribution of Job Types.

Developer jobs have created an attraction for information technology enthusiasts to search and study programming languages related to those jobs. Python is the most popular and easy-to-use programming language in the world [14], but the programming languages needed to become a developer like Java, C/C++, … are always top programming languages and are interesting and sought by many employers [15]. Below is a chart that shows the TOP 5 programming languages that employers are searching for now (Fig. 7):

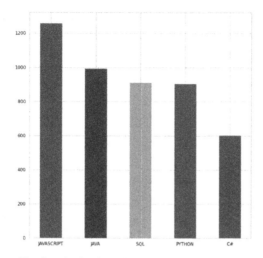

Fig. 7. Distribution of Programming Languages.

3.2 Machine Learning Process

We focused on skill-based employment forecasting in this process. Therefore, several features that weren't helpful in predicting what was best for IT students were eliminated such as company information, company location, salary range, and type of job. We used One-hot Encoding - a popular technique for handling categorical data [16, 17], where each categorical value is converted with one-time encoding to a new column, and the label values are converted to digital (1 or 0) [18], with features to match the model building.

This study aimed to develop a job recommendation system and build an In-formation Technology job graph network with the input being the skills and abilities students have and the output being suitable IT jobs to help students orient their future jobs. To do this, we used libraries in Python to implement several machine learning algorithms. In previous research, we used Machine Learning and Statistical Analysis algorithms such as Feed Forward Neural Network (FNN), Sequential (KNF), K-Nearest Neighbors (KNN), Logistic Regression (LR). After building and evaluating the models, we found that neural network models performed better in predicting the job. So, we continued to use Convolutional Neural Network Model (CNN) and researched other new neural network models to find the suitable model for this recommendation system. Finally, three machine learning algorithms were used to build the model:

- Convolutional Neural Network Model (CNN): CNN has an excellent performance in machine learning problems. Especially in the applications that deal with image data, such as the most significant image classification data set (Image Net), computer vision, and natural language processing (NLP), the results achieved were excellent [19]. Job Recommendation System is a multi-label classification problem. It is a classification that requires predicting more than one class label. In multi-label classification, zero or more labels are required as output for each input sample, and the outputs are required simultaneously. And this system also predicts related jobs based on the skills they have. CNN model is configured to support multi-label classification and can perform well, depending on the specifics of the classification task. Feature extraction of CNN is an effective approach for multilabel classification by removing fully connected layers at the top of the network. Then the output of the final convolutional layer can be used as input to a separate classifier or a multi-label classifier (Fig. 8).

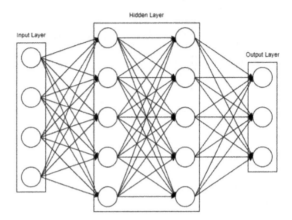

Fig. 8. Convolutional Neural Network Structure.

- Long Short-Term Memory Model (LSTM): It is a deep learning, sequential neural network that allows information to persist [20]. LSTM Model was invented with the goal of addressing the vanishing gradients problem [21]. The key insight in the LSTM design was to incorporate nonlinear, data-dependent controls into the RNN cell, which can be trained to ensure that the gradient of the objective function with respect to the state signal does not vanish [22]. LSTM can be implemented in Python using the Keras library (Fig. 9).

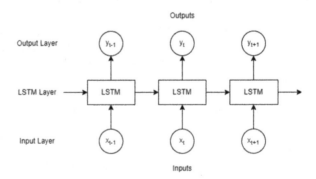

Fig. 9. Long Short-Term Memory Structure.

- Bidirectional Long Short-Term Memory Model (BiLSTM): It is a type of recurrent neural networks [23]. It processes data in two directions: one taking the input in a forward direction, and the other in a backwards direction. This is the main point of divergence with LSTM [24]. BiLSTM effectively increases the amount of information available to the network, improving the context available to the algorithm. BiLSTM has proven good results in natural language processing [25] (Fig. 10).

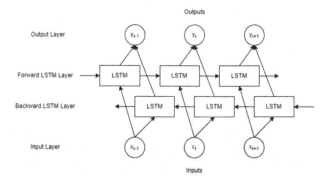

Fig. 10. Bidirectional Long Short-Term Memory Structure.

In addition, we proposed a CNN-LSTM hybrid model combines Convolutional Neural Network Model (CNN) and Long Short-Term Memory Model (LSTM) to leverage the strengths of both architectures for sequential data analysis [26]. This model takes advantage of CNN's ability to extract meaningful features from the input data and the LSTM's ability to model sequential dependencies [27] (Fig. 11).

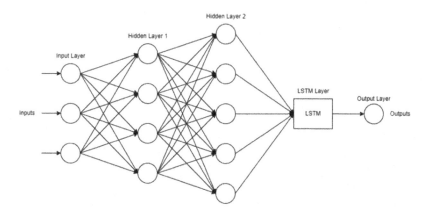

Fig. 11. CNN-LSTM Structure.

3.3 Blockchain Process

SmartCV is an application built by Smart Contracts of Blockchain technology combined with Web3 platform to help students connect with company recruiters quickly and efficiently. Students or company recruiters can use Metamask Accounts to register or login into SmartCV and each person's information is stored on the blockchain to ensure data transparency and security. We build SmartCV on Web3 platform because it brings an enabling set of technologies that has the potential to reshape many different fields. Web3 research and adoption will help it enable new models for capturing, managing, generating, iterating, and deploying research results in ways that were previously complex and difficult [28] (Fig. 12).

Fig. 12. SmartCV – Information User Page.

In SmartCV application, students can design their own beautiful and professional CVs. The information that students declare in their CVs, especially skills information, will be stored as input for the job recommendation system to run and predict IT jobs that are suitable for student's abilities. Then the prediction results of the recommendation system will be displayed on the news feed page so that students can view and choose the job application that is right for them (Fig. 13).

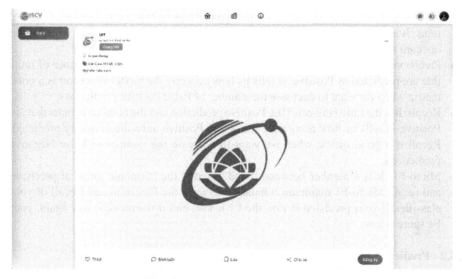

Fig. 13. SmartCV – News Feed Page.

4 Experiments and Results

In this section, we introduce the dataset, train and evaluate neural network algorithms to find the best model for this recommendation system.

4.1 Crawl Data Process

The dataset used in this study was collected by a self- designed crawling system on reputable and quality IT job research website in Vietnam. The total number of records from the crawling system is 7568 rows. When performing data preprocessing, we detected a total of 67 rows of duplicate data and no blank data. We decided to remove them from the dataset using functions including dropna() and drop_duplicates() of the Pandas library to get a clean dataset. The final dataset collected consists of 7534 rows. From the existing clean dataset, we normalize the data using One-hot Encoding. With this technique, the required skills of each job will be converted into data columns with each column name being the name of that skill, each data line representing the job title and each data cell being represented. Denoted as 0 or 1 with 0 being a job that does not require that skill and 1 being a job that requires that skill.

In this experiments, we use the handy train_test_split() function from the Python scikit-learn machine learning library to automatically build the training and evaluation datasets, randomly selecting samples [29]. Use 90% for training and the remaining 10% of the data for validation. Besides, we use the model evaluation metrics of the confusion matrix including accuracy, recall, precision, and micro-F1 in our experiments to evaluate and compare algorithms. Further explanation of the measurements is as follows [30, 31]:

- Accuracy: It is the ratio between correct predictions and the total number of predictions. It is a good performance metric for data that is not imbalanced or when we do not care about class distribution.
- Precision: It is the ratio between True Positive prediction and the number of units that are predicted as Positive. It tells us how accurate the model Precision is a good metric when we want to decrease the number of False Positive predictions.
- Recall: It is the ratio between True Positive prediction and the number of units that are Positive. It tells us how accurately the actual Positive units are correctly predicted. Recall is a good metric when we want to decrease the number of False Negative predictions.
- Micro-F1: It is a number between 0 and 1 and is the harmonic mean of precision and recall. Micro-F1 maintains a balance between the Precision and Recall of your classifier. If your precision is low, the F1 is low, and if the recall is low again, your F1 score is low.

4.2 Predictive Analytics

Four neural network algorithms and others in the previous study were trained and tested to predict the most suitable job for Information Technology students. CNN Model, LSTM Model, BiLSTM Model, and CNN-LSTM Hybrid Model among others were trained using a dataset of 6805 IT jobs to select the best model for the job recommendation system.

Table 1. Comparison Algorithms.

Model	Accuracy	Recall	Precision	Micro-F1
FNN	0.90	0.88	0.85	0.86
Sequential	0.91	0.88	0.84	0.85
KNN	0.92	0.91	0.88	0.89
Logistic Regression	0.91	0.86	0.84	0.85
CNN (Old)	093	0.91	0.88	0.89
CNN (New)	0.95	0.91	0.93	0.91
LSTM	0.88	0.78	0.83	0.79
BiLSTM	0.90	0.84	0.87	0.85
CNN-LSTM	**0.96**	**0.92**	**0.96**	**0.92**

Table 1 shows the evaluation results of the algorithms after training and testing: CNN Model, LSTM Model, BiLSTM Model, CNN-LSTM Hybrid Model, and others in the previous study. According to the results shown in the evaluation table, we can see that improving the quality of the dataset such as collecting data from more sources, and more rigorous preprocessing, … has helped the CNN Model work more effectively in predicting, with accuracy score increased from 0.93 to 0.95 and other stats also increased by about 4–5%. Importantly, the performance of the proposed CNN-LSTM architecture outperforms single machine learning models in predictability, accuracy, and stability, with an Accuracy score is 96%, a Recall score is 92%, a Precision score is 96%, and a Micro-F1 score is 92%.

At the end of our experiments, the CNN-LSTM Hybrid Model gave the best performance. This proved that the combination of these two models worked more effectively and gives better results in predicting IT jobs. So, we decided to use this algorithm to build a model and apply this model to SmartCV to run the job recommendation system.

5   Conclusion

Choosing an IT job that suits your ability is always a dilemma for students of information technology, especially final-year students and fresh graduates because if there is no orientation, specifically, they may go astray. Therefore, the development of an efficient, accurate job recommendation system and information technology job graph network has always been of great interest to employers and candidates in recent years.

This paper presents and implements Machine Learning algorithms, mainly neural network models and especially the combination of Convolutional Neural Network Model (CNN) and Long Short-Term Memory Model (LSTM), to get an effective prediction. In addition, we have also evaluated and compared algorithms with each other through the evaluation indicators of the confusion matrix including Accuracy, Precision, Recall, and Micro-F1. The experimental results showed that the CNN-LSTM Hybrid Model is better than other algorithms for accuracy. Therefore, it can be concluded that the CNN-LSTM Hybrid Model can perform better than other algorithms in predicting.

To make the most accurate and efficient predictions possible in the future, we will keep reviewing and improving the quality of the input data, add some other features, and continue to train and evaluate the algorithms based on other evaluation indicators. Additionally, we will upgrade the programming to predict each job for IT students, such as capacity, level, working position, and salary range. At the same time, the Job Recommendation System will be implemented with more algorithms and researched combining algorithms together to get the most accurate numbers possible and apply them to develop the SmartCV application comprehensively and effectively.

Acknowledgement. This research is funded by Vietnam National University Ho Chi Minh City (VNU-HCM) under grant number DS2022-26-03.

References

1. Hayes, A.: Blockchain facts: what is it, how it works, and how it can be used (2022). https://www.investopedia.com/terms/b/blockchain.asp.
2. IBM, What are smart contracts on blockchain? (2022). https://www.ibm.com/topics/smart-contracts
3. Thuan, N.D., Nhut, N.M., Quan, D.M.: Using blockchain and artificial intelligence to build a job recommendation system for students in information technology. In: 2022 RIVF International Conference on Computing and Communication Technologies (RIVF). IEEE (2022)

4. Lu, J., et al: A hybrid model based on convolutional neural network and long short-term memory for short-term load forecasting. In: 2019 IEEE Power & Energy Society General Meeting (PESGM). IEEE (2019)
5. Agga, A., et al.: CNN-LSTM: an efficient hybrid deep learning architecture for predicting short-term photovoltaic power production. Electr. Power Syst. Res. **208**, 107908 (2022)
6. Daneshvar, H., Ravanmehr, R.: A social hybrid recommendation system using LSTM and CNN. Concurr. Comput.: Pract. Exp. **34**(18), e7015 (2022)
7. Joshi, S., Jain, T., Nair, N.: Emotion based music recommendation system using LSTM-CNN architecture. In: 2021 12th International Conference on Computing Communication and Networking Technologies (ICCCNT). IEEE (2021)
8. Li, J., Li, X., He, D.: A directed acyclic graph network combined with CNN and LSTM for remaining useful life prediction. IEEE Access **7**, 75464–75475 (2019)
9. Nyamathulla, S., et al.: A review on selenium web driver with python (2021)
10. Gundecha, U.: Learning Selenium Testing Tools with Python: A Practical Guide on Automated Web Testing with Selenium Using Python. Packt Publishing (2014)
11. Uzun, E.: A regular expression generator based on CSS selectors for efficient extraction from HTML pages. Turk. J. Electr. Eng. Comput. Sci. **28**(6), 3389–3401 (2020)
12. TopDev, TopDev –Top IT Jobs. https://topdev.vn/
13. McKinney, W.: Pandas: a foundational Python library for data analysis and statistics. Python High Perform. Sci. Comput. **14**(9), 1–9 (2011)
14. Vlasova, A., et al.: Lupa: a framework for large scale analysis of the programming language usage. In: 2022 IEEE/ACM 19th International Conference on Mining Software Repositories (MSR) (2022)
15. Zaveria: Top 10 programming languages in 2023 with the largest developer communities (2023)
16. Farahnakian, F., Heikkonen, J.: A deep auto-encoder based approach for intrusion detection system. In: 2018 20th International Conference on Advanced Communication Technology (ICACT) (2018)
17. Rodríguez, P., et al.: Beyond one-hot encoding: lower dimensional target embedding (2018)
18. Al-Shehari, T., Alsowail, R.A.: An insider data leakage detection using one-hot encoding, synthetic minority oversampling and machine learning techniques (2021)
19. Albawi, A., et al.: Understanding of a convolutional neural network. In: 2017 International Conference on Engineering and Technology (ICET) (2017)
20. Saxena, S.: Learn about long short-term memory (LSTM) algorithms (2021)
21. Sherstinsky, A.: Fundamentals of recurrent neural network (RNN) and long short-term memory (LSTM) network. Phys. D **404**, 132306 (2020)
22. Schmidhuber, J., Hochreiter, S.: Long short-term memory. Neural Comput. **9**(8), 1735–1780 (1997)
23. Schuster, M., Paliwal, K.K.: Bidirectional recurrent neural networks. IEEE Trans. Signal Process. **45**(11), 2673–2681 (1997)
24. Rhanoui, M., et al.: A CNN-BiLSTM model for document-level sentiment analysis. Mach. Learn. Knowl. Extract. **1**(3), 832–847 (2019)
25. Tai, K.S., Socher, R., Manning, C.D.: Improved semantic representations from tree-structured long short-term memory networks. arXiv preprint arXiv:1503.00075 (2015)
26. Parida, L., et al.: A novel CNN-LSTM hybrid model for prediction of electro-mechanical impedance signal based bond strength monitoring. Sensors **22**(24), 9920 (2022)
27. Alhussein, M., Aurangzeb, K., Haider, S.I.: Hybrid CNN-LSTM model for short-term individual household load forecasting. IEEE Access **8**, 180544–180557 (2020)
28. Filipčić, S.: Web3 & DAOs: an overview of the development and possibilities for the implementation in research and education (2022)

29. Garreta, R., Moncecchi, G.: Learning Scikit-Learn: Machine Learning in Python. Packt Publishing Ltd. (2013)
30. B. T, Comprehensive Guide on Multiclass Classification Metrics, Medium (2023). https:// towardsdatascience.com/comprehensive-guide-on-multiclass-classification-metrics-af94cf b83fbd
31. Grandini, M., Bagli, E., Visani, G.: Metrics for multi-class classification: an overview. arXiv (2020). https://doi.org/10.48550/arXiv.2008.05756

A Dataset of Vietnamese Documents for Text Detection

Anh Le[1(✉)], Dang Tran Hai Mai[2], and Thanh Lam[2]

[1] NTT Hi-Tech Institute, Nguyen Tat Thanh University, 300A Nguyen Tat Thanh, District 4, Ho Chi Minh City, Vietnam
leducanh841988@gmail.com
[2] Deep Learning and Applications, Ho Chi Minh City, Vietnam

Abstract. Document analysis and recognition is a crucial technique for automating the input process of forms, receipts, documents at banks, governments, companies. With demands in both research and industry, there are available datasets for Document Analysis and Recognition in English, Chinese, Arabic, and Indic. However, there is no publicly datasets for Vietnamese Document Analysis and Recognition. In this paper, we introduce a new dataset for Vietnamese Document analysis named VNDoc, which aims to set up a standard dataset for researching and developing Vietnamese Document Analysis Systems. The dataset contains 226 documents scanned from mobile phones and scan machines. The documents are collected from diverse categories such as legal and administrations, invoices, resumes, handwriting forms, and so on, which target various applications. At the first stage, we provide ground truth for text lines, which allow performing research in text detection and layout analysis. Moreover, we describe a statistical analysis of text length and bounding box in the dataset and initial experiments for the existing methods for text detection. We are going to provide text transcriptions and available for research communities.

Keywords: Vietnamese document analysis and recognition · dataset · text detection

1 Introduction

With the growth of digital transformation, the demands of process automation have been increasing to save human effort and cost. For example, employees in banks need to input manually many forms and documents form clients every day. We can make autonomous this process to save time for both employees as well as clients. Therefore, document analysis and recognition is the crucial technology to automate the input process from documents.

For Document analysis, text detection, layout analysis, and text recognition are basic tasks. Datasets play a crucial role in training and evaluating new methods for document analysis. As a result, researchers have constructed databases

---

A. Le and D. T. H. Mai—These authors contributed equally to this work.

© The Author(s), under exclusive license to Springer Nature Singapore Pte Ltd. 2023
T. K. Dang et al. (Eds.): FDSE 2023, CCIS 1925, pp. 418–429, 2023.
https://doi.org/10.1007/978-981-99-8296-7_30

in different languages for general tasks of document analysis, such as layout analysis, text detection, and text recognition. For example, the University of Washington (UWASH) dataset [1], PRImA Layout Analysis Dataset [2], Pub-LayNet dataset [3] for English, a dataset for Arabic Printed Character Recognition [4] and so on. Table 1 summaries tasks, languages, annotations on different datasets for the common tasks of document analysis. Most of the datasets are for English. The common tasks are layout analysis, text detection, and recognition. As a result, many publications on those datasets have been published based on the above datasets [8,9].

Table 1. Related languages, tasks, annotation, and size of public datasets.

Dataset	Language	Tasks	Annotation
[1]	English	Layout analysis, text recognition, logical analysis, and font detection	Words, text lines and Paragraphs
[3]	English	Layout analysis	Paragraphs
[4]	Arabic	Text recognition	Words and text lines
[5]	English	Document detection and text recognition	Page transcriptions
[2]	English	Layout analysis	Paragraphs
[6]	Latin	ID card detection and recognition	Text lines
[7]	English	Document understanding	Text lines

The above datasets are useful for text detection and recognition of common languages such as English. For a less popular language such as Vietnamese, the absence of public datasets is a serious problem that directly affects the research outcomes. Researchers do not have samples for training and evaluating and comparing their methods with others. As a result, there are few publications and research outcomes. The Vietnamese language is currently spoken and written by around 100 million people. The demand for applications on document analysis is increasing, since governments, banks, and companies need to optimize human resources on document digitizing and management. We overserve only a few private offline datasets for Vietnamese handwritten characters [10,11], and a public dataset and research for Vietnamese online handwriting (VNonDB) [12, 13]. To speed up the research state and encourage researchers to get involved in the field, building the benchmark dataset is the initial effort.

In this research, we aim to construct a dataset of Vietnamese documents that allow performing research in many tasks such as document image classification, text detection, layout analysis, and text recognition. Moreover, The dataset is collected from diverse contents, which allows building diverse applications of Vietnamese document analysis. Moreover, we test the state of the art text detection methods on our dataset. The initial experimental results and discussion are helpful for future research on this dataset.

The rest of this paper is organized as follows. The dataset design principle and analysis are presented in Sect. 2. The initial experiments on text detection are presented in Sect. 3. Experimental results and discussion are present in Sect. 4, and conclusions are drawn in Sect. 5.

2   Overview of the Dataset

2.1   Dataset Design Principle

Our work aims to provide a standard dataset for Vietnamese document analysis. Therefore, we try to set up a list of requirements to make a general dataset for multi tasks such as document classification, text detection, and recognition. This section presents the requirements for the dataset collection process. The first part is the requirements of image collection:

We define the following requirements since we target multiple applications and multiple tasks.

1) The image must be captured by scan machine or mobile phone, not be in any form or word or pdf converted version, since practical application on document almost input document from scan machines or mobile phones.
2) The image must be in the form of the full document and contain machine printed or handwritten text.
3) The document may contain noises, but the text in the document must be readable.

The second part is the requirements of ground truth:

1) Bounding box and transcription must be provided for every text.
2) The bounding box for text is required to cover the text as well as Diacritical marks (DMs) and minimize overlapping with the neighboring box.
3) To retrieve high-quality images, we used scanned text images to obtain three different sources: companies, schools/universities, the Vietnamese government. We sample the top four main categories: administration, law, contract, and others (publication, CV, handwriting form, ...). The result was 226 images, which are divided into two main groups: camera(using scan application from the mobile phone) and scan(using scan machine). Scanned documents have 195 images, while cameras captured documents have 31 images. The documents are captured from different angles and light conditions to increase the difficulties for the recognition systems. We partitioned the articles randomly into a training set (80%), a development set (10%), and a test set (10%).

2.2   Ground Truth Preparation

We resize all images by setting its short side to 800 and maximal size to 2000 while keeping its original aspect ratio.

We used the LabelImg tool [14] to create the bounding box for text detection. We required three different labels for detection: text label, signature label, and seal label. The label is in the straight rectangle form that covers the whole object. These above objects can be in different sizes and directions so that the bounding boxes have different sizes in both vertical and horizontal directions. During the ground truth preparation process, all of the listed requirements in the previous section must be satisfied.

On each image, the ground truth file contains the following information: folder name, file name, document category, image size, bounding box (xmin, ymin, xmax, ymax) of text, and its transcription. At the current state, we have not provided transcriptions, so we set this tag as "unknown". Figure 1 shows an example of a ground truth format. Figure 2 shows an example of a document and its ground truth bounding boxes.

```
<annotation>
    <folder>camera</folder>
    <filename>camera1.jpg</filename>
    <path>/Users/DeepLearningGroup/camera1.jpg</path>
    <source>
        <database>legal</database>
    </source>
    <size>
        <width>720</width>
        <height>960</height>
        <depth>3</depth>
    </size>
    <object>
        <name>Text</name>
        <Trans>Unknown<Trans>
        <bndbox>
            <xmin>54</xmin>
            <ymin>81</ymin>
            <xmax>285</xmax>
            <ymax>136</ymax>
        </bndbox>
    </object>
    <object>
        <name>Text</name>
        <Trans>Unknown<Trans>
        <bndbox>
            <xmin>307</xmin>
            <ymin>79</ymin>
            <xmax>664</xmax>
            <ymax>105</ymax>
        </bndbox>
    </object>
```

Fig. 1. An example of ground truth format.

2.3 Dataset Analysis

To understand the characteristics of the dataset, we explore different perspectives to evaluate its sustainability for text detection research in the Vietnamese language.

1) Content diversity: In Vietnamese documents, the most popular printed documents are from legal and administrative document types from government and companies. Therefore, the percentage of the documents that belong to

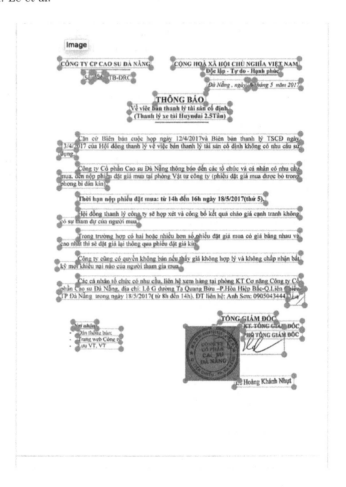

Fig. 2. An example of a document with ground truth bounding boxes.

Table 2. The distribution of document categories

Category	Num of Documents	Ratio
Legal	92	0.41
Administrative	94	0.42
Contract	14	0.06
Recruitment	4	0.02
Others (Handwriting form, CV, and so on)	20	0.09

the legal and administrative groups take into account 42% and 41%, respectively. To maintain the diversity of the dataset, we also collected from other types that are not popular such as invoice, CV, handwriting form.

Table 2 shows the distribution of document categories. This can be used for the document image classification task.

2) Distribution of text objects: The distribution of the number of text lines per document is shown in Fig. 3. We categorize the range into four main ranges: (<20), (20–50), (50–80), (>80) text lines per document. The number of text lines per document is from 10 to 105, since our data set contains various documents from several text lines to more than 100 text lines.

3) Distribution of bounding box size: In the ground truth preparation, we created the rectangle bounding box, which contains the text object. Typically, a bounding box should contain one line of text. However, the direction of the text line is varied from document to document, which leads to the various sizes of the bounding box to satisfy the requirements of ground truth preparation. Figure 4 shows the distribution of the bounding box size of the dataset. This information is useful for design anchor box for object detection based methods such as YOLO, Single Shot Detection.

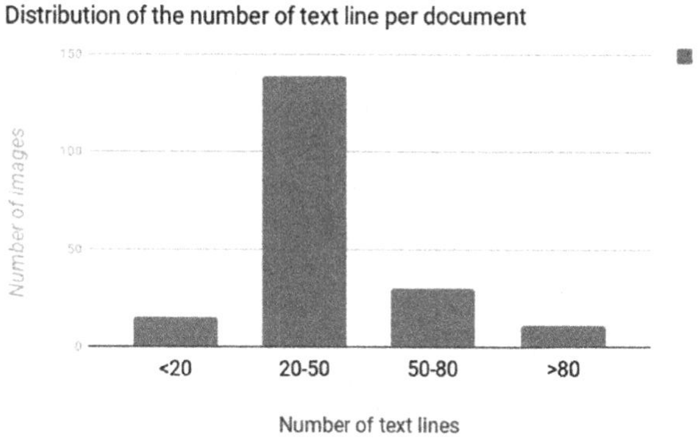

Fig. 3. Distribution of text objects.

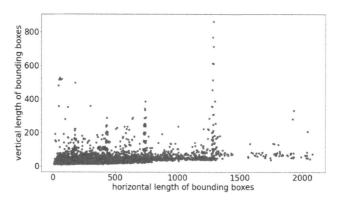

Fig. 4. Distribution of bounding box sizes.

The length and height of bounding boxes are entirely various, but most of them are distributed in the range below 1500 pixels for horizontal length and the range below 70 pixels for vertical length. These values are quite varied because the font size of the text is different from document to document, and it is even different from part to part in one document. Therefore, it will require a robust method to detect multiple size and scale of text lines.

3   Overview of Text Detection Methods for Initial Experiments

We applied some state-of-the-art text detection methods and set up standard evaluation metrics for our dataset. This will be a baseline for future research on our dataset.

3.1   Connectionist Text Proposal Network (CTPN)

CTPN detects a text line by splitting text lines into sequences of fine-scale text proposals [15]. A vertical anchor mechanism that jointly predicts location and text/non-text score of each text proposal was proposed to improve localization accuracy. To improve the performance, they integrate the baseline network with recurrent connectionist text proposals and side-refinement. We followed the architecture presented in the CTPN paper. The pre-trained VGG16 network is used for feature extraction, and three key factors are employed to make text localization more reliable and accurate: detecting text in fine-scale proposals, recurrent connectionist text proposals, and side-refinement. We split bounding boxes of text lines into smaller boxes that have the same width as 10 pixels.

The model loss is optimized using Adam optimization with the initial learning rate 10^{-5} in the first 30K iteration, and the learning rate is reduced with a decay rate of 0.1 after each 30K iteration. To improve the performance, we applied the exponential moving average to adjust neural network weights after each training step. The model was implemented in Tensorflow.

3.2   An Efficient and Accurate Scene Text Detector (EAST)

EAST is a simple pipeline that yields fast and accurate text detection in natural scenes [16]. A Fully Convolutional Network directly predicts arbitrary orientations and quadrilateral shapes of text lines. The intermediate steps, such as candidate aggregation and word partitioning, are eliminated. In the original paper, the authors explored on PVANET, PVANET2x, VGG16 as feature extraction. In our experiment, we followed the same concept but built on a ResNet50 as feature extraction. We used Adam optimizer to optimize dice loss instead of balanced binary cross-entropy loss. The model was trained on 800 epochs with a batch size of 8, an initial learning rate of 10^{-4}, and a decay rate of 0.94. It was implemented in Keras.

3.3   PixelLink: Detecting Scene Text via Instance Segmentation

PixelLink detects text through instance segmentation, where predicted positive pixels are joined together into text instances using positive links [17]. Bounding boxes are then directly extracted from this segmentation result. We followed the same concept and VGG16 as feature extraction. After segmentation, the post-filtering process removes detected boxes whose shorter side is less than 5 pixels or area is smaller than 20. Regarding model optimization, we used Stochastic Gradient Descent with a learning rate of 10^{-3}, a momentum of 0.9, a weight decay of 10^{-4}. The model was implemented in TensorFlow.

3.4   Fast Oriented Text Spotting with a Unified Network (FOTS)

FOTS is a unified end-to-end trainable network for simultaneous detection and recognition [18]. The network learns more generic features through a convolutional neural network, which shares between text detection and text recognition. The backbone of the shared network is ResNet50. There are four main parts: shared convolutions, the text detection branch, ROIRotate operation, and text recognition branch. For our task, we employ only the detection branch. We implemented the same base network and concept from the original paper and trained end-to-end on our dataset. The model loss is optimized using Adam optimization with an initial learning rate 10^{-4} in the first 10K iteration, and the learning rate is reduced with a decay rate of 0.94. The model was implemented in Pytorch.

3.5   Tesseract OCR

Tesseract OCR is a Python tool to read and recognize text from the images [19]. In this experiment, we employ the pretrained Tesseract OCR to test on our test set without any training step.

4   Experiment Results

4.1   Dataset

We train all models and evaluate them on our dataset (except Tesseract OCR, which we just performed on our test set). The dataset is divided into three sets: training, validation, and testing sets, with the ration as 8:1:1, respectively. We scale all images and ground truths to 700×1280.

4.2   Evaluation Metrics

We employed Tightness-aware Intersection-over-Union (TIoU) Metric for evaluation, which has some improvements: completeness of ground truth, compactness of detection, and tightness of matching degree. The harmonic mean of recall and precision is calculated as follows:

$$Hmean = 2 \frac{Recall \times Precision}{Recall + Precision} \tag{1}$$

$$Hmean = \frac{\sum P_{Match_i}}{Num} \tag{2}$$

$$Precision = \frac{\sum P_{Match_{dt_i}}}{Num_{dt}} \tag{3}$$

where $Match_i$ and $Match_{dt_i}$ indicate the result of the match between detection and ground truth rectangles under TIoU conditions.

4.3   Results and Discussion

Fig. 5. An example result from the EAST model.

Table 3 shows the result of CTPN, EAST, Pixel link, FOST, and Tesseract OCR on our dataset. The EAST and FOST achieved 57.6% and 58.4% of TIoU-Hmean. The result of Pixel link is not good since they detect words instead of text lines. The performance of the Tesseract OCR is low since we did not re-train on our dataset.

Figure 5 and 6 show the good results of EAST and FOTS. Although EAST and FOTS provide high performance, we observed that they still have the following disadvantages. For long text lines, the bounding boxes do not cover the left-most and right-most words. Therefore, there is a large room for further improvements in our dataset. These results are the first published detection accuracy results for the VNDoc dataset. We believe that this will serve as a baseline for further research on Vietnamese document analysis and recognition.

Fig. 6. An example result from the FOTS model.

Table 3. The results of text detection.

Methods	TIoU-Recall (%)	TIoU-Precision (%)	TIoU-Hmean (%)
CTPN	44.0	56.7	49.6
EAST	50.8	66.5	57.6
Pixel link	35.7	18.1	24
FOTS	51.7	67.1	58.4
Tesseract OCR	31.8	4.2	7.4

5   Conclusion

The main goal of this paper is to introduce a new dataset for Vietnamese document analysis and recognition. The VNDoc dataset contains 266 documents collected from diverse sources. To the best of our knowledge, this is the first publicly available dataset for Vietnamese document analysis and recognition. Moreover, we employ some state-of-the-art text detection methods to test our dataset. We believe this dataset will help speed up research and application of Vietnamese document processing in the future.

References

1. Phillips, T., et al.: English document database design and implementation methodology. In: Proceedings of the 2nd Annual Symposium on Document Analysis and Information Retrieval, Las Vegas, USA, pp. 65–104 (1993)
2. Antonacopoulos, A., et al.: A realistic dataset for performance evaluation of document layout analysis. In: 10th International Conference on Document Analysis and Recognition (2009)
3. Zhong, X., et al.: PubLayNet: largest dataset ever for document layout analysis. In: 15th International Conference on Document Analysis and Recognition (2019)
4. AbdelRaouf, A., Higgins, C.A., Khalil, M.: A database for Arabic printed character recognition. In: Campilho, A., Kamel, M. (eds.) ICIAR 2008. LNCS, vol. 5112, pp. 567–578. Springer, Heidelberg (2008). https://doi.org/10.1007/978-3-540-69812-8_56
5. Burie, J.C., et al.: ICDAR2015 competition on smartphone document capture and OCR (SmartDoc). In: International Conference on Document Analysis and Recognition (2015)
6. Arlazarov, V.V., et al.: MIDV-500: a dataset for identity documents analysis and recognition on mobile devices in video stream. arXiv:1807.05786 (2019)
7. Jaume, G., et al.: FUNSD: a dataset for form understanding in noisy scanned documents. In: 2019 International Conference on Document Analysis and Recognition Workshops (2019)
8. Liang, J., et al.: UW-ISL document image analysis toolbox: an experimental environment. In: The 4th International Conference on Document Analysis and Recognition (1997)
9. Clausner, C., et al.: Scenario driven in-depth performance evaluation of document layout analysis methods. In: The International Conference on Document Analysis and Recognition, pp. 1404–1408 (2011)

10. Nguyen, D.K., Bui, T.D.: On the problem of classifying Vietnamese online hand-written characters. In: Proceedings - 2008 10th International Conference on Control, Automation, Robotics and Vision, ICARCV 2008, no. December, pp. 803–808 (2008)
11. Tran, D.C.: An efficient method for on-line Vietnamese handwritten character recognition. In: Proceedings of the Third International Symposium on Information and Communication Technology, p. 135 (2012)
12. Nguyen, H.T., et al.: A database of unconstrained Vietnamese online handwriting and recognition experiments by recurrent neural networks. Pattern Recogn. **78**, 291–306 (2018)
13. Le, A.D., et al.: Recognizing unconstrained Vietnamese handwriting by attention based encoder-decoder model. In: ACOMP (2018)
14. LaeblImg tool. https://github.com/tzutalin/labelImg
15. Tian, Z., Huang, W., He, T., He, P., Qiao, Yu.: Detecting text in natural image with connectionist text proposal network. In: Leibe, B., Matas, J., Sebe, N., Welling, M. (eds.) ECCV 2016. LNCS, vol. 9912, pp. 56–72. Springer, Cham (2016). https://doi.org/10.1007/978-3-319-46484-8_4
16. Zhou, X., et al.: EAST: an efficient and accurate scene text detector. In: International Conference on Computer Vision and Pattern Recognition (2017)
17. Deng, D., et al.: PixelLink: detecting scene text via instance segmentation. In: The Thirty-Second AAAI Conference on Artificial Intelligence (2018)
18. Liu, X., et al.: FOTS: fast oriented text spotting with a unified network. In: International Conference on Computer Vision and Pattern Recognition (2018)
19. Tesseract OCR. https://pypi.org/project/pytesseract/

Data Analytics and Healthcare Systems

Personalized Stress Detection System Using Physiological Data from Wearable Sensors

Vinh Pham[1], Yongho Lee[1,2], and Tai-Myoung Chung[1,2(✉)]

[1] Department of Computer Science and Engineering, Sungkyunkwan University,
Suwon, Republic of Korea
{vinhpham,yohlee}@g.skku.edu, tmchung@skku.edu
[2] Hippo T&C, Inc., Suwon, Republic of Korea

Abstract. Thanks to advancements in wearable technologies and biosensors, the accurate collection of physiological data is now more available and convenient than ever before. Thus, it has become more practical to use artificial intelligence technology to analyze physiological data collected from wearable elements. This could be beneficial to a large number of patients suffering from psychiatric disorders who experience high levels of pressure and stress in the modern era, as it allows for timely identification and intervention. Federated learning is a state-of-the-art machine learning paradigm that helps solve the impracticality of collecting personal physiological data, in a privacy respecting and distributed manner, for implementing artificial intelligence-powered healthcare applications. However, healthcare solutions based on federated learning still face accuracy problems as while physiological data varies from person to person, the averaging strategy of general federated learning algorithms cannot converge into an effective one-for-all solution model. To address this issue, we propose a stress detection system that integrates personalized federated learning algorithms. This system tailors the stress detection mechanism to each individual's physiological data, thus improving the accuracy and overall performance of the entire system. To evaluate our proposed system, we conducted extensive simulations using a physiological dataset of drivers who were stressed while driving on crowded streets. The experiment results demonstrated that our proposed system improves stress detection accuracy by more than 5% compared to a typical federated learning system.

Keywords: Physiological Sensors · Wearable · Federated Learning · Artificial Intelligence · Machine Learning

1 Introduction

Stress is considered to be an emotional state deserving of special attention, as it can have harmful effects on human health when experienced over a long period of time. Stress can also lead to general health risks, including headaches, sleep disorders, and cardiovascular diseases. Continuous monitoring of emotions,

T. K. Dang et al. (Eds.): FDSE 2023, CCIS 1925, pp. 433–441, 2023.
https://doi.org/10.1007/978-981-99-8296-7_31

specifically stress stage, can help patients suffering from psychiatric disorders better understand themselves and promote the emotional well-being of the general public. Recent advancements in wearable technologies and biosensors enable a decent level of stress detection.

Due to inherent differences in human physiology, signals obtained from wearable sensors are distinct between individuals. Even if we acquire a sufficient amount of data from various individuals (subject-independent) to construct an AI (artificial intelligence) stress detection model, its performance on data specific to a person cannot be guaranteed. The AI model works best if trained on each individual's data (subject-dependent). However, collecting enough individual data to train an effective AI model is neither practical nor cost-efficient, posing a significant challenge to designing and implementing an AI-empowered stress detection system for physiological data.

In this work, we propose a novel personalized FL (federated learning) stress detection system that initially leverages subject-independent data from multiple users to initialize a common AI detection model, and then allows individual users to fine-tune their respective models using their private data. We conducted experiments using physiological data collected by wearable device sensors from drivers who experienced stress while driving on narrow streets with a lot of red lights, vehicles, pedestrians, motorcycles, bikes, etc., to evaluate our proposed system. The results demonstrate that our system outperforms typical FL systems.

2   Related Work

2.1   Literature Review

Emognition [9] is one of the first systems that employ consumer-grade wearable devices for collecting user physiological data, and then employs AI models for recognizing emotions in everyday life. Ninh et.al. [8] raised a question about the effectiveness and accuracy of two approaches, subject-dependent and subject-independent data collection, for developing machine learning models for stress detection problems.

Incorporating the findings of previous works, we designed and proposed our novel stress detection system [5] based on the FL paradigm. Our system harmonizes the two previously mentioned approaches by allowing multiple users to share their private physiological data in a privacy-preserving manner, jointly improving the accuracy of the stress detection machine learning model.

In this work, we take a step further in improving the performance of our system by upgrading the previous basic FL algorithm to personalized FL algorithms (APPLE [7], Ditto [6], FedAMP [4], FedProto [10], FedRep [1], PerAvg [2]). These algorithms optimize the learning process by favoring each user's own data, thus increasing the stress detection performance on an individual level.

2.2   Dataset

The AffectiveROAD dataset [3] contains 13 sets of physiological data, including but not limited to Blood Volume Pulse (BVP), Electrodermal Activity (EDA), and Body Temperature, collected from drivers as they drove through the same narrow streets with high traffic, which is presumed to induce a high level of stress. Each set of data also includes a continuous stress metric that is self-assessed and validated by the drivers themselves, ranging from 0 (no stress) to 1 (extremely stressful). Figure 1 visualizes the continuous stress metric from the Driver 2 to Driver 6. The metrics over time differ between these drivers, confirming the idea that stress is a subjective feeling and varies from person to person, even with the same stimuli.

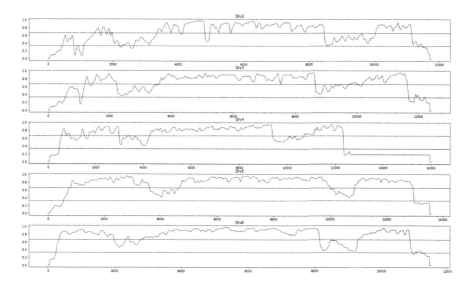

Fig. 1. Stress metric from Driver 2 to 6.

3   System Design

Previously, we introduced our proposed system in [5], which was constructed based on the FL concept. The system monitored the physiological data of each user using sensors embedded inside the wearable device throughout their daily life. The custom mobile application (Fig. 2a) associated with the wearable device was responsible for capturing and processing physiological data. Periodically, the custom mobile application acted as a client in the FL model and collaborated with the server in jointly learning between other clients to enhance the stress detecting performance of their own machine learning model by incorporating newly collected data from the user.

We empower our proposed system with personalized FL algorithms rather than solely employing the canonical FedAvg, which would significantly improve the performance of each client's model on their own user's data (subject-dependent), while still reinforcing the performance of the global model on the majority of aggregation from all user's data (subject-independent).

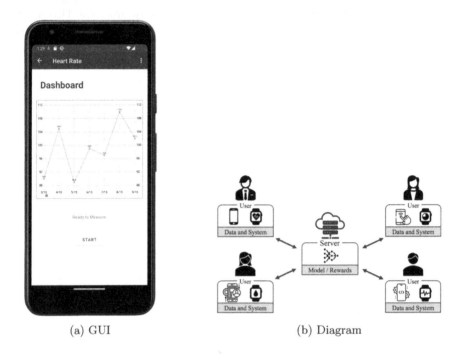

(a) GUI   (b) Diagram

Fig. 2. System overview

4   Experiment

We simulated the joint learning process using multiple personalized FL algorithms to evaluate our proposed system on PyTorch, a machine learning framework, with Python as the programming language. The hardware used for accelerating the training of the machine learning model was an Nvidia GPU RTX 2080 with 8 GB of memory.

4.1   Pre-processing

We applied the same data processing pipeline used in our previous work [5] to the 13 AffectiveROAD datasets. We sweep the window frame, which is a one-minute duration, on the sensor's time series data (BVP, EDA, Body Temperature) and calculate the means, standard deviation, minimum, and maximum values of the data within that window frame.

To maintain consistency with our previous work, we labeled the processed data into three classes, based on the provided self-assessment stress metric of the drivers. The data with stress metrics under 0.33 (i.e. 1/3), between 0.33 to 0.66 (i.e. 2/3), and over 0.66 are labeled as Baseline class, Intermediate class, and Stress class respectively. The threshold value 0.33 and 0.66 are marked as a green line and a red line in Fig. 1. The data distribution respective to each driver's physiological data is presented in Fig. 3.

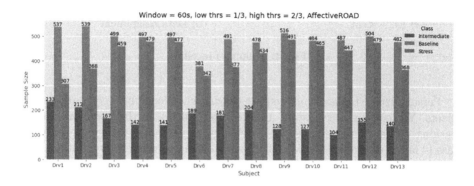

Fig. 3. Data distribution

4.2   Experiment Settings

We conduct the simulation with 12 clients in our federated learning framework (Fig. 4a). Each client represents a user in our proposed stress detection system. We run the simulation 13 times for 600 FL ground each time. We reserve one driver's data as the unseen test then we assign the remaining 12 sets of data to 12 clients (e.g., for the first time execution, we reserve Driver 1 data as unseen test data then assign Driver 2 data to client 1, Driver 3 data to client 2 and so on) in each time. The Fig. 4b describes our data assignment in each simulation time (yellow cell) with the red cell indicating the respective driver (blue cell) whose data will be reserved as test data and the number in the green cell indicates the client who will be assigned the respective data horizontally.

This configuration allows us to evaluate and compare our proposed system in two settings: the Basic setting, in which every client contributes their own client model (trained solely on their own data), and the server aggregates these client models into a global model, which is evaluated on the reserved unseen test data; and the Personalized setting, where all clients split their data into train and test sets and are governed by the server to follow personalized FL algorithms, learning from their own train data and fine-tuning their learned client model with knowledge shared by other clients. The final evaluation aggregates all clients' evaluation results on their own test data.

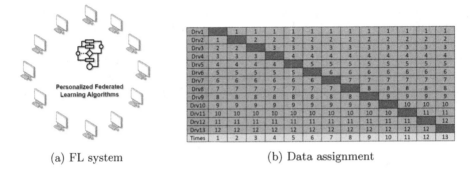

(a) FL system	(b) Data assignment

	1	2	3	4	5	6	7	8	9	10	11	12	13
Drv1		1	1	1	1	1	1	1	1	1	1	1	1
Drv2	1		2	2	2	2	2	2	2	2	2	2	2
Drv3	2	2		3	3	3	3	3	3	3	3	3	3
Drv4	3	3	3		4	4	4	4	4	4	4	4	4
Drv5	4	4	4	4		5	5	5	5	5	5	5	5
Drv6	5	5	5	5	5		6	6	6	6	6	6	6
Drv7	6	6	6	6	6	6		7	7	7	7	7	7
Drv8	7	7	7	7	7	7	7		8	8	8	8	8
Drv9	8	8	8	8	8	8	8	8		9	9	9	9
Drv10	9	9	9	9	9	9	9	9	9		10	10	10
Drv11	10	10	10	10	10	10	10	10	10	10		11	11
Drv12	11	11	11	11	11	11	11	11	11	11	11		12
Drv13	12	12	12	12	12	12	12	12	12	12	12	12	
Times	1	2	3	4	5	6	7	8	9	10	11	12	13

Fig. 4. Training procedure

Personalized FL algorithms require sharing knowledge between participating clients. We employ our custom architecture (Fig. 5) as the common machine learning model of the clients. The architecture contains two components: the base (4 layers on the left) acts as the feature extractor who crafts input data into knowledge representation (which would be shared by the clients and leveraged for fine-tuning client models by the personalized FL algorithms), and the head (4 layers on the right) will learn from the knowledge representation then trying to give the correct stress prediction.

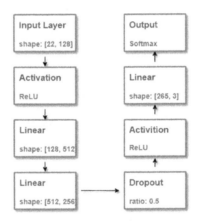

Fig. 5. Model architecture.

## 5	Evaluation

As mentioned above, we evaluate our proposed stress detection system in two settings. In the Basic setting, we look for answering the question of will the subject-dependent strategy works well enough for the stress-detecting problem. The Basic setting mimics the scenario in which a new user initially starts to use our system (and has not collected any own data). The new user receives an initial model (which has been trained on data of the previous user) and begins to assess their stress stage.

In the Personalized setting, we investigate whether the personalized really improves the accuracy of the stress detection machine learning model and which algorithms work best for our stress detection problem. The Personalized setting mimics the scenario in which a new user has collected some of their own data and decides to participate in our personalized system in order to improve the accuracy of their own stress detection machine learning model.

5.1   Basic Setting

The Fig. 6 summarizes the evaluation results in the Basic setting. Visually, the red horizontal line indicates the average accuracy (64.70%) of all 13 test sets. Only 5 subjects (Driver 3, 6, 8, 9, and 10) exceed the considered sufficient accuracy threshold (70%) while 4 subjects (Driver 2, 4, 12, and 13) could not achieve the average accuracy threshold. The 4 remaining subjects are just nearly meeting or a bit passing the average accuracy threshold.

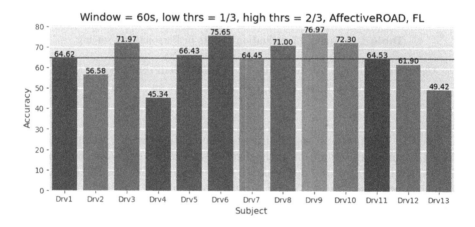

Fig. 6. Evaluation result in the Basic setting.

The evaluation results in the Basic setting demonstrate that stress detection is a subjective problem. Collecting many data does not guarantee that we can establish machine learning that works well for everyone. Hence, personalizing the machine learning model towards the user's private data is a necessary approach and should be always considered in building an AI system not only for specifically stress detection problems but also for general medical or human-related problems.

5.2   Personalized Setting

Different from the Basic setting in which we evaluate the final global model on the only unseen LOOCV (Leave One Out Cross Validation) test data to obtain the result; in the Personalized setting we have to evaluate each client model on its own reserved test set (with the ratio between train and test is 80%-20%) then aggregate all these results to obtain the complete evaluation result.

Firstly, we run the simulation with the canonical FedAvg algorithm, the result of this simulation can be considered as the baseline result because it represents for the evaluation result of the above Basic setting in the Personalized setting. We then run the simulation with 6 different personalized FL algorithms. With each algorithm, we run the simulation 13 times, we also sequentially leave the data of one subject (the driver) at each time to vary the distribution of the training data in order to obtain unbiased results.

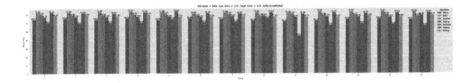

Fig. 7. Evaluation results in Personalized setting.

Table 1. Mean of 13 evaluation results in Personalized setting.

Algorithm	FedAvg	APPLE	Ditto	FedAMP	FedProto	FedRep	PerAvg
Accuracy	<u>67.12</u>	63.70	**72.34***	**69.18**	58.89	**71.52**	**67.76**

The Fig. 7 displays all the results of 13 simulations with 7 algorithms. The Table 1 summarizes the means of those results. As expected, 4 over 6 algorithms did effectively improve the performance of the system with the Ditto algorithm gaining improvement up to 5.22% in terms of accuracy. The other three algorithms (FedRep, FedAMP, and PerAvg) gained improvement of 4.4%, 2.06% and 0.64% respectively. We conjecture the strategy for knowledge representation sharing and fine-tuning of APPLE and FedProto algorithms are not suitable for neural networks designed for working with numeric data (specifically, our physiological data) thus they degrade the stress prediction accuracy compares to the result of baseline FedAvg algorithm.

6   Conclusion

We proposed our novel stress detection works on physiological data collected by wearable device sensors. Our system was designed in FL concept which allows users to contribute their physiological data to gain improvement to their stress-detecting model in a privacy-preserving manner. In this paper, we step ahead by integrating personalized FL algorithms into our system which will help the users fine-tune their model toward their private data thus gaining more accuracy. In the future, we plan to enhance the robustness of the system to cope with heterogeneous data from malfunctioning sensors and user dropouts.

Acknowledgment. This work was supported by the Institute of Information & communications Technology Planning & Evaluation (IITP) grant funded by the Korea government (MSIT) (No. 2020-0-00990, Platform Development and Proof of High Trust & Low Latency Processing for Heterogeneous·Atypical·Large Scaled Data in 5G-IoT Environment) and the Technology Innovation Program (or Industrial Strategic Technology Development Program-Source Technology Development and Commercialization of Digital Therapeutics) (20014967, Development of Digital Therapeutics for Depression from COVID19) funded By the Ministry of Trade, Industry & Energy (MOTIE, Korea).

References

1. Collins, L., Hassani, H., Mokhtari, A., Shakkottai, S.: Exploiting shared representations for personalized federated learning. In: International Conference on Machine Learning, pp. 2089–2099. PMLR (2021)
2. Fallah, A., Mokhtari, A., Ozdaglar, A.: Personalized federated learning with theoretical guarantees: a model-agnostic meta-learning approach. Adv. Neural. Inf. Process. Syst. **33**, 3557–3568 (2020)
3. Haouij, N.E., Poggi, J.M., Sevestre-Ghalila, S., Ghozi, R., Jaïdane, M.: AffectiveROAD system and database to assess driver's attention. In: Proceedings of the 33rd Annual ACM Symposium on Applied Computing, pp. 800–803 (2018)
4. Huang, Y., et al.: Personalized cross-silo federated learning on non-IID data. In: Proceedings of the AAAI Conference on Artificial Intelligence, vol. 35, pp. 7865–7873 (2021)
5. Lee, Y., Lee, N., Pham, V., Lee, J., Chung, T.M.: Privacy preserving stress detection system using physiological data from wearable device. In: Intelligent Human Systems Integration (IHSI 2023): Integrating People and Intelligent Systems, vol. 69, no. 69 (2023)
6. Li, T., Hu, S., Beirami, A., Smith, V.: Ditto: Fair and robust federated learning through personalization. In: International Conference on Machine Learning, pp. 6357–6368. PMLR (2021)
7. Luo, J., Wu, S.: Adapt to adaptation: learning personalization for cross-silo federated learning. arXiv preprint arXiv:2110.08394 (2021)
8. Ninh, V.T., et al.: An improved subject-independent stress detection model applied to consumer-grade wearable devices. In: Fujita, H., Fournier-Viger, P., Ali, M., Wang, Y. (eds.) IEA/AIE 2022. LNCS, vol. 13343, pp. 907–919. Springer, Cham (2022). https://doi.org/10.1007/978-3-031-08530-7_77
9. Saganowski, S., Miszczyk, J., Kunc, D., Lisouski, D., Kazienko, P.: Lessons learned from developing emotion recognition system for everyday life. In: Proceedings of the 20th ACM Conference on Embedded Networked Sensor Systems, pp. 1047–1054 (2022)
10. Tan, Y., et al.: FedProto: federated prototype learning across heterogeneous clients. In: Proceedings of the AAAI Conference on Artificial Intelligence, vol. 36, pp. 8432–8440 (2022)

Vision Transformer for Kidney Stone Detection

Anh-Cang Phan[1]([✉])(ORCID), Hung-Phi Cao[1](ORCID), Thuong-Cang Phan[2](ORCID),
Ngoc-Hoang-Quyen Nguyen[1], and Thanh-Ngoan Trieu[2](ORCID)

[1] Vinh Long University of Technology Education, Vinh Long, Vinh Long, Vietnam
{cangpa,caohungphi,quyennnh}@vlute.edu.vn
[2] Can Tho University, Can Tho, Vietnam
{ptcang,ttngoan}@cit.ctu.edu.vn

Abstract. Kidney stones are unwanted waste products that are deposited in the kidneys, causing complications of urinary tract infection, calyces dilatation, and irreversible renal failure. In some cases, if stones block the urinary tract of both kidneys at the same time, the patient will have urine retention, which can be life-threatening. Therefore, early detection and treatment of kidney stones is essential. In this work, we propose a method to detect and localize kidney stones using deep learning networks such as NASNetLarge, EfficientNetB7, EfficientNetV2L, and Vision Transformer. YoloV7 is proposed to assist in kidney localization. Research results show that the proposed method with Vision Transformer technique achieves a high accuracy of 99%.

Keywords: Vision Transformer · Kidney stones · Deep learning · Coronal CT

1 Introduction

The kidney is a complex organ that acts as a filtering system of the human body [24]. Kidney stones are unwanted waste products that are deposited in the kidneys, interfering with the normal functioning of the urinary system and in some cases, blocking the urine flow, causing pain and discomfort. About 12% of the population worldwide suffer from kidney stones and the incidence has increased over the past few decades [2,18]. Every year, there are about 1.3 million visits and emergency visits related to kidney stones which cause economic losses of up to 5 billion US dollars [10,20]. Kidney stones in young people are disturbing because of the limitations in the treatment methods of this group of patients [23]. Besides, kidney stones can make the patient feel extremely painful When a kidney stone becomes blocked in the ureter. It can block urine flow and lead to kidney swelling [5]. In the presence of large stone obstruction, renal colic is typically the main symptom, with pain radiating to the iliac fossa, accompanied by vomiting and abdominal distension. When the stone moves, the patient may have bloody urine because the stone damages the renal calyx. Late treatment of kidney stones will cause complications of urinary tract infections, calyces dilatation, and irreversible kidney failure. In some cases, if stones block the urinary tract of both kidneys at the same time, the patient will have urine retention, which can be life-threatening [5]. Therefore, the ability to detect kidney stones from medical images is important to give timely treatment, avoiding unwanted complications. The aim of this research is to provide support for kidney stone detection using advanced information technologies in medical imaging. We provide several scenarios with different deep network models and compare the scenarios to give an overview of the suitable network model for the problem. This aids in finding a good and robust model for support systems to help doctors in diagnosis.

Fitri et al. [8] proposed a CNN-based model with 15 layers to classify urinary stones from micro computed tomography (micro-CT) images. The trained model achieved an accuracy of 0.9959 with a classification error of 1.2%. Alper Caglayan et al. [4] proposed a kidney stone detection model using ResNet on CT scans of 455 patients. There were 405 patients diagnosed with kidney stones and 50 patients were not. The accuracy achieved on coronal CT images is 98.2% on the training phase. Irudayaraj [11] proposed to use four specific deep learning algorithms to detect kidney stones. The models included VGG16, ResNet50V2, MobileNetV2, and InceptionNetV3. InceptionNet produced the best classification result in terms of accuracy of 0.862. Yan and Razmjooy [27] proposed a computer-aided kidney stone diagnosis system based on a combination of deep learning and metaheuristic with an accuracy achieved 97.98%. Park et al. [17] proposed a ureter stone detection model by combining deep learning technology (Fast R-CNN) and image processing technology (Watershed). The sensitivity and specificity of the detection model were calculated as 0.90 and 0.91, and the accuracy for their position was 0.84. Islam et al. [12] proposed a method to detect kidney cysts, stones, and tumors on CT scans. Deep learning models were used including VGG16, Inceptionv3, Resnet50, EANet, CCT, and Swin transformer. The results achieve an accuracy of up to 99.30%. Kadir Yildirim et al. [28] proposed to detect kidney stones from coronal CT scans using XResNet-50 with an accuracy of up to 96.82%. Kavoussi et al. [14] proposed to use XGBoost to predict urinary abnormalities from electronic health record-derived data. The accuracy achieved of up to 98%. El Beze et al. [7] proposed a method to detect kidney stone composition based on the InceptionV3 network and achieved a specificity of 99%. Abraham et al. [1] proposed a method to predict kidney stone composition with XGBoost using 24H urine data, EHR-derived demographic, and comorbidity data. The method achieved an accuracy of 91%. Onal and Tekgul [16] presented a method to predict kidney stone composition using a deep learning network (CNN) with the achieved accuracy of 88%.

The rest of the paper is presented as follows. Section 2 presents the basic theoretical background used in this study. Section 3 details the proposed method using deep neural networks for the detection of kidney stone. Section 4 presents the experiments and evaluates the experimental results. Finally, we draw conclusions in Sect. 5.

2 Background

2.1 Kidney Stones

Kidney stones (urinary stones) are hard deposits of minerals and salts that form inside the kidneys [9] (Fig. 1). A kidney stone usually does not cause symptoms until it moves in the kidney or enters one of the ureters. The ureter is the tube connecting the kidney and bladder. Some patients are asymptomatic, while others may experience severe pain (renal colic), or bloody urine. It can lead to complete and irreversible kidney failure. About 1 in 17 adults will develop kidney stones [29]. According to epidemiological data in the United States, the incidence of kidney stones is increasing every year [19] and it is easy to relapse after treatment with a high recurrence rate of 50% [13]. Kidney stone formation is also associated with a higher risk of diseases such as hypertension [15], chronic kidney disease, and end-stage renal disease [3].

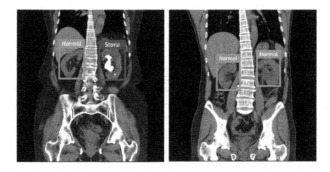

Fig. 1. Kidney stones in CT images extracted from the experimental dataset.

2.2 Network Models

NASNetLarge. NASNetLarge [30] is trained on a large dataset and capable of synthesizing complex image features. NASNetLarge uses a block architecture that adjusts the network topology and hyperparameters automatically through the architecture search process. This architecture allows the model to learn how to build good feature classifiers and optimize hyperparameters to get the best performance on the training dataset.

EfficientNet. EfficientNet [21] is a scaling method that uniformly scales all depth/width/resolution dimensions using a compound coefficient. Unlike conventional practice, EfficientNet carefully balances the width, depth, and resolution of the network with a set of fixed scaling coefficients. EfficientNet transmits well and achieves good accuracy on CIFAR-100 (91.7%) and Flowers (98.8%).

EfficientNetV2L. EfficientNetV2 [22] delivers superior performance over previous models on different datasets including ImageNet, CIFAR, Cars, and Flowers. By pre-train on the ImageNet21k dataset, EfficientNetV2 achieved an accuracy of 87.3% on ImageNet ILSVRC2012.

Vision Transformer. Vision Transformer (ViT) [9] was first applied to the field of natural language processing, which is a type of deep neural network mainly based on self-attention mechanisms. In various visualization standards, ViT-based models perform similarly or better than other types of networks, such as convolutional and recurrent neural networks. With high performance, ViT is receiving more attention from the computer vision community. Due to its lower computational complexity and ability to overcome the limitations of CNNs, ViT outperforms the most advanced CNN models.

2.3   Evaluation Metrics

Accuracy described by Eq. 1 is calculated based on several values such as true positives (TP), false positives (FP), true negatives (TN), and false negatives (FN) in the confusion matrix [25]. Besides, to evaluate the loss of the models when training, we use the Cross Entropy function [10] presented in Eq. 2, where K is the number of classes, y is the actual value, and $\hat{y}$ is the predicted value.

$$Accuracy = \frac{TP + TN}{TP + TN + FP + FN} \tag{1}$$

$$Loss = \sum_{i=1}^{K} y_i log(\hat{y}_i) \tag{2}$$

3   Proposed Method

In this study, we use the transfer learning method on deep learning networks and Vision Transformer to detect kidney stones. The proposed model consists of two phases: training and testing. The details of the phases are shown in Fig. 2.

3.1   Training Phase

Pre-processing. The input dataset will be enhanced by a number of methods such as image rotation and image flip. The data is then passed through YOLOV7 to perform renal extraction and normalized to a size of 224×224.

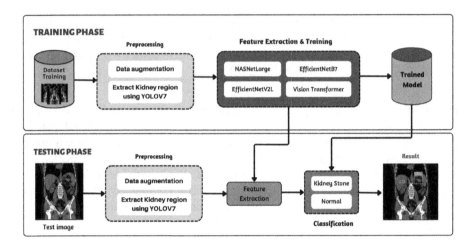

Fig. 2. Proposed approach to detect and classify kidney stones.

Feature Extraction and Training. We conduct feature extraction and training with the proposed networks including NasNetLarge, EfficientNetB7, EfficientNetV2L, and Vision Transformer. For the Vision Transformer model, the input image after being pre-processed will be cropped to patches of 16×16, which limits performance degradation and computational complexity [6], then move to the linear projection stage. In order to avoid image distortion after feature extraction, each patch will be assigned a location and a label. During the Transform encoder stage, the data will be encoded and classified. The result of this process will be an image classified as Stone or Normal. The proposed Vision Transformer network architecture is shown in Fig. 3.

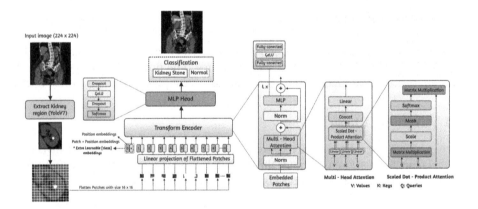

Fig. 3. Proposed vision transformer model.

3.2   Testing Phase

We test the trained models based on the testing dataset. The input data is pre-processed by normalization and passed through YOLOV7 to extract the renal region. YOLOV7 [26] has a good performance in object detection in terms of speed and accuracy. Thus, it is used for the renal segmentation. This region is later passed through trained models to detect kidney stones. The prediction results will give one of two conclusions, Stone and Normal.

4   Experiments

4.1   Installation Environment and Dataset Description

The system is installed in Python language with a configuration of Windows 10, 16GB RAM, and Nvidia Geforce GPU.

Training dataset: Kadir Yildirim et al. [28] introduced a dataset in the study of detecting kidney stones using deep learning techniques. The dataset includes Coronal CT images of patients who were hospitalized at Elazig Fethi Sekin Municipal Hospital in Turkey with 268 of whom confirmed for kidney stones and 165 people were normal. There are a total of 1,799 Coronal CT images including 1,009 normal samples and 790 samples having kidney stones. At least two radiologists reviewed each CT image in the dataset to ensure accurate kidney stone detection and annotation.

Testing dataset: Islam et al. [12] introduced a dataset for detecting renal cysts, stones, and tumors on CT scans including Coronal and Axial CT images. The dataset includes 540 normal images and 410 images of kidney stones. The images were collected from various hospitals in Dhaka, Bangladesh, where the patients were diagnosed with renal tumors, cysts, and stones. The dataset from Dicom format was converted into jpg and was re-verified by radiologists to confirm the accuracy of the data.

4.2   Scenarios

We conduct experiments on four scenarios with the parameters described in Table 1.

Table 1. Scenarios and training parameters

Scenario	Network model	Epochs	Learning rate	Batch size	Image size
1	NASNetLarge	500	0.001	None	224×224
2	EfficientNetB7	500	0.001	None	224×224
3	EfficientNetV2L	500	0.001	None	224×224
4	Vision transformer	500	0.001	16×16	224×224

4.3   Training Results

Figure 4 presents the loss values of the four scenarios during the training phase. The training-validation loss values of scenarios 1 to 4 is 0.0007–0.6332, 0.0012–0.1487, 0.0001–0.05, and 0.0007–0.09, respectively. Observing the figure, it can be seen that the four scenarios all give a higher validation loss value than the training loss. Scenarios 3 and 4 give better results than scenarios 1 and 2 showing that these 2 models perform better than the others.

Figure 5 shows the accuracy of four scenarios during the training phase. The training-validation accuracy of scenarios 1 to 4 are 1.00-0.88, 0.995-0.985, 1.00-0.99, and 1.00-0.99, respectively. Scenario 1 gives validation accuracy of 0.12 lower than training accuracy, which shows that scenario 1 is not working effectively. In scenarios 2, 3, and 4 the deviation between training and validation accuracy is approximately 0.01. Scenarios 3 and 4 have higher accuracy than scenario 2. This shows that these two scenarios perform better than scenarios 1 and 2.

Figure 6 shows the confusion matrix of the four scenarios. Scenario 4 gives better prediction results in two classes than the remaining scenarios. Specifically, in scenario 1, the outcome that the model predicted correctly for the Stone case is 0.79 and the Normal case is 0.92. Scenario 2 predicts correctly the Stone with 0.95 and the Normal case with 1.00. Scenario 3 predicts correctly the Stone case as 0.94 and the Normal case as 1.00. In scenario 4, the outcome that the model predicted correctly for the Stone case is 0.97 and the Normal case is 1.00.

Figure 7 shows the training time of the four scenarios. The training time of scenario 1 is 162.41 min, scenario 2 is 167.57 min, scenario 3 is 167.42 min, and scenario 4 is 936 min. Scenario 1 gives the shortest training time of the remaining scenarios.

4.4   Testing Results

Table 2 presents some experimental results of four scenarios in 3 cases including Stone-Normal (one kidney contains stones), Normal (both kidneys contain no stones), and Stone (both kidneys contain stones). In the case of Stone - Normal, scenario 1 predicts Normal results in both kidneys; scenario 2 gives the predicted result as Normal - Stone, which is not correct; scenarios 3 and 4 give the correct prediction of Stone - Normal. Scenario 4 gives a higher accuracy than scenario 3. In the case of Normal, all 4 scenarios give correct prediction results. Scenario 4 gives the highest accuracy in this case. In the case of Stone, scenarios 2 and 3 predict the results as Stone - Normal, which is incorrect. Scenarios 2 and 3 have errors in predicting stones with small size. In contrast, scenarios 1 and 4 give correct prediction results, however, scenario 4 provides a higher accuracy. Through some experimental results, we can see that scenario 4 gives better results than the remaining scenarios.

Figure 8 presents the average detection time and accuracy on the testing dataset. In Fig. 8a, the detection time of scenario 1 is 3.61 min, scenario 2 is

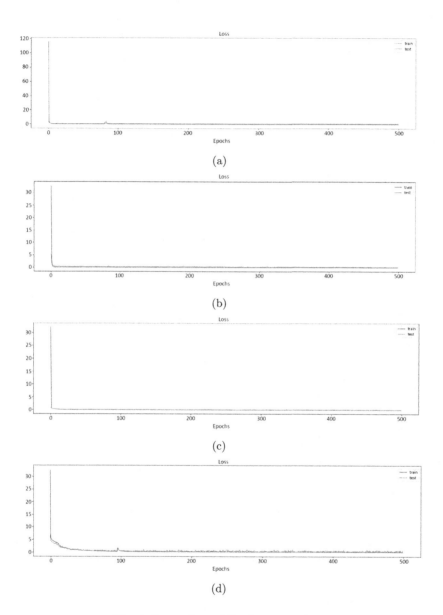

Fig. 4. Loss values of the four scenarios.

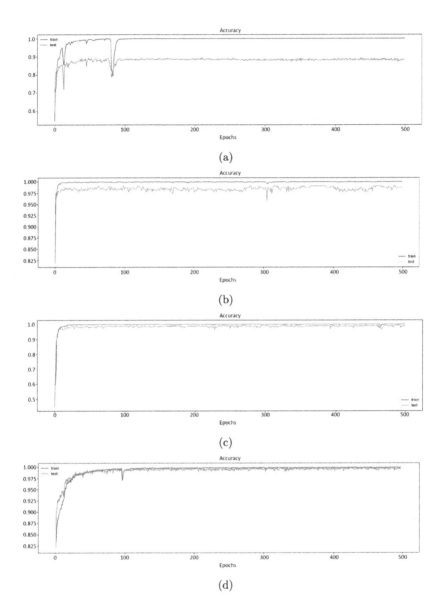

Fig. 5. Accuracy of the four scenarios.

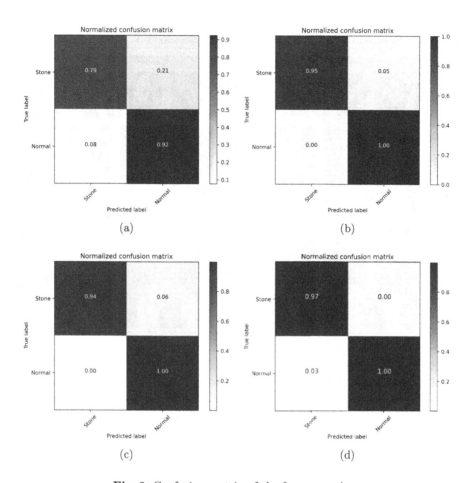

Fig. 6. Confusion matrix of the four scenarios.

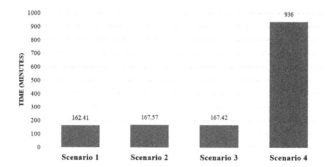

Fig. 7. Training time of the four scenarios.

Table 2. Illustration of classification results from the experimental dataset.

Case	Scenario 1	Scenario 2	Scenario 3	Scenario 4
Stone-Normal				
Normal				
Stone				

3.28 min, scenario 3 is 3.38 min, and scenario 4 is 2.15 min. In Fig. 8b, the accuracy on the testing dataset of scenario 1 is 87.2%, scenario 2 is 98.02%, scenario 3 is 98.03%, and scenario 4 is 99.06%. In terms of time and accuracy, scenario 4 gives better results than the remaining scenarios.

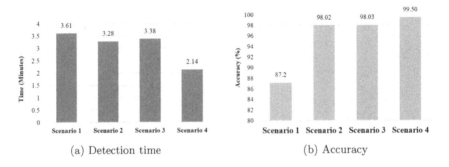

(a) Detection time   (b) Accuracy

Fig. 8. Detection time and accuracy of the four scenarios on the testing dataset.

Figure 9 presents some research results in the detection of kidney stones using deep learning techniques. In this study, we propose kidney stone detection models based on Vision Transformer and deep learning networks such as NASNetLarge,

EfficientNetB7, and EfficientNetV2L with 4 different scenarios. The YOLOV7 is used to extract the renal region from images. This helps to increase prediction accuracy as well as eliminate redundant regions. The training results of the proposed models are up to 99%. The deep learning neural networks in scenarios 1 to 4 are more effective in terms of accuracy compared to the previous research methods presented in Fig. 9 with an accuracy of 99.50% in the testing phase.

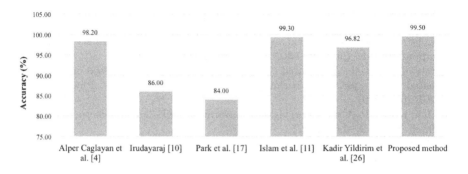

Fig. 9. Comparison on accuracy with several related works.

5 Conclusion

The incidence of kidney stones (urinary stones) has increased over time globally. Late treatment of kidney stones can lead to ureteral obstruction, repeated urinary tract infections, painful urination, and complete kidney failure, which can be life-threatening. Therefore, early detection and treatment of kidney stones is essential. In this work, we propose a method to detect and localize the kidney using deep learning networks such as NASNetLarge, EfficientNetB7. Efficient-NetV2L, and Vision Transformer. YoloV7 is proposed to localize kidney regions. In addition, we present some comparative results between the proposed method and some related studies. Evaluation results contribute to finding and choosing the suitable method so that an accurate detection and localization system can be built to assist doctors in making diagnoses. The research results show that the kidney detection and localization method based on Vision Transformer achieves an accuracy of 99.50%.

References

1. Abraham, A., Kavoussi, N.L., Sui, W., Bejan, C., Capra, J.A., Hsi, R.: Machine learning prediction of kidney stone composition using electronic health record-derived features. J. Endourol. **36**(2), 243–250 (2022)
2. Alelign, T., Petros, B., et al.: Kidney stone disease: an update on current concepts. Adv. Urol. **2018** (2018)

3. Ando, R., et al.: Independent and interactive effects of kidney stone formation and conventional risk factors for chronic kidney disease: a follow-up study of japanese men. Int. Urol. Nephrol. **53**, 1081–1087 (2021)
4. Caglayan, A., Horsanali, M.O., Kocadurdu, K., Ismailoglu, E., Guneyli, S.: Deep learning model-assisted detection of kidney stones on computed tomography. Int. Braz J Urol **48**, 830–839 (2022)
5. Chen, T.K., Knicely, D.H., Grams, M.E.: Chronic kidney disease diagnosis and management: a review. JAMA **322**(13), 1294–1304 (2019)
6. Dosovitskiy, A., et al.: An image is worth 16×16 words: transformers for image recognition at scale. arXiv preprint arXiv:2010.11929 (2020)
7. El Beze, J., et al.: Evaluation and understanding of automated urinary stone recognition methods. BJU Int. **130**(6), 786–798 (2022)
8. Fitri, L.A., et al.: Automated classification of urinary stones based on microcomputed tomography images using convolutional neural network. Phys. Med. **78**, 201–208 (2020)
9. Han, K., et al.: A survey on vision transformer. IEEE Trans. Pattern Anal. Mach. Intell. **45**(1), 87–110 (2022)
10. Hyams, E.S., Matlaga, B.R.: Economic impact of urinary stones. Transl. Androl. Urol. **3**(3), 278 (2014)
11. Irudayaraj, A.A.: Kidney stone detection using deep learning methodologies. Ph.D. thesis, Dublin, National College of Ireland (2022)
12. Islam, M.N., Hasan, M., Hossain, M.K., Alam, M.G.R., Uddin, M.Z., Soylu, A.: Vision transformer and explainable transfer learning models for auto detection of kidney cyst, stone and tumor from ct-radiography. Sci. Rep. **12**(1), 11440 (2022)
13. Kamihira, O., Ono, Y., Katoh, N., Yamada, S., Mizutani, K., Ohshima, S.: Long-term stone recurrence rate after extracorporeal shock wave lithotripsy. J. Urol. **156**(4), 1267–1271 (1996)
14. Kavoussi, N.L., et al.: Machine learning models to predict 24 hour urinary abnormalities for kidney stone disease. Urology **169**, 52–57 (2022)
15. Kittanamongkolchai, W., et al.: Risk of hypertension among first-time symptomatic kidney stone formers. Clin. J. Am. Soc. Nephrol.: CJASN **12**(3), 476 (2017)
16. Onal, E.G., Tekgul, H.: Assessing kidney stone composition using smartphone microscopy and deep neural networks. BJUI Compass **3**(4), 310–315 (2022)
17. Park, J.M., Eun, S.J., Na, Y.G.: Development and evaluation of urolithiasis detection technology based on a multimethod algorithm. Int. Neurourol. J. **27**(1), 70 (2023)
18. Romero, V., Akpinar, H., Assimos, D.G.: Kidney stones: a global picture of prevalence, incidence, and associated risk factors. Rev. Urol. **12**(2–3), e86 (2010)
19. Siener, R.: Nutrition and kidney stone disease. Nutrients **13**(6), 1917 (2021)
20. Strohmaier, W.L.: Economics of stone disease/treatment. Arab. J. Urol. **10**(3), 273–278 (2012)
21. Tan, M., Le, Q.: EfficientNet: rethinking model scaling for convolutional neural networks. In: International Conference on Machine Learning, pp. 6105–6114. PMLR (2019)
22. Tan, M., Le, Q.: EfficientNetv2: smaller models and faster training. In: International Conference on Machine Learning, pp. 10096–10106. PMLR (2021)
23. Tasian, G.E., Kabarriti, A.E., Kalmus, A., Furth, S.L.: Kidney stone recurrence among children and adolescents. J. Urol. **197**(1), 246–252 (2017)
24. Thurman, J.M.: Complement and the kidney: an overview. Adv. Chronic Kidney Dis. **27**(2), 86–94 (2020)

25. Vujović, Ž, et al.: Classification model evaluation metrics. Int. J. Adv. Comput. Sci. Appl. **12**(6), 599–606 (2021)
26. Wang, C.Y., Bochkovskiy, A., Liao, H.Y.M.: YOLOv7: trainable bag-of-freebies sets new state-of-the-art for real-time object detectors. In: Proceedings of the IEEE/CVF Conference on Computer Vision and Pattern Recognition, pp. 7464–7475 (2023)
27. Yan, C., Razmjooy, N.: Kidney stone detection using an optimized deep believe network by fractional coronavirus herd immunity optimizer. Biomed. Signal Process. Control **86**, 104951 (2023)
28. Yildirim, K., Bozdag, P.G., Talo, M., Yildirim, O., Karabatak, M., Acharya, U.R.: Deep learning model for automated kidney stone detection using coronal CT images. Comput. Biol. Med. **135**, 104569 (2021)
29. Zeng, G., et al.: Prevalence of kidney stones in china: an ultrasonography based cross-sectional study. BJU Int. **120**(1), 109–116 (2017)
30. Zoph, B., Vasudevan, V., Shlens, J., Le, Q.V.: Learning transferable architectures for scalable image recognition. In: Proceedings of the IEEE Conference on Computer Vision and Pattern Recognition, pp. 8697–8710 (2018)

Attention Models and Image Pre-processing for Covid-19 Detection Based on Lung Ultrasound Images

Hoa Thanh Le[1,2(✉)], Linh Nguyen[3], and Thao Danh Nguyen[2]

[1] The Ho Chi Minh City University of Theatre and Cinema, Ho Chi Minh City, Vietnam
lethanhhoait@gmail.com
[2] Industrial University of Ho Chi Minh City, Ho Chi Minh City, Vietnam
[3] Department of Mathematics, University of Idaho, Moscow, ID 83844-1103, USA
lnguyen@uidaho.edu

Abstract. This research focuses on developing a practical approach for rapid and accurate COVID-19 detection from lung ultrasound images. We leverage attention models and image pre-processing techniques to enhance the detection process. Deep learning models, including VGG16, VGG19, and ResNet18, are utilized as backbone architectures. The images undergo pre-processing, including denoising, normalization, and contrast enhancement, to improve relevant features and reduce noise.

Additionally, we integrate the Convolutional Block Attention Module (CBAM) to capture informative regions of interest. Experimental evaluations on a dataset containing COVID-19-infected, pneumonia-infected, and healthy lungs demonstrate improved accuracy, sensitivity, and specificity compared to traditional methods. The combined use of attention models and image pre-processing techniques enhances COVID-19 detection from lung ultrasound images, with the CBAM module effectively highlighting significant regions for accurate classification.

Keywords: Attention mechanism · COVID-19 · image pre-processing · convolutional block attention module (CBAM) · deep learning · lung ultrasound · GRAD-CAM · Occlusion Sensitivity Maps (OSMs) VGG · ResNet

1 Introduction

The Coronavirus Disease 2019 (COVID-19) was declared a global pandemic by the World Health Organization (WHO) in early March 2020 [1]. Despite extensive preventive measures, the worldwide count has surpassed 689 million confirmed cases, with 6.88 million reported deaths [2]. COVID-19 and other respiratory infections significantly impact the respiratory system, especially in individuals with comorbidities such as chronic heart disease and diabetes [3]. While most COVID-19 cases present mild symptoms, some progress to severe illness and fatalities. Older adults and those with underlying medical conditions are at a higher risk of severe disease from COVID-19.

© The Author(s), under exclusive license to Springer Nature Singapore Pte Ltd. 2023
T. K. Dang et al. (Eds.): FDSE 2023, CCIS 1925, pp. 456–470, 2023.
https://doi.org/10.1007/978-981-99-8296-7_33

Given the rapid spread of the virus, quick and accurate diagnosis is crucial. The RT-PCR test is widely recognized as an exact method for confirming COVID-19 infection. However, this test is costly and time-consuming, and results may take over 24 h. Moreover, the widespread availability of RT-PCR testing is limited, with only a few accredited clinical laboratories. Alternative methods for COVID-19 diagnosis, such as chest computed tomography (CT), chest X-ray (CXR), and lung ultrasound, have demonstrated potential in complementing RT-PCR testing.

Computed tomography is commonly used to assess disease severity and monitor disease progression. However, it has several limitations, including high cost, radiation exposure to patients, and the need for disinfection and cleaning after large-scale scanning to prevent cross-infection. While X-ray imaging is recommended, studies have shown a relatively low detection rate of abnormal findings in 636 chest X-rays from COVID-19 patients, reaching only 41.7% [4]. In contrast, ultrasound offers several advantages over CT and X-ray. It is a non-invasive, radiation-free, cost-effective, widely available, and repeatable method in most healthcare facilities. Furthermore, the portability of ultrasound devices eliminates the need for patient relocation, thereby reducing the risk of cross-contamination.

1.1 Ultrasound in COVID-2019 Diagnosis

Lung ultrasound is the process of using ultrasound waves to examine the components of the lungs in general. By generating and receiving ultrasound waves, this process allows for the visualization and analysis of lung images to identify related pathologies. The pleura plays a crucial role in detecting abnormal signs. Acute conditions are often associated with changes in the lung surface. Lung ultrasound can effectively diagnose pathologies in the respiratory system, such as injuries, pneumonia, and various other medical conditions. Figure 1 illustrates the common characteristics for detecting these diseases in lung ultrasound. Line A represents horizontal lines indicating a normal lung surface (red arrows in Fig. 1a). Line B is a line with specific features: increased brightness along the vertical axis, synchronized movement with the sliding lung sign, starting from the pleural line to the edge of the screen, erasing the A lines along its path. Figure 1b displays two separate B lines (indicated by red arrows) originating from two discontinuity points on the pleural line (indicated by white arrows). In Fig. 1c, multiple B lines converge to form a white lung image, where the pleural line is interrupted (white arrows). Figure 1d shows a consolidated lung image with a bronchial image containing air (yellow arrow), where the pleural line cannot be identified.

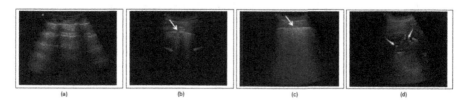

(a)   (b)   (c)   (d)

Fig. 1. Illustrating the imaging features in lung ultrasound

For COVID-19, a common abnormality is related to the interstitial syndrome described as B lines (i.e., three or more B lines present in one lung region, confluent B lines, or a white lung appearance). Multiple B lines in an ultrasound image can be considered a sign of the onset of pneumonia. As the disease progresses, pneumonia spreads and becomes more severe, and the ultrasound image shows the appearance of multiple B lines that cluster together to form a "white lung" image. At this stage, patients usually require mechanical respiratory support. The most severe stage of the disease is characterized by extensive and diffuse lung damage, resulting in significant impairment of gas exchange function, necessitating the use of an extracorporeal membrane oxygenation (ECMO) system. However, a positive trend is observed when repeated ultrasound examinations show a decrease in the number of B lines and the reappearance of A-lines and a regular pleural line.

1.2 Related Work

Deep learning algorithms have demonstrated significant accuracy in the analysis and processing of medical imaging, ranging from object recognition and detection to semantic segmentation. Recent research works have focused on exploring medical image analysis and applying deep learning for classifying lung ultrasound data of COVID-19 patients, attracting considerable attention.

Roberts and Tsiligkaridis [5] conducted a study and presented results on using CNN networks in deep learning for diagnosing COVID-19 based on lung ultrasound images. They employed two networks, VGG16 and ResNet18, and utilized 3,119 frames from 195 ultrasound videos for the training process. The models achieved a performance of 85.9% in detecting COVID-19.

Born et al. [6] introduced a new lung ultrasound dataset comprising 202 videos and 59 images. This dataset is named POCUS [7]. It contains samples from COVID-19 patients, patients with bacterial pneumonia, and healthy individuals. The research team used cross-validation methods to perform classification based on three classes (COVID-19, pneumonia, and healthy). They compared the performance of two neural network architectures: NasNETMobile and VGG16. The results showed that the highest performance achieved by the models was 87.8% for the VGG16 model.

The research team by Diaz-Escobar et al. [8] also utilized the POCUS dataset. The authors conducted cross-validation to perform classification based on three classes, including COVID-19, pneumonia, and healthy. The authors compared the performance of multiple different models, and the VGG19 model achieved an accuracy of 87.8%.

Our paper aims to implement an attention mechanism for deep learning techniques and image pre-processing to diagnose COVID-19 using lung ultrasound images. Our approach is innovative, as previous studies only focused on basic models without incorporating the attention mechanism. The structure of the paper is as follows: Sect. 1 provides an overview of the rationale behind selecting lung ultrasound images for COVID-19 diagnosis and discusses relevant studies. Section 2 describes the image dataset used for training and testing and performs a 5-fold cross-validation on this dataset. Section 3 introduces the pre-processing image technique, presents the Convolutional Block Attention Module (CBAM), and explains its integration into the VGG and ResNet models.

Section 4 compares and presents positive results obtained by combining image pre-processing and the CBAM attention channel in the models. Finally, Sect. 5 contains our conclusion.

2   Dataset

The dataset comprises various lung ultrasound images and videos [7]. These images and videos are obtained using a transducer that emits high-frequency sound waves to capture internal body images, which are then reflected and visualized through medical imaging. Two primary types of transducers are used: linear probes and convex probes. Linear probe: This is a type of ultrasound probe designed with multiple ultrasound crystals arranged in a linear array, connected in a row along the length of the probe. Convex probe: This is a type of ultrasound probe designed with a set of ultrasound crystals arranged in a convex shape.

The dataset consists of 202 videos and 59 images from convex and linear probes. It includes samples from 216 patients with COVID-19, bacterial and viral pneumonia (non-COVID-19), and healthy individuals. The dataset was collected from 41 sources, such as hospitals, academic ultrasound courses, scientific literature, community platforms, open medical repositories, and health-tech companies. As a result, the videos have varying lengths and frame rates, with an average of 160 ± 144 frames and a speed of 2510Hz. Due to the diverse data sources, not all videos contain patient metadata. Only 42% of the data include information about age (with an average age of 41.3 years) and gender (57% male), and 30% have descriptions of symptoms. However, all samples in the database were reviewed and approved by two medical experts, and the diagnosis of COVID-19 was typically confirmed using RT-PCR.

Data from the convex probes include:

- 182 videos (64x COVID-19, 49x bacterial pneumonia, 66x healthy, 3x viral pneumonia).
- 53 images (18x COVID-19, 20x bacterial pneumonia, 15x healthy).

Data from the linear probes include:

- 20 videos (6x COVID-19, 2x bacterial pneumonia, 9x healthy, 3x viral pneumonia).
- 6 images (4x COVID-19, 2x bacterial pneumonia).

Our experiments used 179 videos captured with convex probes and 53 individual images. To prepare the videos and images for analysis, we followed the pre-processing steps outlined in [7], which involved the following procedures:

- LUS videos were divided into individual images at a frame rate of 3 Hz. This means that each second of the video was represented by three consecutive images.
- The images were cropped to a square window, ensuring equal dimensions.
- Finally, the images were resized to a fixed size of 224×224 pixels.

After applying these steps, our dataset consisted of 3257 images, including the individual images. Among these, 1248 images were associated with COVID-19 cases, 704 corresponded to bacterial pneumonia, and 1305 were labeled as healthy.

Due to the relatively small dataset size, to prevent overfitting and have a basis for evaluating model performance, we chose not to use the traditional data split methods (e.g., 80–20 or 70–30 ratios). Instead, we employed cross-validation, which is considered an effective method for assessing models with limited data. To perform cross-validation, the dataset was randomly divided into five distinct folds, with images included only one fold at a time to ensure complete differentiation between the training and testing sets. The training and testing ratios for each fold are shown in Table 1. Additionally, data augmentation techniques such as random image rotation within the range of -10 to $10°$ and random horizontal and vertical shifts within the range of -0.1 to 0.1 times the image size were also applied.

Table 1. Training and Testing Data Split Ratios

Folds	Fold 1	Fold 2	Fold 3	Fold 4	Fold 5
Training set (%)	80	82	84	77	78
Testing set (%)	20	18	16	23	22

3 Methodology

3.1 VGG-Style Base Network

The VGG (Visual Geometry Group) model is a famous and influential deep learning model in image classification. It was introduced by the VGG research group at the University of Oxford in 2014. The VGG model primarily focuses on the structure of deep neural networks, particularly the use of convolutional layers. One notable aspect of VGG is its consecutive use of 3x3 convolutional layers with a stride of 1 and padding to maintain the input size. This helps preserve spatial information during feature extraction. The main structure of the VGG model consists of several convolutional layers and pooling layers, followed by some fully connected layers. The VGG model can have various versions according to the number of layers.

The VGG16 model is composed of 13 convolutional layers, five max-pooling layers, and three fully connected layers. This totals 16 layers with tunable parameters, which gives the model its name. The input image size is fixed at 224×224.

VGG19 is a variation of the VGG model, featuring 19 layers, consisting of 16 convolutional layers and three fully connected layers. The architecture of VGG19 closely resembles VGG16, with an input image size of 224×224, 3×3 kernel size, and a max pooling layer of size 2×2. However, VGG19 differs from VGG16 because it includes an additional convolutional layer in the last three convolutional blocks. Similar to VGG16, VGG19 also includes three fully connected layers. The first two fully connected layers each have 4096 neurons, while the third fully connected layer consists of 1000 neurons, aligning with the number of classes in the ImageNet [9] dataset.

3.2 RESNET-Style Base Network

ResNet was publicly introduced in 2015 and achieved remarkable success by winning the ImageNet ILSVRC 2015 competition with an impressive error rate of 3.57%. It shares similarities with VGG regarding a stacked-layer structure, resulting in a deeper model. However, ResNet is a convolutional neural network that differs from VGG by utilizing small residual blocks.

The key concept behind ResNet is the introduction of skip connections, allowing for skipping one or more layers by establishing connections to the previous layer. Currently, multiple variants of the ResNet architecture are distinguished by the number of layers they contain. Examples include ResNet18, ResNet34, ResNet50, ResNet101, ResNet152, etc. The naming convention for ResNet architectures follows the pattern of "ResNet," followed by a number that denotes the specific number of layers in the model.

3.3 Image Pre-processing Techniques

3.3.1 Noise Filtering Technique

The noise filtering technique reduces noise and removes unwanted noise components from an image to improve quality and preserve valuable information. Noise can occur during image-capturing or transmission through imperfect tools, devices, or environments. There are various noise filtering techniques, among which the highly regarded one is Block-matching and 3D filtering (BM3D). The BM3D noise filtering technique is an advanced and effective method in image processing. It is developed to reduce noise in digital and computational images. BM3D distinguishes itself from traditional methods by combining the concepts of "block-matching" and "3D transform". The BM3D filtering process includes the following main steps: Block-matching, 3D Transform, Noise Information Filtering, Synchronization, and Reconstruction. The BM3D method has demonstrated high efficiency and accuracy in reducing noise in digital and computational images. It achieves good results in preserving essential image details and minimizing image-blurring artifacts. Therefore, BM3D is one of the advanced noise-filtering techniques widely used in image processing.

3.3.2 Contrast Enhancement Techniques

Enhancing the contrast of an image can be achieved through various technical methods. Below are some commonly used techniques for contrast enhancement:

Contrast Limited Adaptive Histogram Equalization (CLAHE) is a method to improve the contrast of a grayscale image by applying histogram equalization to smaller regions within the image. The CLAHE method divides the original image into smaller sub-regions called tiles and applies histogram equalization to each of these tiles. The CLAHE technique improves the contrast of an image by enhancing features and reducing information loss caused by excessive brightness concentration in specific regions. It is widely used in image processing to improve image quality and produce images with better contrast.

EDGE_ENHANCE_MORE filter is one of the filters used in image processing to enhance the contrast of edges in an image. It is a filter that operates through a matrix (kernel) to perform convolution on the input image. The filter increases the contrast of edges in the image, highlighting the boundaries and contours by amplifying the differences between neighboring pixels along the edges.

Our experiment used the denoising and contrast enhancement methods described above for pre-processing the images. After pre-processing, we fed these images into VGG models (VGG16, VGG19) and ResNet (ResNet18) for training. Figure 2 illustrates the pre-processing steps performed on the images before feeding them into the models above.

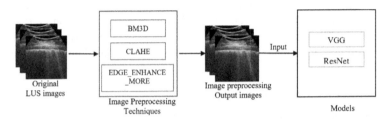

Fig. 2. Illustration of image pre-processing techniques before input into the models.

3.4 Convolutional Block Attention Module

The attention module is employed to enhance the learning process of convolutional neural network models by directing their attention toward relevant information, disregarding redundant and irrelevant details. In tasks like object detection, the important information pertains to the target objects or classes that require classification and localization within an image. Recently, Woo et al. [10] introduced a convolutional block attention module (CBAM) that integrates an attention mechanism. This mechanism guides the neural network model to focus on specific regions of interest, thereby improving the representation of important features. Before delving into the details of CBAM, let's first explore the overall structure of the module (see Fig. 3).

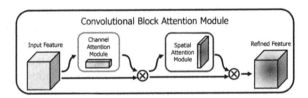

Fig. 3. Convolutional Block Attention Module layout

CBAM consists of two consecutive submodules, the Channel Attention Module (CAM) and the Spatial Attention Module (SAM), which are applied in a specific order. The CAM emphasizes the significant aspects or "what" is important in an input image, while the SAM highlights the informative regions or "where" the crucial parts are located.

These two modules complement each other in the attention mechanism. The authors demonstrate that CBAM is utilized in every convolutional block of deep networks to obtain a refined feature map from the input feature map. The overall attention process can be summarized in Eq. (1).

$$\mathbf{F'} = \mathbf{M_c}(\mathbf{F}) \otimes \mathbf{F},$$
$$\mathbf{F''} = \mathbf{M_s}(\mathbf{F'}) \otimes \mathbf{F'}, \tag{1}$$

where $\otimes$ stands for element-wise multiplication. If the two operands aren't in the same dimension, the valuations are broadcasted (copied) similarly. The spatial attentional valuations circulate along the channel dimension, and the channel attention values are broadcasted along the spatial dimension.

Integration into the VGG16 and VGG19 models: the CBAM attention mechanism integrated into the VGG network is shown in Fig. 4. Two consecutive attention modules (channel and spatial) are added to the activation map $\mathbf{F}$ before the final convolutional layer. The chosen integration point is considered optimal because the number of output channels at this position is the highest, providing CBAM with more choices for important channels. As a result, the model focuses better on crucial places. Subsequently, the refined features are sent to the last convolutional block. Here, AACB (Attention Attached Convolution Block) refers to the convolutional block accompanied by attention, comprising a convolutional block and subsequent attention modules.

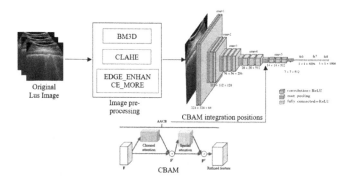

Fig. 4. Pre-processing the input image and integrating CBAM into the VGG model

Integration into the ResNet18 model: The CBAM attention mechanism integrated into ResNet18 is shown in Fig. 5. This figure precisely indicates the location of the CBAM attention module when integrated into a residual block. The CBAM attention module is integrated after all the residual blocks in the ResNet18 model. The chosen integration point is considered optimal because, at this integration point, the model incorporates features from the previous layer, providing CBAM with more information to select from. In addition to proposing the CBAM method, the authors [10] also integrated it into this position in their experiments, and the results demonstrated its effectiveness.

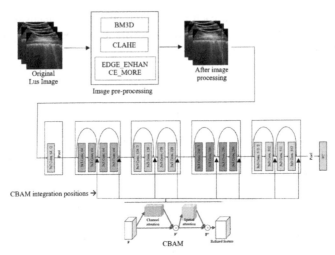

Fig. 5. Pre-processing the input image and integrating CBAM into the ResNet18 model

4 Results

This study employed the Windows 11 operating system with an Intel i5-11400F 6-core, 4.40 GHz CPU, 32 GB memory, and NVIDIA GTX 3060 12 GB VRAM platform. We utilized the Python language and the deep learning framework PyTorch for programming. To assess the performance of our method, we utilized a 5-fold cross-validation approach and reported the maximum metrics obtained. The evaluation metrics used included sensitivity, specificity, precision, F1 score, and accuracy. We terminated at 20 epochs with a batch size of 20 during the training process. The Adam optimizer was employed for each epoch, and the learning rate was set to 1e-4.

We applied the method of preserving the original image to compare different configurations of the attention mechanism, and the results are presented in Table 2. The data in Table 2 shows that without integrating CBAM, the base method VGG16 achieved an overall accuracy of 0.87, which is lower than the integrated CBAM method (VGG16-CBAM) with an overall accuracy of 0.91. For VGG19, the accuracy was 0.91, lower than that of the integrated CBAM method (VGG19-CBAM), which was 0.92. Similarly, the base method ResNet18 achieved an accuracy of 0.87 without integrating CBAM, lower than the accuracy of the integrated CBAM ResNet18 method (ResNet18-CBAM), which reached 0.92.

Table 2. Comparing different configurations of the attention mechanism without image processing

Models	VGG16	VGG16-CBAM	VGG19	VGG19-CBAM	ResNet18	ResNet18-CBAM
Accuracy	0.87	0.91	0.91	0.92	0.87	0.92

For the input image pre-processing using Clahe, we conducted a performance comparison of different configurations of the attention mechanism. In Table 3, we observe that the VGG16 method achieved an accuracy of 0.90, lower than the VGG16-CBAM method with an accuracy of up to 0.94. Similarly, the base VGG19 method yielded an accuracy of 0.92, lower than the accuracy of 0.93 achieved by VGG19-CBAM. For the ResNet18 method, the accuracy was 0.91, lower than that of ResNet18-CBAM, which integrated CBAM and reached 0.93.

Table 3. Comparing attention mechanisms using the Clahe technique

Models	VGG16	VGG16-CBAM	VGG19	VGG19-CBAM	ResNet18	ResNet18-CBAM
Accuracy	0.90	0.94	0.92	0.93	0.91	0.93

When applying the input image pre-processing using the Edge_enhance_more edge enhancement filter, we also compared the performance of different configurations of the attention mechanism. Looking at Table 4, we can see that the base VGG16 method achieved an accuracy of 0.91, lower than the VGG16-CBAM method with an accuracy of up to 0.94. Similarly, the base VGG19 method yielded an accuracy of 0.92, lower than the accuracy of 0.96 achieved by VGG19-CBAM. Additionally, the ResNet18 method without integrating CBAM had an accuracy of 0.92, lower than that of ResNet18-CBAM, which reached an accuracy of up to 0.94.

Table 4. Comparing attention mechanisms using the Edge_enhance_more filter

Models	VGG16	VGG16-CBAM	VGG19	VGG19-CBAM	ResNet18	ResNet18-CBAM
Accuracy	0.91	0.94	0.92	0.96	0.92	0.94

When using the BM3D method for image denoising combined with the Edge_enhance_more edge enhancement filter, we performed a performance comparison of different configurations of the attention mechanism. The results show that VGG16-CBAM and VGG19-CBAM achieved accuracies of 0.95 and 0.97, respectively, higher than their respective base methods, VGG16 (0.93) and VGG19 (0.95). Additionally, the ResNet18-CBAM method achieved an accuracy of 0.96, higher than ResNet18 (0.94). Table 5 demonstrates these results.

Table 5. Comparing attention mechanisms using BM3D in combination with Edge_enhance_more

Models	VGG16	VGG16-CBAM	VGG19	VGG19-CBAM	ResNet18	ResNet18-CBAM
Accuracy	0.93	0.95	0.95	0.97	0.94	0.96

Furthermore, we also generated custom 3 × 3 kernel matrices, as presented in Table 6. The kernel matrices were named K8.6, K8.8, and K9.6, respectively. We performed convolutional operations with the input image that had been denoised using BM3D, and the results are presented in Table 7.

Table 6. Custom 3 × 3 kernel matrix

$\begin{pmatrix} -1, & -1, & -1 \\ -1, & 8.6, & -1 \\ -1, & -1, & -1 \end{pmatrix}$	$\begin{pmatrix} -1, & -1, & -1 \\ -1, & 8.8, & -1 \\ -1, & -1, & -1 \end{pmatrix}$	$\begin{pmatrix} -1, & -1, & -1 \\ -1, & 9.6, & -1 \\ -1, & -1, & -1 \end{pmatrix}$
K8.6	K8.8	K9.6

The results using the K8.6 kernel matrix showed that the VGG19-CBAM model achieved the highest performance with an accuracy of 0.98. When using the K8.8 kernel matrix, the ResNet18-CBAM model achieved the highest performance with an accuracy of 0.97. Finally, in the experiment with the K9.6 kernel matrix, the VGG16-CBAM model achieved the highest accuracy of 0.97. For the baseline models, performance changes were not compared to the BM3D denoising method combined with edge_enhance_more.

Table 7. Comparing attention mechanisms using BM3D in combination with a custom kernel matrix

Models	VGG16-CBAM	VGG19-CBAM	ResNet18-CBAM
Accuracy	0.95	0.97	0.96
Kernel	K9.6	K8.6	K8.8

To evaluate the overall performance of the models, Table 8 summarizes the overall accuracy of each model. The results indicate that combining the BM3D denoising technique and edge_enhance_more demonstrates high performance for the baseline models. For models incorporating CBAM, the BM3D denoising method combined with a custom kernel matrix shows the highest performance.

A comparison of the overall number of parameters of the models was also conducted. The total number of parameters between the VGG16 and VGG16-CBAM models is approximately around 14 million. Similarly, for the VGG19 and VGG19-CBAM models, the number of parameters is about 20 million; for the ResNet18 and ResNet18-CBAM models, it is around 11 million. The number of parameters between the base and CBAM-integrated models is relatively similar, but their accuracies differ. Table 9 clearly illustrates these results.

In addition, we also used Occlusion Sensitivity Maps (OSMs) to observe how the models process and classify images. OSMs were proposed in the paper "Visualizing

Table 8. Summarizing the overall accuracy of each model

Models	Experiment				
	Original image	Contrast enhancement using Clahe	Edge enhancement using Edge_enhance_more	BM3D combined with Edge_enhance_more	BM3D combined with Matrix Kernel
VGG16	0.87	0.90	0.91	0.93	
VGG16-CBAM	0.91	0.94	0.94	0.95	0.97
VGG19	0.91	0.92	0.92	0.95	
VGG19-CBAM	0.92	0.93	0.96	0.97	0.98
ResNet18	0.87	0.91	0.92	0.94	
ResNet18-CBAM	0.92	0.93	0.94	0.96	0.97

Table 9. Comparing the total number of parameters of the models

Models	Parameters
VGG16	14,747,843
VGG16-CBAM	14,814,567
VGG19	20,057,539
VGG19-CBAM	20,124,263
ResNet18	11,209,539
ResNet18-CBAM	11,388,499

and Understanding Convolutional Networks" by Matthew D. Zeiler and Rob Fergus (2014) [11]. The paper introduced a new method called Occlusion Sensitivity Maps to explain how deep learning models process and classify images. It involves systematically occluding parts of the image and measuring the impact of each occluded part on the model's prediction. This method allows observing a model's sensitivity to object changes within an image. The results demonstrate that OSMs are a powerful tool for studying and understanding the behavior of deep learning models.

We can observe the pre-processing of input images when using OSMs in Fig. 6 and Fig. 7. Figure 6(a) is also an image of a COVID-19 patient with an abnormal area shown in the yellow cavity. The OSMs method shows a difference in how the VGG19 model handles focusing on the image region shown in Fig. 6(b) (orange cavity area) compared to VGG19-CBAM in Fig. 6(c). VGG19-CBAM has a stronger reactivity to the abnormal pleural area, showing a red cavity area.

In Fig. 7(a), we see an image of a COVID-19 patient with an abnormal area shown in the yellow cavity. The results are classified as pneumonia when applying the VGG19 model for training. The OSMs method showed that the model did not correctly focus the response on the pleura's abnormal region, as shown in Fig. 7(b). When applying the VGG19-CBAM model to training, the classification results for COVID-19 disease are accurate. Using the OSMs method, it was observed that with the integration of CBAM,

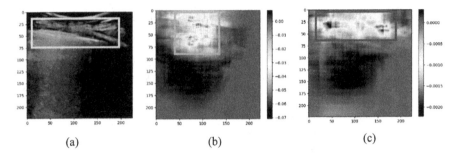

Fig. 6. OSMs with VGG19 and VGG19-CBAM models

the pattern had a strong response to the abnormal area of the pleura and is typically shown in Fig. 7(c) with the red cavity area.

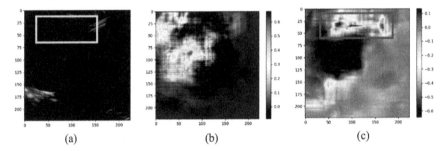

Fig. 7. OSMs with COVID-19 classification model

Furthermore, I utilized Grad-CAM [12] to identify the regions of focus in the ultrasound image captured by the model. Grad-CAM is a technique that provides insights into the decision-making process of a deep learning model by generating a "heat map" highlighting the significant areas of the image that contribute to the classification results. This method proves valuable in analyzing misclassified samples and enhances our understanding of how the model makes decisions based on the image content. We are often only aware of the model's output without knowing which specific regions of the image influenced the predictions. With Grad-CAM, we can identify the specific areas in the image that the model relied on to generate accurate classification results.

For input image processing when using edge_enhance_more edge enhancement filter and applying grad-cam, we can see in Fig. 8 and Fig. 9. Figure 8(a) displays an ultrasound image of a COVID-19 patient. When using the ResNet18 model, which predicts a healthy lung, the model's attention is directed toward the bright areas resembling the A-line, represented by the red cavity area in Fig. 8(b). Likewise, Fig. 9(a) exhibits an ultrasound image of a COVID-19 patient. When utilizing the ResNet18-CBAM model, the results are accurate, and the Grad-CAM method highlights the lung injury area, as depicted in Fig. 9(b) within the red cavity.

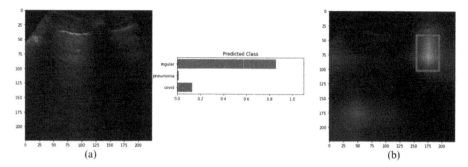

Fig. 8. The Edge_enhance_more, grad-cam with the ResNet18 model

Based on the experimental results, it can be observed that the CBAM-integrated model combined with image pre-processing has achieved higher effectiveness compared to the non-CBAM-integrated model while preserving the original image.

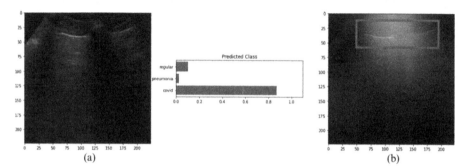

Fig. 9. The Edge_enhance_more, grad-cam with the ResNet18-CBAM model

5 Conclusions

This study presents a method for COVID-19 detection based on image pre-processing, attention mechanism, and transfer learning. This method is considered novel as previous studies only focused on basic models without implementing image pre-processing, especially attention mechanisms. The results show that in small sample sizes, the model achieves the highest effectiveness for the classification task. However, the study also has some limitations that will be addressed in future work. The explanation of the proposed model is complex, and the reasons for its accurate classification results are still unknown. We plan to visualize every stage of the model in the future, exploring further how the model operates. Collecting more COVID-19 ultrasound images and further improving our model to detect specific diseases are also part of our future work. Additionally, we will investigate methods to handle noise in ultrasound images and build specialized deep learning models for medical ultrasound images. We will also expand our model to other medical datasets and improve its performance based on the results.

Furthermore, we intend to integrate ultrasound with other imaging modalities. While ultrasound holds value in COVID-19 assessment, it does have inherent limitations, such as limited depth penetration and challenges in imaging specific structures. Future endeavors can focus on integrating ultrasound with other imaging modalities, such as CT or MRI (if available), to provide a more comprehensive evaluation of COVID-19.

Acknowledgment. Research reported in this publication was supported by the National Institute Of General Medical Sciences of the National Institutes of Health under Award Number P20GM104420. The content is solely the authors' responsibility and does not necessarily represent the official views of the National Institutes of Health.

References

1. WHO, "WHO Director-General's opening remarks at the media briefing on COVID-19 - 11 March 2020, 11 March 2020. https://www.who.int/director-general/speeches/detail/who-director-general-s-opening-remarks-at-the-media-briefing-on-covid-19-11-march-2020. Accessed 31 May 2023
2. Worldometer, " COVID - Coronavirus Statistics - Worldometer,". https://www.worldometers.info/coronavirus. Accessed 31 May 2023
3. Guan, W., Ni, Z.Y., Hu, Y., et al.: Clinical characteristics of coronavirus disease 2019 in China. N. Engl. J. Med. **382**(18), 1708–1720 (2020)
4. Weinstock, M.B., Echenique, A.N., Russell, J.W., et al.: Chest X-ray findings in 636 ambulatory patients with COVID-19 presenting to an urgent care center: a normal chest X-ray is no guarantee. J. Urgent Care Med. **14**(7), 13–18 (2020)
5. Roberts, J., Tsiligkaridis, T.: Ultrasound diagnosis of COVID-19: robustness and explainability 2020. https://arxiv.org/pdf/2012.01145.pdf
6. Born, J., Wiedemann, N., Cossio, M., et al.: Accelerating detection of lung pathologies with explainable ultrasound image analysis. Appl. Sci. **11**(2), 672 (2021)
7. Jannisborn, "covid19_ultrasound/data at master · jannisborn/covid19_ultrasound · GitHub," GitHub, Inc., 21 January 2021. https://github.com/jannisborn/covid19_ultrasound/tree/master/data. Accessed June 2022
8. Diaz-Escobar, J., et al.: Deep-learning based detection of COVID-19 using lung ultrasound imagery, 13 August 2021. https://doi.org/10.1371/journal.pone.0255886. Accessed August 2022
9. Deng, J., Dong, W., Socher, R., Li, L.-J., Li, K., Fei-Fei, L.: Imagenet: a large-scale hierarchical image database. In: Proceedings of the CVPR (2009)
10. Woo, S., Park, J., Lee, J.-Y., Kweon, I.S.: CBAM: convolutional block attention module. In: Proceedings of the European Conference on Computer Vision (ECCV), Munich, Germany, pp. 3–19 (2018)
11. Zeiler, M.D., Fergus, R.: Visualizing and Understanding Convolutional Networks (2014). https://arxiv.org/pdf/1311.2901.pdf
12. Selvaraju, R., et al.: Grad-CAM: Visual Explanations from Deep Networks via Gradient-based Localization (2019). https://arxiv.org/pdf/1610.02391.pdf

Deep Learning Techniques for Segmenting Breast Lesion Regions and Classifying Mammography Images

Nam V. Nguyen[1], Hieu Trung Huynh[1], and Phuc-Lu Le[2(✉)]

[1] Faculty of Information Technology, Industrial University of Ho Chi Minh City,
Ho Chi Minh City, Vietnam
[2] Faculty of Information Technology, Ho Chi Minh City University of Science,
Ho Chi Minh City, Vietnam
`lplu@fit.hcmus.edu.vn`

Abstract. Breast cancer is currently one of the leading causes of death in many countries worldwide. Detecting breast masses early can provide higher chances of survival for patients. However, determining and segmenting benign or malignant breast masses is becoming a challenging issue. Currently, there are a wide range of Convolutional Neural Networks used to address breast mass segmentation and breast cancer classification issues, such as U-Net, SegNet, Mask R-CNN, for segmentation, and Convnet, CNN, ResNet, for classification. However, these solutions are still not effective enough. Therefore, we have solved this problem by applying modern model called Segment Anything Model to predict breast tumor segmentation masks to help doctors identify and evaluate breast tumors and two models EfficientNet B0 combined with Focal Loss and Vision Transformer base to classify breast images as benign or malignant. The experimental results show those modern models achieved high performance with an Intersection over Union score of 96.59% on the CIBS-DDSM dataset. Additionally, the classification model achieved an accuracy of 100% and F1-scores of 100% on the DDSM dataset, outperforming other models. Our technique helps support doctors in identifying breast masses in images and provides reliable predictions for diagnostic purposes, thus improving the effectiveness of breast cancer detection.

Keywords: Deep learning · Breast Cancer · EfficientNet B0 · Segment Anything Model · Vision Transformer · Focal Loss

1   Introduction

According to the WHO, in 2020, approximately 2.3 million women worldwide were diagnosed with breast cancer, and there were 685,000 deaths from breast cancer globally. The exact causes of breast cancer are still not fully understood, although genes and hormones appear to play a major role. Detecting and preventing the development of these cancer cells as early as possible is beneficial not only in increasing the chances of cure but also in improving the quality of life for patients. Currently, imaging techniques such as Magnetic Resonance Imaging (MRI), Single-Photon Emission Computed Tomography (SPECT), Computed Tomography (CT), and X-ray mammography are used for screening and early detection of breast-related abnormalities and breast cancer. The earlier the diseases are detected, the higher the chances of successful treatment. Besides the benefits it brings, X-ray mammography also has certain limitations, including the inability to determine the benign or malignant state of a breast lesion. Moreover, manual image interpretation can lead to subjective results, errors, and burden the healthcare facility. Therefore, recently, image processing techniques combined with Convolutional Neural Networks (CNNs) have been introduced to assist doctors in breast cancer diagnosis. These techniques aim to address the limitations of traditional mammography by providing more objective and automated analysis, aiding in the early detection and accurate diagnosis of breast cancer. However, CNNs require considerable pre-processing to compensate for poor image quality [1]. The usage of low-quality and noisy mammography images can adversely affect the model's performance. Additionally, medical image data, including mammography images, is often scarce, leading to data imbalance between benign and malignant classes, which can bias the model's predictions towards the class with more data. As a result, selecting a suitable model for breast lesion segmentation and mammogram classification becomes one of the major challenges.

In this paper, we utilize the most advanced Segment Anything Model (SAM) model for breast tumor segmentation. This model is built on the largest segmentation dataset up to now, with over 1 billion masks on 11 million licensed and privacy-respecting images [2], making it exceptionally powerful. We performed model fine-tuning on the CIBS-DDSM dataset, starting from pre-trained weights and biases, which improved the breast tumor segmentation performance significantly. In addition, we developed a deep learning method for mammogram classification. We applied data augmentation techniques and utilized YOLOX-s models to remove redundant image regions. Furthermore, we employed mode; EfficientNet B0 combine with Focal Loss and Vision Transformer (ViT) base to classify breast images as benign or malignant tumors. Our solution enables comprehensive and detailed tumor segmentation, providing doctors with valuable insights into breast lesions. Moreover, our classification approach offers reliable predictions regarding the nature of the breast tumor, assisting doctors with trustworthy diagnostic recommendations for the patients.

2 Preliminaries

2.1 Dataset

In this study, we used two datasets for two different purposes. Firstly, we used the CBIS-DDSM dataset (Curated Breast Imaging Subset of DDSM) available at Cancerimagingarchive, and selected only the mass cases, to train the SAM segmentation model with 1,696 images from 892 patients. Secondly, we used the Digital Database for Screening Mammography (DDSM) dataset to train the classification models, which consists of 13,128 images (including the processed, rotated images from the original), here we only used 2,188 raw and unprocessed images. This is available at: https://data.mendeley.com/datasets/ywsbh3ndr8/2.

2.2 Data Preprocessing

To train a good model, preprocessing the images is essential as it significantly impacts the model's performance. We used the CIBS-DDSM dataset in its original Digital Imaging and Communications in Medicine (DICOM) format, which contains important metadata such as brightness, contrast, image features, etc.

Converting DICOM images to PNG images: due to the large file size of DICOM images, this demands high-end hardware while our training on Kaggle with limited hardware resources, we converted the images to PNG format for convenience in processing and inputting them into the models. PNG maintains good image quality and compression capabilities without loss of data compared to other formats like JPEG, TIFF, etc. Additionally, we applied windowing, also known as gray-level mapping, to select specific pixel ranges from the image prior to normalization. This technique effectively increased the contrast between soft tissues and special tissue regions, and also allowed for a larger range when manually adjusting brightness/contrast later on. This technique should be applied when exporting images in PNG format (Fig. 1).

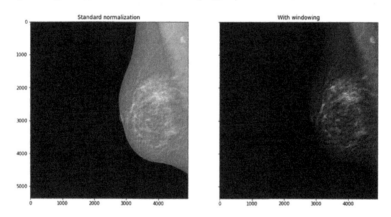

Fig. 1. Comparison of regular image and image using windowing.

Cropping images using the YOLOX model: with the original large-sized mammograms, we only need to extract the region of interest to feed into the model. Cropping and selecting the region of interest help reduce the size and file size of the images and reduce noise.

Recently, with the emergence of YOLOX for accurate lesion detection, we have utilized it for image cropping and resizing with a height of 1024 and a width of 512. YOLOX is a convolutional neural network model designed for object detection, recognition, and classification. Equipped with some recent advanced detection techniques, such as decoupled head, anchor-free, and advanced label assigning strategy, YOLOX achieves a better trade-off between speed and accuracy compared to other models of all sizes [3] (Fig. 2).

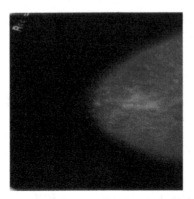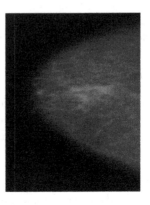

Fig. 2. Images before (left) and after (right) cropped by YOLOX-s.

In this study, we used the YOLOX-s version with 9 million parameters. Additionally, we annotated 1,000 mammogram images to train the YOLOX-s model, which helps improve accuracy in detecting regions of interest.

2.3 Transfer Learning

Transfer learning aims at improving the performance of target learners on target domains by transferring the knowledge contained in different but related source domains. In this way, the dependence on a large number of target domain data can be reduced for constructing target learners [4]. Therefore, this technique is particularly suitable for cases with limited data, especially for the set of mammography images, as models can be pre-trained on large datasets from other related medical image fields and then transfer this knowledge to the task of classifying and segmenting mammography images.

To achieve the best results when applying transfer learning, we should use pre-trained models with a large dataset that is relevant to the new target. This is because these models will have already learned useful features from the large dataset, and they can be used as a foundation for the transfer learning model.

After using the pre-trained model, we can fine-tune the model's parameters to fit the new dataset. This fine-tuning process can help improve the performance of the transfer learning model on the new dataset.

- For segmentation, we utilized the pre-trained SAM model, which was trained on the largest segmentation dataset to date, consisting of over 1 billion masks on 11 million images [2]. This significantly improves the efficiency of breast mass segmentation.
- For classification, we employed two pre-trained models, Vision Transformers and EfficientNet, which were trained on large natural image datasets like ImageNet. The objective was to use the pre-trained weights as a starting point for training the classification model to classify breast mammograms as benign or malignant.

3   Method Details

3.1   Focal Loss

Focal Loss is highly effective in addressing the issue of data imbalance among different classes. It focuses on harder-to-predict examples more than the easier ones. This aids in enhancing the prediction of challenging and hard-to-classify examples. Focal loss incorporates a modulating factor $(1 - p_t)^\gamma$ into the cross-entropy loss, with a tunable focusing parameter $\gamma \geq 0$ [5].

The formula for focal loss is defined as follows

$$FL(p_t) = -(1 - p_t)^\gamma \log(p_t) \tag{1}$$

If in the case of misclassified samples, p_t becomes small, approximately or very close to 1, and the loss function remains largely unaffected. As p_t approaches 1, the modulating factor tends towards 0, thereby down-weighting the loss value for well-classified examples. The focusing parameter γ smoothly adjusts the rate at which easy examples are down-weighted [5]. Subsequently, we add an α-balanced variant of the focal loss, which contributes to slightly improved accuracy compared to the unbalanced form.

$$FL(p_t) = -\alpha_t(1 - p_t)^\gamma \log(p_t) \tag{2}$$

In this study, we use the parameter $\gamma = 2$ and an α-balanced variant of the focal loss with a value of 0.25.

3.2   Balancing Data

Due to the limited and insufficient diversity of the data, we performed data augmentation using techniques such as Horizontal Flip, Vertical Flip, Rotation, and Color Jitter. Additionally, we divided the data into batches with a batch size of 64 or 32, depending on the model. Ensuring data balance within each batch is also an important concern. We increased the frequency of occurrence of classes with fewer samples in each batch. To achieve this, we assigned weights to each image using WeightedRandomSampler in PyTorch.

Initially, we calculated these weights using the formula one divided by the number of occurrences of each class. This way, classes with a higher number of occurrences were assigned smaller weights, while classes with fewer occurrences were assigned larger weights. This approach helped to balance the number of samples from different classes in each batch.

3.3   Vision Transformer Architecture

In this study, we utilized a pre-trained vision transformer model on the ImageNet dataset for benign and malignant classification. Additionally, we employed ensemble learning, which is the combination of multiple models, to further enhance the performance of our model.

Originating from the transformer model used in natural language processing (NLP) with remarkable effectiveness and success on one-dimensional word
tokens, we applied its superior performance to images. To achieve this, we transformed the input images of size (W, H, C) into two-dimensional patches and
flattened them into one-dimensional vectors. This sequence was then considered
as the input sequence for the transformer encoder. The number of patches, N,
was calculated using the formula $N = \frac{HW}{P^2}$, where (P, P) represents the resolution of each image patch. The transformer maintains a constant latent vector
size D across all layers, and thus, we flattened the patches and mapped them to
D dimensions using a trainable linear projection. The output of this projection
is referred to as the patch embeddings [6] (Fig. 3).

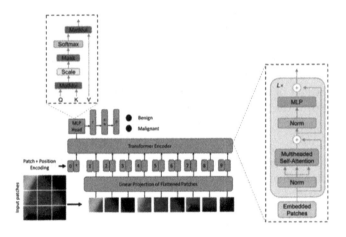

Fig. 3. The vision transformer-based transfer learning architecture for mammogram
breast image detection [7]

The processing pipeline of the model can be summarized as follows: each
image patch is flattened into a vector X_p^n of length $P \times P \times C$, where P is
the patch size and C is the number of color channels, and there are a total of n
image patches. The vectors X_p^n are then mapped to a D-dimensional space using
a learnable linear projection denoted as E. As a result, we obtain a sequence of
embedding vectors with size D. This sequence of embeddings is prefixed with
a learnable class embedding called X_{class}, and the values of X_{class} correspond
to the classification outcomes Y. Finally, the embedding vectors are combined
with the positional embeddings E_{pos} (learned during training) to add positional
information to the input [7]. The concatenated embedding vectors form the final
input z_0, which will be fed into the encoder network of the vision transformer
to perform the image classification process. This processing pipeline enables the

model to understand the spatial structure of the image and classify it based on the embedded information from the image patches and positional information.

$$z_0 = [X_{class}; X_p^1 E; ...; X_p^N E] + E_{pos} \tag{3}$$

Finally, we feed z_0 into a transformer encoder network, which consists of a stack of L identical layers, to perform the classification process. The output of the L_{th} layer of the encoder is then fed into the classification head. Additionally, we use an MLP (Multi-layer Perceptron) with a single hidden layer to further process the classification by employing a single linear layer for the actual classification task. The GELU activation function is used in the MLP as the classification head. In summary, the transformer network helps abstract features from each image, and then the MLP is used for image classification based on the pre-abstracted features.

3.4 SAM Architecture

In this study, we employ SAM for breast tumor segmentation. With training on an extensive dataset, it has enabled the model to perform breast tumor segmentation effectively. SAM is released by the Meta AI Research group. The SAM model architecture consists of three main components: an image encoder, a flexible prompt encoder, and a fast mask decoder.

Image Encoder: We utilize a masked auto-encoder (MAE) [8] pre-trained ViT, which is minimally adapted to handle high-resolution inputs. The image encoder operates once per image and can be employed prior to triggering the model [2].

Prompt Encoder: We consider two groups of prompts: one group consists of sparse prompts (including points, boxes, and text), and the other group comprises dense prompts (including masks). To represent points and boxes, we utilize positional encodings combined with learned embeddings specific to each prompt type. For free-form text, we employ a pre-trained text encoder from the Contrastive Language-Image Pretraining (CLIP) framework. Dense prompts, namely masks, are embedded using convolutions and then element-wise summed with the image embedding.

Mask Decoder: The mask decoder efficiently maps the image embedding, prompt embeddings, and an output token to a mask. Our modified decoder block uses prompt self-attention and cross-attention in two directions (prompt-to-image embedding and vice-versa) to update all embeddings. After running two blocks, we up sample the image embedding and an MLP maps the output token to a dynamic linear classifier, which then computes the mask foreground probability at each image location [2] (Fig. 4).

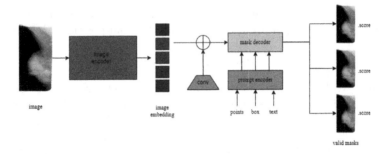

Fig. 4. Overview of SAM Application in Breast Tumor Segmentation.

3.5   Experimental Settings

In this study, our objective is to propose a solution for breast cancer segmentation and classification to aid physicians in diagnosing patients' conditions as benign or malignant. During the experimentation process, we divided our study into two stages. The first stage involved experiments on the SAM segmentation model. In the second stage, experiments were conducted on models EfficientNet B0 combined with Focal Loss and ViT applied for breast tumor classification.

3.6   Implementation Detail

During the model training process, we set the learning rate to 10^{-6} and utilize the AdamW optimizer with a weight decay setting of 0.05, which is an L2 regularization technique aimed at mitigating overfitting by applying a small penalty to the model's weight 'w' during the update process. We employ the Binary Cross-Entropy (BCE) loss function. In the context of the vision transformer model, GELU is employed as an activation function, while for other CNN-based models, we use the Rectified Linear Unit (ReLU). For the SAM model, the Intersection-over-Union (IoU) loss is utilized as the loss function. All experiments are conducted on the Kaggle platform using free GPUs.

4   Results

4.1   Breast Tumor Segmentation Using the SAM Model

In this phase, we utilize the CIBS-DDSM dataset to train the model. We select 1,318 images for the training set and 378 images for the testing set. Additionally, we conduct a pre-training process for the SAM model (Fig. 5).

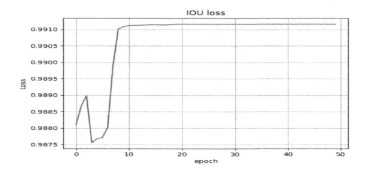

Fig. 5. The loss function during the training process.

The results of the training process with an IoU score exceeding 99% demonstrated that the SAM model adapted very well to the new training dataset. However, we also took the best weights achieved during training to perform evaluation on the test dataset using assessment metrics IoU. Denote S as the IoU values in data set, then we calculated some statistical quantities as follow: Mean is the average of S, $Max = \arg\max_{IoU_i \in S} IoU_i$ and $Min = \arg\min_{IoU_i \in S} IoU_i$ (Table 1).

Table 1. The results on the test sets

Type	IoU
Mean	96.59%
Max	99.4%
Min	53%

There are still some instances where the segmentation model does not perform well, achieving only 53% with IoU. However, overall, the SAM model is demonstrating excellent segmentation performance. It is indeed a valuable tool aiding physicians in detecting breast tumors and identifying any discrepancies during the diagnostic process. Comparison with previous studies (Table 2):

Table 2. The related literature and the method using our SAM model.

Literature	Dataset	IoU
Wessam at al. [9]	CBIS-DDSM	92.99%
Asma at al. [10]	CBIS-DDSM	80.02%
Our results	CBIS-DDSM	96.59%

Finally, compare the results with the state-of-the-art methods and models of previous studies. Our proposed SAM pre-trained model outperforms them (Fig. 6).

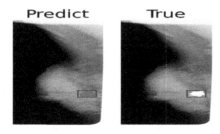

Fig. 6. Segmentation image of breast tumor as predicted by the model and segmentation image of actual breast tumor.

4.2   Classification of Breast Tumors

The results of the model training process for breast tumor classification have been presented in Table 3. Here, we employ two main approaches: (1) the 1st approach involves utilizing the ViT model for training, (2) the 2nd approach incorporates the EfficientNet B0 in conjunction with the Focal Loss function, which helps the model focus on incorrectly predicted samples rather than samples that the model predicts confidently. Both of these approaches yield promising results with Accuracy, Precision, and F1 score metrics all reaching 99.99% on the DDSM dataset.

Table 3. Classification results

Model	Test dataset	Accuracy (%)	Precision (%)	F1 Score (%)	AUC (%)
Efficientnet B0	DDSM	97.2	97.2	97.2	97.2
Efficientnet B0 + Haze Removal + Clahe	DDSM	98.6	98.6	98.6	98.6
Efficientnet B0 + Focal Loss	DDSM	99.9	99.9	99.9	99.9
Vision Transformer (ViT) base	DDSM	100	100	100	100

The following table shows the training time (by second) and weight size (by GB) between various models (Table 4).

Table 4. Model Training Time

Model	Train dataset	Time (s)	Weight size (GB)
Efficientnet B0	DDSM	1638	0.045
Efficientnet B0 + Haze Removal + Clahe	DDSM	9909	0.045
Efficientnet B0 + Focal Loss	DDSM	399	0.045
Vision Transformer (ViT) base	DDSM	604	0.97

We provide two confusion matrices, which are very similar, for two models: EfficientNet B0 + Focal Loss base and (ViT) Base (Fig. 7).

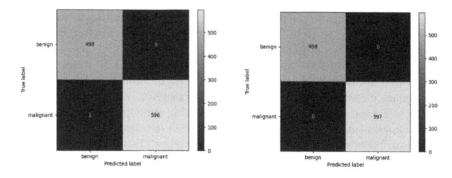

Fig. 7. The confusion matrices of EfficientNet B0 + Focal Loss (left) and ViT Base (right).

To achieve the results, we experimented various methods to select the best approaches. In Table 3, we present the best-performing experiments. Initially, we trained the EfficientNet B0 model on the DDSM dataset, achieving an accuracy of 97.2% and an F1 Score of 97.2%. Subsequently, during the training process, we recognized the pivotal role of data in enhancing model performance (Fig. 8).

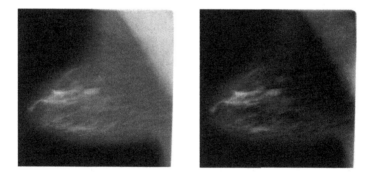

Fig. 8. Images before and after applying Haze Removal and CLAHE techniques

However, accessible data regarding mammographic images is limited. Consequently, we performed data augmentation by employing image processing techniques, namely Haze Removal to enhance clarity by eliminating noise and blurriness, thus sharpening the breast masses. This was combined with the Contrast Limited Adaptive Histogram Equalization (CLAHE) technique to improve contrast and image clarity. As a result, we improved the model by 1.4% in accuracy, achieving 98.6% accuracy and an F1 Score of 98.6%. However, the training time for this model increased sixfold compared to EfficientNet B0.

Subsequently, our proposed method combined EfficientNet B0 with the Focal Loss technique, enabling the model to focus on challenging prediction cases. This led to a significant improvement of 1.3% in performance, resulting in an accuracy of 99.9% and an F1 Score of 99.9%, compared to the (EfficientNet B0 + Haze Removal + CLAHE) method.

Finally, we conducted experiments on a new model, ViT base, achieving nearly 100% accuracy and an F1 Score of 100%. In summary, for the task of breast image classification, we propose the EfficientNet B0 + Focal Loss model and the ViT base model due to their low training time and high performance. All our experiments were conducted on the DDSM dataset. The following is the comparison between our work and the recent studies (Table 5):

Table 5. Related literature and our Proposed Method 1 & 2

Literature	Test dataset	Accuracy (%)	Precision (%)	F1 Score (%)	AUC (%)
Mei-Ling Huang et al. [11]	DDSM	99.93	–	99.92	–
Ribli et al. [12]	DDSM	–	–	–	95
Chougrad et al. [13]	DDSM	97.35	–	–	98
Proposed Method 1	DDSM	99.9	99.9	99.9	99.9
Proposed Method 2	DDSM	100	100	100	100

With our two proposed methods, there are significant improvements in performance metrics such as Accuracy, Precision, F1 Score, and AUC compared to other studies. Our works including source code can be found on the following link: https://github.com/david-nguyen-S16/Segmentation-and-classification-of-mammographic-images.

5   Conclusions and Future Works

In this study, we performed breast mass segmentation on mammographic images using a pre-trained SAM that was fine-tuned with superior performance, achieving an IoU score of 96.59% on the CIBS-DDSM dataset. This supports doctors in detecting abnormal breast masses, with a significantly improved segmentation performance, given a partially pre-trained dataset. Secondly, we conducted the classification of mammographic images as benign or malignant using two proposed methods: EfficientNet B0 + Focal Loss and ViT base. Both models achieved outstanding performance with F1 Scores of 99.9% and 100% on the DDSM dataset, leveraging transfer learning to enhance training. A limitation of this study is the scarcity of mammographic image data, but its impact on model performance is substantial.

In the future, we expect to refine the new methods for mammographic segmentation and classification, while also gathering additional mammographic data to achieve better results across different datasets.

Acknowledgement. We would like to express our gratitude to Mr. Khoi Nguyen (Hajim School of Engineering & Applied Sciences: University of Rochester, USA), have guided and supported us in experimenting and completing this paper.

This article was funded in part by University of Science, VNU-HCM under Grant No. CNTT2022−11.

References

1. Ayana, G., Dese, K., Raj, H., Krishnamoorthy, J., Kwa, T.: De-speckling breast cancer ultrasound images using a rotationally invariant block matching based non-local means (RIBM-NLM) method. Diagnostics **12**(4), 862 (2022). https://doi.org/10.3390/diagnostics12040862
2. Kirillov, A., et al.: Segment anything. ArXiv abs/2304.02643v1. Meta AI Research, FAIR (2023)
3. Ge, Z., Liu, S., Wang, F., Li, Z., Sun, J.: YOLOX: exceeding YOLO series in 2021. ArXiv abs/2107.08430. Megvii Technology (2021)
4. Zhuang, F., et al.: A comprehensive survey on transfer learning. ArXiv abs/1911.02685. IEEE (2020)
5. Lin, T.-Y., Goyal, P., Girshick, R., He, K., Dollár, P.: Focal loss for dense object detection. ArXiv abs/1708.02002 (2017)
6. Dosovitskiy, A., et al.: An image is worth 16×16 words: transformers for image recognition at scale. ArXiv abs/2010.11929v2. Google Research, Brain Team (2020)
7. Ayana, G., et al.: Vision transformer-based transfer learning for mammogram classification. Diagnostics **13**, 178 (2023). https://doi.org/10.3390/diagnostics13020178
8. He, K., Chen, X., Xie, S., Li, Y., Dollar, P., Girshick, R.: Masked autoencoders are scalable vision learners. In: CVPR (2022)
9. Salama, W.M., Aly, M.H.: Deep learning in mammography images segmentation and classification: automated CNN approach. Alex. Eng. J. **60**(5), 4701–4709 (2021). https://doi.org/10.1016/j.aej.2021.03.048. ISSN 1110-0168
10. Baccouche, A., Garcia-Zapirain, B., Castillo Olea, C., et al.: Connected-UNets: a deep learning architecture for breast mass segmentation. Breast Cancer **7**, 151 (2021). https://doi.org/10.1038/s41523-021-00358-x
11. Huang, M.-L., Lin, T.-Y.: Double-dilation non-pooling convolutional neural network for breast mass mammogram image classification. Bahrain Med. Bull. **44**(4), 1144 (2022)
12. Ribli, D., Horváth, A., Unger, Z., et al.: Detecting and classifying lesions in mammograms with deep learning. Sci. Rep. **8**, 4165 (2018). https://doi.org/10.1038/s41598-018-22437-z
13. Chougrad, H., Zouaki, H., Alheyane, O.: Deep convolutional neural networks for breast cancer screening. Comput. Methods Program. Biomed. **157**, 19–30 (2018). https://doi.org/10.1016/j.cmpb.2018.01.011

Development of a Handwriting Drawings Assessment System for Early Parkinson's Disease Identification with Deep Learning Methods

Jieming Zhang[1], Yongho Lee[1], Tai-Myoung Chung[2(✉)], and Hogun Park[1(✉)]

[1] Department of Computer Science and Engineering, Sungkyunkwan University, Suwon 16419, Republic of Korea
hogunpark@skku.edu
[2] Hippo T&C, Inc., Suwon 16419, Republic of Korea
tmchung@hippotnc.com

Abstract. Parkinson's disease (PD) is a prevalent neurodegenerative disorder, and early detection plays a crucial role in timely treatment to prevent further harm to patients. In recent years, researchers have primarily employed machine learning methods using clinical manifestations of PD patients for diagnosis, such as gait rigidity and distorted handwriting. Hand tremors and handwriting difficulties are typical early motor symptoms of PD, making handwriting analysis an important tool for detecting PD. However, previous approaches have limitations in capturing subtle variations in handwriting and often combine other biological signals. This study aims to develop a deep learning-based handwriting drawings assessment system that relies solely on patients' handwriting as vital evidence for early-stage Parkinson's diagnosis. We utilized two publicly available datasets, HandPD and NewHandPD, which contain hand-drawn spirals and meanders from PD patients and healthy participants. We employed EfficientNet-B1, ResNet-34, ResNet-101 and DenseNet-121 deep learning models for the classification task. Experimental results demonstrated that the EfficientNet-B1 network achieved the best performance on patients' meander traced graphics, with a precision and sensitivity of 97.62% and a accuracy of 96.36%. Furthermore, we created a Python Web API based on Flask and a user-friendly Windows application for the assessment system, enabling its use in screening tests for Parkinson's disease diagnosis. This system holds promising potential for aiding early detection and providing valuable support to healthcare professionals in diagnosing Parkinson's disease effectively.

Keywords: Parkinson's disease · Intelligent healthcare · Computer aided diagnosis · Handwriting assessment · Deep learning

1 Introduction

Parkinson's disease (PD) is a prevalent and progressive neurodegenerative disorder characterized by motor symptoms such as tremors, bradykinesia, rigidity, and postural instability [1]. Early and accurate diagnosis of PD is essential for timely intervention and

T. K. Dang et al. (Eds.): FDSE 2023, CCIS 1925, pp. 484–499, 2023.
https://doi.org/10.1007/978-981-99-8296-7_35

personalized treatment strategies to mitigate disease progression and enhance patients' quality of life.

Recent advancements in machine learning and artificial intelligence have offered new possibilities in medical diagnostics, and researchers have begun exploring their potential in aiding in the identification of early-stage PD [2–4]. Among the various motor symptoms associated with PD, handwriting difficulties have shown promise as a potential early indicator of the disease. Handwriting is a complex motor task involving the integration of cognitive, sensory, and motor processes, and its evaluation can provide valuable insights into neurodegenerative conditions [5, 6]. Hand tremors, handwriting difficulties, and other subtle alterations in writing patterns may occur in the early stages of PD, even before other motor symptoms become evident. Therefore, handwriting analysis presents a non-invasive and accessible approach for early PD detection.

Previous studies have attempted to distinguish PD patients from healthy subjects by handwriting. Rosenblum et al. [7] used relevant features such as the average pressure and speed of participants' handwriting, and finally achieved a classification accuracy of 97.5%. Zham et al. [8] proposed to use a tablet computer equipped with a smart pen to obtain the dynamic features of the handwriting process, such as the pressure during writing and the inclination of the pen, and then PD was classified by these features. Drotar et al. [9] collected data by asking participants to perform a variety of different handwriting tasks, and then developed three machine learning models of K-Nearest Neighbors (KNN), Adaboost ensemble model and Support Vector Machine (SVM), and finally achieved an accuracy rate of 81.3%. These studies rely on the integration of additional biological signals, which can introduce complexities and reduce the practicality of the diagnostic process.

Recently, researchers proposed to classify PD directly from handwriting drawings. Ali et al. [10] proposed a novel cascade system named Chi2-Adaboost and experiment results on HandPD dataset showed that the cascaded system achieved classification accuracy of 76.44%. Akter et al. [11] proposed to detect Parkinson's disease from hand-drawn meander images and spiral images of suspected persons, and applied some classification algorithms such as decision tree, Gradient Boosting (GB), KNN, random forest and HOG feature descriptor algorithm. The experimental results show that the accuracy of the GB algorithm reaches 86.67%, and the accuracy of KNN reaches 89.33%. Despite the success of previous attempts to utilize handwriting analysis for PD diagnosis, challenges have been encountered in capturing subtle and intricate variations in handwriting patterns associated with the disease.

In this paper, we propose the development of a deep learning-based handwriting drawings assessment system dedicated to early Parkinson's disease identification. Unlike previous approaches, our system focuses exclusively on handwriting patterns and requires no additional equipment when performing the test, harnessing the power of deep learning techniques to discover subtle meaningful features indicative of PD. We leverage two publicly available datasets, HandPD and NewHandPD, which encompass diverse handwriting samples from both PD patients and healthy controls. By utilizing state-of-the-art computer vision and deep learning models, including EfficientNet-B1, ResNet-34, ResNet-101 and DenseNet-121, we aim to extract discriminative features from hand-drawn images. These features will serve as vital inputs for our deep learning models, enabling accurate and efficient prediction of PD solely based on patients' handwriting. Furthermore, we developed a Python Web Server API based on Flask and a user-friendly Windows application, ensuring the seamless integration of our assessment system into clinical practice. This implementation facilitates PD screening tests and offers valuable support to healthcare professionals in their diagnostic and management efforts.

The rest of this article is arranged as follows. Section 2 describes relevant research in this area. Section 3 focuses on the methods used and how to set up the assessment system. Section 4 presents and analyzes the results obtained. Section 5 summarizes the work.

2 Related Work

In current clinical practice, physicians typically assess Parkinson's disease with the Unified Parkinson's Disease Rating Scale (UPDRS) [12]. However, since the evaluation results of the scale mainly depend on the patient's description and the doctor's visual observation, the diagnosis made may be affected by the doctor's medical level and subjective consciousness, which has certain limitations. Until now, the identification of Parkinson's disease has been a clinically challenging task. Recently, researchers have developed a strong research interest in PD detection using machine learning methods based on gait and handwriting data.

Abnormal gait is a common movement disorder in Parkinson's disease, which usually requires physical examination by a doctor or gait recognition with the help of devices such as sensors. Recently, researchers have favored non-contact, vision-based methods to identify gait abnormalities in Parkinson's disease. Zhang et al. [13] proposed a new spatiotemporal graph convolution based on weight matrix and introduced virtual connections to make up for the lack of Parkinson's gait characteristics expressed by the original physical connections of the body. The final model achieved an accuracy rate of 87.1%. Sabo et al. [14] proposed to predict the clinical score of Parkinson's disease gait from videos of dementia patients, and the macro-mean F1 score of the best model was 0.53 ± 0.03. Guo et al. [15] proposed a Sparse Adaptive Graph Convolutional Network (SA-GCN) to achieve fine-grained quantitative evaluation of skeleton sequences extracted from videos, and the evaluation results confirmed its effectiveness and reliability.

One of the most obvious and common symptoms in the early stage of PD is resting tremor, and the hand is the most obvious part of the patient's tremor, so handwriting assessment is also the simplest and most effective method for early screening. Many studies have shown that handwriting is an effective tool for early Parkinson's diagnosis. Aly et al. [16] performed a statistical spectral analysis of the position signals output by digitized tablets of all participants and compared the power spectra of the control and patient groups to detect the presence of tremor. Saunders-Pullman et al. [17] demonstrated that Archimedean spiral curve analysis can b complement motor assessment in early Parkinson's disease.

3   Methodology

In this paper, we developed a system to assess the PD handwriting drawings and the proposed framework is shown in Fig. 1. We used spiral and meander images to recognize patients, respectively. We implemented data preprocessing firstly, then the various deep learning models were tested to find the best one adopted the specific task. Finally, we built a Python Web API based on Flask and a Windows software to facilitate the clinical use of Parkinson's handwriting assessment system.

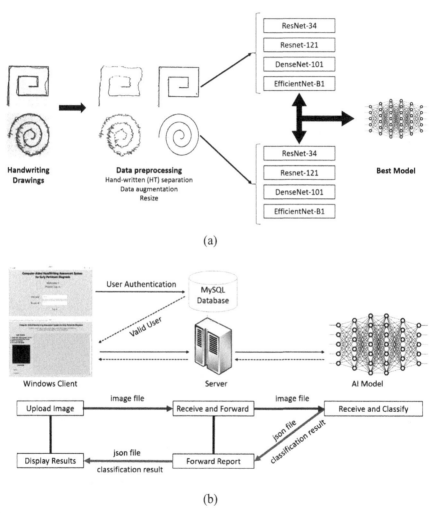

(a)

(b)

Fig. 1. Overall of the proposed system framework. (a) Deep learning model training. (b) Windows application structure.

3.1 Dataset

In our experiments, the research focused on handwritten images of spiral and meander tasks. We combined HandPD [18] and NewHandPD [19], two publicly available handwriting datasets, which were mainly used for the detection of Parkinson's disease.

HandPD is a large dataset containing samples from 92 subjects (18 healthy subjects and 74 PD subjects) performing spiral and meander tasks. It contains a total of 736 images. The NewHandPD dataset was collected by the State University of Sao Paulo, Brazil, and contains data from 66 individuals, including 35 healthy subjects and 31 unhealthy subjects. In our experiment, since 21 healthy subjects in the NewHandPD dataset had very poor handwriting image quality and ambiguous handwriting, we excluded them from the final experimental dataset. The dataset is detailed as shown in Table 1.

Table 1. Dataset details.

Dataset	No. of Healthy subjects	No. of Patient Subjects	No. of Healthy _Spiral Images	No. of Patient _Spiral Images	No. of Healthy _Meander Images	No. of Patient _Meander Images
HandPD Dataset	18	74	72	296	72	296
NewHandPD Dataset	35	31	140	124	140	124
Combined Dataset	53	105	212	420	212	420
Experiment Dataset	32	105	128	420	128	420

3.2 Separation of the Hand-Written Trace (HT)

Before extracting the features of the images, in order to accurately extract the features of the handwritten trace, reduce the influence of the exam template and paper scanning, and capture the subtle changes of the handwritten patterns of Parkinson's patients and normal people, we developed a method to separate the handwritten trace (HT) and the exam template (ET) by using color thresholds. Specifically, we first read the image using cv2.imread function of OpenCV library, and then converted the color space from BGR to HSV (Hue-Saturation-Value) since the HSV color space has the ability to separate the color information from the intensity information. The Hue channel represents the color itself, the Saturation channel represents the purity of the color, and the Value channel represents the brightness. This makes it possible to select a range of colors for a specific color, so that a specific color can be accurately identified according to the color threshold. Finally, in order to remove the noise caused by paper scanning, we only keep the extracted color, and the rest of the pixels are set to white. Figure 2 depicts the separation results.

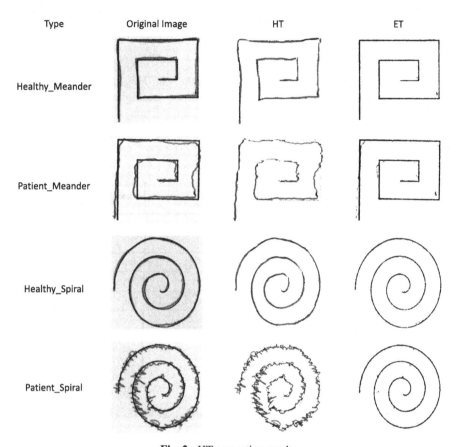

Fig. 2. HT separation results.

3.3 Data Augmentation

Since healthy samples have fewer samples than patient samples, it's essential to augment the data for healthy samples to balance the dataset. Since the handwriting trajectories of normal people are generally stable, it is reasonable that we do not change the attributes of these images, including color and direction, and only scale and translate them to augment them. This process increases the effective size of healthy samples and helps prevent overfitting during neural network training processing.

3.4 Handwriting Assessment Based on Deep Learning Methods

In this study, we propose the utilization of ResNet-34 [20], ResNet-101, DenseNet-121 [21], and EfficientNet-B1 [22] deep learning models for the classification of Parkinson's disease handwriting images, leveraging the advantages of deep learning in extracting deeper-level features compared to traditional CNNs. These models have been pre-trained using the extensive ImageNet dataset. In addition, we use Grad-CAM [23] to visualize the heatmap of the Parkinsonian handwriting features.

Deep Learning Models

ResNet-34 and ResNet-101
ResNet incorporates residual learning to address the vanishing or exploding gradient problem that arises when the network becomes deeper, leading to performance degradation. The key structural feature of ResNet is the introduction of shortcut connections that add input to output, but the residual structures of ResNet-34 and ResNet-101 are different, as shown in Fig. 3.

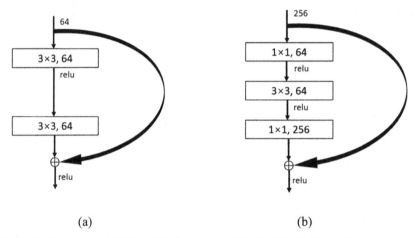

(a)   (b)

Fig. 3. Residual structure. (a) The residual structure of ResNet-34. (b) The residual structure of ResNet-101.

For the residual structure of ResNet-34, the main branch is composed of two layers of 3×3 convolutional layers. The connecting line on the right is the shortcut branch. The output feature matrix shape of the main branch and the shortcut must be the same, and the same output matrix can be added. In the residual structure of ResNet-101, the first layer uses a 1×1 convolutional layer to compress the channel dimension, the second layer is a 3×3 convolutional layer, and the third layer is a 1×1 convolutional layer to restore the channel dimension.
DenseNet-121

DenseNet uses dense connections to connect the feature maps of all layers to the feature maps of each subsequent layer. However, unlike other CNN architectures, the input of each layer in DenseNet comes from the output of all previous layers, allowing the flow of features from the first layer to the last layer. If we denote the data by x and the network layer by H, Eq. 1 shows the output of a traditional network at layer l.

$$x_l = H_l(x_{l-1}) \tag{1}$$

where x_l is the feature map at layer l, and it is obtained by applying the layer operation H_l to the feature map x_{l-1} from the previous layer.

Equation 2 shows the output of ResNet after adding the input from the previous layer.

$$x_l = H_l(x_{l-1}) + x_{l-1} \tag{2}$$

where x_l is obtained by applying the layer operation H_l to the feature map x_{l-1} from the previous layer and adding the feature map x_{l-1} from the previous layer to it. This is known as a residual connection.

Equation 3 shows that in DenseNet, the output layer connects all previous layers as input.

$$x_l = H_l([x_0, x_1, x_2, \ldots, x_{l-1}]) \tag{3}$$

where x_l is obtained by applying the layer operation H_l to a concatenation of all previous feature maps $[x_0, x_1, x_2, \ldots, x_{l-1}]$.

EfficientNet

EfficientNet is developed based on the idea of adjusting the model's depth, width, and resolution, achieving a balance between computational efficiency and performance. We use EfficientNet-B1 which has strong feature representation ability as a classifier. The basic component of EfficientNet is the MBConv module, which is borrowed from MobileNet V2. To further optimize the network structure, EfficientNet has summarized the squeeze and excitation methods from SENet [24].

The EfficientNet network structure consists of a Stem, 16 MBConv modules, Conv2D, GlobalAveragePooling2D, and fully connected layer, where the critical part is the 16 MBConv module. In the MBConv module as shown in Fig. 4, a 1×1 convolution is first used to change the channels of the input features, followed by a depthwise convolution. Then, the channel attention mechanism of SENet is introduced, and finally 1×1 convolution is used to reduce the channels of the feature maps.

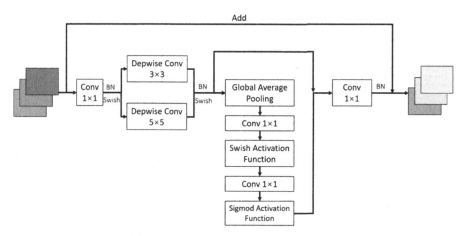

Fig. 4. MBConv module network structure.

The activation function in EfficientNet is designed as a Swish activation function, and the swish function is a Self-Gated activation function, expressed by the Eq. 4.

$$\text{swish}(X) = X\,\sigma(\beta\,X) \tag{4}$$

where σ is the logistic function, the parameters β can be learned or set to fixed hyper-parameters.

Gradient-weighted Class Activation Mapping (Grad-CAM)

Grad-CAM is similar to the CAM algorithm. For a category c, we firstly obtain the weights $w_1, w_2, \ldots w_n$ of each channel of the feature map. Unlike CAM, Grad-CAM uses the gradient of backpropagation to calculate weights. The weight calculation is shown in Eq. 5.

$$\alpha_k^c = \frac{1}{Z}\sum_i\sum_j\frac{\partial y^c}{\partial A_{ij}^k} \tag{5}$$

c represents the category, y_c is the logits value corresponding to the category (that is, the value that has not yet passed SoftMax), A represents the feature map output by convolution, k represents the channel of the feature map, i, j represents the horizontal and vertical coordinates of the feature map, and Z represents the size of the feature map. This process is equivalent to finding the mean value of the gradient on the feature map, which is equivalent to a global average pooling operation.

Then the obtained weights are linearly weighted and summed to obtain a heat map. Grad-CAM adds a Relu operation to the fused heat map, and only retains the area that has a positive effect on category c. As shown in Eq. 6.

$$L_{\text{Grad-CAM}}^c = \text{ReLU}\left(\sum_k \alpha_k^c A_k\right) \tag{6}$$

Evaluation Metrics

We measured our implemented system performance based on precision, sensitivity, F1 score and accuracy using the formulas as shown in Eq. 7 to Eq. 10.

$$Precision = \frac{TP}{TP + FP} \tag{7}$$

$$Sensitivity = \frac{TP}{TP + FN} \tag{8}$$

$$Accuracy = \frac{TP + TN}{TP + TN + FP + FN} \tag{9}$$

$$F1Score = \frac{2 * Precision * Sensitivity}{Precision + Sensitivity} \tag{10}$$

3.5 Application Development for Windows Platform

The application for the Windows platform was developed using C# language within the Visual Studio 2022 integrated development environment. The user interface was constructed using Windows Presentation Foundation (WPF) framework. The backend of the application employed the MySQL database management system to securely store and retrieve user login credentials. This ensured that access to the system was restricted to authorized users only. To handle the application's functionality, the Flask framework, based on Python, was utilized as the backend server. Flask was responsible for reading the uploaded image, loading the pre-trained deep learning model, facilitating the analysis process, and generating responses for the identification results.

4 Experiment

4.1 Experimental Setup

We use NVIDIA GeForce RTX 2080Ti GPU with 12 GB memory, Intel(R) Core (TM) i9-10900 CPU with 2.80 GHz 64 GB RAM to build a deep learning framework using PyTorch in Windows 10 environment. We use CUDA, Cudnn, OpenCV and other required libraries to train and test the PD handwriting classification model.

We use color thresholding to extract images containing only handwritten traces, and then split 10% of the experiment dataset to create a test set. This test set will be used to evaluate the performance of the final model and will only contain the original images, ensuring that the final evaluation is performed on the original images only. Then we apply data augmentation techniques including scaling and translating) to the remaining control group images to increase its diversity and help the model generalize better. After augmentation, we performed the 80:20 split ratio to split into train and validation datasets.

Since we used pre-trained models, we changed the last linear output layer of each model to 2 to classify Parkinson's and normal people. The batch size is set to 32, the optimizer is Adam, the learning rate is set to 0.001, and the epoch is set to 100.

4.2 Early Parkinson's Disease Identification

To assess the performance of various deep learning models for early Parkinson's disease identification based on handwriting drawings, we conducted separate tests on ResNet-34, ResNet-101, DenseNet-121, and EfficientNet-B1. All models were subjected to the same training conditions, including batch size, learning rate, optimizer, and epoch, ensuring a fair comparison.

The experimental results are presented in Table 2.

The results demonstrate the performance of each model for both Meander and Spiral handwriting drawing types. For the Meander drawings, the Efficientnet-B1 model achieved the highest accuracy with 97.62% for the "Patient" class, while the DenseNet-121 model showed highest accuracy with 100% for the "Patient" class. For sensitivity, the performance of the four models for the "Patient" class is not much different, but EfficientNet-B1 has the highest sensitivity for the "Healthy" class, reaching 92.31%. At

Table 2. Experiment results.

Handwriting Drawings Type	Meander				
Model	**Class**	**Precision**	**Sensitivity**	**F1-score**	**Accuracy**
ResNet-34	Healthy	90.91%	76.92%	83.33%	92.73%
	Patient	93.18%	97.62%	95.35%	
ResNet-101	Healthy	90.00%	69.23%	78.26%	90.91%
	Patient	91.11%	97.62%	94.25%	
DenseNet-121	Healthy	100%	76.92%	86.96%	94.55%
	Patient	93.33%	100%	96.55%	
EfficientNet-B1	Healthy	92.31%	92.31%	92.31%	96.36%
	Patient	97.62%	97.62%	97.62%	
Handwriting Drawings Type	Spiral				
Model	**Class**	**Precision**	**Sensitivity**	**F1-score**	**Accuracy**
ResNet-34	Healthy	100%	69.23%	81.82%	92.73%
	Patient	91.30%	100%	95.45%	
ResNet-101	Healthy	91.67%	84.62%	88%	94.55%
	Patient	95.35%	97.62%	96.47%	
DenseNet-121	Healthy	90.91%	76.92%	83.33	92.73%
	Patient	93.18%	97.62%	95.35%	
EfficientNet-B1	Healthy	77.78%	53.85%	63.64%	85.45%
	Patient	86.96%	95.24%	90.91%	

the same time, the F1 score and accuracy of EfficientNet-B1 are the highest among the four models, and the accuracy reaches 96.36%.

Similarly, in the case of Spiral drawings, the ResNet-34 model exhibited the highest precision with 100% for the "Healthy" class, while obtained the poor sensitivity with 69.23% using the same model. For the "Patient" class, the ResNet-101 model achieved the highest precision with 95.35% and F1-score 96.47%. Besides, ResNet-101 achieved the highest accuracy with 94.55%.

Our comparative analysis highlights the potential of deep learning models in early Parkinson's disease identification from handwriting drawings. ResNet-34 demonstrated promising results in both handwriting drawing types, "Meander" and "Spiral," exhibiting high precision and sensitivity values across the healthy and patient classes. Similarly, ResNet-101, with its deeper architecture, showcased commendable performance, yielding competitive precision, sensitivity, and F1-score values. Both ResNet-34 and ResNet-101 models achieved relatively high Accuracy, suggesting their potential as reliable classifiers in Parkinson's disease identification. DenseNet-121, known for its dense connectivity pattern, also exhibited compelling outcomes. While its precision, sensitivity, and F1-score values were commendable, it showcased slightly lower sensitivity compared to ResNet models.

EfficientNet-B1, designed for achieving excellent trade-offs between efficiency and accuracy, displayed promising results, particularly in the "Meander" drawing type. With highest F1-score, accuracy and "Patient" class precision values, this model demonstrated proficiency in distinguishing between healthy individuals and Parkinson's disease patients. Considering the diagnostic application and the goal of this study is to develop an early handwriting assessment system for Parkinson's that is simple and does not require additional equipment, we adopted the EfficientNet-B1 model and meander images as our early screening tools.

Handwriting features in the early stages of Parkinson's disease mainly include hand tremors, handwriting difficulties, and other subtle changes in writing patterns. To assist doctors in making a diagnosis based on Parkinsonian features of writing patterns, we utilize Grad-CAM to visualize the regions in the input image that have the greatest impact on the model's decision-making process. The heatmap in Fig. 5 demonstrates the important regions in each sample. It can be observed that the patient's parkinsonian features are strongly activated, showing a highlighted.

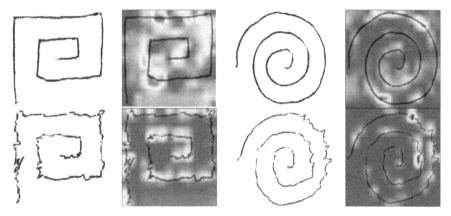

Fig. 5. Heatmap of the Parkinsonian handwriting features. The first row shows the healthy group; second row shows the patient group.

We compared with other studies that also identify Parkinson's from handwritten patterns, and we can find that our method outperforms existing methods. Table 3 shows the comparison.

4.3 Windows Platform Application

The software system interface consisted of several pages, with the initial page serving as the login screen. The purpose of this page was to authenticate users and verify their access rights. This authentication process is crucial in ensuring that only authorized users

Table 3. Comparison with other methods.

	Model	Accuracy	Sensitivity	Specificity
Ali et al. [10] (2019)	Cascade	76.44%	70.94%	81.94%
Akter [11] (2020)	KNN + HOG	89.33%	91.67%	80.33%
Xu et al. [25] (2020)	PCA + Cascade	80.99%	88.98%	76.38%
Wang et al. [26] (2023)	Transformer	92.68%	91.32%	91.15%
Ours	EfficientNet-B1	96.36%	97.62%	92.31%

are granted access to the system, thus safeguarding the server from unauthorized entry and safeguarding valuable computing resources.

Upon successful authentication, users gained entry to the assessment system. Within this system, users had the option to proceed by selecting the "Upload Image" button, which triggered the image upload functionality. Through a designated Web API and the port, the selected images were transmitted to the server for further processing. The server conducted analysis and predictions on the uploaded images, leveraging the pre-trained deep learning model. Moreover, activation maps for each layer were generated, providing insightful visual representations. Subsequently, the analysis results were sent back to the client application for display. The results returned from the server are displayed in the interface, as shown in Fig. 6.

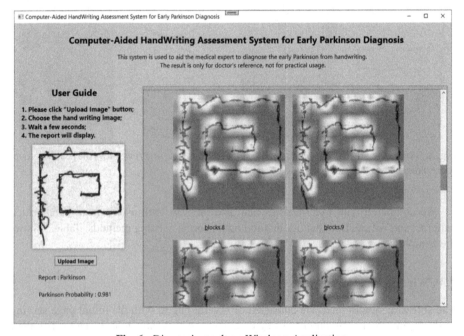

Fig. 6. Diagnosis result on Windows Application.

By presenting the analysis results to medical experts, the application empowered them to conveniently diagnose and evaluate the images. The visualized information aided in making informed decisions and drawing accurate conclusions based on the provided insights.

5 Conclusion

The primary objective of this research is to develop a handwriting drawings assessment system that exhibits high precision and sensitivity in identifying early-stage PD. Through extensive experimental evaluation and performance analysis, we found that the deep learning model of EfficientNet-B1 achieved the best results on meander images, achieving 96.36% accuracy and 97.62% sensitivity, surpassing other models and current research, which demonstrates the effectiveness of our system in detecting early Parkinson's disease.

In addition, the user-friendly application for the Windows platform based on Web API incorporates a secure login process, efficient image uploading, server-side analysis using a deep learning model, and client-side visualization of the results. This comprehensive approach enables effective and convenient image analysis and diagnosis within the medical domain.

Timely PD detection can lead to better disease management and improved patient outcomes. Our system has the potential for broader applications in the field of medical imaging and diagnosis. In the future, we plan to integrate our system to clinical practice, where it can serve as a valuable aid for healthcare practitioners in making accurate and timely diagnoses.

Acknowledgement. This work was supported by the Institute of Information and communications Technology Planning and Evaluation (IITP) grant funded by the Korea government (MSIT) (No. 2020-0-00990, Platform Development and Proof of High Trust and Low Latency Processing for Heterogeneous·Atypical·Large Scaled Data in 5G-IoT Environment) and the Technology Innovation Program (or Industrial Strategic Technology Development Program-Source Technology Development and Commercialization of Digital Therapeutics) (20014967, Development of Digital Therapeutics for Depression from COVID19) funded By the Ministry of Trade, Industry & Energy(MOTIE, Korea).

References

1. De Stefano, C., Fontanella, F., Impedovo, D., Pirlo, G., di Freca, A.S.: Handwriting analysis to support neurodegenerative diseases diagnosis: a review. Pattern Recogn. Lett. **121**, 37–45 (2019)
2. Rosenblum, S., Samuel, M., Zlotnik, S., Erikh, I., Schlesinger, I.: Handwriting as an objective tool for Parkinson's disease diagnosis. J. Neurol. **260**, 2357–2361 (2013)
3. Kotsavasiloglou, C., Kostikis, N., Hristu-Varsakelis, D., Arnaoutoglou, M.: Machine learning-based classification of simple drawing movements in Parkinson's disease. Biomed. Signal Process. Control **31**, 174–180 (2017)

4. Pereira, C.R., et al.: Handwritten dynamics assessment through convolutional neural networks: an application to Parkinson's disease identification. Artif. Intell. Med. **87**, 67–77 (2018)
5. Impedovo, D., Pirlo, G.: Dynamic handwriting analysis for the assessment of neurodegenerative diseases: a pattern recognition perspective. IEEE Rev. Biomed. Eng. **12**, 209–220 (2018)
6. Tseng, M.H., Cermak, S.A.: The influence of ergonomic factors and perceptual–motor abilities on handwriting performance. Am. J. Occup. Therapy **47**(10), 919–926 (1993)
7. Rosenblum, S., Samuel, M., Zlotnik, S., Erikh, I., Schlesinger, I.: Handwriting as an objective tool for Parkinson's disease diagnosis. J. Neurol. **260**(9), 2357–2361 (2013)
8. Zham, P., Arjunan, S.P., Raghav, S., Kumar, D.K.: Efficacy of guided spiral drawing in the classification of Parkinson's disease. IEEE J. Biomed. Health Inform. **22**(5), 1648–1652 (2017)
9. Drotár, P., Mekyska, J., Rektorová, I., Masarová, L., Smékal, Z., Faundez-Zanuy, M.: Evaluation of handwriting kinematics and pressure for differential diagnosis of Parkinson's disease. Artif. Intell. Med. **67**, 39–46 (2016)
10. Ali, L., Zhu, C., Golilarz, N.A., Javeed, A., Zhou, M., Liu, Y.: Reliable Parkinson's disease detection by analyzing handwritten drawings: construction of an unbiased cascaded learning system based on feature selection and adaptive boosting model. IEEE Access **7**, 116480–116489 (2019)
11. Akter, L.: Early identification of Parkinson's Disease from Hand-drawn Images using Histogram of oriented gradients and machine learning techniques. In: 2020 Emerging Technology in Computing, Communication and Electronics (ETCCE), pp. 1–6. IEEE, December 2020
12. Goetz, C.G., et al.: Movement disorder society-sponsored revision of the Unified Parkinson's Disease Rating Scale (MDS-UPDRS): scale presentation and clinimetric testing results. Mov. Disord. Off. J. Mov. Disord. Soc. **23**(15), 2129–2170 (2008)
13. Zhang, J., Lim, J., Kim, M.H., Hur, S., Chung, T.M.: WM–STGCN: a novel spatiotemporal modeling method for Parkinsonian gait recognition. Sensors **23**(10), 4980 (2023)
14. Sabo, A., Mehdizadeh, S., Iaboni, A., Taati, B.: Estimating parkinsonism severity in natural gait videos of older adults with dementia. IEEE J. Biomed. Health Inform. **26**(5), 2288–2298 (2022)
15. Guo, R., Shao, X., Zhang, C., Qian, X.: Sparse adaptive graph convolutional network for leg agility assessment in Parkinson's disease. IEEE Trans. Neural Syst. Rehabil. Eng. **28**(12), 2837–2848 (2020)
16. Aly, N.M., Playfer, J.R., Smith, S.L., Halliday, D.M.: A novel computer-based technique for the assessment of tremor in Parkinson's disease. Age Ageing **36**(4), 395–399 (2007)
17. Saunders-Pullman, R., et al.: Validity of spiral analysis in early Parkinson's disease. Mov. Disord. Off. J. Mov. Disor. Soc. **23**(4), 531–537 (2008)
18. Pereira, C.R., et al.: A new computer vision-based approach to aid the diagnosis of Parkinson's disease. Comput. Methods Programs Biomed. **136**, 79–88 (2016)
19. Pereira, C.R., Weber, S.A., Hook, C., Rosa, G.H., Papa, J.P.: Deep learning-aided Parkinson's disease diagnosis from handwritten dynamics. In: 2016 29th SIBGRAPI Conference on Graphics, Patterns and Images (SIBGRAPI), pp. 340–346. IEEE, October 2016
20. He, K., Zhang, X., Ren, S., Sun, J.: Deep residual learning for image recognition. In: Proceedings of the IEEE Conference on Computer Vision and Pattern Recognition, pp. 770–778 (2016)
21. Huang, G., Liu, Z., Van Der Maaten, L., Weinberger, K.Q.: Densely connected convolutional networks. In: Proceedings of the IEEE Conference on Computer Vision and Pattern Recognition, pp. 4700–4708 (2017)
22. Tan, M., & Le, Q.: Efficientnet: rethinking model scaling for convolutional neural networks. In: International Conference on Machine Learning, pp. 6105–6114. PMLR, May 2019

23. Selvaraju, R.R., Cogswell, M., Das, A., Vedantam, R., Parikh, D., Batra, D.: Grad-CAM: visual explanations from deep networks via gradient-based localization. In: Proceedings of the IEEE International Conference on Computer Vision, pp. 618–626 (2017)
24. Hu, J., Shen, L., Sun, G.: Squeeze-and-excitation networks. In: Proceedings of the IEEE Conference on Computer Vision and Pattern Recognition, pp. 7132–7141 (2018)
25. Xu, S., Zhu, Z., Pan, Z.: A cascade ensemble learning model for Parkinson's disease diagnosis using handwritten sensor signals. J. Phys. Conf. Ser. **1631**(1), 012168) (2020). IOP Publishing
26. Wang, N., et al.: A coordinate attention enhanced swin transformer for handwriting recognition of Parkinson's disease. IET Image Processing (2023)

Breast Cancer Classification on Mammograms Using Vision Transformer

Thuong-Cang Phan[1]([✉])[iD], Anh-Cang Phan[2][iD], and Thanh-Ngoan Trieu[1][iD]

[1] Can Tho University, Can Tho City, Vietnam
{ptcang,ttngoan}@cit.ctu.edu.vn
[2] Vinh Long University of Technology Education, Vinh Long City,
Vinh Long Province, Vietnam
cangpa@vlute.edu.vn

Abstract. Breast cancer is the most commonly diagnosed cancer and the fifth leading cause of death in women. Early detection of this disease not only increases the survival rate but also reduces the cost of treatment. Mammography (X-ray mammography) is the current imaging method to identify and diagnose breast malignancies. In this work, we propose a classification technique based on several network architectures, including NasNetLarge, MobileNetV2, InceptionV3, DenseNet, and Vision Transformer to classify mammograms as normal, benign, or malignant. Experimental results show that the accuracy of the proposed models is up to 99%. The support of mammograms screening containing lesions will help doctors focus more on analyzing results. This helps the accuracy of diagnosis to increase and gives timely treatment direction.

Keywords: Vision Transformer · Breast Cancer · Deep learning · Mammograms

1 Introduction

Breast cancer has become one of the most common cancers in women. Over 2.3 million new cases of breast cancer were diagnosed worldwide in 2020 [3]. By 2023, an estimated 297,790 women in the United States will be diagnosed with invasive breast cancer and 55,720 women will be diagnosed with non-invasive breast cancer[1]. It is estimated that 43,700 deaths from breast cancer will occur in the United States by 2023. Breast cancer in women is the fifth leading cause of death. In practice, mammography is a widely used diagnostic tool for breast cancer diagnosis [17]. Mammography requires exposing the patient's chest to very small doses of radiation - lower doses than usual X-rays. Breast cancer can be identified from mammograms by the different absorption rates of normal and abnormal tissues. Tumors may appear as masses, deformities, asymmetry, or micro-calcifications on

---

[1] https://www.nationalbreastcancer.org/breast-cancer-facts/ accessed on 25 June 2023.

T. K. Dang et al. (Eds.): FDSE 2023, CCIS 1925, pp. 500–512, 2023.
https://doi.org/10.1007/978-981-99-8296-7_36

mammograms [14]. With an increasing number of new cases, it is difficult for radiologists to accurately detect and diagnose breast cancer in a high workload condition. Thus, it is essential to support doctors and radiologists in breast cancer diagnosis on mammograms with advanced technologies.

Gaikwad [7] proposed a model using the SVM classifier to detect breast cancer in mammograms. The method has been implemented in four stages including preprocessing, ROI extraction, feature extraction, and classification. The system achieved an accuracy of 83%. Chougrad et al. [5] proposed a system that uses convolutional neural networks (CNN) to detect breast cancer from public image datasets. The results showed that this work achieves an accuracy of up to 98%. Shamy and Dheeba [16] proposed a model based on k-mean Gaussian Mixture Model (GMM) and CNN. The authors first identify the region of interest and then apply the texture feature extraction method. The accuracy achieved is 95.8%. Vijayam and Lekshmy [22] proposed a model based on deep learning techniques. The author focuses on Lloyd's algorithm for clustering to group similar data points and CNN for classification. An accuracy of 96% was achieved using the proposed model. Aaqib et al. [1] proposed a method for breast cancer identification on an internationally available dataset (DDSM) containing 2,620 mammograms. VGG-16 was used for feature extraction and SSD was used for tumor detection. The results showed an accuracy of 96.2%. Zhong et al. [23] proposed a metastatic cancer imaging classification model based on DenseNet Block, which can efficiently identify metastatic cancer in small image patches taken from larger digital pathology scans. The accuracy of the proposed model during training is up to 98%. Albashish et al. [2] proposed a transformation learning model based on VGG16 to be used to extract features from the BreaKHis histopathological image dataset. The accuracy of the proposed model is 89%. Girish et al. [8] proposed a breast cancer detection model based on microwave images with seven different deep learning network architectures. The results of the models achieved an accuracy of up to 88.41%. Mahmud et al. [13] presented their approach to detect breast cancer using histopathological images using pretrained deep transfer learning models such as ResNet-50, ResNet-101, VGG-16 and VGG-19. The ResNet-50 was outperformed other models, achieving accuracy rates of 90.2%. Asadi and Memon [4] employed a cascade network with UNet for segmentation and a ResNet backbone for classification of breast cancer. The results of the proposed method achieved an accuracy of 98.61%.

2   Background

2.1   Breast Cancer

Breast cancer [19] is cancer that develops from cells in the mammary gland. There are two main types of breast abnormalities: benign and malignant. Benign breast refers to unusual growths or other changes in the breast tissue that are not cancer. It does not spread to nearby structures or distant areas of the body. Benign tumors are often well-defined and slow-growing and most of them are harmless. Breast cancer is a tumor that grows in the mammary gland, but has the ability to invade surrounding tissue, and can spread to other parts of the body. They are often observed and may need to be surgically removed. The local or global dispersion of cancerous cells is uncontrolled and life-threatening without prompt treatment. Figure 1 shows an illustration of breast benign and malignant from out testing dataset.

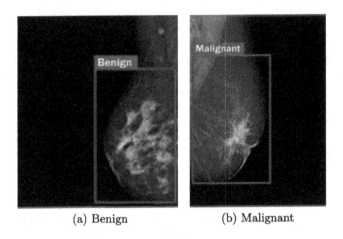

(a) Benign   (b) Malignant

Fig. 1. Illustration of breast benign and malignant from testing dataset.

2.2 Neural Network Models

MobileNet-V2. MobileNet-V2 [15] is one of the neural networks developed to be able to perform on devices with limited resources. This architecture requires a smaller number of parameters than other networks such as VGG [18] and ResNet [9]. This helps in reducing the load on computational resources and memory. With its compact size, the network can perform at high speed on mobile devices and allows the size of the model to be adjusted to fit different application needs.

Inception-V3. Inception-V3 [21] is one of the famous and widely used CNN in the field of computer vision and image processing. It is designed to optimize computational efficiency, help reducing the number of parameters required, and reduce computational complexity. This increases processing speed and reduces network training time. In addition, the network has the reusability characteristic, i.e., the learning weights can be reused for tasks related to different image classifications.

NASNetLarge. NASNetLarge [24] is a CNN that is trained more than a million images from the ImageNet database. It is capable of synthesizing complex image features. NASNetLarge uses a block architecture and each block is supported by a set of popular operations in CNN models with various kernel size. The architecture allows the model to learn how to build good classifier features and optimize hyper-parameters to get the best performance on the training dataset.

DenseNet. DenseNet [12] has a dense connection compared to other models such as VGG and ResNet. Each layer receives additional inputs from all preceding layers and passes its own feature maps to all subsequent layers. This allows for a thinner and more compact network, resulting in fewer channels. In other words, each layer accepts the feature maps of the previous layers as input, and the feature maps of the subsequent layers conveys all the data by explicitly connecting all the layers in the network. DenseNet can reduce the problem of gradient vanishing, improve the spreadability of feature maps, and reduce the number of parameters.

Transformer. Vision Transformer [11] is a neural network used for image processing and classification based on self-attention mechanisms. It is based on the original Transformer model used in natural language processing. In this model, the image is divided into patches and fed to the Transform Encoder for feature extraction. Finally, a classifier is used to predict the label of the image. Dividing images into small patches helps the model to recognize spatial features in an image and the relationship between patches. Information processing is performed based on linear transformations and self-attention mechanisms that do not require convolutions as CNNs. In addition, Vision Transformer can be extended to handle larger images by increasing the number of patches. This helps in handling high resolution images without performance issues. With its low computational complexity and ability to overcome the limitations of CNNs in image processing, Vision Transformer outperforms some of the most advanced CNN models available today [6].

2.3   Evaluation Metrics

Accuracy is calculated based on several values such as true positives (TP), false positives (FP), true negatives (TN) and false negatives (FN) described by Eq. 1. The categorical cross-entropy loss function is presented in Eq. 2 [10], where i is the data label, C is the actual value, and P is the predicted value.

$$Accuracy = \frac{TP + TN}{TP + TN + FP + FN} \tag{1}$$

$$L(C, P) = -\sum_{1} C_i log(P_i) \tag{2}$$

3   Proposed Method

In this work, we use transfer learning method on deep neural networks and Vision Transformer to detect and classify breast cancer. The proposed approach consists of two phases: training and testing. The details of the stages are shown in Fig. 2.

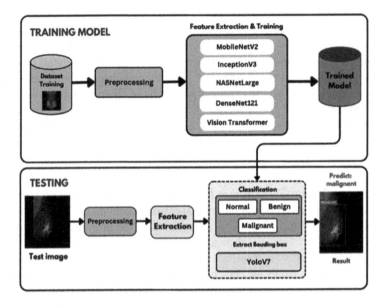

Fig. 2. General model of the proposed method for breast cancer detection and classification.

3.1 Training Phase

Pre-processing. We normalize input images to a size of 224×224 pixels, which is the suitable size to create patches. Then, we enhance the dataset by image rotation and image fliping.

Feature Extraction and Training. Breast cancer features are extracted from mammograms after preprocessing. The training phase uses several deep network models including NasNetLarge, MobileNet-V2, Inception-V3, DenseNet-121, and Vision Transformer. For the Vision Transformer model, the input image after being preprocessed will be divided into patches and passed through a linear projection. Here, we choose the size for each patch to be 16×16 due to its stability to performance degradation and computational complexity [6]. Each patch will be assigned a specific location and label to ensure that the image after extracting the features will not be disturbed. Then, a transform encoder is used to conduct feature extraction encoding, classifying, and localizing benign and malignant tumors. The result of this process is classified images. The proposed network architecture is shown in Fig. 3.

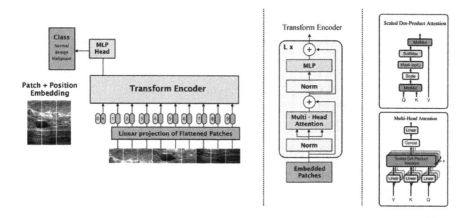

Fig. 3. Proposed vision transformer model.

3.2   Testing Phase

To evaluate the network models, we test the newly trained models using a testing dataset. The input images will be normalized to a size of 224×224, and then passed through YOLO-V7 to determine the mammary area. When the mammary area is determined, it will be put through the trained models for breast cancer prediction. The testing results are one of three conclusions as Normal, Benign, or Malignant.

4   Experiments

4.1   Installation Environment and Experimental Dataset

The system is installed and executed on Windows 10 environment with 8GB RAM configuration and Nvidia Geforce GPU. The libraries that support training network models are TensorFlow and Keras.

The training dataset used in this study was obtained from Mini-MIAS [20] consisting of 322 images containing left and right breast images of 161 patients in three categories: normal, benign, and malignant. There were 208 normal images, 63 benign, and 51 malignant images. To test the accuracy of the training models, we built a testing dataset taken from 150 patients of Can Tho Obstetrics Hospital (Vietnam) including 100 normal images, 100 benign images, and 100 malignant images.

4.2   Scenarios

We conduct experiments on 5 scenarios with the parameters presented in Table 1.

Table 1. Scenarios and training parameters

Scenario	Network model	Epochs	Learning rate	Batch size	Image size
1	MobileNet-V2	100	0.001	default	224 × 224
2	Inception-V3	100	0.001	default	224 × 224
3	NASNetLarge	100	0.001	default	224 × 224
4	DenseNet-121	100	0.001	default	224 × 224
5	Vision transformer	100	0.001	16 × 16	224 × 224

4.3 Training Results

Loss Value. Figure 4 shows the loss values of the scenarios during the training phase. The validation loss of the five scenarios are 0.8354, 0.0836, 0.0059, 0.0062, and 0.0054, respectively. Observing scenarios 1, 2, and 3, we can see that the validation loss values are not stable and higher results than the training loss values. This shows that these training models are not optimal and can lead to bias in the prediction process. In contrast, scenarios 4 and 5 give more optimal results than the above scenarios when the validation loss is equal to the training loss for scenario 4 and the validation loss is lower than the training loss for scenario 5. However, the validation loss value that coincides with the train loss can also be due to underfitting problems. The results show that the model in scenario 5 gives better performance than the models in the remaining scenarios.

Accuracy. Figure 5 shows the accuracy of the scenarios during the training phase. Scenario 1 has an accuracy of 96% and scenario 2 has an accuracy of 96.5%. In the last 3 scenarios, the accuracy is much better than the first two scenarios of 99%. On the other hand, observing scenarios 1, 2, and 3, we can see that the validation accuracy gives lower results than the training accuracy. This shows that these training models are not effective and can lead to errors in the prediction process. In contrast, scenarios 4 and 5 give more optimal results than the above scenarios when the validation accuracy value is equal to the train accuracy value for scenario 4 and the validation accuracy value is higher than the training accuracy for scenario 5. This shows that two models in scenarios 4 and 5 have better predictive ability than the remaining three scenarios.

Training Time. Figure 6 shows the training time of the five scenarios with 39.35 min, 36.18 min, 89.65 min, 42.38 min, and 118.67 min, respectively. It can be seen that scenario 2 gives faster training time than the remaining scenarios and scenario 5 has the longest training time.

4.4 Testing Results

Table 2 presents some experimental results of five scenarios. In the case of Malignant, the tumor is visible on mammogram but scenarios 1 and 4 give a result of

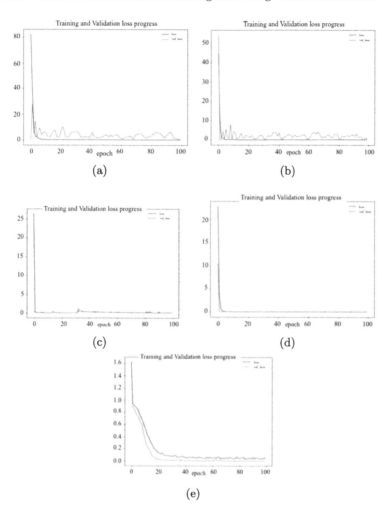

Fig. 4. Loss values of the five scenarios.

Normal, scenario 2 gives a result of Benign, and scenarios 3 and 5 result in Malignant. In the case of Benign, the tumor spots are distributed small throughout the mammary region. The prediction results in scenarios 1, 2, and 4 are Normal, scenario 3 is Malignant, and scenario 5 results in Benign, which is correct to the actual result. In the Normal case, scenarios 1, 2, 4, and 5 give an accurate prediction compared to reality while scenario 3 gives a prediction result of Benign. It can be seen that scenario 5 provides correct results in all three cases of Malignant, Benign, and Normal. This shows that scenario 5 performs better than the remaining scenarios.

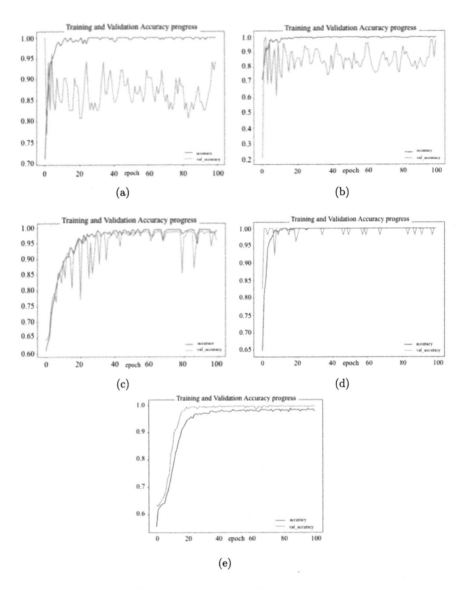

Fig. 5. Accuracy of the five scenarios.

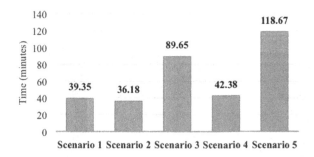

Fig. 6. Training time of the five scenarios.

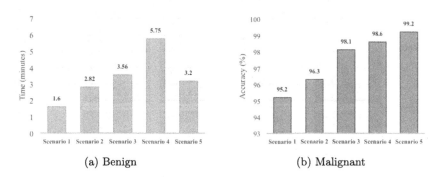

(a) Benign   (b) Malignant

Fig. 7. Detection time and accuracy of five scenarios on the testing dataset.

Figure 7a shows the prediction time on the testing dataset of the five scenarios with 1.65 min, 2.82 min, 3.56 min, 5.75 min, and 3.2 min, respectively. Figure 7b shows the prediction accuracy on the testing dataset of the five scenarios with 95.2%, 96.3%, 98.1%, 98.6%, and 99.2%, respectively. Through the above results, it can be seen that scenario 5 gives faster test training time than scenarios 1 and 4 and slower training time than scenarios 2 and 3. On the contrary, the accuracy of scenario 5 is higher than that of the remaining scenarios. This shows that scenario 5 gives better prediction results than other scenarios.

Table 2. Illustration of breast cancer detection and classification on testing dataset.

5   Conclusion

Breast cancer is the most common and leading cause of death among women. Detecting breast cancer at an early stage and counseling patients for treatment is always essential. In this study, we propose a method to detect and classify breast cancer based on representative feature extraction networks such as MobileNet-V2, Inception-V3, NASNetLarge, DenseNet-121, and Vision Transformer. At the same time, we also collected the biomedical dataset of breast cancer patients for testing. This not only gives objective evaluation results but also proves the effectiveness of the models when making predictions. Besides, we bring some comparison results between the models with the hope to contribute to the evaluation and selection of appropriate models to build a system for breast cancer detection and classification. This will help doctors quickly make diagnosis and conduct timely treatment for patients. Experimental results show that the breast cancer detection model based on Vision Transformer achieves better performance in predicting time with higher accuracy than other deep learning networks such as NASNetLarge and DenseNet-121, which achieved high accuracy on the ImageNet dataset. On the other hand, the accuracy of the proposed model during training is up to 99%.

References

1. Aaqib, M., Tufail, M., Anwar, S.: A novel deep learning based approach for breast cancer detection. In: 2019 13th International Conference on Mathematics, Actuarial Science, Computer Science and Statistics (MACS), pp. 1–6. IEEE (2019)
2. Albashish, D., Al-Sayyed, R., Abdullah, A., Ryalat, M.H., Almansour, N.A.: Deep CNN model based on VGG16 for breast cancer classification. In: 2021 International conference on information technology (ICIT), pp. 805–810. IEEE (2021)
3. Arnold, M., et al.: Current and future burden of breast cancer: global statistics for 2020 and 2040. Breast **66**, 15–23 (2022)
4. Asadi, B., Memon, Q.: Efficient breast cancer detection via cascade deep learning network. Int. J. Intell. Netw. **4**, 46–52 (2023)
5. Chougrad, H., Zouaki, H., Alheyane, O.: Deep convolutional neural networks for breast cancer screening. Comput. Methods Programs Biomed. **157**, 19–30 (2018)
6. Dosovitskiy, A., et al.: An image is worth 16 × 16 words: transformers for image recognition at scale. arXiv preprint arXiv:2010.11929 (2020)
7. Gaikwad, V.J.: Detection of breast cancer in mammogram using support vector machine. Int. J. Sci. Eng. Res. (IJSER) **10**(1), 19–21 (2015)
8. Girish, G., Spandana, P., Vasu, B.: Breast cancer detection using deep learning. arXiv preprint arXiv:2304.10386 (2023)
9. Guan, S., Loew, M.: Breast cancer detection using transfer learning in convolutional neural networks. In: 2017 IEEE Applied Imagery Pattern Recognition Workshop (AIPR), pp. 1–8. IEEE (2017)
10. Gulli, A., Kapoor, A., Pal, S.: Deep Learning with TensorFlow 2 and Keras: Regression, ConvNets, GANs, RNNs, NLP, and More with TensorFlow 2 and the Keras API. Packt Publishing Ltd. (2019)
11. Han, K., et al.: A survey on vision transformer. IEEE Trans. Pattern Anal. Mach. Intell. **45**(1), 87–110 (2022)
12. Huang, G., Liu, Z., Van Der Maaten, L., Weinberger, K.Q.: Densely connected convolutional networks. In: Proceedings of the IEEE Conference on Computer Vision and Pattern Recognition, pp. 4700–4708 (2017)
13. Mahmud, M.I., Mamun, M., Abdelgawad, A.: A deep analysis of transfer learning based breast cancer detection using histopathology images. In: 2023 10th International Conference on Signal Processing and Integrated Networks (SPIN), pp. 198–204. IEEE (2023)
14. Poorolajal, J., Akbari, M.E., Ziaee, F., Karami, M., Ghoncheh, M.: Breast cancer screening (BCS) chart: a basic and preliminary model for making screening mammography more productive and efficient. J. Public Health **40**(2), e118–e125 (2018)
15. Sandler, M., Howard, A., Zhu, M., Zhmoginov, A., Chen, L.C.: MobileNetv 2: inverted residuals and linear bottlenecks. In: Proceedings of the IEEE Conference on Computer Vision and Pattern Recognition, pp. 4510–4520 (2018)
16. Shamy, S., Dheeba, J.: A research on detection and classification of breast cancer using k-means GMM & CNN algorithms. Int. J. Eng. Adv. Technol. **8**(6S), 501–505 (2019)
17. Siegel, R.L., Miller, K.D., Jemal, A.: Cancer statistics, 2015. CA: Cancer J. Clin. **65**(1), 5–29 (2015)
18. Simonyan, K., Zisserman, A.: Very deep convolutional networks for large-scale image recognition. arXiv preprint arXiv:1409.1556 (2014)

19. American Cancer Society's: Breast cancer facts & figures 2019–2020. Technical report. American Cancer Society's (2019)
20. Suckling, J., et al.: Mammographic image analysis society (MIAS) database v1. 21. Technical report, Apollo - University of Cambridge Repository (2015)
21. Szegedy, C., Vanhoucke, V., Ioffe, S., Shlens, J., Wojna, Z.: Rethinking the inception architecture for computer vision. In: Proceedings of the IEEE Conference on Computer Vision and Pattern Recognition, pp. 2818–2826 (2016)
22. Vijayan, V.S., Lekshmy, P.: Deep learning based prediction of breast cancer in histopathological images. Int. J. Eng. Res. Technol. (IJERT) 2278–0181 (2019)
23. Zhong, Z., Zheng, M., Mai, H., Zhao, J., Liu, X.: Cancer image classification based on densenet model. In: Journal of Physics: Conference Series, vol. 1651, p. 012143. IOP Publishing (2020)
24. Zoph, B., Vasudevan, V., Shlens, J., Le, Q.V.: Learning transferable architectures for scalable image recognition. In: Proceedings of the IEEE Conference on Computer Vision and Pattern Recognition, pp. 8697–8710 (2018)

Comparing Performance of Linear Regression Models Trained on Systematic Forest Measurement Datasets to Predict Diameter at Breast Height

Balint Pataki[1], Kinga Nagy[2], and Binh Thanh Nguyen[3(✉)]

[1] University of Sopron, Sopron, Hungary
[2] National Land Centre, Forestry Department, Budapest, Hungary
[3] International Institute for Applied Systems Analysis (IIASA), Laxenburg, Austria
nguyenb@iiasa.ac.at

Abstract. Natural resources in forests are usually estimated through systematic forest measurement programs such as national forest inventories. One of the most important parameters of a tree is diameter at breast height (DBH), which is the base of assessing growth and yield in forests both for stand-level or for regional metrics. However, as most of the forest inventory programs operate with DBH threshold - meaning that only above certain DBH value the trees are measured in a plot -, it leads to missing points in the data. If the sample tree is measured in a cycle of measurement, it might have not been measured in a previous cycle (5 year before) because it might have been below threshold then. The objective of the research is to develop a workflow for predicting these missing DBH values by using machine learning algorithms. First, we integrated the observed data into data warehouse with an ETL (extract-transform-load) process by filtering, data cleaning and transformations. Next, we selected a use case, which is the prediction of the 1st cycle's DBH values based on 2nd cycle's tree- and plot-level data. Afterwards we developed, tested and evaluated three different linear algorithm models for the chosen use case. The evaluation shows that supervised machine learning models trained on tree- and plot-level parameters can help missing data imputation in systematic forest observation datasets. Although the models have promising results but we are aiming to continue our research by exploring other algorithms and use cases. These studies can serve as a stable base for future analysis research as well.

Keywords: forest inventory · diameter at breast height · linear regression

1 Introduction

Decision-making requires accurate information. In the field of forestry, data and information are acquired via forest inventory programs among other measurement programs. The main purpose of forest inventories is to provide estimates

T. K. Dang et al. (Eds.): FDSE 2023, CCIS 1925, pp. 513–527, 2023.
https://doi.org/10.1007/978-981-99-8296-7_37

of means and totals for specific metrics describing forest characteristics, such as growing stock, type of forest or above-ground biomass [14]. Forest inventory programs have been running from the beginning of the 20th century in some countries, but more and more states have decided to start and maintain forest inventory programs during the last couple of decades [5]. Traditionally NFIs concentrated solely on the economic aspect of forestry data (wood supply, production), however there is an ongoing change of focus, currently forest inventories provide information to other areas as well, such as carbon pool calculation or biodiversity metrics [6,9].

Forest inventory programs use systematic sampling methods and extrapolate the data to region and country levels. There are usually forest inventory field sampling crews who do the measurements in a fraction of the whole system in one year and in 5 or 10 years they can cover the whole country. That means the measurements are taken place in the same field points in every 5 or 10 years. The system is similar in most countries, however they can differ in terms of time period between measurements or segmentation in actual sampling circles in the field.

The way we assess forest resources involves statistical sampling methods and monitoring programs, in order to generate region- or country-wide metrics. In the field of forest monitoring, one of the most important factors is diameter at breast height (DBH), which is measured 1.3 m above ground. The metric is applied in various calculations in forestry, like growing stock, basal area, biomass or carbon stock [32]. The more data points a statistical sampling involves, the more reliable the estimation is, because more real values are available. Sampling methods often apply thresholds for DBH that rule the entry barrier for trees in a sampling, in order to avoid measuring all the individual trees on a site. This method can cause cases, when in the first round a tree is not big enough to measure but in the second cycle (e.g. 5 or 10 years later on the same plot) it is big enough and therefore has to be measured. This means missing points in the data cloud, which has a negative effect on the calculation of a periodic growth for individual trees or for certain areas. There is an extensive research in DBH estimation models, such as DBH-height models [20,21,27], LiDAR experiments [2,11,19], or direct DBH models based on forest inventory data [17,23]. There are more and more research activities that combine machine learning and forestry research [12], often with the utilization of neural networks [22,32]. However, there are not many studies focusing on DBH estimation across measurement cycles with machine learning involving categorical features such as relief, wetness class or other site-level parameters for broadleaved tree species in Carpathian basin, especially with the purpose of predicting values for 5 or 10 years period based on forest inventories in order to enrich data cloud. We are aiming to predict DBH by using specific site- and tree-level parameters of the same individual trees in another point in time, with regression models, focusing on Central-European broadleaved tree species. We were provided with the Hungarian Growth Monitoring System (GMS) data, which was active during the 1990s and 2000s, and had three measurement cycles. It was the antecedent of the current Hungarian NFI that is a much more detailed measurement program. Some of the main important differences: there was no segmentation on the sample plots, the radius of the plot circle was varying. Based on the data we have from the 2nd cycle of measurements - where we have DBH, age, height, relief, and other parameters of the site and tree -, we have trained, tested and evaluated different linear regression models with the objective of predicting the missing DBH for the 1st measurement cycle. The model has been developed on a dataset with the five most common tree species that are all broadleaved species. This will enable the enrichment of forest inventory data by using its own measurements, and it can be a useful method to build more precise and reliable predictions, estimations, analysis based on systematic measurements and maybe even to reduce the manual measurement during field surveys. Based on this approach, by reaching a high quality and reliable model, this can be beneficial for predictions aiming growing stock, volume or DBH in the future.

2   Related Work

There are extensive research activities in data integration with missing data. Missing data is usually not a problem in itself, but it can be problematic, how we manage it [18]. If we don't manage it in a proper way, there are three major problems can arise: loss of efficiency, complications in data analysis and bias [13]. There are several patterns on how data can be missing, as described in [3]. In our case, there is one main reason why tree-level data is missing in one of the cycles: it was not measured. There are two specific scenarios: the tree was not measured in the 1st cycle because it was below threshold in terms of DBH, but measured in the 2nd cycle; or it was observed in the 1st cycle but never registered during the 2nd cycle - it could be because of a damage or cutting. In our current research we concentrated on the first scenario, when the 1st cycle's data is missing, and how can we predict the missing DBH value. There are many research studies on DBH estimation. They are mostly based on DBH-height relations [20,21,27], but we are aiming to use other parameters besides sample tree height - even the trees' own DBH data from another measurement cycle. There are solutions for DBH estimation based on plot and tree parameters, such as [17,23], however, our model has more and other type of parameters, and also different tree species that are dominant in Central Europe. Other machine learning research activities in forestry are usually concentrate on LiDAR data [12]. There is a review of imputation methods for forest inventory missing data, which is a similar problem but it concentrates on Nearest Neighbor methods only [7]. Even if it is another machine learning algorithm, it can be useful for our future use cases. The main difference between our contribution and the existing research activities is that we aim to predict DBH based on the same sample tree's data but from another point in time. Another difference is the wide range of parameters we use, the three tested machine learning algorithms, the cycle length (time difference) and the unique group of tree species. Although forest monitoring and inventory programs are similar, they are different in terms of cycle length, observed parameters, sample size and others factors. This makes the current dataset and research workflow unique, therefore a prediction process directly optimized for the observed data is desired. However, this research can lead to more generalized models in the future.

3 Concepts and Methods

We were provided with high quality forest monitoring data based on systematic field measurements, containing both individual tree metrics (such as height, age) and plot-level parameters (such as relief, hydrology) observed on the site. We have chosen a specific case for train, test and evaluate DBH prediction based on the aforementioned parameters.

3.1 Case Study

There are always missing points in the data cloud of different measurement cycles in forest inventories. The following figure shows the problem visually: The figure visualizes the main problem of loosing valuable historical information of individual trees because of applied thresholds. The trees marked with grey are not measured in the first survey but several years later - depending on the actual repeated measurement policy - they are surveyed. This is the problem we are focusing on and we decided to develop a model to predict the DBH values based on site- and tree-specific parameters measured in a later point in time - in a later measurement cycle. The first use case was decided to be a prediction backwards in time. There are individual trees that hadn't been registered during the 1st measurement cycle, but surveyed in the 2nd cycle - mostly because of

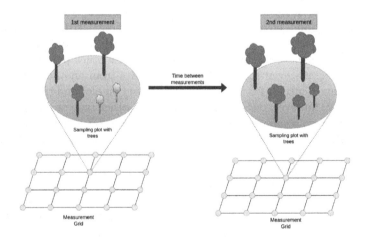

Fig. 1. Simplified view of a theoretical forest monitoring plot in two different points in time in a repeated measurement process with applied threshold for DBH. Colored trees are part of the measurement and grey trees are not. (Color figure online)

the DBH thresholds applied in the measurement policy. Our aim was to predict these missing individual trees' DBH data based on the 2nd cycle data. After data preprocessing, machine learning models have been trained, tested and evaluated in order to predict missing DBH values. Detailed description of the process is described in Data Preprocessing and Regression Models sections. We have been provided many parameters of a tree data point that were considered during the regression as features, such as tree height, tree age, altitude, exposure, slope of the site. Together with NFI experts we identified the five most important and common tree species groups to make predictions for: turkey oak (*Quercus cerris*), beech (*Fagus sylvatica*), black locust (*Robinia pseudoacacia*), sessile oak (*Quercus petraea*), hornbeam (*Carpinus betulus*). The idea behind reducing tree species complexity is to have as many records for a species group as possible and thus, exclude rare species from the analysis that have not enough data to train the algorithms on (Fig. 1).

3.2 Source Data

The data source is based on repeated field measurement program in Hungarian forests, called Growth Monitoring System (GMS). The aim of GMS was to focus on the yield of forest stands, based on individual tree measurements and their statistical evaluation, and observing the change of yield in time. The GMS was launched in 1993 and the data was systematically and continuously collected until 2008 [16]. The network of GMS was built on top of another, pre-existed 4 * 4 km network (Forest Protection Network). Each point of the already existing network was considered as a member of the GMS network, and in addition, each point has been moved 2 km southwards and eastwards, resulting a network twice as dense as the FPN - with a distance of 2.828 km between neighbouring points [28]. There were three measurement cycles, the same plots have been surveyed in each cycle. Within a cycle the number of plots have been equally distributed for five years. The provided field survey data consists of two levels of data: plot-level (like canopy coverage in percentage or environmental conditions such as climate class or hydrology) and tree-level measurements (like diameter at breast height or height).

3.3 Data Preprocessing

Data Warehouse. We built a data warehouse in a relational database management system for OLAP processes to support data analytics. First of all, we needed to develop an ETL process to extract, transform and load the data into the warehouse. An ETL system involves everything between the source and the data warehouse presentation layer. [15] The first step of an ETL process is data extraction from source. We were provided with Excel tables for plot-level and tree-level data, in addition to that, lookup tables were also provided. As the first

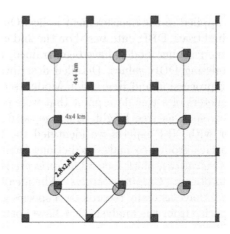

Fig. 2. GMS network overview. Yellow circles: FPN grid points, green squares: GMS grid points [16] (Color figure online).

action, we loaded the raw tables as-is into the relational database management system. The transformation logic is separated into five different types (Fig. 2):

- unioning plot-level data
- finding differences between cycles
- cleaning data
- type conversions
- data modelling

From three different datasets for the three cycles' plot-level data, we developed one dataset including all three cycle's tables. Both in plot-level and tree-level data, there are values which are not subject of change over a 5 or 10 years period, for instance relief, species code or climate category, however, there are values which can change during a cycle's period, such as canopy cover percentage or diameter at breast height on a particular measurement plot. Therefore we increased the number of fields by storing different cycle's data in different columns, to enable direct comparisons between cycles. Based on the discussions with Hungarian NFI specialists, we agreed on the logic that rules how exactly we keep or eliminate values from the data. Our priority was always the 3rd cycle's data, as this was the most cohesive and detailed one, meaning in case of differences between cycles, we always kept the 3rd cycle's value - if this was not present, then the 2nd cycle's value. There were other important parts of the data cleaning process. We identified all the null values with miscoding (for example '0') and converted them to null values, when applicable. The next part of the workflow was to ingest the cleaned data from staging (landing) zone into the data warehouse. In order to start the process, we analyzed the relations across the properties and came up with a star schema model with two fact tables, plot-level and tree-level measurements, and dimension tables that hold the lookup data for categorical values. As the next step, we identified the most suitable data types for each field and applied them on the columns for both tree- and plot-level data. As a preparation and data exploration, first we preprocessed the data before loading it into the data warehouse. This step involved matching the values found in different categories with the provided lookup tables. During data modelling, we did not only separated the dimensions and facts and created the star schema, but also restructured the fact tables not to hold different cycle data in different fields. We created a new field for cycle to enable in-depth analysis with data cubes in the future.

Domain-Specific Data Cleaning. Identifying and handling outliers are always a core part of data analysis research. In our case, there were multiple domain-specific facts we needed to consider during this process. The first step is to make sure we don't have decreasing growth in tree parameters in the future, meaning DBH and height normally cannot be less than 5 years before in another measurement. We eliminated these records from the training data. Based on this equation we excluded all the records where the 1st cycles's DBH value is greater than the 2nd cycle's DBH value plus 5% tolerance. We did similarly for tree height with 8% tolerance: We also addressed DBH to height ratio and identified incorrect records. This means, DBH value in a measurement cycle should be greater or equal than the 50% of the tree height and less than the tree height multiplied by four. The logic applies for both (1st and 2nd) cycle.

Outliers. We identified outliers with this logic: every value is excluded which is above or below 3*standard deviation of the actual feature. We applied this logic for the following features: DBH in 2nd cycle, DBH in 1st cycle, age, volume, canopy closure, altitude, slope.

Correlation Analysis. Next, we started the data exploration by calculating a correlation matrix: The correlation matrix shows that the DBH values between two cycles are highly correlated, however there are other features that has correlation with the DBH. Therefore it is worth training the machine learning model with involving other features in order to find patterns in the dataset and make more accurate predictions.

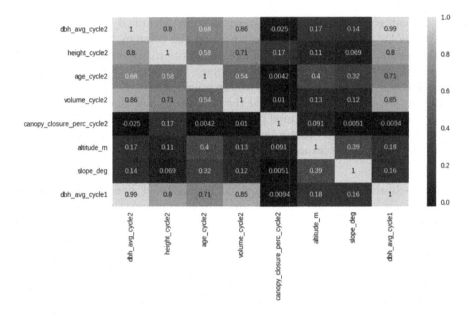

Fig. 3. Correlation Matrix across Continuous Features.

Categorical Features. In the original dataset there aren't just numerical but also categorical variables (such as climate or hydrology categories). In order to successfully fit machine learning (or statistical methods) on the data, numerical representation of features is required [4]. One of the most commonly used solution for this problem is one-hot encoding (OHE) [24]. OHE transforms the categorical variables with n observations and d distinct values, in a way to create d binary variables with n observations. Each observation has the value 0 or 1, indicating the presence or absence of dth variable. During this phase we applied one-hot encoding on the ordinal categorical variables and we didn't use that for nominal variables (Fig. 3).

3.4   Regression Models

The linear regression model is a statistical analysis method for exploring the relationship between variables. Regression analysis is used for predicting values of the dependent variable [31]. There can be multiple independent variables in the data that are used to predict the dependent variable. This method is called Multilinear Regression (MLR) or Multiple Regression [30]. After all preprocessing steps have been performed on the initial data, the algorithm training can be started on a matrix of features and label. The following figure shows a simplified overview of the dataset: The processed dataset has 45.454 records altogether, which have served as an input for the machine learning process. Detailed statistics about the data can be seen below (Fig. 4 and Table 1):

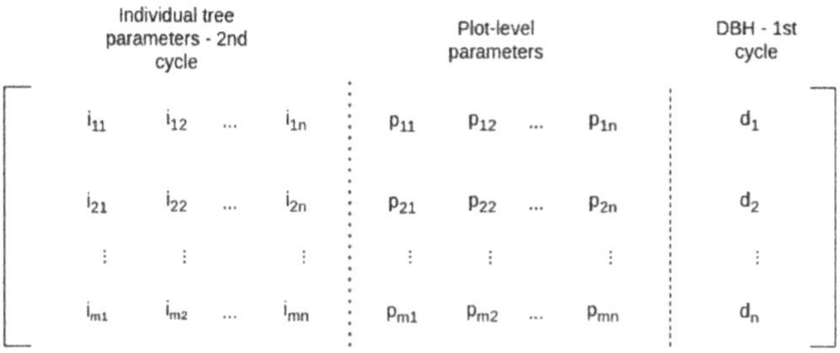

$$\begin{bmatrix} i_{11} & i_{12} & \cdots & i_{1n} & \vdots & p_{11} & p_{12} & \cdots & p_{1n} & \vdots & d_1 \\ i_{21} & i_{22} & \cdots & i_{2n} & \vdots & p_{21} & p_{22} & \cdots & p_{2n} & \vdots & d_2 \\ \vdots & \vdots & & \vdots & \vdots & \vdots & \vdots & & \vdots & \vdots & \vdots \\ i_{m1} & i_{m2} & \cdots & i_{mn} & \vdots & p_{m1} & p_{m2} & \cdots & p_{mn} & \vdots & d_n \end{bmatrix}$$

Individual tree parameters - 2nd cycle | Plot-level parameters | DBH - 1st cycle

Fig. 4. The simplified model of the matrix that has been trained and tested in different regression algorithms. Last column is the label, which is the dependent variable to predict on unseen data.

Table 1. Main statistics of the dataset. C1: 1st Inventory cycle, C2: 2nd Inventory cycle

Statistics	Avg.DBH C2(cm)	Age	Volume	Canopy Closure(%)	Altitude(m)	Slope(deg.)	Avg.DBH C1(cm)
Null count	0	0	0	0	0	0	0
Mean	23.54	58.28	0.75	79.57	291.74	9.43	21.93
Std	11.77	27.14	1.22	14.53	135.38	8.22	11.45
Min	3.87	10.00	0.00	0.00	0.00	0.00	2.87
Max	121.91	336.00	25.89	100.00	900.00	55.00	118.48
Median	21.48	57.00	0.37	80.00	270.00	8.00	19.94
25%	14.87	36.00	0.15	75.00	200.00	4.00	13.37
75%	29.57	77.00	0.85	90.00	360.00	15.00	27.87

We trained and tested three different linear regression models: linear regression with ordinary least squares, lasso regression and ridge regression. Lasso is a special technique of linear regression, where we shrink some coefficients and sets others to 0 [29]. Ridge is another form of regression, where a regularization is added to the model in order to avoid too large coefficients in case of nonorthogonal problems [10].

The model training process starts with separating the label and features - in our case, label is the column of DBH in the 1st cycle. The train to test ratio was 80:20–80% of the dataset was used to train the algorithm and 20% to test it against the actual values. Sometimes features have different magnitudes and this can cause problems in the machine learning phase. Feature scaling is a process where arithmetic operations are applied on the feature values in order to bring them to a similar scale. [26] Then we applied standard scaling for the features. Our decision to use standardization instead of normalization (min-max scaling) was based on the fact that standardization is less affected by outliers [8]. Standardization scaling centers the values around the mean, expressed by the formula below:

$$X' = (X - \mu)/\sigma \tag{1}$$

where:

X': standard score of the sample,
X: sample,
μ: mean of training samples,
σ: standard deviation of training samples [1]

All three linear regression models have been fitted on the transformed feature values and labels, then evaluated based on the comparison with the test dataset.

4   Results and Discussion

Our objective was to develop, train, test and evaluate linear regression models in order to predict missing DBH data based on the available features of the next measurement cycle (environmental/site-specific and tree-specific parameters). Our aim to develop a workflow which can help NFI experts to enrich their already existing field observation dataset through machine learning and statistical methods. We organized the existing data into data warehouse. We cleaned, filtered, transformed the data to prepare it for machine learning techniques. We have chosen a specific case, which is to predict DBH values of the 1st measurement cycle from the 2nd measurement cycle data. To achieve this goal, after data preprocessing, we trained three different regression algorithms on 80% of the data and tested it on 20% of the data.

There are several metrics available for linear regression evaluation purposes. The most widely used performance measure is the Mean Square Error (MSE):

$$MSE(X, h) = \frac{1}{m} \sum_{i=1}^{m} (h(x^{(i)}) - y^{(i)})^2 \tag{2}$$

where:

m: number of instances in dataset,
$x^{(i)}$: vector of all features,
$y^{(i)}$: label vector,
X: matrix of all feature values of all instances,
h: prediction function,
$MSE(X, h)$: cost function [8]

Another important metric is the Mean Absolute Error (MAE). It is better suited when there are many outliers in the dataset.

$$MAE(X, h) = \frac{1}{m} \sum_{i=1}^{m} |h(x^{(i)}) - y^{(i)}| \tag{3}$$

where:

m: number of instances in dataset,
$x^{(i)}$: vector of all features,

$y^{(i)}$: label vector,
X: matrix of all feature values of all instances,
h: prediction function,
$MSE(X, h)$: cost function [8]

R^2-score (coefficient of determination) is another performance measure for regression models:

$$R^2 = 1 - \frac{SS_{res}}{SS_{tot}} \qquad (4)$$

where:

SS_{res}: residual sum of squares,
SS_{tot}: total sum of squares, [25]

Computation of MAE corresponds to the l_1 norm (Manhattan norm). Generally MSE (or the root of MSE, RMSE) is preferred, except in case of many outliers in the data. At this stage of the research we are still exploring the opportunities, therefore we decided to calculate all three performance measures for all three models. This helps us find the best model for future application of the research results. All above metrics can be computed and evaluated with the Python package called Scikit Learn. The followings are the results of the regression model tests (Table 2):

Table 2. Performance metrics of the three evaluated regression models

Model	R^2-score	MAE	MSE
Linear Regression	0.9901	0.7407	1.2757
Ridge Regression	0.9901	0.7407	1.2757
Lasso Regression	0.9896	0.7688	1.3389

The table shows that all three trained and tested models performed relatively good and there isn't any big difference between the models in terms of performance metrics. Linear regression and Ridge regression performed very similarly. We can observe the true and predicted values of 1st cycle DBH in the next figure (Fig. 5):

All three linear regression models show good results as the majority of true and predicted values are close to each other. Having a mean squared or absolute error around 1 cm for diameter at breast height is considered promising for the practical application in the future. However, we would like to highlight that these results are only the first steps in our research objectives.

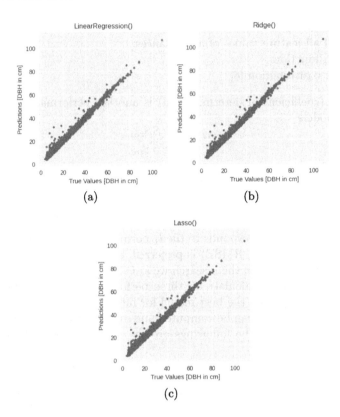

Fig. 5. Results of different regression algorithm tests - diagrams show predicted and true values against each other. (a) Linear Regression (b) Ridge Regression (c) Lasso Regression

The possible real-world application of the model is an automated data pipeline which starts with data preprocessing (cleaning, filtering, transformations), training and testing process, validation and it ends with the prediction of missing DBH values. In order to have a reliable real-world solution, the research has to go deeper and wider to find the best possible solution.

5   Conclusion

The results show that supervised machine learning algorithms can have a role in missing data imputation in systematic forest measurement datasets. Although the first observations show significant progress and promising results, we are planning further steps to find better or more comprehensive connections to predict DBH values. Important to know that tree growth - and therefore DBH increment - is generally not a linear function, however it does not mean that a 5 year long increment cannot be modeled precisely enough with a linear function. Thus, we are planning to explore polynomial regression models for similar type of predictions in the future and estimate for bigger time difference between data points, in order to research the topic from multiple directions. As next steps of the research, we will explore other types of machine learning techniques for similar use cases with longer time distance: we are going to test polynomial models for 10 years time difference between cycles in order to increase the quality and reliability of DBH prediction results. We are planning to use these findings in the current Hungarian NFI as well. There are several areas where this research can be applied in the future after refinement and generalization. Increment models of certain central-european tree species can be improved or validated. The data cleaning and machine learning process can be automated and orchestrated as a generic data pipeline, which then can be customized by end-users (forestry analysts, forest managers or forest inventory professionals) in order to gain more insights of the forestry assets estimated in the future. Specifically in forest inventory programs, such a data pipeline can serve as a decision-support system, thus it can reduce the on-field observation frequency. In those scenarios control-measurements would still be needed but all the plots might not needed to be observed to produce reliable data.

Acknowledgements. We would like to express our gratitude to the whole NFI team work at the Forestry Department of National Land Centre as they provided expertise, valuable insights and high value data through the research process.

References

1. Ampomah, E.K., Nyame, G., Qin, Z., Addo, P.C., Gyamfi, E.O., Gyan, M.: Stock market prediction with Gaussian Naïve Bayes machine learning algorithm. Informatica **45**(2) (2021)
2. Bauwens, S., Bartholomeus, H., Calders, K., Lejeune, P.: Forest inventory with terrestrial LiDAR: a comparison of static and hand-held mobile laser scanning. Forests **7**(12), 127 (2016)
3. Bechny, M., Sobieczky, F., Zeindl, J., Ehrlinger, L.: Missing data patterns: from theory to an application in the steel industry. In: 33rd International Conference on Scientific and Statistical Database Management, Tampa, FL, USA, pp. 214–219. ACM (2021)
4. Cerda, P., Varoquaux, G.: Encoding high-cardinality string categorical variables. IEEE Trans. Knowl. Data Eng. **34**(3), 1164–1176 (2022). arXiv:1907.01860 [cs, stat]
5. Cienciala, E., et al.: Preparing emission reporting from forests: use of National Forest Inventories in European countries. Silva Fennica **42**(1) (2008)
6. Corona, P., Chirici, G., McRoberts, R.E., Winter, S., Barbati, A.: Contribution of large-scale forest inventories to biodiversity assessment and monitoring. For. Ecol. Manag. **262**(11), 2061–2069 (2011)
7. Eskelson, B.N.I., Temesgen, H., Lemay, V., Barrett, T.M., Crookston, N.L., Hudak, A.T.: The roles of nearest neighbor methods in imputing missing data in forest inventory and monitoring databases. Scand. J. For. Res. **24**(3), 235–246 (2009)
8. Géron, A.: Hands-On Machine Learning with Scikit-Learn, Keras & TensorFlow. O'Reilly Media, Inc. (2019)

9. Gschwantner, T., et al.: Common tree definitions for national forest inventories in Europe. Silva Fennica **43**(2) (2009)
10. Hoerl, A.E., Kennard, R.W.: Ridge regression: applications to nonorthogonal problems. Technometrics **12**(1), 69–82 (1970)
11. Huang, H., et al.: Automated methods for measuring DBH and tree heights with a commercial scanning lidar. Photogram. Eng. Remote Sens. **77**(3), 219–227 (2011)
12. Ibanez, C.A.G., et al.: Estimating DBH of trees employing multiple linear regression of the best LiDAR-derived parameter combination in Python in a natural broadleaf forest in the Philippines. ISPRS - Int. Arch. Photogram. Remote Sens. Spat. Inf. Sci. **XLI-B8**, 657–662 (2016)
13. Kaiser, J.: Dealing with missing values in data. J. Syst. Integr. 42–51 (2014)
14. Kangas, A., Maltamo, M. (eds.): Forest Inventory: Methodology and Applications. Managing Forest Ecosystems, vol. 10. Springer, Dordrecht (2006). oCLC: ocm64310708
15. Kimball, R., Ross, M.: The Data Warehouse Toolkit: The Complete Guide to Dimensional Modeling. Wiley, Hoboken (2011). google-Books-ID: XoS2oy1IcB4C
16. László, K.: Erdvédelmi Mérő- és Megfigyelő Rendszer: 1988–2008. Mezőgazdasági Szakigazgatási Hivatal Erdészeti Igazgatóság, Budapest (2009). oCLC: 909726345
17. Lessard, V.C., McRoberts, R.E., Holdaway, M.R.: Diameter growth models using Minnesota forest inventory and analysis data. Forest Sci. **47**(3), 301–310 (2001)
18. Little, T.D., Jorgensen, T.D., Lang, K.M., Moore, E.W.G.: On the joys of missing data. J. Pediatr. Psychol. **39**(2), 151–162 (2014)
19. Liu, G., Wang, J., Dong, P., Chen, Y., Liu, Z.: Estimating individual tree height and diameter at breast height (DBH) from terrestrial laser scanning (TLS) data at plot level. Forests **9**(7), 398 (2018)
20. Lumbres, R.I.C., Lee, Y.J., Seo, Y.O., Kim, S.H., Choi, J.K., Lee, W.K.: Development and validation of nonlinear height-DBH models for major coniferous tree species in Korea. For. Sci. Technol. **7**(3), 117–125 (2011)
21. Lynch, T.B., Holley, A.G., Stevenson, D.J.: A random-parameter height-DBH model for cherrybark oak. South. J. Appl. For. **29**(1), 22–26 (2005)
22. Nguyen Thanh, T., Dinh Tien, T., Shen, H.L.: Height-diameter relationship for Pinus Koraiensis in Mengjiagang Forest Farm of Northeast China using nonlinear regressions and artificial neural network models. J. Forest Sci. **65**(4), 134–143 (2019)
23. Piao, D., et al.: Development of an integrated DBH estimation model based on stand and climatic conditions. Forests **9**(3), 155 (2018)
24. Potdar, K., Pardawala, T.S., Pai, C.D.: A comparative study of categorical variable encoding techniques for neural network classifiers. Int. J. Comput. Appl. **175**(4), 7–9 (2017)
25. Renaud, O., Victoria-Feser, M.P.: A robust coefficient of determination for regression. J. Stat. Plan. Inference **140**(7) (2010)
26. Rouzrokh, P., et al.: Mitigating bias in radiology machine learning: 1 Data handling. Radiol. Artif. Intell. **4**(5), e210290 (2022)
27. Sharma, R., Vacek, Z., Vacek, S., Kučera, M.: A nonlinear mixed-effects height-to-diameter ratio model for several tree species based on Czech national forest inventory data. Forests **10**(1), 70 (2019)
28. Tobisch, T., Kottek, P.: Forestry-related databases of the Hungarian forestry directorate (2013). https://portal.nebih.gov.hu/documents/10182/862096/Forestry_related_databases.pdf/3ff92716-2301-4894-a724-72fafca9d4fc. Accessed 10 July 2023

29. Tibshirani, R.: Regression shrinkage and selection via the Lasso. J. Roy. Stat. Soc.: Ser. B (Methodol.) **58**(1), 267–288 (1996)
30. Uyanık, G.K., Güler, N.: A study on multiple linear regression analysis. Procedia Soc. Behav. Sci. **106**, 234–240 (2013)
31. Weisberg, S.: Applied Linear Regression (2014)
32. Zhou, R., Wu, D., Zhou, R., Fang, L., Zheng, X., Lou, X.: Estimation of DBH at forest stand level based on multi-parameters and generalized regression neural network. Forests **10**(9), 778 (2019)

Detection and Segmentation of Brain Tumors on 3D MR Images Using 3D U-Net

Thuong-Cang Phan[1]([⊠])(iD), Anh-Cang Phan[2](iD), Khac-Tuong Nguyen[2], and Ho-Dat Tran[2]

[1] Can Tho University, Can Tho City, Vietnam
ptcang@cit.ctu.edu.vn
[2] Vinh Long University of Technology Education, Vinh Long City, Vinh Long Province, Vietnam
{cangpa,tuongnk,datth}@vlute.edu.vn

Abstract. A brain tumor is abnormal cells that develop in the brain structure. Brain tumors grow can create pressure and affect the functions of surrounding brain tissues, which is life-threatening. In this work, we propose an approach using deep learning networks to detect and segment brain tumors with 3D U-Net by changing the backbone with MobileNet-V2, ResNet-101, and DensetNet-121. We used the BraTS 2020 dataset for conducting experiments. The results show that the proposed method achieves high accuracy of up to 99%. We use the 3D Slicer tool in modeling 3D brain tumors to effectively support doctors in the early detection and classification of brain tumors for timely treatment.

Keywords: Brain tumors · DenseNet · 3D Slicer · 3D U-Net

1 Introduction

A primary brain tumor is a tumor that begins in the brain. In 2023, an estimation of 24,810 adults in the United States will be diagnosed with primary cancerous tumors of the brain and spinal cord [8]. In 2020, 308,102 people were diagnosed with a primary tumor of the brain or spinal cord. Brain cancer is estimated to be the 10th leading cause of cancer death by 2023 for both men and women of all ages [22]. It is estimated that 18,990 deaths from brain cancer in the United States by 2023. For patients with malignant brain tumors, the relative survival rate after 5 years after diagnosis is 35.7% [1]. The most common primary malignant brain tumor is glioblastoma with only 6.9% of 5-year relative survival. Brain tumors are mostly diagnosed after symptoms appear with magnetic resonance imaging (MRI). Therefore, it is necessary to detect and diagnose brain tumors with advanced information technology for timely treatment.

There are studies on the application of deep neural networks for the detection and classification of brain tumors. Bhalodiya et al. [7] presented a review of

T. K. Dang et al. (Eds.): FDSE 2023, CCIS 1925, pp. 528–541, 2023.
https://doi.org/10.1007/978-981-99-8296-7_38

the methods of brain tumor segmentation based on magnetic resonance imaging (MRI). The finding was that U-Net is cited the most and gives high accuracy with a 0.9 Dice score. Sharif et al. [21] proposed a framework to analyze brain tumors on MR images with four phases. YOLOv2 Inception-V3 was used in the framework, which achieved greater than 0.90 prediction scores in localization, segmentation, and classification. Phan et al. [18] proposed a method of detecting brain hemorrhage on 3D CT scans with Deep Neural Network. The study used U-Net with the transfer learning approach and achieved an accuracy of 92.5%. Pinto et al. [19] presented a differential and fully automated method for segmenting gliomas, using features based on appearance and context. The proposed method was evaluated on the BraTS 2013 dataset, which achieved a Dice score of 0.83, 0.78, and 0.73 for the whole tumor, tumor core, and enhancing tumor, respectively. Mehta and Arbel [15] provided a modified version of 3D U-Net to segment brain tumors. The model was evaluated on the BraTS 2018 dataset and achieved a Dice of 0.706, 0.871, and 0.771 for enhancing tumor, whole tumor, and tumor core, respectively. Ottom et al. [17] presented a framework to segment 2D brain tumors on MR images. The model achieved a high accuracy with a Dice score of 0.96 during model training. Ilhan et al. [13] proposed a method of segmenting brain tumors on MR images. The authors used nonparametric tumor localization and enhancement methods to increase the appearance of tumors and fed to the original U-net, for segmentation. The proposed method achieved good performance with a Dice score of 0.94 on the BrasTS 2012 dataset.

2   Background

2.1   Brain Tumors

A primary brain tumor is a tumor that starts in the brain and is described as low-grade or high-grade. A low-grade brain tumor generally grows slowly while a high-grade brain tumor tends to grow faster. Patients with brain tumors can experience some symptoms such as headache, nausea, vision or speech problems, seizures, etc. [2]. Some signs may be specific to the tumor location such as headache near the tumor, changes in voice speech, hearing, memory, or emotional states, such as aggression [3].

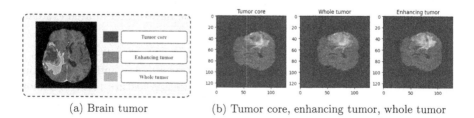

(a) Brain tumor   (b) Tumor core, enhancing tumor, whole tumor

Fig. 1. A brain tumor in MR images from the experimental dataset.

A brain tumor with three parts is shown in Fig. 1. A tumor core is the central region of the tumor, including necrotic and non-enhancing parts of the tumor. Enhancing tumor is the area around the tumor with enhanced image quality, which lies between the tumor core and the whole tumor. The whole tumor is the area around the tumor that has enlargement and swelling due to bleeding or injury. It is the union of the tumor core and the peritumoral edematous region.

2.2 Network Models

In this work, we used 3D U-Net to detect and segment brain tumors by changing the backbone of 3D U-Net with MobileNet-V2, ResNet-101, and DensetNet-121.

3D U-Net. 3D U-Net [6] is a deep neural network architecture used in medical image processing problems, especially in segmentation problems. The architecture is developed based on U-Net with the capability of handling 3D data instead of 2D data. It consists of two main parts, an encoding part and a decoding part. The 3D encoder-decoder architecture is technically trained on image fragments to reduce memory consumption and reduce the impact of unbalanced data. The network has been used in many medical applications such as medical image segmentation, cancer identification, disease classification, and patient outcome prediction.

MobileNet-V2. MobileNet-V2 [20] is a convolutional neural network architecture that works well on mobile devices. The MobileNet-V2 architecture is based on an inverted residual structure, where the input and output of the residual blocks are designed as thin bottleneck layers. MobileNet-V2 uses lightweight depthwise convolutions to filter features in the intermediate expansion layer. In addition, eliminating non-linearities in narrow layers is important to maintain representation power.

ResNet-101. ResNet-101 [11] has greater depth than traditional networks, helping to capture more complex features in the image data. ResNet-101 has been tested and proven to have high performance on many critical image recognition datasets. Despite its great depth, ResNet-101 is still smaller in size compared to some other networks of similar depth. This helps to reduce computational pressure and storage resources when deploying the network on limited systems.

DenseNet-121. DensetNet-121 [12] connects each layer to all other layers in the network directly. This enhances information transmission and creates strong links between layers. Dense connectivity also increases feature reuse and more efficient transmission of information in the network. The DenseNet-121 network significantly reduces the number of parameters compared to traditional networks. Instead of each layer receiving input only from the previous layer, the DenseNet-121 layer receives input from all previous layers. This helps to reduce the repetition of information in the network and significantly reduces the number of parameters that need to be optimized.

2.3 Evaluation Metrics

In the segmentation problems, the Dice score is used to evaluate the similarity between a predicted segmentation mask and the ground truth segmentation mask. The Dice score is calculated as in Eq. 1, where A is the predicted segmentation and B is the ground truth.

$$Dice = \frac{2|A \cap B|}{|A| + |B|} \tag{1}$$

In object detection and classification problems, especially multi-class classification problems, it is necessary to choose appropriate methods for evaluation and comparison. The evaluation metrics used in this study include Accuracy (Eq. 2), Precision (Eq. 3), Sensitivity (Eq. 4), and Loss (Eq. 5), where TP is true positive, TN is true negative, FP is false positive, FN is false negative, K is the number of classes, y is the actual value, and $\hat{y}$ is the predicted value.

$$Accuracy = \frac{TP + TN}{TP + TN + FP + FN} \tag{2}$$

$$Precision = \frac{TP}{TP + FP} \tag{3}$$

$$Sensitivity = \frac{TP}{TP + FN} \tag{4}$$

$$Loss = \sum_{i=1}^{K} y_i log(\hat{y}_i) \tag{5}$$

2.4 3D Models

3D modeling [10] is the process of creating a digitized version of an object, space, or shape in three dimensions. The goal of 3D modeling is to create an accurate and logical digitized model for simulating, displaying, or analyzing three-dimensional objects and spaces. There are different methods for performing 3D modeling in medical imaging. One of them is using a three-dimensional convolutional neural network (3D CNN). 3D CNN extends the concept of a conventional CNN network from two dimensions to three dimensions, allowing spatial and temporal information to be captured in 3D data. 3D Slicer [9,14] is a free and open source software used in the field of medical imaging and medical data analysis. 3D Slicer is a powerful and flexible tool for viewing, processing, and analyzing 3D medical images from various sources such as MRI, CT, PET, and SPECT.

The BraTS2020 dataset consists of multiple brain slices. We use 3D Slicer to convert slices of the same patient from 2D data to a 3D model and change the color of brain tumor areas on the 3D model (as shown in Fig. 2).

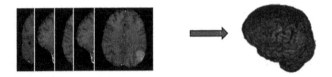

Fig. 2. Changing from MRI slices to 3D model.

3 Proposed Method

Our proposed approach for brain tumor detection and segmentation consists of two phases: the training phase and the testing phase described in Fig. 3.

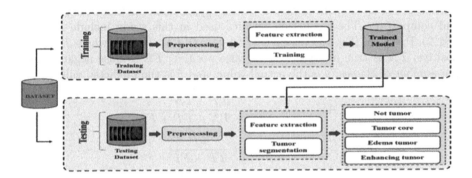

Fig. 3. Proposed approach in the detection and classification of brain tumors.

3.1 Training Phase

Pre-processing. The dataset consists of 4 types of images including FLAIR (T2 Fluid Attenuated Inversion Recovery) removes the signal of fluid in the brain and minimizes contrast between gray matter and white matter; T1 (native T1) provides information about tissue structure and distribution of gray and white matter in the brain; T1 increases the contrast in the brain, T1ce (post-contrast T1-weighted) increases the contrast between the tumor and surrounding areas; T2 (T2-weighted) enhances the signal of the water (as shown in Fig. 4).

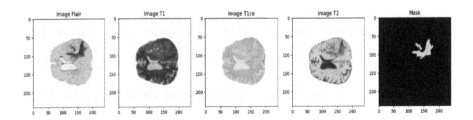

Fig. 4. Illustration of the experimental dataset.

The pre-processing stage will enhance the image dataset through a number of methods such as rotating the image and flipping the image. This is performed by using albumentations - an open-source library for horizontal image flipping, angle rotation, random contrast, and random brightness.

Feature Extraction and Training. We develop deep learning networks for brain tumor detection and segmentation based on 3D U-Net by changing its backbone with several networks including MobileNet-V2, ResNet-101, and DensetNet-121 as shown in Fig. 5.

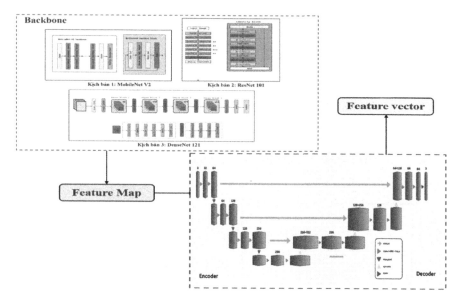

Fig. 5. Proposed model based on 3D U-Net with backbones including MobileNet-V2, ResNet101, and DenseNet 121.

3.2 Testing Phase

The feature extraction stage is performed similarly to that of the training phase. The image will be passed through the trained models to automatically detect, label the tumors, and model the tumors' area.

4 Experiments

4.1 Installation Environment and Dataset Description

The system is installed in Python language and runs on Google Colab Pro environment with a configuration of Intel Xeon 2.00 GHz processor, 32 GB RAM, graphics processor 25.4 GB RAM, and Nvidia Tesla P100 GPU. The library to help train the network model is Tensorflow v1.5.

We use the BraTS2020 dataset [4,5,16] taken from Kaggle. The BraTS2020 dataset (BraTS - Brain Tumor Segmentation) is a medical dataset used in the field of brain cancer research. This dataset contains MR images from 368 brain tumor patients, along with detailed segments of tumors and normal areas of the brain. Each patient has four types of MR images: FLAIR, T1, T1ce, and T2. We divide the experimental dataset into 3 smaller parts. The training dataset includes 249 image files, the validation dataset includes 74 image files, and the testing dataset includes 45 image files.

4.2 Scenarios

Table 1 shows four scenarios that we proposed to conduct experiments.

Table 1. Scenarios and training parameters

Scenario	Network model	Backbone	Learning rate	Epochs	No. class
1	3D U-Net	VGG-16	0.001	100	4
2	3D U-Net	MobileNet-V2	0.001	100	4
3	3D U-Net	ResNet-101	0.001	100	4
4	3D U-Net	DenseNet-121	0.001	100	4

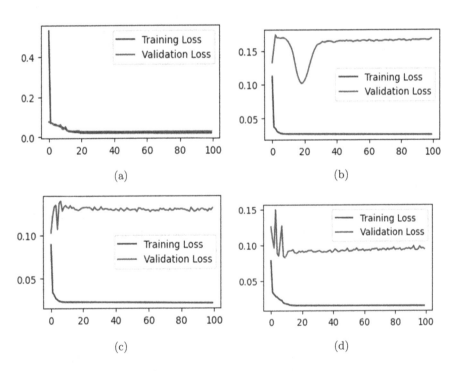

Fig. 6. Loss values of the four scenarios.

4.3   Training Results

The network models will be evaluated with several metrics including Loss, Accuracy, Dice, and training time. Figure 6 shows the training loss and validation loss of the four scenarios. The training-validation loss of scenarios 1 to 4 are 0.02 - 0.02, 0.03 - 0.18, 0.03 - 0.13, and 0.02 - 0.14, respectively. In scenarios 2, 3, and 4, the validation loss is higher than the training loss, whereas scenario 1 has the validation loss approximately equal to the training loss. In terms of loss, scenario 1 gives better results than the remaining scenarios.

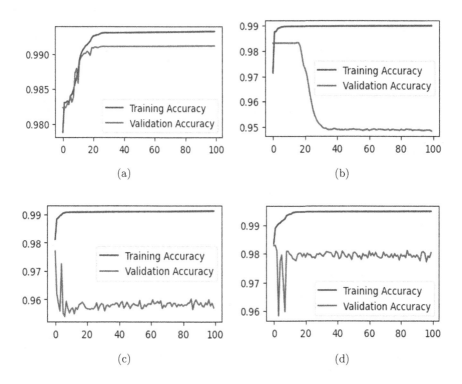

Fig. 7. Accuracy of the four scenarios.

Figure 7 shows the training accuracy and validation accuracy of the four scenarios. The train accuracy and validation accuracy of scenarios 1 to 4 are 0.99 - 0.99, 0.98 - 0.94, 0.98 - 0.95, and 0.99 - 0.97, respectively. In scenarios 2, 3, and 4, the validation accuracy is lower than the training accuracy, whereas scenario 1 has the validation accuracy approximately equal to the training accuracy. In terms of accuracy, scenario 1 gives better results than the remaining scenarios.

Figure 8 shows the training dice scores and validation dice scores of the four scenarios. The training-validation dice scores of scenarios 1 to 4 are 0.58 - 0.58, 0.46 - 0.34, 0.44 - 0.36, and 0.58 - 0.43, respectively. In scenarios 2, 3, and 4, the validation dice coefficient is lower than the training dice coefficient, whereas scenario 1 has the dice scores approximately equal between the training and the validation. Thus, scenario 1 gives better results than the remaining scenarios.

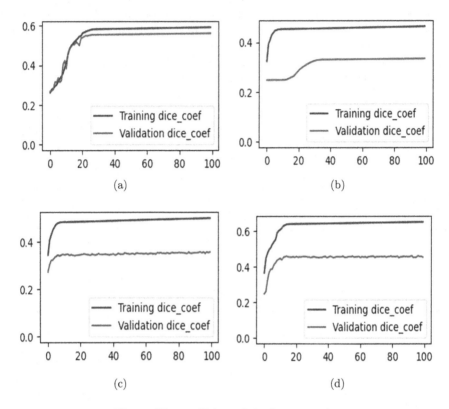

Fig. 8. Dice coefficient of the four scenarios.

In Fig. 9, the training time of scenarios 1 to 4 are 255.43 min, 245.67 min, 249.69 min, and 251.67 min, respectively. Through the above results, it can be seen that model 2 gives the fastest training time in the remaining scenarios while scenario 1 brings the longest training time among the four scenarios.

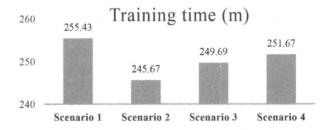

Fig. 9. Training time of the four scenarios.

Table 2 shows the comparison of the four scenarios after the training process. Scenario 1 has a good performance with an accuracy of 0.99, a training loss of 0.02, a dice score of 0.58, a precision of 0.99, and a sensitivity of 0.99. Scenarios 2, 3, and 4 have lower results than those of scenario 1. Scenarios 2 and 3 have lower accuracy, dice score, precision and sensitivity and higher training loss than scenario 1. Scenario 4 has lower precision and sensitivity than scenario 1. The training time of scenario 1 is the longest among the four scenarios. The fastest training time is of scenario 2 with 245.67 min. From the above results, it can be concluded that scenario 1 performs better than the remaining scenarios.

Table 2. Comparison between the four scenarios

Scenario	Accuracy	Loss	Dice	Precision	Sensitivity	Training time
1	0.99	0.02	0.58	0.99	0.99	255.43 m
2	0.98	0.03	0.46	0.96	0.94	245.67 m
3	0.98	0.03	0.48	0.97	0.96	249.49 m
4	0.99	0.02	0.58	0.98	0.97	251.67 m

4.4 Testing Results

Figure 10 presents the average accuracy and prediction time on the testing dataset of the four scenarios. Regarding the accuracy (Fig. 10a), scenarios 1 to 4 have an accuracy of 99.27%, 93.85%, 94.52%, and 97.54%, respectively. The average prediction time (Fig. 10b) of scenarios 1 to 4 is 2.55 min, 2.41 min, 2.46 min, and 2.46 min, respectively. It can be seen that, in terms of time and accuracy, scenario 1 gives better results than the remaining scenarios.

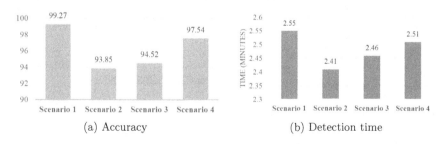

(a) Accuracy   (b) Detection time

Fig. 10. Detection time and accuracy of the four scenarios on the testing dataset.

Table 3 shows the segmentation results on the same slice in the BraTS2020 dataset with 3 types of segmentation including tumor core, enhancing tumor, and whole tumor. In the case of tumor core, scenario 1 clearly shows the center of the tumor, whereas scenarios 2, 3, and 4 do not clearly show the center of the tumor, especially scenario 4. It is the same situation in the case of whole tumor. Scenario 2, 3, and 4 do not clearly show the swelling area, whereas scenario 1 shows it more clearly. In the case of enhancing tumor, all 4 scenarios show the enhancement area, but scenario 1 still gives the best results. Thus, scenario 1 gives the clearest segmentation results among the four scenarios with 3 types of segmentation.

We used the 3D Slicer tool to display the MRI slices of a patient in a 3D model. Figure 11 shows the segmentation results from the 3D Slicer tool. The 3D Slicer's display interface is presented in Fig. 11a. Figure 11b provides the segmentation of the brain tumor with all partitions including Tumor core (Fig. 11c), Enhancing tumor (Fig. 11d), and Whole tumor (Fig. 11e).

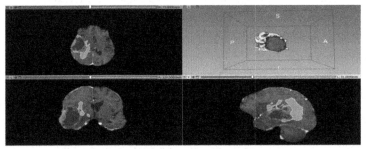

(a) Brain tumor segmentation in 3D Slicer's interface

 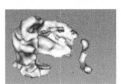 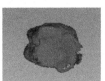

(b) Brain tumor segmentation with all partitions   (c) Tumor core   (d) Enhancing tumor   (e) Whole tumor

Fig. 11. Brain tumor segmentation with 3D Slider

Table 3. Illustration of classification results from the experimental dataset.

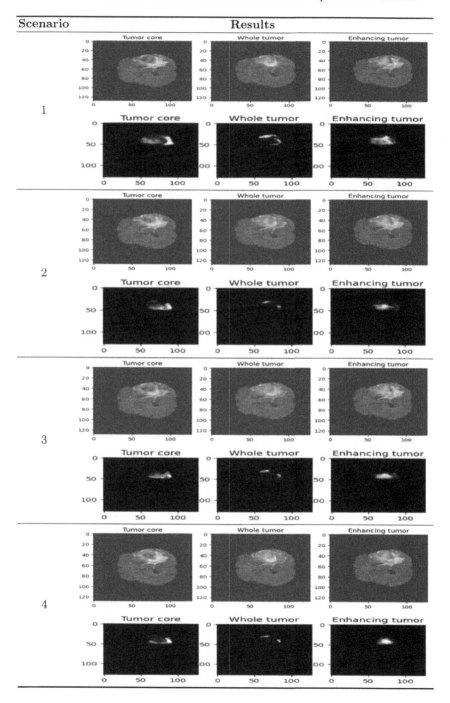

5 Conclusion

Late treatment of brain tumors leads to neurological diseases, reduced quality of life, and even human life-threaten. Therefore, early detection of the disease is essential. In this work, we propose a method to detect and segment brain tumors using 3D U-Net with different backbones including MobileNet-V2, ResNet-101, and DensetNet-121. In addition, we present some comparative results between the network models. The evaluation results can contribute to finding and choosing the suitable method to assist doctors in making a quick and accurate diagnosis. Experimental results show that the proposed detection and segmentation method achieves an accuracy of up to 99%.

References

1. (2023). https://braintumor.org/brain-tumors/about-brain-tumors/brain-tumor-facts/. Accessed 31 July 2023
2. (2023). https://www.nhs.uk/conditions/brain-tumours/. Accessed 19 July 2023
3. (2023). https://www.cancer.net/cancer-types/brain-tumor/symptoms-and-signs. Accessed 19 July 2023
4. Bakas, S., et al.: Advancing the cancer genome atlas glioma MRI collections with expert segmentation labels and radiomic features. Sci. Data 4(1), 1–13 (2017)
5. Bakas, S., et al.: Identifying the best machine learning algorithms for brain tumor segmentation, progression assessment, and overall survival prediction in the BRATS challenge, vol. 10 (2018)
6. Ballestar, L.M., Vilaplana, V.: MRI brain tumor segmentation and uncertainty estimation using 3D-UNet architectures. In: Crimi, A., Bakas, S. (eds.) BrainLes 2020. LNCS, vol. 12658, pp. 376–390. Springer, Cham (2021). https://doi.org/10.1007/978-3-030-72084-1_34
7. Bhalodiya, J.M., Lim Choi Keung, S.N., Arvanitis, T.N.: Magnetic resonance image-based brain tumour segmentation methods: a systematic review. Digit. Health 8, 20552076221074122 (2022)
8. American Society of Clinical Oncology, A.: (2023). https://www.cancer.net/cancer-types/brain-tumor/statistics. Accessed 31 July 2023
9. Fedorov, A., et al.: 3D slicer as an image computing platform for the quantitative imaging network. Magn. Reson. Imaging 30(9), 1323–1341 (2012)
10. Griffey, J.: The types of 3-D printing. Libr. Technol. Rep. 50(5), 8–12 (2014)
11. He, K., Zhang, X., Ren, S., Sun, J.: Deep residual learning for image recognition. In: Proceedings of the IEEE Conference on Computer Vision and Pattern Recognition, pp. 770–778 (2016)
12. Huang, G., Liu, Z., Van Der Maaten, L., Weinberger, K.Q.: Densely connected convolutional networks. In: Proceedings of the IEEE Conference on Computer Vision and Pattern Recognition, pp. 4700–4708 (2017)
13. Ilhan, A., Sekeroglu, B., Abiyev, R.: Brain tumor segmentation in MRI images using nonparametric localization and enhancement methods with U-net. Int. J. Comput. Assist. Radiol. Surg. 17(3), 589–600 (2022)
14. Kikinis, R., Pieper, S.D., Vosburgh, K.G.: 3D slicer: a platform for subject-specific image analysis, visualization, and clinical support. In: Jolesz, F.A. (ed.) Intraoperative Imaging and Image-Guided Therapy, pp. 277–289. Springer, New York (2014). https://doi.org/10.1007/978-1-4614-7657-3_19

15. Mehta, R., Arbel, T.: 3D U-net for brain tumour segmentation. In: Crimi, A., Bakas, S., Kuijf, H., Keyvan, F., Reyes, M., van Walsum, T. (eds.) BrainLes 2018. LNCS, vol. 11384, pp. 254–266. Springer, Cham (2019). https://doi.org/10.1007/978-3-030-11726-9_23

16. Menze, B.H., et al.: The multimodal brain tumor image segmentation benchmark (brats). IEEE Trans. Med. Imaging **34**(10), 1993–2024 (2014)

17. Ottom, M.A., Rahman, H.A., Dinov, I.D.: Znet: deep learning approach for 2D MRI brain tumor segmentation. IEEE J. Transl. Eng. Health Med. **10**, 1–8 (2022)

18. Phan, A.-C., Tran, H.-D., Phan, T.-C.: Efficient brain hemorrhage detection on 3D CT scans with deep neural network. In: Dang, T.K., Küng, J., Chung, T.M., Takizawa, M. (eds.) FDSE 2021. LNCS, vol. 13076, pp. 81–96. Springer, Cham (2021). https://doi.org/10.1007/978-3-030-91387-8_6

19. Pinto, A., Pereira, S., Correia, H., Oliveira, J., Rasteiro, D.M., Silva, C.A.: Brain tumour segmentation based on extremely randomized forest with high-level features. In: 2015 37th Annual International Conference of the IEEE Engineering in Medicine and Biology Society (EMBC), pp. 3037–3040. IEEE (2015)

20. Sandler, M., Howard, A., Zhu, M., Zhmoginov, A., Chen, L.C.: MobileNetv2: inverted residuals and linear bottlenecks. In: Proceedings of the IEEE Conference on Computer Vision and Pattern Recognition, pp. 4510–4520 (2018)

21. Sharif, M.I., Li, J.P., Amin, J., Sharif, A.: An improved framework for brain tumor analysis using MRI based on YOLOv2 and convolutional neural network. Complex Intell. Syst. **7**, 2023–2036 (2021)

22. Siegel, R.L., Miller, K.D., Wagle, N.S., Jemal, A.: Cancer statistics, 2023. CA Cancer J. Clin. **73**(1), 17–48 (2023)

Short Papers: Security and Data Engineering

Towards Automating Semantic Relationship Awareness in Operational Technology Monitoring

Wieland Schwinger[1]([✉]), Elisabeth Kapsammer[1], Werner Retschitzegger[1], Birgit Pröll[1], David Graf[1,2]([✉]), Norbert Baumgartner[2], Johannes Schönböck[3], and H. Zaunmair[1]

[1] Johannes Kepler University Linz (JKU), Linz, Austria
{wieland.schwinger,elisabeth.kapsammer,werner.retschitzegger,
birgit.proll,david.graf,h.zaunmair}@jku.at
[2] Team GmbH, Vienna, Austria
{d.graf,norbert.baumgartner}@te-am.com
[3] Upper Austrian University of Applied Sciences Hagenberg, Hagenberg, Austria
johannes.schonbock@fh-hagenberg.at

Abstract. Critical infrastructures in areas like road traffic management naturally rely on the broad use of *"Operational Technology (OT)"* to ensure efficient and safe *road traffic monitoring (RTM)* through *"OT objects"* like sensors and actuators whereby monitoring OT itself *("OTM")* is evenly crucial. OTM is highly challenging, not least due to *massive heterogeneity of OT, immense complexity and size* and *omnipresence of evolution*. As a consequence, knowledge about *interdependencies between OT objects* in form of *semantic relationships* is often outdated or simply not available. Thus, in case of incidents, detection of cause and effect in the sense of a *situational picture* is missing.

In order to counteract this fundamental deficiency, we aim to *automatically recognize semantic relationships between OT objects* to build up an *ontological knowledge base* as prerequisite for achieving *OT situation awareness*. The contribution of this paper is to sketch out state-of-research w.r.t. real-world challenges *we are facing* and based on that to put forward appropriate research questions, leading to the identification and in-depth discussion of potential concepts and technologies appearing to be useful for our work. Overall, this contribution forms the conceptual framework for a proof-of-concept prototype already realized on basis of real-world OT in the area of road traffic management.

Keywords: Critical Infrastructure · Road traffic management · Operational Technology Monitoring (OTM) · Semantic Relationships · Ontologies

This work is supported by Austrian Research Promotion Agency (FFG) under grant Forschungspartnerschaften 874490.

1 Motivation

Efficient and safe operation of critical infrastructures like electricity grids, communication networks or traffic management systems is naturally based on *"Operational Technology (OT)"* [30] (see (1) in Fig. 1). OT comprises a broad range of *"objects"* like sensors, actuators and various hardware and software backend systems and devices, commonly employing the IoT-paradigm [12, 30]. It is evident that monitoring these OT objects themselves *("OTM")* is evenly crucial (see (2) in Fig. 1), not least due to *massive heterogeneity of OT* being grown over decades, their *inherent geographical distribution* resulting in *immense complexity and size* and last but not least their *omnipresent evolution* [15]. Considering, e.g., the area of *road traffic management (RTM)*, the national highway network we focus on is geographically distributed over 2.220 km and 165 tunnels, comprising more than 100.000 OT objects of more than 200 different types, ranging from simple sensing and actuating devices (e.g., traffic jam detectors, CO-sensors or variable message signs) to more complex backend systems (e.g., video and audio surveillance) consisting of many devices of various types [17].

This challenging real-world setting is the main reason that state-of-the-art OTM usually provides information about current *isolated states* of *individual OT objects* only [32], i.e., whether a certain device works properly or not (see (3) in Fig. 1). The reason is that in practice, knowledge about interdependencies between OT objects and their semantics in form of so-called *semantic relationships* is often outdated or simply not available – primarily at *instance-level*, usually, however, also at *type-level* [13, 25, 35, 36]. As a result, in case of incidents, a detection of cause and effect in the sense of an automated creation of a *situational picture for "OT incident chains"* as well as effective maintenance strategies together with predictions of criticality and potential future incident evolutions are missing [15, 36]. For example, in case a tunnel has been closed for safety reasons because of interrelated incidents of OT objects, the expected time when the tunnel can be reopened again can normally not be estimated [15].

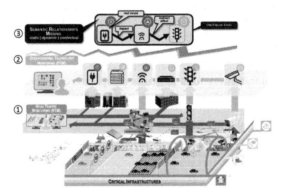

Fig. 1. OTM in Practice – Isolated OT Object States due to Lack of Semantic Relationships

To counteract this fundamental deficiency, we aim to *automatically recognize seman-tic relationships between OT objects* to build up an *ontological knowledge base* as pre-requisite for achieving OT situation awareness [15]. The contribution of this paper is to first discuss the state-of-research w.r.t. real-world challenges and based thereupon to put forward appropriate research questions in Sect. 2. For these research questions, we sketch out the necessary building blocks of a research roadmap, starting in Sect. 3 with a *semantic OT meta model*, followed by a discussion of a *hybrid knowledge acquisition method* for its population in Sect. 4 and finally, reasoning on *OT evolution techniques* in Sect. 5. A summary, a sketch of a proof-of-concept prototype on basis of real-world OT in RTM and an outlook on future work is given in Sect. 6.

2 Operational Technology Monitoring – State-of-the-Art

In critical infrastructures like RTM, OTM is highly challenging (see Fig. 2). This is not least since (i) massive *heterogeneity of OT* at different granularity levels is omnipresent, due to various manufacturers, evolving standards, diverse capabilities and legacy com-ponents [23], (ii) the *large scale of OT* multiplies the problem, since hundred thousand OT objects are geographically distributed [29] and finally (iii) the *dynamic nature of OT* is immanent, being *un-intendedly* and *intendedly* changed [38].

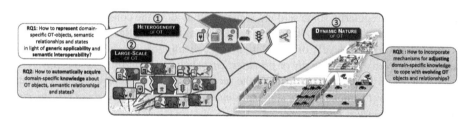

Fig. 2. OTM Challenges and Research Questions

These challenges lead to the following deficiencies in practice and form the basis for three research questions setting the scope of our work.

2.1 Conceptual Representation Challenged by OT's Heterogeneity

A major necessity w.r.t. the massive heterogeneity of OT is to establish a conceptual OT representation [15], required to provide (i) *generic modeling mechanisms* to be broadly applicable to the large variety of heterogenous OT objects, while being able to cover *domain peculiarities* as well, (ii) *interoperability mechanisms* to achieve awareness about incident chains across system boarders, (iii) *state replication mechanisms* allowing continuous monitoring and updates of an OT object's state and finally (iv) *semantic mechanisms* to allow for fine-grained representations of interdependencies.

Regarding related research, a broad variety of efforts for conceptual representations of OT exists, ranging from *IoT-ontologies* [45], via industry standards like *OPC UA* [41] to the *digital twin paradigm* [46]. Nevertheless, an integrative conceptual model for OT and their semantic relationships coping with the requirements mentioned is not yet available [4]. One reason is, that concepts such as *IoT-ontologies* are often a composition of existing upper ontologies being quite generic, lacking, however, domain specific concepts as well as semantic interoperability and state update mechanisms [16].

Consequently, this situation leads to our first research question: *RQ1: How to represent domain-specific OT objects, semantic relationships and states in light of generic applicability and semantic interoperability?*

2.2 Knowledge Acquisition Challenged by OT's Large-Scale

Manually modeling OT objects with their semantic relationships at instance-level is fairly time consuming and keeping them up to date, above all, is not feasible, especially in the light of the sheer size of employed OT [15]. Thus, automatisms for knowledge acquisition about OT objects are needed being most commonly based on OT log files, leading, at the very end, to an initial conceptual representation of all OT objects, their semantic relationships and ideally, also their continuously updated states.

Promising approaches already exist [1, 2, 1–2, 29], being highly challenged, however by the fact that in our domain [18] (i) log files contain a mixture of *state messages* about OT objects (i.e., warnings and failures) and *service messages* (i.e., environmental monitoring results), (ii) a stream of ten thousands messages per hour is recorded in several logs, (iii) the amount of log messages strongly depends on OT object's type – some reporting regularly, some seldom, some never at all in the considered time period and finally probably most challenging, (iv) a semantic differentiation of relationships is needed at different levels of abstraction (e.g., distinguish a generic *workTogether* relationship from a *powerSupply* or *providesSensorValueForControl* relationship).

Consequently, this situation leads to the second research question addressed by our work: *RQ2: How to automatically acquire domain-specific knowledge about OT objects, semantic relationships and states?*

2.3 Evolution Support Challenged by OT's Dynamic Nature

Critical infrastructures as in the area of RTM are subject to constant change [38], needing to deal with *(i) intended changes* due to constant OT maintenance during operation, i.e., OT objects being removed or added at will, as well as *(ii) unintended changes*, since such environments are subject to unforeseen incidents and direct/indirect impacts. In this context, it is required [15] that (i) the kind of evolution is identified and explicated, i.e., weather an OT object and/or relationship emerged, disappeared or changed and (ii) already existing information about the OT object is adjusted in our knowledge base at instance-level and potentially also at type-level.

Considering related work, some approaches are able to *adjust to evolution*, only, i.e., they produce meaningful output despite changes of the underlying system, such as the work of [22, 26, 29], others go beyond in terms of providing at least first steps towards *identification and explication* of changes of the underlying system [20, 34, 44].

Consequently, this situation leads to the third research question addressed by our work: *RQ3: How to incorporate mechanisms for adjusting domain-specific knowledge to cope with evolving OT objects and semantic relationships?*

3   Semantic OT Meta Model

In order to overcome heterogeneity, the first building block of our research roadmap is to develop a *semantic meta-model* which can be further on employed as guidance and target template for an automatic population of OT objects and semantic relationships, thereby building-up an *ontological knowledge base* (see (1) in Fig. 3). In the following, the research road map and the rationale behind establishing this semantic meta model is discussed by identifying promising concepts and approaches.

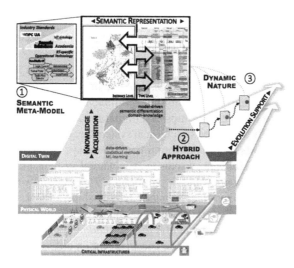

Fig. 3. Basic Building Blocks of our Research Roadmap

3.1   IoT Ontologies for Ensuring Genericity

In order to conceptually represent OT objects and relationships in a *generic way*, there already exists a plethora of proposals in the area of semantic technologies in terms *of IoT ontologies* (for an overview, see [4, 11, 43]). For our work, especially so-called *upper ontologies* seem to be promising, since providing a set of generic concepts which can be further on extended with domain specifics. To be more concrete, one suitable building block is the W3C ontology for *Semantic Sensor Networks (SSN)* [21] being the de-facto standard for representing sensors, their observations, actuators and contextual information where many other existing IoT-ontologies are built upon. Being an instantiation and extension of SSN, and therefore also suitable for our purposes, *IoT-Lite* [7] puts forward a lightweight ontology especially developed to discover sensor data in heterogeneous IoT platforms as is the case in our domain.

3.2   OPC Unified Architecture for Establishing Semantic Interoperability

Complementing the efforts of IoT ontologies, the *Open Platform Communications Unified Architecture (OPC UA)* [41] is a widely used service-oriented, platform-independent standard for industrial IoT, also widely used in road traffic management [15]. It is not only a communication protocol, i.e., addressing interoperability on the transport layer, but it has its strength compared to other IoT-protocols like DDS, ROS or MQTT [33] in describing the semantics of resources in a machine-interpretable way, i.e., addressing *interoperability on the semantic layer* [33, 41]. Precisely this aspect is relevant for our work in terms of OPC UA's meta model [41], comprising, for instance, the concepts of (i) *OPC UA objectType*, (ii) *UPC UA referenceType*, and (iii) *OPC UA object*, which might be suitable to be used as super classes for an appropriate IoT ontology to achieve an interoperable semantic representation of OT objects in our domain.

3.3 Digital Twin for Runtime State Explication

While our employment of *IoT ontologies* and parts of the *OPC UA meta model* focus on *conceptually* representing OT *at design-time*, we intend to employ the *digital twin paradigm* to focus on state representations at *run-time*, i.e., mapping the states of real-world OT objects and their relationships to a digital model [8, 37, 46]. Overall, while digital twins are initially developed for physical systems, e.g., in terms of a virtual counterpart of production lines, their application field nowadays is highly diverse, ranging from cyber-physical and software systems to even natural systems [46].

For our approach, the *digital shadow paradigm* [37] is especially relevant for explicating states of OT objects and their semantic relationships, in that information about real-world OT is automatically processed as an input for the digital representation. In particular, the *conceptual meta model of a digital shadow proposed by* [5] might provide a valuable basis comprising suitable concepts, e.g., a differentiation in *structural, behavioral and configuration classes* as pivotal customization hook.

3.4 Semantic Relatedness as Core for Achieving OT Situation Awareness

Since semantic relationships between OT objects are our central focus as crucial prerequisite for OT situation awareness, the concept of *semantic relatedness* [25] is most relevant, not least since allowing to *incorporate domain specifics* into rather generic concepts provided by the basic building blocks of our approach as mentioned above.

For our approach, first of all we intend to distinguish according to [25] in *(i) taxonomic relationships*, i.e., generalizations/specializations, in that *similar objects* are related because of shared, internal features, and *(ii) non-taxonomic relationships*, i.e., associations, in that *dissimilar objects* are related because different features co-occur in some external context (temporal, spatial, or linguistic). Regarding non-taxonomic relationships we propose to incorporate, besides some basic properties like *direction, multiplicity* and *criticality* [3] also a differentiation between *structural, behavioral* and *contextual* relationships [14], to cope with our use case of determining an incident's external root cause. Finally, besides semantic relationships between OT objects, relationships *between OT events* are highly relevant as proposed by [40] in terms of distinguishing *mereological relationships*, i.e., event aggregation, *causal* ones, i.e., event cause and effect, and *correlations*, i.e., two events having some common cause.

4 Hybrid Knowledge Acquisition for OT

In order to address the size of large-scale IoT-based environments and the specific domain challenges we mentioned before, we aim on a *hybrid approach for OT knowledge acquisition* and the *automatic population* of an ontological OT knowledge base. This means, we focus on *data-driven approaches* on the one hand side, using *OT log files* to automatically derive knowledge about OT objects and their interdependencies [26, 29] and on *model-driven approaches* on the other hand side, using *domain knowledge* to further enhance results of solely data-driven approaches by incorporating additional semantics [8, 42]. Thus, *signal intelligence* will be combined with *human intelligence*.

4.1 Data-Driven Approaches to Gain Knowledge from Log Files

Promising work regarding data-driven approaches can be found in various areas, most relevant for our purposes being (i) *event log mining* in IT networks to reason about resource interdependencies [26, 29], (ii) *organizational process mining* to extract knowledge about workflows [27] and (iii) *complex event processing* dealing especially with the streaming aspect in such environments [2].

Regarding techniques used by these approaches, the wide-ranging field of *machine learning* plays an important role, such as traditional *clustering and semi-supervised classification techniques* [24] or *rule-based machine learning* [28]. Beyond that, however, especially *statistic-based approaches* [26] adhering to temporal coincidences of events like [29] are suitable since, based on the time stamps of log entries, they can be employed to detect OT incident chains.

4.2 Model-Driven Approaches to Add Knowledge from the Domain

Overall, enhancing data-driven approaches with additional domain knowledge should allow for a more precise and semantically richer representation of OT. Domain knowledge can be either added at type-level, at instance-level, or at both [8], whereby we focus on type-level domain knowledge, simply because of the scale of our domain.

Related work covers (i) *semantic annotation* focusing, however, most often unstructured (text) data sources (e.g., [24]), being therefore only widely related and (ii) *process mining* being more closely related, being also often based on semi-structured log files [42]. In this context, the approach of [6] populates an event ontology's A-Box grounded on processes in heterogeneous IoT networks enriched with semantic meta-data about the monitored environment's life cycle. They mine, however, solely relationships between events, but not between OT objects. Most interesting is the survey of [42], putting forward a taxonomy of the distinguishing features of domain knowledge incorporation and their characteristics thereby defining the design space of our own solution.

5 OT Evolution Support

In order to face the dynamic nature of OT, we target *evolution support* allowing the adjustment of our ontological knowledge base. Dealing with the dynamic nature of OT is addressed in various areas like *(i) process mining* focusing on so-called *concept drifts* [39], *(ii) community mining*, identifying changes of the underlying structure [31] and *(iii) context- and self-aware systems* adapting themselves to evolution [10]. Out of these three areas, in the following, promising approaches are identified, distinguishing between simple adjustment to evolution and identification/explication of evolution.

5.1 Implicit Adjustment to Evolution

A first step to tackle system evolution is an approach's ability to at least, *"implicitly" adjust to evolution*, i.e., to produce meaningful output despite changes of the underlying system, such as the work of [22, 26, 29]. It is intended, however, to complement this quite simple form of evolution support by more sophisticated mechanisms in order to identify certain kinds of evolution together their explication (see below).

5.2 Identification and Explication of Evolution

Beyond *implicit adjustment* to evolution, approaches provide first steps towards change identification, being aware, to some extent, that evolution takes place. In particular, their focus is on *(i) accumulation of intermediate results* [34], *(ii) calculation of change ratios* in order to identify change points [20, 44], *(iii) recording provenance information*, i.e., keeping track of data processing and its results, thus allowing to identify changes at the input side resulting from potential changes of the underlying system [9].

6 Summary and Outlook

Critical infrastructures urgently demand for techniques to *automatically recognize semantic relationships between OT objects* to build up an *ontological knowledge base* as prerequisite for OT situation awareness, thus enhancing OTM. This paper discusses the state-of-the-art w.r.t. real-world challenges and provides a first research roadmap, especially targeting the establishment of a semantic meta model to overcome heterogeneity, the employment of hybrid knowledge acquisition techniques to cope with large scale OT and finally evolution support mechanisms to deal with OT's dynamic nature.

In the context of this research roadmap, a *first proof-of-concept prototype* has been already realized and evaluated based on real-world OT log data (two sections of a highway tunnel comprising around 70.000 OT messages of 485 OT objects of 66 types within one year) [15–20]. Our initial focus was on establishing a first version of the hybrid knowledge acquisition mechanism, thereby adhering to a *statistic-based mining approach* [29] allowing to compute the probability of functional correlations between temporally co-occurring messages of OT objects, being either in a *cause-effect* or a *working-together* semantic relationship. Second, we enhanced this data-driven mining method with a first version of a *semantic meta model*, describing core IoT concepts and their interdependencies in a generic way reusing concepts from the IoT-ontologies SSN [21] and IoT-Light [7], the OPC UA meta model [41] and semantic relatedness approaches. Third, initial efforts have been made to enhance instantiation of the semantic meta model's instance-level concepts (A-Box), aimed at by our log mining-driven ontology population approach, through incorporation of type-level concepts (T-Box) during the population in terms of not only an extensive generic type system, but also packages of domain-specific types plugged in as subclasses.

Future work is planned in three different directions: First, our mining approach should be enhanced towards recognizing more coarse-grained semantic relationships, involving not just pairs of OT objects but whole incident chains. Second, promising digital twin approaches should be integrated to enhance the current structural representation of OT with runtime state representations being continuously updated. Finally, evolution awareness should be realized, starting with the integration of provenance.

However, in the very end, from a practical point of view, in order to support system operators w.r.t. OT situation awareness, it will be necessary to incorporate methods and techniques in OTM solutions provided by system manufacturers of different domains.

References

1. Alam, I.E., et al.: A survey of network virtualization techniques for Internet of Things using SDN and NFV. ACM Comput. Surv. (CSUR) **53**(2), 1–40 (2020)
2. Alevizos, E., et al.: Probabilistic CE recognition: a survey. ACM CSUR **50**, 1–31 (2017)
3. Ali, N., Hong, J.-E.: Failure detection and prevention for CPS using ontology-based knowledge base. Computers **7**, 68 (2018)
4. Bajaj, G., et al.: 4w1h in IoT semantics. IEEE Access **6**, 65488–65506 (2018)
5. Becker, F., et al.: A conceptual model for digital shadows in industry and its application. In: Ghose, A., Horkoff, J., Silva Souza, V.E., Parsons, J., Evermann, J. (eds.) Conceptual Modeling. ER 2021. LNCS, vol. 13011, pp. 271–281. Springer, Cham (2021). https://doi.org/10.1007/978-3-030-89022-3_22
6. Belkaroui, R., et al.: Towards events ontology based on data sensors network for viticulture domain. In: Proceedings of the 8th International Conference on the Internet of Things. ACM (2018)
7. Bermudez-Edo, M., et al.: IoT-Lite: a lightweight semantic model for the IoT and its use with dynamic semantics. Pers. Ubiquit. Comput. **21**, 475–487 (2017)
8. Brauner, P., et al.: A computer science perspective on digital transformation in production. ACM Trans. Internet Things **3**, 1–32 (2022)
9. Carata, L., et al.: A primer on provenance. Commun. ACM **57**(5), 52–60 (2014)
10. Chen, T., Bahsoon, R., Yao, X.: A survey and taxonomy of self-aware and self-adaptive cloud autoscaling systems. ACM Comput. Surv. (CSUR) **51**, 1–40 (2018)
11. De, S., et al.: Ontologies and Context Modeling for the WoT. Morgan Kaufmann, San Francisco (2017)
12. Finogeev, A., et al.: Intelligent monitoring system for smart road environment. J. Ind. Inf. Integr. **15**, 15–20 (2019)
13. Flentge, F., Beyer, U.: The ISE meta model for critical infrastructures. In: Goetz, E., Shenoi, S. (eds.) Critical Infrastructure Protection. ICCIP 2007. IFIP International Federation for Information Processing, vol. 253, pp. 323–336. Springer, Boston, MA (2007). https://doi.org/10.1007/978-0-387-75462-8_23
14. Genova, G., Llorens, J., Fuentes, J.M.: UML associations: a structural and contextual view. J. Object Technol. **3**, 83–100 (2004)
15. Graf, D., Retschitzegger, W., et al.: Towards OTM in ITS. In: Proceedings of the 11th International Conference on Management of Digital EcoSystems (MEDES), pp. 237–241, ACM, Limassol (2019)

16. Graf, D., Retschitzegger, W., et al.: Cutting a path through the IoT ontology jungle – a meta survey. In: Proceedings of the International Conference on IoT & Intelligence Systems. IEEE, Bali (2019)

17. Graf, D., Retschitzegger, W., et al.: Event-driven ontology population. In: Rocha, Á., Adeli, H., Dzemyda, G., Moreira, F., Ramalho Correia, A.M. (eds.) Trends and Applications in Information Systems and Technologies . WorldCIST 2021. AISC, vol. 1366, pp. 405–415. Springer, Cham (2021). https://doi.org/10.1007/978-3-030-72651-5_39

18. Graf, D., Retschitzegger, W., et al.: Bridging Signals and Human Intelligence. In: Memmi, G., Yang, B., Kong, L., Zhang, T., Qiu, M. (eds.) Knowledge Science, Engineering and Management. KSEM 2022. LNCS, vol. 13369. Springer, Cham (2021). https://doi.org/10.1007/978-3-031-10986-7_46

19. Graf, D., Retschitzegger, W., et al.: Semantic-driven mining of functional dependencies in large-scale SoS. In: Rocha, Á., Ferrás, C., Méndez Porras, A., Jimenez Delgado, E. (eds.) Information Technology and Systems. ICITS 2022. LNNS, vol. 414, pp. 344–355. Springer, Cham (2022). https://doi.org/10.1007/978-3-030-96293-7_31

20. Graf, D., Retschitzegger, W., et al.: Towards message-driven ontology population. In: Rocha, Á., Adeli, H., Reis, L., Costanzo, S., Orovic, I., Moreira, F. (eds.) Trends and Innovations in Information Systems and Technologies. WorldCIST 2020. AISC, vol. 1159, pp. 361–368. Springer, Cham (2022). https://doi.org/10.1007/978-3-030-45688-7_37

21. Haller, A., et al.: The SOSA/SSN ontology: a joint WEC and OGC standard specifying the semantics of sensors observations actuation and sampling. Semantic Web 1, 1–19 (2018)

22. Harper, R., Tee, P.: A method for temporal event correlation. In: IFIP/IEEE Symposium on Integrated Network and Service Management (IM), pp. 13–18. IEEE (2019)

23. Hazra, A., et al.: A comprehensive survey on interoperability for IIoT: taxonomy, standards, & future directions. ACM Comput. Surv. 55(1), 1–35 (2023)

24. Jayawardana, V., et al.: Semi-supervised instance population of an ontology using word vector embedding. In: Proceedings of the International Conference on Advances in ICT, pp. 1–7. IEEE (2017)

25. Kacmajor, M., Kelleher, J.D.: Capturing and measuring thematic relatedness. Lang. Resour. Eval. 54(3), 645–682 (2020)

26. Kobayashi, S., Otomo, K., Fukuda, K., Esaki, H.: Mining causality of network events in log data. IEEE Trans. Netw. Serv. Manag. 15, 53–67 (2017)

27. Matzner, M., Scholta, H.: Process mining approaches to detect organizational properties in CPS. In: Proceedings of the 2nd European Conference on Information Systems (ECIS), Tel Aviv (2014)

28. Mehdiyev, N., et al.: Determination of rule patterns in complex event processing using machine learning techniques. Procedia Comput. Sci. 61, 395–401 (2015)

29. Messager, A., et al.: Inferring FCT. Connectivity from time-series of events in large scale network deployments. Trans. Netw. Serv. Mang. 16(3), 857–870 (2019)

30. Murray, G., et al.: The convergence of IT and OT in critical infrastructure. In: Proceedings of the 15th Australian Information Security Management Conference, pp. 149–155 (2017)

31. Peng, H., et al.: Streaming social event detection and evolution discovery in heterogeneous information networks. ACM Trans. KDD 15(5), 1–33 (2021)

32. Pliatsios, D., et al.: A survey on SCADA systems: secure protocols, incidents, threats and tactics. IEEE Commun. Surv. Tutor. 22(3), 1942–1976 (2020)

33. Profanter, S., et al.: OPC UA versus ROS, DDS & MQTT: performance evaluation of industry 4.0 protocols. In: Proceedings of the International Conference on Industrial Technology, Melbourne (2019)

34. Psorakis, I., et al.: Inferring social network structure in ecological systems from spatio-temporal data streams. J. R. Soc. Interface. 9, 3055–3066 (2012)

35. Puuska, S., et al.: Nationwide critical infrastructure monitoring using a common operating picture framework. Int. J. Crit. Infrastruct. Prot. **20**, 28–47 (2018)
36. Rinaldi, S., et al.: Identifying, understanding, and analyzing critical infrastructure interdependencies. IEEE Control. Syst. Mag. **21**, 11–25 (2001)
37. Rivera, L.F., Jimenez, M., Villegas, N.M., Tamura, G., Muller, H.A.: Toward autonomic, software-intensive digital twin systems. IEEE Softw. **39**, 20–26 (2022)
38. Russell, L., et al.: Agile IoT for critical infrastructure resilience: cross-modal sensing as part of a situational awareness. IEEE Internet Things J. **5**(6), 4454–4465 (2018)
39. Sato, D., et al.: A survey on concept drift in process mining. ACM CSUR **54**(9), 1–38 (2021)
40. Scherp, A., et al.: A core ontology on events for representing occurrences in the real world. Multimed. Tools Appl. **58**(2), 293–331 (2012)
41. Schiekofer, R., et al.: A formal mapping between OPC UA and the semantic web. In: Proceedings of the 17th International Conference on Industrial Informatics (INDIN), pp. 33–40. IEEE (2019)
42. Schuster, D., van Zelst, S.J., van der Aalst, W.M.: Utilizing domain knowledge in data-driven process discovery: a literature review. Comput. Ind. **137**, 103612 (2022)
43. Sethi, P., et al.: IoT: architectures, protocols, & applications. J. Electr. Comput. Eng. **2017**, 1–25 (2017)
44. Song, Y., et al.: Topology tracking of dynamic UAV WLANs. J. Aeronaut. **35**(11), 322–335 (2021)
45. Szilagyi, I., Wira, P.: Ontologies and semantic web for the IoT – a survey. In: Proceedings of the 42nd Conference of the IEEE Industrial Electronics Society, pp. 6949–6954 (2016)
46. Wen, J., et al.: Toward digital twin-oriented modeling of complex networked systems and their dynamics: a comprehensive survey. IEEE Access **10**, 66886–66923 (2022)

Feature Fool Exploitation for Lightweight Anomaly Detection in Respiratory Sound

Kim-Ngoc T. Le[1], Sammy Yap Xiang Bang[1], Duc-Tai Le[2], and Hyunseung Choo[1,2,3(✉)]

[1] Department of AI Systems Engineering, Sungkyunkwan University, Seoul, South Korea
{ltkngoc0228,sammyyap98,choo}@skku.edu
[2] College of Computing and Informatics, Sungkyunkwan University, Seoul, South Korea
ldtai@skku.edu
[3] Department of Electrical and Computer Engineering, Sungkyunkwan University, Seoul, South Korea

Abstract. Respiratory sound auscultation with digital stethoscopes is a common technique for identifying lung disorders, however, it requires a qualified medical expert to interpret the sounds, and inter-listener variability results from subjectivity in interpretations. To improve diagnostic accuracy and enhance patient treatment, there is a growing need for automated detection of lung diseases. Deep neural networks (DNNs) have demonstrated substantial potential in addressing such challenges. However, DNNs demand a significant amount of data, and the largest available respiratory dataset, ICBHI, comprises only 6898 breathing cycles, which is insufficient to train a satisfactory DNN model. To address the issue, we propose a robust and lightweight model that employs a feature fool exploitation technique to identify respiratory anomalies. Next, we deploy two evaluation approaches to evaluate its performance: random 60/40 splitting and 5-fold cross-validation, against state-of-the-art methods, using the ICBHI dataset. Remarkably, our scheme outperforms existing approaches up to 18.26%, achieving impressive accuracy rates of 72.36% and 89.46%, using the two respective train/test splitting methods. The results show a significant improvement from our method over existing approaches, suggesting its promise for future respiratory healthcare technology research.

Keywords: anomaly detection · respiratory sound · feature extraction · lightweight · ICBHI dataset

1 Introduction

The diagnosis of respiratory diseases is primarily reliant on a method known as respiratory sound auscultation. This practice involves the use of stethoscopes to detect and interpret lung sounds, often indicative of underlying pathological

T. K. Dang et al. (Eds.): FDSE 2023, CCIS 1925, pp. 556–563, 2023.
https://doi.org/10.1007/978-981-99-8296-7_40

conditions. Auscultation, being a non-invasive procedure, is widely used in clinical settings for initial assessment and monitoring of lung diseases. However, it is largely contingent upon the expertise and insight of the medical professional conducting the examination, thus introducing a significant element of subjectivity into the diagnostic process.

Automated analysis is developed to reduce the variability associated with human interpretation and provide a more uniform and objective diagnosis. Recently, the use of deep learning methods has gained traction in this domain. Deep Neural Networks (DNNs), in particular, have shown promise in automating the analysis of respiratory sounds [1]. DNNs learn intricate patterns in high-dimensional data, making them ideally suited for the task of identifying anomalies in respiratory sounds, which are inherently complex and non-linear. Several studies have explored the state-of-the-art architectures, such as ResNet [1–3], and CNN-MoE [4], to achieve effective anomaly detection in respiratory sound.

One primary concern is the requirement of DNNs for large amounts of data to learn effectively. The largest publicly available dataset for respiratory sounds, the International Conference on Biomedical Health Informatics (ICBHI) dataset, contains only 6898 breathing cycles [5]. Given the complex nature of respiratory sounds and the diversity of pathological conditions that they represent, this dataset is markedly insufficient for training robust DNN models. The paucity of data fails to capture the full spectrum of variability and complexity inherent in respiratory sounds, thereby limiting the ability of DNNs to learn effectively. Moreover, a common caveat with many deep learning models is their specialization for specific types of data, such as image or audio signals. This specificity often means that while they excel in their designated domains, they may falter when applied to different types of data or tasks. This issue stems from the inherent learning mechanism of these models. They are designed and trained to recognize and capitalize on patterns and features within a given dataset that are pertinent to a specific task.

In light of these challenges, this study presents a novel model designed to optimize feature fool exploitation for the purpose of identifying respiratory anomalies. The proposed method is a model combining machine learning-based feature extraction and deep learning-based classification techniques for respiratory anomaly detection. This aims to provide a robust and lightweight solution to the data limitation issue and data specificity issue encountered with conventional DNN models, thereby pushing the boundaries of automated respiratory sound analysis. Our proposed model consists of two main components: a front-end feature exploitation part that exploits seven types of features and a back-end neural network classifier that utilizes multi-layer perceptron. We evaluated the performance of the proposed scheme using two different evaluation approaches: random 60/40 splitting and 5-fold cross-validation. It achieves 72.36% and 89.46% for the two evaluation approaches, respectively, outperforming other state-of-the-art models. The results demonstrate that our method offers a significant improvement over existing approaches, indicating a promising direction for future research in this crucial area of healthcare technology.

This paper is structured as follows. Section 2 presents a detailed description of our respiratory anomaly detection scheme. Next, in Sect. 3, we provide the experimental setup, including the ICBHI 2017 dataset and evaluation metrics, and present the results of our experiments. Finally, in Sect. 4, we summarize our findings and conclude the paper.

2   Respiratory Anomaly Detection Scheme

In this section, we detail a lightweight and robust model for respiratory anomaly detection. The architecture of the proposed scheme is illustrated in Fig. 1, comprising two main components: front-end feature exploitation and back-end neural network classifier. The process begins by converting respiratory cycles from lung sound signals into mel-spectrogram representations. These spectrograms serve as input to the scheme, which classifies them as either normal or abnormal patterns.

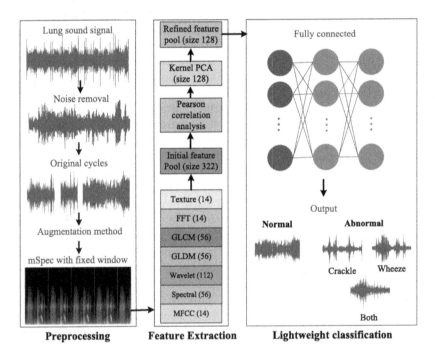

Fig. 1. The overall process of the proposed scheme

The objective of our study is to detect respiratory anomalies by classifying the four types of cycles into two groups: normal and anomaly sounds. The anomaly group consists of cycles exhibiting crackles, wheezes, or both, while the normal group represents cycles characterized by normal breathing. Our focus lies in accurately identifying and distinguishing these two groups for effective respiratory anomaly detection.

2.1 Preprocessing

The recordings in the dataset have varying sampling rates, ranging from 4 kHz to 44.1 kHz. In order to standardize the dataset, we downsample all the recordings to 4 kHz. Additionally, we apply a band-pass filter to preserve frequencies within the range of 50–2000 Hz, effectively removing unwanted noise such as heartbeat sounds and background speech [3]. To maintain consistency throughout the dataset, we establish a maximum duration of 8 s for respiratory cycles as the majority of cycles, approximately 99.8%, already fall within this duration [6]. For cycles that surpass the 8-second limit, we truncate them to include only the initial 8 s. Conversely, for cycles that are shorter than 8 s, we duplicate them to match the desired duration.

The ICBHI dataset exhibits a class imbalance, with the normal class representing 53% of the samples. To address potential overfitting issues, we conducted experiments using an augmentation technique described in [3]. This technique involves generating additional samples for a specific class by randomly selecting and concatenating two samples from within that class. The implementation of this augmentation scheme yielded significant improvements in the classification accuracy of abnormal classes. Once the audio signal has been appropriately preprocessed, we convert it into a time-frequency representation Mel-spectrogram with 64 Mel filterbanks, a window size of 1024 over a hop size of 512, with a minimum and a maximum frequency of 50 and 4000 Hz respectively, because wheezes and crackles are in this interval [7]. This Mel-spectrogram representation serves as the input for the feature exploitation block.

2.2 Feature Exploitation Phase

Our feature exploitation phase principally comprises two integral components: feature extraction and feature reduction. Feature extraction initiates with an original set of measured data and builds upon it by generating derived values. These derived values are designed to be informative and non-redundant, thereby facilitating subsequent learning and generalization processes. Once this expansive pool of features is extracted, we then move on to the feature reduction phase to avoid the issue of multicollinearity.

The feature extraction process we employed in our model is thorough and multi-faceted, resulting in a rich set of features that capture various aspects of the lung sound signals. Specifically, we extracted a total of 322 features for each mel-spectrogram, which is the representation of each lung sound signal. This set includes 14 texture features, 14 Fast Fourier Transform (FFT) features, 56 Gy-Level Co-Occurrence Matrix (GLCM) features, 56 features Gray Level Dependence Matrix (GLDM) features, 112 wavelet features, 56 spectral features, and 14 features derived from Mel-Frequency Cepstral Coefficients (MFCC).

Next, we conduct a Pearson correlation analysis on the initial feature set to investigate the correlation coefficients between features. This step is critical in identifying and eliminating features that exhibit strong correlations with others to avoid the issue of multicollinearity [8]. Multicollinearity can inflate the variance of the model's parameter estimates, leading to unreliable and unstable estimates. To further refine our feature pool and address the issue of high dimensionality, we employ Kernel Principal Component Analysis (Kernel PCA). PCA is an unsupervised statistical technique widely employed to reduce the dimensionality of datasets [9]. In our study, we leverage kernel PCA to transform our initial feature pool of 322 features into a refined, reduced set of 128 features. By doing so, we maintain the intricate relationships within the data while reducing its complexity. This process not only improves the computational efficiency of our model but also enhances its ability to learn and generalize from the given respiratory sound data.

2.3   Lightweight Detection Phase

Having obtained the refined feature pool, the subsequent step is to employ a classification model capable of performing anomaly detection based on these features. Various models can serve this purpose, including deep convolutional neural networks laden with intricate elements. These advanced models are renowned for their ability to learn intricate patterns and dependencies. However, these models come with their own set of limitations. In particular, they demand considerable computational power and memory capacity due to their complex architectures. This requirement poses a significant hurdle, especially when real-time detection is desired. Moreover, the high computational and memory demands of these models could potentially negate the effort put into reducing the feature pool size, as they might still require substantial resources to operate.

Therefore, to address these challenges and ensure the practical applicability of our model, we opt for a more lightweight and compact solution-a multi-layer neural network. This network is designed to be streamlined yet effective, comprising seven hidden layers and a softmax activation decision layer. The hidden layers are responsible for capturing the relationships and patterns in the input data, while the decision layer classifies the data into normal or anomalous based on these learned patterns. The aim of this simplified yet robust architecture is to perform efficient and accurate anomaly detection on lung sound signals. By making this choice, we strike a balance between model complexity and computational efficiency, ensuring that our model remains practical for real-world, real-time applications while retaining a high level of performance. The training was conducted for 100 epochs, employing binary cross-entropy as the loss function, and the Adam optimizer with a learning rate of 10^{-5}. We utilized a mini-batch size of 128 and a dropout rate of 0.1 to optimize computational efficiency and prevent overfitting.

3   Experimental Setting and Performance Evaluation

3.1   Dataset and Evaluation Metrics

Our evaluations are conducted using the ICBHI scientific challenge respiratory sound dataset, which consists of 5.5 h of recordings. This dataset encompasses a total of 6898 respiratory cycles, with durations ranging from 0.2 s to 16.2 s. On average, the respiratory cycles have a duration of 2.7 s. Within the dataset, there are 3642 respiratory cycles characterized by normal breathing, 1864 cycles exhibiting crackles, 886 cycles exhibiting wheezes, and 506 cycles containing both crackles and wheezes. These respiratory cycle categories are distributed across 920 audio samples obtained from 126 subjects.

By the official ICBHI 2017 challenge [5], we employ the same evaluation metrics. The evaluation score (S_c) is calculated as the arithmetic mean of the sensitivity (S_e) and specificity (S_p) scores. This approach enables us to comprehensively assess the performance of our model by considering both true positive and true negative rates. S_e and S_p scores are computed using the following formulas:

$$S_e = \frac{P_c + P_w + P_b}{T_c + T_w + T_b}; \quad S_p = \frac{P_n}{T_n}; \quad S_c = \frac{S_e + S_p}{2}.$$

where P_c, P_w, P_n, P_b represent the numbers of correct predictions for the crackle, wheeze, normal, and both classes, respectively, while T_c, T_w, T_n, T_b correspond to the total number of instances of each class.

3.2 Experiment Results

In this study, we evaluate two commonly used methods for train/test splitting found in the literature [2]. The first approach is random 5-fold cross-validation, while the second approach follows the 60/40 splitting recommendation from the ICBHI challenge. We compare the performance of our proposed framework against state-of-the-art systems [1–4] to determine its effectiveness in anomaly sound classification. By examining the results obtained from different train/test splitting methods, we aim to gain insights into the impact of the splitting strategy on the overall performance of the classification model.

Regarding respiratory anomaly detection, the proposed method demonstrates superior performance compared to other systems, as evidenced by the overall ICBHI score. However, it may not necessarily outperform them simultaneously for both subcomponents, namely specificity, and sensitivity. Notably, as presented in Table 1, our method exhibits a significant improvement over state-of-the-art (SOTA) methods, with an increase of over 8% and 5% in terms of Sc for the 60/40 and 5-fold train/test splitting, respectively. Furthermore, similar to many medical datasets, the ICBHI dataset suffers from a considerable class imbalance, with the normal class representing 53% of the samples. We observe that the use of 5-fold cross-validation, yielding a result of 89.46%, outperforms the 60/40 data splitting, which achieves a result of 72.36%. This improvement can be attributed to the 5-fold approach's ability to maintain approximately balanced class frequencies in both the training and test sets.

Deep learning (DL) models have extensive applicability in real-world scenarios, but they come with certain drawbacks, such as a high number of parameters that demand substantial computational resources. Additionally, DL models typically require longer training times compared to machine learning (ML) models, often 2 to 3 times longer. Interestingly, our experiments reveal that increasing the

Table 1. Performamce comparison between the proposed scheme and SOTA schemes following the random data split (Highest scores are highlighted in bold)

Methods	Train/test	S_p	S_e	S_c	Parameters
ResNet-Att [1]	60/40	71.44	51.4	61.42	–
CNN-MoE [2]	60/40	72.4	37.5	54.1	4M
ResNet50 [4]	60/40	**79.34**	50.14	64.74	23M
Our	60/40	68.62	**76.10**	**72.36**	**774,050**
CNN-MoE [2]	5 folds	**90.0**	78.0	84.0	4M
RespireNet [3]	5 folds	80.90	73.10	77.0	21M
Our	5 folds	88.22	**90.70**	**89.46**	**774,050**

number of parameters in DL models does not necessarily lead to improved performance. For example, even though ResNet101 has twice the number of parameters compared to ResNet50, its performance remains lower. This suggests that a deep and dense neural network is not essential for our respiratory anomaly detection task. In this study, our model achieves high accuracy with significantly fewer parameters, specifically 774,000 parameters for training, resulting in reduced training time.

4   Conclusion

This paper introduces a robust and lightweight framework specifically designed to enable accurate respiratory anomaly detection from lung auscultation recordings, even with limited dataset sizes. Through the utilization of novel feature exploitation techniques, our proposed method surpasses the state-of-the-art (SOTA) by achieving improvements of over 8% and 5% in terms of Sc for the 60/40 and 5-fold train/test splitting, respectively. Moreover, this study highlights the effectiveness of employing 5-fold cross-validation, which contributes to a notable 17% improvement in S_c. It is important to note that the current model is trained on only binary classes, namely normal and abnormal lung sounds, while real-life scenarios involve a range of respiratory diseases that require consideration. Thus, for future research, we recommend that the scientific community prioritizes the acquisition of larger datasets while addressing the challenges outlined in this paper.

Acknowledgement. This work is supported by an IITP grant funded by the Korean government (MSIT) under the ICT Creative Consilience program (IITP-2023-2020-0-01821), Artificial Intelligence Innovation Hub (IITP-2021-0-02068), and AI Graduate School program(IITP-2019-0-00421).

References

1. Mukherjee, H., et al.: Automatic lung health screening using respiratory sounds. J. Med. Syst. **45**, 1–9 (2021)

2. Pham, L., Phan, H., Palaniappan, R., Mertins, A., McLoughlin, I.: CNN-MoE based framework for classification of respiratory anomalies and lung disease detection. IEEE J. Biomed. Health Inform. **25**(8), 2938–2947 (2021)
3. Gairola, S., Tom, F., Kwatra, N., Jain, M.: Respirenet: a deep neural network for accurately detecting abnormal lung sounds in limited data setting. In: 2021 43rd Annual International Conference of the IEEE Engineering in Medicine & Biology Society (EMBC), pp. 527–530. IEEE (2021)
4. Nguyen, T., Pernkopf, F.: Lung sound classification using co-tuning and stochastic normalization. IEEE Trans. Biomed. Eng. **69**(9), 2872–2882 (2022)
5. Rocha, B.M., et al.: A respiratory sound database for the development of automated classification. In: Maglaveras, N., Chouvarda, I., de Carvalho, P. (eds.) Precision Medicine Powered by pHealth and Connected Health. ICBHI 2017. IFMBE Proceedings, vol. 66, pp. 33–37. Springer, Singapore (2018). https://doi.org/10.1007/978-981-10-7419-6_6
6. Moummad, I., Farrugia, N.: Supervised contrastive learning for respiratory sound classification. arXiv preprint arXiv:2210.16192 (2022)
7. Jakovljević, N., Lončar-Turukalo, T.: Hidden Markov model based respiratory sound classification. In: Maglaveras, N., Chouvarda, I., de Carvalho, P. (eds.) Precision Medicine Powered by pHealth and Connected Health. IP, vol. 66, pp. 39–43. Springer, Singapore (2018). https://doi.org/10.1007/978-981-10-7419-6_7
8. Bang, S.Y.X., Le, K.N.T., Le, D.T., Choo, H.: Feature pool exploitation for disease detection in fundus images. In: 2023 17th International Conference on Ubiquitous Information Management and Communication (IMCOM), pp. 1–4 (2023). https://doi.org/10.1109/IMCOM56909.2023.10035647
9. Rosipal, R., Girolami, M., Trejo, L.J., Cichocki, A.: Kernel PCA for feature extraction and de-noising in nonlinear regression. Neural Comput. Appl. **10**(3), 231–243 (2001). https://doi.org/10.1007/s521-001-8051-z

Multiple Vehicles Detection and Tracking Using Ground and Aerial Images for Vehicular Management System

Sardar Jaffar Ali[1]([⊠]), Muhammad Omer[2], Syed Muhammad Raza[3], and Hyunseung Choo[1,3]

[1] Department of AI Systems Engineering, Sungkyunkwan University,
Seoul, South Korea
`sardar.jaffar.ali@gmail.com, choo@skku.edu`
[2] Department of Computer Science and Engineering, Sungkyunkwan University,
Seoul, South Korea
[3] Department of Electrical and Computer Engineering, Sungkyunkwan University,
Seoul, South Korea

Abstract. Vehicle Management Systems (VMSs) are crucial in location-based services for optimizing transportation efficiency, traffic flow, and overall mobility for individuals and businesses. To further enhance their performance, smart VMSs must leverage existing traffic data it gathers by detecting and tracking vehicles periodically. However, despite recent advancements in traffic monitoring, there remains a need for an efficient and up-to-date system, especially in dense traffic or situations requiring aerial monitoring. This paper focuses on the importance of detecting and tracking multiple vehicles in such systems, presenting a two-way validation architecture that integrates CCTV and drone images to enhance accuracy and authenticity. The architecture utilizes the YOLO pretrained model for CCTV images, which is subsequently fine-tuned for drone images. Results demonstrate an accuracy of 99% and a mean average precision of up to 97%. Lastly, the proposed architecture is used for two real-time applications of vehicle counter and lane detection which shows its validity and ability in aforementioned situations.

Keywords: Vehicle Management System (VMS) · vehicle detection and tracking · Ground and aerial monitoring · vehicle counter · lane detection

1 Introduction

Effective Vehicular Management Systems (VMSs) are crucial for vehicle fleet-dependent businesses and organizations. Vehicle detection and tracking play a vital role in VMSs, improving safety, reducing fuel consumption, preventing theft, and ensuring regulatory compliance, resulting in higher revenues. Developing and enhancing vehicle detection and tracking have a significant impact on fleet-dependent businesses' success and profitability. Methods for improvement fall into two categories: reactive approaches use real-time traffic data for adaptive traffic light control [1], traffic flow management [2], and congestion detection

© The Author(s), under exclusive license to Springer Nature Singapore Pte Ltd. 2023
T. K. Dang et al. (Eds.): FDSE 2023, CCIS 1925, pp. 564–571, 2023.
https://doi.org/10.1007/978-981-99-8296-7_41

[3], while proactive approaches analyze extensive traffic data to develop strategies based on movement characteristics and traffic flow trends [4,5]. Leveraging these methods allows businesses to optimize their vehicle management systems for enhanced operational efficiency and overall success.

One of the best approach for vehicle management task is to detect and track the vehicle and maintain a database. This information can be used both in real-time and in future to perform the necessary analysis and actions. A good model would be the one which is capable of performing detection and tracking of multiple vehicles simultaneously [6]. Besides ground surveillance using CCTV, it is also important to take aerial view into account for better and efficient detection and tracking. Several researchers have proposed their respective models to carry out the same task. For the detection purposes most popular approaches include the use of You Only Look Once (YOLO) [7] and Faster RCNN [8].

This study proposes a unified solution that can provide tasks of detection, classification, counting, and tracking of multiple vehicles simultaneously. For this, we first use CCTV images which are trained on YOLO model. In the next step, aerial images are used to retrain the same model in the Darknet architecture. The proposed solution achieves the accuracy of 99% with the mean average precision (mAP) of 97%. Moreover, all the collected information is appended in to a database which is to be used periodically to train the model. Lastly, in order to validate the practicality of the proposed unified solution, two test cases are used as applications; vehicle counter and lane detection.

The rest of paper is organized as follows. We discuss some recent development in vehicle detection and tracking in Sect. 2. In Sect. 3, we present our proposed scheme that includes ground and aerial surveillance. We conduct extensive experiments to verify performance of the proposed scheme in Sect. 4. Moreover, two use-cases are also implemented and are displayed in Sect. 5. Finally, we claim our work and plan for our future research in Sect. 6.

2   Related Work

YOLO is a real-time object detection system. The first three YOLO versions were launched in 2016, 2017, and 2018 consecutively. After that, YOLO v4, YOLO v5, and PP-YOLO [9] are three significant versions of YOLO that were published in 2020. The problem with YOLO is that it is not trained for aerial images like drones. Faster RCNN uses the Region Proposal Network (RPN), which is more cost-effective than RCNN and Fast R-CNN [10] in sharing full-image convolutional features with the detection network. However, the problem with this algorithm is that it extracts all of the items. For that the algorithm must pass through the image many times which consequently increases the computational cost. As there are several systems operating simultaneously, the performance of the systems depends on how well the prior systems performed.

Authors in [9] have presented a model by the name of Deep Simple Online and Realtime Tracking (DeepSORT) which is capable of object tracking. It's a SORT extension, which is an online tracking method. Re-identification and occlusion are two major problems associated with DeepSORT algorithm. The next is Recurrent YOLO (ROLO) [10] which is a combination of Recurrent Neural Network and YOLO. Despite of concrete research, to the best of our knowledge there is no specific application that stores the information which is used to allow any specific category or density of vehicle. Moreover, the phenomena of taking aerial images for detection purposes has not been explored in depth.

3   Proposed Approach

In this study, a dynamic technique is used that have two approaches for detecting the vehicles. In the first approach CCTV images are used for detection and tracking which uses pretrained YOLO v4. After that, aerial images are used to retrain YOLO in Darknet architecture on vehicle aerial imaging from drone dataset. Later, collectively, this information can be managed and used by the applications that requires tracking or location services of vehicles. Both the approaches (ground and aerial surveillance) are explained below.

For ground surveillance, we employ the state-of-the-art DeepSORT model, which excels in multiple object tracking. This model combines the strength of YOLO, capable of accurately detecting bounding boxes for various objects, with advanced techniques like Sort (Kalman filter) and ReID (re-identification model) to link and maintain object tracks effectively. As shown in Fig. 1, the process starts by identifying vehicles in CCTV images using YOLO. Each detected vehicle is then assigned a unique ID for tracking. If a vehicle re-enters the line of sight within a specified time frame after being out of sight, it retains the same ID. However, if the time limit expires, a new ID is assigned to the vehicle. This process ensures continuous and consistent tracking of vehicles as they move within the surveillance area.

To further enhance the ground surveillance model's accuracy and bolster the confidence of our system, we tackle the issue of YOLO not being trained on drone images. To accomplish this, we implement a solution by retraining the YOLO v4 model using the Darknet architecture and a drone image dataset, as depicted in Fig. 1. By training the model on drone images, it becomes adept at detecting vehicles in aerial views, complementing the ground-based detection. Incorporating a new tracker class for multiple object tracking in the retrained YOLO v4 model allows us to handle each detected vehicle independently. Information related to each vehicle is stored within its respective object in the tracker class, enabling detailed analysis and tracking in aerial imagery. This integration ensures a seamless transition between ground and aerial surveillance, presenting a holistic view of vehicle movements.

The data generated by our proposed framework is stored in two convenient formats: object-wise data in CSV format and frame-wise data in .txt format. This organization allows for flexible data analysis and supports various traffic-related studies. The wealth of data collected through this technique can serve as a valuable resource for researchers and traffic management professionals in understanding and optimizing vehicular movement patterns. In conclusion, our dynamic approach integrates ground and aerial surveillance, capitalizing on the

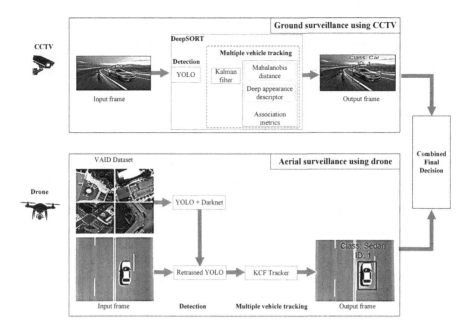

Fig. 1. Proposed combined approach for ground and aerial surveillance.

strengths of both CCTV and drone images. By incorporating the DeepSORT model and retraining YOLO v4 on drone images, we create a powerful system for accurate vehicle detection, tracking, and location services. The structured data generated through this process holds significant potential for advancing traffic analysis and contributing to future research in this field.

4   Evaluation and Discussion

4.1   Dataset Description and Experimental Setup

For the validation of the proposed approaches, Vehicle Aerial Imaging from Drone (VAID) dataset is used. This dataset consists of 6000 drone images, captured in different illumination environments, viewing angles from different places in Taiwan. The images are taken with the resolution of 1137 * 640 pixels in JPG format. The VAID dataset comprises of seven classes of vehicles, namely 'sedan', 'minibus', 'truck', 'pickup truck', 'bus', 'cement truck', and 'trailer'. Moreover, the distribution of each class is shown in Table 1. Figure 2 below illustrates different classes of VAID dataset.

Table 1. Class wise distribution in VAID dataset.

Class name	Sedan	Minibus	Truck	Pickup	Bus	Cement truck	Trailer
Score	40330	501	3189	3011	580	190	804

Fig. 2. Top view of vehicle classes in VAID dataset.

In this study, Python 3.0 was utilized as the programming language in Visual Studio Code and Sublime. The YOLO model was retrained on a machine equipped with an Nvidia GeForce RTX 2060 super GPU. The training process took 36 h for 160 epochs, and a learning rate of 0.0001 was set. For model training and testing, the dataset was split to 80% and 20% respectively. To validate the model's performance, several evaluation metrics are used. For class-wise performance of vehicles, accuracy is used. To evaluate the overall performance of the model, precision, recall and F1 score are used as the dataset is partially imbalanced. Lastly, mean Average Precision (mAP) is used for the performance of the detection.

4.2   Results and Discussion

The results represented in Table 2 reflect the samples we have from Table 1. For cement truck, we have lesser number of samples which corresponds to lower accuracy as shown in Table 2. For the rest of the classes the accuracy is greater than 90%. Table 3 show the overall performance of retrained model. o assess the accuracy of object detectors, the mAP metric is widely used, and we employed it to measure the detection performance. Remarkably, the proposed model achieved an impressive score of nearly 97% mAP on the test dataset. It is important to note that the VAID dataset exhibits a significant class imbalance, with the Sedan class accounting for 83% of the dataset. Consequently, we employed recall, precision, and F1-score to evaluate the dataset, and the proposed model demonstrated excellent performance on this highly imbalanced dataset.

Table 2. Class wise accuracy.

Class name	Sedan	Minibus	Truck	Pickup	Bus	Cement truck	Trailer
Accuracy	98.49%	96.04%	96.44%	97.2%	97.03%	57.2%	98.45%

Table 3. Overall performance (YOLO and DeepSORT Combined).

Metrics	mAP	Precision	Recall	F1 score
Score	96.9%	94.4%	97%	96%

The study addresses the limitation of the current version of YOLO which is not trained on drone images, by retaining the YOLO v4 model using an aerial view dataset known as VAID. The proposed framework employs multiple vehicles detection and tracking to count the number of vehicles class-wise, their directions, and the total number of vehicles. The manual counting of vehicles is labor-intensive and error-prone. Therefore, deploying AI-based systems that automatically analyze video frames to identify and count vehicles with almost the same accuracy as humans is highly desirable. The proposed framework can achieve this objective with high accuracy while requiring fewer resources compared to manual counting. The proposed framework's excellent performance makes it highly suitable for real-time traffic analysis applications.

4.3   Applications for Vehicle Management System

The proposed approach is utilized for two main applications for its validation and feasibility. These applications include vehicle counter and lane detection. However, the potential of this data can be further explored for other traffic-related applications as well. Following Fig. 3 and 4 show the working of the application for counting vehicles and lane detection respectively. The former could help monitoring teams to tackle congestion issues in areas where traffic is dense and only ground surveillance is not sufficient. In the next application of lane detection, the stored vehicles' data are used to draw the lines on the road where the vehicles have intercepted. Next, the dilation technique was applied to merge all the lines, followed by the Skeleton method to obtain a single line. Finally, pruning was used to remove any branches from the line, as illustrated in Fig. 4.

Fig. 3. Application as Vehicle counter showing detection of various vehicle classes.

Fig. 4. Application as Lane detection for vehicle tracking.

5   Conclusion

In conclusion, this study presented novel models for both ground surveillance using CCTV and aerial surveillance using drones. The DeepSORT model was utilized for CCTV camera video analysis, while the YOLO model was retrained on the VAID dataset for accurate detection in drone images. Additionally, the inclusion of the KCF Tracker enabled effective vehicle tracking. The results were highly promising, with accuracy rate of up to 99% and a mean absolute precision of up to 97%. Moreover, the feasibility of the proposed approach was confirmed through the implementation of two real-time applications: a vehicle counter and a lane detection system. These applications showcased the practicality and real-world utility of the proposed methodology.

Acknowledgement. This work was supported by IITP grant funded by the Korea government (MSIT) under Artificial Intelligence Graduate School (No. 2019-0-00421), and Artificial Intelligence Innovation Hub (No. 2021-0-02068) and the ICT Creative Consilience Program (IITP-2023-2020-0-01821).

References

1. Yang, S., Tan, J., Lei, T., Linares-Barranco, B.: Smart traffic navigation system for fault-tolerant edge computing of internet of vehicle in intelligent transportation gateway. IEEE Trans. Intell. Transp. Syst. (2023)
2. Liu, C., Ke, L.: Cloud assisted internet of things intelligent transportation system and the traffic control system in the smart city. J. Control Decis. **10**(2), 174–187 (2023)

3. Li, X., Hao, T., Jin, X., Huang, B., Liang, J.: Fine traffic congestion detection with hierarchical description. IEEE Trans. Intell. Transp. Syst. **23**(12), 24439–24453 (2022)
4. Xiao, Z., et al.: Next-generation vessel traffic services systems-From "passive" to "proactive". IEEE Intell. Transp. Syst. Mag. **15**(1), 363–377 (2022)
5. Malik, S., Khattak, H.A., Ameer, Z., Shoaib, U., Rauf, H.T., Song, H.: Proactive scheduling and resource management for connected autonomous vehicles: a data science perspective. IEEE Sens. J. **21**(22), 25151–25160 (2021)
6. Chen, L., et al.: Deep neural network based vehicle and pedestrian detection for autonomous driving: a survey. IEEE Trans. Intell. Transp. Syst. **22**(6), 3234–3246 (2021)
7. Redmon, J., Divvala, S., Girshick, R., Farhadi, A.: You only look once: unified, real-time object detection. In: Proceedings of the IEEE Conference on Computer Vision and Pattern Recognition, USA, pp. 779–788 (2016)
8. Ren, S., He, K., Girshick, R., Sun, J.: Faster R-CNN: towards real-time object detection with region proposal networks. In: Advances in Neural Information Processing Systems, vol. 28 (2015)
9. Wojke, N., Bewley, A., Paulus, D.: Simple online and realtime tracking with a deep association metric. In: 2017 IEEE International Conference on Image Processing (ICIP), pp. 3645–3649. IEEE, China (2017)
10. Ning, G., et al.: Spatially supervised recurrent convolutional neural networks for visual object tracking. In: 2017 IEEE International Symposium on Circuits and Systems (ISCAS), pp. 1–4. IEEE, USA (2017)

Deep Learning Approach for Tomato Leaf Disease Detection

Nguyen Thai-Nghe, Tran Khanh Dong, Hoang Xuan Tri, and Nguyen Chi-Ngon[✉]

Can Tho University, 3-2 Street, Can Tho City, Vietnam
{ntnghe,ncngon}@ctu.edu.vn

Abstract. In Vietnam, where agriculture is the main source of income for the majority of the population, effectively combating crop diseases and increasing crop yield are very important. Plant diseases can cause significant damage to agricultural productivity and product quality. Early detection of diseases could minimize losses for agricultural sector, thereby fostering tangible benefits for rural communities and overall economic. This paper introduces an approach, leveraging from the VGG-19 architecture, to detect plant leaf diseases by analyzing images of crop leaves. The approach was tested on a dataset comprising approximately 18,000 tomato leaf samples. The model was designed to automatically learn important features from tomato leaf images and classify them into different disease categories. Experimental results show that the model achieved a classification accuracy of 93% on the test set. In addition, after building the prediction model, we has also developed an application that allows users to quickly identify diseases on tomato leaves by capturing or uploading images to the application.

Keywords: Tomato leaf disease detection · plant disease detection · CNN · VGG-19 · deep learning

1 Introduction

One of the nation's main economic sectors in Vietnam is agriculture. However, global warming, climate change and environment pollution cause many effects, e.g., plant diseases in agricultural. In Vietnam, where agriculture is the main source of income for the majority of the population, effectively dealing with crop diseases and increasing crop yield are very important. Plant diseases can cause significant damage to agricultural productivity and product quality. Thus detection of diseases could minimize losses for agricultural sector, thereby fostering tangible benefits for rural communities and overall economic.

One of the primary problems farmers encounter when cultivating is leaf disease. The farmers invest a lot of time, effort, and money in identifying and treating leaf diseases. Using deep learning models for disease classification is one way to speed up disease detection and treatment while also lowering costs. Through image processing, deep learning models are able to learn and identify the traits of several leaf diseases.

© The Author(s), under exclusive license to Springer Nature Singapore Pte Ltd. 2023
T. K. Dang et al. (Eds.): FDSE 2023, CCIS 1925, pp. 572–579, 2023.
https://doi.org/10.1007/978-981-99-8296-7_42

This study aims to present an approach for tomato leaf disease detection using deep convolutional neural networks. The proposed approach incorporating the VGG-19 architecture [12]. In addition, we have also developed an application that allows users to quickly predict diseases on tomato leaves by capturing an image or uploading a tomato leaf image to the application.

2 Related Work

In recent years, there has been a growing interest in the application of deep learning techniques for plant disease detection. Several studies have explored the use of deep convolutional neural networks (CNNs) for accurate and efficient identification of diseases in tomato leaves. In the study [1], the authors present a comparative analysis of machine learning models such as SVM, KNN, and CNN. Three different models are described and studied in this article, and they can detect eight different types of diseases on plant leaves. The CNN model achieved the highest accuracy of 96% when trained with a dataset of soybean leaf diseases, surpassing the KNN and SVM models with accuracies of 64% and 76%, respectively.

In the study [2], the authors describe a Disease Recognition model supported by leaf image classification. To detect diseases on plants, the research team employed image processing with a specially designed Convolutional Neural Network (CNN) to handle the input images and used it for image recognition. The authors in [3] introduce a method for classifying tomato leaf diseases using a Convolutional Neural Network (CNN) with high accuracy. In the study [4], the authors summarize the important role of agriculture in Mexico's economy, particularly tomato cultivation, the country's most exported agricultural product. In [5], the authors discuss the economic value of tomato plants and the importance of detecting tomato leaf diseases to produce healthy yields. In recent years, many studies have used deep learning models for automatic tomato leaf disease detection. It employs transfer learning to extract deep features from the last fully connected layer of the CNN networks to obtain more compact and high-level representations. Then, it combines the features from the three CNN networks to leverage the strengths of each CNN structure. Next, it applies a feature selection and combination method to generate a comprehensive feature set with reduced dimensions. Six classifiers are then used to detect tomato leaf diseases.

In the study [6], the authors address the challenges of identifying and diagnosing diseases on plants to improve agricultural productivity. The research utilizes a dataset compiled from publicly available datasets on Kaggle, containing 14,531 tomato leaf images with 10 different disease classes. The study proposes a 2-D Convolutional Neural Network (CNN) model with 2 Max Pooling layers and a fully connected layer to classify tomato leaf diseases. The model is compared with other classification models such as SVM, VGG16, Inception V3, and MobileNet CNN. The test results show that the proposed model can detect diseases with an accuracy of 96%. In [7], the authors describe the significance of tomato plants in agriculture and the need to diagnose and classify tomato leaf diseases to increase productivity. In the study [8], the authors discuss the use of deep learning techniques for detecting and classifying diseases on tomato plant leaves in agricultural fields. Tomatoes are a widely cultivated and popular vegetable worldwide;

however, various diseases affect the quality and quantity of tomato production. The article presents a strategy based on a CNN model with two convolutional layers and two pooling layers to detect and classify diseases on tomato leaves.

In the study [9], the authors discuss the impact of plant diseases on the quality and quantity of crop yields, emphasizing the importance of early detection. Tomatoes are one of the commercially important crop plants, and several diseases significantly affect the growing seasons. The article presents the use of two Convolutional Neural Network (CNN) models, namely GoogLeNet and VGG-16, for disease classification on tomato leaves. The aim of this proposal is to find the best solution for disease detection on tomato leaves using deep learning methods. VGG-16 achieves an accuracy of 98%, while GoogLeNet achieves 99.23% on the Plant Village dataset containing 10,735 leaf images. The proposed system can be used in tomato cultivation to detect diseases early and prevent yield loss. In [10], the authors discuss the CNN model based on transfer learning is proposed for identifying diseases on tomato leaves. The model performs disease detection by using real-time images and stored tomato plant images. Furthermore, the model's performance is evaluated using optimization algorithms such as Adam, SGD, and RMSprop [11].

While these studies have made significant advancements in leaf disease detection using deep CNNs, there is still a need for further research to improve the efficiency and accuracy of detection models as well as an application that can help the farmers. In our work, we aim to contribute to this growing body of knowledge by proposing an approach using the VGG-19 architecture for tomato leaf disease detection. By leveraging the capabilities of deep learning and the extensive dataset, we aim to enhance the early detection and prevention of tomato diseases, ultimately contributing to increased crop productivity and improved agricultural practices.

3   Proposed Approach

For building the model and an application for tomato leaf disease detection, this work is carried out through several steps as the following:

- Step 1: Data collection, preprocessing including shuffling, image flipping, resizing images to 256 × 256 pixels.
- Step 2: Model training. In this work, we used a 16-layer model of the VGG-19 (Fig. 1) as follows:

    i. resize_and_rescale: A data processing layer to resize and rescale the images.
    ii. Conv2D(32, kernel_size = (3,3), activation = 'relu', input_shape = input_shape_cnn): A convolutional layer with 32 filters, a filter size of 3 × 3, ReLU activation function, and the input shape of the model.
    iii. MaxPooling2D((2, 2)): A layer that reduces the size of the output from the convolutional layer by performing max pooling with a window size of 2 × 2.
    iv. Repeated convolutional and pooling layers for a total of 5 times, with different filters and sizes to extract features from the images.
    v. Flatten(): A layer that flattens the output from the last convolutional layer.
    vi. Dense(64, activation = 'relu'): A fully connected layer with 64 units and ReLU activation function.

vii. Dense(n_classes, activation = 'softmax'): A fully connected layer with the number of units equal to the number of classes in the input data (10), and softmax activation function to compute probabilities for each output class.

- Step 3: During the training process, the hyperparameters were uploaded to the neptune.ai system for convenient reference and future adjustments.
- Step 4: After the completion of training, the models were saved locally in different versions and automatically uploaded to the neptune.ai system.
- Step 5: FastAPI was utilized to build the REST API to serve the user application.
- Step 6: ReactJS and Flutter were used to develop the user application. The data, after users look up information, would be stored on Firebase. Users can have a user interface where users can drag and drop or take photo of tomato leaf with diseases, and the system will automatically predict and return results.

After training the model, we built an application so that the users/farmers can use it easily. In this application, several libraries and frameworks are used for online processing, as presented in Fig. 1.

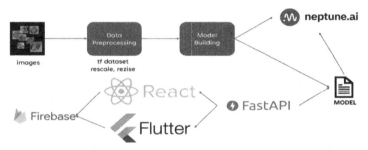

Fig. 1. Integrating the classification model to build an online application

4 Experiments

4.1 Data Set

To train and validate our tomato leaf disease detection model, we collected a dataset of tomato leaf images from the online Plant Village Project[1]. The dataset consists of 18,000 images, divided into 10 different disease categories as in Fig. 2. In order to ensure proper evaluation and generalization of the model, we further divided the dataset into three subsets: a training set (70% of the images) has 12,600 images, a validation set (20% of the images) with 3,600 images, and a test set (10% of the images) with 1,800 images. To ensure consistency in input dimensions, we performed data preprocessing by resizing each image to a unified dimension of 224 × 224 pixels. This step guarantees that all images in the dataset have the same size, enabling effective processing by the VGG-19 model.

---

[1] https://www.kaggle.com/datasets/mohitsingh1804/plantvillage.

Fig. 2. Sample images of ten diseases

4.2   Model Training and Evaluation

The training process involved the following steps:

1. Mini-Batch Creation: The training dataset was divided into mini-batches, with each batch containing a fixed number of images. This allowed us to process the data in smaller chunks, making the training process more efficient.
2. Forward Pass: Each mini-batch of images was fed into the VGG-19 model, and a forward pass was performed. The forward pass involved passing the images through a series of convolutional and pooling layers, followed by fully connected layers, to extract meaningful features from the input images.
3. Loss Computation: After the forward pass, the predicted outputs were compared with the ground truth labels using a suitable loss function, such as categorical cross-entropy. The loss function quantified the discrepancy between the predicted and actual labels, serving as a measure of how well the model was performing.
4. Backward Pass and Parameter Update: The gradients of the loss function with respect to the model parameters were computed using backpropagation. These gradients were then used to update the model weights and biases through an optimization algorithm, such as stochastic gradient descent (SGD) or Adam. The learning rate determined the step size of the parameter updates.
5. Iterative Training: Steps b to d were repeated for a predefined number of epochs. In this study, we trained the model for 20 epochs to ensure sufficient learning and parameter adjustment.

By performing multiple epochs, the model had the opportunity to learn and adjust its parameters iteratively, enhancing its ability to detect tomato leaf diseases. To evaluate the performance of the proposed approach using the VGG-19 model for tomato leaf disease detection, we conducted a comprehensive comparison with other methods commonly used in the literature. In addition to our VGG-19 model, we also trained a CNN model to evaluate its effectiveness in this task. Several key metrics were considered for the comparison, including accuracy, precision, recall, and F1 score. As shown in Table 1, the proposed approach has better performance than the CNN model. We also report the confusion matrix of the proposed approach as in Fig. 3.

Table 1. Comparison of Performance Metrics

Model	Accuracy	Precision	Recall	F1 Score
Proposed approach	**0.95**	**0.94**	**0.96**	**0.95**
CNN	0.93	0.92	0.94	0.93

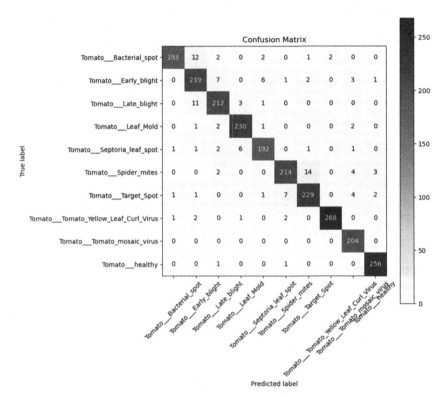

Fig. 3. Confusion matrix of the proposed approach

4.3 System Interface

After building and testing the disease classification model, we have built an application for applying this model as presented in Fig. 4. To begin the process, the user selects an image by dragging it to the system. Then, our system performs disease detection and provides the corresponding result.

Through our proposed method, we can effectively detect and diagnose various diseases affecting tomato plants by analyzing leaf images. These results demonstrate the potential of our approach in assisting farmers and researchers in timely disease identification and management for enhanced crop productivity.

Fig. 4. A snapshot of the application for tomato leaf disease detection

5   Conclusion

In this work, we presented a study on the disease detection of tomato leaf using deep convolutional neural networks, specifically employing the VGG-19 architecture. By replacing manual inspection, our deep learning-based model enables rapid and automated disease diagnosis, saving valuable time and resources for farmers and agricultural experts. By implementing our proposed approach, farmers and crop management authorities can promptly detect and respond to plant diseases, leading to improved crop health, increased productivity, and reduced economic losses.

In future work, we explore the integration of real-time monitoring systems and remote sensing technologies to create a more comprehensive and efficient disease detection framework. Additionally, expanding the dataset to include a wider range of tomato leaf diseases and exploring transfer learning techniques could further enhance the accuracy and generalization capabilities of the model.

References

1. Nikitha, B.V., Keerthanb, N.K.S., Praneeth, M.S., Amrita, T.: Leaf disease detection and classification. Procedia Comput. Sci. **218**, 291–300 (2023)
2. Shelar, N., Shinde, S., Sawant, S., Dhumal, S., Fakir, K.: Plant disease detection using CNN. In: ITM Web of Conferences, vol. 44, p. 03049 (2022)
3. Brahimi, M., Boukhalfa, K., Moussaoui, A.: Deep learning for tomato diseases: classification and symptoms visualization. Appl. Artif. Intell. **31**, 299–315 (2017)

4. Guerrero-Ibañez, A., Reyes-Muñoz, A.: Monitoring tomato leaf disease through convolutional neural networks. Electronics **12**(1), 229 (2023)

5. Attallah, O.: Tomato leaf disease classification via compact convolutional neural networks with transfer learning and feature selection. Horticulturae **9**(2), 149 (2023)

6. Pushpa, B.R.: Tomato leaf disease detection and classification using CNN. Math. Stat. Eng. Appl. **71**(4) (2022). ISSN: 2094-0343 2326-9865

7. Trivedi, N.K., et al.: Early detection and classification of tomato leaf disease using high-performance deep neural network. Sensors (Basel) **21**(23), 7987 (2021)

8. Sakkarvarthi, G., Sathianesan, G.W., Murugan, V.S., Reddy, A.J., Jayagopal, P., Elsisi, M.: Detection and classification of tomato crop disease using convolutional neural network. Electronics **11**(21), 3618 (2022)

9. Kibriya, H., Rafique, R., Ahmad, W., Adnan, S.M.: Tomato leaf disease detection using convolution neural network. In: 2021 International Bhurban Conference on Applied Sciences and Technologies (IBCAST) (2021)

10. Thangaraj, R., Anandamurugan, S., Kaliappan, V.K.: Automated tomato leaf disease classification using transfer learning-based deep convolution neural network. J. Plant Dis. Prot. New Ser. **128**(4) (2020)

11. Thai-Nghe, N., Tri, N.T., Hoa, N.H.: Deep learning for rice leaf disease detection in smart agriculture. In: Dang, N.H.T., Zhang, Y.D., Tavares, J.M.R.S., Chen, B.H. (eds.) Artificial Intelligence in Data and Big Data Processing. ICABDE 2021. LNDECT, vol. 124, pp. 659–670. Springer, Cham (2022). https://doi.org/10.1007/978-3-030-97610-1_52

12. Simonyan, K., Zisserman, A.: Very deep convolutional networks for large-scale image recognition. In: Proceedings of the 3rd International Conference on Learning Representations, San Diego, CA, USA, pp. 1–14, 7–9 May 2015

Invasive Ductal Carcinoma Classification from Whole Slide Image Based on BRISQUE and Convolutional Neural Networks

Le Nhi Lam Thuy⬤, Vu Ngoc Thanh Sang⬤, Pham The Bao$^{(\boxtimes)}$ ⬤, and Tan Dat Trinh$^{(\boxtimes)}$ ⬤

Information Science Faculty, SaiGon University, Ho Chi Minh City, Vietnam
{ptbao,trinhtandat}@sgu.edu.vn

Abstract. This research aims to improve the performance of an invasive ductal carcinoma (IDC) classification system by examining how input image quality affects the dataset. To achieve this goal, we utilized the Blind/Referenceless Image Spatial Quality Evaluator (BRISQUE) method to assess image quality and divided the dataset into subsets for training, cross-validation, and testing of the proposed Convolutional Neural Network (CNN) architecture. The study evaluated various subsets of the training dataset to determine the optimal option, which was then used to identify the appropriate training parameters and evaluate the system's performance. The results demonstrated that the proposed approaches outperformed the standard methods for IDC classification.

Keywords: Invasive Ductal Carcinoma Classification · Whole Slide Images · Blind/Referenceless Image Spatial Quality Evaluator · Convolutional Neural Network

1 Introduction

One of the world's most severe diseases is cancer. The most frequent kind of cancer in women is breast cancer, which has been and continues to be one of society's most challenging concerns. Around two million individuals worldwide receive a breast cancer diagnosis each year, and 600,000 people worldwide pass away from the condition [1]. Invasive ductal carcinoma (IDC), which accounts for about 80% of all diagnoses, is the most prevalent form of breast cancer [2]. Whole pathology glass slides can now be converted into whole slide images (WSI) because of technological advancement [3]. On WSI obtained from patients with IDC, areas of cancer risk are identified, allowing pathologists to assess the degree of disease progression as well. This procedure forecasts patient outcomes and suggests potential therapy trajectories. Our goal is to develop a system that can automatically classify whether WSI images include IDC cancer cells. Numerous studies using various methods, including handcraft features, machine learning, and deep learning, have been investigated on IDC classification based on medical images [4].

T. K. Dang et al. (Eds.): FDSE 2023, CCIS 1925, pp. 580–589, 2023.
https://doi.org/10.1007/978-981-99-8296-7_43

Author in [4] proposed CNN-based approach to classify ematoxylin and eosin-stained breast biopsy images. The feature vector which was extracted from the input images via CNN was considered as input to SVM classifier. An intelligent breast cancer diagnosis system was proposed by authors in [5] that combines the Pareto optimum technique and a multilayer perceptron neural network based on an improved non-dominated sorting genetic algorithm (NSGA-II). A convolutional neural network-based classification (CNN) method for breast cancer histopathology images was shown in the study [6]. The BreaKHis dataset was used to test the proposed method, which shows great accuracy. The study [7] suggests utilizing CNNs to automatically detect invasive ductal carcinoma (IDC) in the whole slide images. The algorithm exhibits great accuracy and sensitivity in detecting IDC after being trained and validated on a large dataset of breast cancer tissue samples. The CNN-based approach performs better than conventional machine learning algorithms. In [8], authors introduced a convolutional neural network (CNN)-based system for classifying breast cancer histopathology images that includes a tiny SE-ResNet module. The proposed approach performs well in categorizing breast tissue samples as benign or malignant using a publically BreakHis dataset. In [9], authors proposed a weakly-supervised and transfer learning-based breast invasive ductal carcinoma (IDC) classification method for the whole slide images. The proposed system is trained and evaluated on a large dataset of breast tissue samples and achieves high accuracy in detecting IDC.

In [10], authors introduced the StackBC method for IDC classification. Specifically, they employed deep learning models such as CNN, Long Short-Term Memory (LSTM), and Gated Recurrent Unit (GRU). The GRU model, which outperformed its counterparts, was designated as the meta classifier to differentiate between Non-IDC and IDC breast images. Authors in [11] introduced a CNN-based diagnostic method for IDC classification. They integrated transfer learning (TL) and data augmentation (DA) strategies to enhance the model's predictive results. In [12] authors constructed binary machine-learning models to discern between the early and late phases of IDC. These models utilize RNA-seq gene expression profiles from 610 IDC patients, sourced from The Cancer Genome Atlas (TCGA). They trained and assessed various supervised learning algorithms, augmented by diverse feature selection approaches.

In this study, we investigate an IDC classification system by evaluating the impact of input image quality on the dataset. We apply BRISQUE method to evaluate the quality of an image and divide the dataset into subdatasets. Then, these subsets are used for training, cross-validation, and testing the model based on the proposed CNN architecture. To determine the best option, we trained the proposed CNN model on various subsets of the training dataset, followed by further training of the selected option to identify the appropriate training parameters, and evaluate the system's performance.

2 Proposed Method

In this paper, we develop an IDC recognition system based on investigating the effect of input image quality on the dataset to enhance performance of system. This involves evaluating and choosing the best training dataset. To investigate the effectiveness of the identification system, a CNN model is used as a classifier. We separate the original dataset into two sub-dataset A and B based on the DMOS (Different Mean Opinion Score) scale via the BRISQUE method [13]. The purpose of the step is to evaluate the image quality. The quality score of an image corresponds to the DMOS scale ranging from 0 to 100. The lesser the DMOS score of an image, the better the quality is. Sub-dataset A includes images that have DMOS scores between 0 and 100. Otherwise, sub-dataset B includes images that have DMOS scores outside of the range [0, 100]. Because the images in subset B are below the BRISQUE method's acceptable threshold, we assume that they are of poor quality, contain complex structures, or are affected by noise. In our experiments, we trained the CNN model on different subsets of the training dataset to select the best one, which was then further trained to find appropriate training parameters for evaluating the performance of the system. Figure 1 shows the flowchart of our IDC recognition system.

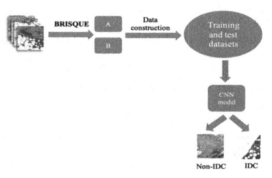

Fig. 1. Our process for the IDC recognition system.

2.1 Image Quality Evaluation Based on the BRISQUE

The Blind/Reference-less Image Spatial Quality Evaluator (BRISQUE) [13] is one of the Image Quality Assessment (IQA) methods that can evaluate the quality of an image without a reference. This contrasts with other methods such as SSIM (Structural Similarity Index), PSNR (Peak Signal-to-Noise Ratio), and VIF (Visual Information Fidelity). The correctness of BRISQUE is often evaluated by comparing its predictions with human-annotated quality scores or subjective assessments. The BRISQUE algorithm is computationally efficient and can quickly assess the quality of images, making it suitable for real-time or large-scale image processing applications.

The BRISQUE algorithm includes three steps: Natural Scene Statistics (NSS) extraction, feature vector computation and image quality score estimation. The natural scene statistics (NSS) features that capture the image's statistical characteristics are obtained by BRISQUE through a feature extraction step. Using a support vector regression (SVR) model [13] that has been trained on many distorted images and their accompanying quality scores, these features are then mapped to a quality score.

Mean Subtracted Contrast Normalization (MSCN) can be used to normalize an image. The MSCN coefficients are computed as follows [13]:

$$\hat{I}(i,j) = \frac{I(i,j) - \mu(i,j)}{\sigma(i,j) + C} \tag{1}$$

where $i \in \{1, 2, .., M\}, j \in \{1, 2, .., N\}$, , M is the height and N is the width of the image, I(i,j) is the intensity of the pixel at location (i,j); $\mu(i,j)$ and $\sigma(i,j)$ are local mean value and local the standard deviation value, respectively. The small constant C is used to prevent division by zero. The local mean and local standard deviation calculated by [13]:

$$\mu = \sum_{k=-K}^{K} \sum_{l=-L}^{L} w_{k,l} I_{k,l}(i,j) \tag{2}$$

$$\sigma = \sqrt{\sum_{k}^{K} \sum_{l=-L}^{L} w_{k,l} I_{k,l}((i,j) - \mu(i,j))^2} \tag{3}$$

where $w_{k,l}$ is the weight of the filter with size of K = 3, L = 3.

Moreover, the difference between normal images and distorted images is not only limited to the distribution of pixels but also the relationship between each pixel and its 4 neighbors: Horizontal (H), Vertical (V), Diagonal-Left (D1), Diagonal-Right (D2). These pixels will be normalized as follows [13]:

$$\begin{aligned} H(i,j) &= \hat{I}(i,j)\hat{I}(i,j+1) \\ V(i,j) &= \hat{I}(i,j)\hat{I}(i+1,j) \\ D1(i,j) &= \hat{I}(i,j)\hat{I}(i+1,j+1) \\ D2(i,j) &= \hat{I}(i,j)\hat{I}(i+1,j-1) \end{aligned} \tag{4}$$

2.2 The IDC Recognition Based on the CNN

Convolutional neural networks (CNNs) were applied successfully and significantly in image classification and medical image processing [2–4, 14–19]. In this study, our model is designed for IDC classification based on the idea of the CNN architecture in [2]. The network architecture we proposed is described in Table 1. We introduce a CNN architecture with 10 layers. This model is easy to design but still delivers high performance. The model consists of 04 convolutional layers, 03 maxpooling layers, 02 fully connected layers and softmax layer. The first convolutional layer employs a 5×5 filter, and the subsequent layers utilize 3×3 filters with a stride of 1. A Dropout of roughly 50% is used in the last convolutional layer to reduce some unnecessary connections to deal with overfitting problem. The ReLU non-linear activation function is applied to each convolutional layer to learn the preactivation feature maps. The feature maps after the first three convolutional layers will be normalized and reduced in size through each maxpooling layer with filter size of 2×2 and a stride of 2. In our experiments, we use softmax loss or categorical cross-entropy loss to train the network. We train our network using the Adam optimizer [20] with cyclic learning rate via the backpropagation algorithm.

Table 1. Our CNN architecture for IDC classification.

Layer type	Filter size	Stride	Activation function	Pooling
Input Layer	-	-	-	-
Convolutional Layer 1	5×5	1	ReLU	-
Max-Pooling Layer 1	2×2	2	-	2×2
Convolutional Layer 2	3×3	1	ReLU	-
Max-Pooling Layer 2	2×2	2	-	2×2
Convolutional Layer 3	3×3	1	ReLU	-
Max-Pooling Layer 3	2×2	2	-	2×2
Convolutional Layer 4	3×3	1	ReLU	-
Max-Pooling Layer 4	2×2	2	-	2×2
Fully Connected Layer 1	-	-	ReLU	-
Fully Connected Layer 2	-	-	ReLU	-
Output Layer (Softmax)	-	-	Softmax	-

3 Experiment Results

3.1 Dataset and Analysis of the Experiments

We conduct the performance evaluation of our method on the public Breast Histology Images dataset [7, 21]. The dataset comprises 5547 image patches of 50×50 pixels each, which were selected from 162 whole-mount slide images of breast cancer specimens that were scanned at 40x magnification. Among the total of 5547 images, 2788 images have been labeled as 1 (IDC class), while the remaining 2759 images belong to the 0 class (non-IDC class). The size of each color image is 50×50 pixels. Figure 2 shows some images from the experimental dataset.

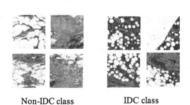

Non-IDC class   IDC class

Fig. 2. Some images from the Breast Histology Images dataset [7].

We applied the BRISQUE method to divide the dataset into two sets, A and B. Due to the imbalanced distribution of data when divided by BRISQUE, we constructed subsets A1, A2, A3, and A4 to make balanced data for experiment evaluation. A1 and A2 are subsets of dataset A, with A1 comprising 90% of randomly chosen images from A and A2 comprising the remaining 10%. Notably, the ratio of Class 0 (Non-IDC) to Class 1 (IDC) images remains the same for these subsets. In addition, A3 dataset is a combination of images from A1 and B, resulting in a total of 5036 images. On the other hand, A4 dataset merges images from A2 and B, generating a dataset of 952 images. We implemented our model using the tensorflow framework. The model was trained on a computer with Intel(R) Core (TM) i5-11400H @ 2.70 GHz, 2.69 GHz, 8 GB RAM. The accuracy, recall, precision, f1-score were used to evaluate the performance.

$$Recall = \frac{TP}{(TP + FN)} \tag{5}$$

$$Precision = \frac{TP}{(Tp + FP)} \tag{6}$$

$$F1 - score = \frac{2 * Precision * Recall}{(Precision + Recall)} \tag{7}$$

$$Accuracy = \frac{(TP + TN)}{(TP + TN + FP + FN)} \tag{8}$$

where true positives (TP) are correctly predicted positive instances, false positives (FP) are incorrectly predicted positive instances, true negatives (TN) are correctly predicted negative instances, and false negatives (FN) are incorrectly predicted negative instances.

3.2 Results

We first evaluate the results on the original dataset. Second, we evaluate the results on the dataset that has been evaluated for image quality using BRISQUE (with IQA). We use the k-fold cross-validation method to train and evaluate the model (k is chosen to be 10) without applying data augmentation. Table 2 shows the performance of proposed method and baseline CNN [22] on our dataset.

From Table 2, we can see that the proposed model achieves better results than the CNN model in [22] in most cases. Specifically, in the case of the full dataset, our method achieved an accuracy of 82%, with a precision of 85%, a recall of 81%, and an F1-Score of 83%, while the baseline CNN model achieved an accuracy of 76%, with precision, recall, and F1-Score all at approximately 76%. Furthermore, under different subsets of the dataset (A, A1, A3), the proposed method consistently outperformed the baseline CNN model. Overall, the proposed method, especially when incorporating image quality assessment using BRISQUE, is generally outperforming the baseline CNN model across different scenarios. We compare the proposed method without data augmentation to the CNN method using data augmentation on the original dataset as described in Table 2. The experimental results confirm that the proposed method can enhance the recognition performance on our dataset and achieves better performance than baselined CNN without data augmentation. In our experiments, we use the subdatasets A, A1 and A3 as training

Table 2. Comparison of proposed method and CNN [22] using k-fold cross-validation.

Experiments	Training data	Validation data	Method	Accuracy	Precision	Recall	F1-score
Full dataset (without IQA)	90% #images from (A + B)	10% #images from (A + B)	Proposed	0.82	0.85	0.81	0.83
			CNN	0.76	0.76	0.77	0.76
Image Quality Assessment using BRISQUE	90% #images from (A)	10% #images from (A)	Proposed	0.82	0.87	0.79	0.83
			CNN	0.79	0.78	0.83	0.80
	90% #images from (A1)	10% #images from (A1)	Proposed	0.85	0.88	0.83	0.85
			CNN	0.80	0.81	0.83	0.82
	90% #images from (A3)	10% #images from (A3)	Proposed	0.83	0.82	0.82	0.82
			CNN	0.79	0.82	0.76	0.79
Without data augmentation	90% #images from (A + B)	10% #images from (A + B)	Proposed	0.82	0.85	0.81	0.83
Data augmentation	90% #images from (A + B)	10% #images from (A + B)	CNN	0.80	0.77	0.84	0.80

and validation data based on 10-fold cross-validation technique. The performance of the trained model is evaluated on test subdataset such as A2, A4 and B. Table 3 shows the performance of the proposed method and baseline CNN [22] using data augmentation and k-fold cross-validation.

Table 3 shows that our method outperforms the CNN approach in all cases. Our model performs better even on the low-quality dataset B. Our method achieves higher accuracy, particularly in the range of 1% to 4%, and higher F1-score, particularly in the range of 1% to 12%. However, our model achieves lower results on subdataset B. Because the quality or complex structure of the images in dataset B can reduce the performance. From these tables, we claim that the proposed model achieves the best performance when using subdataset A3 as the training data and subdataset A2 as the test data. Table 4 shows the performance of our model in different training epochs. The accuracy of the model generally increases as the number of training epochs increases, indicating that the model is learning and improving its ability to classify instances correctly. Finally, the performance of the well-known CNN models and proposed model are shown in Table 5. The proposed method demonstrates the highest accuracy among the compared models, achieving an accuracy of 84%. The F1-score of 85% reflects a balanced trade-off between precision and recall. Despite having fewer network design layers, our model ensures higher performance and greater stability.

Table 3. Comparison of proposed method and CNN [22] on our test data.

Experiments	Training data	Validation data	Test data	Method	ACC	Precision	Recall	F1-score
Image Quality Assessment using BRISQUE and k-fold cross-validation	90% #images from (A)	10% #images from (A)	B	Proposed	0.83	0.74	0.67	0.70
				CNN	0.82	0.78	0.50	0.61
	90% #images from (A1)	10% #images from (A1)	A2	Proposed	0.81	0.84	0.81	0.82
				CNN	0.78	0.78	0.80	0.79
		10% #images from (A1)	B	Proposed	0.83	0.75	0.67	0.71
				CNN	0.81	0.75	0.48	0.59
		10% #images from (A1)	A4	Proposed	0.82	0.77	0.78	0.77
				CNN	0.79	0.77	0.70	0.73
	90% #images from (A3)	10% #images from (A3)	A2	Proposed	0.82	0.86	0.81	0.83
				CNN	0.79	0.79	0.83	0.81
Full dataset (Without IQA) using k-fold cross-validation	80% #images from (A + B)	10% #images from (A + B)	A + B (10%)	Proposed	0.80	0.84	0.78	0.81
				CNN	0.76	0.78	0.76	0.77
Full dataset (Without IQA) using hold-out method	80% #images from (A + B)	10% #images from (A + B)	10% #images from (A + B)	Proposed	0.79	0.76	0.82	0.79
				CNN	0.77	0.78	0.76	0.77
Image Quality Assessment using BRISQUE and hold-out method	A1	A2	B	Proposed	0.79	0.85	0.58	0.69
				CNN	0.82	0.79	0.48	0.60
	A1	B	A2	Proposed	0.77	0.77	0.78	0.77
				CNN	0.77	0.78	0.80	0.79

Table 4. Performance of the proposed model in different training epochs using data augmentation and k-fold cross-validation on the training data A3 and the test data A2.

#Epochs	Accuracy	Precision	Recall	F1-score
25	0.80	0.85	0.80	0.82
30	0.82	0.86	0.81	0.83
40	0.83	0.87	0.82	0.84
50	0.84	0.88	0.82	0.85
200	0.84	0.87	0.83	0.85

Table 5. Performance comparison of the well-known CNNs and proposed model.

Method	Accuracy	Precision	Recall	F1-score
Proposed	0.84	0.88	0.82	0.85
ResNet-50 [25]	0.66	0.5	0.8	0.59
VGG-16 [24]	0.53	1.0	0.53	0.69
AlexNet [23]	0.75	0.85	0.73	0.79

4 Conclusion

In this study, we introduce the IDC classification system based on the CNN model, which provides high performance. Our classification system produces different results for different data when using the BRISQUE method to divide the data. The specific results, measured by ACC, Precision, Recall, and F1, are 84%, 88%, 82%, and 85%, respectively. In the future, we will focus on researching and developing an algorithm to evaluate the structural complexity of histological images to enhance the performance of the system.

Acknowledgements. This research was supported by Sai Gon University under Fund Grant No. CSB2022–39.

References

1. Ferlay, J., et al.: Global cancer observatory: cancer today. Lyon: International Agency for Research on Cancer (2021). https://gco.iarc.fr/today. Accessed 17 June 2021
2. Wang, J.L., Ibrahim, A.K., Zhuang, H., Ali, A.M., Li, A.Y., Wu, A.: A study on automatic detection of IDC breast cancer with convolutional neural networks. In: 2018 International Conference on Computational Science and Computational Intelligence (CSCI), pp. 703–708. IEEE (2018)
3. Kanavati, F., Tsuneki, M.: Breast invasive ductal carcinoma classification on whole slide images with weakly-supervised and transfer learning. Cancers **13**(21), 5368 (2021)
4. Araújo, T., et al.: Classification of breast cancer histology images using convolutional neural networks. PLoS One **12**(6), e0177544 (2017)

5. Ibrahim, A.O., Shamsuddin, S.M.: Intelligent breast cancer diagnosis based on enhanced Pareto optimal and multilayer perceptron neural network. Int. J. Comput. Aided Eng. Technol. **10**(5), 543–556 (2018)

6. Spanhol, F.A., Oliveira, L.S., Petitjean, C., Heutte, L.: Breast cancer histopathological image classification using convolutional neural networks. In: 2016 International Joint Conference on Neural Networks (IJCNN), pp. 2560–2567. IEEE (2016)

7. Cruz-Roa, A., et al.: Automatic detection of invasive ductal carcinoma in whole slide images with convolutional neural networks. In: Medical Imaging 2014: Digital Pathology, vol. 9041, p. 904103. SPIE (2014)

8. Jiang, Y., Chen, L., Zhang, H., Xiao, X.: Breast cancer histopathological image classification using convolutional neural networks with small SE-ResNet module. PLoS One **14**(3), e0214587 (2019)

9. Kanavati, F., Tsuneki, M.: Breast invasive ductal carcinoma classification on whole slide images with weakly-supervised and transfer learning. Cancers **13**(21), 5368 (2021)

10. Haq, A.U., et al.: Stacking approach for accurate invasive ductal carcinoma classification. Comput. Electr. Eng. **100**, 107937 (2022)

11. Haq, A.U., et al.: DEBCM: deep learning-based enhanced breast invasive ductal carcinoma classification model in IoMT healthcare systems. IEEE J. Biomed. Health Inform. 1–12 (2022)

12. Roy, S., Kumar, R., Mittal, V., Gupta, D.: Classification models for Invasive ductal carcinoma progression, based on gene expression data-trained supervised machine learning. Sci. Rep. **10**(1), 4113 (2020)

13. Mittal, A., Moorthy, A.K., Bovik, A.C.: No-reference image quality assessment in the spatial domain. IEEE Trans. Image Process. **21**(12), 4695–4708 (2012)

14. Krizhevsky, A., Sutskever, I., Hinton, G.E.: ImageNet classification with deep convolutional neural networks. Commun. ACM **60**(6), 84–90 (2017)

15. Dat, T.T., Truong, N.N., Vu, P.C.L.T., Sang, V.N.T., Vuong, P.T.: An improved CRNN for vietnamese identity card information recognition. Comput. Syst. Sci. Eng. **40**(2), 539–555 (2022)

16. Miranda, E., Aryuni, M., Irwansyah, E.: A survey of medical image classification techniques. In: 2016 International Conference on Information Management and Technology (ICIMTech), pp. 56–61. IEEE (2016)

17. Kim, H.E., Cosa-Linan, A., Santhanam, N., Jannesari, M., Maros, M.E., Ganslandt, T.: Transfer learning for medical image classification: a literature review. BMC Med. Imaging **22**(1), 69 (2022)

18. Yadav, S.S., Jadhav, S.M.: Deep convolutional neural network based medical image classification for disease diagnosis. J. Big Data **6**(1), 1–18 (2019)

19. Thuy, L.N.L., Trinh, T.D., Anh, L.H., Kim, J.Y., Hieu, H.T.: Coronary vessel segmentation by coarse-to-fine strategy using U-Nets. BioMed Res. Int. (2021)

20. Kingma, D.P., Ba, J.: Adam: a method for stochastic optimization. In: Proceedings of the 3rd International Conference on Learning Representations (ICLR) (2015)

21. Janowczyk, A., Madabhushi, A.: Deep learning for digital pathology image analysis: a comprehensive tutorial with selected use cases. J. Pathol. Inform. **7**(1), 29 (2016)

22. Malm, R.: Cancer Image TensorFlow CNN 80% Valid. Acc. (2018). https://www.kaggle.com/code/raoulma/cancer-image-tensorflow-cnn-80-valid-acc. Accessed 20 Feb 2021

23. Li, S., Wang, L., Li, J., Yao, Y.: Image classification algorithm based on improved AlexNet. In: Journal of Physics: Conference Series. vol. 1813, no. 1, p. 012051. IOP Publishing (2021)

24. Khan, H.A., Jue, W., Mushtaq, M., Mushtaq, M.U.: Brain tumor classification in MRI image using convolutional neural network. Math. Biosci. Eng. MBE. **17**(5), 6203–6216 (2020)

25. Sarwinda, D., Paradisa, R.H., Bustamam, A., Anggia, P.: Deep learning in image classification using residual network (ResNet) variants for detection of colorectal cancer. Procedia Comput. Sci. **179**, 423–431 (2021)

Robust and Accurate Automatic License Plate Recognition System

Anh Le[1]([✉]), Dung Pham[2], and Thanh Lam[2]

[1] NTT Hi-Tech Institute, Nguyen Tat Thanh University, 300A Nguyen Tat Thanh, District 4, Ho Chi Minh City, Vietnam
leducanh841988@gmail.com
[2] Deep Learning and Applications, Ho Chi Minh City, Vietnam

Abstract. Inspired by the recent successes of deep learning on Computer Vision, we propose a deep learning-based system for Automatic License Plate Recognition (ALPR). The recognition system has two main modules: license plate detection (LPD) and license plate recognition (LPR). We employ anchor clustering, generalized IoU, and focal loss for improving YOLO based license plate detection and a method to generate synthesis license places to improve character recognition. The experiments on UFPR-ALPR and VN-ALPR datasets show that our recognition system achieved 94.06% and 96.00% for the ALPR task, respectively. Moreover, our recognition system achieves real-time processing at 30–32 FPS.

Keywords: Automatic License Plate Recognition · YOLO · Attention-based encoder-decoder

1 Introduction

Automatic License Plate Recognition (ALPR) has been focused recently since it plays an important role in building many applications such as automatic toll collection, smart parking, road traffic monitoring, and so on. This task is a complex problem due to the following reasons: blurry images, poor lighting conditions, weather conditions, moving cars/bikes. The demands from practical applications require a robust Automatic License Plate Recognition system that works various conditions while maintaining high accuracy and fast speed. An ALPR can divided into two main stages: License Plate Detection (LPD) and License Plate Recognition (LPR). In LPD, the system detects the bounding box containing a license plate. In LPR, the system recognizes characters in license place. Character recognition methods can be character segmentation or character segmentation free based methods.

In this research, we aim to build an robust ALPR with high accuracy and real-time speed. To achieve the high accuracy, we employ YOLO (a recently fast object detection) for LPD and attention based character recognition (character segmentation free based method) for LPR. Moreover, we employ anchor

T. K. Dang et al. (Eds.): FDSE 2023, CCIS 1925, pp. 590–597, 2023.
https://doi.org/10.1007/978-981-99-8296-7_44

clustering and focal loss for improve license plate detection and a method to generate synthesis license place to improve the character recognition. For achieve real-time speed, we adjust the architecture of the neural networks to balance between accuracy and speed. The rest of this paper is organized as follows. The related works is overviewed in Sect. 2. The overview of the ALPR system, the proposed LPD and LPR are presented in Sect. 3. The experimental results are presented and discussed in Sect. 4, and the final conclusions are presented in Sect. 5.

2   Related Works

Many approaches have been proposed for ALPR during the last two decades. In the following, we review a few recent approaches developed in academia and industry, which employed deep neural networks.

Elihos et al. [1] utilized Single Shot Multi-Box Detector to localize and to recognize license plate characters. They finetuned the pre-trained model on their license plate dataset. They also employed some rules to improve the accuracy of the recognition system.

Lee et al. [2] presented an LPR system based on denoising and rectification by CNN on low-quality images. The system was trained as an end-to-end system that optimizes the auxiliary tasks. The experiments demonstrate the effectiveness of the system in recovering the high-quality license plate image from the low-quality.

Yang et al. [3] presented a set of techniques such as edgedetection to quickly detect the candidate plates, augmentation, incorporating SIFT features into the CNN network to improve a CNN classification. The experimental results demonstrate that the recognition system can accurately recognize license plate in real-time under various levels of illumination and noise.

Laroca et al. [4] present an efficient and layout-independent ALPR system based on the YOLO object detector to detect license plate and classify layout and improve the recognition results using post-processing rules. The proposed system achieved a recognition rate of 96.8% in various public datasets.

OpenAPLR [5] is a commercial service for APLR. They provide APLR service run in locally hosted PCs and cloud servers. The service supports plate recognition over 70 countries.

3   Overview of ALPR

The overall architecture of the ALPR is shown in Fig. 1. It has two stages: a YOLO object detection [6] for detecting license places and an attention model based recognition system [7] for recognizing characters in license places. These modules are described in turn in the following sections.

AXV 8804

Fig. 1. The overall architecture of the ALPR system.

3.1   YOLO Based License Plate Detection

YOLO is one of the breakthroughs of deep learning in object detection. Yolo has three versions, and the speed and accuracy have been improved after each version. In this research, we employ YOLO3, which has many improvements to compare with the previous versions, such as pyramid feature maps to detect small objects. To improve the performance of YOLO, we employ focal loss, generalized Intersection Over Union (IoU), and clustering anchor box.

Focal Loss: cross-entropy loss treats the losses of background and foreground similarly. Since we have more anchor for background than plates, the cross-entropy loss will bias to background class. To solve this, we add a balanced weight between classes.

$$CE(p_t) = -\alpha_t \log(p_t) \tag{1}$$

where CE is the cross-entropy, p_t is the probability of predicting the current anchor belongs to class t, and $\alpha_t \in [0, 1]$ is the balanced weight between classes. In this research, we have two classes: plate and background, so that we use $\alpha_{background} = 0.3$ and $\alpha_{plate} = 0.7$ to balance the loss between them. Another problem is that cross-entropy loss can not distinguish easy/hard objects. Easy objects achieve high confidence scores faster than hard objects. Focal loss adopts another approach to reduce the loss of well-trained classes. When the model is good at detecting background, it will reduce its loss and reemphasize the training on the plate class. $\gamma \in [0, 0.5]$ is the focusing parameter.

$$FL(p_t) = -\alpha_t(1 - p_t)^\gamma \log(p_t) \tag{2}$$

Generalized IoU: IoU is the most popular evaluation metric used in object detection. IoU can be used as a distance for bounding box regression. However, in the case of nonoverlapping bounding boxes, IoU does not reflect the distance between the predicted box and the ground truth. Generalized IoU has proposed to solve this problem by adding a penalty to reflect the distance between two boxes.

$$\text{GIoU} = \text{IoU} - \frac{C(A \cup B)}{|C|} \tag{3}$$

where A and B are the predicted and ground truth boxes, C is the smallest convex hull that encloses both A and B. Finally, we used GIoU as Loss for Bounding Box Regression by the following equation.

$$L_{\mathrm{GIoU}} = 1 - \mathrm{GIoU} \tag{4}$$

Clustering Anchor Boxes: If we set a good initialization for anchor boxes, the network can learn easily to predict good detections. Instead of choosing priors by hand, we run K-means clustering on the training set bounding boxes to find a good initialization for anchor boxes. We set K = 9 anchor box and employ $(1 - \mathrm{GIoU})$ as the distance metric for K-mean. Then, we set the initial size for anchor boxes by the center of 9 clusters. Figure 2 visualizes the result of clustering anchor boxes.

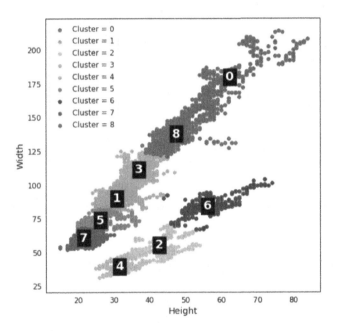

Fig. 2. The result of clustering anchor boxes.

3.2   Attention-Based License Plate Recognition

Our License Plate Recognition is based on the attention model. The architecture of our recognition system is shown in Fig. 3. It contains two modules: a Densely Convolutional Neural Network for feature extraction and an LSTM Decoder with an attention model for generating the target characters.

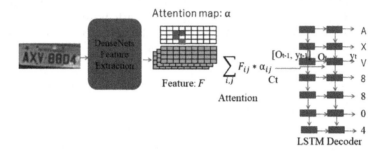

Fig. 3. The architecture of attention-based encoder-decoder.

Encoder: we employ DenseNet as feature extraction. DenseNet has direct connections from any preceding layers to succeeding layers. Densely connections help the network reuse and learn features cross layers and make the backpropagation faster.

Decoder: The LSTM decoder generates one character at a time. At each time step t, the decoder predicts symbol y_t based on the embedding vector of the previous decoded symbol $E_{y_{t-1}}$, the current hidden state of the decoder h_t, and the current context vector c_t calculated by attention model.

$$p(y_t) = \text{softmax}(W_E \times E_{y_{t-1}} + W_h \times h_t + W_c \times c_t) \tag{5}$$

where W_E, W_h, W_c are learnable parameters. We reused the network settings on our previous research [7] for the implementation.

Synthesis License Place Generation: Since the UFPR-ALPR dataset contains only 150 unique license plates, the attention model will be easily overfitting. Moreover, the number of training samples is small, data generation will help us to overcome the above problems. First, we randomly generate a string of a license plate. Then, we draw the string into a paperlike background. Finally, we employ blur, rotation, and distortion to generate the final image. Figure 4 shows examples of generated license plates.

4   Evaluation

We employed UFPR-ALPR dataset and our collected dataset. The UFPR-ALPR dataset contains 4,500 images taken from inside a vehicle driving through regular traffic in Brazil. The images were obtained from 150 videos and the number of unique license place is 150. We prepared a new dataset collected license place of bike in Vietnam. The dataset contains 2000 LP images. The images are collected in parking area in various conditions of light. As the above mentioned, UFPR-ALPR contained only 150 unique license place, we need generate more place to train attention model. We generate images of car and bike license place by employing the method in Sect. 3.2. The numbers of training, validation, testing,

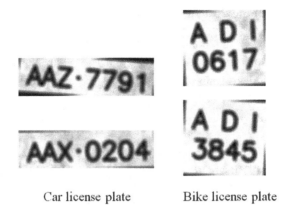

Car license plate   Bike license plate

Fig. 4. Synthesis license plates by our method.

and generated data of UFPR-ALPR and our dataset are shown in Table 1. We resize the image into (416×416) and (128×128) for LPD and LPR, respectively. For LPD we get a bounding box of the plate when the confident score larger than 0.3. We consider a detection as the correct detection when its IoU with the ground truth is greater than 0.6. For LPR, a correct recognition if all characters are recognized correctly.

Table 1. The number of images UFPR-ALPR and VN-ALPR datasets.

Dataset	UFPR-ALPR	VN-ALPR
Training	1800	1600
Validation	900	200
Testing	1800	200
Generated data	18000	18000

The first experiment was for evaluating the LPD by YOLO3 with/without our improvements. The result is shown in Table 2. The License Plate Detection is improved by our proposed methods. We improve 21% of Recall, 28.6% of Precision, 24.7% of mAP on UFPR-ALPR dataset and 21% of Recall, 28.6% of Precision, 24.7% of mAP on VN-ALPR dataset. This result shows the effectiveness of our proposed methods.

The second experiment evaluated the attention-based LPR. We train the recognition system by the training sets and with/without generated datasets, as described in Table 1. The result is shown in Table 3. Since the UFPR-ALPR dataset has only 150 unique license plates for training, the attention model is overfitted to the training set, so it can not recognize license plates in the testing set. By employing the generated dataset with 18000 unique license plates, we

Table 2. Results of license plate detection.

Dataset	Method	Precision	Recall	F1
UFPR-ALPR	YOLO3	70.4	70.5	70.4
UFPR-ALPR	improved YOLO3	91.4	99.1	95.1
VN-ALPR	YOLO3	93.5	93.5	93.5
VN-ALPR	improved YOLO3	99.5	99.5	99.5

achieve 98.22% on UFPRALPR and 98% on VN-ALPR. This verified that our generated data is helpful for training attention based LPR system. The diversity of the training set is necessary to train the attentionbased encoder-decoder which contains a strong language model in the decoder.

Table 3. Results of license plate recognition.

Dataset	Training datasets	Accuracy
UFPR-ALPR	Without synthesis plates	0.00
	With synthesis plates	98.22
VN-ALPR	Without synthesis plates	88.50
	With synthesis plates	98.00

The third experiment evaluate the overall recognition system. The results are shown in Table 4. We achieved 96.00% on VNALPR and 94.06% on UFPR-ALPR. We also compare our proposed system with other academia and commercial systems in UFPR-ALPR dataset. Our proposed system outperforms Sighthound, OpenALPR, and Laroca et al. by 21%, 12%, and 4%, respectively.

Table 4. Comparision of different system of license plate recognition.

Dataset	Systems	Accuracy
UFPR-ALPR	Our system	94.06
	Montazzolli et al. [4]	63.18
	Sighthound [4]	73.13
	Laroca et al. [4]	90.00
	OpenALPR [5]	82.2
VN-ALPR	Our system	96.00

In Table V, we report the average processing time of our system on the two datasets. We assume that the network weights are already loaded. The processing time for LPD is around 12–13 ms, while that for LPR is around 18.4–20.1 ms. The overall processing time is around 30.4–33.1 ms. Our system achieves real-time processing at 30.2–32.9 FPS, since cameras generally record videos at 30 FPS.

5 Conclusion

We presented here a method for ALPR. Our method detects license plates by YOLO and recognizes license plates by attention-based encoder-decoder. The accuracy of YOLO is improved by integrating anchor clustering, generalized IoU and focal loss while the accuracy of attention-based encoder-decoder is improved by generated license plates. The experimental results on UFPR-ALPR and VN-ALPR datasets show the effectiveness of our proposed methods. Our system achieved 94.06% and 96.00% for ALPR tasks on UFPR-ALPR and VNALPR, respectively. In addition, the processing time of the recognition system achieves real-time at 30–32 FPS.

Acknowledgment. We thank Dr. Dung Duc Nguyen, Institute of Information Technology, Vietnam and Rayson Laroca, Vision, Robotics, and Imaging Research Group, the Federal University of Parana for providing the VN-ALPR and UFPR-ALPR datasets, respectively.

References

1. Elihos, A., Balci, B., Alkan, B., Artan, Y.: Deep learning based segmentation free license plate recognition using roadway surveillance camera images. arXiv:1912.02441 (2019)
2. Lee, Y., Lee, J., Ahn, H., Jeon, M.: SNIDER: single noisy image denoising and rectification for improving license plate recognition. In: 2019 IEEE International Conference on Computer Vision (ICCV) Workshop (2019)
3. Yang, X., Wang, X.: Recognizing license plates in real-time. arXiv:1906.04376 (2019)
4. Laroca, R., Zanlorensi, L.A., Goncalves, G.R., Todt, E., Schwartz, W.R., Menotti, D.: An efficient and layout-independent automatic license plate recognition system based on the YOLO detector. arXiv:1909.01754 (2019)
5. OpenALPR. https://www.openalpr.com/
6. Redmon, J., Divvala, S., Girshick, R., Farhadi, A.: You only look once: unified, real-time object detection. In: IEEE Conference on Computer Vision and Pattern Recognition, pp. 779–788 (2016)
7. Le, A.D., Nguyen, H.T., Nakagawa, M.: An end-to-end recognition system for unconstrained Vietnamese handwriting. SN Comput. Sci. **1**, 7 (2020). https://doi.org/10.1007/s42979-019-0001-4

Community Detection for Personalized Learning Pathway Recommendations on IT E-Learning System

Nguyen Dinh Thuan[1,2](✉), Tran Man Quan[1,2], Dang Nguyen Phuoc An[1,2], and Nguyen Minh Nhut[1,2]

[1] University of Information Technology, Ho Chi Minh City, Vietnam
thuannd@uit.edu.vn, nhutnm.17@grad.uit.edu.vn
[2] Vietnam National University, Ho Chi Minh City, Vietnam

Abstract. Since COVID-19, technology's rapid growth and remote learning's increased demand have led to the evolution of online education. Platforms like Udemy, Coursera, and Skillshare offer free and paid courses. However, the abundance of scattered content overwhelms learners. Amidst hundreds of studies on E-Learning websites, self-learners need a specific learning plan and procedures tailored to everyone's abilities. Recognizing this need, we aim to enhance existing online learning systems by constructing an advanced recommendation system that elevates the personalized learning experience for individuals. We employ a method of community detection within social networks to segment the programming knowledge dataset into specific communities. Subsequently, based on the user's existing skills, we place each user in the right neighborhood for them and provide a roadmap accordingly. Algorithms used for clustering include Louvain, SLPA, LFM, and combined forms like SLPA-Louvain, SLPA-LFM, and LFM-Louvain. Closeness centrality measures are also used to propose related courses.

Keywords: Personalized learning path · e-learning recommendation system · Overlapping community detection · Social network analysis · Online course

1 Introduction

According to a recent Global Market Insights, Inc. Research report, the online learning market will be valued at around 325 billion USD by 2025 [1]. Online education is a highly potential market to tap into and expand. However, one challenge for learners is more motivation to participate in courses [2]. The utilization of these platforms might not be practical, as only about 10% of online learners complete their courses [3]. Most learners need help to self-direct, leading to system non-completion due to needing assistance in the learning process. Thus, providing consistent inspiration and guidance for learners significantly enhances the sustainability of Massive Open Online Courses (MOOCs) [4].

We aim to create a learning path suitable to each person's current orientation and abilities through an input survey of each student, suggesting what topics they should

T. K. Dang et al. (Eds.): FDSE 2023, CCIS 1925, pp. 598–605, 2023.
https://doi.org/10.1007/978-981-99-8296-7_45

study, how they should look, and what level of priority. We will provide learning content corresponding to the roadmap outlined for each student. Besides, we also suggest courses related to the content that users have learned. The scope of this research focuses on the IT field.

Our methodology focuses on community detection algorithms and using closeness centrality measures in social networks for content-based recommendations. Community detection uncovers structures and interconnections within networks using Stack Overflow[1] and roadmap.sh[2] data. We create an IT sector network dataset to explore language-skill links. Algorithms used include Louvain, SLPA, and LFM, often combined for better outcomes (e.g., SLPA and Louvain). Modularity, coverage, and conductance guide network model selection. The combined SLPA and Louvain model proves most compatible with our findings.

The study's structure is as follows: Sect. 2 reviews related works. Section 3 explains the methodology. Section 4 presents experimental results and evaluation criteria. Finally, Sect. 5 concludes with findings and future directions.

2 Related Works

To identify relevant papers, we used the following search terms: "personalized E-learning system," "e-learning recommendation system," "social network analysis in recommendation systems," and "overlapping community detection." The outcome yields a multitude of relevant studies.

Since 2018, the number of research studies related to e-learning systems in educational institutions has increased significantly due to the substantial impact of the COVID-19 pandemic on global education [1]. Souabi et al. [5] highlight effective recommendation systems for improving learner performance and knowledge.

Researchers discuss e-learning recommendation systems and their construction techniques. Khanal et al. [6] research reveals that clustering algorithms are the most widely used in hybrid recommendation systems. Clustering is an unsupervised learning technique in which items are grouped into clusters to group things with similar characteristics into the same set using distance metrics. The similarity between learners is determined based on distance measurements. In the realm of E-Learning, for behavior identification and participation assessment, and cooperation of learners to improve teaching quality, S. Yassine et al. [7] have identified three leading techniques for community and cluster detection: K-Means Clustering, Cliquen Analysis, and the Louvain algorithm, which can classify users into different groups. Meanwhile, X. Li et al. [8] studied student behavior using the Louvain algorithm for its intricate dataset.

In another study by J. Xie et al. [9], a new overlapping community detection algorithm named SLPA was proposed. This algorithm outperformed community detection algorithms like Copra, LFM, and Cfinder in various social network datasets. J. Scripps et al. [10] compared multiple community detection algorithms to identify the most optimal,

---

[1] https://stackoverflow.com/questions.

[2] https://roadmap.sh/.

high-quality, and user-desired algorithm. Through diverse datasets in various fields, algorithms, including Agglom, Cfinder, Ahn, SLPA, and Oslom, were compared, consistently highlighting the excellent performance of the SLPA algorithm.

Additionally, Gasparetti et al.'s study [11] on social recommendation systems indicated the widespread use of the LFM algorithm in complex networks. On the other hand, J. Zhang et al.'s research [12] explored various popular community detection algorithms in complex networks, with the LFM algorithm recognized for its early detection of communities and simultaneous identification of overlapping and hierarchical structures.

The research above provides a foundation for employing community detection algorithms in this project, including Louvain, SLPA, and LFM.

3 Methodology

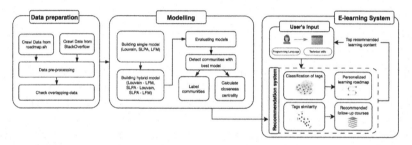

Fig. 1. Process of the proposed method

The proposed method's process is outlined in Fig. 1 through the following steps:

Step 1: Gather training data from tech websites.

Step 2: Preprocess and verify the social network model structure.

Step 3: Construct and evaluate both single and combined models. Assess using practical measures. Choose the best model for community detection.

Step 4: Label IT fields for each community from step 3 and calculate closeness centrality. Apply to the recommendation system to identify the user's skill field and suggest routes based on community. Use closeness centrality to propose further courses. Specifically, we apply the content-based recommendation system as follows:

For roadmap suggestion: Users who log in for the first time will have their known skills gathered through a short survey. Then, the system determines which knowledge community the user's input skills belong to, thereby proposing a learning path corresponding to that community, thanks to the roadmap.sh dataset.

For course suggestion: Related courses use the closeness centrality measure. The graph dataset is built from skill programming language tags that many users in the Stackoverflow community often mention. When a user studies a course with this tag, the system uses the closeness centrality index in the recommender to suggest other methods closest to the current tag for which a user is looking.

3.1 Data Collection

The study used Selenium to collect data. Information was obtained from StackOverflow and roadmap.sh to support building a learning path and course recommender.

The Stack Overflow Dataset

Stack Overflow, a programming community website, lets members post tagged questions for categorization. These tags are keywords related to information technology, such as programming languages or skills, and are used to categorize user questions with similar ones [13]. Stack Overflow, a programming community website, provides a rich dataset with approximately 105,000 IT-related questions. These questions are tagged with keywords related to programming languages and skills. For instance, questions tagged with "Laravel" often include "PHP," creating connections among tags. This dataset captures the social network structure of the IT field, featuring over 21,455 unique tags after data cleaning. Tags were further grouped into pairs, resulting in over 200,000 data entries representing connections between various tags.

The Roadmap.Sh Dataset

We also conducted research and collected data from the website *roadmap.sh*. This open-source project offers detailed learning paths for various IT domains, contributed to by thousands of experts worldwide.

It was ranked sixth on GitHub with 242k stars, roadmap.sh provides valuable data on learning paths, programming languages, and skills. This aids in crafting detailed, intuitive learning paths for programmers. The collected data spans six IT domains: FrontEnd, BackEnd, Android, DevOps, Flutter, and Blockchain.

3.2 Data Preprocessing

Data from both StackOverflow ("dataset 1") and Roadmap.sh ("dataset 2") was collected, preprocessed, and visualized, as depicted in Fig. 2.

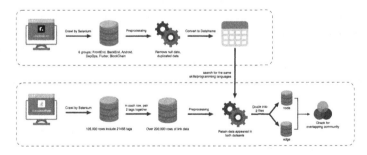

Fig. 2. Overview of the data preparation process.

Steps included removing duplicates and empty entries. To accomplish the tasks mentioned above, Dataset 2 was cross-referenced with Dataset 1. The objective was to filter and retain only those programming skills and languages in both datasets while discarding rows exclusive to either dataset. Subsequently, Dataset 1 was partitioned into smaller datasets called "node" and "edge."

Consider the social network as a graph, where "node" represents data containing information about the nodes within the social network (or the vertices of the chart), and "edge" stores the relationships between these nodes (i.e., the graph's edges). Therefore, the "node" dataset comprises a single attribute column named "names," which stores various tags.

The "edge" dataset consists of three attribute columns: "source," "target," and "value." The "source" and "target" columns store pairs of tags that have been pre-associated (e.g., the pair "html - css" has "HTML" as the source and "CSS" as the target). The "value" column represents the number of times the tag pair is duplicated across all data rows, referred to as the weight of the link. A higher weight indicates a stronger connection between the tags.

After preprocessing, the datasets yielded the following outcomes: For dataset 1, the node file contained 253 data entries, and the edge file contained 2764 data entries. As for dataset 2, our data consisted of 610 rows with four attribute columns: Group, MainType, Skill, and Value.

Subsequently, we needed to pinpoint its community structure to choose the best clustering algorithm for dataset 1. Social networks can have diverse facilities like discrete and overlapping ones [14]. So, the Louvain algorithm [15] was used here to define the structure of the community. Dataset 1 showed an overlapping community structure. It means nodes could belong to multiple communities [16].

3.3 Model Construction and Evaluation

In this part, we aim to swiftly recognize the right community for learners when they input their skills. This helps the system suggest fitting learning paths based on that community. Using closeness centrality, we also recommend relevant courses in that community. We've delved into Python-based community detection algorithms in social networks. Coupled with our earlier community analysis, we've chosen five suitable algorithms for the model: Louvain, SLPA, and LFM.

After building social network community detection algorithms, we found that single methods might miss crucial aspects, causing accuracy issues and ignoring network complexities. To address this, we've chosen practical combined algorithms – like Louvain-SLPA, Louvain-LFM, and SLPA with LFM. This aims to enhance detection and offer a complete community view. By leveraging each method's strengths and combining them, we improve accuracy and ensure consistency, reducing errors compared to individual plans.

Additionally, combining these algorithms allows us to handle particular situations, such as community detection in overlapping social network models or other more complex models [17].

After constructing the community detection models in social networks using the algorithms above, we used metrics such as the Number of Communities, Modularity, Coverage, Conductance, and Execution time to evaluate the effectiveness of the models.

3.4 Community Labeling and Closeness Centrality Calculating

After detecting communities, we labeled them by comparing elements within each with skills and programming languages from six domains in the roadmap.sh, dataset. Each community can belong to multiple domains due to skills overlap. We counted elements per domain to label and chose the most common one. Then, we calculated the graph's closeness centrality for course suggestions based on current courses.

3.5 Applying Model

After labeling each community, the next step is proposing learning paths. Users share their skills and desired programming languages. The system calculates compatibility with communities and suggests learning paths in compatibility levels. For personalized learning, it tracks path progress based on initial skills the user inputs and the courses they have taken. It recommends vital languages and abilities, too. When a path is chosen, the system calculates closeness centrality to suggest the following methods. Using completed or ongoing course tags to be centered, it identifies the closest markers via closeness centrality and offers related courses.

4 Experiment and Results

We have built three single community detection algorithms and three community detection algorithms combined and tested them to suggest learning paths for students and related courses. Table 1 compares the effectiveness of those algorithms.

Table 1. Comparison of the effectiveness between models.

Model	No. Communities	Execution time	Modularity	Coverage	Conductance
Louvain (Lv)	7	0.049526s	0.394	0.434	0.566
SLPA	2	0.399544s	0.544	1	0
LFM	4	0.250086s	0.069	0.931	0.069
Lv + SLPA	8	0.008240s	0.691	0.368	0.632
SLPA + LFM	6	0.312809s	0.203	0.457	0.543
Lv + LFM	6	0.048229s	0.20	0.457	0.543

In Table 1, the comparative results of the six algorithms that we use are described as follows: Louvain algorithm, SLPA algorithm, LFM algorithm, Louvain algorithm combined with SLPA algorithm, SLPA algorithm combined with LFM algorithm, and Louvain algorithm combined with LFM algorithm. At the results, we can see that the combination of Louvain and SLPA algorithms gives better results than other algorithms with the number of communities found at 8, a running time of approximately 0.00824 s, a Modularity score is about 69%, the Coverage score is about 36%, and the Conductance score is about 63%. It shows that with this combined model, there is quite a good clustering; the number of members in the social network is evenly distributed into different clusters, and there is a cross-association between these communities.

The Louvain algorithm also achieved almost the same value with the number of communities found of 7, running time of approximately 0.05 s, Modularity score of roughly 40%, Coverage score of about 43%, and Conductance score. Approximately 56%.

At the end of our experiment, the model applying the community detection algorithm between Louvain and SLPA brought the most suitable performance.

5 Limitations and Future Works

The system faces challenges, including limited data diversity, where suitable learning pathways may be missing due to data variety constraints. Resource and time consumption are also concerns, especially with a growing database. To address these issues, we plan to enhance the algorithm and gather more diverse data from various fields within and outside the IT industry.

6 Conclusion

Improving E-Learning is vital for enhancing online education, expanding learning opportunities, and increasing access to knowledge in the digital era. This study focuses on implementing social network community detection algorithms to identify communities in the dataset. Various algorithms are compared based on community count, runtime, Modularity, Coverage, and Scalability metrics. Results favor the Louvain algorithm combined with SLPA for community identification. Each community is labeled, and user skills are used to suggest personalized learning paths. Additionally, centrality index calculations aid in recommending suitable courses, making online learning more tailored to individual needs. This approach facilitates a smoother learning journey for online students.

Acknowledgments. This research is funded by Vietnam National University HoChiMinh City (VNU-HCM) under grant number DS2022–26-03.

References

1. Aulakh, K., Roul, R.K., Kaushal, M.: E-learning enhancement through educational data mining with covid-19 outbreak period in the backdrop: a review. Int. J. Educ. Dev. **101**, 102814 (2023). https://doi.org/10.1016/j.ijedudev.2023.102814
2. Zhou, M.: Chinese university students' acceptance of MOOCs: a self-determination perspective. Comput. Educ. **92**, 194–203 (2016). https://doi.org/10.1016/j.compedu.2015.10.012
3. Aldahmani, S., Al-shami, S.A., Adil, H., Sidek, S.: A review paper on MOOCs development stages, types, opportunities and challenges. System. Rev. Pharm. **11**(12), 172–179 (2020)

4. Hone, K.S., Said, G.R.E.: Exploring the factors affecting MOOC retention: a survey study. Comput. Educ. **98**, 157–168 (2016). https://doi.org/10.1016/j.compedu.2016.03.016

5. Souabi, S., Retbi, A., Idrissi, M.K.K., Bennani, S.: Recommendation systems on e-learning and social learning: a systematic review. Electron. J. e-Learn. **19**(5), 432–451 (2021). https://doi.org/10.34190/ejel.19.5.2482

6. Khanal, S.S., Prasad, P.W.C., Alsadoon, A., Maag, A.: A systematic review: machine learning based recommendation systems for e-learning. Educ. Inf. Technol. **25**(4), 2635–2664 (2019). https://doi.org/10.1007/s10639-019-10063-9

7. Yassine, S., Kadry, S., Sicilia, M.: Detecting communities using social network analysis in online learning environments: systematic literature review. WIREs Data Min. Knowl. Discovery **12**, e1431 (2021). https://doi.org/10.1002/widm.1431

8. Li, X., Yu, Q., Zhang, Y., Dai, J., Yin, B.: Visual analytic method for students' association via modularity optimization. Appl. Sci. **10**(8), 2813 (2020). https://doi.org/10.3390/app100 82813

9. Xie, J., Szymanski, B.K., Liu, X.: SLPA: uncovering overlapping communities in social networks via a speaker-listener interaction dynamic process. In: 2011 IEEE 11th International Conference on Data Mining Workshops, pp. 344–349. Vancouver, BC, Canada (2011). https://doi.org/10.1109/icdmw.2011.154

10. Scripps, J., Trefftz, C., Kurmas, Z.: The difference between optimal and germane communities. Soc. Netw. Anal. Min. **8**, 1–19 (2018). https://doi.org/10.1007/s13278-018-0522-1

11. Gasparetti, F., Sansonetti, G., Micarelli, A.: Community detection in social recommender systems: a survey. Appl. Intell. **51**, 3975–3995 (2020). https://doi.org/10.1007/s10489-020-01962-3

12. Zhang, J., Ma, Z., Sun, Q., Yan. J.: Research review on algorithms of community detection in complex networks. In: Journal of Physics: Conference Series, vol. 1069(1), p. 012124 (2018). https://doi.org/10.1088/1742-6596/1069/1/012124

13. Beyer, S., Macho, C., Penta, D.M., Pinzger, M.: What questions do developers ask on stack overflow? A comparison of automated approaches to classify posts into question categories. Empir. Softw. Eng. **25**(3), 2258–2301 (2019). https://doi.org/10.1007/s10664-019-09758-x

14. Fortunato, S., Newman, M.E.: 20 years of network community detection. Nat. Phys. **18**(8), 848–850 (2022). https://doi.org/10.1038/s41567-022-01716-7

15. Singh, D., Garg, R.: Ni-Louvain: a novel algorithm to detect overlapping communities with influence analysis. J. King Saud Univ. Comput. Inf. Sci. **34**(9), 7765–7774 (2022). https://doi.org/10.1016/j.jksuci.2021.07.006

16. Cherifi, H., Palla, G., Szymanski, B.K., Lu. X.: On community structure in complex networks: challenges and opportunities. Appl. Netw. Sci. (2019). https://doi.org/10.1007/s41109-019-0238-9

17. Dahlin, J., Svensson, P.: Ensemble approaches for improving community detection methods—arXiv preprint arXiv:1309.0242v1 (2013). https://doi.org/10.48550/arXiv.1309.0242

Improving Warped Planar Object Detection Network for Automatic License Plate Recognition

Nguyen Dinh Tra, Nguyen Cong Tri, and Phan Duy Hung[✉]

FPT University, Hanoi, Vietnam
{trandhe140661,trinche141519}@fpt.edu.vn, hungpd2@fe.edu.vn

Abstract. The Warping Object Detection Network (WPOD-Net) is a model designed to detect license plate contours in images. This study aims to enhance the performance of the original WPOD-Net model by incorporating knowledge about edges in the image through feature engineering. By leveraging edge information, the proposed approach improves the accuracy of license plate contour determination. The Sobel filter has been selected experimentally and acts as a Convolutional Neural Network layer, the edge information is combined with the old information of the original network to create the final embedding vector. The proposed model was compared with the original model on a set of data that we collected for evaluation. The results are evaluated through the Quadrilateral Intersection over Union value and demonstrate that the model has a significant improvement in performance.

Keywords: Convolutional Neural Network · WPOD-Net · License plate · Edge Detection · Sobel filter

1 Introduction

Convolutional Neural Network (CNN) is technically deep learning used effectively in feature extraction of images, widely use in Computer Vision to solve problems: Object Detection [1], Image segmentation [2], Recognition [3], Tracking [4] and Alignment [5] and has significant performance compared to using traditional machine learning. This article focuses on real-life license plate detection and recognition. One primary approach when it comes to domain transfer problems is using Warping Planer Object Detection Network [6].

The problem of license plate (LP) detection is not a new problem with many different methods, but when applying the CNN model, specifically YOLO [7] in the Object Detection problem, the accuracy increases compared to using machine learning. However, there is a limitation of this method that Object Detection only results in the area containing the license plate. If the license plate is at a non-front angle, the results can affect the extraction of license plate information.

In order to effectively detect objects such as license plates above when the input image is tilted too much, using WPOD-net is the first choice to detect the license plate area. This study gives an idea to improve that machine learning model architecture by adding information to the embedding vector. The edge information will be added as a CNN layer and the results will be compared with the original model on a set of data that we collected for evaluation.

2 Related Works

Sergio et al. designed WPOD-Net based on the idea of YOLO, SSD [8], STN (Spatial Transformer Network) [9]. As mentioned above YOLO and SSD only return 1 bounding box in the license plate regardless of the surrounding space. STN can detect non-rectangular regions, but it cannot handle multiple transformations at the same time, instead performing a single spatial transformation across the entire input. WPOD-Net return bounding box area surrounds the license plate and brings the number plate to the front view.

In the paper published in 2021 [10], Sergio et al. present a method to improve WPOD model by add more convolutional layer in the end of model.

Vincent et al. in the paper [11] present a commonly used digital image processing technique to find the contours of an image object. The author explained edge point: a pixel is considered an edge point if there is a rapid or sudden change in gray level (or color). Boundary: a set of consecutive boundary points. Edge detection is an image processing technique used to find the edges of objects in an image or can understand finding areas with a continuous loss in brightness (areas where there is a sharp difference in brightness).

In another paper published in 2009 [12], Vincent et al. use a Gaussian filter to remove noise, smooth the image first to make the edge detection algorithm work better.

3 Methodology

This section presents the improved architecture, loss function and evaluation metric. The model is then used for license plate detection. Using image processing algorithms to find edges helps us to extract more information from the image. We can consider the Sobel filter as a special layer in the CNN model, more specifically the WPOD-Net that increases the accuracy of the License Plate detector.

3.1 The Architecture

The WPOD-net architecture is proposed using insights from [7–9]. The Fig. 1 shows how the WPOD-Net works. From input image through the forward process, we get output features maps include: 8 channels in which the first 2 channels are probability with/without license plate and remaining 6 channels are parameters to calculate the transformation matrix. To extract the license plate area, the authors consider a fixed size square part with white border around the cell in the output features map. If the probability of the cell's object is greater than threshold then the values of the cell's remaining 6 channels will calculate the transform matrix from square part to license plate area. The matrix can be used to bring the license plate to the front view. From this idea, the authors give the WPOD network architecture.

From the original model, with the idea that adding edge information to the embedding vector can potentially increase the performance of the model, we have proposed a new architecture as shown in the Fig. 2.

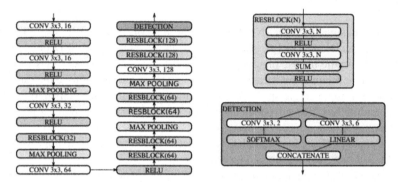

Fig. 1. WPOD Network Architecture

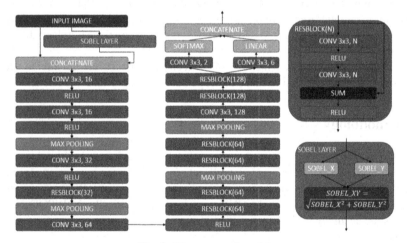

Fig. 2. The proposed model

The Sobel filter is based on convolving an image with a set of pre-determined 3x3 kernels. It is an example of a gradient-based edge detection algorithm. The first kernel computes the horizontal gradient at each pixel (SOBEL_X in the Fig. 2), while the second kernel computes the vertical gradient (SOBEL_Y in the Fig. 2).

These kernels can be used to compute the horizontal and vertical gradients at each pixel, and the resulting gradients can then be combined to determine the edge strength at each pixel (SOBEL_XY in the Fig. 2).

3.2 Loss Function

In this work, the mean-squared-error (MSE) loss is used to estimate the error between a warped version of the canonical square and the normalized annotated points of the LP. The binary-cross-entropy (BCS) loss is used to handle the probability of having/not having an object at each pixel in final feature map.

The location loss, as defined by Sergio et al. in the WPOD net [10], is given by the following equation:

$$f_{location}(m, n) = \sum_{i=1}^{4} (T_{mn}(\boldsymbol{q}_i) - A_{mn}(\boldsymbol{p}_i))^2$$

Confidence loss as follow:

$$f_{confidence}(m, n) = \log \text{loss}(\mathbb{I}_{obj}, v_1) + \log \text{loss}(1 - \mathbb{I}_{obj}, v_2)$$

The total loss function is a combination of the location loss and confidence loss, and can be expressed as:

$$\text{Total\_loss} = \sum_{m=1}^{M} \sum_{n=1}^{N} \left[\mathbb{I}_{obj} f_{location}(m, n) + f_{confidence}(m, n) \right]$$

where $\mathbb{I}_{obj}$ is the object indicator function that returns 1 if there is an object at point (m, n) or 0 otherwise.

3.3 Evaluation Metric

The Quadrilateral Intersection over Union (qIoU) is used to evaluate the accuracy of the detection model.

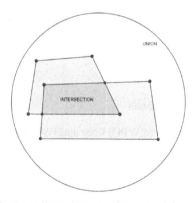

Fig. 3. Quadrilateral Intersection over Union (qIoU)

In the Fig. 3, we can see how to calculate qIoU, higher qIoU proves that the model is more effective for detecting license plates.

4 Implementation and Evaluation

4.1 Implement

This CNN model is implemented in Tensorflow [13]. Whole experiments were performed on an NVIDIA GeForce RTX 3090 GPU.

The model is trained by using a per-batch training strategy and use Adam's algorithm with learning rate 10–3, batch size 64 for 300,000 iterations.

4.2 Dataset

We create a training dataset of 363 images, including some images taken from the AOLP dataset [14], some data of Vietnamese car and motorbike license plates we collected from Internet. Specifically we have: 50 images from the AOLP dataset, 105 images of cars, and 208 images of motorbikes. An independently generated test data, 175 images include: 25 images from the AOLP dataset, 50 images of cars and 100 images of motorbikes.

For each image, we manually annotated the 4 corners of the LP in the picture. A few samples are shown in the Fig. 4.

Fig. 4. Examples of the LPs in the training dataset

4.3 Comparison to Other Methods

Model performance is compared to WPOD-net and iWPOD-net [14].

WPOD-net, iWPOD-net and the proposed model are trained by the same dataset, loss function, optimization algorithm, hyper parameters. The results in Table 1 show that the improved model gives slightly better results in qIoU (from 1 to 1.5%) than the original model when evaluated on our dataset.

Table 1. Quantitative evaluation

Method	qIoU
WPOD-net	84.81%
iWPOD-net	84.32%
Proposed Model	*85.81%*

5 Conclusion and Future Works

This paper proposes a method to improve the performance of WPOD network by adding edge knowledge to the embedding vector of the network. The results of the article show that when applied to the license plate detection problem, the quality of license plate detection is slightly improved.

Accurate object detection, especially in cases where the subject image is tilted, will help better in the subsequent information extraction. The paper can serve as a valuable reference for machine learning applications, particularly in the field of object detection [15, 16]. It provides insights and techniques that can be applied to various relevant problems within this domain.

References

1. Zou, Z., et al.: Object detection in 20 years: a survey. arXiv:1905.05055 (2019)
2. Haralick, R.M., Linda, G.S.: Image segmentation techniques. Comput. Vision Graph. Image Process. **29**(1), 100–132 (1985)
3. Logothetis, N.K., David L.S.: Visual object recognition. Ann. Rev. Neurosci. **19**(1), 577–621 (1996)
4. Bewley, A., Ge, Z., Ott, L., Ramos, F., Upcroft, B.: Simple online and realtime tracking. In: Proceedings of the IEEE International Conference on Image Processing (ICIP), pp. 3464–3468 (2016)
5. Richard, S.: Image alignment and stitching: a tutorial. Found. Trends® Comput. Graph. Vision **2**(1), 1–104 (2007)
6. Silva, S.M., Jung, C.R.: License plate detection and recognition in unconstrained scenarios. In: Proceedings of the European Conference on Computer Vision (ECCV), vol. 11216, pp. 580–596 (2018)
7. Redmon, J., Divvala, S., Girshick, R., Farhadi, A.: You only look once: unified, real-time object detection. In: Proceedings of the IEEE Conference on Computer Vision and Pattern Recognition (CVPR), Las Vegas, NV, USA, pp. 779–788 (2016)
8. Liu, W., et al.: SSD: single shot multibox detector. arXiv:1512.02325 (2016)
9. Jaderberg, M., Karen S., Andrew Z.: Spatial transformer networks. In: Advances in Neural Information Processing Systems, vol. 28 (2015)
10. Silva, S.M., Jung, C.R.: A flexible approach for automatic license plate recognition in unconstrained scenarios. IEEE Trans. Intell. Transp. Syst. **23**(6), 5693–5703 (2022)
11. Torre, V., Poggio, T.A.: On edge detection. IEEE Trans. Pattern Anal. Mach. Intell. **PAMI-8**(2), 147–163 (1986)
12. Vincent, O., Folorunso, O.: A descriptive algorithm for Sobel image edge detection. In: Proceedings of the InSITE 2009: Informing Science + IT Education Conference (2009)

13. Abadi, M., et al.: TensorFlow: a system for large-scale machine learning. arXiv:1605.08695 (2016)
14. Hsu, G.-S., Chen, J.-C., Chung, Y.-Z.: Application-oriented license plate recognition. IEEE Trans. Veh. Technol. **62**(2), 552–561 (2013)
15. Hung, P.D., Su, N.T.: Unsafe construction behavior classification using deep convolutional neural network. Pattern Recognit. Image Anal. **31**, 271–284 (2021)
16. Su, N.T., Hung, P.D., Vinh, B.T., Diep, V.T.: Rice leaf disease classification using deep learning and target for mobile devices. In: Al-Emran, M., Al-Sharafi, M.A., Al-Kabi, M.N., Shaalan, K. (eds.) ICETIS 2021. LNNS, vol. 299, pp. 136–148. Springer, Cham (2022). https://doi.org/10.1007/978-3-030-82616-1_13

Author Index

Printed in the United States
by Baker & Taylor Publisher Services